NEW OXFORD HISTORY OF MUSIC

VOLUME I

THE VOLUMES OF THE
NEW OXFORD HISTORY OF MUSIC

I. Ancient and Oriental Music
II. Early Medieval Music up to 1300
III. Ars Nova and the Renaissance (1300–1540)
IV. The Age of Humanism (1540–1630)
V. Opera and Church Music (1630–1750)
VI. Concert Music (1630–1750)
VII. The Age of Enlightenment (1745–1790)
VIII. The Age of Beethoven (1790–1830)
IX. Romanticism (1830–1890)
X. The Modern Age (1890–1960)

KRISHNA PLAYING A FLUTE

Relief from a temple at Belūr (Deccan). Hoyśala Dynasty, 12th century

ANCIENT AND ORIENTAL MUSIC

EDITED BY

EGON WELLESZ

OXFORD NEW YORK
OXFORD UNIVERSITY PRESS

OXFORD
UNIVERSITY PRESS
Great Clarendon Street, Oxford OX2 6DP
Oxford University Press is a department of the University of Oxford
It furthers the University's objective of excellence in research, scholarship,
and education by publishing worldwide in
Oxford New York
Athens Auckland Bangkok Bogotá Buenos Aires Calcutta
Cape Town Chennai Dar es Salaam Delhi Florence Hong Kong Istanbul
Karachi Kuala Lumpur Madrid Melbourne Mexico City Mumbai
Nairobi Paris São Paulo Singapore Taipei Tokyo Toronto Warsaw
with associated companies in Berlin Ibadan
Oxford is a registered trade mark of Oxford University Press
in the UK and in certain other countries
Published in the United States
by Oxford University Press Inc., New York

Reprinted 1999

ISBN 0-19-316301-2
Printed in Great Britain
on acid-free paper by
Biddles Short Run Books
King's Lynn

GENERAL INTRODUCTION

THE present work is designed to replace the *Oxford History of Music*, first published in six volumes under the general editorship of Sir Henry Hadow between 1901 and 1905. Five authors contributed to that ambitious publication—the first of its kind to appear in English. The first two volumes, dealing with the Middle Ages and the sixteenth century, were the work of H. E. Wooldridge. In the third Sir Hubert Parry examined the music of the seventeenth century. The fourth, by J. A. Fuller Maitland, was devoted to the age of Bach and Handel; the fifth, by Hadow himself, to the period bounded by C. P. E. Bach and Schubert. In the final volume Edward Dannreuther discussed the Romantic period, with which, in the editor's words, it was 'thought advisable to stop'. The importance of the work—particularly of the first two volumes—was widely recognized, and it became an indispensable part of a musician's library. The scheme was further extended in the new edition issued under the editorship of Sir Percy Buck between 1929 and 1938. An introductory volume, the work of several hands, was designed to supplement the story of music in the ancient world and the Middle Ages. New material, including two complete chapters, was added to volumes i and ii, while the third volume was reissued with minor corrections and a number of supplementary notes by Edward J. Dent. The history was also brought nearer to the twentieth century by the addition of a seventh volume, by H. C. Colles, entitled *Symphony and Drama, 1850–1900*.

Revision of an historical work is always difficult. If it is to be fully effective, it may well involve changes so comprehensive that very little of the original remains. Such radical revision was not the purpose of the second edition of the *Oxford History of Music*. To have attempted it in a third edition would have been impossible. During the first half of the present century an enormous amount of detailed work has been done on every period covered by the original volumes. New materials have been discovered, new relationships revealed, new interpretations made possible. Perhaps the most valuable achievement has been the publication in reliable modern editions of a mass of music which was previously available only in manuscript or in rare printed copies. These developments have immeasurably increased the historian's opportunities, but they have also added heavily to his responsibilities. To attempt a detailed survey of the whole history of music is no longer within the power of a single writer. It may even be doubted whether the burden can be adequately shouldered by a team of five.

The *New Oxford History of Music* is therefore not a revision of the older work, nor is it the product of a small group of writers. It has been planned as an entirely new survey of music from the earliest times down to comparatively recent years, including not only the achievements of the Western world but also the contributions made by eastern civilizations and primitive societies. The examination of this immense field is the work of a large number of contributors, English and foreign. The attempt has been made to achieve uniformity without any loss of individuality. If this attempt has been successful, the result is due largely to the patience and co-operation shown by the contributors themselves. Overlapping has to some extent been avoided by the use of frequent cross-references; but we have not thought it proper to prevent different authors from expressing different views about the same subject, where it could legitimately be regarded as falling into more than one category.

The scope of the work is sufficiently indicated by the titles of the several volumes. Our object throughout has been to present music not as an isolated phenomenon or the work of a few outstanding composers, but as an art developing in constant association with every form of human culture and activity. The biographies of individuals are therefore merely incidental to the main plan of the history, and those who want detailed information of this kind must seek it elsewhere. No hard and fast system of division into chapters has been attempted. The treatment is sometimes by forms, sometimes by periods, sometimes also by countries, according to the importance which one element or another may assume. The division into volumes has to some extent been determined by practical considerations; but pains have been taken to ensure that the breaks occur at points which are logically and historically justifiable. The result may be that the work of a single composer who lived to a ripe age is divided between two volumes. The later operas of Monteverdi, for example, belong to the history of Venetian opera and hence find their natural place in volume v, not with the discussion of his earlier operas to be found in volume iv. On the other hand, we have not insisted on a rigid chronological division where the result would be illogical or confusing. If a subject finds its natural conclusion some ten years after the date assigned for the end of a period, it is obviously preferable to complete it within the limits of one volume rather than to allow it to overflow into a second. An exception to the general scheme of continuous chronology is to be found in volumes v and vi, which deal with different aspects of the same period and so are complementary to each other.

The history as a whole is intended to be useful to the professed student of music, for whom the documentation of sources and the bibliographies are particularly designed. But the growing interest in the music of all periods shown by music-lovers in general has encouraged us to bear their interests also in mind. It is inevitable that a work of this kind should employ a large number of technical terms and deal with highly specialized matters. We have, however, tried to ensure that the technical terms are intelligible to the ordinary reader and that what is specialized is not necessarily wrapped in obscurity.

J. A. WESTRUP
GERALD ABRAHAM
EDWARD J. DENT
ANSELM HUGHES
EGON WELLESZ

CONTENTS

ILLUSTRATIONS

KRISHNA PLAYING A FLUTE *Frontispiece*

Relief from a temple at Belūr (Deccan). Hoyśala Dynasty, twelfth century. *Reproduced by courtesy of the Bollingen Foundation.*

I. PRIMITIVE INSTRUMENTS *between pp.* 232 *and* 233

(*a*) Xylophone. Ten flat wooden keys with gourd resonators, two strikers, and fibre cord for hanging. Baluba of Lake Moero, Congo.

(*b*) Slit drum, hollowed from one piece of wood, terminating at each end with a woman's head showing artificial cranial deformation. Struck with a wooden stick. Made by the Mangbetu of East Sudan.

(*c*) Zither made from bamboo, with eight strips slit away from the surface and bridged to form strings, the hollow bamboo acting as a resonator. Dyak, Borneo.

(*d*) Wooden rattle, enclosing small stones, representing the raven, sparrow-hawk, and a demon absorbing through his tongue from the frog the power of working spells. Painted blue, red, and black. Haida Indians, North-West America.

(*e*) Zansa with eight iron keys and gourd resonator. The hands are put through the slots and the keys plucked by the thumbs. Ibo of Onitsha Province, Nigeria.

Reproduced by courtesy of the Curator of the Pitt Rivers Museum, Oxford.

II. PRIMITIVE WIND INSTRUMENTS

(*a*) Side-blown trumpet carved from elephant tusk. West Africa.

(*b*) Bone vertical flute with three finger-stops and one thumb-stop drilled by stone borer. Ancient Peruvian, Chancay.

(*c*) Conch-shell trumpet, side-blown (*Triton giganteus variegatus*). Nares Bay, Admiralty Islands, Pacific.

(*d*) Whistle made of a reindeer phalanx. One blows between the two nearer articular condyles against the edge of the hole. Upper Palaeolithic, about 20,000 years old, from the cave of La Madeleine, Dordogne, France.

(*e*) Globular gourd flute with two stops. Jarawa, Northern Nigeria.

Reproduced by courtesy of the Curator of the Pitt Rivers Museum, Oxford.

III. CHINESE INSTRUMENTS

(*a*) Seven-stringed zither (*guuchyn*); dorsal aspect, showing the seven silk-gut strings and the thirteen mother-of-pearl studs marking the nodes. The tassels are decorative extensions of the looped silk cords which pass through the tuning pegs to secure the strings.

(*b*) The same; ventral aspect, showing the seven tuning pegs, the two knobs round which the ends of the strings are tightly twisted, the two sound holes ('Dragon Pool' and 'Roc Lake'), the personal name of the instrument: 'The Dragon's Purr', and the seal of the engraver.

(*c*) Globular flute (*shiun*). Three finger-holes are visible; two thumb-holes are present on the side away from the camera. This is a modern replica made to the specifications of the present Bureau of Rites and Music.

(*d*) Two globular flutes of Tarng date in the form of human heads. The eyes are the finger-holes.

(*e*) Mouth-organ (*sheng*). The apparent length of the pipes is not in every case the effective length; holes on the inner face of the pipes may shorten the length of the air column. The pipes speak only when the finger-holes visible near the base are closed. The instrument is held with the pipes almost horizontal. This is a Japanese instrument.

(*f*) Detail of the same. This shows the ends of two bamboo pipes removed from the wind chest; one still carries a thin sheet of copper (white with verdigris) in which a rectangular free reed has been cut. The frequency of vibration has been adjusted by means of the small blob of wax near the free end.

(*g*) Vertical six-holed flute (*shiau*). One of a pair of instruments from Yuhbiing, a famous centre for flutes.

(*h*) Detail of the same. The blow-hole is cut in the nodal diaphragm, and the wall bounding its outer rim is trimmed to a sharp edge. The embouchure is not fixed (as in a Western recorder, for example), and practice is required to make the *shiau* speak.

(*i*) Clay whistle flute in the form of a bear, from Shandong. The blow-hole is in the forehead. The stream of air strikes a sharp edge bounding the lower margin of the air-exit on the dorsal side.

(*j*) Bamboo 'whistle' from Shandong. Two bamboo free reeds are let into the wall of each of two short bamboo tubes, closed at both ends. On the side away from the camera, two small mouth-pieces are let into the larger tubes. The reeds are tuned about a semitone apart and are set in motion simultaneously by blowing into the mouth-pieces.

IV. (*a*) CHINESE PLAYERS OF MOUTH-ORGAN, *SHENG*, AND PERCUSSION-CLAPPER, *CHONGDWU*.

From Prince Ju Tzayyuh, *The Handbook of Music* (1596).

(*b*) CHINESE SONOROUS STONES, *CHINQ*, ASSOCIATED WITH LAUDATORY DECLAMATION, TOGETHER WITH THE HAND-DRUM, *TAUR*.

From Prince Ju Tzayyuh, op. cit.

V. (*a*) CHINESE ROC-HEADED VERTICAL HARP WITH EIGHTEEN STRINGS

From Chern Yang, *Yueh Shu* (13th-14th century).

(*b*) CHINESE SEVEN-STRINGED ZITHER TABLATURE

From the end of the twelfth century. This is a song with zither accompaniment and an interlude for zither alone. Reading from right to left the columns are: first the title, and then alternately tablature and text. The tablature is described on page 99 and transcribed as example 186. The interlude extends from the sixth to the eighth column. From the Syhbuh Tsongkan edition.

VI. CHINESE AND OTHER FAR-EASTERN INSTRUMENTS

(*a*) Two-stringed Manchurian fiddle.

(*b*) Mouth-organ in use among the Chingmiau near Anshuenn, Gueyjou Province, China. The free reeds of the six pipes are of copper and are lancet-shaped. They are tuned with blobs of wax. In this instrument the wind chest is of wood.

(*c*) Jew's harp of three tuned elements in use among the Lihjiang Lolo in Yunnan Province, China. The three elements are gripped between thumb and closed fingers of the left hand and set in motion by plucking the projecting 'keys' with the fingers of the right hand.

(*d*) Toy Jew's harp played by Minjia children in Shiijou, near Dahlii, Yunnan Province, China. The vibrating tongue is much thicker below the forked tip than elsewhere. It is set in motion by jerking a silk-gut cord attached to the lower end in the photograph.

(*e*) Three-stringed idiochordic bamboo tube-zither from Borneo. The strings are slivers of bamboo raised from the surface of the tube.

(*f*) Mouth-organ from Borneo. The wind-chest is a gourd.

(*g*) Detail of the same. Two of the free reeds are shown in pipes removed from the wind chest. Each reed is a rectangular tongue cut in a thin sheet of bamboo let into the wall of the pipe. Near the free end of each there is a thickening, comparable to that on the tongues of Minjia and Lolo Jew's harps (figures (*c*) and (*d*)). This figure should be compared with Plate III, figures (*f*) and (*j*).

Figures (a), (e), (f), and (g) are reproduced by courtesy of the Curator of the Cambridge University Museum of Archaeology and Anthropology.

VII. (*a*) INDIAN VÎṆÂ PLAYER

A representation of the *Râgiṇî Syâma Gûrjarî*. This *râgiṇî* is said to belong to the rainy season and should be sung in the early hours of the morning, expressing a mood of sadness and melancholy. See page 214. (Bodleian Library MS. Laud. Or. 149 fo. 33^{v}.)

(*b*) A BURMESE ORCHESTRA, *SAING* TYPE

For theatrical and other performances on a large scale. Melodic instruments: oboes with detachable brass bell-mouths; a graduated scale of drums played with the hands; a graduated scale of brass gongs played with wooden strikers tipped with disks of buffalo hide. Instruments for rhythm and emphasis: a bass drum struck with the fist, and four drums played by the hands; drums beaten with sticks; cymbals; wooden spring clappers. *Pictures copied from E. J. Colston, 'A Monograph on Tanning and Working Leather in the Province of Burma' (Rangoon, 1903), by courtesy of the Curator of the Pitt Rivers Museum, Oxford.*

VIII. MESOPOTAMIAN INSTRUMENTS

(*a*) Assyrians playing lower-chested harps (reign of Ashur-nāṣir-pal, 883–859 B.C.). *Reproduced by courtesy of the Trustees of the British Museum.*

(*b*) Harp from Ur (twenty-fifth century B.C.). *Reproduced by courtesy of the Trustees of the British Museum.*

(*c*) The royal Elamite orchestra, showing upper and lower-chested harps, double reed-pipes, and drum (reign of Ashur-bāni-pal, 668–626 B.C.). See pages 237–8. *Reproduced by courtesy of the Trustees of the British Museum.*

IX. EGYPTIAN INSTRUMENTS

(*a*) Lower-chested harp and flute (Eighteenth Dynasty, *c.* 1570–1310 B.C.). *Reproduced by courtesy of the Director of the Rijksmuseum, Leiden.*

(*b*) Harp, lute, and double reed-pipe (*c.* 1475 B.C.). From the tomb of Amenemhet, Thebes. *Reproduced by courtesy of the Trustees of the British Museum.*

X. GREEK INSTRUMENTS

(*a*) A kithara player singing.

An Athenian vase *c.* 480 B.C. *Reproduced by courtesy of the Museum of Fine Arts, Boston.*

(*b*) A Greek Music School.

The instructor is playing on a lyre and singing; about him are youths playing double *auloi*, and holding flutes and lyres. Athenian vase of the early fifth century B.C. *Reproduced by courtesy of the Trustees of the British Museum.*

XI. ROMAN INSTRUMENTS

(*a*) A Priest of Cybele.

Relief showing cymbals, tympanum, and twin Phrygian pipes. (*c.* A.D. 150.) See p. 405.

(*b*) Roman Musicians at the Circus

Showing the *tuba, hydraulus* (with female player), and *cornu.* From a mosaic at Zliten (late first century A.D.).

XII. A ROMAN CONCERT

Showing twin pipes and *kithara.* See page 413. From a fresco at Herculaneum. *Reproduced by courtesy of the Museo Nazionale, Naples.*

XIII. ARABIC INSTRUMENTS

From the *Kitāb al-Adwār* of Ṣafī al-Din 'Abd al-Mu'min (d. A.D. 1294)

(*a*) Lute of five double strings (Bodleian Library MS. Marsh 521, fo. 157ᵛ. A.D. 1333–4).

(*b*) Psaltery of thirty-two strings (from the same MS., fo. 158).

(*c*) Harp of thirty-four strings (Cairo MS. f. j., 428. A.D. 1326–7).

The Arabic in figure (*a*) gives the names of the parts of the instrument, whilst that in figures (*b*) and (*c*) indicates the tuning. See pages 462–3.

XIV. ARABIC MUSIC MANUSCRIPTS

(*a*) British Museum MS. Or. 2361, fo. 32. Late thirteenth century.

(*b*) British Museum MS. Or. 136, fo. 38ᵛ. Late thirteenth century.

For a transcription of these see pages 454–5.

Reproduced by courtesy of the Trustees of the British Museum.

The Glossary of Chinese characters, pp. 190–4, was written by Dr. Tsaur Tian-Chin, sometime Fellow of Gonville and Caius College, Cambridge.

INTRODUCTION TO VOLUME I

THE second edition of the *Oxford History of Music* had an Introductory Volume edited by Percy C. Buck which dealt primarily with those facts and forms which preceded the rise of polyphony, and included other subjects which had been omitted in the first edition. Explaining the scope and content of the volume, Buck stated 'that the understanding of any subject can only be derived from the study of how it came to be what it is'. This aim was not fully realized in the Introductory Volume, because its chapters were not designed to form a unity, but to fill the gaps in the main body of the work. It has needed the replanning and rewriting of the whole history of music as delineated in the 'General Introduction' to make it possible to approach Buck's far-sighted postulate.

During the two decades that separate the publication of the Introductory Volume and the planning of the *New Oxford History of Music* musicological research has made great progress in the field covered by the present volume. Phonograph and gramophone have made it possible to study the music of remote and primitive peoples. The methods of transcribing the music have improved. Comparative musicology, that new branch of musical research, regarded in its beginnings some fifty years ago as a side-line, has enlarged its scope and developed its methods. Orientalists have taken an ever-increasing interest in writings about music and passages in historical works referring to it. Students of comparative liturgiology have given the initiative to an investigation of the relationship between Jewish and Christian chant, and their work has led to the examination of the passages on music in the Holy Scriptures in a new light.

The present volume takes into account this widening of the field of musicological studies, which has created a new outlook. The first chapter gives an introduction to the essentials of all kinds of primitive music. The main part of the volume, Chapters II–VIII, gives a historical survey of the music of the East. The next section, Chapters IX–X, contains a survey of Greek and Roman music, and the last, Chapter XI, deals with the music of the Islamic world.

It has been clear to the Editor from the beginning that the treatment of such vast and divergent material in a single volume must be carried out on different principles from those applied to the other volumes of the *History*. There, as pointed out in the General

Introduction, music is seen as an art, closely connected with various trends of our Western civilization. Such treatment not only permits but enforces the application of the so-called 'historical method' which aims at describing the single work of art as a product of the creative mind of a composer; or, where this is impossible, at description of the creative tendencies of a group or school of composers who remain anonymous.

When we come to deal with non-European music, however, we cannot apply the same criteria as we use in studying and appreciating the music of the West. In the East music has—or at any rate had until recently, when social changes, radio and the gramophone have so much altered the whole outlook—still preserved its ritual, even its magic character. The factor of time which governs the structure of Western music plays hardly any part in Oriental music. An Arabic song may last more than an hour, the performance of a Chinese opera stretch out over several days. To the Western musician conciseness of expression, clearly shaped form, and individuality are the highest criteria by which a work of art is judged; the attitude of the listener is an active one: he listens to what the composer has to say. The Eastern musician likes to improvise on given patterns, he favours repetition, his music does not develop, does not aim at producing climaxes, but it flows; and the listener becomes entranced by the voice of the singers, by the sound of the instruments, and by the drumming rhythms.

All this makes it difficult to apply our critical values to music which is so essentially different from our own. For example, in judging Chinese music, we are in the same position as the Chinese listeners to whom, as Amiot relates in his *Mémoire sur la musique des Chinois* (Paris, 1779), French missionaries played music of Rameau: it meant nothing to them. We have also a report from the nineteenth century of the effect of songs by Schubert on a Chinese audience; they liked the music as a play of notes, but objected that it did not move the heart.

How, one may ask, can one hope to acquire any knowledge of Oriental music, if such a cleavage exists in structure and expression between the music of the East and that of the West? And one may add, that objection applies to an even higher degree to our understanding and appreciation of primitive music, with which the present volume opens.

It is here that the work of the comparative musicologist begins. The student of this most recent branch of our studies will not confine himself to describing the peculiarities of each tribe whose music has been recorded. That kind of research precedes his work which, in the same way as the ethnologist's, must consist in showing the function of music in primitive life. Such studies must remain within the scope of general statement, derived from the material which precedes historical research.

A similar though more specialized approach must be applied to Oriental music. Here one must rely to a great extent on the judgement of those experts who have devoted themselves to the study of the music of a particular part of the civilized world from enthusiasm and a peculiar inclination, fully equipped with the knowledge of the language, the customs, rites, and ceremonies of the people whose music they investigate, and the experience of having heard the music performed in the surroundings in which it was created and to which it belongs. Some of the music, like that of India, Java, Bali, Laos, and Indochina, for example, appeals to the Western mind directly; that of China and Japan, however, needs a more thorough acquaintance before it is appreciated and before it is possible to distinguish between old and modern instrumental music; folk-songs on the one hand, and ceremonial and ritual music on the other. The main obstacle for the European listener in appreciating Far Eastern music comes in the beginning from the different method of voice-production. For the European, singing is a kind of elated speech; for the Far Eastern musician singing is opposed to speech: the voice is used like a highly strung instrument.

For the study of the Ancient Orient, of which no music has survived, we must turn to the visual arts to learn which instruments were used, and to literary sources to discover what those who wrote about their national music thought of it. In this case the task of the scholar will be similar to that of the historian: to state what he has read about the music, and to convey to the reader the impression that he has gathered from his sources.

To deal with Jewish and Islamic music and that of Greece and Rome a different approach has been felt to be necessary. Systematic studies in Jewish music are of recent date and are based upon the methods of comparative musicology. It has been necessary to determine how far the oral tradition can be traced back, and to what extent time and cultural changes have altered the character of the music. The result of these studies has been more positive perhaps than one dared to expect. For example, recordings of the religious music of Jewish communities who have lived for centuries separated from their neighbours have shown that they are still related to the common source and, furthermore, that their psalm-tunes and many other liturgical chants are closely related to, if not identical with, those of the Christian churches, both Eastern and Western, who took them over in the early days of Christianity. Thus a new basis for the study of Christian chant has been established.

The approach to the music of Islam and the methods employed in investigating its character and history have been the same. Here again the integration of these studies into the history of Western music will shed new light on some problems which are still under discussion. With the chapter on Greek music we enter a field of studies which, since the days of Humanism, has been favoured by classical scholars. We need only recall Meursius's edition of the theoretical treatises of Aristoxenus, Nicomachus, and Alypius, printed in Amsterdam in 1616, followed by the more comprehensive edition of Meibom in 1652 and of Ptolemy's *Harmonicorum libri tres*, printed at Oxford in 1682. Bellermann's edition of *Die Hymnen des Dionysius und Mesomedes* in 1840 aroused the interest of musicologists in Greek music, and from that time its investigation has been an important subject of musicological research.

However, the study of Greek music has shown also the difficulties with which one is faced in studying the music of a period from which only a limited number of musical documents have survived. From the writings of Greek poets, philosophers, and theorists Greek music seems familiar to us. In fact, the music itself, when we read or hear it, seems to offer no problems to our understanding from the formal or aesthetic point of view. We find in it those qualities which appeal directly to our mind: clarity of shape and conciseness of expression. But how can we attempt to comprehend Greek music as a whole from the few fragments which have come down to us?

Hermann Abert, a musicologist of the former generation, whose book on the *ethos* of Greek music has become a classic, discussed this question in a lecture on Greek music, given to the Prussian Academy in 1923. He asked his audience to visualize the position of a musicologist who, 2,000 years from now, would try to give a picture of our music with the following documents as the only material from which to draw his conclusions: three bars from the St. Matthew Passion, a drinking-song from the eighteenth century, a Mass by Bruckner, half a dozen modern pieces for the piano; but, in addition, a great many theoretical works from J. J. Fux's *Gradus ad Parnassum* to a modern textbook on harmony. Would he be able to give an adequate picture of our music from these sources?

Such is our position in relation to the material of Greek music at our disposal. But we may ask further: even if we had enough documents to enable us to make an historical approach, should we be any nearer to a real understanding of its aesthetics or to a knowledge of the effect it had on the audience for which it was written?

This question may well be asked about Oriental music also. We must face the fact that the music which we read, or even hear on records, can give us only a faint idea of what it means to the people who live with it. This may be illustrated by a few examples, taken from personal experience.

During the concerts given for the members of the first Congress of Arabic Music at Cairo in 1932 we heard a Persian singer who sang of his sorrow at leaving his friends. The audience, which consisted mostly of Egyptians, became so excited that they forgot they were listening to a song and shouted: 'Stay with us, do not leave us.' One felt at once that the artificial barriers which in the modern concert hall separate the singer from his audience had been broken down. For his audience the plaintive song of the singer had become reality. I was reminded of the Greek classical play in which the *personae dramatis* were for the audience not the actors in the role of the heroes of the past, but actually the shadows of the dead heroes, conjured up from Hades by the priest of Dionysus to perform their deeds once more.

On another occasion we saw the solemn ritual of the 'dancing dervishes'. It was impossible to believe that old men who had performed the whirling movement for more than an hour could sit down when the dance came to an end without breathing more heavily, if one did not assume that the music had produced a state of trance in which the normal physical reactions were suspended. One was reminded of the writings of the Platonists and Gnostics which describe the sacred dances as the symbols of the movements of the moon, the sun, and the stars, and music as a supernatural power, as an *ἐπανόρθωσις τῶν ἠθῶν*, as a means to improve the character.

Finally we saw the dance of Egyptian sorceresses, who danced to an exciting music of flutes, fiddles, and drums round the imaginary body of a sick man. Here one felt at once: such was the kind of music to which Plato refers in his *Laws* (790 d) when he speaks of the 'female healers of Corybantic troubles'.

These examples, taken from the music of the Islamic world, could easily be supplemented by a great number of others, all demonstrating the magic effect of music. They would lead from travellers' descriptions of the rituals of primitive tribes to the writings of the sages of Ancient China about the power of music to organize or disrupt the order of the State.

This brings us to an explanation of the plan of the present volume. The reader may object to the separation of the chapters on Hebrew and Jewish music in this volume from those on 'Early Christian Chant' in Volume II; with our growing knowledge of the development of Christian from Jewish liturgy, one might have expected to find both sections side by side. For similar reasons one might object to the placing of Greek and Roman music in the first volume, because both belong to European civilization and particularly because Greek and Roman musical theory had a decisive influence upon medieval theorists.

There is, however, a unifying idea in the volume. It deals with the music of the non-Christian world: a world in which music is regarded as a power creating a magic effect upon the listener. This magic character of music ranges, according to the state of civilization of the people who produce it, from totemistic connotations to music which represents a certain rite or a certain ceremony and creates in the listener the proper mood to participate in it. Considering the emotional character of such music, one may well understand the many warnings of the Fathers of the Church in the early days of Christianity against any kind of singing which creates such an effect. Even St. Augustine, brought up in the classical tradition and, as one knows from the famous passage in his *Confessions*, enjoying music 'which is pleasing to the ear', advises that the chanting of the psalms should be nearer to recitation than to singing—*pronuncianti vicinior esset quam canenti*—and says in another place: 'We sing with our voice to be excited, we sing with our heart to please God' (*Enarratio in Ps. 147*, 5).

This rigid attitude of the Church in its first centuries shows that she was aware of the magic power of music in the surrounding pagan world. When the Christian faith was established as the acknowledged religion all over the Roman Empire, it was no longer necessary; the magic spell was broken. Music could now be used primarily as *laus Dei*, to heighten the splendour of the service, and, in our Western civilization, the way was opened for its development as an art.

EGON WELLESZ

ACKNOWLEDGEMENTS

ACKNOWLEDGEMENTS are due to the following for permission to reproduce music examples from the works cited: Librairie Delagrave, Paris (A. Lavignac and L. de la Laurencie, *Encyclopédie de la musique*); Paul Geuthner, Paris (A. Gailhard, *Théâtre et musique modernes en Chine*); Breitkopf and Härtel, Wiesbaden (E. Fischer, *Beiträge zur Erforschung der chinesischen Musik*); the Sven Hedin Foundation, Stockholm (*Reports from the Scientific Expedition to the North-Western Provinces of China*); W. W. Norton & Co., Inc., New York (Curt Sachs, *The Rise of Music in the Ancient World*, including two examples after Frizzi (Peri)); T. Howard Somervell ('The Music of Tibet' from the *Musical Times*); Colin McPhee (*Angkloeng Gamelans in Bali*, *A House in Bali*, and 'The 5-tone Gamelan Music of Bali'); the Editor of *Anthropos*, Poisieux; Mezhdunarodnaya Kniga (*500 kazakskikh pesen*); Dr. Jaap Kunst (*De enheemse muziek in N. Guinea*, 'Music in Nias', *A Study on Papuan Music*, and *Over zeldzame fluiten*); Cha Fu-Hsi (extracts from recordings in the Library of Congress, Washington); G. Schirmer, Inc. (article by Colin McPhee, 'The 5-tone Gamelan Music of Bali', in *Musical Quarterly*, April 1949); Österreichische Akademie der Wissenschaften (R. Lach, *Gesänge russischer Kriegsgefangener*); the National Museum of Canada (Jenness and Roberts, *Eskimo Songs*); the Smithsonian Institution (Bulletins of the Bureau of American Ethnology); the Editor, *Journal de la société des Américanistes*; the Finno-Ugrian Society (A. Kannisto, *Wogulische und ostjakische Melodien*); University Museum, Philadelphia (Speck-Sapir, *Ceremonial Songs of the Creek and Yuchi Indians*); the Syndics of the Cambridge University Press (*Reports of the Cambridge Anthropological Expedition to Torres Straits*, ed. A. C. Haddon); the Oxford University Press (P. Kirby, 'Bushmen', in *Bantu Studies*); and George Allen & Unwin Ltd. (a translation by Arthur Waley of four lines from *The Book of Songs*).

Chapter I was translated by Stanley Godman.

I

PRIMITIVE MUSIC

By MARIUS SCHNEIDER

COMPARATIVE MUSICOLOGY

UNTIL a few decades ago the term 'history of music' meant merely the 'history of European art music'. It was only by degrees that the scope of music was extended to include the indispensable foundation of non-European and, finally, primitive music. Since only a few relics of primitive music survive in European folk-music, to get any idea at all of primitive music scholars had to turn first to the primitive tribes still living in the Stone Age. At the same time the study of more highly developed non-European cultures, which had begun much earlier, was revived and a new branch of musicology concerned exclusively with non-European music came into being. This new discipline was called 'comparative musicology', its primary aim being the comparative study of all the characteristics, normal or otherwise, of non-European art. This study led to the establishment of connexions between European and non-European music.

It must be emphasized that the methods of the musical ethnologist are entirely different from those of the historian. For the student of primitive music Europe has played only a very small part in the total framework of human history. But he has to attempt to rediscover the bridges between European and non-European music which certainly once existed and to reconstruct them, theoretically at least, by means of comparative ethnology. The aim of the present chapter is to describe the music of the hunting, pastoral, and peasant peoples whose historical position is bounded at one end by the earliest primitive cultures and at the other by the beginnings of more advanced cultures. At the extreme end are those pastoral and peasant peoples, for example the Caucasians, who already show the marked influence of a highly developed culture and must be included because their tradition, still alive today, provides the key to the understanding of those ancient civilizations which can now be investigated only by purely archaeological methods.

Although all the material dealt with here is of recent origin, we shall use the term 'historical development' as understood by the ethnologist who attempts to bring into historical order the medley of primitive, transitional, and advanced cultures which still exist side by side in the world today. 'Higher development' simply means a general historical process and is in no way intended as a criterion of musical value.

MELODY AND MANKIND

Primitive music is a separate field of its own, but to a much greater extent than art music it is bound up with everyday life and with many special factors: psychological, sociological, religious, symbolic, and linguistic. Some songs must be performed only by a certain individual; others must be sung only by men or women. The same melodies may have a quite different psychological meaning, according to whether they are sung falsetto, or with a nasal or chest voice. For a proper understanding of any given musical phenomenon direct contact with the singers and their surroundings is therefore indispensable. The conception that we can get from the written version of a simple melody is quite inadequate (and may even be entirely misleading) unless we have this practical experience. In particular we need to be acquainted with the method of performance of the people concerned and the tone quality they produce, in order to hear the song correctly. It is a simple matter of experience that the actual transcription of a melody will vary essentially according to whether it is made from a direct hearing and seeing of the singer or only indirectly from a gramophone record. In the first instance the rhythm of the song as a whole will be more accurately transcribed; in the second the melodic details will be better reproduced. A primitive melody is always the musical expression of an idea. Primitive man sings only when he has something definite to express. Since his singing is the *spontaneous* expression of his thought, song and speech are often mingled in the course of his performance. If one tries to introduce a primitive man to a new tune (without the foreign words which he cannot understand) he will never stop asking what the song is about. For him the thoughts expressed in the song are at least as important as the melody itself. But if he hears a melody that pleases him, the words of which he does not understand, he will at once add words of his own. Even his instrumental melody and his whistling are the expression of definite ideas. Thus the roots of programme-music reach down into the earliest strata of instrumental music. Whether the simple sing-song of certain kinds of children's songs and lullabies is entirely bereft of ideas has still to be proved. The idea need not be clearly formulated in words;

it may consist of a vaguely defined thought, felt rather than conceived, expressed directly in sound without the mediation of an intelligible sequence of words. It may also happen that the logical thought and the musical motive pass little by little from the indefinite to the definite in the course of the song, as if the initial dream-state were gradually yielding to waking consciousness. Many of the supposedly nonsensical syllables to which a melody is sung also have a magic significance. Thus the syllable *hee* often serves to express the shooting of an arrow and *hoo* has a medical value. Such syllables serve to evoke a spirit or frighten it away. Just as one cannot sound a medicine-rattle heedlessly or merely for fun without falling ill, so one must not sing thoughtlessly to oneself, for every note summons up a spirit. Melody has a great significance for primitive man, a magic power which must not be squandered or abused. The agreement of sounds is always a symbol of identity or at least of mutual understanding. In the Solomon Islands, when an invitation is sent to a neighbouring tribe it is customary to send the measurements of the tribal panpipes so that the guests can tune theirs beforehand, thus ensuring the greatest agreement in the mutual musical greeting. When young men are singing, and it suddenly occurs to one of them to strike up so high a melody that the other singers cannot follow him, sometimes a young girl will take up the melody in this high register and continue it. When this happens, it means that the two young people are in love.[1]

A melody is not a chance combination of notes but an organic and dynamic whole, a form which is more than the simple sum of the notes of which it consists. A succession of single notes artificially put together is ineffectual because it is a synthetic product, not a living one. The aboriginal describes a melody of that kind as 'powerless' because it is not in a position to offer a dwelling-place to a spirit. Primitive melody, which is scarcely more than a continually repeated and varied motive, is regulated essentially by the tension between the beginning of the motive and its final note. All the notes between are determined by conscious striving towards the last note. Both the motive and the series of its repetitions *grow* according to definite patterns which can assume the most varied forms according to the particular culture or the ideas and feelings expressed.[2]

This growth of melody is undoubtedly one of the main reasons why music is so significant in the life of primitive peoples. Music and dancing create a movement which generates something that is more

[1] M. Leenhardt, *Arts de l'Océanie* (Paris, 1947), p. 58.
[2] See infra, p. 24.

than the original movement itself. As he sings and dances, man discovers in himself an all-pervading element whose intensifying, liberating, or healing power is unknown to him in everyday life. Music which has such an intensifying effect grows to the point of ecstasy. The quietly and regularly flowing rhythms lead to a great inward release. I have myself observed the liberating and healing power of music in the case of a native of Uganda who, at the funeral of a brother (killed by a spirit), at first broke into a terrible howl of rage and then, beginning to sing, gradually defeated the black demon of despair by the soothing power of song.

The effects of musical rhythm are especially strong when singing is accompanied by dance movements or by the singer's own playing on an instrument. Of course this purely instinctive, primitive music-making has at this stage nothing to do with art. Nevertheless, even in the oldest cultures we find the preconditions of art: the mastery and more or less conscious shaping of the medium of expression. Where the singer who is at the same time dancing tries to achieve a certain regularity in his movements, his singing takes on regular musical forms. The pure play-instinct certainly has a great part in this shaping of the melody into regular phrases. On the other hand it must be noted that even ecstatic songs and dances often exhibit very rigid phrase-structure.

This regularity of tectonic structure is even more striking when the community takes part as a choir. But the participation of a choir not only helps the regularity of the rhythmic movement: it also contributes materially to the unification of the melodic line. The African pygmy dances in Father P. Schebesta's collection[1] usually begin with a wild cry for all the singers out of which a comparative unison gradually emerges. The melodic lines and the various rhythms of the opening gradually adjust themselves to one another and in the end there emerges a completely regular community chant.

The powerful influence of collective performance on the development of primitive music can be seen from the fact that even funeral music and love-songs are also very largely choral. The life of the individual is so strongly bound up with the community that the latter will not relax its guardianship even during the short hours of the wedding night, which it celebrates with continual singing.

The collective consciousness, however, does not lead at all to a musical 'levelling'. The distinction between soloist and chorus is always maintained. This hierarchy is expressed both by different

[1] In the Phonogramm-Archiv of the Berlin Museum für Völkerkunde.

methods of performance and by the degree of ecstasy to which the singers gradually abandon themselves in the ritual songs. The soloist is the master, the choir are his 'assistants'. Even when both sing the same song the soloist performs it sharply and abruptly, the choir in a more *cantabile* (*arioso*) manner. The soloist dances; the choir forms a magic protective circle around him. The soloist intensifies his rhythms more and more in order to penetrate into the land of spirits. But this he can do only with the help of the chorus, whose singing and hand-clapping set him in motion and lead him to a state of ecstasy. When the movement is in full swing, the relation between singer and song seems to be completely reversed, for the dancing soloist, who is the initiator of the melody, is now borne along by the song. The music is a vehicle, a ship or a road, transporting the mortal to another land. All movements become reflexes. While the dancer adorned with dangling rattles abandons himself to the mysterious powers of the rhythmic sounds, he senses that out of this game that he himself has created something is growing that is greater than he. He grows with the song and entwines himself about it until the moment when he identifies himself with it and becomes a human rattle. Then his soul ascends into the land of the spirits, while the chorus guard his body until the soul returns to it.

THE ORIGIN OF MUSIC

According to the old European theory, music begins at the point where clearly distinguishable intervals appear. In contrast, speech is regarded as a succession of variations of pitch. This distinction is not applicable to primitive music, however, or to non-European art music, because these involve the use of all the vocal resources, including whispering, speaking, humming, singing, and even yelling. In the same way, at some time or other any implement capable of producing a rhythm becomes a 'musical instrument' in the hands of a savage.

It is very difficult to say anything definite about the origin of music, because the phenomenon is quite outside the range of our observation. Even in those primitive civilizations that still exist there is no race so primitive that it can be considered a relic of the very beginning of human culture. Naturally there is no lack of theories about the origin of music. Charles Darwin attributed song to the imitation of animal cries in the mating season. Against this, it is to be noted that while it is true the imitation of animal cries plays a big part in the oldest civilizations known to us, love-songs are very rare and usually mythological rather than erotic in character. Rousseau, Herder, and Spencer[1] argued that speaking with a raised voice was the beginning of song; and a kind of 'speech song' or chant-like recitative is indeed to be found in many primitive cultures. Whether this style is derived from speech seems very doubtful, however, in view of the many nonsense syllables (without verbal significance) which form the 'text' of these songs. Wallaschek[2] stresses the importance of rhythm in the origin of music. Buecher[3] even traces its beginnings to occupational rhythms, overlooking the fact that occupational songs belong to a very late stage of cultural history.

According to Father W. Schmidt[4] and Carl Stumpf[5] music arose, like speech, from the need to give signals by sound. A loud cry led to lingering on a note of definite pitch. With this basic idea Stumpf linked his theory of consonance: if the cry was uttered simultaneously by men and women so that it sounded in two different pitches at once ditones resulted, preference being necessarily given to octaves, fifths and fourths owing to their high degree of blending. If such sounds were then sung successively, instead of together, an interval resulted and its progressive breaking up into smaller parts led to the formation of melody. In Stumpf's view, the real step towards the development of music was the breaking up of the original ditone into successive notes and the transposition of 'cry' notes and musical motives. This theory conflicts, however, with the fact that in many primitive cultures the motives are often made up of very small intervals and motive-transpositions usually occur at very close intervals.

Although we must reject the hypothesis that speech is protomorphic music, it is still possible to speculate whether the very ancient 'sound-languages' may not represent the common source of both speech and music. In these languages, which will be dealt with more fully later,[6] the meaning of a syllable depends on the pitch at which it is uttered. Thus such a language is itself musical. If it is sung, music merely gives a more *arioso* effect to the melodic speech-curves already determined by etymology; it merely strengthens the existing musical element. It is, of course, possible that the whole

[1] The theories of Darwin and Spencer, no longer tenable today, were first discussed in detail by Stumpf in 'Musikpsychologie in England', *Vierteljahrsschrift für Musikwissenschaft*, i (1885), pp. 261–349.

[2] *Primitive Music* (London, 1893).

[3] *Arbeit und Rhythmus* (Leipzig, 1924).

[4] 'Über Musik und Gesänge der Karesau-Papuas', *Kongressbericht der internationalen Musikgesellschaft* (Vienna, 1910).

[5] *Die Anfänge der Musik* (Leipzig, 1911).

[6] See infra, p. 32.

language is merely a sort of levelled-down music; but it is more likely that the sound-language is the older element from which developed both speech and song, speech striving towards free rhythm and music towards a more regulated one. The greatest difficulty in the way of this new theory is that at present we know too little about the languages of the so-called primitive cultures. It is true that various pygmy races display the elements of 'sound-languages' but so far only a small number of examples have been collected. For this reason my own researches have so far been confined to the African Ewe languages and to Chinese songs. Some songs of the pygmy Batswa, of the Congo, recently recorded by the Rev. Father Hulstaert and discussed by F. Tegethoff in a still unpublished Cologne dissertation, however, show such marked agreement of musical and speech sounds as to appear to support the theory of the common origin of music and speech.

It is idle to discuss the relative merits of these theories because the primitive material available exhibits features which support one as much as another. In the primitive cultures known to us speaking, shouting, imitation of animals, and the rhythms of movement all tend to musical forms whenever man feels the need of a more beautiful or more effective means of communicating his impressions or wishes. By so communicating them man frees himself from the impressions which accumulate in his inner consciousness. Even a simple shout—to a fellow human or to a higher being—expressing a desire for action, betokens a liberation. The way it is used in war shows, however, that it also serves to dispense strength. If the shout is followed by additional sounds which are not strictly necessary, the psychic relief is even greater; for by such growth the song not only releases but actually unfolds the emotion which has hitherto been confined or seeking expression.

In music there emerge very quickly hard-and-fast, conventional melodic forms which by reason of their indeterminate significance can easily become vehicles of the most varied subjective feelings; so the objective formula, generally recognized and accepted, combines quickly and easily with the subjective feelings of the singer. In this way music has a unifying effect in human society. Melody liberates and gives objective form to feelings that to begin with were amorphous, ultra-subjective, or exaggerated.

Singing allows innumerable repetitions of the same words, repetitions which, apart from magical utterances, seem meaningless or clumsy in ordinary speech; it also enables things to be said or hinted at which it would be difficult to express in sober speech. To the uninitiated the words of such songs are for the most part completely unintelligible; but the aboriginal knows exactly what the few, apparently quite disconnected words mean in association with a particular melody. In some way or other music throws a neutralizing veil over that which is individual and realistic, giving it the appearance of something objective and universally valid or typical, without prejudicing its subjective emotional value. It is easier to sing a love-song than to speak a declaration of love. A musical motive, which when performed in a certain way is regarded as a formula of scorn, seems more indirect than plainly spoken abuse. An idea set to music is more formal, more general, or more ambiguous than the same idea expressed in words alone because it is subject to a regular rhythm. In language something of the same kind occurs in the proverbs which, for the same reason, are so popular with primitive peoples.

Besides this spontaneous musical invention—of which sing-song, as an expression of the simple play-instinct, is another example—the imitation of natural sounds plays an important part. Admittedly Schaeffner, disinclined as he is to generalize, is perfectly correct in saying: 'Toute une fausse optique de l'art musical découle d'une idée abusive de l'imitation.'[1] When a savage beats a piece of wood it is a spontaneous act not necessarily originating in any intention of imitation, and although many songs and dances do imitate animal noises, it is unnecessary to trace particular forms, such as the dialogue or the alternation of solo and chorus, back to similar phenomena in the animal world, since human society arrives at such forms unaided. In any case there is no reason why animals should have 'invented' such forms more easily than human beings.

Nevertheless, the purely realistic (and also the approximately musical) imitation of natural sounds forms an important constituent of the music of the oldest primitive hunting and food-gathering peoples among whom totemism is an individual affair, that is, not yet the basis of society.

TOTEMISTIC MUSIC

To grasp the significance of totemistic cultures in the history of music it must be remembered that the totemistic conception of the world is anthropomorphic. The natural world is animated by a variety of good and evil spirits, more or less endowed with voices, whose continual interaction determines the course of the world. The sounds

[1] André Schaeffner, *Les Origines des instruments de musique* (Paris, 1936), p. 14.

of nature are the voices of the spirits who dwell in natural objects. All objects and living things in the world were created by the totem gods (the mythical ancestors of mankind), created, moreover, in such a way that every totem-god during his sojourn on earth called into being only *one* particular kind of object or creature, i.e. one definite totem, by means of songs and war-dances: the kangaroo-god, the kangaroo; the cloud-god, the cloud; the flute-god, the flute. In Australian mythology these mythical ancestors, having finished their work and taught men the rites and songs necessary for the maintenance of Creation, sank down exhausted in a cave, died, and became petrified or turned into bull-roarers. Their 'mystical' bodies survive in their totems but they left to man the actual care of maintaining things. In view of this fact men began to divide the task between them, in each tribe entrusting one person or group with the care of a particular totem and the worship of the corresponding god (or ancestor). As each object (each kind of stone, plant, animal, wind, musical instrument, &c.) represents a particular totem, in theory the totemistic order of society constitutes a complete reflection of the world. In practice, however, and possibly as a later development, the animal totem predominates.

The connexion with the totem or the mystic ancestor is established by the person concerned imitating the particular object which it is his duty to maintain, that is, his own totem. If the totem is a tiger or a snake, he must behave like a tiger or a snake and if need be even have direct intercourse with one of the creatures. For example, if the tiger-man has a drum he must not play it in the usual way, but must bite and scratch it as would his totem animal. If, to take another example, he has been assigned to the wind or storm, he will fulfil his task by means of a corresponding pantomime, like influencing like. But the essential part of the imitation is the simulating of sounds, for of all the available means of imitation the human voice is far and away the best. The form and movements of the human body can be brought to resemble the outward appearance of the totem only to a limited degree with the aid of dancing, masks, and other adornments. The voice, on the other hand, can imitate so well as really to deceive. One must have heard them to realize how extremely realistically aboriginals are able to imitate animal noises and the sounds of nature. They even hold 'nature concerts' in which each singer imitates a particular sound (waves, wind, groaning trees, cries of frightened animals), 'concerts' of surprising magnificence and beauty.

In totemism the voice has much the same significance as, on a smaller scale, numbers had for the Pythagoreans. It is a mysterious bond uniting all things in the universe. If a man is capable of reproducing exactly the croaking of the frog or the hissing of the snake, it is because his mystic ancestor was the totem-god of the frog or the snake. When he imitates the voice of his totem with the greatest realism, he imagines he is obliterating the boundary between subject and object and identifying himself with his totem. Whoever croaks like a frog, *is* a frog. By vocal assimilation he 'recognizes' the object and in that moment becomes the thing recognized. He becomes in fact a sound-symbol. This symbol, perhaps the oldest in the history of human culture, which presupposes no technical or material skill, is the voice of a dead ancestor, whose mystic body survives in the totem. The song represents the dwelling of the dead ancestor, or is itself the dead ancestor, who, together with all the other ancestors, forms the substance of the world.[1] Vocal imitation is the strongest form of mystic participation in the surrounding world.

Here we come upon one of the oldest forms of magic. By singing the name, or the song, the acoustic substance of the totem-god, or by playing his flute in the presence of the corresponding mask, one recognizes him and forces him to sound in the singer's breath, in the mask or in the flute, that is, to become substantially (acoustically) present. Just as one can make an open string vibrate by sounding its own note on another nearby instrument, so one can conjure up a spirit by providing it with its mystic station. Evidently the voice or the sound ranks as the ultimate indestructible substance of each object. This substance leaves the body of a man at death by escaping through his mouth in the form of the death-rattle, or through his nose as the sound of his breathing, and carries his soul away. 'You are blind but your ears are not deaf! Listen to me!' said a Bakango chieftain, rattle in hand, at the grave of a famous hunter. The idea of the acoustic nature of the soul, which survived into the Middle Ages in Europe (*symphonalis est anima,* said Hildegard von Bingen) and was taken up again by the German Romantics (notably by Friedrich Schlegel), is manifest among primitive peoples particularly in the belief that, even after the disappearance of the last mortal remains, the soul of a dead man (that is, the substance of the human being) survives as an essence (spirit) which is perceptible only in sound.

Every human being has his own sound or *is* a particular melody. To stop a magician (magicians are capable of imitating the otherwise inimitable) from imitating this melody and so getting its bearer

[1] See infra, p. 43.

into his power, primitive man thinks it necessary to keep his own melody as secret from sorcerers as his 'real' name.[1] (The intonation of the name is closely related to that of the melody.) Among the Gogodara each clan has its own death-songs which must be kept secret even from the other clans, because they contain the names of the ancestors. The assumption that sound forms the mystic substance of the human being explains the belief that two people having the same name represent merely the dual expression of the same individual.

This leads to the question of the widespread 'personal song' which is often identical with an individual's medicine-song or totem-song. It may be sung only by the person to whom it belongs. Only after its owner's death may a friend or relative venture to sing the dead person's song at the funeral. This song honours the deceased but it has real magic power only when sung by the 'song-father'. The melody of a personal song need not be an original composition but may well belong to the current repertory of the tribe. What makes the melody a personal song is the individual manner of performance. The term 'personal song' refers not to the melody as such but to something almost inimitable in the method of performance, the timbre of the voice, the particular rhythm the singer gives to the song. The concept of the 'personal sound' seems to lie still deeper. It is to some extent the primary substance out of which the 'personal song' is formed and it seems specially closely connected with the timbre of the voice.

As the substance of every being is revealed in rhythmic sound, it is obvious why the timbre of the voice plays such a crucial part in the individual totem system in deciding a man's mystic descent. Similarity of voice betokens a fundamental relationship. From this it follows that it is only at puberty, that is, when his voice breaks, that a young man is finally named, assigned to the totem, and introduced to his ritual duties. At this time, too, his real musical education begins; he learns the ritual songs and the use of the sacred musical instruments.

The idea of sound as the substance of things may derive from the daily experience of the primitive huntsman as he tries to get animals in his power by imitating their cries and by the use of magic words of terror. But here too, perhaps, age-old mystical traditions regarding the true essence of the natural world are at work. At any rate imitation among primitive peoples is a form of mystic participation which enables a man in everyday life to 'invoke' and entice a natural object

[1] i.e. the name which best reflects phonetically the essence of the human being. Primitive peoples usually give their children a great number of names. The name by which the child is normally called is unimportant.

and, by adapting himself to it, to subjugate it or assimilate it to himself—an end unattainable by force.

CULTURE AND RACE

To obtain a reasonably comprehensive picture of the various peoples and cultures of the world, ethnologists have adopted a classification of races according to the predominant forms of their economy and the state of their culture (which probably corresponds to these forms). They distinguish between primitive food-gathering, hunting, pastoral, and agricultural peoples, although there are many races which do not clearly belong to any one of these groups, either because they are culturally or economically in a state of transition, preserving many archaic elements from lower stages of civilization, or because they have been subject to cultural influences which (theoretically) do not correspond to their normal way of life. Thus totemism appears to belong to the early hunting stage, although there are strong traces of it in the middle farmers' cultures and a particular late form has developed among some cattle-breeding tribes.

The primitive food-gatherers include in particular the pygmies and pygmean races. Hunting, pastoral, and agricultural races are usually divided into lower, middle, and higher groups. The lower groups comprise the totemistic patriarchal hunters, the agricultural and matriarchal civilization based on two classes, and the patriarchal nomadic shepherds. A late stage of hunting civilization is found among former cultivators who have been forced out of their domiciles and have turned to hunting from necessity. The middle pastoral peoples develop cultures dependent on saddle-animals. The middle farmers use a more developed form of hoeing, while the late farmers use the plough and, like the shepherd-warrior group, show very many megalithic and even later influences from high cultures. This theoretical order, which is mainly due to the Vienna school,[1] may be represented by the so-called inverted pyramid of civilization:

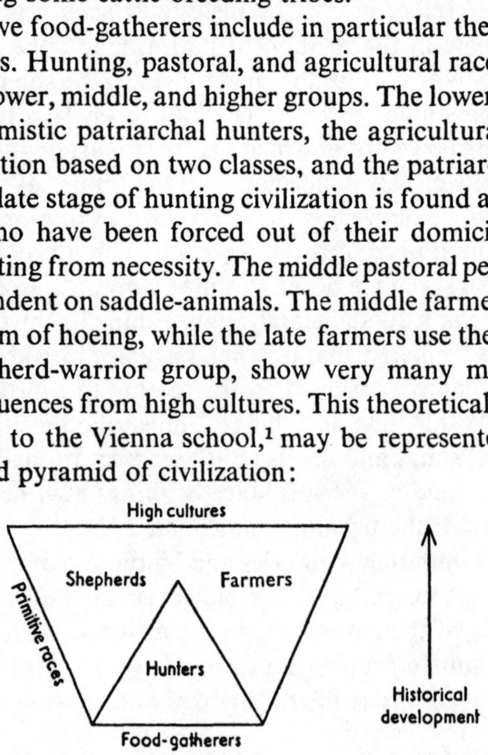

[1] The reader will find a concise summary in O. Menghin, *Geschichte der Steinzeit* (Vienna, 1931).

To this ethnographic classification there is a corresponding musical one. If one considers the material so far available[1] the three main groups (hunters, shepherds, and cultivators) may be distinguished, theoretically, as follows. Among the hunters, musical performance is interspersed with much shouting, is formed from free speech-rhythms, and has little tonal definition. Among the cultivators, however, an *arioso* style of performance prevails; the style is tonally regulated and the form is rounded off. The pastoral cultures occupy a middle position. With the hunters, metre is the strongest factor in determining form and is the expression of a very individual kind of music-making, while with the cultivators the collective note and the balance between metre and melody are more important.

This scheme which can be no more than a first attempt to organize the wealth of material, is naturally to be taken *cum grano salis*, since over each of these theoretical strata (based on the 'pure' cultures) are laid others which do not always agree with the first and may even be of quite a different nature, in fact with no cultural connexions at all. Thus, for example, within the same culture, historically considered, the singing of the woman is naturally more *cantabile* than that of the man. Very often we find coexistent modern, archaic, and foreign styles reflecting the historical development. The hunting songs of farmers who have been formerly hunters are always more authentic than those sung on the hunting expeditions of farmers pure and simple. The true hunting song is rooted in the mystique of the hunt, whereas the late hunting song is merely for entertainment.

If one considers the predominant cultural role of the man in hunting and pastoral societies and that of the woman in agricultural societies the following scheme results:

Hunters———Shepherds———Cultivators

Man	Woman
Predominance of Metre	Predominance of Melody
Polyphony	Harmony

The concepts of polyphony and harmony naturally apply only to the narrowly bounded regions in which part-singing occurs.

Racial characteristics in music are easily detected when one actually hears a singer, but they cannot be described in words. Race shows itself by timbre, by the general rhythm of movement, and by types of melody, in so far as these exhibit particularly individual forms.[2] Deliberate screaming or abrupt transition from high falsetto

[1] To which the present writer would add his unpublished transcriptions from the Phonogramm-Archiv of the Berlin Museum für Völkerkunde. [2] See infra, p. 24.

to chest and abdominal voices do not enter the category of racial characteristics, however, because they represent ideals of performance belonging to specific cultures and are acquired by conscious effort.

THE FORMATION OF SCALES

Up to now the question of the formation of a tonal system[1] has been answered, notably by Hornbostel and Robert Lachmann,[2] by the assertion that a fixed scale was impossible without instruments giving clearly defined intervals. As such instrumental tunings are a product of late civilizations, a real tonal system could not be produced by primitive races. Strangely enough these two scholars, to whom comparative musicology owes such a great debt, hardly took any account of the fact that the very oldest instrumental tonal systems (which led Hornbostel to the 'blown fifths' theory[3] now refuted by Bukofzer and others) do not use the natural (pure) fifths, although in the vocal music of primitive peoples these intervals not only frequently determine the tonal framework of the individual motives but are everywhere found to have the greatest influence in the formation of scales. In fact tonal systems are formed without the help of instrumental tunings. They grow progressively in primitive vocal music out of fanfare-like formations or out of the elementary fourth and fifth relationships which are found above or below a melody of narrowly restricted range (Exs. 10, 14, 53, 61, 67, 68, 79, and 80).[4] These intervals are even all the clearer and more definite for being free from any influence of instrumental music. The natural tone-system is built up entirely of consonances, the only exception—especially in primitive and middle cultures—being those notes which are derived from the harmonic division of a consonant melodic interval. Where, however, rows of overtones (Ex. 63) or slightly flattened fifths or widened seconds are sung, we may take this as evidence of the direct influence of instrumental tunings (musical bow[5] or panpipes).[6] When the same song is performed simultaneously

[1] Marius Schneider, 'Ethnologische Musikforschung', in 2nd edition of Preuss and Trimborn, *Lehrbuch der Völkerkunde* (Stuttgart, 1956).

[2] *Musik des Orients*, ii, 1 (Breslau, 1929).

[3] According to this theory the oldest tone-systems arise from a succession of over-blown fifths, i.e. they are formed by slightly flattened fifths. See E. M. von Hornbostel, 'Musikalische Tonsysteme', in Geiger and Scheel's *Handbuch der Physik*, viii (Berlin, 1927); Manfred Bukofzer, 'Kann die Blasquintentheorie zur Erklärung exotischer Tonsysteme beitragen?', *Anthropos*, xxxii (1937), p. 241; Ll. S. Lloyd, 'Hornbostel's Theory of Blown Fifths' in *The Monthly Musical Record*, lxxvi (1946), pp. 3 and 35; J. Kunst, *Around von Hornbostel's Theory of the Cycle of Blown Fifths* (Amsterdam, 1948).

[4] The musical examples to this chapter are grouped on pp. 61–82.

[5] P. Kirby, 'The Musical Practices of the Bushmen', *Bantu Studies*, x (1936), p. 381.

[6] E. M. von Hornbostel, 'Die Musik auf den nordwestlichen Salomo Inseln', in R. Thurnwald, *Forschungen auf den Salomo Inseln* (Berlin, 1912).

or alternatively by voices and instruments, the melody proceeds in two different tunings. The instruments perform it in their own scale, the voices in theirs (built from natural fifths).

As songs with or without a definite tonal organization are often found side by side in the same culture, we must distinguish two kinds of primitive vocal music. The first, which is perhaps the older, is closely related to speech, to the realistic imitation of natural sounds, and to emotional outbursts of only slight musical form. It is manifest not only in recitative, tonally very free recitative (Exs. 5 and 6), but also in songs of abuse and laments. In religious songs it may even be traced well into the late cultures. These songs are by no means limited to a narrow compass; among the American Indians they even extend to an astonishing range (up to 2½ octaves), particularly when motives are freely transposed.

Nevertheless, even in these freely intoned songs there is a recognizable tendency to use a clearly defined fourth or fifth as the basic melodic formula and to group the other tonally indefinite notes more or less freely around it. If these formulae are transposed, at least one of the two basic notes is generally found to have a consonant relationship to the first exposition of the motive. In Exs. 18, 19, 22, and 25 this transposition and consonant relationship have a direct influence on the development of the tonal system for, although the motives are only small, and only their basic notes are tonally definite, yet by reason of the transposition of the basic intervals the whole song already displays in its broad outlines a succinct tonal order. Yet, in view of the fact that transpositions of the smallest motives are to be found in very early stages of cultural history at distances of a second or third (Exs. 17 and 20), neither the pentatonic scale consisting of seconds and thirds nor the form interspersed with semitones can be considered older than the six- or seven-degree scale.

With the extension of the consonant relations there emerges a tone-structure which may be traced back in the field of primitive music as a rule to a more or less large extract from the series of fifths (B flat) F, C, G, D, A, E, B (F sharp). The fact that the keys formed from the series of fifths are so much closer than most of the primitive instrumental tunings to our European musical sense can probably be explained only by supposing that the vocal tone-system has been evolved in a natural and specifically musical fashion, whereas in the tuning of instruments (which are an artificial product) quite different principles were applied—such as, for example, the breadth of the thumb as the standard for the space between flute-holes. It is true that there are frequent departures from the system of natural fifths but in many cases the significance of such notes may have been overestimated. It seems very doubtful whether the measurement of vocal pitches will ever lead to useful results, unless account is taken of the difference between what the singer intends and what he actually achieves. Measurements taken by the writer from a native of Uganda showed that a high note which seemed diatonically too low became quite pure in a second recording in which the song was pitched lower. Moreover, such departures are sometimes quite deliberate. For example, from the above-mentioned measurements it became clear that a note was intentionally taken too low in order to represent the 'weeping note'.

The essence of musical functions is probably best grasped by considering in the first place not the individual modes, but the whole system of relations of the fifths to one another and by regarding different 'keys' only as specific extracts from the series of fifths. In a melody the functional tension (which can, of course, be essentially increased or diminished by the metre) is intensified by increasing the relative distance of the individual notes within the series F, C, G, D, A, E, B. Moreover, the notes F, C, G, and D appear the strongest, probably because they are the most fundamental. (We are assuming that the corresponding melodies are all transposed to a pitch involving the least possible use of accidentals.) In fact it appears that the tonal relationships in the F or C mode are much less complex than in the G, D, A, or E mode. If we take for the primitive motive, in so far as it has a tonal character, F as the fundamental note and F–A or D–F as the germ cell, we find apart from the second above or below the tonic, the fourth below (Exs. 61 and 86) or the harmonically or diatonically divided fifth above (Exs. 80, 82, 83, and 84) as the main function. The augmented fourth above (tritone melodies: Exs. 85, 87, and 113) is probably a late phenomenon.[1] On the other hand, melodies in the C mode (Exs. 10, 13, 22, 26, 37, and 52), in addition to the tonic and its neighbours, stress particularly the fourth, that is the 'subdominant' F. Songs in the G mode (Exs. 15, 32, and 49) emphasize both the subdominant C and the double subdominant F. Songs in the D mode lay stress on G, C, and F (Exs. 19, 33, and 48). The A and E modes are even richer in relationships (Ex. 21). In other words, the number of functional relationships grows as the fundamental note of the mode advances from F through C and G to D, A or E, for these relationships seem to grow not out of the brilliance

[1] J. Kunst, *Music in Nias* (Leiden, 1939), p. 7; *Music in Flores* (Leiden, 1942), p. 35.

of the dominants but out of the dark depths of the subdominants F, C, G, and D. This is, naturally, not to say that in the last-named modes one cannot have a phrase of the greatest functional simplicity; but in these modes the functional *possibilities* are far greater than in the simple ones of F and C. The scales of all modes can also have seven degrees but the number of notes of real functional importance is limited in the F and C modes to a few notes, while the more highly developed modes (G, D, A, and E) include all the functions of the modes *preceding* them. This may be expressed in the following table in which the vertical lines represent the progressive increase in functions of subdominant origin:

f mode		c	d	[e]	⟨f⟩	[g]	a	(b)	$\underline{c}$	d	e	f		
c „	[b]	⟨c⟩	[d]	e	f	$\underline{g}$	a	b	⟨c⟩					
g „			d	e	[f]	⟨g⟩	[a]	b	c	$\underline{d}$	e	f	g	
d „		[c]	⟨d⟩	[e]	f	g	$\underline{a}$	b	c	⟨d⟩	e			
a „				e	f	[g]	⟨a⟩	[b]	c	d	$\underline{e}$	f	g	a
e „			[d]	⟨e⟩	[f]	g	a	$\underline{b}$	c	d	e			

⟨ ⟩ Tonic; || Subdominant; — Dominant; [ ] Note next to tonic

This theory, put forward by the writer in 1934,[1] is confirmed in vocal polyphony in which the tonal relations sketched above—according to mode—are apparent in the selection and nature of the concords.

STRUCTURE OF THE MELODIC AMBIT

The tonal functions discussed above are expressed within a given ambit. The number of patterns which determine the main outlines of a composition is very great and it would be a hopeless undertaking to attempt to enumerate and describe them all here. We will therefore confine ourselves to mentioning the normal patterns which have been most important in the historical development of music. In considering the structure of the ambit we shall take the motive or theme as the given point from which the development of the ambit proceeds. It must be admitted that the separation of the theme from its continuation is in many cases very problematical, but the mass of available musical material enables us to discern definite norms. Apart from this, the musical structure can often be determined from the words. Owing to lack of space, however, it is possible to include the words in the musical examples only in the most important cases.

[1] M. Schneider, *Geschichte der Mehrstimmigkeit*, i (Berlin, 1934).

The main principle in the continuation of a given theme consists of varied repetition. In this repetition many melodies remain persistently within the tonal ambit given by the motive in the first place. This applies not only to narrow two- or three-note melodies but also to more broadly constructed ones (Exs. 1, 2, 3, 7–9, 75–84, and 87–93).

There is a very common tendency gradually to diminish the compass with which a melody has begun. Some songs consist merely of a short introductory motive whose final notes are repeated at such lengths that they represent the greatest part of the piece (Exs. 10 and 14). With themes of wider range one would be inclined to attribute the progressive lowering of the top notes to fatigue. But it occurs just as much with quite short motives of limited compass as with longer songs (Exs. 11–13, 15, 16, 52, 72–74). Often at the end only the rhythm of the theme, instead of the melodic line, is repeated in the cadence notes (Ex. 21). In Ex. 71 the first note of bars 2, 4, and 6 is lowered each time.

An essential part in the determination of ambit is played by the attack of the first note and by the form of cadence. Sometimes a song is introduced by a long high note giving the effect of a shout (Ex. 86). Very often the singer's voice is heard sliding down glissando-fashion from a high note, musically almost indefinable, to the first tonally defined note of his song (Ex. 4). On the other hand, the end of a song may also consist of a loud cry (Ex. 12) or a short high motive. An upward swing is rare at the beginning of songs of narrow compass, but quite common when the motive is based on a fourth or fifth, although it is much commoner in later cultures than in early (Exs. 45, 49, 51, 58, and 66).

Simple transpositions of motive occur even in quite primitive cultures. They are often simple displacements of the tonal centre within the same melody (Ex. 27). The Australians, the Marind-anim of New Guinea, and the inhabitants of the Torres Straits use a model in which a short motive descends stepwise at each repetition. By this means the motives are joined to form a unified line (Ex. 17). Where the motives are longer or the transposition intervals wider, the repetitions are more clearly separated. At the same time, the motive can be repeated exactly or freely (Exs. 18 and 19), with smaller (Exs. 21 and 22) or wider (Exs. 25–26) intervals. If the motive is transposed only once, the 'two-zone song' results; this is found in its simplest form among the Copper Eskimos (Ex. 53). In the later development of this pattern, the repetition of the theme either merely follows the shape of the original statement or answers the exposition. The answer is often only metrically related to the theme, while the melodic line goes its own way. Instead of varied repetition, the theme is 'developed' (Ex. 108).

The tonal ambit can also be extended by giving more emphasis to the lower notes of the motive in the second exposition or by stretching the melodic material so that in the repetition the closing note is lower than it was in the original statement (Exs. 27–29, and 32). The extended form of the motive obtained by the lowering of the cadence (Ex. 30–48) can then be carried further by transposition (Exs. 31, 38, and 39). Often a progressive breaking away from the motive sets in, so that the last repetition may contain a completely new component phrase (Exs. 32, 35, 40, and 42). The arrangement of Exs. 30–51 shows the increasing intervals between the cadence notes.

In another pattern the voice, while repeating motives of narrow compass, takes a sudden upward or downward leap (Exs. 54–56). These newly acquired notes lead in some cultures to forms of yodelling (Exs. 62 and 134), in others they are linked with the melodic basis in a more continuous fashion (Exs. 57–60). Such patterns may in many cases have led to the songs constructed on the triad. That such forms can also originate independently, however, is shown by the occurrence of fanfare-melodies in cultures in which this pattern does not exist (Exs. 63–65). Here too we find transpositions (Ex. 66) and repetitions within diminished compass (Exs. 72–74). Exs. 67–70 also use motives in contrary movement which divide the song into two parts within the narrowest range. In general these patterns, like the 'triad' forms (Exs. 75–82), are not very favourable to a concentration of functions. In these structures based on thirds, fourths, or fifths there is a tendency to utilize the functions contained in the limits imposed by the motive only when the wide-leaping movement becomes somewhat more restricted. Exs. 75, 83, and 84 introduce the upper fifth by a stressed second above it. In fourth-motives the relation between the third and fourth is emphasized (Exs. 92 and 93). In fifth-motives the relation between fourth and fifth, or third and fourth, becomes structurally important (Exs. 88–91). This structural wealth within a constant compass seems to represent the highest development of these limited melodies.

Apart from the upward transpositions of motive and the rising curves at the beginning of the 'triad' forms, both comparatively rare, upward extension of compass is an historically late product (Exs. 95–97). In early cultures such upward extension is generally very small. But it increases when it is introduced by means of a new phrase, i.e. a new motive (Ex. 94). If this second phrase is followed by the repetition of the first we have the ternary form ABA. Rising melody is generally richer in functions than falling. Some patterns are arch-shaped (Exs. 98–102); others widen their compass by exceptionally wide leaps (Exs. 103–7).

The last phrase of a song often has a special significance in the structure. Besides the elastic repetition of the final notes or the transformation of the last exposition of the theme into a free phrase, a concentric condensation of the thematic substance is common (Exs. 36 and 37). Of particular importance is the cadence in form of an ostinato motive (Exs. 8, 15, 51, 65, 88, and 145–9), which, unlike the other sections, is not varied when the stanza is repeated, is often sung polyphonically, and sometimes slows up the tempo by a third (Exs. 65 and 147).

ORIGIN OF POLYPHONY

All these patterns which develop the compass by progressive variants lead to polyphonic forms when they occur *simultaneously* with the theme. Polyphony originates when two singers—consciously or not—perform the same theme in different forms (within a given pattern). In many cases the varying of the theme is paralleled by a variation of the words[1] (Ex. 147). Primitive melody does not grow out of harmony; harmony is rather the product of melodic variants. The attempt to trace the origin of vocal polyphony to chance observation of consonant intervals emitted by sounding objects must be rejected for three reasons. First, consonances occur in a perfectly natural way when the same melody is sung simultaneously by men and women or children. The frequent alternation of unison with octave, fifth and fourth, is due to the extent to which these intervals blend. It seems very doubtful whether an organic polyphony could develop from these forms, because its geographical distribution suggests that it cannot be any older than canon and the heterophonic variation (Ex. 110) which exhibits a great number of dissonant intervals. It would seem that strict parallel motion is devoid of all possibility of development. For this reason it is found quite unchanged in primitive and late cultures alike. Secondly, even if consonance were a necessary precondition for the creation of polyphony, its discovery could not have been due to musical instruments, since melodic instruments are historically far younger than vocal polyphony.

[1] M. Schneider, 'Gesänge aus Uganda', *Archiv für Musikforschung*, ii (1937), p. 185, ex. 29.

The distribution of polyphonic singing also shows that (apart from chance parallelism and the musically undeveloped drone) the 'chance discovery' of consonance must have been confined to the white and black races, while it is just in those regions where gongs originated—to whose simultaneous sounding the beginnings of harmony have often been traced—that no vocal polyphony exists. Thirdly, such an organic structure as canon could never have arisen from the chance observation of consonance; yet canon is one of the most primitive forms of polyphony. These things arose spontaneously and cannot be explained in a mechanical fashion. Canon, which develops from the idea of following and hunting, was still called *chasse* or *caccia* in medieval Europe. Song and bodily movement are so closely related among primitive peoples that it seems completely misguided to attempt to explain their spontaneous musical creation by speculative methods.

Ex. 110, belonging as it does to a very primitive cultural stratum, proves that the oldest polyphony occurs without the use of consonant intervals at all. This kind of polyphony exhibits a special development, springing from strong emphasis on the individual. Acoustically it aims rather at the fusion of noises than at the pure concord of definite notes. In the concerted imitation of natural sounds (see p. 9) each singer adopts the voice of his own totem quite independently of the other performers, yet the total impression is entirely pleasing to the ear and just as 'harmonious' as when we hear simultaneously the song of birds, the buzz of insects, and the rippling of a stream. Atonal polyphony achieves a special form in concerted instrumental music.

Canon is one of the oldest patterns of vocal polyphony. Among the Kenta (pygmies of the Malay Peninsula, cf. Ex. 112) the imitation is usually very strict. The same applies to their neighbours, the Sakai. The African pygmies and bushmen use a more or less free imitation (Exs. 111 and 114). On the island of Flores, where many remnants of ancient Papuan tribes survive, the canon is sometimes worked out over a third free part or over a drone (Ex. 113)—the *pes* of the canonic forms of medieval Europe. In contrast with the small intervals before the imitative entries in these examples, among the Badiki of the primeval African forest (Ex. 115), in the head-hunting songs of the Naga (Ex. 117), in the Congo, in the Solomons and in Samoa (Ex. 116) we find forms in which the voices enter at longer distances.

If the theme is repeated simultaneously (instead of canonically) and strictly, parallel parts result (Exs. 118–20). Often two voices first proceed in unison until they separate through each placing a different functional interpretation on a certain note. The extremely wide geographical distribution of parallelism in fourths and fifths may go back to the ancient Negroid patriarchal (old Sudanese) cultures. Among the pygmy and hunting tribes and in the Solomons it is usually mixed with elements of descant (Exs. 124, 127, and 128–30). Parallelism asserts itself throughout history with the utmost tenacity and we still find it in the Caucasus and in Europe (Exs. 121, 122, and 127). It may be doubted whether parallelism in thirds is really so recent as is generally supposed, since it occurs in the middle cultures (Exs. 126 and 133). Parallelism in seconds possibly represents the debased product of a highly developed culture[1] (Ex. 125). The alternation of fourths and thirds (Exs. 131–3) is extraordinarily widespread, as is also parallelism within tonal limits, i.e. a vocal parallelism interrupted at the points where its bitonal implication would disturb the unity of the phrase by introducing notes foreign to the tonal system. The harmonic system which has developed particularly strongly in Africa is closely connected with the development of the tonal system. The new notes which are added by polyphony to the *canto fermo* represent functional variants of the melodic notes within the given key; and just as every mode contains in itself the melodic functions of the preceding 'key' (see p. 17), so also every 'key' comprises the harmonic possibilities of the preceding scale.[2]

Intervals *f mode.* Notes				(2)4(56) c	34(57) d	(e)	235 [f]	234(5) g	34 a		c
c mode.	(2)4(56) g	34(57) a	(b)	235 [c]	234(5) d	34 e	235 f	g			
g mode.	235 (g)	234(5) a	34 b	235 c	(2)4(56) d	34(57) e	235 f	235 [g]	234 a	b	c
d mode.		(2)4(56) a	34 (b)	235 c	235 [d]	2345 e	235 f	4 g	234 a		

If the simultaneous repetition of the melody is varied by contrary motion, a kind of descant appears (Exs. 134 and 135) which gradually develops into higher forms (Exs. 136–9). According to whether the linear or the harmonic element is predominant, polyphonic or chordal forms arise. In the Caucasus a choir is often contrasted with a solo yodeller. Broad series of triads are found in Indo-China, in the Caucasus, and in Europe (Exs. 140–3). In the primitive and middle cultures the endings of the songs often show a striking consistency, while the other sections vary greatly in each verse. These closes—

[1] M. Schneider, *El origen musical de los animales simbolos* (Barcelona, 1946), p. 239.

[2] The bracketed intervals are found less often.

ostinato-like in effect—are very often accompanied by the choir (Exs. 144, 145, and 148) or left to it entirely. If this ostinato overlaps with the solo voices a special form of polyphony results, as seen in Ex. 146. A further development, suggesting a primitive form of chaconne, is shown in Exs. 150–2 which are taken from the shepherds of Ruanda, the Ossetes of the Caucasus, and from medieval polyphony (Còdex de Las Huelgas).[1]

The very ancient drone form (Exs. 153–9) is as persistent as parallel harmony but with greater possibilities of development. To this too, an element of descant is very soon added. The long note held by the choir (Exs. 160 and 161), as well as the short, repeated motive, appears also in instrumental music (Ex. 162). The drone of the bagpipe, however, belongs to the higher civilizations.

VARIATION AND TYPES OF MELODY

The patterns described above appear in different forms according to the musical energies which pervade them. These different aspects must now be described in greater detail from the point of view of variation and types of melody. The term 'variation' will be used to cover all methods of continuing a given theme, although in later cultures a kind of thematic development is already found alongside the original variation form. By using the term 'variation' in this wider sense we shall absolve ourselves from a hopeless attempt to establish the extremely fluid boundary beyond which a given phrase can no longer be regarded as a mere variant (a^1) of a theme (*a*) but must be interpreted as a new phrase (*b*). It is particularly difficult to define this boundary in primitive music because the purely rhythmic element is so much more important than the *specifically* melodic. What is really repeated or developed in the continuation is the rhythm of the motive. In early and middle cultures the simple repetition of the metrical pattern takes second place and that of the melodic line third. Therefore in analysing primitive melodies the varied repetition (a^1) of the motive (*a*) must be interpreted more freely than in many songs found in highly developed cultures. A motive, the rhythm or melodic line of which is considerably modified in the repetition, must not be interpreted too hastily as a really new phrase (*b*) since the essence of continuation in primitive music consists in variation and in *progressive* breaking away from the given motive rather than in the thematic contrast of the phrases.

[1] The examples are published in full in M. Schneider, 'A propósito del influjo árabe', *Anuario musical del Instituto Español de Musicología*, i (1946), exs. 61 and 61*a*.

The melodic type is determined by the dynamic expressed in the subject and its continuation. The variation reinforces and develops in the continuation the thought presented by the theme; how this is done depends on the particular type of melody. Although some types of melody are very closely connected with certain forms of movement (time) or patterns (space) (Exs. 46 and 47), the metrical or linear aspects of a theme do not determine the type of melody to which it belongs, nor does the ambit. The typological affinity of two melodies often becomes *more apparent* only when similar metrical patterns and melodic curves join the same dynamic (Exs. 99 and 100). But the type is revealed above all in performance and in the particular way in which metre and melodic line coalesce in the rhythm. On paper it can be grasped only incompletely, but the ear detects it immediately. The same melodic idea, appearing simultaneously in the music of two different peoples, can be used by each of them in a different type (Exs. 148 and 149).[1] On the other hand, the same type may appear in two different melodies although the actual notes may have little in common. Just as, for example, pastorales, gigues, or spiritually kindred human beings emit the same kind of atmosphere, so typological affinity between different melodies is based on a common atmosphere which cannot be defined by the actual notes or by weight or measurement, but which any musician should be able to recognize.

The subject broached here offers one of the most important fields for future research in comparative musicology. Hitherto, melodic types have been defined according to 'the most obvious characteristics of the particular melody' (Hornbostel). The criteria employed have included that of compass ('narrow' melodies, melodies in fourths, 'triad' forms) or spatial concepts (steplike melodies, terraced melodies, leaping melodies). But these designations cover only part of what is understood by the whole complex of a melodic type. Thus Hornbostel by 'narrow melody' (*enge Melodik*) really meant only the narrowest *primitive* melodies performed in a fairly free rhythm. 'Fanfare melody' means a particular style found among pygmies, but it does not include by any means every kind of fanfare-like song. With a few exceptions (for example, in tritone melodies) interval-structure is a bad criterion for determining melodic type, because it is too general. In the present description of primitive music the concept of space has therefore been excluded in defining types of melody.

[1] A few years after the publication of the essay on 'Wandernde Melodien' in *Archiv für Musikforschung*, iii (1938), p. 363, the author played the melody of Ex. 148 to a Ewe man on the gramophone. As soon as the Negro heard the song, he claimed to know it very well and sang Ex. 149.

Since metrical pattern is equally inadequate as a criterion, all we can do in the present stage of research is to collate melodies which appear to be related dynamically in some way or other[1] and to abstain from a specific terminology. It might be useful, however, to revert to the Indian conception of *râgas*,[2] according to which a type of melody is defined not by technical criteria but by its locality and definite poetic mood-content. The criteria proposed by Dincser[3] for the classification of variants:

Isomelodic—isorhythmic—isochronic—isometrical—or
heteromelodic—heterorhythmic—heterochronic—heterometrical

exclude any such fusion of musical and extra-musical elements. This attempt to establish a uniform terminology and an exhaustive classification of types of melody is to be welcomed. But the classification suggested is too formal: it separates things that essentially belong together. And its categories are too rudimentary for serious research. They cover only the external characteristics and omit the most important aspect of all: the dynamic nature, in other words, the quality of the melody.

Since acoustic feeling has no terminology of its own but has to borrow concepts usually applied to the other senses (we have to speak of sounds as being light or dark, hard or soft) this terminology is bound to encroach on non-musical fields. Taking *fellah* songs as an example, I have shown[4] how in different melodic expressions of the same basic type the intensity may fluctuate or remain constant, how some variants may have strong or weak tonal relief, and how some parts may be constant in all versions and others continually varied; this was an attempt to work out the various forms of expression of a qualitative (dynamic) kind that are possible within a given type of melody, bearing in mind, however, that the growth of a melody is absolutely biological. It is only from such criteria that we can infer the nature of the type by which the variants are determined. By adopting this kind of terminology one is not escaping into a 'foreign range of ideas inapplicable to music' but merely accepting a makeshift which it is impossible to do without unless one is prepared to rest content with purely external, quantitative (and therefore, from a

[1] Cf. W. Wiora, 'Alpenländische Liedweisen der Frühzeit' in *Festschrift für John Meier* (Lahr, 1949); and M. Schneider, 'Lieder ägyptischer Bauern', in *Festschrift für Kodály* (Budapest, 1942) and 'A propósito del influjo árabe' and 'La canción de cuna' in *Anuario musical*, i (1946) and iii (1948).

[2] See Chap. IV.

[3] O. Dincser, *Die Probleme der Varianten in der Volksmusikforschung* (Geneva, 1947).

[4] M. Schneider, 'Lieder ägyptischer Bauern', in *Festschrift für Kodály*.

typological standpoint, secondary) criteria of form. The term 'iso-melodic' which Dincser suggests using for two similar (typologically identical) melodies, the notes of which are different,[1] is misleading since it ignores the most important thing of all: the existence of characteristic turns of phrase (variants) which are different in two songs although they belong to the same type. The great difficulty in all typology is establishing the dividing-line beyond which the variant of a melody deviates qualitatively so forcibly from the model that it can no longer be assigned to the same type.

Although the all-important acoustic impression cannot be reproduced here, an attempt must be made to show by a few obvious examples how the various types fashion the theme and its continuation in their own particular way. (If in the following lines examples of similar compass are grouped together, despite earlier insistence that compass is inessential, this is done in order to show the great differences that can exist within the same model.) Even in the most primitive cultures two basic forms of melody are to be found. The one proceeds from a clearly defined melodic idea which it varies in the course of the song. In the second form it is impossible to separate the primary idea from the variation since the entire song does not proceed from an idea clearly expounded at the beginning but expresses in constantly changing forms an idea that is never absolutely stable (Ex. 92). If the idea is clearly and concisely formulated at all, this formulation often occurs only during, or at the end of, the song.

The more primitive the models, the less differentiated they will be in type and in the working out of the musical idea. Songs such as Exs. 1, 2, and 27 occur very frequently in early cultures. In rather more developed cultures they often take on a definite metrical form (Exs. 3, 9, and 28), but both styles persist side by side right into advanced cultures. The same is true of purely recitative 'songs' (Exs. 5 and 6).

If one studies how different principles of continuation are applied in the various models, one often finds only a slight typological relationship between melodies based on the same model. In the examples where the compass is abbreviated (Exs. 10–16 and 72–74) only Exs. 13 and 14 or 72 and 73 seem to be related typologically. The songs of which the compass is formed by transposition or lowering the cadence (Exs. 17–52) fall into various groups. There seems to be a dynamic relationship between Exs. 17, 18, and 21; 30 and 31; 19, 32, 33, and (to some extent) 107. On the other hand Exs. 50 and

[1] Dincser, op. cit., p. 85.

51 differ completely in their rhythmic patterns although they follow the same model so far as compass is concerned. Exs. 20, 34, and 58 are closely related although the last belongs to a different model. Exs. 25, 26, 39, 40, and 47 also belong to each other so far as type is concerned. Ex. 40 which, in pattern, is very much like Ex. 39, nevertheless belongs to the same type as Ex. 41. Exs. 23, 42, and 65 (which last belongs to another ambit-group) form a separate dynamic group of their own. Despite the very similar melodic outlines, Exs. 81 and 82, and 83 and 84, are not related dynamically. On the other hand, there is a typological relationship between Exs. 78 and 79; 80 and 81; 59 and 88; 56 and 68; 69 and 70; 72 and 73. Despite the similarity of the models on which Exs. 54, 55, 57, 59, and 60 are based, only the first two seem to show some typological affinity. The dynamic relationships are closer in the extended melodies of Exs. 92 and 93, 99 and 100, 103 and 104, 105 and 106.

It seems as if the more intensely specialized melodic types are bound up with certain racial factors; otherwise it is difficult to explain the coincidence of identical types found in America and Asia, Europe or Australia, the relationships between Bushmen and Lapps or the similarity between songs found in Indo-China and India proper, Pamir, Afghanistan, and Central Asia and songs from Europe and the Caucasus. It is difficult to accept the theory of cultural exchange as an explanation, since the geographical distribution of these songs coincides more with areas of similar race than with those of similar culture. In fact, the innermost essence of the more intensely specialized types of song cannot be transmitted at all, that is to say, cannot be imitated, since the dynamic and the vocal timbre which is inseparably bound up with it cannot be acquired by learning. However note-perfectly a European may sing a Bedouin song, he will still be unable to reproduce the essence of the type since the notation merely represents the *last* and external result of the type. The European will inevitably reproduce the song in one of the types with which he is familiar. How deeply the type is rooted in men's constitution can be seen by the fact that even within the confines of the Iberian Peninsula a Spaniard from the north is incapable of singing correctly the highly specialized *cante jondo* of Andalusia. Admittedly there are particularly gifted *individuals* of great adaptability who succeed, after year-long contact with a foreign musical culture, in acquiring its songs to a high degree. But the expert will never mistake such an outsider for a native singer.

The virtuosity of a few foreign individuals exerts only a very small influence on folk-music. Melodic types migrate only when the people themselves migrate. It is certainly a great error to imagine that, wherever some foreign utensil or cultural object has been introduced, the corresponding music must inevitably have been adopted as well. Songs do not travel as easily as carpets, vases, or ornaments, because they are bound up much more intensely with the 'owner'.

The composition of a primitive song is also closely connected with the melodic type. There is no doubt that a song proceeds from a particular individual. Nevertheless almost every primitive composition is still in some way a collective work, since the folk-musician composes very much in accordance with definite moulds. In Exs. 92 and 93 it is the fourth and the strongly accented leading note, in Exs. 46 and 47 the metre which provides the model. The writer once observed three Duala Negroes composing a song together. One of them invented a short motive and also the words: 'The stranger has invited us to drink.' To begin with, the motive had a fixed metre but little melodic shape. Then all three sang the motive, each in a somewhat different melodic shape, and very gradually, after endless repetitions, a quite charming motive emerged. The three following phrases were then quickly added, since they merely varied the motive. When the song was finished it represented no more than a fresh melodic expression of a familiar metrical formula. In his book on the Andaman Islanders, A. R. Brown writes: 'A man composes his song as he cuts a canoe or a bow or as he paddles a canoe, singing it over softly to himself, until he is satisfied with it.'[1]

HISTORICAL DEVELOPMENT

It is very difficult to discern a historical process at work in any given primitive race; at best one can do so only for a comparatively short period. A song considered 'as old as the world' often turns out to be no more than two generations old. If the whole range of primitive music is studied in the context of the early cultural development of mankind, however, the results are more promising. In any given people there is hardly ever a straightforward process of development, with primitive forms being displaced by higher ones. In the 'pyramid of civilization' the various elements are superimposed on one another rather than progressively displaced. Admittedly, a particular stratum can become completely forgotten but normally what happens is that as the variety of musical forms and styles increases each layer is allotted a certain place where it can continue to thrive. In the middle

[1] A. R. Brown, *The Andaman Islanders* (London, 1933), p. 132.

cultures where the new forms are usually secular songs, the old songs pass into the religious field or become children's or women's songs.

Native elements and those borrowed from other cultures often exist side by side within one tribe. Nevertheless, foreign forms are not adopted so much as is generally supposed. Even when two races of different culture are in constant economic or military contact there is little evidence that they adopt each other's musical forms. It is true that a tribe that is stronger economically or militarily often uses musicians from subject tribes for its festivities (for example, the pastoral tribes of Ruanda make use of pygmies), but the degree of reciprocal influence appears to be relatively small. Even when foreign musical instruments are adopted, the relevant literature seems to be taken over only to a small extent or in mutilated form.

If the whole complex of primitive music is surveyed, a number of historical characteristics can be discerned according to the degree of cultural development. Most of the ambit-patterns appear in early cultures but their application is at first limited, gradually developing later. The dynamic element which gives life to the pattern determines the type of melody and thereby the special historical and geographical development of the elementary model. Thus, according to the culture in which it occurs, a pattern which circles round a central note may become a recitative which is interrupted now by a high note, now by a low one (Exs. 53–55), or it may develop into a gently oscillating song (Exs. 59, 60, and 88). In the evolution of the more highly specialized types, certain patterns will be highly developed while others will fall into the background. Thus the 'transposition' pattern is far more significant in Australia and America than in Africa. Among the Red Indians double or triple transposition is one of the commonest methods of continuation, while the Negroes (in so far as they use the method at all) usually content themselves with a single transposition (Ex. 22). On the other hand, they use not only successive but simultaneous transposition, producing polyphony (Exs. 119 and 120). Where the patterns are realized in a primitive fashion, the European generally finds them easy to understand since they reflect rudimentary musical thought. On the other hand, where they are used within a highly specialized type of melody, the idea that music is an internationally comprehensible language is exposed as an utter illusion; such melodies can be approached only by way of careful analysis.

The absolutely unlimited wealth of rhythm revealed in the songs of primitive cultures is very striking. In later cultures, however, there is a strong tendency to organize the rhythm by devising definite metrical schemes. Fixed metrical formulas become to a certain extent moulds into which the melodic material is forced. These schemes can sometimes be so complicated and extensive (Exs. 51 and 101) that they appear to be free rhythms; but close observation of the repeated stanzas will show that the rhythmic patterns are in fact organized.

There is no evolutionary relationship between tonal and atonal music. Both forms occur very early side by side. It is true that atonal is gradually displaced by tonal music, but even in highly developed cultures it survives in recitative and in songs in praise of the dead or of animal gods.

In the phrase-construction the form *a a′ a″* predominates. To the modest extent that primitive music allows, the development to *ab*, *abc*, and *aba* forms is already found in early cultures. The form *ab* appears to develop quite as much from a phrase *a* with an epilogue in the form of a shout or ostinato, as from the progressive differentiation of the repetitions of the motive. Fundamentally all musical forms are present in embryo in primitive cultures. Evolution proceeds essentially by the extension of the application of the given principles. The original patterns are moulded in many different ways: the rhythms extend over longer phrases or become more regular, the melodic phrases are given a wider span. The bi-partite Exs. 69 and 70 show concisely what Ex. 108 exhibits over a wider area. The transposition of Exs. 17 and 18 appears in an extended form in the numbers that follow. The progressive condensation of the series of functional parts is particularly important. Primitive themes are mostly very even, functionally, since their melodic lines often persist in the same function for a long time or because the contrast between two functions is only rarely emphasized by a metrically distinguished place. Even the different positions in which the motive appears when transposed are not always able to break up the dead level of the series of functional parts. The close series of melodic functions is best developed in melodies in which the compass is medium and constant in range (Exs. 87–93), or in spacious ascending melodies (Exs. 96 and 97). In the songs of late cultures the individual phrase is usually longer, and divides itself into two sub-groups.

It is only very slowly that the short motive with its varied repetition is replaced by a real theme developing consistently in the course of the song and leading to a new phrase which can be called the complement or answer. It is true that a tendency towards this process appears very early on (Exs. 69, 70, and 94) but it is not really applied until comparatively late (Exs. 95–97 and 101).

Since some scholars have attempted to make a widening of the compass a criterion of historical progress it must be emphasized that wide and narrow compasses are found in almost all cultures. It must also be remembered that wide fanfare-like melodies and transposition are found in very early cultures. An attempt to classify the music of primitive races according to the concept of cultural cycles has been published by Werner Danckert.[1]

MUSIC AND SPEECH

There is no doubt that in the earliest cultures words and music are closely associated. The few reliable transcriptions of melodies and words available show that—except in purely syllabic songs—the smallest alteration in the words leads to a modification in the melody. In recitative and the mythological narratives, in which the melody often has a stronger curve, the relationship between music and words is different because the text predominates and the musical form is of secondary importance. A certain balance between music and words is sometimes attained by interpolating mystic syllables in the text, thus dividing the song into regular periods.

Often the text consists of merely a few words repeated over and over again, like the motive itself. In Ex. 13 the words 'The frog leaps' are constantly reiterated. Certain vowels or sonorous consonants sometimes take the place of actual words. A shout, or a few words expressing a wish, a surprise, a name or a short proverb, often constitute the entire text of a song. The result is that in primitive cultures the musical form is often more highly developed than that of the text. The whole emotional content of the text seems to be sustained entirely by the rhythm of the music. The broader the melodies and the words, the more the realistic expression of the words through song gives way to purely musical line-drawing and the close connexion between words and music is relaxed. Strophic forms or different words set to the same melodies are found particularly where the repetition of the melody is not very consistent. The Chippewa take the view that new words may not be set to old melodies unless the subject-matter is the same.[2]

Many of the texts are quite unintelligible to the uninitiated because they often presuppose the knowledge of some story, event or custom. When the Californian witch doctor says 'In Dalmona I dig up the earth and find nothing but rotten turnips', one has to know that

[1] *Anthropos*, xxxii (1937), p. 1.

[2] Frances Densmore, *Chippewa Music*, i (Bureau of American Ethnology Bulletin 45), (Washington, 1910), p. 2.

rottenness stands for disease and that in Dalmona the earth and the sick are both beaten with a digging stick.[1] Frances Densmore has published a song[2] sung by a grandmother to a child: 'Say to me *m m m* and that I belong to you.' Here the consonant *m* is a sign of love.

A very special relationship between music and speech occurs in the sound-languages[3] where the meaning of a word stem depends on the level and direction of the intonation in which it is spoken (for example, be = to hide oneself; bè = to speak; bé = to take out). My researches on Ewe texts,[4] Chinese songs and those of the African Batswa, have led me to the conclusion that there is certainly a direct correspondence between the high, medium, and low notes in speech and in music, though established rules may in many cases destroy it. Where there is a direct correspondence, the musical intervals move in the same direction as the speech intervals but differ in size. Normally the intervals are wider in song. Moreover, the tonal basis (from which the concepts 'high' and 'low' are derived) may be transposed in the course of the song (Ex. 43). An uninterrupted succession of high notes in speech will either keep to the same level in music or form a slowly ascending melodic line. In the case of low notes exactly the reverse applies. The most important rule is that notes that are high in speech can be low in music, if they coincide with a metrically emphasized point in the song. Similarly, low notes of speech can be high in music if they come on an unaccented beat in the song (Ex. 16).

INSTRUMENTAL 'LANGUAGE'

The 'language' spoken by flutes, drums, and horns also appears to be closely connected with sound-language. Herzog[5] gives the melody played on an African horn (Ex. 174) in which speech curves are reproduced. The Bubi of Fernando Po speak into a calabash on which they are able to reproduce five tones of their language.[6] The whistle language (on mouth pipes)[7] which Baumann regards as an

[1] J. d'Angulo and E. d'Harcourt, 'La Musique des Indiens de la Californie du Nord', in *Journal des Américanistes*, xxiii (1931), p. 203.

[2] F. Densmore, *Nootka and Qulleute Music* (Bureau of American Ethnology Bulletin 124) (Washington, 1939), pp. 277–8.

[3] G. Herzog, 'Speech Melody and Primitive Music', in *Musical Quarterly*, xx (1934), p. 452.

[4] M. Schneider, 'Phonetische u. metrische Korrelationen bei gesprochenen u. gesungenen Ewe Texten' in *Archiv für vergleichende Phonetik*, vii (1941 ?), and 'La relation entre la musique et le langage dans la chanson chinoise', *Anuario musical*, v (1950), p. 62.

[5] Op. cit., p. 455.

[6] G. Tessmann, *Die Bubi auf Fernando Po* (Darmstadt, 1923), p. 31.

[7] J. Beecham, *The Ashanti* (London, 1841), p. 168; Biblioteca Canaria, *El lenguaje*

element of hunting cultures[1] and the flute music which represents the beginning of programme music both reproduce speech rhythms and modulations in musical form. R. S. Rattray[2] has established that the difference in pitch between two skin-drums used for transmitting news corresponds to the high- and low-pitched vowels of ordinary speech. Eboué also considers that drum language is an exact imitation of speech rhythm[3] (Ex. 175). Heinitz has emphasized the significance of the reproduction of the 'dynamic profile' of the spoken phrase, and I myself have drawn attention to the differentiation of vowel-sounds and the connexion with the sound-laws which condition the relationship between speech and melody-function.[4] There are evidently also pure ideograms such as those of the Nor-Papuas published by Father J. G. Schmidt[5] (Ex. 176). It is probable that these speech forms originally represented some kind of secret language or language of respect. In any case it is significant that the African Twi and Ewe do not utter the praise-names of their gods in speech but only beat them on their drums.[6]

THE MUSICAL INSTRUMENTS (see plates 1 and 2)

The rhythmic articulation of time by means of an instrument of some kind is far older than the construction of a true musical instrument. Any object that primitive man happens to pick up when singing or dancing becomes a sound-producing 'musical instrument'. Implements used exclusively as musical instruments and for no other purpose develop only very slowly. Many instruments (for example, the pot-drum) are merely adaptations of already existing utensils.

As the instruments used by primitive man have already been investigated more thoroughly than his vocal music it will suffice to describe only the most important types. The ideas associated with

silbado en la Gomera; R. Ricard, *A propos du langage sifflé des Canaris* (Hesperis, 1932), p. 140.

[1] H. Baumann, 'Afrikanische Wild- und Buschgeister', in *Zeitschrift für Ethnologie*, lxx (1938), p. 226.

[2] R. S. Rattray, *The Ashanti* (Oxford, 1923), pp. 242–86.

[3] M. Eboué, *Les Peuples du Oubanghi-Chari* (Paris, 1933), pp. 80 and 94; H. Labouret, 'Le Langage tambouriné et sifflé', *Bulletin du comité d'études de l'Afrique occidentale française*, (1923), pp. 120–58.

[4] W. Heinitz, 'Probleme der afrikanischen Trommelsprache', *Beiträge zur Kolonialforschung*, lv (1942), p. 69; M. Schneider, 'Zur Trommelsprache der Duala', *Anthropos*, xlvii (1952), p. 235.

[5] J. G. Schmidt, 'Neue Beiträge zur Ethnologie der Nor-Papuas', *Anthropos*, xxviii (1933), p. 330.

[6] D. Westermann, 'So, der Gewittergott der Ewe', *Zeitschrift für Ethnologie*, lxx (1938), p. 154.

them will be dealt with later.[1] Curt Sachs's *History of Musical Instruments*[2] gives a classification on morphological lines, and the same author has described the cultural and geographical distribution and morphology of primitive instruments in greater detail in his *Geist und Werden der Musikinstrumente.*[3] In his *Origines des instruments de musique,*[4] Schaeffner has given a classification based on the materials used in their construction, while Montandon has preferred to classify them according to the method used in playing them.[5] Kirby's *The Musical Instruments of the Native Races of South Africa*[6] contains the richest collection of primitive instrumental music published so far.

Idiophones. The practice of beating the body with the hands or with some object appears to be transferred very early to the beating of horizontal tree-trunks and bamboos and to stamping on the ground. Jumping on or beating a springy plank ('dancing tree') or an animal skin laid across a hole in the ground is an early specialization of the process. If a tree-trunk is split open and hollowed out lengthwise like a canoe, the result is a slit-drum (often carved in the likeness of a man) which is played either with the feet or with two sticks. The ritual significance of the slit-drum will be discussed later. Its secular purpose is the transmission of news ('drum language'), and to obtain the necessary variations of pitch, the drum is beaten in different places or tongue-shaped strips of different thicknesses are detached from the side. In the course of evolution, instruments originally made 2 to 7 metres long are reduced to hand-drums and finally to wooden bells.[7]

Stamping on the ground leads to the construction of special 'stamping sticks', which are used to beat the ground during a dance, and thin bamboo tubes which are commonly used in pairs of different length, thus producing different notes. When struck against a sheet of water, they produce a loud and sombre sound. Another way of producing sounds is by scraping the rough parts of sticks, tubes, or receptacles against some suitable object; human and animal bones, bamboo reeds, and shells are used for preference.

Idiophones can not only be beaten or scraped; they can be shaken. Shaking has led to the construction of the extremely numerous types of rattle. To make the rhythm of the dance audible, various small, hard objects, such as sea-shells, bones, teeth, coconut-shells, are strung together and hung on the human body. Rattles are also made

[1] See p. 51.
[2] New York, 1940.
[3] Berlin, 1929.
[4] Paris, 1936.
[5] G. Montandon, *La Généalogie des instruments de musique* (Geneva, 1919).
[6] Oxford, 1934.
[7] Sachs, *Geist und Werden*, p. 47.

by filling the rinds of gourds, animal skins, or clay vessels with grains of corn, stones, or magic objects and fixing handles to them. The rattling objects may also be strung on a ring or enclosed in a hollow staff. Priests use rattle-staves of this kind as a token of authority and they are also used in dancing. In Indonesia staves filled with grain are used as seed-drills.[1] Small bells made from the bodies of animals or fruit rinds are closely akin to rattles. Only small types of metal bells are found in primitive cultures; they are often used in pairs connected by a ring.

Whereas plucking as a sound-producing method for idiophones has led only to the jews' harp and the African *zansa* (which consists of strips of wood or iron fastened to a board, keyboard fashion, and plucked), the evolution of percussion has resulted in the construction of a much greater range of instruments. These include two sticks beaten against each other, wooden bats, and bell-like objects struck against each other; cymbals were probably first adopted from more highly developed cultures. The earliest forms of xylophone are also found in primitive cultures. The prototype consists of two pieces of hard wood which the player, seated on the ground with legs extended and spread, places on the upper part of his thigh and beats with two clubs; later on, two banana stems are used instead of the thigh. Holes in the ground or gourds under the wooden bars act as resonators. The xylophone is used not only to accompany but also to play instrumental works in one or more parts (Exs. 164 and 169); it seems to be regarded as an all-purpose instrument, rather like the modern piano, for its literature includes many arrangements of songs and pieces for drums and flutes;[2] it is also used for programme music.[3] Of the other percussion instruments, only the lithophone is found in early cultures. The gong, which has been developed by higher cultures, represents an advanced element in the later farming cultures.

Membranophones. The oldest forms are produced by stretching a skin over a tube, coconut, gourd, or bowl. All the early types are struck by hand only. In comparatively early cultures we find a drum the narrow middle section of which is spanned by a handle. This one-skin drum, shaped like an hour-glass, perhaps originally looked like a funnel or mortar. The two-skin drum of this type was not developed until later. The skin stretched across a round, hexagonal, or oval wooden frame is often found in the hands of witch-doctors, hence the name '*shaman* drum'. The wooden hoop, which sometimes has

[1] Ibid., p. 121. [2] Kirby, op. cit., p. 56.
[3] S. Nadel, *Marimbamusik* (Vienna, 1931).

a handle, is criss-crossed by strings. The skin is struck with a beater, often made in the shape of a knife. Cask-like receptacles made of clay, covered by a skin stretched across with strings, are always beaten with the hands, whereas the bellied wooden drums, whose skins are nailed on, are played with sticks. They are usually fixed to a post or hung up on a cross-beam. Their side-handles and the fact that they are occasionally filled with rice, suggests that the instrument was originally used for a practical, not a musical purpose. In the case of the friction drum, the sound is produced either by a stick fixed on the skin, or by rubbing with damp fingers a string knotted through it. Drums usually reproduce the general rhythm of a song (Exs. 11, 12, and 21). But in many cases they have a tempo of their own (Exs. 50 and 150), or some formula completely independent of the song (Ex. 153).

The last membranophone to call for mention is the mirliton ('kazoo'). This is a fine membrane which vibrates in front of the mouth or at the open end of a pipe through which the player speaks, sings, or blows.

Chordophones. String instruments are very little developed in primitive cultures. Sachs derives the oldest form—the earth-zither—from a thinned-out wooden pole, beaten with a stick.[1] Actually the oldest type of earth-zither is a 4-metre long rattan reed stretched horizontally across the ground and joined in the middle with a membrane, which lies above a small hole in the ground; the player beats the string with two little sticks (Ex. 163). The earth-bow is a genuine hunting implement. Its string, which is plucked or struck, is fastened at one end to a springy stick or tree and at the other to a piece of bark over a hole in the ground. In the ordinary bow (Ex. 162) the two ends of a flexible stick are connected by a string which is sometimes cut directly from the outer surface of the stick. To intensify the extremely soft sound a gourd or earthen pot is usually attached or the string is held in the mouth. The string is plucked, struck, or scraped with a stick.

A 'reed zither' is made by taking a narrow strip from the surface of a halved bamboo reed to form a string, of which only the two ends remain connected with the reed. The tension of the string is maintained by some object placed underneath and it is struck with two little sticks. In a more highly developed form, strings from the reed itself are replaced by strings from other sources, stretched across a board or a bowl. Lyres, lutes, and harps do not appear until the late farming cultures and then very often in backward forms.

[1] Sachs, *Geist und Werden*, p. 60.

Aerophones. The bull-roarer consists of an oval or rectangular wooden board, the upper end of which is fastened to a cord. When the instrument is swung in a circle, it also revolves on its own axis and as the speed increases an extraordinary variety of noises is produced.

The most primitive flutes are made of bones and have up to four finger-holes. The mouth-hole in front or at the side is made by the insertion of a plug into the pipe. When two pipes are combined into a double flute, they are of different length. A flute in which the breath is sent not through a pipe but through a small convex vessel is very widely distributed; the player blows through a round unnotched hole. On the other hand, the round flutes made of clay, which are filled with water, are always notch flutes. The vertical flutes with notches can be divided into three types, according to whether the lower end is open or stopped or whether the stopped end has a hole through the middle. Curt Sachs conjectures that the stopped flutes, which are sometimes as long as 1½ metres, are the oldest.[1] The simple vertical flute with no special blowing appliance is historically later than the fipple and notch flutes. The transverse flute stopped at the lower end has some very archaic features. It may be as long as 6 metres and it has a maximum of three finger-holes. To make a double transverse flute, a mouth-hole is bored on both sides of the nodule of a bamboo reed. In many districts vertical, transverse, and vascular flutes are blown through the nose. The flute took a long time to develop into a really melodic instrument. Its primitive forms are scarcely capable of anything beyond signal-calls. The melody is also usually very indefinite in rhythm and somewhat irresolute (Exs. 170–3). Panpipes, on the other hand, exhibit far more definite musical forms. The reeds are sometimes arranged in a single more or less symmetrical row, sometimes they are tied in a bundle or in two rows (Exs. 166 and 168).

In the trumpet family the longish tuba made of wood or reed and the snail- or mussel-shells with a mouth-hole probably represent the oldest types. In the tuba the lips rest directly on the edge of the bore-hole; the player does not so much blow as shout into the pipe. The instrument may also be made from bottle-gourds instead of wood, or, like the alphorn, from a hollow branch of a tree wrapped in bark (Ex. 167). The animal horns which are played in Africa as transverse trumpets, are also very widely distributed (Ex. 174). The oldest clarinets have no finger-holes and are often quite long. The mouth-piece is usually inserted in a gourd or horn.

Singing is often accompanied by a rattle, a drum, a flute (Ex. 173),

[1] Ibid., p. 81.

panpipes, or xylophone. The combination of drum with conch, pipe, horn, flute, or clarinet may be considered 'classical'. Choirs are often formed of similar instruments. In the drum orchestra (normally four to six instruments) each drum has its own motive (Ex. 175), which usually takes the form of a comment on the idea propounded by the biggest drum. Kirby[1] gives the following South African example of the widely distributed panpipe orchestras: 1. Four to six small reeds, all tuned to the same pitch and played by one performer. 2. Three reeds (the same pitch, one performer). 3. Six reeds (the same pitch, one performer). 4. The player has one or two pipes in his hand. 5. This reed gives the pitch to all the other pipes. Its name means 'Weeping'. 6. A single pipe, whose name means 'weeping afterwards'. 7. A single pipe, meaning 'the cow'. 8. A single pipe. 9. The pipe with the lowest sound.

Ex. 168 gives a specimen of an orchestral hocket.

REPERTORY

Since primitive man sings much more spontaneously than civilized man, the repertory of primitive tribes is considerably more varied than that of art music. As it reflects the whole of life, most of it is 'occasional' or 'utility' music. Primitive man sings to call out, to play, to mock, to greet someone, to give thanks at the end of a meal. Many of the songs are improvised. Songs can even be sung before a judge; if two men quarrel or a couple want a divorce the contestants will plead alternately in words and more or less improvised songs. Whenever anything unusual happens—whether it be a boatman's oar falling into the water or a domestic animal running away—primitive man at once gives vent to his feelings in an improvised song.

He also sings at his work. When road-making, working in the fields, or rowing, however, the working man usually confines himself to the ostinato. Often a musician will keep the rhythm of the work going with a drum or oboe instead of song; he is not thought of as an idler but as an important helper. Most of the so-called working-songs are, however, intended for amusement; only a few show any direct connexion with the rhythm of labour. A special genre of working song has evolved among ploughmen, who address their horses or oxen in song.

In love charms the magic formulas are sung. The jocular love-song does not appear till very much later. Songs which celebrate the beauty of the loved one and are often accompanied on the flageolet (Exs. 104

[1] Op. cit., p. 138.

and 172) are closely connected in style with the songs of praise sung in honour of the tribal chieftain; both types often refer in their words to mythological events. But in the market-place even the small man gladly pays for a song of praise about himself, improvised by a musician in a voice loud enough for all who pass by to hear. Needless to say, all popular merrymakings are accompanied by music and dancing.

There is a very extensive repertory of children's songs, cradle songs, songs to accompany games, songs which describe dreams, and songs containing riddles or proverbs. All the rites relating to birth, circumcision, marriage, hunting, war, weather, medicine, and death are permeated with musical elements. Among the funeral songs, the women's laments and the songs which men sing in praise of the dead deserve special mention.

In primitive cultures it is very difficult to distinguish musically the various kinds of song since there is still so little differentiation of form. Often the type of voice used determines the character of a melody. Funeral songs and erotic songs are often sung in a nasal voice; love-songs are accompanied by a significant play of the lips. In more highly developed cultures formal differentiation is usually determined by the various layers of tradition. An archaic style survives in animal-songs and hunting-songs, and also in children's songs, funeral songs, epic songs, and in medicine and weather charms. Lamentations have a style appropriate to their own nature. In songs of praise the melodic line tends either to rise emphatically or to start very high.

It should be noted, however, that the 'literary' approach to song-classification is not altogether satisfactory. Not every song sung during a rain ceremony represents a true rain-song, since such ceremonies are very complex. They include introductory songs, mythological recitatives, interludes, sacrificial songs, and songs of praise, and only a small part of the ceremony is occupied by the song that is intended directly to influence the rain. In the same way, war-songs are not necessarily intended to incite the listeners to battle; they may also be protective songs or individual medicine songs. In any attempt to discover the stylistic qualities of particular types of song, the words must first be studied very carefully. The relation between the musical style and the content of the song (i.e. the words) lies not in the external occasion (rain, war) but in the prevailing psychological tension. If the witch doctor implores the spirit of disease to release his patient, the song will be friendly; if he fights it with his spear, the song will be warlike; yet both will be medicine songs.

THE IMPORTANCE OF THE MUSICIAN

The many-sided role which music plays in the life of primitive races explains the personal importance of the musician. No girl wants to marry a man unless he can play on the hunter's bow,[1] and any girl is particularly proud of her man if he has been victorious in a singing contest. That singer is most highly esteemed who can sing a proverb or saying at the right moment. The arrival of a musician often turns a whole village upside down, and his departure is often accompanied by scenes of lamentation, especially among the women. Scandals between visiting musicians and married women are also a common occurrence.

In spite of all that, good musicians often receive invitations from neighbouring tribes. It is also customary for the musicians to lead a village community when it pays an official call on a neighbouring community and the latter presents the singers and instrumentalists with gifts. The musicians are very often feared, for their song is dangerous. Even if a singer is punished or banished for a satirical song, the effect of the song cannot be checked. Many chieftains take singers into their personal service in order to confirm their authority with a repertory of songs of praise of themselves. Here we have the beginnings of music as a profession.

Songs often represent real capital. When the girls of the Little River Woman Society reach the age limit of 18 years and have to resign, they sell their 'Society songs' to their successors and receive a horse or a dress of buffalo-hide in return.[2]

The distinction between higher and lower musician appears to go back to the very beginnings of musical history. In the primitive community of the Andaman Islands everyone is allowed to compose his own songs but not everyone is authorized to recite the tribal legends.[3] Among the peoples of central Asia the narrator of the tribal myths is often also a *shaman*. The priest-musician endowed with medical knowledge, whose songs reach the world of the gods, has a distinct role in such communities. Mythological songs must not be paid for in money; in return for their own legends, the Uitotos ask for another sacred legend.[4] In the transition to more advanced cultures, musical specialization leads to the distribution of musicians among various

[1] Kirby, op. cit., p. 233.

[2] Densmore, *Mandan and Hidatsa Music* (Bureau of American Ethnology Bulletin 80) (Washington, 1923), p. 97.

[3] A. R. Brown, op. cit., p. 187.

[4] Theodor Preuss, *Religion und Mythologie der Uitoto*, i (Leipzig, 1921), p. 15.

classes of society. In the Sahel and the western Sudan,[1] society is divided into five castes: aristocrats, bondsmen, smiths, bards, and inferior musicians. The bards (*dialli*) are the custodians of lofty epic art and rank as great warriors. The inferior musicians, on the other hand, devote themselves to popular entertainment and their task in war is to goad on the mass of fighting men with their shouts and songs. Like the court jester of later times, the *dialli* are privileged to tell their masters things which others are forbidden to say, whereas the lower musicians are held in very low esteem. The musician represents the spiritual world. He is the 'blacksmith' of song and in West Africa he sometimes wears a costume not unlike that of a smith. In Togo the singer (who is quite distinct from the poet-composer) carries a horse-tail in each hand as a badge of authority. He is naked to the waist and his robe is fastened round the loins.[2]

In general the musician is highly esteemed while practising his art, because he is regarded as the possessor of a higher power. But he is also feared, or despised. He is honoured in public but avoided in private. That he is able to traffic with the world of spirits makes him a somewhat sinister figure, and the more intensely a community feels his power the more it tries to keep him at arm's length. Since it also needs him, it cannot banish him completely; so it acknowledges him secretly or openly, yet rejects him because it cannot forgive his superior powers.

SPIRITUAL CULTURE

So many writers have remarked on the astonishing unity of basic religious conceptions which underlies all the varied manifestations of primitive culture in so many different times and places that there is no need to emphasize it again here. Universal predispositions of spirit and the same fundamental observations have presumably resulted everywhere in similar conceptions; myths, symbols, and social organizations have been the clearest expression of these universal ideas. The progressive development of the physical and metaphysical conception of the world can be clearly traced from the earliest cultures right into the Megalithic Age, and the systematic symbolism of that age underlies the religious systems of the highly developed cultures. Some tentative efforts to combine the now disconnected remnants of these ancient conceptions into an organic whole have already been made.[3] An attempt must be made here to represent the specifically

[1] L. Frobenius, *Atlantis*, vi (Jena, 1921), p. 261.
[2] P. Witte, 'Lieder und Gesänge der Ewe-Neger', *Anthropos*, i (1906), pp. 66–67.
[3] Schneider, *El origen musical de los animales símbolos* and *La danza de espadas y la*

musical part of this ancient conception of the world, excluding as far as possible the contribution of the highly developed cultures, although it is very difficult to separate these latter elements since, on the one hand, the religious conceptions of the highly developed cultures include many primeval constituents and, on the other, many late elements have been assimilated by primitive cultures.

Music is the seat of secret forces or spirits which can be evoked by song in order to give man a power which is either higher than himself or which allows him to rediscover his deepest self. This is true of 'religious' and 'secular' music alike, for no distinction between the two kinds exists for primitive man, whose whole thinking is essentially religious or magical. When primitive man sings at his work, the music serves both to lighten his labour and to appease the spirit of the felled tree or the gods of the water he is crossing. It is only in later cultures that the working-song serves a purely practical end.

It has already been mentioned in connexion with totemistic ideas[1] that every being has its own sound or its own song, the timbre and rhythm of which embody the mystic substance of the owner. Just as the 'personal song', which develops the sound-substance of the bearer to magical power, is not the melody itself but the personal way in which it is sung, so here too the term 'sound' is to be understood not so much as a clearly defined note as a particular inflexion or characteristic tone-quality. This rhythmical sound is the clue to the nature and quality of an object. From merely hearing a voice we know whether it is the voice of a human being and we can even identify the particular human being and tell whether he is happy or sad, resolute or undecided, bold or reserved. If we strike a tree or a stone, the sound produced tells us not only the nature but also the condition of the tree or stone. We can also tell by merely hearing the blows of an axe how well it has made its mark.

The mystical sound-substance inherent in all things, manifesting itself now directly, now indirectly, exists everywhere, even beyond the range of the normal human ear. The fact that primitive man easily attributes non-acoustic impressions to acoustic sources (owing to the unity of his sense-perceptions, or to the priority of his sense of hearing?) substantially widens the field of the rhythmic sound-substances

tarantela (Barcelona, 1946 and 1948); 'Los cantos de lluvia', *Anuario musical*, iv (1949). Recent studies by the present writer after the completion of this section have strengthened the arguments here given. Cf. Schneider, 'Die Bedeutung der Stimme in den alten Kulturen', *Tribus* (*Jahrbuch des Linden Museums*) ii-iii (Stuttgart, 1953), *Singende Steine* (Kassel, 1955), and *La philosophie de la musique chez les peuples non européens* (Paris, 1956).

[1] See p. 8.

which can be grasped indirectly. This is particularly facilitated by his psychological disposition to observe dynamic phenomena more intensely and to rate them much higher than static ones. When the sombre sounds and violent rhythms of a tempest convert the waves of the sea or the bushes of the forest into the likeness of the trampling and the swaying backs of a herd of animals stampeding down a hillside, the Duala Negro feels that these three phenomena are dynamically related and is at once able to reduce them to a common acoustic denominator by a suitable drum-song. Where the same sounds or rhythms appear, there also analogous beings are at work.

In view of the inconstancy of the world of form, primitive man questions the reality of static (spatial) phenomena and believes that transient (temporal) dynamic rhythms are a better guide to the substance of things. Hence he calls the *same* animal or the *same* tree by *different* names (i.e. rhythmic sounds) according to its age, condition, colour, and so on. Even one and the same person represents entirely different beings according to whether he acts in anger or kindness, as friend or foe, or moves like a child or an old man. The primitive conception of nature has a psychological basis. To the primitive mind the phenomena here called 'rhythms' are spirits, the audible souls of the dead ancestors who created all things[1] and in which they constantly reincarnate themselves. They are the physical and metaphysical reality which is the source of all life and all magical song.

In contrast to stones and plants the rhythms and sounds of which are monorhythmic and therefore have only one meaning, man is distinguished by his polyrhythmic constitution. The animals come between these two groups. It is true that man too has his own unequivocal basic sound, corresponding to the resonator of his outward appearance, but since his resonating surface is not so limited as that of inanimate nature, he is not only able to produce the sound peculiar to his own nature but also to *imitate* non-human rhythms and sound-colours. In addition, he can imitate sounds artificially since he makes musical instruments. Thanks to all these abilities, man is able to develop enormous power; for anyone who knows and can imitate the specific sound of an object is also in possession of the energy with which the object is charged. The purpose of magic is to utilize this indwelling energy (*orenda*, *mana*, *sila*, *manitu*, *kami*, &c.) in some way. The words *orenda*, *mana*, and so on denote the power of the sound-substance which an object emits audibly or otherwise. *Orenda* is the growth or the special curative power of plants, the purifying

[1] See p. 9.

power of water, the dynamic power inherent in a song. It becomes a magic energy whenever it appears to any exceptional degree. The resourceful magician gifted with special vocal powers can control this energy because he can imitate the sound-substance of the *orenda*; for, although it is emitted by spirits or particularly outstanding human beings, the *orenda* is an impersonal force which can be communicated, especially by exhalation or by shooting, to other people or suitable objects, such as musical instruments, and then withdrawn again. It is not confined to its bearer.[1]

By sound-imitation the magician can therefore make himself master of the energies of growth, of purification or of music without himself being plant, water, or melody. His art consists first of all in localizing the object in sound[2] and then co-ordinating himself with it by trying to hit the right note, that is, the note peculiar to the object concerned. He may attempt to do this by way of a rhythm in the cadence of its original murmur, by briefly shaking a rattle or by singing a short musical motive, thereby relating himself to the object or spirit by sympathetic vibration. If the contact between subject and object has led, by such musical analogy, to a mystic fusion of both parts, the sound or the motive will gradually develop into a song. Through the correct intonation, the spirit is held captive in the magicians' body and sings through his mouth. But it is the song which the magician makes from the sound-substance of the spirit and the corresponding visible rites that determine the dynamic and the course of action which the magician attempts to force on the spirit. The spirit can be localized and allured by its own personal sound but it can only be captured, appeased, or overwhelmed by the song developed from its sound-substance. Admittedly, the visible rites may include analogical actions, such as the representation of the spirit by a mask, but their essential purpose is to act on the spirit which the sound-analogy has evoked. This activity may be expressed by the brandishing of a magic spear or sword, but it may also be limited to the words which envelop the sound-substance.

To understand this action of imposing the will on a spirit, it has to be remembered that for primitive man the world consists of an interaction of spirits which think and act like human beings. The spirits are conceived as fabulous beings (often in the shape of animals) dwelling in rain-clouds, springs, crevices, dark caverns, under heavy

[1] R. H. Codrington, *The Melanesians*, vii (Oxford 1891), p. 119; J. N. B. Hewitt, 'Orenda', *American Anthropology*, iv (1902), p. 33.

[2] On localization in rain-ceremonies see Densmore, *Papago Music* (Bureau of American Ethnology Bulletin 90) (Washington, 1929), pp. 154–5.

stones, in old trees, or in bamboo reeds. As a particular spirit is responsible for every disease and a particular healing-song exists to cure every disease,[1] the doctor, after he has localized the cave-dwelling or the note of the spirit by examining the patient, must try to establish the name of the spirit, so that he can name it in the magic song. By means of a song pleasing to the spirit, by shaking a rattle, or by singing abusive and mocking songs, he entices the spirit from its dark dwelling-place (that is, from the recesses of the patient's body). If the spirit appears, that is, if the doctor is possessed by the spirit, the spirit must be forced to 'confess'. It must name its name, that is, sacrifice its substance and become a song. Although this sacrifice is entirely in the nature of the sound, the spirit makes it only on condition that a return service is offered in the form of a song or a sacrifice and that the patient patiently endures the suffering involved in the treatment.

The spirit which gives its sound and its name to the healing-song emerges from the dark cavern into the light, like sound escaping from a resonator. All the dark dwellings from which the spirits 'look out', that is to say, emerge *in sound*,[2] are symbols of the sleep that brings health and purification, of the potential concentrated energy of the womb and ultimately of the fruitful sacrificial energy of the dead spirits which are the givers of all life. The ordinary man and the medicine man both receive their healing songs as a rule from a dead ancestor who is revealed to them in a dream. When the *shaman* sings a healing song, the spirit says to him: 'You are singing a song which pleases me. It is *my* song. Therefore I will give you also my power. If you will care for me, I will care for you. If I hear your song, I will come.'[3] Spirit and medicine man need one another. The *shaman* receives his strength from the song, but the ancestor (i.e. the spirit which causes the disease and takes it away again) also needs to sound in song. By drawing the sounds of spirits from the dream-cavern and bringing them to light in the form of a song, the medicine man carries the spirit, becomes the singing cave, the 'drum', the 'ship', the 'wagon', or 'bird'. The usual expression for this is: 'He carries the tune.'

In view of the fact that sound represents the original substance of the world, the singing dream-cavern (which is also symbolized by

[1] G. Speck, *Ceremonial Songs of the Creek and Yuchi Indians* (Philadelphia, 1911), p. 211; Densmore, *Papago Music*, p. 88; *Music of the Indians of British Columbia*, p. 18. (Bureau of American Ethnology Bulletin 90 and 136) (Washington, 1929 and 1943); Schneider, *La danza de espadas y la tarantela*, p. 47.

[2] See p. 49, n. 5.

[3] D'Angulo, op. cit., p. 201.

the moon or by water) constitutes not only the source of musical inspiration but also the source of Creation. In his *Religion und Mythologie der Uitoto* Preuss writes:

There is an inexplicable substance which seems to be a phantom and yet exists in a form hidden from the senses and perceptible only in dreams. The world came into being when God touched this unreal substance and as a result of a dream held it fast by a dream-thread which passed through *the breath of his mouth.* As he dreamt, he held the substance fast, stamped on the deceitful ground, and settled on the substance which he had dreamt, and created heaven and earth by secreting their elements from his body.[1]

To produce a sound, however, an effort has to be made. The bowstring has to be stretched and the breath must impinge on a sharp resisting edge. The 'ground' must be 'stamped down'. All life arises solely from stamping, from the tension or friction of two opposing factors, which have to sacrifice their strength and, if need be, their life for the birth of new life. All new life comes from sacrifice and, ultimately, from death. Since sound forms the substance of life, the spirits—that is, the sounding souls of the dead—are the real givers of life and preservers of the world. The dream-cavern is both the entrance to the underworld and the source of life. When the cavern sings or shouts, or the cloud thunders, each is sacrificing and emptying itself, like a fruit when it reaches maturity. But by giving their fruitful waters to frightened man, they liberate and regenerate themselves. When man offers his song or his shout, he purifies himself from the overripe guest of the cave and thereby helps it (the spirit) to achieve its full existence, to become sound. Sound is the material expression of the mutual sacrifice that is enacted between the living and the dead.

The experience that concentration and effort are necessary for every creative act led in ancient Indian philosophy to the cosmic idea of sacrifice. According to this, the world arose from the expiration of a light-sound, the 'friction' (sacrifice) of which created the gods and the stars, until it finally 'expanded' into matter. According to the Brihadâranyaka Upanishad this original sound was a song in praise of death or hunger which made all things grow or 'swell'. The fasting ascetic acts analogously when he offers the breath of life in singing or reciting from the 'cavern of his heart and lungs'. The sacrifice or 'friction' is the path or wagon on which man overcomes the dualism of the world. Since the world can be preserved only by the mutual sacrifices of the living and the dead, the ascetic can exert the same

[1] Op. cit., i, p. 27.

kind of compulsion on the gods as they exert on man.[1] In the practical magic which has developed among primitive races from similar ideas, the idea of a balance between the living and the dead is much less pronounced. For primitive man the dead are always the more powerful and he is therefore not afraid to feign sacrifices to mislead the spirits, or to sing them flattering or plaintive songs in order to achieve the desired result.

Although primitive races are not acquainted with the idea of sacrifice in the strict and theoretical form in which it appears in advanced cultures, there is—quite apart from the fact that they are continually making food-offerings, performing ritual war-dances, castigating themselves and fasting—sufficient evidence to suggest that for primitive man, too, light-sound (in particular lightning and thunder), sacrifice, and an immanent dualism are recognized as the beginning of all things. When the gods were still wandering on earth they sang and drummed (= lightened and thundered) in order to create all things in the war-dance (sacrificial dance). These 'gods' are probably only sounds or vibrating objects conceived in the forms of human beings or animals. The Australian creator-god created the solid earth by beating the original seas with a reed. At the sound the waters divided and the death-gods came forth from their caves and created men and things.[2] In European folk-lore the tradition of the beating of the water is ascribed to witches. The Marind-anim of New Guinea say that God lit a fire of bamboo wood to warm the first freezing (semi-human, semi-fishlike) creature; at the first crackling of the fire the creature's ears were opened, at the second its eyes, at the third its nostrils, at the fourth its mouth: so man gradually came to life.[3] (It is very significant that hearing was the first sense to be created.) The father-god of the Uitoto created the primeval waters by beating the hollowed-out tree-drum (he was probably one himself).[4] The first crocodile created the harmony of the world when it drummed on its hollow belly with its tail.[5] Theodor Preuss has already shown that the gods are thought to have produced all created things from their own bodies and, more especially, from their own mouths. Created things are apparently released from the caverns of the divine bodies, just as sound is released from a drum or thunder from a thunder-cloud.

[1] Schneider, 'Die historischen Grundlagen der musikalischen Symbolik', *Die Musikforschung*, iv (1951), p. 113.

[2] C. Strehlow, *Die Aranda und Loritjastämme*, i (Frankfurt, 1907), p. 3.

[3] P. Wirz, *Die Marind-anim*, i, 2 (Hamburg, 1922), p. 185.

[4] Preuss, op. cit., p. 29.

[5] M. Granet, *Danses et légendes de la Chine ancienne*, i (Paris, 1926), pp. 263 and 326.

Music not only creates the world; it also cultivates and preserves it. On the island of Er they say that the first settlers, the original ancestors Pop and Kod, who were probably twins, dwelt in a hollow coral-tree (Erythrina) and made a song; then they climbed down to earth and 'had connexion on the ground'.[1] The custom of promoting the growth of fruit with such instruments as bull-roarers, panpipes, and flutes is very widespread. According to a story told in the Aleutian Islands a girl raised a man from the dead by singing.[2] In the language of the Ewe the word *lo* means both 'to sing' and 'to weave'.

The idea of sacrifice is particularly marked in the cosmic myths according to which the world was created by the self-castigation or self-fertilization of a bisexual god. Sometimes the god is the god of lightning and thunder, sometimes a drum-, tree-, or cave-god. This immanent dualism is also represented by a fighting pair of twins, whose flashing swords and thudding shields produce the creative sound. The idea that this sound can develop only from fighting, castigation, and sacrifice dominates all religious music in primitive cultures. Song is a sounding sacrifice of the breath of life. Women beat the abdomen rhythmically; men beat their arms until the blood spurts. Stretched ox-hides are beaten with an ox-tail. The sound of the drum acquires magic power only when it is 'heated' by special songs[3] or has been smeared with blood. Often, the drum must be beaten until the skin bursts. Many instruments have to be made from parts of sacrificed animals or human beings (bones or skin) in order to acquire magic power. A legend from the Sudan tells of a musician who acquired a lute from a blacksmith. But the lute 'did not sing'. The smith said, 'This is a piece of wood. It cannot sing if it has no heart. You must give it a heart. You must take it into battle with you on your back. The wood must resound at the blow of the sword; the wood must soak up dripping blood; blood of your blood, breath of your breath. Your pain must become its pain, your fame its fame.'[4]

From painful darkness self-sacrificing man reaches the joyful light, as sound enters the light of day from the darkness of the cave. On the Andaman Islands it is said that the ancestor of the tribe once crushed between the palms of his hands the grasshopper sacred to the lightning and thunder god Biliku; the creature groaned like a human being and

[1] *Reports of the Cambridge Anthropological Expedition to Torres Straits*, vi (Cambridge, 1908), p. 19.

[2] E. Ermann, 'Ethnographische Wahrnehmungen auf den Küsten des Berings-Meeres', *Zeitschrift für Ethnologie*, iii (1871), p. 212–13.

[3] Densmore, *Menominee Music* (Bureau of American Ethnology Bulletin 102) (Washington, 1932), pp. 154–5; Preuss, op. cit., i, p. 140.

[4] L. Frobenius, *Spielmannsgeschichten der Sahel* (Jena, 1921), pp. 56–57.

darkness fell; then the ancestor taught men songs and dances which continued till the light returned.[1] Like night and sleep, music is the dark giver of power which leads to the light. That is why the cavern of night is the right time for music-making. It preserves life in the darkness and every morning is a new act of creation through which dark sound is brought to radiant light. In the mythology of the Pawnee Indians the morning star repeats the act of creation every day, by appearing as a warrior (beside its little brother) and bringing up a dark ball (the sun). Reddening, it throws the ball in the air and sings: 'This I did, when I became angry in order that in the future the earth might be formed.'[2] (Ex. 52.)

The luminous nature of sound, which in Indian tradition is based on the similarity between *svar* (light) and *svara* (sound), recurs in the creation myth of the Navaho. Originally all mankind lived in a cave in the heart of a mountain. Their light glimmered only for a few hours a day but two flute-players enlivened the darkness with their music. Accidentally one of the players hit his flute against the roof of the cave. A hollow echo resulted and the men decided to bore a hole in the direction from which the sound came. The flute was held against the roof and the boring continued until they reached the outside of the mountain. Then a wind arose which dried out the sea and the people climbed out of the cave and played their favourite song 'Patole'. Then they built the sun and moon and entrusted the two flute-players with the conduct of these lights.[3] The association of the light-producing explosion of the bamboo nodules with the origin of man has been mentioned earlier.[4] Jakob Grimm held that the original etymological affinity between 'peeping', 'string', and 'piping'[5] indicated that the idea of the association of light and sound also existed in ancient Europe.

Music for worship consists in a repetition of the act of creation. Admittedly it has not the creative power which enabled the divine ancestors to call forth matter from nothing by their shining songs and war-dances, but its power is analogous and has the power to renew life. The sound produced by sacrifice or battle establishes the connexion between heaven and earth. In many legends the sky formerly

[1] A. R. Brown, op. cit., p. 215.

[2] Densmore, *Pawnee Music* (Bureau of American Ethnology Bulletin 93) (Washington, 1929), p. 20.

[3] E. Fuhrmann, *Tlinkit und Haida* (Hagen, 1923), p. 18.

[4] See p. 47.

[5] Grimm drew attention particularly to the English words 'peep' and 'pipe' and to the German word *svegel* which means both 'pipe' and 'light'. See *Deutsche Mythologie* (Göttingen, 1844), pp. 706–8.

hung so close to the earth that it was possible to come and go between the two on an intervening rope (or tree). The obvious inference is that the string of the earth-bow stretched between the bough of a tree and a hole in the ground was the musical symbol of this rope. In any case, sound nourishes and preserves both gods and men. In the sky resound sun and moon, lightning and thunder, which give man sunshine and rain. The sounds of earth, human songs of praise, nourish the celestial spirits. Since heaven and earth are regarded as analogous spheres, though with opposite values, all earthly sorrow is a joy in heaven and all earthly joy a heavenly sorrow. In accordance with this inversion of values, the lamentations in which primitive music abounds serve to attune the spirits to a happy, therefore favourable, mood.

The sound symbols developed from these ideas are very diverse. Recitative bridges the dualism of the world by its psalmodizing balance between music and speech, or a tremolo-like oscillation between two notes (a third, fourth, or fifth apart). Perhaps singing in parallel seconds (Ex. 125) also goes back to the same source. Other forms attempt to reach their goal by inversion. On earth-bows sighs are produced which resemble those of the human voice. If a funeral song does not sound completely realistic, it progresses mainly in descending semitones.[1] Among the Duala piercing cries are regarded as arrows, and even today in Andalusia in the night of Good Friday the *saeta* (from *sagitta*) is still sung in a high falsetto, with hands clenched. In the advanced culture of India the syllable *om* (arrow) (which is pitched very high in the *udghita* song) is the 'nail' which pierces the whole world and holds it together. The expression 'to fire off a song' is also very widespread.

The long sustained (non-rhythmical) drone also appears to represent a particular mystic force. In West Africa (Baule) it is thought to be the expression of 'female strength'. Among the Menominee it is sung by the women to help the men.[2] In the Caucasus it is associated with a melody used in healing the sick.[3] Among the Indians of western Brazil a woman utters persistent piercing cries, while the men sing a solemn communal song.[4] In the South African panpipe bands the drone is called the 'weeping note'. Since the nose conveys the breath of life among the living and has phallic significance among the dead,

[1] The thirteenth-century theorist Elias Salomonis still calls the semitones below B flat, C and F, 'lamented' notes. See Gerbert, *Scriptores*, iii (St. Blaise, 1784), p. 18.

[2] Densmore, *Menominee Music*, pp. 161–2.

[3] V. Belaiev, 'The Folk-Music of Georgia', *The Musical Quarterly*, xix (1933), p. 423.

[4] T. Koch-Grünberg, *Zwei Jahre unter den Indianern N. W. Brasiliens* (Stuttgart, 1923), p. 55.

erotic and funeral songs are often sung in a nasal tone. Piping during the night is usually interpreted as the voice of one recently dead. Among the Duala eating is stopped even in daytime whenever a passer-by whistles, lest the spirit of a dead man settle on the food. The sound of the bowstring represents a compressed force. The harsh sound of the scraper justifies the obstinate survival of this most unmusical of all primitive instruments since it represents the act of sacrifice most vividly as a process of 'friction'.

In view of the significance of sound it is not surprising that certain sounds constantly associated with some process or other are considered the most important constituent of the process. The superior power of the rattle-spear, the setting stick, or priest's staff is based on the specific noise they make. Deafening noise is particularly important. The roaring waterfall from which the spirit of great Manitou speaks, and any noise that proceeds from stone or iron frightens away evil spirits because—by definition—they shun the act of sacrifice. Noises are specially contrived in rain charms and at change of moon; noise keeps off the evil spirits which attempt to arrest the rain-laden clouds or prevent the birth of the new moon. At funerals the soul (which still cleaves to the earth for the first weeks after death) is banished as an evil spirit, until it is released from this world and transformed by the sacrifice of banishment into a good spirit. A systematic abstention from noise (prohibition of speaking and singing, pounding rice, and beating down nuts) is also recommended as a means of misleading the spirits.

Sound is regarded as just as much the substance of the powers of darkness as their dwelling-place. For primitive races sound is a wholly concrete expression of the spiritual world. In West Africa a series of identical musical phrases is likened to a string of pearls. In Uganda, where the soloist often breaks off in the middle of the theme and leaves the rest to the chorus, the chorus is said to 'catch' the melody (like a ball).[1] Among the Nyamwesi, parallelism of voices is called going arm in arm. The expression 'to carry a tune' indicates that the singer is thought of as the seat, wagon, ship, or cavern of the sound.

The musical instrument and in particular the sound-box also represent a kind of sacrificial cavern. The ideas associated with instruments are largely conditioned by two factors: firstly, by the ideas connected with the surrounding world from which the material of the instrument comes and secondly, by the way in which the

[1] Schneider, 'Über die Verbreitung afrikanischer Chorformen', *Zeitschrift für Ethnologie*, lxix (1937), p. 88.

outward shape of the instrument conditions the antagonism of forces, thereby making the sound possible. Because of the place where it is found, the conch is closely associated with the life-giving ocean of death; its outward shape is thought to express the idea of bisexuality. Since the sound-substance of the world is produced by a dual being who overcomes (i.e. converts into sound) the immanent dualism by self-castigation or self-fertilization, so originally every sound-producer must be thought of as bisexual. The African drum which, in a moment of danger, speaks of its own accord; the tree-drum which is the seat of the deity and which beats itself to create the primeval waters; the crocodile which beats itself with its own tail: all these embody the immanent dualism. But where a male or female player approaches the instrument, the immanent dualism may disintegrate into two separate elements (instrument and player). Yet the two parts are related like horse and rider, who always form a unity in symbolism.

By this conception of the basically dual nature of musical instruments the writer differs from the view held by his revered teacher, Curt Sachs, who tries as far as possible to attribute a male or female character to each instrument. There is no doubt that in many instruments the accent is on one sex or the other but instruments seem to resemble the bisexual cave-god who is very often divided into two persons and is therefore sometimes thought of as male, sometimes as female (the god of spring or *Magna Mater*). If a predominantly female instrument is played by a man, the bisexuality is maintained in the relationship between instrument and player. The player, the instrument, and the sound are related as father, mother, and child. If a woman plays a predominantly female instrument, however (for example, a drum), or a man a predominantly male one (for example, a flute), the player acts only as the outward shape or even merely as the technique of the instrument and the sound of the drum is masculine and that of the flute feminine—a relationship which again recalls the self-fertilization of the mythical dual being or of the ascetic whose 'wife' (sound-box) resides in his own nature and whose 'child' (sound) represents his spiritual renewal.

In fact the idea that the present division of the sexes has gradually developed from an original unity, by way of a hybrid being and a pair of twins (the marriage of brother and sister), is already found in the old hunting civilizations.[1] Usually this mythological figure is a bisexual forest god or a fabulous creature who manifests himself in the echo, in the whizzing of the bull-roarer or in the complaining note

[1] Baumann, op. cit., p. 208.

of the bamboo trumpet. He is half man and half tiger or partly stone and partly straw or bees-wax. Sometimes he is also thought to be a grandmother or a hunter whose bow is carried by a brother or a mourning leopard (the transition from the hybrid to the pair of twins). The dualism is also expressed in psychological terms when the gloomy hunter indulges in some wild sport, killing or seriously injuring men and then healing them and teaching them medicine-songs. His close association with the rustling of the forest and the buzzing of insects suggests that the drone represents one of his most essential symbols. He too lives in hollow trees, and, as he is moreover lord of the dead, it is probable that the bisexual forest god is an anthropomorphic formulation of the dream- and resonance-cavern.

In order to understand the dual conception of instruments properly the *whole* man or the *whole* of nature as represented anthropomorphically must be taken into account, not merely the sexual aspect. Man and nature are tripartite beings. Heaven, intervening world (humanity), and earth correspond to the head, the trunk and the lower part of the body or, alternatively, to the mouth and nose, the heart and the digestive organs, the sexual parts and the feet. The body is often thought of as a circle, so that mouth and feet touch one another. When a man stamps in the rhythmic dance, or offers his sperm, he creates new physical life. In the sacrificial meal he mediates between heaven and earth, by passing on celestial food to the earth through the 'digestive fire'. When he gives his breath, his speech, and his song, he creates spiritual values, analogous to heaven. These three zones represent the three aspects of the creative sacrifice. They are analogous to one another, but hierarchically ordered. A given symbol can be valid in all three zones. In Europe this tripartition survived in music right into the Middle Ages, when three kinds of music were distinguished: *musica mundana*, *musica humana*, and *musica instrumentalis*. As a mere *tool*, the instrument belongs to the third zone. The fact that it is essentially a sounding instrument, however, means that it cannot represent primarily a sexual symbol but belongs rather to the first zone (head, heaven). The player or the sound-board belongs to the second zone. The musical instrument therefore belongs to all three zones, but as used by man its specific task is to connect the third and first zones. And the power to do this comes to it from the 'cavern' of the second zone. If lightning and rain are usually interpreted as the product of the marriage of heat and cold (sun and cloud, drumstick and drum),[1] this simply means that an obvious aspect of dualism is

[1] Sachs, op. cit., p. 35.

being transferred to the first plane. The terms 'masculine' and 'feminine' (instead of fire and water, day and night, &c.) are therefore used below for all three zones in order to express as simply as possible the dualism that runs through all three levels.

The conch which Sachs, too, regards as bisexual,[1] is a clear example of the dual structure and the three levels on which it is expressed. Because it dwells in the sea and is spiral, it is thought to contain all the seeds of life. Its role in the first zone as propagator of the breath of life is apparent in creation myths, in its use as a call-signal, in its ritual fixing on the forehead, and in its combination with ear and nose shells. Its war-call or sacrificial call is used particularly in rain charms. From the second zone downwards, it is used increasingly as a simple implement besides its function as a musical instrument. It is heard in fertility rites, but in libations and cures it is used predominantly as a container. On the third plane it is closely associated with the worship of the dead, since conches are at the same time sexual symbols, dwellings of the dead, and burial places, from which new life springs. On all three levels the conch is a sacrificial cavity, but its fertility is spiritual in the first zone, physical in the second, and metaphysical in the third.

Rattles consisting of hard objects strung together, and hung round the body, turn the dancer himself into a rattle, into the *homme-sonnaille* (to use Schaeffner's expression) from which the spirit speaks. In the vessel form the dual structure is indicated by magic carvings (for instance, of birds and aquatic animals) though it is already symbolized to some extent in the combination of handle and hollow ball. The first of the three planes is shown by its significance in the 'cloud festivals' (i.e. rain ceremonies) in which each dancer wears a tall head-ornament of feathers (representing clouds), to which a rattle is attached.[2] Its use in field and medicine rites corresponds to the second zone, as does probably also the interpretation of spherical rattles as female breasts.[3] According to Frances Densmore a different rhythm is beaten for every illness.[4] The third zone appears to be specially indicated by wearing the rattle in the region of the knee. Characteristically, the *orenda* of the rattle is also connected with that of the cricket and the dragonfly, both of which are creatures of the underworld.[5]

[1] Schneider, 'Los cantos de lluvia', *Anuario musical del Instituto Español de Musicologia*, iv (1949). [2] Wirz, op. cit., iv, p. 60.

[3] Densmore, *Pawnee Music*, p. 18. [4] *Papago Music*, p. 102.

[5] Preuss, op. cit., i, pp. 35, 80, and 128; *Die Nayarit-expedition*, i (Leipzig 1912), pp. 75 and 81.

The idea of sacrifice which is expressed in the conch and the rattle by the friction of the breath against the mouth-hole or the grains rubbing against one another in the hollow inside of the rattle, is symbolized in other instruments by the skin taken from a living body. When the skin is stretched over a pit or a hollow vessel, a drum results. Its specific effect depends on the quality of the sound it produces, that is, on the sound of the animal or person from whom the skin is taken. The dry hard sound of a goatskin attracts thunder, because the mountain goat is a thunder animal. Cow-hides bring rain. Although the low or belly-shaped drums 'speak' (in the first zone) they seem to belong predominantly to the second, i.e. the animal zone; they are regarded as mothers, cows, or frogs and are practically simple 'caverns'. On the other hand, the skin that produces the sound is thought of as the head. The *ngoma*-drum of the Venda seems, however, to extend over all three zones; it is called 'egg of an ostrich'; the side-handles are called 'a frog's knee'; the opening at the bottom is termed 'vagina'; the head, 'the skin of a man'; the smooth hairless circular portion in the centre of the head, 'a baby's fontanelle'; the pegs which secure the head, 'the fingers'; the drumstick, 'the hand of a person'.[1] The skin of these drums is often rubbed with sacrificial foods, and sacred stones or bones of the dead lie inside the instrument. If the skin bursts, no one is allowed to look inside.

It seems doubtful whether the friction-drum represents the sexual act, as is generally assumed. Its use in initiation ceremonies in the spring and at the winter solstice and also the term 'menstruation drum' seem rather to point to puberty.[2]

While the low barrel-shaped drum represents fertility as a crouching figure, longitudinal instruments express it in the upright or recumbent position of the mystic dual being. Since the self-fertilization typical of this dual deity is performed by most trees, it is not surprising that the deity also appears as a tree god. The corresponding musical symbols are the springy dance-tree (with a crocodile's or woman's face) and the slit-drum. The hollow interior of the slit-drum is the dwelling of the dual deity (or the deity itself) and the home of dead or still unborn souls. It was its 'word' that created the primeval waters when the father-god beat the slit (or himself) with the drum-stick. The Uitoto connect this sacrificial act with the darkened moon. It is characteristic that the slit of the anthropomorphic drum is often

[1] Kirby, op. cit., p. 36.

[2] Marius Schneider, 'Zambomba und Pandero', *Spanische Forschungen*, i, 9 (1954), p. 13.

found on the back, not on the front. The beating or whipping by a power *behind* (that is, invisible) clearly shows that fertilization is not conceived in specifically sexual terms. The head-hunters of the Naga place captured skulls on these sounding ancestral figures, tree-men, forest spirits[1] or soul containers. Gigantic drums are laid or hung horizontally in a house specially built for the purpose or they are hung on a tree (usually in a sloping position). In this position they have quite exceptional power because they are thought to be suicides,[2] i.e. beings who have become especially powerful spirits owing to their self-sacrifice.

Since the original types of flute were very large, like the earliest drums, the tree or the long reed seems to have determined their original symbolic form. Among the Tlinkit, flutes are carved in the shape of ancestral figures or supplied with figures of eagles or fishes (symbolizing fire and water). The dualism is also expressed by double flutes or pairs of flutes. (In the creation myth of the Navaho mentioned above,[3] the two flutes correspond to the sun and moon.) In the initiation ceremonies of the Nor-Papuans the lads are laid on the drum and beaten until the voice of the spirit Brag sounds in the two flutes, of which the male is 1·5 metres and the female 1·25 metres long.[4] It is said of the Parak flute, which holds the secret of life and death, that it forms the veil in which the god Wunekau has enveloped the mystery of procreation.[5] The flute is primarily the carrier of wind and breath. 'I have reared a bird' means 'I have made a big bamboo flute.'[6] If the face of the totem-god, to whom the instrument belongs, is known, the flute is provided with the corresponding head.[7] Or when the spirit is evoked a corresponding mask is held ready,[8] so that the totem-god can manifest itself vocally as well as bodily. Flutes are also played to promote the growth of the fruits of the field.

The flute is related to the drum in a number of ways. Neither instrument must be played indoors since both give rise to thunderstorms.[9] Both 'speak' not only alone but to one another. In such dialogues the flute assumes the symbolic role of the drumstick. This relationship

[1] A. Steinmann, 'Über anthropomorphe Schlitztrommeln in Indonesien', *Anthropos*, xxxiii (1938), p. 244.

[2] Ibid., p. 243. [3] See p. 49. [4] J. G. Schmidt, op. cit., p. 344.

[5] R. F. H. Mayer, 'Sonnenverehrung in Neu-Guinea', *Anthropos*, xxviii (1933), p. 48.

[6] P. A. Schaeffner, 'Zur Initiation im Wagi Tal (Bismarck Archipelago)', *Anthropos*, xxxiii (1938), p. 401.

[7] K. Koch, 'Totemismus und Zweiklassenkultur in Neu-Guinea', *Zeitschrift für Ethnologie*, lxxi (1931), p. 325.

[8] J. G. Schmidt, op. cit., pp. 341 and 666.

[9] J. Kunst, *Music in Flores* (Leyden, 1942), p. 127; R. F. W. Arndt, 'Die Religion der Nad'a', *Anthropos*, xxvi (1931), p. 356.

seems to be confirmed by the fact that in later cultures the flute is predominantly a male instrument and the drum female. Among the Banoro the sexual relationship between flute and drum is expressed in the longitudinal bisection of the spirit house. In the flute section (opposite the drum section) of the house, the bride is deflowered by one of her father-in-law's kinsmen.[1] According to a story told by the Mandan and the Papago a boy saw his grandmother (the moon) take a full pot into bed with her every night, and the pot was empty in the morning. One day he found a snake in it and killed it. The snake (the sun) was the grandfather. The woman buried him (the grandfather) in a lake, took the stalk of a sunflower (or a reed from the lake) and made the boy a flute with which he could summon snow and rain.[2]

The high notes of the flute are particularly effective in sexual magic and a special style of singing has developed in association with this instrumental sound-symbol. The special songs sung while a flute is being made, which still survive in some European folk-customs, may also be connected with this. The reeds which grow on graves and betray the name of the murderer, the singing bones and the tomb-flutes close the life-circle by letting new life sound from the sacrifice of the old.

The power which springs from dualism is particularly obvious where a tree or a stick has been bent by an opposing force. The easily bent slit-drum or the sighing spirit-voice of the bow, with which the player holds converse, arises in this way. Even though the musical bow seems to be an earlier development than the hunter's bow, the ideological relationships between the two cannot be overlooked. According to a legend of the Hehe, the musical bow sprang from a girl thrown into the water; her head became the calabash, her backbone the stick, and her limbs strings.[3] According to a legend of the Marind-anim, however, the hunter's bow is also a human being, sometimes even a pair of human beings. The stick is the man, the string the woman. When the Papuan goes hunting he conjures the 'wife' to clasp her 'husband' firmly so that the string shall not break.[4] The Washambula believe that men whose strings break while they are playing the bow will not get wives.[5]

The harp, which derives historically from the bow, often appears

[1] Koch, op. cit., p. 328.
[2] Densmore, *Mandan and Hidatsa Music*, p. 81; *Papago Music*, p. 61.
[3] Sachs, op. cit., p. 63.
[4] P. Wirz, op. cit., i, 2, p. 128; iii, p. 106–9.
[5] Sachs, op. cit., p. 63.

among primitive races as the retrogressive form of an instrument from an advanced culture. It is the fish-hook of the death- and water-spirits or a man whose back is bent with sorrow and care. Because of its long neck it is also called crane, goose, or swan.[1] With this identification with the swan (the ship of the dead) is probably connected the later 'swan song'.[2] In the outward shape of the harp, the hunter's bow, and the easily bent tree-drum, one can detect the mystic shape of the ship which, like the cry, the arrow, the path, the wagon, the waning moon, and man is a symbol of sacrifice. According to totemistic myths, the canoe is a human corpse which has been stamped into shape.[3] According to other traditions, the drum is a forest spirit which originally stood at the bow of a princely ship.[4] Schaeffner has already drawn attention to the connexions between the construction of a harp and of a ship.[5]

The bull-roarer also appears to be a small boat. Many Australian legends tell of the circular voyages of the totem-gods who left their caves after the dividing of the waters, singing and dancing with spears, and set out to create all things. Then they taught men the songs on which the preservation of the world depends, returned to their caves, and turned into bull-roarers. These instruments represent the 'mystical body' of the totem-god and renew its creative energy as soon as they begin to travel, that is, as soon as they begin to whiz in the air. As carvings representing the journeys of the totem-gods or ancestral figures (in animal forms) are often found on Australian bull-roarers,[6] the whizzing of the bull-roarer appears to represent a revival of the voice and ritual journeys of the cave-gods. The bull-roarer which a grandfather carves out for a child is kept in a cave before the child is born and returned there after its owner's death. It confers on its owner the joy of mystic communion with his ancestors so long as he hides it from the women. It is customary to give the sick a few shavings from the wood as medicine.[7]

The bow or the tree-man that has been painfully bent into a circle or oval forms the framework of the *shaman* drum. It is used particularly in medicine, rain rites, and soothsaying. The victim (reindeer or horse) which gave its skin for the drum, is the lord of this 'singing

[1] A. O. Vaisaenen, *Wogulische und ostjakische Melodieen* (Helsinki, 1937), p. 22; Sachs, *Handbuch der Musikinstrumentenkunde* (Leipzig, 1920), p. 231.

[2] *The Rigveda*, iii, 53, 10 and ix, 97, 8 also requires the singers to sing like the swans who perform the prelude to the hymns.

[3] Wirz, op. cit., i, pp. 122 and 176.

[4] Steinmann, op. cit., p. 244.

[5] Op. cit., pp. 164–5.

[6] Strehlow, op. cit., pls. 1 and 2.

[7] Ibid., ii, p. 79.

bow tree'.[1] Since the doctor's original implement is a bow and arrow[2] (medicine is 'shot'), it is not surprising that the drum, which replaces the bow, is also called 'bow' and the drumstick 'arrow'. Among the Shor of the Altai mountains the six 'horns' on the frame of the drum are used to attack, and the six iron rings (ring-mail) to ward off, evil spirits. The 'iron bow-string' runs right across the frame and beside it is the 'sword' (six knife-shaped iron plates).[3] Like all symbols of sacrifice, the frame-drum represents a way or a means of transport by which the *shaman* travels to the world of spirits. If the drum is a horse, the drumstick is a whip.[4] The skin, on which blood or libations are poured, is often decorated with symbolic drawings (of the sun, moon, drums, or animals) which represent 'the whole world'.[5] The number-symbolism of Samoyed drums[6] probably points to a very late cultural development. On the other hand, the description of the drum as 'grandfather' and the Lapp custom of never bringing the instrument into a tent through the main entrance but only through the small 'sacred door' through which the hunters crawl[7] are probably of earlier origin. Since the drum is a dead man it is worth mentioning in this context the custom of carrying the dead out of the house through a small door that is usually kept shut.[8]

A dark god also speaks out of the hourglass-drum and is even depicted on it occasionally. Two similar, approximately triangular but inverted sections form the body of the drum. These outlines, which occur in many archaeological representations as the body of the tightly-girdled dancer (and later, in the shape of Shiva), represent the inversion brought about by sacrifice. The same significance attaches to the depiction of the waxing and waning crescents of the moon. The conches and the whale or crocodile jaws at the lower end and the resonant skin at the upper end of the instrument symbolize, like lizards and snakes, the dualism of water and fire.

In the transition to the higher farming and pastoral cultures many of the ideas touched on here undergo considerable extension or specialization. They become more and more the esoteric preserve of

[1] E. Emsheimer, 'Zur Ideologie der lappischen Zaubertrommel', *Ethnos*, ix (1944), p. 142.

[2] Ibid., p. 143.

[3] L. Menges and P. Potapov, *Materialien zur Volkskunde der Turkvölker des Altay* (Mitteilungen des Seminars für orientalischen Sprachen) (Berlin, 1934), p. 62.

[4] Emsheimer, op. cit., p. 147.

[5] Menges and Potapov, op. cit., p. 64.

[6] E. Emsheimer, 'Schamanentrommel und Trommelbau', *Ethnos*, ix (1946), p. 173.

[7] Emsheimer, 'Zur Ideologie', p. 162.

[8] Baechtold-Staeubli, *Handwörterbuch des deutschen Aberglaubens*, v (Berlin, 1932/3), p. 1134.

individuals; the people as a whole only partially continue the old tradition and usually lack any deeper understanding of it. But in the depths of the subconscious the ideas continue to be active. No art fascinates primitive man more than music; he is as vividly aware of its dynamic fluctuations between light and darkness as he is of the mysterious relationship between life and death.

A 1. Asia: Wedda (Wertheimer)

2. America: Tierra del Fuego, Small black Albatross (Hornbostel)

3. Asia: Moluccas, Rowing song (Tauern)

4. Indonesia: Kŭbŭ (Hornbostel)

5. America: Taulipang, Cure of the sick (Hornbostel)

6. Australia: Yuna, Initiation into tribal laws (Schneider)

7. New Guinea: Sialum (Kolinski)

8. New Guinea: Kai (Kunst)

9. Europe: Votyak, Love song (Lach)

B 10. Asia: Semang (Kolinski)

11. New Guinea: Laŭkanŭ (Kolinski)

13. America: Menominee, Frog-dance (Densmore)

14. America: Pawnee, Song of Buffalo (Fletcher)

15. Africa: Acooli (Schneider)

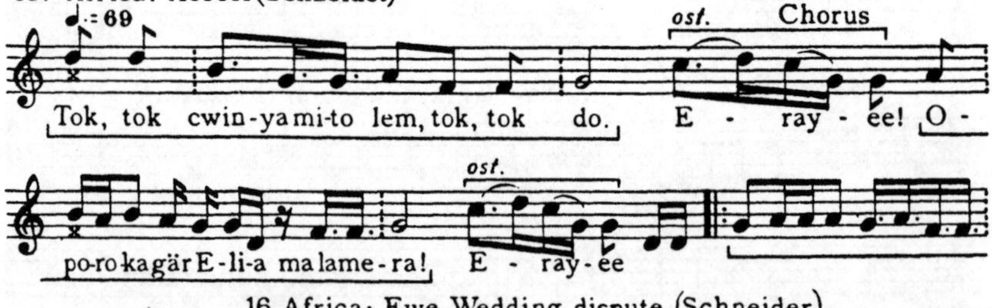

16. Africa: Ewe, Wedding dispute (Schneider)

C 17. Torres Straits: Murray, Death song (Myers)

18. America: Osage, Song to water spirits (la Flesche)

19. New Guinea: Bukaua (Kolinski)

20. Asia: Vogul, Bear song (Kannisto)

21. America: Chippewa, Owl medicine song (Densmore) Drum:

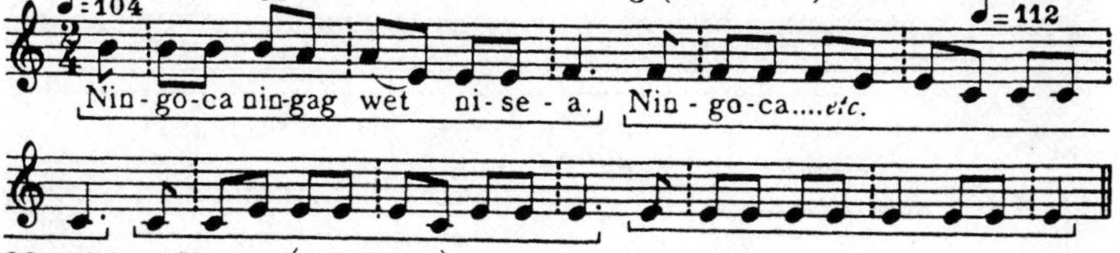

22. Africa: Hausa (Schneider)

23. Africa: Nyamwesi, Travel song (Hornbostel)

24. Caucasus: Kartvelia (Dirr)

25. Europe: Cheremiss (Lach)

26. America: Omaha, Scout song (Fletcher)

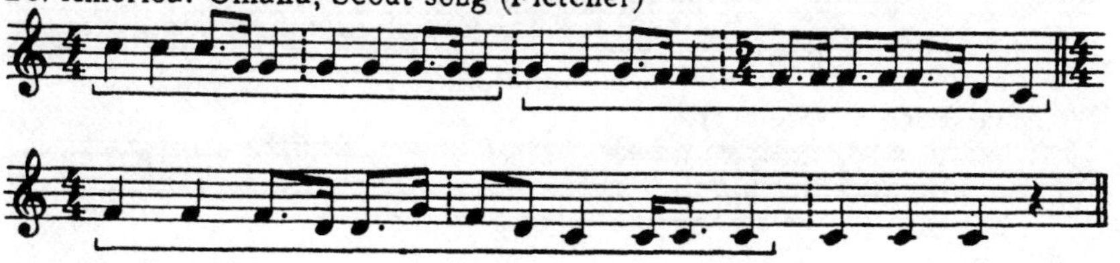

D
27. America: Yamana, Song of bird (Hornbostel)
28. Asia: Malabars, Prayer (Hornbostel)
♩.=112
29. America: Patagonian (Fischer)
♩.=92
30. America: Ojibway (Hoffmann)
31. Torres Straits (Myers)
♩=60
etc.
32. New Guinea: Sialum (Kolinski)
33. Bismarck Archipelago:
♩=100
Barriai (Schneider)
34. Asia: Vogul, Mythological spirit song (Kannisto)
♩=186
35. Asia: Buryat (Stumpf)

36. Asia: Seram, Rowing song (Tauern)

37. America: Chippewa, Lullaby (Densmore)

38. America: Makŭrap (Schneider)

39. America: Omaha (Fletcher)

40. Africa: Masai, War song

(Schneider)

41. Africa: Wahehe, Dance (Schneider)

42. Africa: Tanganyika, Hunting song (Molitor)

Andantino

43. Africa: Ewe, Incantation (Schneider)

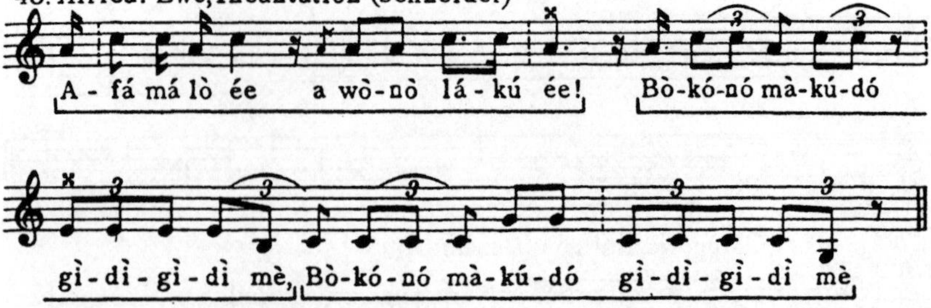
A - fá má lò ée a wò-nò lá - kú ée! Bò-kó-nó mà-kú-dó
gì - dì - gì - dì mè, Bò-kó-nó mà-kú-dó gì - dì - gì - dì mè

44. Asia: Flores (Kunst)

Chorus

45. Asia: Ostyak (Kannisto)

46. America: Creek, Skunk dance (Sapir)

♩ = 184

47. Europe: Cheremiss (Lach)

♩ = 162

48. America: Nootka, Rain song (Densmore)

♩ = 72

49. Asia: Karakirgiz, Lament (Zataevič)

♩ = 132

50. America: Pawnee, Buffalo dance (Densmore) Drum ♩ = 132 & 116

51. Africa: Uganda (Schneider)

52. America: Pawnee, Mythological song (Densmore)

E 53. America: Copper Eskimo, Dance song (Roberts)

54. America: Copper Eskimo, Dance song (Roberts)

55. America: Creek, Medicine song (Sapir)

56. America: Shasta, Girl initiation (d'Harcourt)

57. Asia: Burma, Prayer (Schneider)

58. Asia: Vogul, Bear song (Kannisto)

59. America: Makuschi, Women at work (Hornbostel)

60. Europe: Children's song

61. Torres Straits: Death song (Myers)

62. Asia: Pamir (Schneider)

63. Africa: Bushman (Kirby)

64. Africa: Bakango (Schneider)

65. Africa: Cameroons, Work song (Schneider)

66. Asia: Toba-Batak, Rowing song (Schneider)

67. New Guinea: Awembiak (Kŭnst)

68. America: Ashumawi, Puberty song (d'Harcourt)

69. Europe: Lapp (Schneider)

70. Africa: Bushman, Dance (Schneider)

71. Africa: Schillŭk, Dirge (Schneider)

72. America: Menominee, War song (Densmore)

73. America: Menominee, Hunting medicine (Densmore)

74. America: Nootka, Lullaby (Boas)

75. Bismarck Archipelago: Mioko (Schneider)

76. Asia: Engano (Schneider)

77. America: Cocopa, Song concerning the Diver (Densmore)

78. Asia: Semang (Kolinski)

79. Bismarck Archipelago: Baining (Schneider)

80. Africa: Hehe, Dance (Schneider)

81. Africa: Bakongo (Schneider)

82. America: Iroquois, Medicine society song (Roberts)

83. America: Cape York Eskimo, Spirit song (Schneider)

84. New Guinea: Hube, Spirit song (Schneider)

H 85. Africa: Central Congo, Medicine song (Schneider)

86. Asia: Dyak, Borneo (Schneider)

87. Asia: Buryat (Schneider)

88. America: Makŭschi, Women's song (Hornbostel)

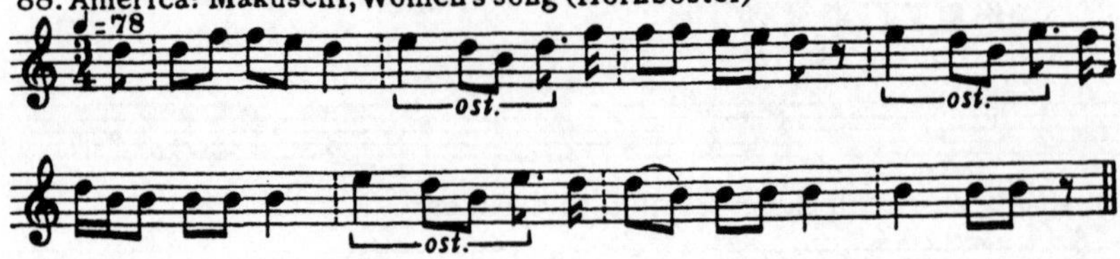

89. Caucasus: Kartvelia, Love song (Lach)

90. Asia: Karakirgiz (Zataevič)

91. Africa: Hehe, Dance (Schneider)

92. Africa: Egyptian Peasant (Schneider)

93. Europe: Spain (Schneider)

94. America: Jabuti, Dance (Schneider)

95. Africa: Fipa (Schneider)

96. Europe: Cheremiss (Lach)

97. Asia: Flores (Kunst)

98. Oceania: Nissan, Lament for the dead (Hornbostel)

99. Asia: India, Beggar's Song (Schneider)

100. Europe: Spain (Torner)

101. Africa: Sudan, Kerŭmbe (Schneider)

102. Africa: Acooli, Hero song (Schneider)

103. America: Chippewa, Love song (Densmore)

104. America: Menominee, Love song (Densmore)

105. Asia: Karakirgiz, Lament (Zataevič)

106. Asia: Ortos, Lament over lost horse (Oost)

107. Asia: Eastern Mongolia (Emsheimer)

J 108. Asia: Pamir, Love-song (Schneider)

109. Europe: Cantigas de S. Maria (13th century) (Anglès)

K 110. Asia: Wedda (Schneider)

111. Africa: Bambŭtti (Schneider)

112. Asia: Kenta (Kolinski)

113. Asia: Flores (Kunst)

114. Africa: Bushman (Kirby)

115. Africa: Badiki (Schneider)

116. Oceania: Samoa, Song on a volcano (Kolinski)

117. Asia: Naga, Headhunters' song and rice stamping (Schneider)

118. Africa: Bashlengwe (Schneider) 119. Africa: Wanicha (Schneider)

120. Africa: Karanga (Schneider)

121. Caucasus: Ossete (Lach)

122. Europe: 12th century (Trope) Adsit Johannes 123. Africa: Nyamwesi (Hornbostel)

124. Africa: Wabali (Schneider)

125. Oceania: Hŭrea, Feast song (Schneider)

126. New Guinea: Sepik (Schneider)

127. Caucasus: Mingrelia (Lach)

128. Africa: Kindiga (Schneider)

129. Africa: Batswa-Pygmy (Schneider)

130. Oceania: Solomon Islands (Hornbostel)

131. Africa: Chewa, War song (Schneider)

132. Africa: Ngoni (Schneider)

133. Africa: Ngoni (Schneider)

M

134. Oceania: Solomon Islands, Kongara (Hornbostel)

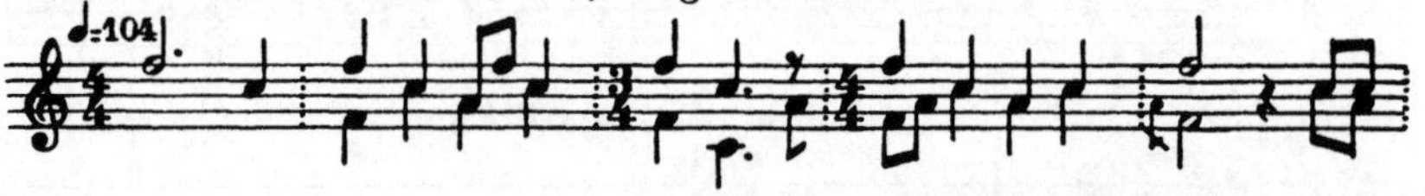

135. Oceania: Solomon Islands, (Hornbostel)

136. Asia: Naga (Schneider)

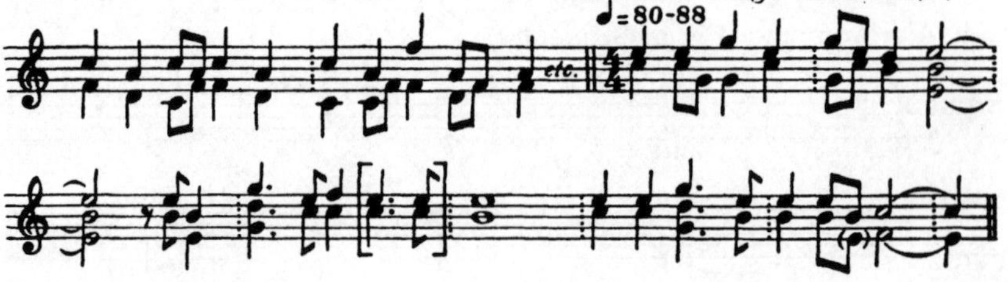

137. Oceania: Raiatea, Religious song (Schneider)

♩=104
138. Africa: Bashlengwe
(Schneider)
♩=126
etc.
139. Africa: Nyassa (Schneider)
N
140. Caucasus: Svanetia, Dance (Dirr)
♩=72
etc.
141. Portugal (Sampaio)
♩=54
142. Portugal (Sampaio)
143. Europe: Worcester 13th century (Hughes) Dulciflua
O
144. Bismarck Archipelago: Barriai (Schneider)

145. Africa : Chagga (Schneider)

146. Africa: Masai, war song (Schneider)

147. Africa: Acooli, Mocking Song (Schneider)

148. Africa: Sobo (Schneider)

152. Europe (medieval): Codex Las Huelgas. Clama (Anglès)

153. Africa: Bakango (Schneider)

154. New Guinea: St. Mathias, Death song (Schneider)

155. Oceania: Rennell Island (Burrows)

156. Oceania: Marquesas (Schneider)

157. Asia: Sema Naga, Women's song (Schneider)

158. Caucasus: Abkhaz (Lach)

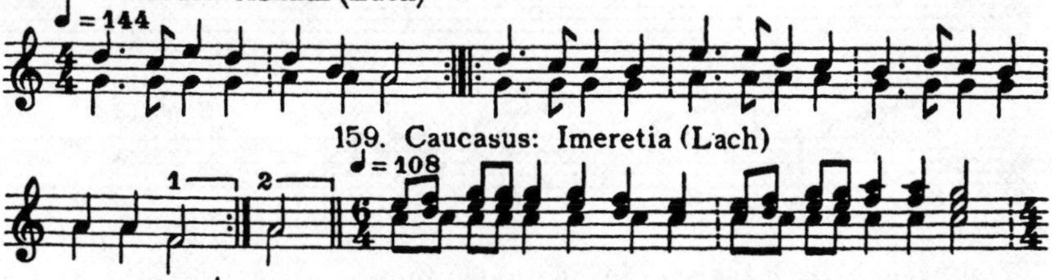

159. Caucasus: Imeretia (Lach)

160. Caucasus: Georgia, Dirge (Dirr)

161. Europe: Codex Las Huelgas, Verbum Patris (Anglès)

162. Africa: Bushman, Musical Bow (Kirby)

163. Indonesia: Earth-zither (Brandt-Bŭys)

164. Asia: Flores, Xylophone (Kunst)

165. Africa: Ivory Coast, Hunting song with sansa accompaniment (Schneider)

166. Africa: Bamalete, Reed flute ensemble (Kirby)

167. America: Bark trumpet (Alphorn) (Vegas)

168. Africa: Bechuana, 4 reed flutes (Kirby)

169. South Africa: 2 Xylophones (Kirby)

170. Africa: Ubangi Chari, Shepherd's flute (Schneider)

(original a minor 3rd higher)

171. Africa: Chwana, Flute (Kirby)

172. America: Menominee, Flute, Love-medicine (Densmore)

173. Asia: Eastern Mongolia, The blue banner (Emsheimer)

174. Africa: Liberia, Horn (Herzog)

175. Africa: Duala, Drum orchestra (Schneider)

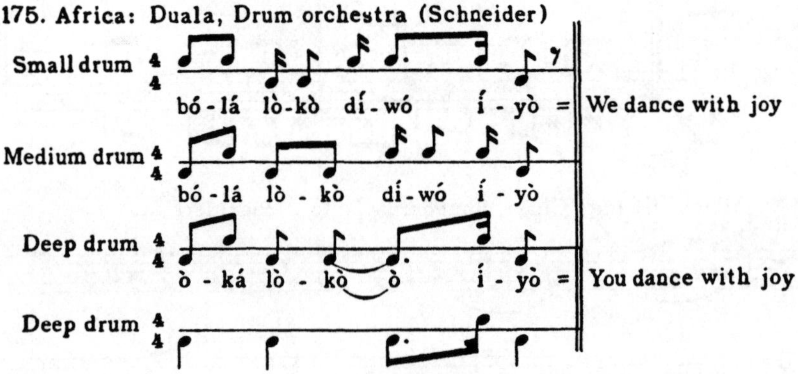

176. New Guinea: Nor-Papua, Drum signal (Schmidt)

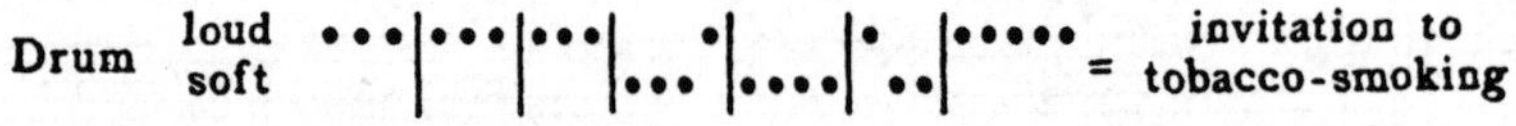

II

THE MUSIC OF FAR EASTERN ASIA

1. CHINA[1]

By LAURENCE PICKEN

INTRODUCTION

IN spite of considerable differences between the musical practices of one locality and another, the vast territory of Far Eastern Asia—China, Mongolia, Tibet, Shinjiang (1),[2] Shikang (2), Korea, Japan, Indo-China, Siam, Burma, Malaya, Java, Bali, &c.—can be regarded, with respect to its musical culture, as a unit, to be compared and contrasted with India perhaps on the one hand and western Europe on the other. A wave of musical culture seems to have swept over China to the seaboard of the great land-mass of Asia and beyond, so that there survive at the present time, on the periphery, types of orchestras and habits of polyphonic treatment which have vanished almost entirely from the central region.

[1] Recent general accounts of Chinese music are: Kenneth Robinson, 'Chinesische Musik, I. Geschichtliche Entwicklung von der Frühzeit (Shang-Dynastie) bis zum Ende der Han-Zeit (1523 a. Chr. bis 206 p. Chr.) (Deutsche Übs. und Bearb.: Hans Eckardt)', *Die Musik in Geschichte und Gegenwart*, ii (ed. Friedrich Blume) (Kassel und Basel, 1952), columns 1195–1205. This account is based directly on the Chinese sources. H. Eckardt, 'Chinesische Musik, II. Vom Ende der Han-Zeit bis zum Ende der Sui-Zeit (220–618). Der Einbruch westlicher Musik', ibid., columns 1205–7; 'III. Die T'ang-Zeit (618–907). Die Rolle der westländischen (Hu-)Musik. Die Zehn Orchester. Die Musik der Zwei Abteilungen. Akademien und Konservatorien', ibid., columns 1207–16; P. C. Crossley-Holland, 'Chinese Music', *Grove's Dictionary of Music and Musicians* (ed. E. Blom), ii (London, 1954), pp. 219–48. Dr. Eckardt's bibliography includes a valuable selection of recent Japanese publications, and materials on central Asian music and East-West musical interchange. Mr. Crossley-Holland's bibliography is virtually complete for works in European languages.

[2] Figures in brackets refer to serial entries in the Glossary of Characters, p. 190. The system of Romanization adopted here is that primarily due to Professor Jaw Yuanrenn of the University of California. Its main feature is that the tones are inherent in the spelling as they are in the spoken word. Knowing the system, the Romanized form can be read in its correct tone, thus reducing ambiguity. Typographically this system has the advantage that it avoids the use of all aspirates, diacritic signs, and superscript numerals. Some familiar words appear in new guise: Jou = Chou^{1}, Hann = Han^{4}, Wey = Wei^{4}, Tarng = T'ang^{2}, Sonq = Sung^{4}; chyn = ch'in^{2}, pyipar = p'i^{2}-p'a^{2}, shiau = hsiao^{1}, seh = sê^{4}; Symaa Chian = Szŭ^{1}-ma^{3} Ch'ien^{1}, Ju Shii = Chu^{1} Hsi^{3}. Again, the two types of pitch-pipes, previously written alike as lü, but pronounced in two different tones: lü^{3} and lü^{4}, are differentiated as leu and liuh. A guide to the system will be found in W. Simon, *The New Official Chinese Latin Script, Gwoyeu Romatzyh* (London, 1944).

This interpretation of the total musical picture of the Far East is to a considerable extent explicit in the surveys of Far Eastern music made by Sachs.[1] Though the course of the exposition adopted here has been largely determined by this interpretation, it must not be accepted as more than a working hypothesis.

PREHISTORY AND ETHNOLOGY OF THE FAR EAST

China is to be regarded as a continent apart, turning her back on the rest of Eurasia, more isolated even than India; and it is this geographical setting which has determined the main features of Chinese history.[2] Behind her natural barriers there developed a culture of such integrity that when, in the fourth century, invaders and conquerors came, it was they who were absorbed; and thus it has always been. The Chinese of Tarng (3) times was an entirely different person, ethnically speaking, from the Chinese of Chyn (4) and Hann (5) times, because of this constant absorption of invaders from the north and conquered peoples in the south.[3]

Palaeolithic sites have been found in the Ordos region, and it is known that neolithic civilizations flourished in Mongolia as well as throughout the Yellow River valley. At the time of the development of high civilization at the turn of the third millennium B.C., the Chinese, or rather, the Proto-Chinese, differed from surrounding peoples in the superior organization of their agriculture rather than in physical character. Even at the present time they have linguistic relatives all over the Far East; indeed it is customary to recognize a Sino-Tibetan language-group which includes, on the one hand, Chinese and the various Thai languages of southern China and Indo-China and, on the other, the Tibeto-Burman languages of Tibet and Burma and (in China proper) of the Luoluo (6) and Mosuo (7) peoples of Yunnan (8) and Syhchuan (9). This group does not by any means embrace all the mongoloid peoples of China, however. Not included in it are the Turco-Mongols of the Gobi Desert, and the Miau (10) and Yau (11) peoples of southern and south-western China; the linguistic affinities of the two latter are still uncertain.

The invasions of north China in historic times all came from

[1] *The History of Musical Instruments* (New York, 1940); *The Rise of Music in the Ancient World, East and West* (New York, 1943).

[2] R. Grousset, *L'Asie orientale des origines au XVe siècle* (Paris, 1946), p. 139.

[3] G. Haloun, 'Die Rekonstruktion der chinesischen Urgeschichte durch die Chinesen', *Japanisch-Deutsche Zeitschrift für Wissenschaft und Technik*, iii (Kobe, 1925), pp. 243–70.

Mongolia or Manchuria, never from Shinjiang (Turkestan); that is to say, the invaders were always barbarians, never bearers of high civilization, such as were the merchants or pilgrims, transmitters of cultural gifts of the highest importance—mathematics, Buddhism, music, &c.—who passed along the Silk Road or the Buddhist Pilgrim route.

This pressure from the north provided an incentive to the progressive sinicization of southern China and perhaps led to the constant movement southwards of earlier offshoots of the mongoloid stock, the Proto-Chinese or, more generally, the palaeomongoloids. Among these one may perhaps include the Proto-Malays. The Japanese are also sometimes grouped with the palaeomongoloids. A number of characters suggest that they are a branch of the mongoloids separated off at a very early date; it is known that they are not the original inhabitants of much of the territory they now occupy.

Coming south to Indo-China and Indonesia, it is certain that the present ethnic complexity of this region goes back to prehistoric times. In addition to Negritos, the most ancient inhabitants seem to have included relatives of the present inhabitants of Australia, New Guinea, and Melanesia. A second and later wave of prehistoric immigrants to this region brought the Proto-Malay element, to be found in the present Bataks and Dyaks of the islands, and in the Cham and other vanished peoples of the mainland. These folk are in many respects mongoloid; their ethnological position is uncertain, but they may perhaps be placed at the base of the mongoloid stock. They have a bamboo culture, and this fact may perhaps be important as an indication of affinity with the third wave of immigrants, the brachycephalic mongoloids, who also have to some extent a bamboo culture. These entered across the north-west frontier of Indo-China, and it is possible that they brought with them the first Bronze Age culture to reach Indo-China. As compared with Europe this culture arrived comparatively late.

At the time of the unification of China at the end of the third century B.C., the southern limit of Chinese territory scarcely extended beyond the Yangtz (12) River. Not until Hann times was southern China added to the Chinese domain; but by 111 B.C. Annam, in Indo-China, had been annexed. The Chinese continued to dominate this region during Hann times and from then until the tenth century. As early as the second and third centuries of our era, however, the colonization by the Hindus of Burma, Siam, Indonesia, and the coast of Indo-China, had begun and reached a peak in the fourth and fifth centuries,[1] so that from the earliest times there has been a clash of cultures in this area.

The presence of the Ainu in northern Japan must not be forgotten even in this brief sketch of Far Eastern ethnology. They are not mongoloids and have existed in their present position since before the arrival of the Japanese.

Considering the 'continent' of China, Indo-China, and Indonesia as a whole, evidence points to a constant movement southward of more or less mongoloid peoples. To diffusion in other directions may be ascribed the colonization of the American continent: the Eskimos, and the Indians of North and South America are mongoloids whose affinities with the Pacific area, in the widest sense, is exhibited, among other characters, in their armoury of musical instruments. With the exception of a few instruments of universal occurrence all these (or their close relatives) are to be found exclusively in China, the territory between China and India, the Malay Archipelago, and the Pacific Islands. Of the instruments used by American Indians 50 per cent. occur in the Burmese hinterland and adjacent countries.[2]

In the light of this short account of ethnological relationships in the Far East, it is surely not surprising to find a marked uniformity in musical culture over the whole area, particularly with respect to more primitive features. It is known that primitive characteristics of musical culture are often preserved with great tenacity by peoples otherwise at a high cultural level: European folk-song, for example, retains extremely primitive features.[3] The persistence in China proper, in spite of constant contact with other musical cultures (via Turkestan), of the characteristic minor third pentatonic genus, with the fourth as the dominant melodic unit, is the expression in musical terms of that vigour in her autochthonous culture to which, at the beginning of this section, her powers of absorbing conquerors and conquered were ascribed.

THE PLACE OF MUSIC IN CHINESE CIVILIZATION

The views on music held by the Chinese in antiquity were remarkable in that its essence was conceived to be not sound but a transcendent power. To a considerable extent this view of the nature of music survives even to this day. The music of the seven-stringed zither (p. 90) tends constantly towards imagined sounds: a vibrato is

[1] G. Coedès, *Les États hindouisés d'Indochine et d'Indonésie* (Paris, 1948), pp. 36, 81.
[2] Sachs, *The History of Musical Instruments*, p. 203.
[3] Sachs, *The Rise of Music in the Ancient World*, p. 296.

prolonged long after all audible sound has ceased; the unplucked string, set in motion by a suddenly arrested glissando, produces a sound scarcely audible even to the performer. In the hands of performers of an older generation the instrument tends to be used to suggest, rather than to produce, sounds.

As early as the date of compilation of the *Joulii* (13) (*The Ceremonial of the State of Jou*) in the third century B.C., a system relating musical sounds to the order of the Universe had been worked out. Its elaboration forms part of that scientific systematization of knowledge which took place between the fifth and the third centuries B.C. (the period of the Warring States), after the decay of the feudal system and at a time when the process of fusion to form states[1] had already begun. At a very early date, at least as early as the *Leu Shyh Chuenchiou* (14) (*The Spring and Autumn of Leu Buhwei* (15)), 239 B.C., a theory was devised by which the notes of the Chinese musical world could be derived from a fundamental pitch-pipe by simple arithmetical operations. The orderly generation of sounds from a fundamental by this procedure was equated with other types of order in the Universe: with the four directions, with the categories of substance, with the orderly sequence of the seasons.[2]

(F) Autumn
(C) Spring
(G) Winter
(D) Summer

This system was extended and worked out in a manner analogous to that of similar systems in India, Islam, ancient Greece, and the Christian Middle Ages.

In an attempt to preserve the harmonious correspondence between their system of sounds and the order of the Universe, the Chinese were early faced with the problem of fixing an absolute pitch. The pitch-pipes were not only of standard length but of standard capacity, and it is understandable that the Imperial Bureau of Music became part of the Imperial Bureau of Weights and Measures.

The belief in the power of music to sustain (or if improperly used to destroy) Universal Harmony was but an extension of the belief in the magic power of sounds. As a manifestation of a state of the soul, a single sound had the power of influencing other souls for good or ill. By extension, it could influence objects and all the phenomena of Nature. Symaa Chian (16) (163–85 B.C.) describes two zither tunes of

[1] Haloun, op. cit., pp. 243–6.
[2] Sachs, *The Rise of Music*, p. 110.

magic power:[1] when the first was played, two groups of eight black cranes appeared at the opening strain; at the second strain, they stretched out their necks and cried, extended their wings and began to dance.

The conditions under which the zither might be played (up to fifty years ago) were originally of magical significance, but gradually their significance was forgotten until they became merely symbolic of the ideal way of life of the *literatus*.[2] In Ming (18) times the playing of the zither was forbidden to women (though that did not prevent their playing it), and it was forbidden to perform before any but cultured persons. The fact that the zither became the favourite instrument of Taoist and Buddhist monks meant that it exchanged its more ancient magical associations for those of the monastery, but that it retained at all times the power to command a respectful hearing.

The categories of hieratic and popular music are to be distinguished in most cultures, in antiquity as in recent times, but China is perhaps unique in the extent to which ritual music came to be regarded as an effective regulator of the harmony of the Universe in general and of the State in particular, so that the first duty of the Ruler was to look to the perfect maintenance of tradition in the execution of the music and ritual of the State.

CHINESE MUSICAL INSTRUMENTS

The earliest Chinese documents (*c.* 1300–1050 B.C.) are inscriptions on fragments of bone recording the decisions of the tortoise-bone oracle. A number of these contain characters either certainly or possibly depicting musical instruments, and it has been suggested that they provide evidence for the use of drums struck by a drum-stick, bells on a wooden stand struck by a stick, suspended triangular stones struck by a padded stick, and a horn struck with a stick.[3]

Excavations on the famous Shang (19) sites in the plain of north-east China at Anyang (20) have yielded sonorous stones (*chinq*) (21) (pl. 4 (*b*)) and a globular flute (*shiun*) (22) (pl. 3 (*c*) and (*d*)). The former are L-shaped slabs of calcareous stone which (according to the pictographs in bone inscriptions) were hung from a frame and struck with a padded stick. The *shiun* from the Shang site is barrel-shaped and about 2½ inches high, carved with an ogre-mask. Hollow, with

[1] Symaa Chian, *Shyyjih* (17), xxiv, fo. 37 v°. Translated in R. H. van Gulik, *The Lore of the Chinese Lute* (Tokyo, 1940), p. 137.

[2] R. H. van Gulik, op. cit., pp. 134–48.

[3] E. H. Gibson, 'Music and Musical Instruments of Shang', *Journal of The North China Branch of the Royal Asiatic Society*, lxviii (Shanghai, 1937), pp. 8–18.

an apical blow-hole and five finger-holes in the side, it is said to produce the note-series: *do re mi fa sol.*[1]

In many of the folk-songs and dynastic songs from the Book of Songs (*Shyjing*) (23)—often said to have been selected by Confucius, but probably only used by him for purposes of instruction—references to music occur specifically mentioning some of the instruments supposed to be represented in the bone characters or found in Shang sites. According to Sachs's tentative chronology of primitive instruments, flutes with holes, and drums, such as are mentioned in these songs, belong to the middle neolithic stratum; they occur in neolithic sites and are distributed over several continents. The sonorous stones are also included among neolithic instruments. In some songs there are references to bells; these are the Bronze Age counterpart of sonorous stones.

Whistle flutes of clay, with or without finger holes, occur in China as children's toys. One type from Shandong (51) without finger holes and in the form of a bear is shown in pl. 3 (*i*). In Shikang there is a whistle flute with four finger holes in the form of a frog; and there are specimens with two finger holes from Gueyjou (24) in the form of a bird. The fact that in each case the whistle has the shape of an animal may well be significant. Such clay whistle flutes are also to be found in central America and may be a legacy from a late neolithic substrate. A bamboo whistle-flute is reported to have been seen in funeral processions fifty years ago.[2]

The Shang were overthrown by the Jou (25) about 1050 B.C., and many songs in the *Shyjing* suggest a considerable increase in the number of instruments used by the Jou (1050–255 B.C.). In addition to sonorous stones and stone-chimes, bells and bell-chimes, their idiophones include the percussion clapper (*chongdwu*) (26) (pl. 4 (*a*) the trough (*juh*) (27) resembling a rice-pounding mortar with pestle; and the tiger (*yeu*) (28), with a serrated strip of wood along its back, thrice scraped to mark the end of the music. Scrapers (according to Sachs) are idiophones reaching back to the earliest neolithic stratum; there is some evidence that they have a life-giving significance as charms. The Jou armoury of instruments also included chordophones, for the existence of which in Shang times there is no evidence. Thus the first of the songs (in the traditional order) refers to welcoming the noble lady: 'With *chyn* (29) and *seh* (30) we hearten

[1] H. G. Creel, *The Birth of China* (New York, 1937), p. 99.

[2] A. C. Moule, 'A List of the Musical and other Sound-Producing Instruments of the Chinese', *Journal of the North China Branch of the Royal Asiatic Society*, xxxix (1908), pp. 1–160.

her.' The two instruments referred to are both half-tube zithers (using Sachs's nomenclature) of which the former (or a descendant) is still in use as the classical seven-stringed zither (*chyn*) (pl. 3 (*a*) and (*b*) and the latter (*seh*) survives in a descendant with thirteen brass strings, the *jeng* (31). New aerophones include the mouth-organ, *sheng* (32) (pl. 3 (*e*) and (*f*), and pl. 4 (*a*)), two cross flutes, *yoh* (33) and *chyr* (34), a double pipe, *goan* (35), and the panpipes, *shiau* (36). (The modern *shiau*, a vertical flute, is shown in pl. 3 (*g*) and (*h*). Several sorts of drum, including one of earthenware, are mentioned.

From the *Yilii* (37) (*Rites and Ceremonies*), edited at the latest in the third century B.C., we have the following description of the distribution of the orchestra at the great archery tournament:

> On the day before the shoot are suspended, for the musicians, to the east of the eastern steps, facing west, the sonorous stones associated with the mouth-organs; south of these are the bells (*jong*) (38) associated with the mouth-organs, and south of these are other bells (*boh*) (39): all these are arranged in order towards the south. West of the eastern steps a drum is set up; it is beaten from the south. The answering drum (*byi*) (40) is to the east of this; it is struck from the south. To the west of the western steps are the sonorous stones associated with laudatory declamation; they face east. To the south of these are bells (*jong*) and to the south of these are other bells (*boh*); these are all arranged in order towards the south. To the south of all these a drum is set up; it is struck from the east. To the north of this is the starting drum *byi*. A drum is set up to the east of the western steps, it faces south. In the space between the set-up drums are the bamboos [flutes and mouth organs, presumably]. The hand-drum, *taur* (41) [struck by two buttons on two strings] rests on the western cords supporting the sonorous stones associated with laudatory declamation.[1] (See pl. 4 (*b*).)

The *chyn* probably had but five strings originally, the number being later increased to seven. The *seh* had twenty-six strings of silk-gut. The *jeng*, which survives particularly in southern and south-western China,[2] has thirteen brass strings and seems to be a small version of the *seh*; it is the only one of the half-tube zithers which includes the bamboo determinative in its ideograph. This may perhaps be regarded as support for the theory that it was originally made from an internode of bamboo divided down the middle into two half-cylinders.

The mouth-organ, *sheng*,[3] is always symbolized by a gourd (as the

[1] *Yilii*, vii.

[2] R. H. van Gulik, 'Brief Note on the Cheng, the Chinese Small Cither', *Tōyō Ongaku Kenkyū*, ix (Tokyo, 1951), pp. 10–25.

[3] F. W. Eastlake, 'The "Sho" or Chinese Reed Organ', *China Review*, xi (Hong Kong, 1882–3), pp. 33–41; L. C. Goodrich, 'The Chinese Shêng and Western Musical Instruments', *China Magazine*, xvii (New York, 1941) pp. 10, 11, 14; L. M. Traynor and S. Kishibe, 'On the Four Unknown Pipes of the Shō (Mouth Organ) used in Ancient Japanese Court Music', *Tōyō Ongaku Kenkyū*, ix (Tokyo, 1951), pp. 22–53.

shiun is by clay, and the flutes by bamboo) and at some period a gourd formed (and in some places still forms) the wind-chest; among a number of primitive peoples playing the instrument today, however, the wind-chest is made of wood, and in China and Japan it is often made of lacquer. Thirteen or so slender bamboo pipes, differing in length, are arranged so that each opens into the wind-chest by an aperture covered by a free reed of copper (pl. 3 (*f*)). A small hole in the pipe near the reed is stopped at will, so that a sufficient back pressure can be produced for the reed to be set vibrating when the pressure in the wind-chest is raised or lowered by blowing into or sucking the mouth-piece. The reed may be tuned by weighting with wax (pl. 3 (*f*)). The number of pipes has varied considerably in China at different epochs, and among non-Chinese tribes the number is much less at the present time (see pl. 6 (*b*) and (*f*)). They are so arranged that the lower notes can be accompanied by their octave or fourth or fifth. The *tessitura* of the modern Chinese instrument is soprano, but it is very probable that the early forms were of considerably lower pitch. It is known from late Bronze Age figured drums, probably of the fourth century B.C.,[1] found in northern Annam,[2] that the *sheng* in use at that time closely resembled the large forms found among the tribes-people in southern China at the present day, and accordingly must have had a range approximating to D–d.

Mention must also be made of the *jiun* (42), a stringed instrument used by the Jou for determining the pitch of bells; it consisted of strings mounted on a resonating table, 7 feet long.

The political unification of China brought about between 250 and 220 B.C. by King Jenq (43) of Chyn (*Chyn Shyy Hwangdih*) (44) was followed by the downfall of the unifier's dynasty and the succession to power of the Hann, during whose reign extensive contacts with various nomadic peoples on the north-western frontier of the Chinese empire, as well as with central and western Asia and India, led to the appearance of new musical instruments in Chinese orchestras. Chief of these was the *pyipar* (45), a short lute. It is reported to have been played on horseback[3] and seems to have been a short-necked instrument with a circular body, four strings, and twelve frets.

[1] B. Karlgren, 'The Date of the Early Dong-so'n Culture', *Bulletin of the Museum of Far Eastern Archaeology*, xiv (Stockholm, 1942), pp. 1–28.

[2] V. Goloubew, 'L'Âge du bronze au Tonkin et dans le Nord-Annam', *Bulletin de l'école française de l'extrême orient*, xxix (Hanoy, 1929), pp. 1–46.

[3] Liou Shi, *Shyhming* (46). See L. E. R. Picken, 'The Origin of the Short Lute', *Galpin Society Journal*, viii (1955), pp. 32–42.

Jing Farng (47), Imperial Secretary in 45 B.C., devised a stringed instrument after the fashion of a *seh*, the *joen* (48), in function resembling the *jiun* of the Jou, for it was used to fix the sound of the sixty notes into which Jing Farng divided the octave (p. 96).

Some of the earliest representations of zithers, stone chimes, *sheng*, vertical flutes, panpipes, and the drum known as *ingguu* (49) occur in the shallow bas-reliefs from Hann times on the walls of the Wuu (50) family tombs in Shandong (51) province.[1] On other Hann reliefs cross-flutes occur. In some of these Hann scenes the *chyn* is shown with but five strings.

By late Wey (52) times, that is, some two centuries after the overthrow of the Chinese empire in the third century A.D. by mercenaries settled on the northern frontier, the *pyipar* begins to appear in bas-reliefs as a four- or five-stringed, pear-shaped, bent-necked lute and may have resembled the *gaku biwa* of the Japanese court orchestra—an instrument over 3 feet in length.

A vertical angular harp also came to China in late Wey times, and representations are to be seen in the frescoes at Duenhwang (53) and on many stelae of the sixth century A.D.[1] According to size the harp had sixteen to twenty-five strings and is referred to in Chinese texts as *konghour* (54) (pl. 5 (*a*)). It did not establish itself in China as did other instruments originally imported in court orchestras from abroad.

The Shoosooin (Nara, Japan) preserves several Chinese *pyipars* of Tarng date (A.D. 600–900). This was an era of extensive intercourse between China and central Asia. Many new instruments and many types of orchestra were introduced, usually associated with their own dancers, jugglers, or acrobats, characteristically costumed. The size and composition of these orchestras is known from Tarng frescoes in the Thousand Buddha Caves at Duenhwang and from the Tarng histories.

Toy globular flutes with two finger holes occur in Tarng kiln-sites in the neighbourhood of the provincial capital of Syhchuan. Two specimens are shown in pl. 3 (*d*); both have the form of quasi-human heads. They furnish an instance of the survival as toys of ancient musical instruments whose ritual use has been forgotten.

Relatives of the *pyipar* in use at the present time, and possibly introduced in Tarng times, are the *yuehchyn* (55), a four-stringed flat

[1] H. E. Fernald, 'Ancient Chinese Musical Instruments', *Museum Journal* (Philadelphia, 1936). Reprinted in Hsiao Ch'ien, *A Harp with a Thousand Strings* (London, 1944), pp. 395–440.

lute, the strings of which are said to be tuned in pairs a fifth apart; and the *sanshyan* (56), a three-stringed flat lute, played with a jade plectrum; the strings are tuned: *do fa do* or *do re la*.

To the same period of importation probably belong the various bowed instruments, of which a considerable variety are in use in China today. Bowed instruments are first mentioned in Persia in the ninth century,[1] and a reference to a bowed zither, related to the *jeng*, occurs in a Chinese account of a Khitan orchestra playing at the Chinese court about A.D. 900. An instrument of this kind was in fairly common use in Pekin up to fifty years ago.[2]

Bowed lutes (that is, fiddles) arose at a slightly later date, and all varieties found in China are known collectively as *hwuchyn* (57) ('barbarian' *chyn*), suggesting that the instrument came to China from central Asia. The *ellhwu* (58) is perhaps the commonest form of *hwuchyn*.[3] It has a hexagonal tubular wooden body a few inches long, one end of which is covered with snakeskin, the other end is open; the whole acts as a resonator. The handle is inserted into the body at right angles to its long axis. There are two strings of silk-gut tuned a fifth apart, stopped by the fleshy part of the fingers, and the hair of the bow passes between the strings. The instrument is played with constant vibrato and glissandi and has a veiled tone of great beauty.

It is interesting to note that a dulcimer in use in south China today bears the name of *yangchyn* (59), the 'foreign' zither. It resembles the Persian dulcimer known as *santir*, but its distribution on the south-eastern seaboard suggests that it reached China from the sea rather than from central Asia.

HISTORY OF THEORY AND NOTATION

The writings of Leu Buhwei from 239 B.C. contain an account of the making of the pitch-pipes by Ling Luen (60): *ling* means music or musician, *luen* is a rule or to rule.[4] The name and the person were invented in the course of that scientific reconstruction by the Chinese of their own prehistory which occurred in the period of the Warring States already referred to (p. 87). There are no grounds for regarding

[1] Sachs, *The History of Musical Instruments*, p. 216.

[2] A. C. Moule, op. cit., p. 120. In relation to a number of points in the history of Chinese instruments see T. Norlind, 'Beiträge zur chinesischen Instrumentengeschichte', *Svensk Tidskrift för Musikforskning*, xv (1933), pp. 48–83. See also: F. A. Kuttner, 'The Musical Significance of Archaic Chinese Jades of the *Pi*-Disk Type', *Artibus Asiae*, xvi 1/2 (Ascona, 1953), pp. 25–50.

[3] A *hwuchyn* leads the ensemble in *The History of Music in Sound*, i, side 3 (*b*).

[4] G. Haloun, *Tocharer und Indogermanen* (Leipzig, 1926), pp. 156 ff.

the passage so often quoted from Leu Buhwei as other than a rationalization; it does not concern a historic figure nor does it include any precise geographical indications—the terms usually translated as place names are in fact general terms for geographical features:

> He [Music Ruler] gathered bamboos in a valley on a mountain pass, taking those grown of uniform bore and thickness, and cut between two nodes; the length of the piece being three inches and nine tenths, he blew it, making this to be the *do* of Yellow Bell [the fundamental of the Chinese system].[1]

At the present time the scale most characteristic of the Far East (as defined at the beginning of this chapter) is pentatonic without semitones, consisting of three whole tones and two minor thirds, the thirds being separated by one or two whole tones. The scale has the form:

do re mi sol la.

The ancient names for this series, as pronounced today, are:

gong shang jeau jyy yeu. (62)

The evidence for the existence of five-note melodies in early Jou times is confined to references to the 'five degrees', and to the names of the five notes in texts compiled in the third or fourth centuries B.C. The same texts contain references to the seven sounds or the seven 'beginnings', and it has been supposed that these indicate that a seven-note scale with two semitones was known even in Jou times. The first definition of the notes is that given by Symaa Chian in the second century B.C.

The process by which the lowest note (Yellow Bell) engendered the rest of the notes in the Chinese system is also described in the writings of Leu Buhwei: 'To the three parts of the generator add one part, making the superior generation. From the three parts of the generator reject one part, making the lower generation.'[2] The interpretation of this passage is that the complete note-series (of which the names are also given) was obtained by cutting bamboo tubes (of the same diameter) to lengths calculated by alternately subtracting and adding one-third of the length of the preceding tube, so that the ratio of the length of any pipe to that of the next in the series was as 3:2 or as 3:4. The notes given by pipes two-thirds of the length of their predecessors in the series were said to belong to the inferior generation; these are

[1] *Leu Shyh Chuenchiou*, v. *Guu Yueh* (61).
[2] *Leu Shyh Chuenchiou*, vi. *Inliuh* (63).

the six female *leu* (64), made (according to legend) from the singing of the female roc. The six remaining notes were said to belong to the superior generation; these are the six male *liuh* (65) made (according to legend) from the singing of the male roc. Theoretically this procedure yielded a chain of ascending fifths and descending fourths:

C D E F♯ G♯ A♯
F G A B C♯ D♯

and, if arranged in ascending order, the note sequence: F, F♯, G, G♯, A, A♯, B, C, C♯, D, D♯, E.

The *liuhleu* (66) (the complete note-series) was not a 'chromatic scale', but an array of all the notes in the Chinese musical firmament of the third century B.C. The process of generation described in the writings of Leu Buhwei presumably provided an approximate theory, satisfying the desire for order of those engaged at that time in systematizing the sum total of human knowledge. Similarly, the two 'whole-tone scales' of the male and female *liuh* (both *leu* and *liuh* are referred to collectively as the twelve *liuh*) were the result of a classification of the series into two groups by origin; there is no evidence that the Chinese musical genius at any time found expression in melodies referable to whole-tone scales.

It is certain that melodies making use of various scales must have existed before the *liuhleu*. The latter provided a theoretical means of deriving an array of notes, any one of which (again in theory) could act as *do* (that is, *gong*) in the five-note series. A pentatonic scale has five loci of modal inversion: that is, the series may begin (and end) on each of the five notes in turn, giving five modes. Each mode takes the name of the note which is *finalis*, which ends melodies in that mode. It is probable that the fact that different melodies were in different modes had been recognized at a very early date, and that transposition of the modes, changing the *liuh* selected as tonic, was practised.

Obviously, variation in the unit of length on which the length of the fundamental pitch-pipe was based at different times must have meant that absolute pitch was never attained. Under the Jou the minimal length of the Yellow Bell pipe is estimated to have been 20 centimetres. Europeans have accepted pitches of F (Amiot), E (Courant), D (van Aalst), E (Mahillon).[1] For convenience the value of F will be adopted here.

The fact that so many of the *liuhleu* bear the name of *jong* (bell) suggests that part of the original note-series may have been a set of

[1] For references see Bibliography, pp. 482–3.

bells (like the celestas or kettle-gong chimes in the Balinese orchestra). It is known that by 500 B.C. bells were cast in sets of six or seven members bearing, in some cases, names similar to those of bells in the *liuhleu* series. It is also possible that the names of the *liuhleu* were originally applied to a note-series differing from the *liuhleu* of Leu Buhwei.

Hann Dynasty (206 B.C.–A.D. 220) *to Swei Dynasty* (581–618)

While references in *Hwainantzyy* (67) suggest that a scale of seven notes was known in the second or first century B.C., there can be no doubt as to its use in the time of Jing Farng in 40 B.C.; nor can there be any doubt about the practice of transposition. Jing Farng gives an exact definition: 'At the Winter solstice one takes F (Yellow Bell) as *do*, G as *re*, A as *mi*, C as *so*, D as *la*, E as *si* (becoming *do*) and B as *fe* (becoming *so*), as the notes of the scale. Since the *liuh*(s) corresponding to the day act in turn as the fundamental, *re* and *so* follow (the fundamental) in accordance with their nature.'[1]

It was under the Hann emperor Wuudih (68) (141–87 B.C.) that the Imperial Bureau of Music (*Yuehfuu*) (69) was founded. This was responsible for supervising rites, ceremonies, and music of all kinds (foreign, court, and folk-music); for preparing archives of national melodies; and for establishing and maintaining the correct pitch of the *liuhleu*. In an attempt to bring the last note in the cycle of the *liuh* nearer to coincidence with the octave of the fundamental, Jing Farng in 40 B.C. increased the number of *liuh* from 12 to 60. But even when continued through five cycles, the twelfth fifth of the fifth cycle would still differ from the octave of the fundamental—always supposing that a stringed instrument such as Jing Farng used (the *joen*) could be made to produce accurately the sixty theoretical *liuh*.

That some notation or tablature existed in early Hann times is clear from the beginning of the story, already referred to (pp. 87–88) of Duke Ling (70) of Wey, recounted by Symaa Chian. Ling heard a zither tune played by spirits and requested his music master, Jiuan (71), to write it down for him. Jiuan did so and asked for time to practise it. Symaa Chian, writing in the second century B.C., was therefore familiar with some method of zither notation.

The decay of the practice of ritual transposition during the next three or four hundred years may perhaps be correlated with the disturbed state of the empire during the period of the Three Kingdoms.

[1] Maurice Courant, 'Essai historique sur la musique classique des Chinois' in *Encyclopédie de la musique* (Lavignac and La Laurencie), 1re partie, i (Paris, 1913), p. 94.

Not until the Swei (72) dynasty (581–618) do we again find explicit reference to transposition in relation to the lunar calendar.

In the early part of the sixth century a further theoretical extension of the series of *liuh* took place, the cycle of fifths being extended to 360 *liuh*; but while some attempt seems to have been made to put into practice the system of Jing Farng, the system of 360 *liuh* was undoubtedly of theoretical interest only.

In 587, Jenq Yih (73), Duke of Peh (74), in a memorial on the subject of ancient and contemporary musical practice, showed how to vary the tuning of the *pyipar* ('twisting the string-posts', that is, the tuning-pegs) so as to extend the range available, and make 'twelve *yunn* corresponding to the twelve *liuh*'; and the subsequent formation of eighty-four *systems* by transposition, each of the twelve *liuh* serving as initial.[1] The term 'system' (*diaw*) (75) includes both mode and key in the Western sense; that is to say, for the Chinese as for the Greeks the notion of a change of mode and a change of pitch were inseparable. The twelve keys (F, F♯, G, G♯, A, A♯, B, C, C♯, D, D♯, E) are known in Chinese as the twelve *yunn* (76); the seven modes are the seven *diaw* (the seven different kinds of systems) and this expression is identical with that used for the total number of different systems (scales in the Western sense) possible, $12 \times 7 = 84$ *diaw*. If this appears confusing, it is so even to the Chinese. This is due to the confusion between a change in key and a change in mode, which arises because on an instrument with a fixed scale (a bell-chime, for example), a change in mode must also mean a change in pitch, that is a change in key. In due course the proposal made by Jenq Yih was accepted, the legitimacy of the seven-note scale was recognized, and the practice of transposition was re-established, although this did not receive imperial favour and take effect until the next dynasty, that of the Tarng.

Tarng Dynasty (618–907)

In 628, the emperor Taytzong (77) approved the eighty-four systems: the seven notes from below upwards 'form a scale: *yunn*. In general, the twelve systems of *do* (that is the *do* mode in its twelve keys) all have the true fundamental, they have no sound lower than the fundamental. . . . The twelve systems of *re* all contain a note lower than the initial, this is the fundamental. The twelve systems of *mi* have two notes lower than the initial; these are the fundamental

[1] Courant, op. cit., p. 96, mistranslates. For further discussion of central Asian influence in Chinese music see H. G. Farmer, 'Reciprocal influences in music twixt the Far and Middle East', *Journal of the Royal Asiatic Society* (1934), pp. 327–42.

and *re*.'[1] Each *liuh* starts a scale of the type: F, G, A, B, C, D, E, F, and each of these twelve scales is called a *yunn*. Each *liuh* also acts as each degree of the standard scale in turn, forming the initial to seven systems (modes in the Western sense) known as *diaw*. Sixty of the *diaw* are principal systems founded on the five points of modal inversion corresponding to the five-note scale; the remaining twenty-four are complementary systems founded on the auxiliary notes. The different systems are defined by naming the *liuh* which is *do*, followed by the degree which names the mode. Thus 'Yellow Bell (F) *do*' is the *do* mode on F, that is, with F as initial (and fundamental); 'D♯ *re*' is the *re* mode on D♯, that is, with D♯ as fundamental (*do*) and *re* of the scale of D sharp (E♯) as initial.

A single Tarng music manuscript has been found in the famous Thousand Buddha Caves at Duenhwang.[2] It includes 'Emptying-the-cup Music' and is apparently written in a tonal notation, some elements of which are indistinguishable from numerals. This notation has not as yet been deciphered. It has affinity with the Sonq (78) notation used by *Jiang Kwei* (79) (p. 109) and with that of Ju Shii (80) and other Sonq writers, as well as with the *gaku biwa* notation of the Japanese court orchestra (p. 147). The structure of this composition will be considered later (p. 105). A tune of this name is mentioned in the section on rites and music in the Tarng History (190).

Sonq (960–1126) *and Southern Sonq* (1127–1279) *Dynasties*

From the end of the ninth century onwards, the imperial music again fell into disorder, and a statement made in 959 reveals that only seven notes, forming the Yellow Bell scale, are in use; the other eighty-three systems have disappeared. Of many hundreds of melodies in the eighty-four systems only nine survived and all of these were attributed to Yellow Bell (F) *do*. During the decline of the Sonq, the invading Tartars were practising a simplified version of Tarng ritual music, basing their tuning on the *pyipar*. The Jin (81), who conquered the Sonq, made use of a set of twelve hymns for all ritual circumstances, comparable to the twelve hymns of the Tarng. In the thirteenth century the Mongol invaders were again practising ritual transposition.

In addition to the *pyipar* notation already mentioned, the Sonq

[1] Courant, op. cit., p. 97.

[2] Bibliothèque nationale de France; Collection Pelliot, No. 3808 v°. Professor In Faaluu of Pekin National University possesses a photographic copy which I have examined and of which I possess a written copy.

poet and musician, Jiang Kwei,[1] made use of another notation, probably of very great antiquity, namely that of the names of the *liuh*. In four of his songs he also uses two notes sharpened by one or two commas, thereby extending the scale to nine notes (p. 110). In all cases the fractional tones are approached from, and quitted for, the note below, so that they are heard as a microtonal sharpening of two of the notes of a seven-note scale.

Jiang Kwei is also the first composer for the seven-stringed zither whose work survives in a contemporary tablature (pl. 5 (*b*)). This is based on these principles: each string is represented by one of the numerals from one to seven (82); the action of the right hand—whether the string is plucked with a forward or a backward motion, and which of the fingers 1–4 is performing the operation—is indicated by abbreviated characters written over, under, or embracing the number of the string concerned; the string may be open—indicated by an abbreviated character written over the complex—or stopped, in which case the finger of the left hand doing the stopping, and the point of stopping in relation to the nodes of the string, are indicated; the position adopted when playing harmonics is indicated by a prefatory character, as is the return to the usual position. The tablature of Jiang Kwei differs from that in use today in the very restricted use of ornaments and of ligatures, both of which are produced by shifting the position of stopping after the string has been set in motion. Jiang Kwei's tablature is transcribed and the work described on p. 111.

The notation most widely used for flute music and songs, up to the end of the empire and the founding of the republic in 1912, first appeared in China in Sonq times. Ju Shii makes use of this notation, taken from books of popular music, and equates it with the other Sonq notation already referred to, possibly developed for the *pyipar*.

Yuan Dynasty (84) (1271–1368)

In the first Mongol dynasty of the Yuan, the ritual music was carefully preserved and the practice of transposition cultivated. It was under this dynasty that the diatonic major scale was introduced into China as the main mode, and it is in the flute notation associated with this scale that all music of the theatre is written to this day. The characters for the note-series: c′ d′ e′ f′ g′ a′ b′ c″ d″, are given in the Glossary of Characters (84*a*); alternative forms are omitted.

In the latter part of the Yuan dynasty, and from the rise of the

[1] *Bairshyr Dawren Gecheu, Syhbuh Tsongkan* (83) (Shanghai, 1929).

Ming onwards, the practice of ritual transposition again fell into disuse.

Ming Dynasty (1368–1628)

During the Ming dynasty there appeared what is perhaps the most remarkable of Chinese theoretical works on music: *The Handbook of Music* (85),[1] by Prince Ju Tzayyuh (86) of the house of Jenq (87). This work, running into nineteen volumes, is a complete survey of music, dance, and ritual in ancient China. It attempted a reconstruction of the music of Jou times, providing full scores of many ritual hymns, and proposed an equal-tempered chromatic scale a hundred years before Werckmeister made the same proposal in Europe. Not content with establishing a just scale, Ju Tzayyuh reached the concept of equal temperament and succeeded in calculating values for the length and diameter of a series of equally tempered *liuh*: an equal-tempered chromatic scale of two octaves.

This dynasty saw the publication of superb collections of zither tunes in tablature.[2] The number of abbreviated characters in use had increased considerably from Sonq times, judging by the single example of Sonq tablature from Jiang Kwei. This was due to the development of the finger technique and to the increased use of ornaments and ligatures of various kinds.

Ching Dynasty (88) (1644–1911)

At the beginning of the eighteenth century, in the reign of Kangshi (89), the ritual music was restored, and the practice of transposition reintroduced. It was also at this time, Tzayyuh forgotten, that the octave was divided into fourteen steps, in an attempt to combine the process of derivation through the cycle of fifths with the octave standard. This scale differed from that of the flutes and chimes on the one hand and of the stringed instruments on the other, and the official melodies of the Ching cannot be played on an equal-tempered keyboard instrument without gross distortion.

At the present time, the ritual music survives only, if at all, in the Confucian temple at the home of Confucius at Cheufuh (90). Knowledge of the systems has decayed until a majority of the melodies in the modern repertoire of the seven-stringed zither are in the *do* mode on F. Even among zither players, who as a class are knowledgeable in the old music, confusion exists between a tuning, a key, and a mode.

[1] *Yuehliuh Chyuanshu* (85).
[2] R. H. van Gulik, op. cit., p. 85.

In addition to staff notation imported from the West, the Chinese also make use of a sort of sol-fa system developed by the Japanese, representing the notes of the diatonic scale by the numerals 1–7. For homophonic music this is typographically simpler than staff notation. Practically all collections of popular songs published in the past ten years in China have been written in this notation. The first four bars of Ex. 209 (p. 127) would be written as follows:

5|5 65 4 42|5 0 45|5 65 4 42|5 0

HISTORY OF THE MUSIC

Jou and Chyn Dynasties (*before* 206 B.C.)

No specimens of music survive in any text earlier than Tarng times, so that our knowledge of early and late Jou music is limited to descriptions of orchestras, names of songs associated with a particular ritual or with particular occasions, &c. A passage from the *Shujing* (91), the *Canon of Documents*, provides support for the view that Chinese music was essentially 'logogenic' in character at a time considerably earlier than the period of classical opera, in describing which Sachs makes use of this term.[1] In Shuenn's *Code* (92) we read: 'Poetry expresses the will; song prolongs the expression; music depends on the prolongation.' In a subsequent chapter[2] we are given some idea of the nature of ritual music:

> Kwei [the director of music] said, when the sonorous stones are struck lightly or heavily, when *chyn* and *seh* are struck lightly or heavily, and their sounds alternate with human voices, the spirits of the ancestors come: the guest of Yu [the emperor Shuenn] takes his place, the crowd of princes display their virtue in mutual courtesy. Down below, the flutes [double vertical flutes] and the small drums play together as soon as the signal is given by the wooden trough and cease as soon as the signal is given by the tiger-scraper. The mouth-organs and the bells play in the intervals.

Prince Tzayyuh, writing before 1595, chose the 'Hymn for the Sacrifice to Confucius', as played in the sixteenth century, to illustrate the ancient practice of transposition. The melody dates from the fourteenth century and may retain something of the character of the corresponding hymn performed in Tarng times. To suppose, as did Tzayyuh, that it represents the music of the Jou, 2,000 years before his time, would appear unwise. The hymn illustrates not only transposition into five keys other than the initial key (each key being one

[1] *The Rise of Music in the Ancient World*, p. 137.
[2] *Shujing, Yushu Yihjyi* (93).

tone higher than the preceding key) but also the constant distance of a fourth between the accompanying orchestra and the voices. By a brilliant emendation of a passage from the *Joulii* which, though it made cosmological sense as it stood, made no musical sense, Tzayyuh produces the following formula: 'The instruments play in F, the chant is in A sharp . . . for the sacrifice to the celestial spirits. For the sacrifice to the terrestrial spirits the instruments play in G, the chant is in C. . . .'[1] Sachs points out the similarity of this practice to that of one type of medieval organum: the organum (originally an instrument) accompanied the cantus at the fourth or fifth below.

Ex. 177

This is the first stanza of the hymn quoted by Tzayyuh; the bar lines mark the ends of the four-word lines and the commas mark the rhymes. In this type of transposition the melody is transposed in the Western sense, without change in mode. But Tzayyuh also gives an example of transposition involving a change in mode as well as in pitch. While the evidence that the Jou did anything of the kind is slender, the effect is enchanting, as the following example shows. It is the 'Hymn for the Sacrifice to the Imperial Ancestors', first in its original form (*do* mode on F) and then in the first modal transposition (*mi* mode on D):[2]

Ex. 178

Ex. 179

[1] Courant, op. cit., p. 102. [2] Ibid., pp. 114, 115.

One of the most remarkable aspects of the work of Tzayyuh is his reconstruction of the orchestral accompaniment to the ritual melodies, based on his own interpretations of ancient texts and on those of the Sonq Confucian philosopher, Ju Shii. Of this reconstruction perhaps the most brilliant feature is the elucidation of the ancient practice of prolonging a note, on plucked stringed instruments (such as *chyn* and *seh*) whose sound quickly decays, by means of a rapidly executed figuration—the procedure known as *tsawmann* (94). In a phrase used by performers of his day to tune their instruments, the Prince discovered what he believed to be the vestiges of the old *tsawmann*: the intervals of the octave and the fifth were played in succession to words meaning 'the moon is bright, the wind is soft'. The following example sets out in score the opening line of the second stanza of the 'Hymn from the Temple of the Ancestors'. The figuration differs in minor details from that given by Courant, and the mouth-organ part has been converted into chords of octave and fifth or fourth. The pitch of the mouth-organ may well be an octave lower than that at which it is written.[1]

Ex. 180

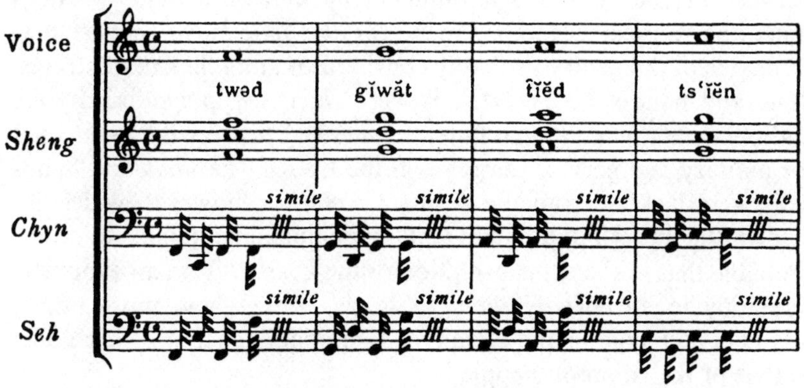

In addition to the ritual orchestra already described, there was a military orchestra, which included many varieties of drums, bells, and cymbals; this was also used in various exorcistic rites.

Hann Dynasty (202 B.C.–A.D. 220)

The imperial orchestra of Hann times comprised four different

[1] G. E. Moule, 'Notes on the Ting-chi, or half-yearly sacrifice to Confucius', *Journal of the North China Branch of the Royal Asiatic Society*, xxxiii (Shanghai, 1901), pp. 37–73, may be consulted for an account of the Confucian ritual as it survived at the turn of the century.

sections and employed more than 800 musicians. A great increase in the number and variety of drums in use as compared with the previous dynasty is to be noted; their designation by local names suggests that regional music was played.

During this period occurred the first stages in the evolutionary process which led finally to the development of Chinese opera. As in the evolution of Greek drama, a performance originally of religious and even of magical significance came to be repeated for the sake of its value as entertainment. In Jou times there had existed a ceremony of exorcism performed by a wizard, the *fangshianq* (95): this consisted in dances and songs executed by a troop of performers masked as animals and led by the wizard. It was made use of on two occasions: in the annual *nuo* (96) ceremony for driving away disease; and at funerals, to drive away the ghost. In Hann texts there appears for the first time the expression *koeileei* (97) used, apparently, as a synonym for *fangshianq*, and this term survives to the present (though written with graphic variants) as a term for marionettes of all kinds (98). What is unusual in the history of the Chinese theatre is the importance of the puppet theatre as an intermediate step between ceremony and entertainment by human actors.[1] In Hann times the musical accompaniment for the *fangshianq-koeileei* performance of the gentry probably consisted of an orchestra of strings, flute, and handbells. The strings were *chyn*, *seh*, *pyipar*, and *jeng*, and the flute was a vertical flute, *shiau* (99). This was the band used for military and general purposes in the Court. The *shiau* and handbells were lacking from the popular orchestra, however, which included the mouth-organ and the cross-flute, *dyi* (100). It seems probable that in the transformation of the *koeileei* from an exorcistic ceremony to an entertainment of songs, dances, and music, there was also a change in the status of its music from that of the court to that of the common people.

Tarng Dynasty (618–907)

The only specimen[2] of Tarng music supposedly transcribed from a contemporary document, and having some claim to be regarded as authentic, is the melody for the first song in the *Book of Songs*, printed by Prince Tzayyuh in 1596. According to Tzayyuh the melody was taken from the edition of the classics engraved on stone in the ancient

[1] Souen K'ai-ti, 'L'origine et le développement du théâtre des marionnettes chinoises', *Bulletin du centre franco-chinois d'études sinologiques*, i (Pekin, 1944), pp. 81–105 (summary in French) (194).

[2] The melodies preserved by Ju Shii may perhaps be included here. See p. 109.

capital, Shi An (101), in Tarng times. Engraving began in 835 and was finished in 837.[1]

This melody is one of those which Tzayyuh scores for drum, clapper, *seh*, sonorous stones, and voice. Another score is for voice, *chyn*, *seh*, two sorts of bells, sonorous stones of two kinds, clapper, mortar, tiger, drum, and small drum. The tune is remarkable in that it constantly avoids *re* but makes frequent use of both the auxiliary notes, *fe* and *si*. The chords supplied by Tzayyuh use only notes in the mode. Each four-syllable line of the poem is separated from the next by two bars of percussion, and there are 3½ bars of percussion at the end of each of the five stanzas. The first stanza only is quoted here. In Waley's translation the text runs:

'Fair, fair', cry the ospreys
On the island in the river,
'Lovely is this noble lady,
Fit bride for our lord'.[2]

The mode is *mi* on F. The voice sings the top part.

Ex. 181

An indisputably authentic relic of Tarng music survives in the manuscript from the Thousand Buddha Caves at Duenhwang already referred to (p. 98). From external features this is a suite in eight movements, headed as follows: 'Emptying-the-Cup Music; another slow tune; another tune; quick tune; another tune; another slow tune; quick tune; another slow tune.' These terms may well have a technical significance.[3] With the exception of the first section ('Emptying-the-Cup Music') and the last, each movement includes a repeat and a

[1] Professor E. G. Pulleyblank, Professor of Chinese Language and History in the University of Cambridge, has recently (November 1954) examined the stone-engraved ninth-century text of the *Book of Songs* in Shi An on my behalf. He reports that there is no trace of notation on the stones. This discrepancy between Prince Tzayyuh's ascription and the surviving stone-text at Shi An has also been noted by Professor Yang Inliou of the Central Institute for Musicological Research, Pekin. Thus the authenticity of Prince Tzayyuh's 'Tarng' melody remains unconfirmed.

[2] A. Waley, *The Book of Songs* (London, 1937), p. 81.

[3] This is undoubtedly the case for the term here translated as 'quick', which survives as a designation for final movements in the suites that form part of the repertoire of the Imperial Musicians of the Japanese Court (p. 147). (See H. Tanabe, *Nihon Ongaku Kōwa* (Tokyo, 1926), pp. 534 ff.). It would be of the greatest interest to compare the surviving part-books of the Japanese versions of the 'Emptying-the-Cup Music' with the Tarng manuscript.

coda. In the Tarng History this work (or a work with this title) is specifically referred to as a *dahcheu* (102) and is said to consist of at least ten movements.

The structure of this work corresponds to some extent with what is known from other sources of the structure of the 'extended melody' (*dahcheu*) of Tarng and Sonq times.[1] These orchestral compositions consisted of a number of movements (*piann*) (103), each of which might be divisible into several subsections. The character of these varied in the different types of *dahcheu*. The Tarng poet, Bair Jiuyih (Po Chü-I) (105) refers to: 'free prelude', 'middle prelude', and *poh* (106) or 'broaching the theme'. Some types include as many as twelve different movements. This structure has been compared with that of the suite in western Europe; but a more direct comparison would seem to be with the structure of Indian *rāgas*, with the Turkish *fasıl*, and with the *nūba*, as it survives in Morocco and Algeria.[2]

With regard to this last type of composition, it is interesting to note that the *dahcheu* occasionally included vocal movements. It is surely not without significance that the extended melodies of the seven-stringed zither repertoire are always referred to today as *dahcheu*. As we shall see, their structure offers points of resemblance to the structure of Tarng and Sonq *dahcheu* as inferred from literary sources, and it is reasonable to suppose that the zither compositions of the present day, lasting twenty to thirty minutes, echo an instrumental form which flourished from the seventh to the twelfth centuries.

From the period of the northern Chyi (107) (550–77) to the end of the Tarng (905), the music current in court circles on all but state occasions was known as *hwuyueh* (108): barbarian music. The fact that this foreign music was associated with the life of the court makes it improbable that the foreign styles had as yet become current among the people, though some influence cannot be excluded even at this early date. Since the popular music was essentially secular, it is not described in any of the records; but it seems probable that the musical accompaniment of the *koeileei* performances in Tarng times was a survival of the court military orchestra of Hann and Wey times.[3]

The Tarng emperor Shiuantzong (109) (713–55) maintained a troop of 300 actors, founded by himself in 714 and referred to as the Pear Garden; and to this period are traditionally ascribed certain melodies

[1] In Faaluu, 'Tarng-Sonq Dahcheu jy Laiyuan jyi chyi Tzuujy', *Wuuchang Hwajong Dahshyue Gwoshyue Yanjiou Luennwen Juankan*, i. 4 (Dahlii, 1945) (104).

[2] See p. 98 and Sachs, *The Rise of Music in the Ancient World*, p. 290. A comparison with the Turkish *fasıl* is in some respects closer than with the *peşrev*, instanced by Sachs.

[3] Souen K'ai-ti, op. cit.

still current in the Chinese theatre. The following example is part of a duet with accompaniment for cross flute, drum, and gong, transcribed from a gramophone record and ascribed to Shiuantzong himself.[1] It occurs in the opera, *The Little Shepherd*:

Ex. 182

The purely pentatonic character of this and other operatic melodies has been regarded as evidence of their antiquity, but as the examples of the Tarng (?) melody '"Fair, fair", cry the ospreys' and the Sonq melodies of the next section show, it is questionable whether any such deduction is legitimate. One would not expect the music of the Court of the time of Shiuantzong to be purely pentatonic. On the other hand such a melody might well be an echo of the popular *koeileei* music of

[1] G. Soulié de Morant and A. Gailhard, *Théâtre et musique modernes en Chine* (Paris, 1926), p. 134. See M. Granet, *Fêtes et chansons anciennes de la Chine* (Paris, 1919) for commentary (p. 269) and translation.

Tarng times, which indeed seems to have provided the basis for the development of classical opera (largely pentatonic) in Sonq times.

TABLE SHOWING THE COMPOSITION OF VARIOUS *TARNG* ORCHESTRAS

(after *In Faaluu*, op. cit.)

Instruments / Orchestra	*Yannyueh* (116)	*Chingshang* (199)	[*Gansuh*] (200) *Shiliang* (201)	[India] *Tianjwu* (202)	[Korea] *Gaulih* (203)	[*Shinjiang*] (1) *Jioutzy* (204) (Kutcha)	[Bukhara] *Angwo* (205)	[*Shinjiang*] *Shuleh* (206) (Kashgar)	[Samarkand] *Kanggwo* (207)	[*Shinjiang*] *Gauchang* (208) (E. of Turfan)
Sonorous stones .	1	..	..	..	..	..	..	..	..	..
Stone-chimes .	..	1	1	..	..	..	..	..	..	..
Bells . . .	1	..	2	2	..	2	1	..	2	..
Bell-chimes .	..	1	1	..	..	..	..	..	..	..
Iron chimes .	1	2	..	..	..	..	..	..	..	..
Conches . .	2	..	1	1	1	1	..	..	..	..
Copper horns .	..	..	..	..	..	..	..	..	..	1
Long vertical flutes . .	1	2	1	..	1	..	..	..	2	..
Short vertical flutes . .	1	..	1	1	..	1	1	1	..	2
Cross flutes .	1	2	1	..	1	1	1	1	..	2
Chyr flutes .	..	2	..	..	..	..	..	..	..	..
Free reeds .	1	2	1	..	1	1	..	..	..	..
Other reeds .	2(1)	1	2(1)	1	3(1)	1	1	1	..	2
Halftube- and board-zithers .	1	4(1)	1	..	2(1)	..	..	..	..	..
Lutes . .	1	1	1	1	1	1	1	1	1	2
Vertical harps .	2(1)	1	2(1)	1	3(1)	1	1	1	..	1
Drums . .	3(2)	1	3(1)	3(1)	4(1)	8(1)	2(1)	5(1)	2(1)	4(2)

The number of each sort of instrument used is shown in the appropriate column. Where a figure in brackets is given, this is the number of each of as many *kinds* of instrument as are shown by the number *outside* the bracket. Thus, under 'Drums', the *Jioutzy* orchestra contained one of each of 8 different types of drum; this is indicated in the form: 8(1). The category 'Other reeds' includes both oboe- and clarinet-type reeds.

Though practically nothing of the music of Tarng times has survived, a great deal is known from contemporary accounts of the nature of the orchestras employed in the palace, the number of performers taking part, the costumes they, and the dancers and jugglers associated with particular orchestras, wore, and the names of the melodies they played.[1] The composition of these orchestras has recently been reviewed[2] and the table above is modified from a table

[1] H. Trefzger, 'Das Musikleben der Tang-Zeit', *Sinica*, xiii (Stuttgart, 1938). See also Courant, op. cit., p. 192, Sachs, *The Rise of Music in the Ancient World*, p. 150, and Waley, *The Life and Times of Po Chü-I* (London, 1949), pp. 150–5. [2] In Faaluu, op. cit.

in this review. Foreign orchestras in China during this dynasty included orchestras from India, Bokhara, East Turkestan, Cambodia, Burma, Annam, Tibet, and Mongolia.

Sonq Dynasties (960–1279)

This is the first period in the history of Chinese music from which printed music of the time survives to the present. The famous Sonq Confucian philosopher Ju Shii, whose ideas exhibit some affinity with the monadology of Leibniz and who may indeed have directly influenced Leibniz,[1] left twelve melodies for twelve songs from the *Book of Songs*.[2] The following is a setting of the first song, of which we have already seen what is possibly a Tarng version (p. 105):[3]

Ex. 183

This melody is in several respects remarkable. It is heptatonic considered as a whole, but the first stanza is entirely pentatonic and the last stanza is pentatonic except for the last line: the mode is stated to be *re* on D sharp but is in fact a mixture of this and *do* on F. Ju Shii ascribes all twelve melodies to a Tarng source and to the reign of the emperor Shiuantzong, Kaiyuan (713–741).

A figure from Sonq times deserving of much more attention than he has as yet received, either from Chinese or from Western scholars, is the poet and composer, Jiang Kwei, the White Stone Taoist. His works include *Nine Songs for Yueh* (111) (Yueh is the ancient name for Jehjiang and Jiangshi Provinces) written in *liuhleu* notation; a song with zither accompaniment and interlude (p. 111); and a number of tunes in the Sonq *pyipar*(?)-notation which, though they have received some attention,[4] have not as yet been transcribed.

[1] E. R. Hughes, *The Great Learning and the Mean-in-Action* (London, 1942), p. 167.

[2] Ju Shii, *Yilii Jingjuann Tongjiee Shyyueh Pian* (110). Reprinted in the *Yueh Dean* (168) of Hwang Tzuoo (1692).

[3] Stanza-divisions following Waley, *Songs*, p. 81.

[4] Shiah Cherngdao, 'Bairshyr Gecheu Parngpuu Biann', *Yannjing Shyuebaw* (113) (Peiping, 1932). According to a recent report from Pekin (*Dahgong Baw*, 7. ix, 1954), this notation has now been deciphered; and a substantial body of Sonq music in the same notation has also been discovered.

Of the nine songs for the people of Yueh, the first six make use of only the seven notes of the diatonic scale, the mode being *do* or *re* in various keys. The text of the following example describes the singer awaiting the goddess of the Wuuchang Gulf (112), pouring a libation and riding the waves. The bar-lines mark the end of the lines (determined from the sense and from the verse-form); the comma indicates the caesura; and the double bar marks the ends of the stanzas. The mode is *re* on G sharp.

Ex. 184 The Spirit of the Billows

Four of the songs of Jiang Kwei make use of fractional tones (p. 99). In this example the mode is *la* on C. Fractional tones are indicated by diamond-shaped notes, following Levis.[1]

Ex. 185 General Parng

The single song with zither accompaniment by the same composer is prefaced by explicit directions for tuning the seven strings to the scale: F G A B d e g. The song is entitled 'Old Regrets'. It is a woman who sings, considering with bitterness the passing of her beauty. After the first stanza there is an interlude in harmonics for zither alone; at the end of this the normal position is resumed and the voice enters once more. In the transcription below (Ex. 186) the tablature has been emended, where necessary. All notes not a direct transcrip-

[1] J. H. Levis, *The Foundations of Chinese Musical Art* (Peiping, 1936), p. 175.

tion from the text are printed small in the transcription.[1] The bar-lines mark the end of the lines (determined from the sense); the double bar marks the end of the stanzas (explicit in the layout of the text); and the comma marks a caesura. The tablature does not indicate the duration of the notes; the minim values are supplied on the principle that a note at the end of a line is likely to be prolonged for at least two beats of the basic note-value. A change in the direction of the stems of successive notes at the same pitch, but played in different positions, indicates that the timbre is changed. Though the finger technique is rudimentary compared with later zither technique, the variety of positions in which the same note is taken, and hence the variety of timbre, is very considerable. If the example is played on the piano, the sustaining pedal and *una corda* should be depressed until the end of each 'bar', and as much variety in touch as possible should be given to notes at the same pitch. The voice presumably reduced the zither part to the range of one octave.

Ex. 186

From various sources it is known that the street performances of the *koeileei* in Sonq times were accompanied by the music known as *chingyueh* (114).[2] This was the term used by Swei and Tarng writers to cover the old-style (non-ritual) music of Hann and Wey times; the term persisted until Sonq times and was used in contrast to *hwuyueh*

[1] Versions in the *Syhbuh Tsongkan* and in the *Cheangtsuen Tsongshu* have both been utilized in making this transcription. See pl. 5 (*b*).

[2] Souen K'ai-ti, op. cit.

(barbarian music). The *chingyueh* orchestra included several instruments lacking in the imperial band of Sonq times, such as the *fangsheang* (115) (a chime of sixteen pieces of iron),[1] *sheng*, *dyi*, &c. It seems it was in Sonq times that the evolution from the puppet to the human theatre occurred, and that this development took place through an intermediate step of living puppets, that is, of children dressed as adults. Two separate types of performance developed from the street entertainment of the 'flesh puppets'; each consisted of dances and songs. They differed with respect to the origin of their music and of the texts of their songs. One type made use of the *words* of songs originally belonging to the repertoire of secular entertainments in the palace—the *yann* (116) (banquet) music of Tarng and Sonq times, but their music was the *chingyueh*, in which the cross-flute, *dyi*, was the chief melodic instrument supporting the voice; this type is known as *Nancheu* (117) (Southern Songs) in the repertoire which survives to this day as classical opera. The other type made use of the *words and music* of *yannyueh* songs, and the chief instrument supporting the voice was the *pyipar*. This was the origin of the *Beeicheu* (118) (Northern Songs) of the repertoire of classical opera. The names of the two genres are understandable, since the Northern Songs were strongly influenced by foreign music reaching China from the north, while the Southern Songs reflected the musical atmosphere of the more conservative south.

If anything of the music of these entertainments survives, it has undoubtedly undergone constant revision at the hands of successive generations of performers. The following three 'overtures' are supposed to be of pre-Yuan date.[2] They are entirely pentatonic and might well belong to the *Nancheu* tradition, but there is no documentary evidence of their antiquity.

Ex. 187

[1] A. C. Moule, op. cit., p. 146.
[2] Soulié de Morant and Gailhard, op. cit., p. 121.

The lyrics of *Nancheu* and *Beeicheu* were written in a special verse form, the *tsyr* (119), in which the lines are of irregular length and the syllables succeed each other in an ordered pattern of *tones*. The Chinese language is essentially monosyllabic, and since there are no double or triple initial consonants and only two finals in the northern dialect (for example), the sound equipment is poor. The number of different monosyllables is increased to something less than 1,400 by pronouncing each syllable with four different varieties of melodic accent (in the northern dialect)—the *four tones*. They have been represented in staff notation by Courant[1] as follows:

Ex. 188

The melodic accents are functionally neums,[2] and the types of melodic movement displayed in the four *sheng* (120) (the tones) are described as level, rising, falling, and entering. Shen Iau (fifth century) (121) was the first to make deliberate use of a pattern of accents, level and oblique (*pyng* (122) and *tseh* (123)), in a new style of poem, the *liuhshy* (124), in lines of five or seven syllables. At the end of the Tarng dynasty, one of the types of poem making use of a conscious neum-pattern was the *tsyr*.[3] The length of line is irregular in this type, and the poem is held together by the repetition, with variations, of a number of different unit patterns of tonal accents. If we represent the level tones by – and oblique tones (rising, falling, and entering) by / the structure of a poem of this kind can be displayed diagrammatically as shown overleaf.

The melody of many Chinese songs is but an exaggeration of the tonal accents and is inherent in the first *pyngtseh* draft of the poem; a melody devised according to the *pyngtseh* scheme shown here, by

[1] M. Courant, *La Langue chinoise parlée* (Paris, 1914), p. 19.
[2] J. H. Levis, op. cit., pp. 21 ff.
[3] A. Hoffmann, *Die Lieder des Li Yü* (Cologne, 1950), pp. 105 ff.

the Ching poet-composer, Shieh Yuanhwai (125), is transcribed on p. 125. The importance of the *tsyr* form in the history of Chinese music lay in its providing a great variety of types of melodic structure of considerable subtlety which could be used as moulds for new poems.

```
– – – / /
– – / – /
– – / / – – /
– – – / /
– – / /
– / / /
– / / – – /
– – / / – – /
– – – / /
```

The *cheu* was a quasi-popular development of the Sonq *tsyr*; it adhered less strictly to the tonal and rhythmic structure of the original *pyngtseh* draft; it was less 'classical' in its language and often betrayed local dialectical peculiarities in its tonal structure.

Yuan Dynasty (1271–1368)

Although there existed in Sonq times a type of theatrical performance known as *Tzarjiuh* (126) (literally 'Variety'), it was not until Yuan times that complete operas, comprising action, declamation, and songs, were devised.[1] The *Yuancheu* (127), as these works are known collectively, are of high literary quality and are the first representatives of the dramatic genre in the history of Chinese literature. While the importance of the *Yuancheu* as literature has been recognized by Western writers,[2] the fact that these were operas, not plays in the Western sense, has tended to be overlooked, and their very remarkable musical structure is virtually an unexplored field for future study.

At the time of the coming to power of the Yuan, two schools of opera were already established, the northern and southern schools of the Sonq dynasty; their differences reflect differences between the two regions in temperament and in contacts, and affect versification, music, and style in the broad sense. Musically the schools differed in that the southern school was strictly pentatonic and used the cross-flute as the chief accompanying instrument (if strings were used they

[1] Chiang Un-kai, *K'ouen K'iu — le théâtre chinois ancien* (Paris, 1932).

[2] A. P. L. Bazin Aîné, *Théâtre chinois* (Paris, 1838); *Le Siècle des Youen* (Paris, 1854).

were secondary); while the northern school made use of the heptatonic scale, with free use of semitones, and the accompanying instrument was a stringed instrument. At the beginning of the Yuan, the northern school was particularly active and works composed entirely in the northern style were known by the same name as the Sonq 'variety' theatre, that is, as *tzarjiuh*.

One of the most fascinating musical features of these early operas (a feature still characteristic of Chinese opera) is the use of a label, the *cheupair* (128) or song-label, for each verse-form. The *cheupair* is a fragment of a *cheu* poem, usually consisting of three characters, and its function is to recall to the reader the structure of that particular verse-form. Its function may be compared with that of the metrical formulas in hymnals in the West which indicate to what type of melody a hymn text can be sung or for what texts a given tune is suitable. Very often the author was guided by association in his choice of a particular *cheupair* in a particular situation. Thus he might use the *cheupair: shii shiangferng* (129) ('delights in conjunction') if he felt a correspondence between the situation to be presented and the spirit of this *cheupair*. Since a particular *cheupair* was limited to a particular mode, this system tended to reinforce the association of that mode with a particular verse-form and a particular emotional situation. The number of different melodies current was (and still is) far smaller than the number of lyrics. A casual opera-goer, who did not happen to know a particular lyric, would nevertheless have some clue to the emotional situation, if he were familiar with the tune. This is still true at the present time and is essential to the average person's enjoyment of opera, since the lyrics are written for the most part in a language too literary to be comprehended by the ear alone.

Up to 1297 the northern was the more important of the two schools, but after this date mixed works, including acts in both northern and southern styles, were written, and by the end of the Yuan the southern school had become dominant. Five works of the ancient southern school survive, of which the most famous is the *Pyipar Jih* (130), *The Story of the Lute*, by Gau Ming (131). These were written at the end of the Yuan or at the beginning of the Ming. At the present time they are better known from private reading than from stage performance and are often played by amateurs *en famille*.

Ex. 189 is an overture said to date from the end of the thirteenth century and often made use of in *The Little Shepherd* (p. 107). A note outside the mode occurs in bars 15 and 16.[1]

[1] Soulié de Morant and Gailhard, op. cit., p. 121, no. 4.

Ex. 189

Ex. 190 is an intermezzo (*guohmen* (132); literally, 'crossing the threshold') said to date from the fourteenth century and chosen on account of its free-flowing line. A B♭ outside the mode occurs frequently:[1]

Ex. 190

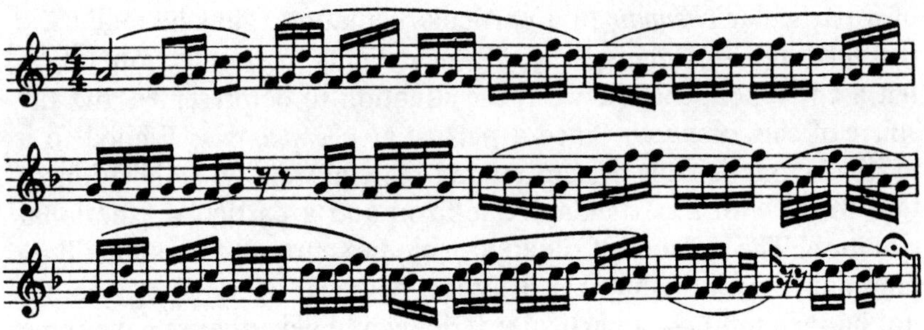

A most interesting feature of Chinese opera is the use of a characteristic theme or *yeadyi* (133) (literally, 'elegant flute') as a leitmotive in certain situations, or to express certain feelings. Three instances, possibly earlier than the thirteenth century, are given in Exs. 191, 192, and 193:[2]

Ex. 191

Ex. 192

[1] Soulié de Morant and Gailhard, op. cit., p. 123, no. 4. [2] Ibid., p. 124.

Ex. 193

A collection of Yuan melodies for zither, only one of which has been transcribed, is contained in the *Sehpuu* (*Music for the Seh*) of Shyong Pernglai.[1] This includes four volumes of tunes in both *liuhleu* and flute notation. One volume consists of twelve tunes identical with those of Ju Shii previously considered (p. 109); two volumes are entitled *New Tunes for the Songs* (that is, for songs from the *Book of Songs*), and a fourth is devoted to the Confucian ritual.

Ming and Ching Dynasties (1368–1911)

(i) *Seven-stringed zither*. The tablatures of seven-stringed zither tunes, printed in sumptuous large-paper copies and published in the Ming period, were one of the less conspicuous products of that unparalleled craftsmanship which has made the name of this dynasty a household word in the West. It will be convenient to treat the period from 1368 to the end of the Ching and even to the present day without further subdivision. The most famous zither tunes (with but few exceptions) were already in existence at the beginning of the Ming, but they are played today in Ching versions.

The nature of the development which the tunes have undergone between early Ming and Ching editions, is clear from successive versions (Exs. 194, 195, and 196) of the prelude from the tune 'Clouds over the Rivers Shiau and Shiang', ascribed to the Sonq composer, Guo Mean (134). Wherever a group of notes occurs in the early version which also occurs in the tune as played today, it has been given the same rhythmic structure in transcription as in current performance, so that the similarity between the versions is emphasized. The three preludes are in harmonics throughout.

[1] Shyong Pernglai, *Sehpuu* (198). See Yang Inliou, *Jonggwo Inyueh Shyygang* (Shanghai, 1953), p. 194.

Ex. 194

Ex. 195

Ex. 196

Ex. 194 is the prelude as it appears in the *Rare and Valuable Secret Treatise of an Emaciated Immortal*[1] (135), dated 1425. It bears the title: 'Mist and Rain on the Donqtyng Lake.' The text contains one complex which does not make sense; in its place a single note has been supplied to complete the phrase. The slur indicates that the

[1] *Chyushian Shernchyi Mihpuu* (135), by the Prince of Ning.

repeated notes are all played on the same string. Ex. 195 is taken from the *Wugaang Chynpuu* (136) of 1546. It has undergone amplification by extension and repetition of its members, and by interpolation. In this edition the prelude no longer carries a subtitle. One note has been supplied where the tablature seems to be faulty. The third version of the prelude is that current today. It differs but little in line from the seventeenth-century version in the *Chingshan Chynpuu* (137) (1673) though the notes are frequently produced in different positions. The transcription is made from a manuscript copy from an unknown source. The note-values approximate to those adopted by Shyu Yuanbair (138), one of the virtuosi of the present day. The prelude has now become an extended melody which, even when it finishes, leaves the way open for more to follow. Interest is maintained by a continual shifting of the tonal centre.[1]

From the *cheu* structure of the classical operatic melody to that of the seven-stringed zither tune, the difference is one of degree rather than kind. The smaller tunes (*sheaucheu* (139)) are essentially *cheu* melodies; the words usually survive and are commonly sung by the performer as the tune is played. This is so for the tunes 'Faang Tzyychyi' (140) ('Visiting Tzyychyi'), and 'Yangguan San Dye' (141), ('Three Repetitions of the tune: "The Yang Pass"'), which will be referred to later. The larger tunes or *dahcheu* (102) are purely instrumental, and their structure is that of a melody of higher order; they are for the most part rondos, in which the returns of the main tune are transposed up or down by one or more octaves—necessarily with change in timbre, or presented in different 'registration'—in harmonics or in a different position, without change in pitch but with change in timbre. The importance of timbre in this music is such that any transcription into staff notation can give but a faint impression of the original.

The larger tunes almost invariably begin with a prelude in slow time, often on the open strings, but frequently in harmonics. The prelude may include a characteristic turn of the main melody, as in the Ching version of 'Meihua San Nonq' (142) ('Three Repetitions of the tune: "Plum Blossom"') which is here transcribed from Ja Fuhshi's (143) recording in the Library of Congress[2] (Ex. 197). Versions of this tune occur in Ming tablatures of 1530 and 1546. The first six notes of the prelude are related to the central phrase in the

[1] Library of Congress, Music Division, Mr. Cha playing Chinese music, Order No. 1095, 4 sides: 4B, 5A, 5B, 6A. A slightly different version from that of Mr. Shyu.

[2] Library of Congress, Music Division, Mr. Cha playing Chinese music, Order No. 1095, 3 sides: 3A, 3B, 4A.

Ex. 197

main tune; the latter appears three times in harmonics, always in a different position. The following example is a transcription of the tune at its third appearance, again as played by Ja. This is one of the most immediately engaging tunes in the zither repertoire.

Ex. 198

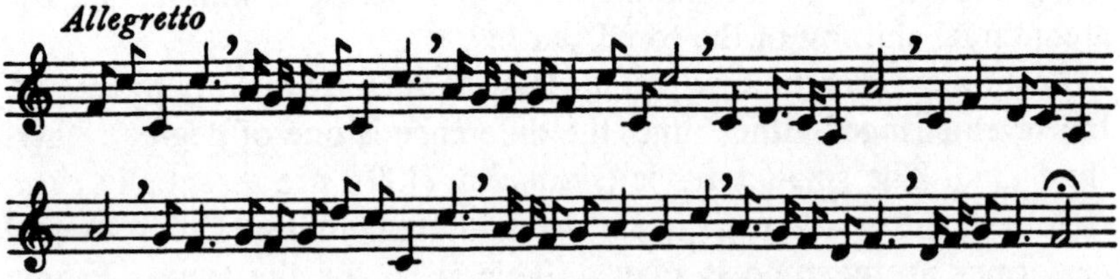

A prelude of unusual type, echoing Buddhist cantillation, is that to the famous tune 'Pụuan Jow' (144) ('The Spell of Puuan'):

Ex. 199

Puuan was an Indian Buddhist of the twelfth century, but the tune of this name was probably not composed before the seventeenth century. The prelude opens with octaves, one string being caused to produce a succession of sounds by shifting the finger after plucking. The second section of the prelude is in harmonics (beginning at the change of clef in the example). Although in many respects a work *sui generis* it deserves mention here because of its great popularity with zither players. Its square-cut rhythms recall Pekin opera-tunes and folk-songs of the north-western border.[1]

The climax of a zither tune is frequently marked by a passage in harmonics. If the work is of considerable extent there may be more than one such—as in 'Meihua San Nonq', for example. These passages are felt to be of the greatest emotional tension: at these moments the music leaves the earth.

Most of the zither tunes, whether short or long, end with a coda in harmonics. This may be very short, or it may contain a reference to the main tune and summarize the whole work, as in the coda to 'Yangguan San Dye' ('Three Repetitions of the tune: "The Yang Pass"').[2]

Ex. 200

This includes a reference to the second phrase of the opening melody. The whole of the first section, including the thrice repeated refrain is transcribed in Ex. 201.

Ex. 201

The pass referred to in the title is that in the north-west through which so many have travelled to real or virtual exile. A Northern Song to the same words is transcribed in Ex. 210 (p. 127). It is not unusual for the last note of the coda to be a note other than the expected tonic, as in Ex. 200. Another example is provided by the end of a short tune

[1] Also recorded by Cha under the title 'Universal Benediction', Library of Congress, Music Division, Order No. 1095, 3 sides: 1B, 2A, 2B.

[2] A transcription of the opening phrases of a version of this work is printed by F. Bose in *Musikalische Völkerkunde* (Freiburg i. Br., 1953) as No. 50 of the musical examples, taken from a recording: Overseas Branch Rec. 17–2954, collected by Reinhard.

peculiar to Syhchuan Province, 'Visiting Tzyychyi'. The harmonics begin at the change to the treble clef.

Ex. 202

Successive appearances of the main tune are usually at different pitches but in the same key. Modulation in the sense of a change of key is relatively infrequent. It occurs commonly, however, in the sense of a shift in the tonal centre, even in the course of one and the same melody, as shown in Exs. 196 and 201; the melody temporarily behaves as if some other note in the note-series of the mode were the tonic. Occasionally a true modulation to the dominant occurs, as in the following example from 'Puuan Jow'.

Ex. 203

This is the passage in harmonics at the climax of the work. Two arpeggios of harmonics bring about a modulation to the dominant and there follows a pause on the dominant. Where the clef changes to the bass clef in Ex. 203, the normal position and the key of the tonic are resumed. Another example, in a work predominantly 'minor' in colouring, occurs in the short tune 'Yih Guhren' (145) ('Remembering a Friend'[1]) in which transition to the new key is prepared through the mediant. In this example the B is flattened throughout (Ex. 204).

[1] Library of Congress, Music Division, Mr. Cha playing Chinese music, Order No. 1095, 2 sides: 9B, 10A; under the title 'In Memory of a Deceased Friend at a Lonely Hill'.

Ex. 204

Occasionally a note outside the mode may be introduced with overwhelming effect. Towards the end of 'Shiau-Shiang Shoei Yun' (146) ('Clouds over the Rivers Shiau and Shiang') such a note occurs; it is sometimes interpreted as a monastery bell.

Ex. 205

(ii) *Pyipar and Jeng*. Of the instruments introduced into China in historic times, only the *pyipar* can compare with the *chyn* in the extent of its repertoire and the virtuoso skill attained by its finest exponents. Published transcriptions of *pyipar* music[1] are atypical inasmuch as it is characteristic of this music that the melody is frequently accompanied by a simple bass—perhaps a single note repeated as a pedal point, and that considerable use is made of repeated chords. On the whole, music for the *pyipar* is even more frankly descriptive than that for the *chyn*. One of the finest performers, Yang Dahjiun (147), executes a battle-piece that includes imitations of the groans of the wounded and dying, and a moving version of the famous tune, 'Geese Descend on the Level Sands', with astonishingly birdlike noises.

In recent years Liang Tzaypyng (148) has travelled extensively in the mountainous interior of Fwujiann (149) Province, collecting *jeng* tunes from elderly performers and studying their technique. In the south-west, and particularly in Kuenming (150), there is a vigorous group of amateurs of this instrument, and itinerant performers are to be heard in Cherngdu (151), the capital of Syhchuan Province. One of the most memorable tunes is entitled 'Cold Crows Playing with Water'.

[1] E. Fischer, *Beiträge zur Erforschung der chinesischen Musik* (Leipzig, 1910), also in *Sammelbände der internationalen Musikgesellschaft*, xii (1911), pp. 153–206. Other transcriptions will be found in A. Dechevrens, 'Étude sur le système musical chinois', *Sammelbände der internationalen Musikgesellschaft*, ii (1901), pp. 484–551.

CHINESE INSTRUMENTAL HETEROPHONY

A few transcriptions from phonograph recordings demonstrating Chinese polyphonic practice have been made. The first example is from a *sheng* recording.[1]

Ex. 206

The second is for cross-flute (*dyi*) and fiddle (*yuehchyn*). The conclusion only is quoted. The *yuehchyn* accompaniment is largely a variation on the flute melody at the fourth below. The interest of this combination for a Chinese ear lies in the simultaneous presentation of theme and variant, not in their incidental clashes.[2]

Ex. 207

[1] E. Fischer, *Beiträge*, p. 1.
[2] Ibid., p. 11.

THE STRUCTURE OF CHINESE INSTRUMENTAL MUSIC

From an analysis of nine recorded works, all popular in character, it is clear that both binary (or quaternary) and ternary types of construction occur.[1] In their formal organization the pieces analysed reveal a high level of development; indeed, many of the formal complexities encountered can be paralleled in the procedures of the Netherland school of the fifteenth century. The structure of these nine pieces is generally as follows: after an introduction, a complex of groups of phrases is repeated several times with variation. Among the different types of variation the following may be mentioned; a group of phrases may be lengthened or diminished, or entirely omitted, or varied with such freedom that the variant is only recognizable as such because it retains some characteristic turn. Within a group, several bars may be transposed to the fifth or fourth; they may be arranged in a different order or they may be replaced by others. Transposition of entire themes to the fifth or fourth is fairly common, and two-part writing in parallel fifths or fourths, comparable to early medieval Western practice, is frequent.

In one instance a comparison has been made between recorded performances (on *sanshyan* and on the large *hwuchyn*, p. 93), by two different performers, and the noted version supplied by one of the performers.[2] The tune in question has been subjected to detailed analysis and in spite of its seeming simplicity is plainly anything but artless in construction. Its title, 'Visiting the Son of Heaven,' goes back at least to early Ching times; but the particular tune analysed is not one of the tunes of this title printed in the great Palace Collection of *tsyr* of 1747.

A TSYR MELODY

In his study of *The Foundations of Chinese Musical Art*, Levis analysed four *tsyr* melodies by the Ching composer, Shieh Yuanhwai, written in 1848 according to the tonal structure followed by the Tarng or Sonq author of the *tsyr* in question. The pattern of one of these Sonq *tsyr* was given earlier, on p. 114. The following example is Shieh Yuanhuair's realization of the neums, transcribed by Levis:

Ex. 208

[1] E. Fischer, op. cit., p. 29.

[2] E. M. von Hornbostel, 'Ch'ao-t'ien-tze (Eine chinesische Notation und ihre Ausführungen)', *Archiv für Musikwissenschaft*, i (1919), pp. 477–98.

OPERA

At the beginning of the Ming dynasty the southern school of opera became divided into many small schools, working in different regions and making use of local dialects in their scripts. Towards the middle of the sixteenth century, a native of Kuenshan (152) in Jiangsuh (153) Province, Liang Borlong (154), wrote the script of *The Story of the Laundress of Fine Textiles* which was set to music by a fellow countryman from a neighbouring town, Wey Liangfuu (155), who had invented a new style of singing. The result of their collaboration was immensely successful. The school which they founded at first bore the name of *Shoeimodiaw* (156) (literally: 'song ground in water') but it gradually assumed the name of *Kuencheu* (157): The songs of the men from Kuenshan. The collaborators proceeded to revise the works of the southern school, and their revisions were generally approved and accepted as models. The name *Kuencheu* as used at the present time, however, includes not only works of the southern school written subsequent to the collaboration of Liang Borlong and Wey Liangfuu, but also all the works of the Yuan period, particularly those revised by Wey himself. The *chwanchyi* (158) was the characteristic form developed by the school of Kuenshan and differed in length from the Yuan *tzarjiuh*. While the latter had consisted of but four acts and a single singing role, the *chwanchyi* were composed of thirty to fifty acts of which perhaps four-fifths were in the southern style and the rest in northern; several acts might be mixed in style. From the point of view of the arrangement of the acts according to style, the seventeenth-century opera *Charngsheng Diann* (159) ('The Hall of Long Life') by Horng Sheng (160) is today regarded as a model. *Chwanchyi* also differed from *tzarjiuh* (p. 114) in the number of singing roles; the former recognized six chief types whose identification by the audience was (and is) facilitated by their characteristic costumes and maquillage.

Each act of a classical Chinese opera comprises both declamation and measured song. An important character, entering at the beginning of an act, will declaim a prologue in prose explaining the situation. This will be followed by a poem, which in turn will be followed by a monologue in prose. Each act is given a pithy title such as the following, taken from the *Pyipar Jih*: 'Marriage by Imperial Command'; 'Help to the Hungry'; 'Difficulties in Maintaining Parents-in-Law'; 'Sale of Hair to Bury Parents-in-law'; 'Entire Family Decorated'.

A single act will generally include ten *cheu*, all in the same mode and key, either all in the southern or all in the northern style or with some in each style. Generally speaking the *cheupair* (128) are so chosen that all are suitable for the expression of the same quality of feeling, and the individual *cheu* patterns normally succeed each other in the order of their classification in the mode.

Exs. 209 and 210 are melodies of the southern and northern schools respectively:

Ex. 209

Ex. 210

These (and Ex. 208) are the only examples of Chinese vocal melody so far quoted that display melismatic as opposed to syllabic structure. All Sonq and Yuan melodies known from contemporary documents are syllabic, as were (so far as is known) the most ancient Chinese melodies; but it is to be remembered that none of the surviving melodies is popular in character, and it may well be that a proportion of the *koeileei* melodies of Tarng times were at least partly melismatic.[1]

Whereas in the past twelve flutes, each at the pitch of a different

[1] Exs. 209 and 210 are transcribed from T'ung Fei, *Fundamentals of Chinese Music*, ii (Shanghai, 1927) (195), pp. 19, 20.

liuhleu, were used to accompany *kuencheu*, only a single flute is used today. The largest number of modes now used in any tonality is four, and two tonalities are represented by a single mode only. Each mode or system is associated with a definite character—fresh and distant, sighing and afflicted, rapid and varied, fierce and melancholy, elegant and reserved, &c. It is perhaps worth recalling that similar feeling about modal quality was current in Europe at least as late as the sixteenth century.

The essential accompanying instrument in *kuencheu* performances is the cross-flute, *dyi*, but other wind instruments—flute, mouth-organ, oboe-type reed instruments—may be added; strings—*sanshyan* and *pyipar*—may support the *dyi*; and a body of percussion is indispensable—indeed, the hoop-drum, *bangguu* (161), leads the ensemble. Changes of scene, and the beginning and end of the acts, are indicated by vigorous interludes for percussion alone. There may be some trace of Indian or at least central Asian influence in these interludes, though Chinese drumming never approaches the rhythmic complexity of that of India.

In Nanking or Pekin one may hear professional performances of *kuencheu*; but the operas to be heard all over China, even in small country towns, belong to the new northern style developed in the nineteenth and early twentieth centuries. The style is associated with the Manchu capital, Pekin, and operas of this type are often referred to collectively as *jingshih* (162) (plays of the capital). Provincial opera merits greater attention than it has hitherto received.[1] Like the classical northern opera (of which it is to a certain extent the descendant) *jingshih* makes use of a stringed instrument (a *hwuchyn* of some kind) as the chief instrument supporting the voice. Superficially the most obvious difference between *kuencheu* and *jingshih* lies in the rejection of the *tsyr* form of lyric and the abundance of symmetrical melodies. While *kuencheu* makes use of only two rhythms: a 2/4 with the first beat strongly accented, and a 4/4 with the first beat strongly accented and the third beat divided into two quavers, *jingshih* makes use of a considerable number of rhythms, both regular and irregular.

The following example is transcribed from *The Kingfisher-Feather-Screen-Mountain* (*Tsueypyng Shan*) (163), a *jingshih* opera of the genre *bangtzyy* (164). The vocal line in 2/4 time is accompanied by a fiddle in 3/4 time, a sonorous wooden block beaten in 3/4 time

[1] Chao Wei-pang, 'Yang-ko, the Rural Theatre in Ting-hsien, Hopei', *Folklore Studies*, iii (Peiping, 1944), pp. 17–40.

(the *bangtzyy* from which the genre takes its name), and a hoop-drum:[1]

Ex. 211

As an example of a leitmotive of much later date than those given on p. 116, the following is of considerable rhythmic interest; it depicts complete intoxication (Ex. 212).[2]

[1] Soulié de Morant and Gailhard, op. cit., p. 137.
[2] Ibid., p. 125.

Ex. 212

Evidence of the remarkable accuracy of the oral tradition in Chinese opera is provided by the nearly complete agreement between the *kuencheu* recording in Hornbostel's record-series *Musik des Orients*, and the printed edition of 1792.[1] The intervals agree almost entirely, but there are slight rhythmic deviations—a crotchet in the edition of 1792 may become a dotted crotchet in the recorded version.

FOLK-SONG

The scientific study of Chinese folk-music has scarcely begun, for though many collections are now being made, no collector, so far as is known, has as yet made recordings in the field; all depend on the ear. From personal observations made during a brief stay in central China it seems probable that traces of other and older types of scalar structure survive in the folk-music. This is suggested by street-cries collected in Syhchuan and Gueyjou Provinces. The enharmonic tetrachord (a fourth built up from a major third and a minor second) of the Japanese modes *hirazyoosi*, *kumoizyoosi*, and *iwatozyoosi* (p. 145) is rare in classical Chinese music and *jingshih*; it occurs, however, in the following street-cry:

Ex. 213

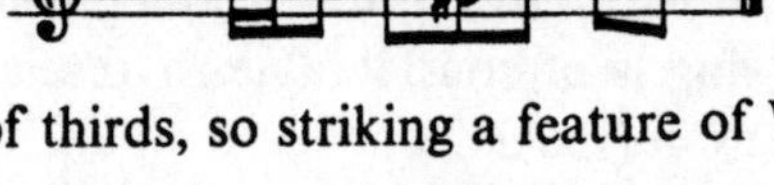

Again, chains of thirds, so striking a feature of Western, African,

[1] Wang Kwang-chi, 'Über die chinesische klassische Oper 1530–1860', *Orient et Occident, Bibliothèque Sino-Internationale* (Geneva, 1934).

Polynesian, and American Indian music, rarely occur in classical Chinese music, so strong is the tendency for a minor third to form a unit by adding a major second; yet Exs. 214 and 215 (also street-cries) are both expanded triads:

Ex. 214

Ex. 215

Ex. 215 illustrates a primitive stage of the 123 scale[1] (E♭, F, G, B♭) in which two superposed thirds form a pentachord and the lower third is filled in (123. 5). Ex. 216 is interesting in that the fourths are only acciacaturas:

Ex. 216

One feature of everyday life in China which impresses the stranger is the singing of the coolies; when pulling or carrying loads, they improvise a seemingly continuous chant, which has the function of co-ordinating activities and maintaining the rate of working at the optimum pace set by the leader. It is in fact an antiphon between leader and gang, in which statement and answer tread so closely on each other's heels that the sound is effectively continuous. Ex. 217 might be sung (to the vowel sound 'ah') by men pulling a loaded cart up hill.

Ex. 217

[1] Sachs, *The Rise of Music in the Ancient World*, p. 123.

Ex. 218, on the other hand, might be sung by men trotting with a load slung on poles.

Ex. 218

In such improvised antiphons it is the leader alone who varies his utterance with successive repetitions. The answer frequently overlaps the statement. Sometimes one hears 'shanties' such as the following:

Ex. 219

An excellent short collection of popular Chinese songs, many of them folk-songs, has been published by C. H. and S. H. Chen.[1] The collection merits praise not only for the notable accuracy of its transcriptions but for the quality of the accompaniments devised by C. H. Chen. In themselves they provide useful material for studying melodic variation and heterophony in Chinese music.

Ex. 220 is a well-known folk-song, sung to different words in different districts.[2] It is a good example of the pure pentatonic genus, still characteristic of Chinese melody in spite of the constant infiltration of other genera from central Asia. Another purely penta-

[1] C. H. and S. H. Chen, *The Flower Drum and other Chinese Songs* (New York, 1943). Other folk-tunes are to be found in A. G. Jacobs, *The Chinese-American Song and Game Book* (New York, 1944), and S. M. Graves and M. F. Farley, *Min River Boat Songs* (New York, 1946).

[2] For another version of this tune see Hsiao Shusien, 'La chanson populaire chinoise', *Sinologica*, i (Basel, 1947), pp. 65–86.

tonic folk-song is shown in Ex. 221, taken from a setting by Liu Shea-An [*sic.*][1]

Ex. 220

Ex. 221

Within the last few years many popular collections of folk-songs from all provinces have been printed in China, transcribed in the numerical notation (p. 101). Though popular in character, these collections are of the greatest value and already enable us to determine the regions of transition to types of melody resembling those of western Asia.

BUDDHIST MUSIC

The music of the Buddhist office as practised in Chinese monasteries deserves special attention, since it embodies many features at first sight foreign to the Chinese musical genius. While some of these may well be due to Indian and Tibetan influence, some may echo that more primitive stratum of folk-music revealed in the street-cries already discussed. In a small monastery in Anshuenn (165), Gueyjou Province, novices in their teens have been heard chanting the scriptures in thirds (cf. the English and Scandinavian *gymel* of the twelfth century). The range of cantillation was a fourth, and the result could be placed alongside Lachmann's juxtaposition of the German folk-song 'Laterne, Laterne!' and Hornbostel's Macusi Indian melody,[2]

[1] Liu Shea-An, *Three Songs* (Tokyo, 1935).

[2] R. Lachmann, 'Musik der außereuropäischen Natur- und Kulturvölker', *Handbuch der Musikwissenschaft* (Potsdam, 1929), p. 8; quoted by Sachs in *The Rise of Music in the Ancient World*, p. 40.

as an example of the survival in China of tendencies observable in very primitive musical cultures elsewhere. At a funeral in a small country town, Meitarn (166) in Gueyjou Province, Buddhist priests were heard singing, to the accompaniment of cymbals and triangle, a metrical chant of that infectious gaiety so common in India and so rare in China. The aspect of Buddhist music which most merits study, however, is the singing of the office by precentor and novices. The instrumental accompaniment is provided entirely by idiophones and membranophones; the instruments include a large drum, a large bell, a gong, cymbals, a triangle, a small bell, and a wooden fish. The office begins with intoned statements and responses by precentor and novices, with occasional interruptions by single instruments. As the service proceeds the speed of recitation increases, and the precentor no longer waits for the novices to end their response before recommencing; as the overlapping antiphon develops, the frequency of percussive interruptions increases.[1]

Concerning the Taoist office no information is available. Several hymns making use of a notation unlike any other Chinese notation are printed in the Ming *Dawtzanq* (167). They have not been transcribed.

Note on the Zither-Transcriptions

To avoid excessive use of leger lines and signatures, the transcriptions on pp. 118–23 are made throughout as if the third string were tuned to F, so that in the commonest tuning the seven open strings will yield the series: C D F G A c d. In the hands of different performers, and on different instruments, the sounding pitch of the third string will range from F to B♭ (below 'cello bottom C).

[1] See also A. Stanley, 'Putoshan', *Journal of the North China Branch of the Royal Asiatic Society*, xlvi (1915), pp. 1–18.

III

THE MUSIC OF FAR EASTERN ASIA

2. OTHER COUNTRIES

By Laurence Picken

MONGOLIA

A considerable range of music recorded in eastern Mongolia has been published in transcription.[1, 2, 3] The tunes are mostly pentatonic, with tetrachords consisting of a major second and a minor third. Major third scales, in which the tetrachords each consist of a major third with a minor second above, have been reported in melodies from the Buryat Mongols,[4] but the material from eastern Mongolia does not afford a single example of this type. The melodies are often less than an octave in range and fall into two main groups: those in free rhythm and those which are measured. The first type is illustrated by the following example for male voice from the Chipchin tribe, 'Bargas' (an old tribal name) 'of the Holy Mountain'.[2]

Ex. 222

The second example, the 'Song of Chingis Khan'[2] (male voice) from the Jalait tribe, is a symmetrical tune with a strong major flavour imparted by the arpeggioed triad in the first bar (Ex. 223).

[1] N. de Torhout and Humbert-Sauvageot, 'Dix-huit chants et poèmes mongols', *Bibliothèque musicale du musée Guimet*, 1re série, iv (Paris, 1937).

[2] H. Haslund-Christensen and E. Emsheimer, *The Music of The Mongols* (Stockholm, 1943). Several small collections of Mongolian tunes have been published in China in recent years. The tunes are all of the measured, symmetrical type.

[3] Chūichirō Takeda, 'Songs of the Mongols, Notations and Explanations', *Tōyō Ongaku Kenkyū*, ix (Tokyo, 1951), pp. 147–54, and x–xi (Tokyo, 1952), pp. 67–73.

[4] C. Stumpf, 'Mongolische Gesänge', *Sammelbände für vergleichende Musikwissenschaft*, i (1922), pp. 107–12.

Ex. 223

A third example, a flute solo from the Khorchin tribe,[1] is Chinese in character.

Ex. 224

Many of the songs have flute, fiddle, or 'guitar' accompaniments. Descriptions are given of four-stringed and two-stringed fiddles (pl. 6 (*a*)); a zither resembling the Chinese *jeng*; three types of 'guitar' (lute), one of which is the same as the Chinese *sanshyan*; and cross-flutes of the *dyi*-type.[1] The resemblance between the square-cut type of Mongolian melody and many of the tunes of Pekin opera is striking.

SHINJIANG (CHINESE TURKESTAN)

The material collected by Haslund-Christensen in the region of Urumchi (Dyihuah) (169)[2] has not as yet been published. This was taken from members of the Torgut tribe and should be of great interest. From a brief account of a troupe of dancers and musicians from Chinese Turkestan who visited Shanghai it seems that[3] their practices show marked parallels to those of Tarng times. Thus

[1] Haslund-Christensen and Emsheimer, op. cit., p. 37.
[2] Figures in brackets refer to serial entries in the Glossary of Characters, p. 190.
[3] In Faaluu, 'Tsorng Lihshyy-shanq Luenn Shinjiang Gewuu', *Shanqhae Jongiang Ryhbaw* (Shanghai, 12 Dec. 1947) (172).

dancers, dances, and instruments correspond to descriptions in the Tarng poet Bair Jiuyih and in poems from early anthologies (*Yuehfuu Shyji*) (170); and their music displays structural features fitting the descriptions of Tarng *dahcheu* (p. 106). One of their tunes has been identified with the seven-stringed zither tune known as 'Jaujiun's Lament' (171). It is remarkable that such an identification should have been made precisely in the case of this particular zither tune, since Jaujiun was the lady bestowed on the Hunnish Khan by the Emperor and carried away to Mongolian territory in 33 B.C. This account suggests that study of the music of this region may throw light on Chinese music of Tarng times and may lead to the identification of those tunes or parts of tunes in early zither handbooks which date from Tarng times. Chinese workers have begun to collect folk-songs in Shinjiang, and some of the material collected has now been published. A high proportion of these tunes are symmetrical, measured and heptatonic.

TIBET

The availability in recent years of a small number of recordings of Tibetan music made in Lhasa has transformed the picture of the music of Tibet based on earlier accounts.[1] A recent review[2] includes a number of examples transcribed from these recordings and brings together for the first time a wealth of information on Tibetan music and musical instruments and on the functions of music in Tibetan culture. The instruments described include a vertical flute with bell and whistle-mouth-piece (*gliṅ bu*); a conical oboe similar to the Chinese *suoonah* (*rgya gliṅ*); bone trumpets (*rkaṅ duṅ*); large copper horns, in some cases extensible like telescopes to a length of 3 metres (*rag duṅ*); and percussion: braced copper kettle-drums and nailed drums, including an hour-glass drum made from two human skulls.

The recordings show that at least three distinct types of music, exclusive of folk-music, are practised in Lhasa. These are: (1) Sino-Mongolian music resembling Chinese provincial opera. This may be religious or secular. The following example is part of a hymn sung in perfect unison by two nuns (Ex. 225).

[1] A. H. Francke, 'La musique au Thibet' in *Encyclopédie de la musique* (Lavignac and La Laurencie), 1re partie, v (Paris, 1922), pp. 3084–93.

[2] P. C. Crossley-Holland, 'Tibetan Music', *Grove's Dictionary of Music and Musicians*, viii (London, 1954), pp. 456–64.

Ex. 225

All the Lhasa recordings of this type are in binary rhythms. The secular songs may be accompanied by flute, fiddle, zither (*jeng*), lute, and percussion. (2) Liturgical chanting. The voices in approximate unison and lowest register move in small, often microtonal, steps with an occasional step of a minor third, to the accompaniment of single metallophones, drums, and at times a horn-pedal. Instruments and voices may be rhythmically independent of each other, or they may coincide and proceed together in an unstressed rhythm of equal pulses, as in the following example.

Ex. 226

The vocal range in this recording is a diminished fifth, approximately subdivided into three minor seconds and a minor third. In the instrumental interludes for oboes, trumpets, pedal horns, and percussion, the melodic line may have a range of as much as an augmented sixth and resembles the vocal line of the third type (q.v.) Several observers comment on the constant use of drones during choral singing, and it has been suggested that this practice is due to Indian influence.[1] Two horns, in unison, or a third or a fifth apart, may sustain a drone for several minutes; this usage is comparable to that of the large curved horns of India (*raṇa śṛiṅga*). The drum and cymbal rhythms, maintained by the orchestra, even when other instruments are silent, are Indian in character.[2] (3) Overlapping antiphonal singing; this style occurs in the recordings of historical dramas. The melodic line is non-Chinese in character, unmeasured, with arpeggioed triads (both major and minor) and major-third cadential tetrachords with the semitone above, as shown in Ex. 227: 'Su-ki-nyi-ma (Lady, bright as the sun).'[3]

Ex. 227

There is no supporting melodic instrument, and perhaps for this reason the pitch gradually drifts in the course of this type of singing. The overlaps may occur at the unison, but sustained major seconds and major and minor thirds are also to be heard. The partners in the antiphon are not always of equal importance; the 'confidant' may prolong the ends of the 'protagonist's' melismata. In the following example: 'Da-we Sing-ge (The lion of the moon)', the cadences of

[1] Sachs, *The Rise of Music in the Ancient World, East and West* (New York, 1943), p. 145.
[2] Ibid., p. 139.
[3] Kyumu-Lunga Troupe (Lhasa); H.M.V. Recording, N. 16678 (Calcutta).

the soloist are supported by a divided chorus, and there is a rhythmic accompaniment of drum and struck cymbal.[1] In contrast to the purely vocal antiphons for two voices, this example is measured.

Ex. 228

All the recorded examples in this style are sung in falsetto; this may be related to the need to secure maximum audibility in open-air performance. The style has some affinity with Tibetan working songs (Ex. 229); examples of these have been noted in which (as in Ex. 228) two- and three-note chords are formed on sustained finals.[2]

Ex. 229

In contrast to Exs. 227 and 228, the voices here are of equal standing. The similarity to the antiphonal working chants of the Chinese (p. 131) is striking and merits closer examination, as does the parallel

[1] Kyumu-Lunga Troupe (Lhasa): H.M.V. Recording, N. 16623 (Calcutta).
[2] Francke, op. cit., pp. 3090, 3092.

with songs for solo-voice and one-note chorus from Sarawak (Borneo) (p. 178).

It seems probable that musics from different cultural strata, and possibly from different cultural groups, co-exist in the Tibetan area. This view is supported by a brief report from a traveller who entered Tibet from Nepal.[1] The existence of a non-Chinese element in Tibetan folk-music is indicated by the whistled arpeggios of common chords, diminished sevenths, and fragments of whole-tone scales recorded. The following example is of interest in relation to tetratonic, anhemitonic melodies from Indonesia (p. 170) where, however, the range is a tritone.

Ex. 230

A primitive three-note melody, consisting of two superimposed fourths, sung as a duet for men's voices has been transcribed.[2] It may be compared with Japanese Buddhist cantillation, or with the vocal line of the Noo drama (p. 148).

Ex. 231

None of the recordings available exhibits the type of melody in ternary rhythm illustrated by Francke. Such rhythms, however, are common in Kashmiri music;[3] their presence in Francke's material may be due to border-conditions. One tune from Francke's article is interesting in view of the occasional major-third tetrachords noted in the dramatic duets; but it must be emphasized that no Lhasa recording as yet shows a tune of this symmetry and rhythmic regularity with ascending major-third tetrachords having the semitone above.

Ex. 232

[1] T. H. Somervell, 'The Music of Tibet', *Musical Times*, lxiv (1923), p. 108.
[2] Sachs, *The Rise of Music*, p. 38.
[3] Teachers' Training College, *Kashmiri Mūsiqi*, i (Srinagar, no date) (in Urdu).

A single specimen of lamaist music in score has been reproduced in facsimile.[1] Superficially it is similar to the Taoist notation already mentioned (p. 134). This notation may have been brought to China with Mahayana Buddhism and borrowed by the Taoists, in the elaboration of their ritual.

KOREA

From the most extensive surveys[2] of Korean music available, it is clear that a distinction must be made between the ritual music, directly derived from the Chinese Confucian or Buddhist ritual, and the secular music of the court and of the people. The latter differs markedly from Chinese music, either popular or classical, in that it makes almost exclusive use of 3/4 and 6/8 rhythms.

Korea acquired the Confucian orchestra early in the twelfth century, and instruments bearing the names of those in the Jou orchestra survive to this day. Some of the instruments preserved date from the fourteenth century. A number of variants of Chinese instruments also survive, several unique to Korea; there are, for example, six different types of half-tube zithers (*chyn*, *seh*, *jeng*, &c.). There is an interesting description of the completely mechanical performance of the ritual music: the fact that bells in a chime are hanging in the wrong order is of no importance; a difference of half a tone between bell-chime and stone-chime occasions no discomfort. The most valuable part of Eckardt's account is the description of the instruments and the sketch of Korean musical history; the description of the music leaves many questions unanswered; but on the whole Keh's transcriptions confirm Eckardt's findings.

Ex. 233, the beginning of the 'Hymn for the Sacrifice to Confucius', dates perhaps from the introduction of the ritual orchestra in the fourteenth century.[3] The first four bars may be a distortion of Ex. 177, p. 102:

Ex. 233

[1] L. A. Waddell, *The Buddhism of Tibet or Lamaism* (Cambridge, 1934) p. 433. See also P. C. Crossley-Holland, op. cit., p. 458.

[2] A. Eckardt, 'Koreanische Musik', *Mitteilungen der deutschen Gesellschaft für Natur- und Völkerkunde Ostasiens*, xxiv B (Tokyo, 1930); C. S. Keh, 'Die koreanische Musik', *Sammlung musikwissenschaftlicher Abhandlungen*, xvii (Strasbourg, 1935).

[3] Eckardt, op. cit.

The official adoption of the Confucian orchestra and ritual dates from 1114; but it is certain that Chinese instruments (and presumably music too) were imported in Tarng times. The vertical angular harp is known to have existed in Korea.

A second example, in this case of funeral music, is rhythmically not unlike some of the works given in full score by Prince Tzayyuh in his 'Rustic Dances', quoted by Courant.[1]

Ex. 234

Eckardt reprints Courant's[2] transcription of a piece for the black zither (*hyon kum*) (173) which he checked against the performance of a Korean musician. The last eleven bars are quoted here for their rhythmic variety and to show the use of ornaments:

Ex. 235

The following is part of one of the folk-songs noted: 'The Song of the Rising Sun and the Abiding Moon.' This is Keh's transcription.[3]

Ex. 236

[1] M. Courant, 'Essai historique sur la musique classique des Chinois avec un appendice relatif à la musique coréenne' in *Encyclopédie de la musique*, 1re partie, i (Paris, 1913), pp. 135 ff.

[2] Ibid., p. 215.

[3] Cf. C. S. Keh, op. cit., p. 7 of the musical examples.

The folk-songs include the following, a 'National Song', exhibiting major-third-plus-minor-second tetrachords.[1]

Ex. 237

It seems probable that many more vestiges of the Tarng and Sonq Chinese theatre survive in Korea than in China.

JAPAN

A substantial body of information concerning Japanese music has been available to the Western reader for more than half a century. The following short account is based largely on Sachs,[2] Piggott,[3] Courant,[4] and Harich-Schneider.[5]

It might be expected that Japanese music would exhibit considerable Chinese influence; but it is perhaps somewhat surprising that it also exhibits features of which only traces are to be found in the music of China.

Pentatonic scales predominate, though there is a constant tendency for these to become heptatonic, as in Chinese music. The 'Chinese' modes are displayed in folk-song, as well as in more sophisticated

[1] Eckardt, op. cit., p. 60.

[2] Sachs, *The Rise of Music*, p. 122.

[3] F. T. Piggott, *The Music and Musical Instruments of Japan* (Yokohama and London, 1893 and 1909).

[4] Courant, 'Japon: Notice historique', *Encyclopédie de la musique*, 1re partie, i (Paris, 1913), pp. 242–56.

[5] Eta Harich-Schneider, 'The Present Condition of Japanese Court Music', *The Musical Quarterly*, xxxix (New York, 1953), pp. 49–74.

music, and it does not seem justifiable to assume that their usage dates only from the beginning of Chinese influence in late Wey and Tarng times. The tunings of the Japanese *jeng* (p. 90), the *soo no koto* (31), as used in the Imperial Ceremonial Orchestra, cover a range of six Chinese pentatonic modes.[1] Three of these are *so* modes on A (e f♯ a b c♯′), d (a b d′ e′ f♯′) and e (b c♯′ e′ f♯′ g♯′) (using the Chinese nomenclature; see p. 94); these are the *ritusen* (174) (female forms) and on the whole are preferred to the three *ryosen* (175) (male forms), the *do* modes on d (d e f♯ a b), e (e f♯ g♯ b c♯′) and g (g a b d′ e′). Occasionally other Chinese modes occur in Japanese music, as in Ex. 238, a 'Fisherman's Song' collected by the late Dr. Takeo Kamada of Tokyo University. This is in the *re* mode on C. Many other examples will be found in the recently published survey of folk-songs of Tokyo and district.[2]

Ex. 238

Though the *re*, *sol*, and *la* modes are usually thought of as modal inversions of the 123.56 scale, the *ritu*-type scale cannot have been derived from *ryo*: the latter, undoubtedly ancient, is based on the fifth and lacks the fourth; the former is based on units of a fourth.[3]

In contrast to the 'Chinese' scales, the 'national' scales, though pentatonic, have semitone steps. Like *ritu*, they are scales built up from units of a fourth, but the tetrachords consist of major third plus minor second. This is the type of tetrachord already met with in certain Tibetan and Korean melodies and occasionally encountered in fragments of Chinese folk-music (p. 130). While the Tibetan and Korean melodies do not exhibit scales exclusively built up from two tetrachords of this type, Japanese music offers abundant examples of melodies with pure 'major third' scales. Three principal modes are in use. The first mode, *hirazyoosi* (176), may be represented by the series: A B C E F A. Ex. 239 is a cowherd's song.[4]

[1] Ibid., p. 56. [2] Y. Saionji, *Nihon Minyō Taikan, Kantō-hen* (Tokyo, 1953).
[3] Sachs, *The Rise of Music*, p. 124.
[4] Y. Matsudaira, *Seven Japanese Folk Songs from Nambu District* (Tokyo, 1937).

Ex. 239

The second mode, *kumoizyoosi* (177), may be represented by the series: E F A B C E. Its plagal form is shown in Ex. 240, a Furuma dance song.[1]

Ex. 240

The third principal major third mode is *iwato*; it may be represented by the series: B C E F A B.

It is clear that modulation from one mode to another occurs frequently. The following example exhibits modulation from *kumoizyoosi* (disjunct tetrachords) to *hirazyoosi* (conjunct tetrachords):[2]

Ex. 241

[1] Y. Kiyose, *Six Japanese Folk Songs from Shinano District* (Tokyo, 1937).

[2] N. Peri, 'Essai sur les gammes japonaises,' *Bibliothèque musicale du musée Guimet*, 2e série, i (Paris, 1934), p. 54, quoted by Sachs, *The Rise of Music*, p. 126.

Both 'Chinese' and 'Japanese' pentatonic scales tend to be converted to heptatonic forms; the former, by inserting a sharpened fourth and a major seventh, yielding the typical Chinese heptatonic scale: F G A (B) C D (E) F; the latter, by dividing the major thirds into two major seconds: A B C (D) E F (G) A. Music in the 'Japanese' scales frequently alternates between 'major' and 'minor' variants of the mode.[1]

It is of the greatest importance for the study of Far Eastern music that there survives in Japan, albeit in modified form, music of the Tarng dynasty, introduced from China, along with Korean and Indian music, between the seventh and the tenth centuries.[2] Treatises on this old music written in the thirteenth, sixteenth, and seventeenth centuries are still available. Since the oral tradition of performance is comparatively little concerned with the written parts, it is probable that the latter, preserved in three different notations for flute, mouth-organ, and bass lute, are authentic relics. This is also suggested by the notations themselves, which have Tarng and Sonq parallels. As an example of the melodies inherent in the written parts, but only to be recognized with difficulty in the music as performed today, Ex. 242 gives mouth-organ and *biwa* (p. 92) parts of the first phrase of the 'Martial Virtue Music' as transcribed from the Japanese notation, printed in facsimile by Harich-Schneider in an admirable first-hand account of Japanese court music.

Ex. 242

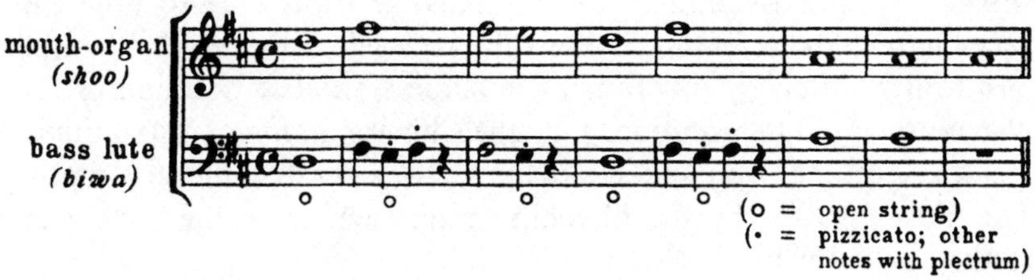

Ex. 242 only shows the notes as written; it does not include percussion, also shown in the original; nor does it indicate the figured-bass-like expansion of the *biwa* part or the mouth-organ chords erected on each degree of the scale. Ex. 242 may be compared with the full score prepared by Harich-Schneider. The resulting elaborate heterophony was first displayed in score by Mueller[3] who was able to test

[1] See examples in Piggott, op. cit., p. 103. [2] Harich-Schneider, op. cit., p. 65.

[3] L. Mueller, 'Einige Notizen über die japanische Musik', *Mitteilungen der deutschen Gesellschaft für Natur- und Völkerkunde Ostasiens in Tokio*, i 6 (Tokyo, 1874), pp. 13–20, i 8 (1875), pp. 41–48, i 9 (1876), pp. 19–35.

each performer separately. A version of the ceremonial 'Etenraku' (180) ('Music coming through from Heaven') for a Western orchestra has been prepared,[1] and a number of modern studies of the vestiges of Tarng and Swei music surviving in Japan are available.[2]

On the whole, the Chinese musical instruments of Japan are those of the Tarng court orchestras rather than those of the Confucian ritual. There seems to be no counterpart in Japan of the Jou orchestra preserved in Korea, for example, though a number of very early Chinese instruments have survived in the incomparable treasure-house of the Shoosooin at Nara. This collection includes a Chinese *chyn* of the fifth century.[3] What is perhaps the most ancient Japanese music—that of the temple dances and of the *Noo* (182) plays—makes use of flute or flutes and drums only, and seems to point to an even earlier musical substratum than that associated with the Shang culture in the Yellow River valley in the second millennium B.C.

Of considerable musical interest is the structure of the archaic lyric drama known as *Noo*, which reached the peak of its development in A.D. 1500, though in its use of masks and stylized expression it seems to hark back to a period earlier than the fifteenth century. The *Noo* orchestra consists of one stick-beaten and two hand-beaten drums and a cross-flute. While the drums maintain a regular rhythm, the voice moves to a large extent arhythmically and is only rarely supported by the flute, which for the most part provides interludes. Certain standard melodic patterns are introduced into a chant otherwise at one pitch—though this may change from time to time.[4] A very characteristic feature is the shift in level of the voice by steps of a fourth, often by two fourths in succession. The notation of the *Noo* music is a flute notation. Like the Chinese drama of Yuan times, the texts of the *Noo* repertoire have considerable literary merit. The most famous, by the fifteenth-century writer Seami, have been studied extensively.[5]

The music for the solo instrument known as the *yamada koto* (178), essentially a large *jeng* with thirteen silk strings, has been the subject[6]

[1] H. and N. Konoye, *Etenraku* (Tokyo, 1935).

[2] K. Hayashi, *Swei-Tarng Yannyuehdiaw Yanjiou* (181) (Shanghai, 1936) (Chinese translation); H. Tanabe, *Nihon Ongaku Kōwa* (Tokyo, 1926).

[3] R. H. van Gulik, *The Lore of the Chinese Lute* (Tokyo, 1940), pp. 181–9.

[4] Sachs, *The Rise of Music*, p. 136.

[5] N. Peri, 'Études sur le drame lyrique japonais', *Bulletin de l'école française de l'extrême orient*, ix (Hanoy, 1909), pp. 251, 707; also succeeding volumes. A. Waley, *The Nō Plays of Japan* (London, 1921).

[6] Piggott, op. cit., p. 88.

of a special study. This is the most highly developed of the many Japanese board-zithers and its music is largely in the various major third modes. The style was fully elaborated in the seventeenth century, when a blind musician, Yamazumi, created the various modern forms. The same constructional principles are to be detected in slighter, less elaborate and more popular melodies.[1] A short phrase of perhaps five notes serves as the basis of the entire composition, undergoing transposition and every kind of variation in the process of elaboration. This is music conceived largely in terms of the instrument and arising out of its mechanical properties; in particular the extended form known as *danmono* (179) is purely instrumental. An attractive feature is the use of arpeggios of the set of thirteen strings tuned to the characteristic major third scales. The following is from the first verse of 'The Plum Branch':[2]

Ex. 243

When accompanying the voice, the *koto* approximately follows the voice and maintains the rhythm if the voice sustains a note; it may supply two-note intervals—octaves, perfect or diminished fifths, fourths, thirds and seconds—to increase sonority.

An excellent account of Japanese Buddhist cantillation is available.[3] The music is undoubtedly Chinese in origin, but elaborate ornamentation leads to a single syllable being sung to a group of notes instead of to a single note, as in the Chinese Confucian hymns. The notation (of which there are various forms) includes symbols indicative of the pitch of the main note to which a syllable is sung, and more or less graphic neums indicating voice movements during the execution of the ornaments about the main note. In the following fragment the numerals mark the essential degrees of the scale (Ex. 244).

[1] Ibid., p. 102. See also Tokyo Academy of Music, *Collection of Japanese Koto Music*, (Tokyo, 1888).

[2] Ibid., p. 90.

[3] P. Demiéville, *Hōbōgirin* (Tokyo, 1930); see article '*Bombai*' *Tōyō Ongaku Kenkyū*, xii–xiii (Tokyo, 1954), is largely devoted to essays on Buddhist music.

Ex. 244

MIAU

Leaving the peoples of countries bordering on north China, we must now consider the music of various non-Chinese peoples living in southern China and the highlands of Burma and Indo-China. The anthropological and ethnological relationships of these peoples are complex, and no attempt will be made to classify them.

The Miau (10) are a large group of tribes scattered over southern China and the highlands of Annam. To them are related the Yau (11) and perhaps some of the Thai-speaking peoples of Haenan (183) and the border country of China and Indo-China. In certain respects their culture presents features reminiscent of the earliest records of Chinese civilization. The antiphonal courtship songs of the Miau have been compared with similar songs in the *Book of Songs* (*Shyjing*)[1] but this comparison has not gone unchallenged.[2]

The most striking feature of the music of the Miau tribes is the use of large mouth-organs resembling the Chinese *sheng*. Among the Chingmiau (184) of Gueyjou Province the *sheng* have six pipes, the

[1] M. Granet, *Fêtes et chansons de la Chine ancienne* (Paris, 1926), p. 147.

[2] B. Karlgren, 'Glosses on the Kuo Feng Odes', *The Museum of Far Eastern Antiquities Bulletin No. 14* (Stockholm, 1942), pp. 71–247. See p. 75.

longest of which may be 4 feet in length (pl. 6 (*b*)). In other tribes still larger specimens occur, up to 13 feet in length, but the largest forms often have only three pipes. The free reeds are cut from thin copper. The six-pipe *sheng* of the Chingmiau is fairly accurately tuned to the scale D F G A C D, beginning on the D below middle C; this is the Chinese *la* mode on F. A small blob of wax may be stuck on to the tongue to modify the frequency of vibration.

At least two men play at a time and while playing they lead an open, square, or round dance with the women following. The pace of the music is always a leisurely andante, even when the performers are leaping about with considerable speed and energy. The effect is grave and moving; this is a music with none of the uncertain pitch of Chinese opera or flexible rhythm of Chinese zither music.

Since the six pipes are played in groups of two or three at a time, as with the Chinese *sheng*, it is understandable that the music has a very limited melodic range. Ex. 245 was written down from a performance by members of the Chingmiau tribe a few miles outside Anshuenn in Gueyjou.:

Ex. 245

The alternation of sucking and blowing is approximately indicated by the accents. A change in timbre between chords produced in these two ways adds to the quality of the music in a manner which cannot be guessed from the score. The phrasing suggested is not authentic; it is merely the sort of phrasing of which the performers made use. Since the pipes used for producing the middle voice in Ex. 245 (that is, A, G, and F) and the lowest pipe, D, are those with greatest resonance, the middle voice stands out in performance. Variety is obtained by varying the middle part; wherever possible, fourths and fifths are added above and below, as shown in the example.

In one dance the rhythm of the steps only coincided with that of the music to the extent that twenty steps were fitted to twenty quavers of Ex. 245. The distribution of accented stamping steps in the twenty-step unit (checked repeatedly during the performance) was as follows:

$\bar{1}$ 2 $\bar{3}$ 4 5 $\bar{6}$ 7 $\bar{8}$ 9 10 11 12 13 14 15 16 17 18 19 20

At times the second quaver of the ligatures was dotted, giving a 'Scottish snap' to the movement. The players tended to break off on the interval $\frac{C}{G}$.

While this is the music played at the New Year Mating Festival in the second fortnight of February, corresponding to the Old Style Chinese New Year, music of another kind may be heard on market days, when the Miau come into the Chinese towns from their villages. The following is a fragment of a melody played in unison on two six-holed cross-flutes by two men who stood facing each other; it contains a major third tetrachord and would be converted into the Japanese mode *hirazyoosi* if the octave G were added:

Ex. 246

Ex. 247 is a remarkable three-note tune[1] from the Yau people of Lienyang in Canton Province:

Ex. 247

Some of the Miau tribes use a Jew's harp;[2] though no description of this instrument is given, many of the peoples of countries bordering on southern China have a bamboo Jew's harp, and it is certain that this is one of the very ancient instruments common to the whole area (p. 185).

The fourteen-pipe mouth-organs of the people of Laos in northern

[1] Hwang Yeoudih, 'Lienyang Yauren-di Inyueh', *Minswu*, i (4) (Canton, 1942), pp. 28–35.

[2] F. Savina, *Histoire des Miao* (Hong Kong, 1924), p. 25.

Annam are made in three sizes: mezzo-soprano, contralto, and baritone, and in sweetness and clarity they are said to surpass both Dyak mouth-organ and Chinese *sheng*. Ex. 248 ('The Possessed') is written on three staves, but whether played by three instruments is not clear:[1]

Ex. 248

Some of the examples show that the instrument may also be used entirely melodically: to play a one-line melody without chords or with only occasional chords or a pedal-point.[1,2]

In the highlands of Burma and the country of the Yunnan-Burma

[1] M. Humbert-Lavergne, 'La Musique à travers la vie laotienne', *Zeitschrift für vergleichende Musikwissenschaft*, ii (1934), pp. 14–19.

[2] G. Knosp, 'Histoire de la musique dans l'Indo-Chine', *Encyclopédie de la musique*, 1re partie, v (Paris, 1922), pp. 3100–46. See p. 3145.

border are the Karen people, possibly related to the Miau and possibly (though doubtfully) belonging to the Sino-Tibetan language-group. They make use of mouth-organs not inferior in size to those of the Miau,[1] though differing from these in that they lack a mouthpiece a foot or more in length.

LUOLUO AND MINJIA

While the Miau and Karen are only doubtfully included in the Sino-Tibetan language-group, the Luoluo (6) are unquestionably members of the Tibeto-Burman branch. Those in the vicinity of Lihjiang (185) in south-western Yunnan, belonging to the Mosuo (7) group, have been studied by Professor Fuh Mawji (186) formerly of Hwajong (187) University, to whom I am indebted for specimens of their bamboo Jew's harps and of their tunes.[2] The first type consists of a single vibrating tongue, cut in a length of bamboo; it vibrates in a long narrow slit and is set in motion by jerking the end of a short length of silk-gut attached to one end, while holding the other firm by a loop of silk. The instrument is held across the mouth, in front of but not touching the parted lips. By varying the shape and capacity of the mouth-cavity, selected partials of the fundamental are reinforced—as in playing all types of Jew's harp.

A more interesting type of Jew's harp consists of three tuned vibrators, each yielding a note of fixed pitch. In this case the vibrators are excited by plucking a slender projection on the free end (pl. 6 (*c*)). The three notes are, judged by ear, from above down: F sharp, D sharp (both above middle C) and the G sharp below middle C; they are clear and musical in quality.[3] The player not only changes the shape of the mouth but alters the position of the tongue, as if articulating the words. Young men and women are able to exchange messages using this instrument as a generator of sound, modified by the changing properties of the mouth cavity as a resonator, as in speech.

Two popular three-note tunes, played on the triple Jew's harp, have been written down by Professor Fuh. The first, in ternary measure, is called 'The Bees Fly across the Golden Sand River':

Ex. 249

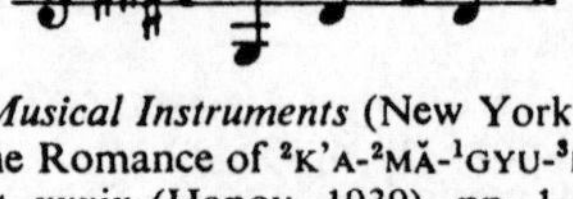

[1] Sachs, *The History of Musical Instruments* (New York, 1940), p. 184 and pl. X d.

[2] See also J. F. Rock, 'The Romance of ^{2}K'A-^{2}MĂ-^{1}GYU-^{3}MI-^{2}GKYI', *Bulletin de l'école française de l'extrême orient*, xxxix (Hanoy, 1939), pp. 1–152; in particular pp. 2–5, 7–13, and 122.

[3] Another specimen is tuned F sharp, D sharp, and C sharp.

The second, in common time, is 'A Dog Follows a Deer'. The unit is repeated over and over again, sometimes at great speed.

Ex. 250

Among the Lihjiang Mosuo the Jew's harp plays an important part in the courtship pattern of the community.[1] With another Tibeto-Burman people, the Minjia (188),[2] now considerably sinicized, living about a hundred miles south of Lihjiang, on the Eelhae (189), the Jew's harp is only a children's toy. It is a small version of the first type described from the Mosuo, but with a cloven tongue (pl. 6 (*d*)).

NAGAS

Away to the west, over the southern continuation of the Himalaya range, are people who belong to the central and southern Assamese division of the Tibeto-Burman family: the Nagas. Their musical instruments include a bamboo Jew's harp with a single vibrating unit, almost identical with those of the Lihjiang Mosuo and of the Minjia, and played in the same way; a flute; a fiddle,[3] and slit-drums—the last often of gigantic size.[4, 5] The Sema Nagas have no slit drums, though they make use of various struck or shaken idiophones for non-musical purposes, but they have a two-holed cross-flute and a bamboo Jew's harp. The following example is a three-part chorus sung by these people.[6]

Ex. 251

[1] See Rock, op. cit.

[2] For a general account of this people (not, however, of any musical interest) see C. P. Fitzgerald, *The Tower of Five Glories* (London, 1941).

[3] C. von Fürer Haimendorf, *The Naked Nagas* (Calcutta, 1946), fig. 49.

[4] Ibid., figs. 38, 39. [5] Sachs, *The History of Musical Instruments*, p. 30 and pl. Ib.

[6] J. H. Hutton, *The Sema Nagas* (London, 1921), p. 370.

ANNAM[1]

The urban music of Annam is very largely sinicized.[1,2] In the towns the instruments in use are Chinese, or variants of Chinese instruments, and (with the exception of single sonorous stones or metal slabs) all belong to the 'modern' category, that is, they are instruments imported into China in Tarng times or later. The instruments of the Confucian orchestra survive only as illustrations in early books, or as rare specimens, no longer played, in the imperial palace; even the *sheng* has been forgotten in Annam.

Of the tunes and fragments available, none exhibit any trace of the major third scale noted in Tibet, Korea, and Japan; with one exception all are 'Chinese', and all but two are strictly pentatonic. While the *do* mode is the most frequent, examples in other modes also occur. The following is a popular fiddle tune (for a fiddle of *ellhwu*-type, p. 93) entitled 'Running Water':[3]

Ex. 252

A tune of unusually regular sequential structure is the following 'Spring Breeze'[4] (Ex. 253).

[1] Knosp, 'Histoire de la musique dans l'Indo-Chine' p. 3100.

[2] G. de Gironcourt, 'Recherches de géographie musicale en Indochine', *Bulletin de la société des études indochinoises, Nouvelle Série*, xvii, No. 4 (Saïgon, 1942), pp. 7–174.

[3] Knosp, op. cit., p. 3104.

[4] Ibid., p. 3105.

Ex. 253

Knosp gives an interesting account of improvisation and examples of characteristic turns of phrase, including the following with its chain of fourths :[1]

Ex. 254

All the examples so far quoted are in duple or quadruple time. A remarkable specimen is the following hexatonic tune in triple time; this tune is more Indian in character than Chinese:[2]

Ex. 255

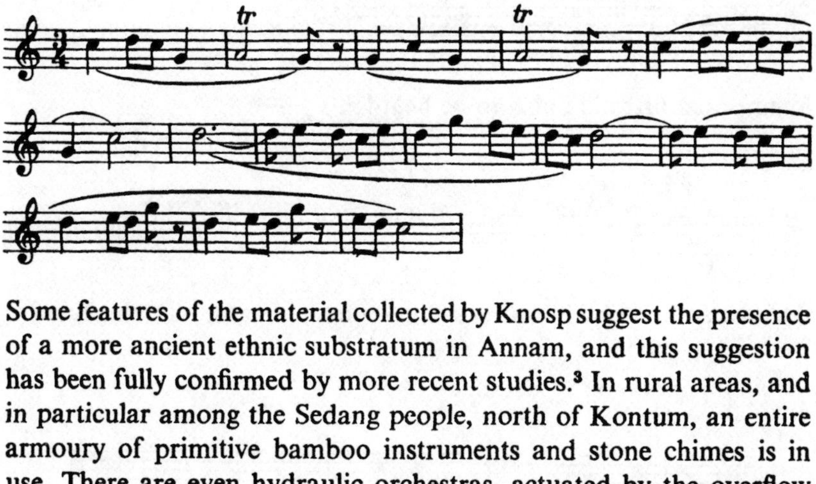

Some features of the material collected by Knosp suggest the presence of a more ancient ethnic substratum in Annam, and this suggestion has been fully confirmed by more recent studies.[3] In rural areas, and in particular among the Sedang people, north of Kontum, an entire armoury of primitive bamboo instruments and stone chimes is in use. There are even hydraulic orchestras, actuated by the overflow from irrigation channels, including slit-drums, clappers, xylophones, stone-chimes, and a bowed gourd; two or more instruments, playing rhythmically and melodically differentiated parts, are mechanically co-ordinated so as to play continuously. To this list of archaic

[1] Knosp, 'Histoire de la musique dans l'Indo-Chine', p. 3106.
[2] Ibid., p. 3103.
[3] G. de Gironcourt, op. cit.

instruments may be added two forms of ground-zither, played by men only and used to accompany courtship-songs.[1]

The specimens of rural music available display archaic features as striking as the instruments. The following example is the antiphonal vocalization of a waterman and his wife, as heard at dusk on the Hue River.[2] It makes use of four notes only, distributed over a range of one and a half octaves; the repeated drop of a fourth is striking:

Ex. 256

Superposed fifths are also to be heard:[3]

Ex. 257

Pure expanded-triad melodies occur, such as, for example, this lullaby from Phuc-tho:[3]

Ex. 258

Even in urban music there are traces of an early substratum in funeral music. The following example is played on a double-oboe with reeds made from the pupal skin of a certain insect; the two components are tuned so that each 'note' is an interval of a minor second. This

[1] Knosp, 'Histoire de la musique dans l'Indo-Chine' p. 3117.
[2] Ibid., p. 3126. [3] G. de Gironcourt, op. cit.

instrument is doubled by a true oboe. The fragment is repeated indefinitely:[1]

Ex. 259

The 'fanfared' character of this example (p. 178) suggests that it derives from the same ancient substratum as Ex. 258. Such expanded triad melodies are characteristic of certain primitive peoples in New Guinea. The existence in Annam of many ancient instruments, including two of the oldest chordophones known, and of a great variety of non-Chinese types of melodic utterance, is compatible with what is known from other sources of the ethnological complexity of this region. It is of interest that one type of ground-zither preserved in Annam occurs also in the southern Sudan among the Nuer.[2]

CAMBODIA

One account of Cambodian music[3] records that these people neither sing in the street nor play single instruments, though they possess a sonorous orchestra of instruments of superb workmanship. It may be, however, that this author was unfortunate in his contacts, since there is available from another source a collection of fifty-four songs, both words and music, from all the provinces of Cambodia.[4] More recently a further collection of twenty-one songs, and a number of specimens of rural music (work-songs, &c.), and also of aboriginal music from the most primitive inhabitants, have been published.[5]

Although the Khmers, ancestors of the Cambodians, were raised to a high cultural level for a thousand years by Indian colonists reaching Cambodia at the beginning of our era, the musical culture of their descendants, unlike that of Burma, shows very little Indian influence.

Of the fifty-four songs transcribed,[4] two only are based on major third scales; half of the remainder are purely pentatonic minor third scales, half are hexatonic with minor third tetrachords; only a few are heptatonic. Some of those in the hexatonic group make only occasional use of the semitone. With few exceptions they are all in common time.

[1] Knosp, 'Histoire de la musique dans l'Indo-Chine', p. 3109.

[2] A. N. Tucker, *Tribal Music and Dancing in the Southern Sudan* (*Africa*) (London, n.d.), p. 13.

[3] Knosp, op. cit., p. 3129.

[4] A. Tricon and Ch. Bellan, *Chansons cambodgiennes* (Saigon, 1921).

[5] G. de Gironcourt, op. cit.

The following example exhibits the plagal form of the mode *hirazyoosi* (to use the Japanese name); the upper tetrachord is occasionally filled in. This and other examples appear to be syllabic:

Ex. 260 'Dâmbang dèk' ('Iron Rod' or 'Small and Tender')

The first part of the next example is in plagal *iwato* with the lower tetrachord occasionally filled in; in the tenth bar it modulates to a different genus and key, returning to a major third tetrachordal structure in the last two bars:

Ex. 261 'Peak prầmpel' ('Seven Words')

A number of the songs in the collection have four equal notes to the bar throughout, dotted notes or notes of two or three times the unit value being absent or few, as in the following example:

Ex. 262 'Bok srou' ('Rice-pounding Song')

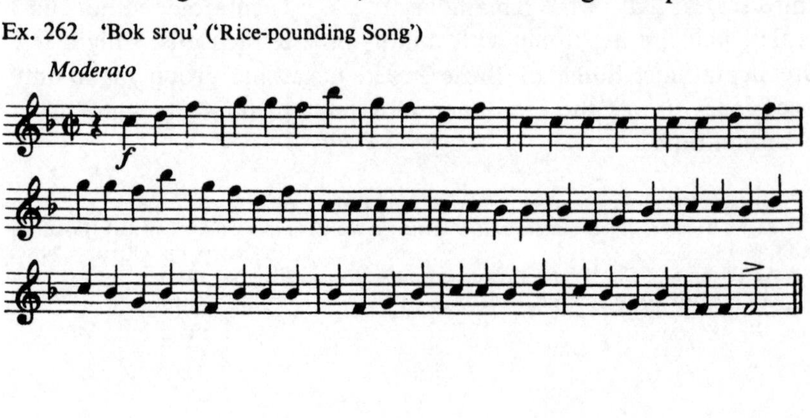

The following four bars resemble the most ancient surviving Chinese melodies:

Ex. 263

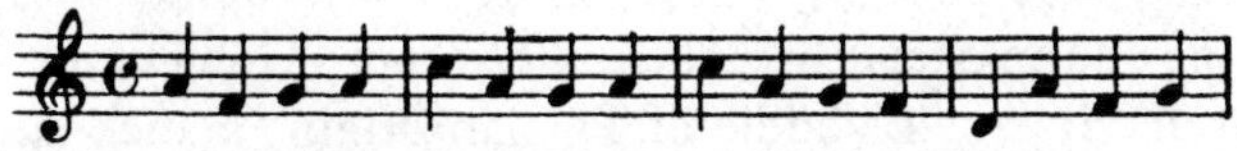

In most of the songs, however, dotted ligatures replace single notes here and there, though the four-beat rhythm is maintained.

Ex. 264

The following is a more highly organized tune:

Ex. 265

Ex. 266 is a royal funeral chant sung antiphonally by soloist and chorus accompanied by oboe and two drums:[1]

Ex. 266

While popular rural tunes may show major-third tetrachords and occasionally 'filled-in' tetrachords, the aboriginal music in some instances exhibits pure 'fanfared' melodies.[1]

Cambodia has been included in the group of countries of eastern Asia where chime-instruments tend to have an equal-tempered octave

[1] G. de Gironcourt, 'Motifs de chants cambodgiens', *Bulletin de la société des études indochinoises, nouvelle série*, xvi, No. 1 (Saïgon, 1941), pp. 51–105.

of seven equidistant notes, each of which can serve as a locus of inversion for pentatonic scales.[1]

The 21 instruments in use in Cambodia include 2 xylophones of 21 and 17 keys respectively and a chime of 21 bronze plates; 2 gong chimes, the one an octave higher than the other; 3 long lutes; 3 fiddles, of which one is a spike-fiddle of Persian origin; a stick-zither with a gourd as resonator; an oboe and a flute; cymbals, 4 different types of drum, and clappers of wood.[2] The striking difference, as compared with the Annamese orchestra, is the presence of various chimes. The stick-zither is not an orchestral instrument; it is unquestionably of great antiquity, like the ground-harp and zither of the Annamese.

There are 2 court orchestras, one of male, the other of female, performers. In the former, out of 11 instruments, 5 are chimes (gongs and xylophones are the chief melodic instruments), 2 are flutes, one is a spike-fiddle and the rest are percussion. To the 5 chimes, the women's orchestra adds 6 different stringed instruments. The following 3 bars illustrate in short score a point at which heterophony becomes harmony:[2]

Ex. 267

SIAM (THAILAND)

Not until the end of the fourteenth century did Siam become a political unit under the leadership of Thai conquerors from the border country adjoining Yunnan, but by the end of the following century the new unit had conquered Cambodia and annexed the Malayan Peninsula. Prior to the end of the fourteenth century, the area later to become Siam was occupied by a group of states all strongly influenced by Indian culture; in certain regions this influence was predominantly Hindu, but for the most part it was Buddhist.[3]

[1] Sachs, *The Rise of Music*, p. 132. [2] Knosp, op. cit., p. 3131.
[3] J. Auboyer, 'L'Indochine' in *L'Asie orientale des origines au XVe siècle* (R. Grousset) (Paris, 1941), pp. 378 ff.

The tonal system of the Siamese was one of the first Far Eastern systems to receive attention from the West.[1] It may even be said that Siam achieved a certain notoriety among musicologists when it was discovered that the system of the Siamese tends towards equal temperament of an unusual type: the octave is divided into seven equal parts. Generally speaking their tunes do not make use of all seven steps but of five only, skipping two to produce pentatonic scales that the Western ear interprets as 'Chinese' pentatonic scales of major seconds and minor thirds. Three modes are used, corresponding to the Chinese *do*, *sol*, and *la* modes.

When subjected to physical measurement this tempering is found to be far from accurate, and singers appear to take little notice of instrumental temperament. One recording includes a passage in which the singer makes use of almost Western intervals, but alternates with an orchestra playing in the tempered scale.[2] In this recording the singer is never accompanied but alternates with orchestral ritornelli.

The Siamese orchestra seems to be almost identical with that of Cambodia.[3] An entire composition was transcribed by Stumpf[4] and has been reprinted by Davison and Apel.[5] Ex. 220, taken from Seelig,[6] is a tune (No. 17(*b*) in that collection) entitled 'The Slim Cambodian'.

Ex. 268

[1] A. J. Ellis, 'Musical Scales of Various Nations', *Journal of the Society of Arts* (27 March 1885); C. Stumpf, 'Tonsystem und Musik der Siamesen', *Sammelbände für vergleichende Musikwissenschaft*, i (1922), pp. 129–77.

[2] Sachs, *The Rise of Music*, p. 133.

[3] Phra Chen Duriyanga, *Siamese Music* (Bangkok, n.d.).

[4] Stumpf, op. cit., pp. 171 ff.

[5] A. T. Davison and W. Apel, *Historical Anthology of Music*, i (Cambridge, Massachusetts, 1947), p. 4.

[6] For a collection of 150 melodies see P. J. Seelig, *Siamesische Musik* (Bandoeng, 1932).

BURMA

From such transcriptions as are available[1] and from the constitution of Burmese orchestras, there seems little doubt that Indian influence predominates in the music of Lower Burma. The characteristic Burmese orchestra is that accompanying plays in which the shadows of two-dimensional puppets are projected on a screen. It consists of two pairs of clappers, two pairs of cymbals, a gong-chime (like those of Siam and Cambodia), a drum-chime, a large drum, and two oboes (see pl. 7 (*b*)).[2] Omitting the gong-chime, this is the sort of instrumental ensemble to be met with in southern India. It may be mentioned that Burmese orchestras were known to the Tarng court, and that the *Tarngshu* (190) contains an account of Burmese music.

The Burmese apply the term 'Chinese' to their pentatonic melodies;[1] and these form but a small part of the repertoire. The following is interesting in relation to some of the Cambodian tunes: if the rests are filled in with repeated notes the resulting melody closely resembles Ex. 262 (p. 160):

Ex. 269

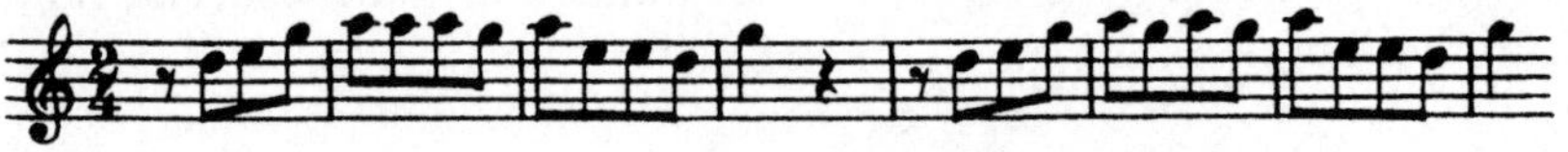

Another 'Chinese' tune differs from classical Chinese tunes in the way it is built up in a square, predictable manner:

Ex. 270

Practically all the tunes quoted are symmetrical in structure; some of them have that exciting rhythmic quality which one associates with Indian drumming. Here is a tune with a conspicuous major third–minor second tetrachord, but with the semitone above (Ex. 271).

[1] G. Knosp, 'La Birmanie' in *Encyclopédie de la musique*, 1re partie, v (Paris, 1922), pp. 3094–9. See also F. Bose, *Musikalische Völkerkunde* (Freiburg i. Br., 1953), p. 129 and examples 53 and 54.

[2] Sachs, *The Rise of Music*, p. 153.

Ex. 271

The melody has a non-Far-Eastern character in that the strong accent falls almost invariably on a note of the tonic chord of D major.

JAVA, SUMATRA, AND NIAS

The music of Java has been the subject of several memoirs of outstanding importance.[1] No part of the world, other than Japan, shows such a predilection for major third scales as does the Malay Archipelago; and in west Java (culturally the most primitive part of the island) singers perform in scales with two disjunct major third tetrachords, comparable to the Japanese mode *kumoizyoosi.* Instruments and whole orchestras are tuned to scales which include one or more major thirds, as in Exs. 272 (Sachs) and 273 (Groneman and Land); this major third pentatonic genus, *pelog*, is to be found not only throughout Java, but in Bali as well:

Ex. 272

When the pitch of successive notes in these scales is accurately measured, it is found that, on the same instrument, one third is not the same size as another, and seconds may be of several sizes. The reason for this is that the orchestras consist almost exclusively of idiophones tuned by comparison with standard metal bars kept by the gong-founders. Neither the cycle of fifths nor the harmonic division of strings is known to these people; their scales are duplicated, not constructed.[2]

[1] J. Groneman and J. P. N. Land, *De Gamĕlan te Jogjâkartâ* (Amsterdam, 1890); D. de Lange and F. F. Snelleman, 'La Musique et les instruments de musique dans les Indes orientales néerlandaises', *Encyclopédie de la musique*, 1re partie, v, pp. 3147–78. Jaap Kunst, *De Toonkunst van Java* (The Hague, 1934); *Music in Java* (The Hague, 1949); M. Hood, *The Nuclear Theme as a Determinant of Paṭet in Javanese Music* (Groningen and Djakarta, 1954).

[2] Sachs, *The Rise of Music*, p. 129.

In order to allow more than one mode to be played within the same range, the idiophones of the *pelog*-orchestras are given seven notes; this series may be approximately represented as follows, starting from E: E F G A B C D. Although there were originally three 'female' (*pelog*) modes, *nem*, *lima*, and *barang*, much of the *lima*-material now available shows *nem*-characteristics.[1]

Ex. 273 *pelog patet nem*[2]

Corresponding to the Chinese minor third pentatonic genus, the Javanese also have a 'masculine' genus, *salendro* or *slendro*, taking its name from the Indian dynasty of the *Śailendra* which ruled Java from the end of the eighth until the end of the tenth century. The two genera—*pelog* and *slendro*—are played by different sets of instruments in different orchestras. In effect, melodies in *slendro* sound to the Western ear like Chinese pentatonic melodies; but the octave in fact tends to be divided into five equal steps. The tuning of old instruments excavated in Java suggests, however, that there was a time when the octave was divided into steps approaching three major seconds and two minor thirds. It has been suggested that, whereas in the West, equal temperament arose from the need for freedom of transposition, in Java, it arose from the attempt to play melodies in different modes in the same range on instruments of fixed pitch.[3]

A recent study[4] has shown that both *slendro* and *pelog* are essentially non-equidistant scale-systems. The results imply that the tendency to equal temperament has been overstressed. Furthermore, contrary to earlier views, *pelog* and *slendro* modes can be distinguished by their structure—by the position of tonic and dominant, and by their characteristic cadences, themselves determined by the limited range of the dominant chime-idiophone. The parallel with cadential formulae in the Tarng (?) melodies of Ju Shii (p. 109) is striking.

The following example is in the *slendro* mode *nem*.[2]

Ex. 274

[1] Hood, op. cit., pp. 194 ff.

[2] De Lange and Snelleman, op. cit., p. 3156; taken from Groneman and Land, op. cit., pp. 57 and 78.

[3] Sachs, *The Rise of Music*, pp. 131, 132.

[4] Hood, op. cit.

It seems probable that the names for the modes were invented in relation to the major third pentatonic genus *pelog* and it is now accepted that this is the older genus.

Like Cambodian and Siamese orchestras, the Javanese orchestra or *gamelan* includes the Persian spike-fiddle known as the *rebab*; this instrument leads and is responsible for the prelude and for announcing the melody which forms the basis of the whole composition. The Javanese also have a solo reed instrument, a type of oboe, the *selompret*, but this does not form part of the *gamelan*.

In addition to the gong-chimes the Javanese make use of a number of celesta-like metallophones constructed on a plan similar to that of Indo-Chinese xylophones, but with flat metal plates replacing the wooden slats of the former. Both gong-chimes and at least one type of celesta (the *gendèr*) incorporate tuned resonators in their structure. As in the orchestras on the mainland, several solitary gongs of large size are also used. The *gamelan* includes one instrument not represented in the Cambodian armoury; this is a board zither of fourteen strings tuned to a *pelog* scale of two octaves.

In west Java a number of primitive instruments occur. The chime-idiophones among these are all made of wood; some are suspended xylophones of tubes or laths of bamboo. In those made with tubes, these are closed below and cut away at the open end until only a long, more or less flat, vibratile tongue, tuned to the pitch of the tube, remains. This form of tube is the same as that found in the other type of idiophone, the *angkloeng*. In this, two or more tubes tuned at the octave are arranged in a wooden frame in such a way that they can slide in slots, and are caused to emit their characteristic notes by striking against the end of the slots; a number of such frames, each of two or three tubes, may be arranged in a chime.

In Java occurs the first example we have met of a primitive zither constructed entirely of bamboo. This is the tube-zither, *ketoeng-ketoeng*.[1] It consists of an internode of bamboo together with its two adjacent nodes. Round the periphery of the cylinder are a number of 'strings' formed by lifting up strips of the outer layers of the tube itself, and tuned by inserting small blocks of wood under the 'string' at each end. A hole is cut in the wall of the tube, so that the cavity acts as a resonator (pl. 6 (*e*)). Another primitive instrument is the set of panpipes, consisting of ten or twenty reeds, closed below, and

[1] The figure in de Lange and Snelleman, op. cit., p. 3168 is wrongly labelled *soeling*; the *soeling* is a vertical flute, cf. ibid., p. 3149.

assembled in such a way that their open ends can be blown across in sequence.

A full score of an entire composition for a *gamelan* of twelve different instruments has been prepared;[1] it includes ten distinct melodic voices. Except for a greater range, the theme itself is indistinguishable from Prince Tzayyuh's examples of the earliest Chinese ritual music (p. 102). It is as follows:

Ex. 275

Two bars of the full score are shown in Ex. 276.

Recent work has revealed a correspondence between the vibration frequencies of certain early Javanese metallophones and the vibration frequencies of particular modes on reed pipes.[2] The results suggest that some of these early metallophones must have been tuned to a note series generated by a pipe. The suggestion is of the greatest importance, not only because it implies that at some period in the past the Javanese had a means of generating scales instead of copying them, but also because it raises the question whether pentatonic genera of some kind necessarily precede hexatonic and heptatonic genera in time.

In striking contrast to Javanese orchestras, none of the four different orchestras of northern Sumatra contains idiophonic chimes; all have single idiophones (gongs), percussion and a solo instrument of some kind—flute, clarinet, rebab, or other fiddle. This suggests Arab or Indian influence and might perhaps be correlated with the early conversion of this part of the island to Islam. Marco Polo records the existence of a Mohammedan state in west Sumatra as early as 1292.[3] Among the more primitive peoples of the island, the idiophonic chime occurs in the form of a xylophone of bamboo laths; there is also a bamboo tube-zither, a two-stringed short lute, and a bamboo Jew's harp resembling those of the Naga, Mosuo and Minjia.

[1] De Lange and Snelleman, op. cit., pp. 3160–4; taken from Groneman and Land, op. cit., p. 105.

[2] Kathleen Schlesinger, *The Greek Aulos* (London, 1939), pp. 334ff.

[3] *The Travels of Marco Polo*. Book III, ch. xi.

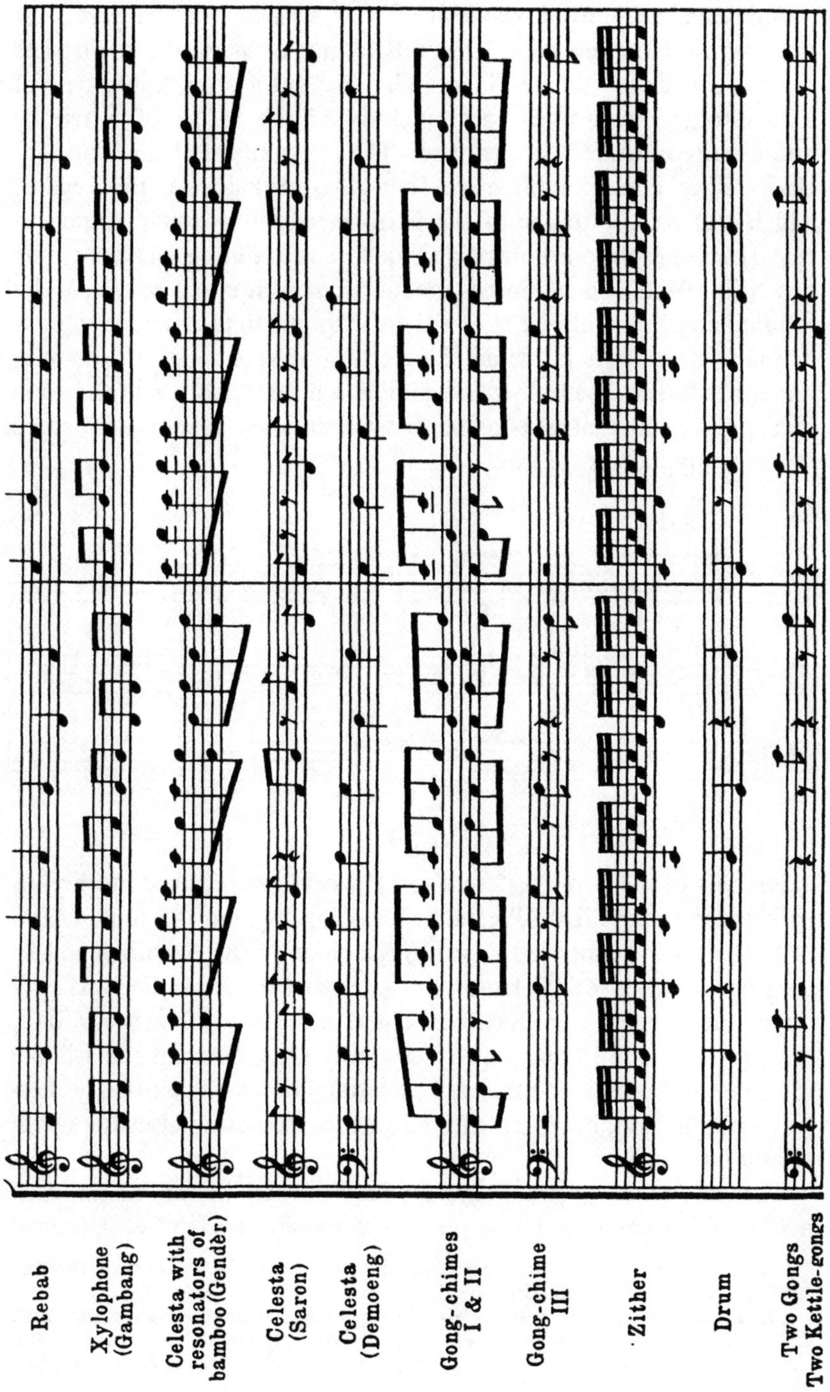
Rebab
Xylophone (Gambang)
Celesta with resonators of bamboo (Gendèr)
Celesta (Saron)
Celesta (Demoeng)
Gong-chimes I & II
Gong-chime III
Zither
Drum
Two Gongs
Two Kettle-gongs

A detailed account of the music of Nias, an island off the west coast of Sumatra, has been given.[1] The inhabitants of the southern districts are closely related to the Nagas. They exhibit a remarkable type of anhemitonic, tetratonic, vocal melody of the range of a tritone and usually in three-beat measures. The instruments of the island include single gongs; a three- or four-keyed xylophone, the keys of which rest on the thighs of the performer sitting over a trench; a remarkable aerophone consisting of a bamboo 'tuning fork', the tube of which selects and reinforces the fourth or fifth upper partial of the fundamental; idiochordic tube-zithers with one to four strings, struck or plucked; a Jew's harp; an idioglottal free-reed pipe; a nose-flute and other flutes. The following example is a transcription of the gong music played in central Nias on festal occasions. The original score includes three drums:

Ex. 277

BALI

No part of the non-Western musical world has received more sympathetic treatment from Western musicologists than the small island of Bali, next in sequence to Java in the chain of the Archipelago.[2] In contrast to Java which, from contact with Muslim India, was predominantly under the influence of Islam in the fifteenth century, Bali, having rejected Buddhism at a very early date, escaped the Islamic influence and remains to this day essentially Hindu. The ritual orchestras make no use, however, of instruments associated elsewhere with Hindu influence.

The classical orchestra, originally used only in the ceremonies connected with cremation, is composed almost exclusively of idiophones;

[1] Kunst, 'Music in Nias', *Internationales Archiv für Ethnographie*, xxxviii (Leiden, 1940), pp. 1–89 and p. 26 in particular.

[2] J. Kunst and C. J. A. Kunst-Wely, *De toonkunst van Bali* (Weltevreden, 1925). C. McPhee, 'The Balinese *wajang koelit* and its music', *Djawa*, xvi (Jogjåkartå, 1936); '*Angkloeng gamelans* in Bali', *Djawa*, xvii (Jogjåkartå, 1937); *A House in Bali* (New York, 1944).

the only non-idiophonic instruments are the drums. The scale of the instruments is of four notes only. In many of the classical orchestras (*gamelans*) the idiophones are entirely metallophones; but in certain parts of Bali the classical *gamelan* includes wooden idiophones: *angkloengs* and two types of xylophones. Even when *angkloengs* are absent the classical *gamelan* is referred to as *gamelan Angkloeng*.[1]

The keyed metallophones are of two types: those in which the keys are suspended freely over the resonators; and those in which they rest on some damping material over the resonators. The former are the *gendèrs*, the latter, the *gangsas*. On the whole it is the *gendèr* type which is used in *gamelan Angkloeng*. Each *gendèr* has four keys within the range of an octave, and there are large, medium, and small *gendèrs*, tuned an octave apart. The *gamelan* includes a pair of the largest size and four (two pairs) of each of the other two sizes. The members of these pairs are tuned so that there is a difference in pitch —which may be as large as three-eighths of a tone in the large instruments—between corresponding keys; the effect of this is to give a bell-like sonority to the higher registers and a throbbing intensity to the lower.[2]

The remaining metallophones are the *réjongs* and gongs. A *réjong* is a pair of tuned kettle-gongs mounted one at each end of a wooden handle, and tuned a second or a minor third apart. They are played in pairs by two players, who between them cover the whole of the four-note scale. It is known from bas-reliefs that such *réjongs* existed in Java at least as early as the fourteenth century. Each *gamelan* also has a single gong, lower in pitch than the lowest note of the large *gendèrs* and tuned to a note which is not of the scale, but which roughly converts the four-note scale into a pentatonic scale. Thus if the scale is G A B D, the gong might be any note between E♭ and F♯. A second small gong is tuned to one of the notes of the scale but at a high pitch. Cymbals and two small drums, tuned a second apart, complete the *gamelan*.

Remarkably enough, the scale of the *gamelan Angkloeng*: G A B D, the 123.5 sequence of the commonest Chinese mode, common to so many primitive peoples, is considered by the Balinese to be identical with the four chief notes produced by a Jew's harp, *gènggong*: G B♭ C D, that is 134.5, and tunes for the one are played on the other.[3]

[1] McPhee, '*Angkloeng gamelans* in Bali', p. 122. [2] Ibid., p. 128. [3] Ibid., p. 127.

The nature of the parts played by the different instruments is as follows.[1] Lowest in pitch is a *canto fermo* played on the largest *gendèrs*. This is in minims with a gong stroke at every ninth minim. Above this the higher pitched *gendèrs* play a melody in quavers based on the *canto fermo*, and above this the *réjongs* play a two- or three-part figuration in semiquavers. In the classical *gamelan* the line based on the *canto fermo* may disappear, and the higher pitched *gendèrs* may assist the *réjongs* in the figuration. The following example illustrates this figuration and its relation to the *canto fermo*:[2]

Ex. 278

The type of melody developed from the *canto fermo* is shown in the next example:[3]

Ex. 279

In bars three and four the *gendèrs* occasionally split into two voices a fifth apart; because of their greater sonority the fifths stand out as a cross-rhythm in relation to the movement of the *canto fermo*. Similar fifths arise in the *réjong* figuration and give life to the music, just as does syncopated drumming within a fixed framework. There is a certain similarity between Balinese drumming technique and that of *réjong* playing; and also similarity in form between *réjongs* and Indian (and Japanese) hour-glass drums.[4] It is possible that the polyrhythm of the figuration is not Far Eastern but Indian.[5]

The composition of an old-style *gamelan Angkloeng* is as follows.

[1] McPhee, '*Angkloeng gamelans* in Bali', pp. 128 ff.
[2] Ibid., p. 131. [3] Ibid., p. 135. [4] Ibid., p. 129.
[5] Sachs, *The Rise of Music*, p. 139.

The usual four-note metallophones and a single set of *réjongs* are supplemented by two small *gangsas*, four *angkloengs*, and two different kinds of xylophones: the *grantang* with *angkloeng*-like keys, and a simple xylophone without resonators, the *tjoengklik*. In this *gamelan* the *réjongs* and *angkloengs* are responsible for the figuration, the lowest *gendèrs* give out the *canto fermo* and the other keyed metallophones play the melody in unison. *Grantang* and *tjoengklik* each produce a different paraphrase of the melody. Only four of the nine staves of the original score are quoted here, omitting two staves of *angkloengs*, one of *réjongs*, one of cymbals, and one of drums.[1] The third note of the series is a B♭ in this example; this deviation is accepted as a mere change in intonation:

Ex. 280

[1] McPhee, '*Angkloeng gamelans* in Bali', p. 138.

Yet another tuning is found in a different *gamelan*. One of the melodies played by this *gamelan* is as follows:[1]

Ex. 281

The following two bars in full score (Ex. 282) illustrate the texture of another type of orchestra, the old-style ceremonial *gamelan Gong*, consisting exclusively of metallophones and drums.[2] Here the gong-chime expounds a flowing five-note *pelog* melody (scale: G♯ A C♯ D E) and the cantus of the *gendèrs* receives a first amplification from the *gangsas* in double octaves. This example illustrates the extraordinary harmonic quality imparted by the punctuating gongs.

The pieces played by the *gamelans* nearly always consist of two sections: a 'body' (*pengawak*) followed by an Allegretto (*pengètjèt*).[3] Each is introduced by a solo (the *pengawit*): a statement of the musical material which it introduces. Whereas the 'body' is a complete statement which does not require repetition, the Allegretto is meant to be repeated; its closing note is the note on which it opens, and it is in fact an *ostinato* of at least a dozen repeats. The *pengawit* intimates what piece is to be played and sets the pace.

Since the sixteenth century, the vowels of the five names of the notes (*ding*, *dong*, *deng*, *doeng*, and *dang*) have been used in Bali to record melodies. Though time values are not indicated, the metres are named.

[1] McPhee, '*Angkloeng gamelans* in Bali', p. 141.

[2] McPhee, 'The Five-tone Gamelan Music of Bali', *The Musical Quarterly*, xxxv (New York, 1949), pp. 250–81.

[3] McPhee, '*Angkloeng gamelans* in Bali', p. 132.

Ex. 282.

Ceremonial *Gamelan Gong*, Old Style

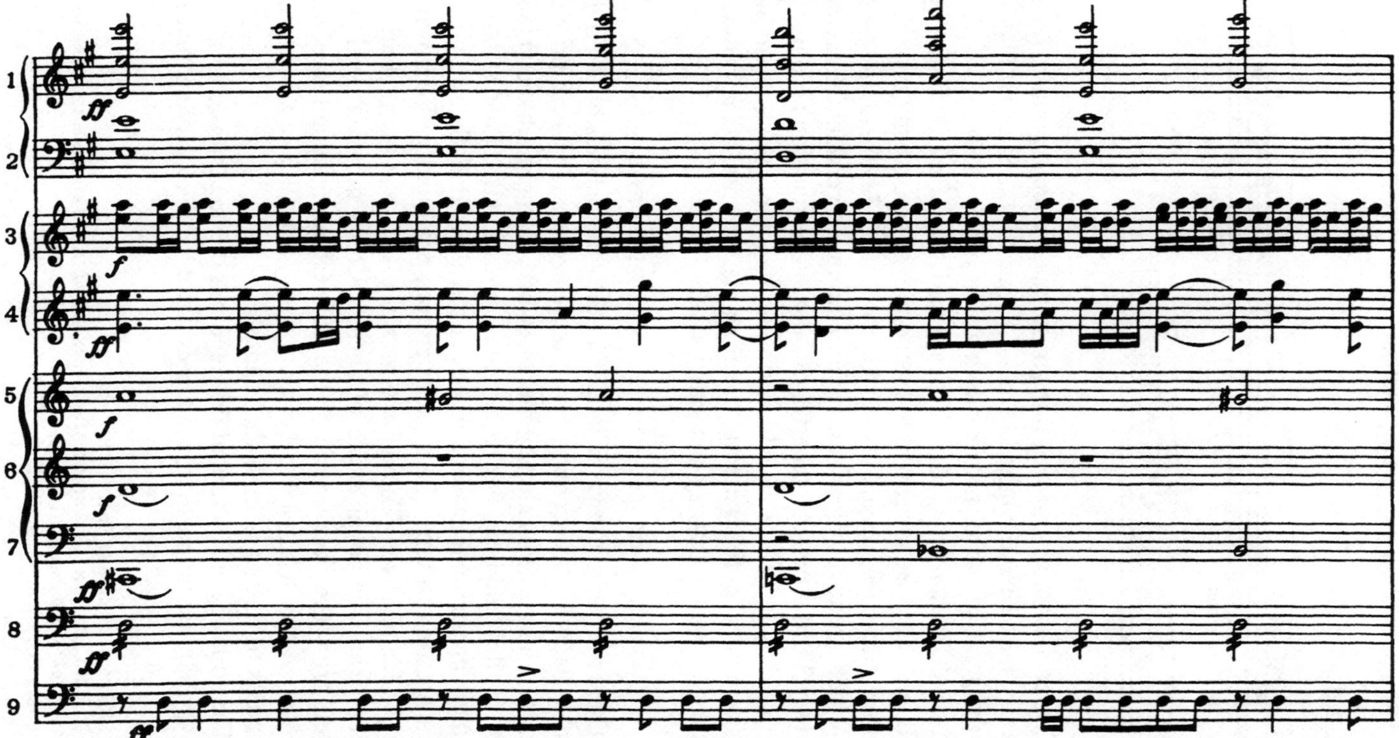

1. metallophones, *gangsa* type; 2. metallophones, *gendèr* type; 3. 4-note *réjongs*, 1st and 2nd players; 4. gong-chime, *trompong* soloist; 5, 6, and 7. punctuating gongs; 8. cymbals; 9. drums.

The last example is an improvised *pelog* tune:[1]

Ex. 283

Three admirable transcriptions of Balinese *gamelan* music, for two pianos, have been published.[2] One—'Music for the Shadow Play'—is in the genus *slendro*: the other two are in *pelog*.

In Bali, Indian types of orchestra, consisting of rebab, flutes, cymbals, &c., are used for two purposes: one type accompanies the classic drama, *Gamboeh*, played in fourteenth-century Javanese, the themes of which are taken from romantic or mythical versions of Javanese history;[3] and a similar orchestra of flute and percussion accompanies *Ardja*, a type of drama which draws to some extent on modern Chinese tales. In the latter the use of an instrumental accompaniment seems to be a relatively modern usage.[4]

OTHER ISLANDS OF THE INDIAN ARCHIPELAGO

There are two reasons for including the other islands of the Indian Archipelago in this account. First, there are islands where primitive forms of instruments already met elsewhere in more refined versions survive; it would be wrong to give the impression that the distribution of these instruments ceases abruptly in Java and Bali. Secondly, there are traces in this area of a musical culture profoundly different from that so far reviewed. Though the music of China at the present time differs from the ritual music of ancient China quite as much as it differs from the ritual music of the Balinese *gamelan*, all three have greater affinity with each other than they have with certain musical elements to be met with in the islands.

The ethnological picture of this region is of the utmost complexity; in New Guinea alone, there are hundreds of tribes of varying mixtures

[1] McPhee, *A House in Bali*, p. 210.

[2] McPhee, *Balinese Ceremonial Music transcribed for Two Pianos, Four Hands: Pemoengkah; Gambangan; Taboe teloe* (New York, 1940).

[3] B. De Zoete and W. Spies, *Dance and Drama in Bali* (London, 1938), pp. 134 ff.;

[4] Ibid., p. 196.

of races with many and various cultural strata superimposed. The evidence supports the view that there are in this area traces of a different main stem of mankind, of a people more different from the Mongoloids and the Proto- and Deutero-Malays than are these from each other; and it is suggested that this fact is reflected in the total musicological picture of this region. The most important work in this field from the standpoint of comparative musicology is that of Kunst,[1] though valuable information regarding instruments and the music of certain tribes is to be found scattered through the anthropological literature of this part of the world. A brief survey of the instruments of the islands with some account of musical practices is included in de Lange and Snelleman's article previously mentioned.

While many of the instruments recorded are such as we have already encountered, there are others (many idiophones, certain flutes, certain free aerophones) which are new and which are obviously primitive instruments (in the sense of Sachs's classification). From the distribution of various instruments in this area, it is clear that New Guinea and the adjacent islands constitute a region in which a high proportion of these primitive instruments occurs. It is also in this region that a type of music becomes conspicuous of which in this survey only traces have hitherto been encountered.

Before coming to discuss the music of the Papuans, the occurrence in Madagascar of stick-zithers with resonators (both plucked and tapped), and of tube-zithers, should be mentioned; they were taken thither by a Malay people (the Hovas) some time in the fifteenth century.[2] The tube-zither of the Hovas (*valiha*) has the strings tuned for the most part in thirds (D F A, E G B) in a manner recalling one tuning of the Japanese *yamatogoto* or *wagon* (191) (d A D G B E), claimed by the Japanese as an entirely national instrument and said to have been derived from six long-bows tied side by side.[3] Chords of thirds or sixths are frequently used in playing the *valiha*.

From Borneo (Sarawak) songs of great interest have been recorded and transcribed;[4] in some instances these combine an upper minor-

[1] Kunst, *A Study on Papuan Music* (Weltevreden, 1931); *Over zeldzame Fluiten en veelstemmige Muziek in het 'Ngadaen Nageh-Gebied (West-Flores)* (Batavia, 1931); 'Music in Nias'; 'Music in Flores', *Internationales Archiv für Ethnographie*, Supplement to xlii (Leiden, 1942).

[2] A. Sichel, 'Histoire de la musique des Malgaches' in *Encyclopédie de la musique*, 1re partie, v, pp. 3226–33. See also Sachs, 'Les instruments de musique de Madagascar', *Travaux et mémoires de l'institut d'ethnologie*, xxviii (Paris, 1938).

[3] For a recent account see E. Harich-Schneider, op. cit, p. 57.

[4] C. S. Myers, 'A Study of Sarawak Music', *Sammelbände der internationalen Musikgesellschaft*, xv (1914), pp. 296–308.

third tetrachord with a lower major-third tetrachord with the semitone above. The following example, from the Long Kiput tribe is of particular interest in relation to the style of antiphonal singing described from Tibet (p. 139):

Ex. 284

The major-third tetrachord with the semitone below is also displayed in music from Sarawak. Ex. 285 is a Kenyah dance-tune played on a six-pipe mouth-organ (*keluri*). The triple rhythm and pendulating tonic-dominant harmony are both noteworthy.

Ex. 285

The Papuans of the Nassau Range in New Guinea know no other musical instrument than the Jew's harp, but they possess two entirely different types of melody.[1] While the greater part of their melodies are primitive in the sense that their range does not as a rule exceed a fourth, others have a range of as much as an octave and are 'fanfared': that is to say, they are expanded common chords. Recordings from the Kauwerawet people of the Van Rees Mountains on the one hand, and from pygmoid tribes of the Central Mountains on the other, also reveal two completely different types of melody. The following example is from the Kauwerawet; melodies of this kind are characteristic of Australian culture:

Ex. 286

[1] Kunst, *A Study on Papuan Music*, pp. 24 ff.

The next example is from the Awembiak, one of the Central tribes; it is fanfared and has a range of an octave and a half:

Ex. 287

Certain coastal melodies, such as those of the Waropen, seem to betray Malayan influence, judged by their *pelog* character. The following is an example:

Ex. 288

Other coastal melodies are triadic in character but not fanfared. This suggests that the fanfared melodies are correlated with the persistence of the Negrito civilization in those regions most sheltered from foreign influence: the mountain ranges of the interior of New Guinea. It is assumed by some authorities that fanfared tunes can arise only in regions where wind-instruments are, or have in the past been, played; but fanfared melodies also occur in Formosa among the Vusun[1] aboriginals and are there clearly linked with the use of the musical bow. With this instrument the fanfare is derived from the upper partials of the fundamental, selectively reinforced by the mouth cavity. Similarly, the Jew's harp may be the source of the Negrito fanfares; for any instrument producing sounds in which the harmonic series of overtones is conspicuous may serve as a source of a fanfared series (2nd, 3rd, 4th, and 5th overtones), when coupled with the mouth cavity as a selective resonator. It may be argued that the Negrito civilization, although comparatively primitive, stands on a higher level, from a musical point of view, than does the younger component, represented by the 'Australian' melodies. This superiority in musical culture is paralleled by the general cultural superiority

[1] Takatomo Kurosawa, 'The Musical Bow of the Bununs[*sic*] Tribe in Formosa and Suggestion as to the Origin of the Pentatonic Scale', *Tōyō Ongaku Kenkyū*, x–xi (Tokyo, 1952), pp. 18–32.

of the Negritos as compared with coastal peoples, in whom the proportion of Australian and Melanesian blood is higher.[1]

Although the extreme type of fanfared melody seems to be confined to central New Guinea and certain of the islands off the coast, melodies of a pronouncedly triadic character have been recorded from the coastal regions of New Guinea, among the Semang in central Malaya, in Flores (east of Bali in the chain of islands), and in Samoa among the central Polynesian Islands.[2] It is understandable that canons in unison may arise from the antiphonal singing of triadic melodies, and such have been transcribed from recordings made among the Semang.[3] The most remarkable canons are those recorded in west Flores.[4] One of these is a two-part canon in unison sung by two women over a drone bass of tonic and fifth sustained by two men; a third man proposes a chromatic variant on the melody (against the drone) while the women interrupt their canon.[5] The following is another (partial) canon on a tonic pedal held by two voices:[6]

Ex. 289

CULTURAL INTERRELATIONS

It remains now to consider the interrelations of musical cultures over Far Eastern Asia, both in time and space. First, in contrast to

[1] Kunst, *A Study on Papuan Music*, pp. 24 ff. [2] See Exs. 44 and 78.

[3] F. M. Kolinski, 'Die Musik der Primitivstämme auf Malaka usw.', *Anthropos*, xxv (1930), pp. 585–648. [4] See Ex. 113.

[5] See Sachs, *The Rise of Music*, p. 51, ex. 29. The complete canon will be found in Kunst, 'Music in Flores', p. 77. [6] Kunst, *Over zeldzame Fluiten*, p. 78.

the condition observable in what has been defined here as the Far Eastern area, orchestras of idiophonic instruments have never (so far as we know) been a feature of the musical life of India. This statement may require revision when more is known of the musics of primitive Indian peoples. It remains true, however, that the whole tendency of cultured Indian music is towards chamber music: a singer is accompanied by a double drone on the *tambura*, or by two fiddles and a pair of hand-beaten drums, or by *vîṇâ* (a stick-zither), fiddle, and drum.[1] Such ensembles obviously have more affinity with the Chinese theatre orchestra than with the ritual orchestra described in the *Yilii* (p. 90) or with the orchestras of Siam, Cambodia, Java, and Bali. The ritual music of Bali introduces us to a very different musical world, a world with almost no point of contact with the orchestras of present-day India and almost without contact with the music of present-day China; but it resembles, to some extent, the world of ancient Chinese ritual.

If we survey rapidly the present distribution of 'idiophonic' orchestras, that is, of orchestras including a high proportion of chime-idiophones, we find, first, a few ritual orchestras surviving in China, rarely, if ever, played. In Korea we find stone-chimes, bell-chimes, celestas of iron plates, surviving in their ancient Chinese form and still played. In Annam a few instruments survive in the palace, unplayed, but as we have seen (p. 157), in rural Annam both stone- and bamboo-chimes and orchestras are to be found. In Cambodia and Siam we meet with a functional orchestra of gong-chimes, celestas, and bamboo xylophones, with flutes and drums as the only non-idiophonic components. In Java we observe a division of the celesta-like metallophones into forms with and without resonators; flute and sometimes rebab are used as leading solo instruments—perhaps a trace of Islamic dominance. Then comes the classical Balinese orchestra of idiophonic instruments and drums only; next the wooden chime-idiophones scattered over the islands, sometimes united as orchestras, sometimes used as single instruments; and finally there are the single wooden idiophones, simple as opposed to compound, flung far out over the Pacific Islands even to the Americas: the slit-drums and drum-substitutes made from bamboo tubes.

Were there no chime-idiophones in Korea and China one might define an Indonesian musical culture centred on Java, fading out in Annam in contact with China, in Burma in contact with India, in the islands in contact with Australian and Negrito elements. But the

[1] Sachs, *The Rise of Music*, p. 192.

existence of chime-idiophones as the first-named components of the Jou ritual orchestra, surviving to this day in Korea, necessitates a different assessment: their existence suggests that that cultural element in Indo-China, in Indonesia, and in the Pacific islands, which is responsible for the existence of chime-idiophones today, was still actively shaping Chinese musical culture at the time of the Warring States in the third century B.C.

We might suppose that Chinese influence in our own era had imposed this chime-idiophone culture on Indo-China and Indonesia. But this is out of the question. Annam, for example, the region most obviously under Chinese influence, was an integral part of the Chinese empire from 111 B.C. until A.D. 939; it was again held by the Chinese for a brief period in Ming times. Yet in spite of a deliberate attempt by the Annamite dynasty to foster Confucianism in 1007, and a fierce persecution of Buddhism in favour of Confucianism by the Chinese in Ming times,[1] there is almost no trace of the ritual orchestra in urban Annam at the present time. Indeed, chime-idiophones only survive in regions least exposed to Chinese influence.

A second possible channel of Chinese influence was established later: Khubilai Khan, Mongol emperor of China, attacked Java in 1292. His offensive was repulsed; but from this time onwards Chinese influence in Java grew until, at the end of the fifteenth century, it is noticeable in the treatment of landscape in temple bas-reliefs.[2] The contact was established too late, however. It is not to be supposed that Chinese influence in Yuan times led to the development of an orchestra in some respects more primitive than the ritual orchestra of Jou times.

In Siam and Cambodia, on the other hand, the chief formative cultural influence is usually held to have been Indian—either Sivaist or Buddhist; yet the music of Siam and Cambodia is characterized by the use of orchestras of chime-idiophones with the rebab as the sole Indian (or Islamic) borrowing. From bas-reliefs on the great *stupa* at Borobudur in Java (750) it is known that orchestras of the time included all the instruments of ancient India.[3] The evidence suggests that in Java, at any rate, Indian musical influence was at one time paramount in court and ritual orchestras; it renders even more striking the fact that Java now shows so little trace of this influx of foreign instruments. If one assumes that Siam and Cambodia were at one time no less Hinduized than was Java, it is remarkable that

[1] J. Auboyer, op. cit., pp. 396 ff.
[2] Ibid., p. 412. [3] Sachs, *A History of Musical Instruments*, p. 235.

they also exhibit so little Indian influence in their current musical practices.

An alternative explanation would seem to be that in the remote past the inhabitants of the great plain of the Yellow River included an ethnic element closely related to that now distributed all over southern China, Farther India, Indo-China, Indonesia, and the Archipelago. A number of cultural parallels have in fact been adduced at different times in support of the idea of an ancient community of culture over Far Eastern Asia. One such is the parallel between ceremonies in different regions in which protective animals participate. Attention has been drawn to the resemblance of the Balinese *Barong* to the lion-dancers in Hokusai's album *Daily Exorcisms*;[1] and the *Barong* has been compared with the Chinese lion that dances in the street at the New Year.[2] To these may be added the Tibetan lion dancers. It must be admitted, however, that the common factor in these parallels may be Tantric Buddhism of Indian origin.

There are, however, certain other features, so far unconsidered, common to the musical cultures of the different peoples in this area. One of these is the importance of the bamboo plant. The Javanese myth of the origin of music is described by Raffles in the following terms: 'the first music of which they have any idea was produced by the accidental admission of the air into a bamboo tube, which was left hanging on a tree . . . the *angkloeng* was the first improvement upon this Aeolian music.'[3] Here, as in the Chinese account of the making of the pitch-pipes (p. 94), bamboo is of primary importance.

A second point in relation to bamboo concerns the curious mixture of names of bells and of pipes in the Chinese names for the series of pitch-pipes, the *liuhleu* (p. 95). This mixture of names has functional parallels in Indonesia. In the quotation from Raffles an idiophonic instrument is regarded as the descendant of a wind-instrument; conversely one finds wind-instruments (*goembang*) in *gamelans* in West Java, which functionally replace single gongs and are in fact bass flutes; other examples of such instruments are to be found on other islands—on Flores, for example.[4]

The functional equivalence of struck xylophones and struck metallophones can be observed all over Indo-China and Indonesia. Moreover, in the area of the islands many of the simple struck idiophones are resonating bamboo tubes; for a *tube* may either be struck or

[1] De Zoete and Spies, op. cit., p. 95.

[2] M. Covarrubias, *Island of Bali* (London, 1937), p. 356.

[3] Quoted by McPhee, '*Angkloeng gamelans* in Bali', from T. S. Raffles, *The History of Java*, i (London, 1817), p. 472.

[4] Kunst, *Over zeldzame Fluiten*, op. cit., p. 14.

blown to yield a note. The observation, then, that names of bells and names of bamboo tubes were freely mixed in naming a series of pitch-pipes in ancient China, is surely less surprising when one finds: (1) blown pipes functionally replacing struck metallophones; (2) bamboo xylophones existing side by side with metallophone chimes; and (3) a living tradition to the effect that, although a blown pipe produced the first music, a struck tuned pipe (the *angkloeng*) was the first improvement on such a system.

Considerable interest has been aroused among musicologists by the parallels between Chinese and South American panpipes.[1] In surviving specimens of Chinese panpipes, the pipes are divided into the two sets, the *liuh* and the *leu*, arranged symmetrically on either side of the instrument. In ancient Peru the two sets of panpipes (in 'raft'-form, as in China), played by two players, were connected by a cord. This arrangement still exists in Bolivia and among the Karen in Burma. Now the two sets of pipes in the Chinese instrument are the male and female portions of the series (p. 95); and, as if echoing Chinese practice, among the Cuna Indians of Panama, the player has two sets of panpipes, a fifth apart, referred to as man and wife and connected by a cord. These instruments seem to point to the possibility that a knowledge of the properties of pipes is a part of the most ancient cultural heritage of a people distributed in the course of time from the Yellow River valley to the Burmese hinterland and Central and South America.

The whole position of the bamboo plant in early Chinese civilization is of importance in the discussion of cultural affinities. It seems reasonable to assume that, whatever elements may have coexisted or been added at a later stage, there must have been a considerable bamboo-cultural element in the people who made and played and sang about mouth-organs (in the *Book of Songs*) in the eighth century B.C. Elephant and buffalo, as well as the bamboo rat, *Rhizomys*, were known to the people of Anyang in Shang times, and the climate in general was milder and more humid then than later.[2] Though large bamboos do not grow today in the region of Anyang they may well have grown there in the second millennium B.C. The presence of such a bamboo-cultural element would make understandable the preoccupation of these people with the properties of pipes as sound-producing organs of all types, both as wind-instruments and as

[1] Sachs, *A History of Musical Instruments*, p. 178.

[2] P. Teilhard de Chardin and Pei Wen-Chung, *Le Néolithique de la Chine* (Pekin, 1944). See pp. 15-20.

struck-idiophones. Furthermore it seems likely that a relationship between struck-idiophones and free aerophones, such as one observes in this area, could only have been discovered in a bamboo culture, since bamboo is unique among natural products in mechanical properties and in conformation.

Various wooden idiophones have been known in China since ancient times: the tiger (a scraped idiophone), the percussion clapper, and the trough (a struck-idiophone) were used in the Jou orchestra; the wooden fish, still in use among Taoists and Buddhists, is a slit-drum. By this armoury of simple wooden idiophones, China is linked with many peoples of south-eastern Asia; and one of these ancient idiophones, of the dimensions of a toy, distributed at the present time almost universally over central Asia, Siberia, China, Indo-China, Assam, Indonesia, and Melanesia, is the Jew's harp.

The position of the Jew's harp among musical instruments is remarkable. It is, following Sachs's classification, a plucked idiophone, that is, an instrument of naturally sonorous material requiring no additional tension (as do strings or membranes) to convert it to a substance of high elastic modulus. But in the form in which it occurs among the Naga, Mosuo and Minjia, for example, it is only a step removed from the free reed of the mouth-organ. There is evidence that the free reed has always been recognized by the Chinese as an instrument distinct from the mouth-organ in which it occurs. It is referred to in the *Book of Songs* as *hwang* (192) written with the bamboo determinative, and this is nowadays identified with the metallic free reed of the mouth-organ: Waley[1] translates, for example, 'Blow my *shêng*-pipes, trill their tongues', where 'tongue' is '*hwang*'. Although the free reeds are of thin copper in the Miau mouth-organs (p. 150), as they are in the Chinese instrument, in those from other peoples of south-eastern Asia—from the Dyaks of Borneo, for example—the free reeds are cut in thin bamboo and let into the wall of the pipe (pl. 6 (*f*) and (*g*)). From the photograph it can be seen that in construction these reeds are miniature Jew's harps, with the thickening near the free end of the tongue carved in the substance of the reed, as in the Jew's harps (pl. 6 (*c*) and (*d*)). 'Whistles' from Shandong may consist of two short tubes of bamboo into the walls of

[1] *The Book of Songs* (London, 1937), p. 192. This is the usual interpretation of this passage; but it is worth noticing that there is a suggestive change in the verb in the Chinese. A literal translation would be: 'Blow *sheng*; strike *hwang*.' Van Gulik (R. H. van Gulik, *Hsi K'ang and his Poetical Essay on the Lute* (Tokyo, 1941)) has indeed suggested that the *hwang* was a separate instrument—in his opinion a variety of *sheng*. It may have been a plucked or struck idiophone.

which two bamboo free reeds are inserted, as in the Dyak instrument (pl. 3 (*j*)).

From accounts of the Jew's harp-technique in eastern Asia,[1,2] it is clear that although this is a plucked idiophone, and the mouth-cavity acts as a loosely coupled variable resonator, the amplitude of vibration of the tongue is influenced by the manner in which the breath is expelled against it. The Jew's harp is not so far removed from the free reed, activated by the breath and closely coupled with a tuned resonator, as one might suppose. The frequent use of a large, loosely coupled resonator with the Jew's harp in Java,[3] for example, narrows still further the gap between free reed and Jew's harp. Only in bamboo, however, is a continuous transition possible, in the same material, from struck or plucked macro-idiophone to a plucked micro-idiophone (a Jew's harp) and from this to a breath-activated micro-idiophone (a free reed). This is because of the special properties of bamboo; its stiffness is greater than that of any other wood and it occurs naturally in the form of resonators.

One remarkable aspect of the Jew's harp technique in various regions of the Far East is its use to imitate animal or human sounds;[2] similar use is made of its relative, the free reed. We have seen how the Jew's harp is used by the Lihjiang Mosuo in China to imitate speech during courtship (p. 154). The *koouchyntzyy* (193) (a free reed 'whistle') is used in Pekin puppet plays today for imitating animal and human sounds—hens and infants, for example; and there is a Sonq account of a man rendered mute who successfully used a 'whistle' for purposes of communication, 'as do the puppet players'.[4] In Bali there is a Jew's harp orchestra which not only plays music of the ritual orchestra, but also provides an accompaniment of animal noises for certain dances: in particular, noises of toads for a pantomime toad chase.[5] Lastly, tribes of the Nassau Range in central New Guinea 'symbolise consciously certain animals by means of the Jew's harp. . .'.[6]

Even the onomatopoeic names for the Jew's harp, current in widely separated regions of eastern Asia, appear to be related. The Balinese *gènggong* recalls the *gonggina* of the Garos in Assam,[7]

[1] McPhee, '*Angkloeng gamelans* in Bali', op. cit., p. 127.

[2] Emsheimer, 'Über das Vorkommen und die Anwendungsart der maultronmmel in Sibirien und Zentral-Asien', *Ethnos*, vi (Stockholm, 1941), pp. 109–27.

[3] Kunst, *Music in Java* (The Hague, 1949), pp. 360 and 443.

[4] Souen K'ai-ti, 'L'origine et le développement du théâtre des marionnettes chinoises', *Bulletin du centre franco-chinois d'études sinologiques*, i (Pekin, 1944), pp. 81–106 (summary in French) (194).

[5] De Zoete and Spies, op. cit., pp. 249 ff.

[6] Kunst, *A Study on Papuan Music*, p. 8.

[7] A. Playfair, *The Garos* (London, 1909), p. 44.

the *kunka* of the Golds (lower Amur, eastern Siberia)[1] and the *qoŋgoŋ* of the Gilyaks (lower Amur[1] and Sakhalin). The Chinese *hwang*, for the free reed—derived (according to Karlgren[2]) from an ancient form *g'wâng*, may also be related to these.

The coming of the Bronze Age to the Far East meant the translation of stone or bamboo idiophones, both simple and compound, into bronze. The free reeds, we may suppose, were translated at this time to metallic free reeds; and the Jew's harp has also undergone translation into terms of metal. Bronze Age culture undoubtedly reached the various regions of the Far East at very different times: although it was advanced, for example, in the plain of the Yellow River by 1500 B.C., it does not seem to have reached northern Annam until the fourth century before our era (p. 91). In rural areas on the mainland and in some of the islands of south-eastern Asia, the translation of bamboo idiophones into metallophones has never occurred.

We have seen (p. 87) that the five notes of the Chinese scale were anciently correlated with various aspects of the cosmos. A similar correlation exists in Bali, where the five notes are associated with the gods of the five directions: North, East, South, West, and Centre.[3] The Centre is the realm of Batara Siva (whose colour is white) and is equated with the first note of the series, *ding*. Each of the four directions has its colour and is equated with one of the notes. It may be that this system is Indian in origin, but it has not been possible to find an Indian correlation of a five-note scale with the properties of the cosmos. Moreover, even before the third century B.C.,[4] the Chinese were certainly familiar with the Five Rulers of the Earthly Regions, each with his characteristic colour. At the time of the compilation of the *Liijih Yuehlinq* the following equation had been established between the notes and the directions.[5]

Note	*Direction*
mi	east
sol	south
do	centre
re	west
la	north

[1] Emsheimer, 'Über das Vorkommen und die Anwendungsart der Maultrommel in Sibirien und Zentral-Asien'.

[2] B. Karlgren, *Compendium of Phonetics in Ancient and Archaic Chinese* (Stockholm, 1954), p. 319.

[3] McPhee, *A House in Bali*, p. 40.

[4] G. Haloun, 'Die Rekonstruktion der chinesischen Urgeschichte durch die Chinesen', *Japanisch-Deutsche Zeitschrift für Wissenschaft und Technik*, iii (Kobe, 1925), pp. 243–70.

[5] Courant, 'Essai historique sur la musique classique des Chinois', *Encyclopédie de la musique*, 1re partie, i, p. 93.

From McPhee's brief statement it is not possible to be certain what are the Balinese correlations of notes, colours, and directions, except in the case of the tonic, *ding*, which is the Centre and is white. In the Chinese system the Centre is yellow; but correlations varied. Symaa Chian,[1] for example, quotes a system with *re* and *la* reversed. The existence of such a correlation in Indonesia, even though the terms correlated differ, merits investigation.

Looking back now over the whole of the Far Eastern area, we may surely regard it, with some justification, as a unit. From what centre an ancient common musical culture spread throughout the area under review cannot as yet be determined; nor are we in a position to do more than note the possible significance of cultural parallels recently established between the Balkans and south-eastern Asia, parallels which suggest a far closer connexion between the Far East and the lands of the Pontine Basin in the first millennium B.C. than has hitherto been envisaged;[2] but that the 'chime-idiophone' substratum is of great antiquity is clear from the recent discovery in southern Annam of stone-chimes knapped in the manner of neolithic flints from the Bacsonian of Indo-China and tuned to a pentatonic scale close to the *pelog* scales of Indonesia.[3]

In spite of the foreign instruments and music which began to invade China from Hann times onwards, and in spite of the one time dominance of Indian instruments and music in Indo-China and Indonesia, we are never likely to confuse Chinese, Siamese, Cambodian, or Indonesian music with Indian music, so strongly marked is the individuality of the music of Far Eastern Asia. In some of the islands of the Archipelago, however, we meet a different musical culture; there, melodies take the form of expanded triads or fanfares. Pure fanfared melodies also occur, as we have seen, in rural Annam and in Cambodia. Their occurrence on the mainland accords well with the general picture of population dynamics in south-eastern Asia; anthropological studies also suggest the presence in parts of Indo-China of

[1] See M. Granet, *La Pensée chinoise* (Paris, 1934), p. 377.

[2] Kunst, 'Kulturhistorische Beziehungen zwischen dem Balkan und Indonesien', *Mededeling No. CIII, Afdeling Culturele en Physische Anthropologie, No. 46, Koninklijk Instituut voor de Tropen* (Amsterdam, 1953).

[3] Schaeffner, 'Une importante découverte archéologique: Le lithophone de Ndut Lieng Krak (Vietnam)', *La Revue de Musicologie*, xxxiii° année, N.S.: Nos. 97–98 (Paris, 1951), pp. 1–19; G. Condominas, 'Le lithophone préhistorique de Ndut Lieng Krak', *Bulletin de l'école française de l'extrême orient*, xlv (Paris, 1951), pp. 359–92. See, however, F. A. Kuttner's criticism in 'Nochmals die Steinzeit-Lithophone von Annam', *Die Musikforschung*, vi (1953), pp. 1–8.

negritoid peoples.[1] The possible relationship of certain peoples of south-eastern Asia to African peoples must not be lost sight of; and here again studies of music and musical instruments already offer significant pointers.[2] Finally, there is reason to anticipate that traces of other, and possibly earlier, musical strata than the common substratum will be found throughout the Far Eastern area; it is for the future to confirm their existence and determine their ethnological significance.

[1] W. Nippold, *Rassen- und Kulturgeschichte der Negrito-Völker Südost-Asiens* (Göttingen, 1936), pp. 109–35.

[2] Kunst, 'A Musicological Argument for Cultural Relationship between Indonesia—probably the Isle of Java—and Central Africa', *Proceedings of the Royal Musical Association*, lxii (1936), pp. 57–76.

1 新疆
2 西康
3 唐
4 秦
5 漢
6 羅羅
7 麼些
8 雲南
9 四川
10 苗
11 猺
12 揚子江
13 周禮
14 呂氏春秋
15 呂不韋
16 司馬遷
17 史記
18 明
19 商
20 安陽
21 磬
22 壎
23 詩經
24 貴州
25 周
26 春牘
27 柷
28 敔
29 琴
30 瑟
31 箏
32 笙
33 籥
34 箎
35 管
36 簫
37 儀禮
38 鐘
39 鎛
40 鼙
41 鼗
42 均
43 政
44 秦始皇帝
45 琵琶
46 劉歆釋名
47 京房
48 準
49 應鼓
50 武
51 山東
52 魏
53 燉煌
54 箜篌
55 月琴
56 三絃
57 胡琴
58 二胡
59 洋琴

(46): For *shin* read *shi* of *Kangshi* (89).

60 伶倫
61 古樂
62 宮商角徵羽
63 音律
64 呂
65 律
66 律呂
67 淮南子
68 武帝
69 樂府
70 靈
71 涓
72 隋
73 鄭譯
74 沛
75 調
76 均
77 太宗
78 宋
79 姜夔
80 朱熹
81 金
82 一二三四五六七
83 白石道人歌曲四卷四部叢刊
84 元
84 合四一上尺工凡六五
85 樂律全書
86 朱載堉
87 鄭
88 清
89 康熙
90 曲阜
91 書經
92 舜典
93 虞書益稷
94 操縵
95 方相
96 儺
97 魁櫑
98 傀儡
99 簫
100 笛
101 西安
102 大曲
103 遍
104 陰法魯唐宋大曲之來源及其組織武昌華中

大學國學研究論文專刊
105 白居易
106 破
107 齊
108 胡樂
109 玄宗
110 朱熹儀禮經傳通解詩樂篇
111 越九歌
112 洞庭
113 夏承燾白石道人歌曲旁譜辨燕京學報
114 清樂
115 方響
116 燕
117 南曲
118 北曲
119 詞
120 聲
121 沈約
122 平
123 仄
124 律詩
125 謝元淮
126 雜劇
127 元曲
128 曲牌
129 喜相逢
130 琵琶記
131 高明
132 過門
133 雅笛
134 郭沔
135 臞仙神奇秘譜
136 梧岡琴譜
137 清山琴譜
138 徐元白
139 小曲
140 訪子期
141 陽關三疊
142 梅花三弄
143 查阜西

144 普菴咒
145 憶故人
146 瀟湘水雲
147 楊大鈞
148 梁在平
149 福建
150 昆明
151 成都
152 崑山
153 江蘇
154 梁伯龍
155 魏良輔
156 水磨調
157 崑曲
158 傳奇
159 長生殿
160 洪昇
161 梆鼓
162 京戲
163 翠屏山
164 梆子
165 安順
166 湄潭
167 明道藏
168 黃佐樂典
169 地化
170 樂府詩集
171 昭君怨
172 陰法魯 從歷史上論新疆歌舞 上海中央日報
173 玄琴
174 律旋
175 呂旋
176 平調子
177 雲井調子
178 山田琴
179 段物
180 越天樂
181 林謙三 隋唐燕樂調研究
182 能
183 海南
184 清苗

185 麗江
186 傅懋勣
187 華中
188 民家
189 洱海
190 唐書
191 和琴
192 簧
193 口琴子
194 孫楷第傀儡戲考源中法漢學研究所漢學第一輯
195 童斐中樂尋源
196 宋陳暘撰樂書宋刻元印本
197 明高明撰琵琶記明尊生館刻本
198 元熊朋來瑟譜
199 清商
200 甘肅
201 西涼
202 天竺
203 高麗
204 龜茲
205 安國
206 疏勒
207 康國
208 高昌

IV

THE MUSIC OF INDIA

By ARNOLD BAKE

INTRODUCTION

THE term 'Indian music' embraces a very wide and varied field of musical phenomena. Classical theory was formulated in detail as early as the second century B.C., the date now accepted for Bharata's *Nâṭyaśâstra*, the earliest surviving treatise. This is actually a work on stagecraft, but includes six chapters on music. On the subject of religious chanting there are even older texts, like the *Rkpratiśâkhya* (fourth century B.C.?), and the oral tradition of that kind of music goes back at least a thousand years more.

Apart from this historically developed and theoretically defined system, one has to take into consideration the numerous ways in which the different peoples and tribes of India give vent to their musical impulses, which vary according to their respective stages of culture. This wide range of musical activities has not escaped the notice of the indigenous authors on music; they mention its existence but do not take it into account when formulating the classical theoretical system.

When we examine the system which the Indian writers themselves have built up, we see that we are confronted with something closely related to that of Ancient Greece. The conclusion reached by Antoine Meillet in respect of the metres of Ancient Greece and India: 'Le nombre et la précision des concordances du védique avec le grec sont trop nets pour qu'une rencontre fortuite soit vraisemblable',[1] is equally applicable when comparing the systems of music of the two ancient civilizations.

The music of India is the easternmost representative of a large group of interrelated musical phenomena, in the same way as Sanskrit is the easternmost representative of a large group of Indo-European languages. On the northern and eastern border of India this group meets, but does not intermingle with, the basically different conceptions of the Chino-Tibetan and the Far Eastern tone-systems. It is

[1] Antoine Meillet, *Les Origines indo-européennes des mètres grecs* (Paris, 1923), p. 76.

true that one finds strains of a composite nature in the folk-music of Nepal, northern and eastern Bengal, Assam, and down into the Chittagong Hills, but the official system does not acknowledge them, nor are they found anywhere outside these very definite border-regions.

CULTURAL AND PHILOSOPHICAL IMPORTANCE

It is impossible to divorce Indian music from the whole structure of Indian culture and philosophy with which it is interwoven in a number of ways from the earliest times of which we have records.

A remarkable feature of Indian culture is its ability to integrate many different and seemingly divergent tendencies against the background of a unifying philosophical thought. From an Indian standpoint there is nothing strange in the fact that the *Saṃgîtaratnâkara* (The Ocean of Music), a treatise dating from the thirteenth century, should begin with a detailed cosmogony, gradually narrowing its scope to the human body and the stages of pregnancy from month to month, before it gets down to what we should consider the subject of music proper. To the Indian student, music is not an isolated phenomenon but one directly and inextricably linked with philosophy and religion, and of cosmic importance. The right kind of music—that is to say, the only kind of music worth considering—is that which deserves the epithet *vimuktida* (bestowing liberation), that is the music which, when properly practised, serves to break the cycle of birth, death, and rebirth. The eminent French Sanskritist Sylvain Lévi once said: 'On ne sait pas assez le rôle immense qu'a tenu la musique dans les civilisations anciennes comme un élément intégrant de la vie religieuse et politique.'[1] To look into that aspect of the matter well repays the trouble.

In the finished system, as found in the texts of the classical, pre-Islamic period, such as the *Saṃgîtaratnâkara*, we find the central notion of *nâda* (sound) which has, of course, a musical connotation, but, apart from this musical meaning, a physical as well as a metaphysical aspect.

In music—the Sanskrit term for which, *Saṃgîta*, includes vocal music, instrumental music, and dance—vocal music is considered to be pure sound, sound *per se*, in contrast to instrumental music which is described as a manifestation of sound. Dance, the third

[1] In a letter to the Director of the Kern Institute of Leyden University (25 November 1929).

component of the triad, is dependent on both vocal and instrumental music, so that music as a whole is dependent on sound.[1]

This definite distinction between the nature of vocal music and that of instrumental music seems strange from a rationalistic standpoint. Why should the one be pure sound in itself and the other a secondary manifestation? It seems that at the time when these theories were first formulated the function of the vocal chords was unknown. Thus it is easily understandable that the miracle of the change from silent life-breath (*prâṇa*) into sounds of meaning and beauty, without the aid of any visible or perceptible agent, came to be considered as a spontaneous manifestation of sound itself, basically different from the sound produced by a man-made instrument.

That the function of the vocal chords was unknown, or at least considered to be irrelevant, we may conclude from the description of the five stages of this spontaneous manifestation:[2] 'This *prâṇa* then, stirred by the fire of the body, goes gradually upwards and produces an extremely subtle sound in the navel, a subtle sound in the heart, a strong sound in the throat, a weak sound in the head, and in the mouth a sound with the qualities of art.'

On the physical plane the entire human society is dependent on sound, as explained by the following reasoning:[3] 'By sound the letter is formed, by letters the syllable, by syllables the word, by words this daily life. Hence this human world is dependent on sound.'

It must be borne in mind that the sound that rules the world by means of speech is the same spontaneous manifestation which produces the musical phenomena.

The metaphysical theory of sound, set forth in the *Saṃgîtaratnâkara*, shows the position of music in the religious system of India. It probably represents a medieval attempt at explaining the actual religious importance of music which struck the philosophers of those days, but had its roots in much earlier, even prehistoric periods.

[1] Śârngadeva, *Saṃgîtaratnâkara* (referred to later as *SR*) *Ânandâśrama Sanskrit Series*, 2 vols. (Poona, 1896), i. 2. 1; Dâmodara, *Saṃgîtadarpaṇa* (referred to later as *SD*) (Paris, 1930), i. 13:

gîtam nâdâtmakam vâdyam nâdavyaktyâ praśasyate
taddvayânugatam nṛtyam nâdâdhînam atas trayam

[2] *SR*, i. 3. 3-5a. *SD*, i. 34, 35:

pâvakapreritaḥ so'tha kramâd ûrdhvapathe caran
atisûkṣmam dhvanim nâbhau hṛdi sûkṣmam gale punaḥ (34)
puṣṭam śîrṣe tvapuṣṭam ca kṛtrimam vadane tathâ
avirbhâvayatîty evam pañcadhâ kîrtyate budhaiḥ. (35)

[3] *SR*, i. 2. 2; *SD*, i. 14:

nâdena vyajyate varnaḥ padam varnât padâd vacaḥ
vacaso vyavahâro 'yam nâdâdhînam ato jagat.

The metaphysical explanations are principally concerned with vocal sound, as being primary in nature. This, as we have seen above, was produced by the gradual upward surge of the *prâṇa* or life-breath. In its course the *prâṇa* passes different mystical centres of power, bearing the name of *cakras* (circles), portrayed as lotuses with a varying number of petals. Two of those *cakras* have special importance from the musical point of view, namely the *anâhatacakra* situated in the heart, and the *viśuddhacakra* in the throat. The latter, having sixteen petals, is considered as the seat of speech and of all the musical notes with their divisions and variations.[1]

The sound alluded to so far is only the *âhatanâda* (struck or manifested sound), which cannot exist without its ideal counterpart, the *anâhatanâda* (unstruck or unmanifested sound). It is this dual nature of sound as *âhata* and *anâhata*, which brings it right into the centre of religious-philosophical speculations, because the unmanifested sound, the *anâhatanâda*, is identified with the creative principle of the universe in its transcedental form of Shiva himself, as well as in its immanent form as the syllable *OṂ* which is said to reside in the heart. Hence the name of the centre of power placed there, the *anâhatacakra*:[2]

> In the heart is a lotus with twelve petals, called *anâhata*, belonging to Shiva in his aspect of the syllable *oṃ*, a beloved object of adoration.
>
> There the wise revere the unmanifested sound according to the instructions of the preceptors, the sound that is for liberation but not for enjoyment. That sound, however, when manifested in the world, serves for enjoyment, but also to break the cycle of existence.

In this context the breaking of the cycle of existence means the merging of the individual self with the creative principle of the Universe.

It is now easy to see how music was held to serve as a means to that ultimate bliss. Sound, in its unmanifested aspect, was identical with the divine creative principle of the Universe, not only in its transcendental aspect, but also with that aspect which dwells in one's heart. So it remained for the individual to find the right way to realize the connexion between the latter aspect of the unmanifested sound and the manifested sound, in order to be brought into direct contact with the divine creative principle of the universe itself, which amounted to the desired liberation. The obvious means to this end was music,

[1] *SR*, i. 2. 199 ff. *SD*, i. 18–25a.

[2] *SR*, i. 2. 164b–165. *SD*, i. 16–17a:

tatrânâhatam nâdam tu munayaḥ samupâsate
guropadiṣṭa-mârgena muktidam na tu rañjakam (16)
sa nâdas tvâhato loke rañjako bhavabhañjakah.

and preferably vocal music, which by its own nature was pure sound itself.

On the physical plane the power of music was easily grasped when one understood that, on the one hand, sound regulated human society through its power to form letters, syllables, and words, and that, on the other hand, vocal music was that very sound in its spontaneous form. The ideal means to influence and regulate the course of human existence would thus naturally be a combination of words and musical sound, that is to say the intoned formula, or *mantra,* which we actually find used for that end in every form of religion on Indian soil.

In the above philosophical construction of *âhata* and *anâhatanâda,* we find consequently the crystallization of the ancient Indian belief that music has a well-defined power to influence the course of human life in this world, and that it even can lead to the ultimate bliss of the merging of the self with the divine principle of the universe, in other words that it can bring about the breaking of the cycle of existence. Hence it fully deserves the epithet *vimuktida* (bestowing liberation), given to it in the Sanskrit texts.

VEDIC MUSIC

The notion that the power of music, especially the intoned word, can influence the course of human destiny and even the order of the Universe, goes back to the very oldest surviving form of Indian music, namely, the music of the Vedas. The intoned formula is the pivot of the whole elaborate structure of Vedic offerings and sacrifices. It is the power of the words, enunciated with the correct intonation, that determines the efficacy of the rites: a mistake may destroy everything. The priests claim that by their activity they not only uphold the order of human society, but maintain the stability of the universe. By means of well-conducted ceremonies they have compelling power over the Gods themselves. The instrument that conveys that power is the word. It is impossible to overlook the connexion between *Brahman,* in the sense of divine principle, and *brahman* in the sense of sacrificial formula or incantation.

The Vedic offerings comprise a great many actions: altars are built, fires are lit, butter and other substances are poured into the flames, and animals are sacrificed. Sometimes these activities may continue for a year or longer, but none of them have any value unless accompanied by the prescribed recitations, uttered with exactly the right intonation. Musically those recitations are of great interest, as in their successive forms they represent the development from ordinary speech to elaborate singing, with a compass ranging from one or two notes to an octave. The *bhâṣikasvara* (speech tone) has the narrowest compass and is employed, according to tradition, in reciting the formulas of the (White) *Yajur Veda*. It is an even recitation without variation in pitch. A greater compass, however, is found in the *Rigveda*, the basis of all the texts used at the Vedic offerings. It contains the hymns to the different deities as they were composed by the sages of old who are known by name, but about whose date nothing is known with certainty. Opinions range over a couple of thousand years, one school placing them in the fourth millennium B.C., another about the middle of the second millennium.

The way of chanting the Rigvedic hymns has definite musical importance, as the three accents employed, the *udâtta*, the *anudâtta*, and the *svarita*, denote a distinct difference in pitch. There is some controversy as to the original meaning of these accents and their relationship to the *pracaya* (multitude)—a term denoting a succession of unaccented syllables. As we find the practice of Rigvedic recitation in our days—and examples collected by Haug in 1874[1] and Felber in 1912[2] seem to indicate that at that time the same system was followed—the accents indicate a compass of a minor or major third, the middle note being the *udâtta*, the lower the *anudâtta*, and the upper the *svarita*. The *pracaya* coincides with the *udâtta*, which, as a matter of fact, is itself unmarked in the Vedic texts. The *anudâtta* is indicated by a horizontal line under the syllable, the *svarita* by a perpendicular line over it:

Ex. 290

nā - rā - ya-ṇam ma-hā-jñe-yam viś-vāt-mā-ṇam pa-rā-ya-ṇam

(*Taittirīya-âraṇyaka* X. 11, as sung by Manjeri Ramakrishna Iyar, Allepey, Travancore.)

The melodic line follows the text in every detail; the words prescribe the rhythm and the flow; there is one note to each syllable, pitch is independent of duration. One might say that the melody only supports the words.

The *Rigveda* is extensively used, not only during the great Vedic

[1] Martin Haug, *Über das Wesen und den Werth des vedischen Accents* (Munich, 1874); see also Fox Strangways, *Music of Hindostan* (Oxford, 1914), p. 247.

[2] E. Felber-Geiger, *Die indische Musik der vedischen und klassischen Zeit* (Vienna, 1912).

sacrifices, but also during the lesser ceremonies in everyday life in the house. A large measure of similarity in tradition over a very wide area would thus point to a great antiquity and bear witness to a tenacity of custom not surprising in a field where deviations from the prescribed method were believed to have dire spiritual and material consequences. Adherence to the hereditary style would last as long as faith in the efficacy of the rites in question persisted. That faith has not yet died in India in spite of the onrush of modern civilization.

In the *Sâmaveda*, which, in contrast to the *Rigveda*, is used exclusively in connexion with the larger offerings and sacrifices, we find a complete reversal of the rules laid down for the recitation of the *Rigveda*. To begin with, the compass used is much wider, and some schools of Sâmavedic chanting are said to use the full octave (the texts give the names of the seven notes, originally counted from the highest note downwards) but even if, as among the Nambudiris of the Malabar coast who follow the Jaiminîya tradition, the compass of only a second is used, the tendency is to deviate as far as possible from ordinary speech or even chanting. The words are broken up in an arbitrary fashion and often the periods start in the middle of a word; vowels are lengthened beyond recognition, and syllables without rational importance are inserted in the text. In most cases the basis of the Sâmavedic chants is a hymn from the *Rigveda*, but it is overlaid and changed to such an extent that the original is usually well hidden. The object of this procedure is purely liturgical. By the very minutely prescribed changes the spiritual efficacy of the formula is heightened and the success of the sacrifice ensured.

The limitation of the use of the *Sâmaveda* to the actual offerings and sacrifices is the cause of its much greater rarity, and it would be useless to look for a sound tradition of the chanting of this *Veda* in parts of India where, owing to social changes, these larger ceremonies seldom take place: for instance, in northern India where continuous foreign invasions have shaken the very basis of Hindu society. It is in south India that the tradition according to the different schools is carried on, handed down from teacher to pupil, as has been the case for centuries. Priestly families in which the tradition is known to have persisted unbroken for twenty generations are not uncommon.

Research in this field, except by members of the priestly class itself, is greatly hampered by the secrecy that surrounds this type of singing, which is not meant to be heard, much less written down or recorded, by uninitiated persons. This is hardly surprising when one realizes the supernatural effect attributed to the correct reproduction of the melodies.

At the actual sacrifices a hymn is executed by three priests who sing its seven divisions alone or in chorus. The priests to whom the singing of the *Sâmaveda* is allotted are the *Udgâtar* with his two acolytes, the *Prastotar* and the *Pratihartar*. The introductory part, the *Huṃkâra* (the singing of the syllable *huṃ*), is done by the three together. Then follow: 2, the *Prastâva*, or prelude, sung by the *Prastotar*; 3, the *Udgîtha*, or main theme, by the *Udgâtar*; 4, the *Pratihâra*, the first responsorium, by the *Pratihartar*; 5, the *Upadrava*, second responsorium, again by the *Udgâtar*; 6, the *Nidhana*, or final chorus, by the three priests in unison; and finally, 7, the *Praṇava*, the chanting of the syllable *oṃ*, also in chorus, which seals the hymn like our Amen.

For purposes of study or practice, however, the hymns are sung by one person only according to the song-books, the *Gânas*, of which there are four. The different schools of Sâmavedic chanting all use these four books, but sing them to quite different melodies. Even in one and the same school the differences are sometimes considerable:

Ex. 291

Kauthuma Sâmaveda (Chidambaram and Trichinopoli) S.V. I[66a]

Ex. 292

Kauthuma Sâmaveda (Baroda)

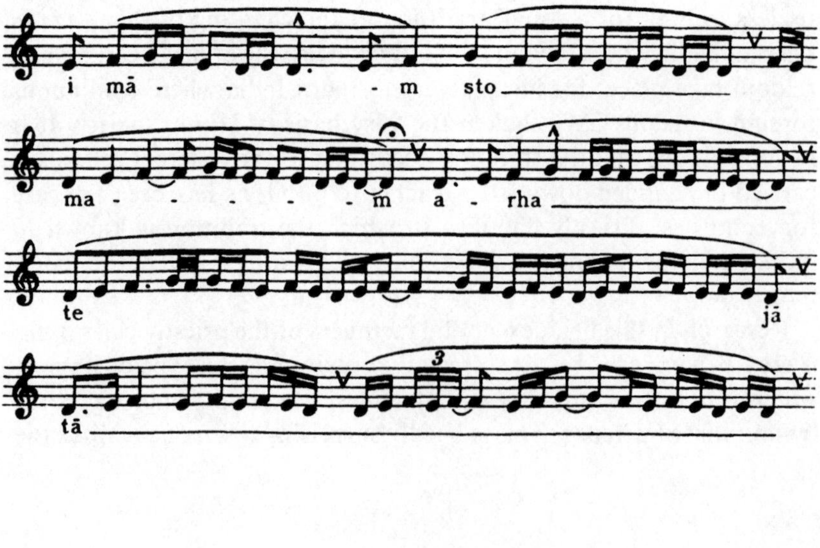

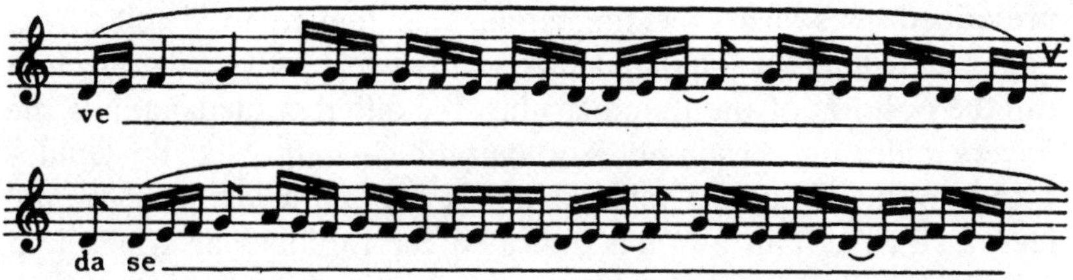

It should be mentioned that the tradition of the *Kauthumas*, as observed in Trichinopoly and Chidambaram, both centres of south Indian orthodoxy, shows no differences at all, apart from those that might have resulted from individual uncertainties of one singer or the other. The totally different style of the example from Baroda which called itself *Kauthuma* too, may be due to the very influence indicated above—the foreign invasions and their cultural consequences—and bears traces of the flourishes of the later, purely secular, musical style, strongly influenced by Moslem practices.

One can see that the claim made by the classical Indian theory of music, that the proper use of this art leads to salvation, has its roots in the Vedic practices. It is true that the object of the Vedic ceremonies, built on the proper enunciation of the intoned word, is not salvation, in the later spiritual sense, but the upholding of the order of the world and, by extension, of the universe. But in both cases the sole aim is to get in touch with the powers of the world of the gods, an aim that has perpetuated itself through the centuries, varying only as to the nature of the gods and the nature of the desired contact.

The second component of the triad comprised in the word *Saṃgîta*, namely, instrumental music, has perhaps not such direct and clear connexions with the Vedic ceremonies as vocal music. Instruments are mentioned in the *brâhmaṇas*, the treatises that describe the procedure of the ritual, and drums and cymbals must have made their appearance at a very early date. However, seeing the paramount importance of the spoken or intoned word, it is but natural that instrumental music should occupy the second place. In any case it is more than probable that the development and perfection of instrumental Indian music is of much later date than that of the vocal art.

As to the third component of *Saṃgîta*, dance, which shares the epithet *vimuktida* with vocal and instrumental music, its links with Vedic ceremonies are very direct and clear. We find that the chanting was accompanied by movements of the hands, and perhaps also by prescribed steps when executing certain tasks that involved going from one place to another. The hand movements were partly mnemo-technical, the position of the thumb against the different phalanges of the fingers indicating certain notes or figurations—rather like the Guidonian hand in Gregorian music—and partly had a textual meaning, inasmuch as certain postures indicated certain ideas or symbolized certain deities, thus approaching a sign-language that accompanied, followed, and intensified the meaning of the chanted text. These sequences of hand-postures and their development into a kind of sign-language are the basis of the most classical form of all Indian dancing, the *Bharatanâṭya* of southern India, and, to a lesser extent, of the Hindu forms of north Indian dancing, as well as of the mimed dramas of the coast of Malabar, the *Kathâkali* and the *Yakṣagâna*.

As these movements are an integral part of the Vedic ceremonies and share the holiness of everything that belongs to revealed religion, one sees how they are by rights the third component of *Saṃgîta*, in so far as they have their roots in the practices of the Vedic ritual.

In actual life it is not improbable that at times the third component of the triad had a more prominent position than the other two. As mentioned above, the oldest data about the theory of music are found in the *Bharatanâṭyaśâstra* (*c.* 200 B.C.). This has thirty-six chapters, of which only chapters 28–33 deal with music.

It seems doubtful whether, outside the ritual sphere, the spiritual importance of music was always fully realized. After all, the *âhatanâda* was said to be for enjoyment as well as for the breaking of the cycle of existence, and one cannot wonder that the accent was often laid on the first function rather than on the second. Still, many traces of the original sanctity are preserved, for instance in movements of adoration and obeisance which one sees musicians and actors perform even nowadays and, more especially, in the attitude of the pupil towards his music-master, which is to a great extent that of a novice towards his spiritual guide. It is not forgotten that—if the latter understands his task properly—he ought to lead his pupil on the way to salvation.

THE CLASSICAL SYSTEM

Quite apart from its religious importance, the classical system of Indian music deserves attention in its own right. It explains every aspect of construction and technique in great detail, from the notes of the scale and their subdivisions onwards.

The Octaves

The basis of the classical system—as represented in the *Saṃgîtaratnâkara,* for instance—is the octave and its division into tones and semitones, closely akin to our system. The number of octaves recognized is three, one in each register, the low being the breast register, the middle octave the throat register, and the high octave the head register. This classification is another proof of the primarily vocal conception of music in India.[1]

Consonance

The division of the notes of the octave is accomplished according to the laws of consonance, three intervals being recognized as such, namely, the octave, the fifth, and the fourth. Only they are consonant (*saṃvâdî*). Dissonant (*vivâdî*) are only the semitones. All the others are assonant (*anuvâdî*).

Śrutis

For the definition of what constitutes consonance or otherwise, the Indian theory has recourse to a tonal subdivision smaller than the West has taken into consideration for the construction of its scales. This microtonic unit is called *śruti,* a word derived from the root *śru* (to hear) and it is defined as follows:[2] 'The sound that is just perceptible as such by the ear, without reverberation (i.e. harmonic connexion) is called *śruti.*'

There are twenty-two *śrutis* in the octave and the question has been asked whether they are mathematically alike. Sir William Jones, the first European scholar to interest himself in the matter, in the late eighteenth century, maintains that they are not, but are intended to be alike in a general way. He points out that mathematics do not enter into the subject at all as far as the writers of the Indian treatises are concerned.[3] Bosanquet recognizes a general alikeness in the conclusion of his article 'On the Hindu division of the Octave',[4] a conclusion with which Rao Sahib P. R. Bandharkar

[1] *SR,* i. 3.7:

vyavahâre tvasau tredhâ hṛdi mandro 'bhidhîyate
kaṇṭhe madhyo mûrdhni târo dviguṇaścottarottaraḥ.

[2] *SD,* i. 49:

svarûpamâtraśravanân nâdo'nuraṇanam vinâ
śrutir ity ucyate bhedâś tasmâd dvâviṃśatir matâḥ.

[3] 'On the musical modes of the Hindus', in *Asiatic Researches,* iii (1792), p. 55. Reprinted in S. M. Tagore's *Hindu Music* (Calcutta, 1882), pp. 123 ff.

[4] *Proceedings of the Royal Society,* xxvi (1877).

agrees.[1] Fox Strangways, however, attributes three definite mathematical values to the *śruti*:[2] (*a*) the difference between a major and a minor tone, 22 cents, called *pramâṇaśruti*; (*b*) the difference between a minor tone and a semitone, 70 cents; and (*c*) the difference between a semitone and the *pramâṇaśruti*, 90 cents. Reasoning along altogether different lines, a German scholar, Dr. B. Breloer[3] arrives at the values, 24, 66, and 90 cents, practically identical with Fox Strangways's conclusion. A more recent publication, however, A. Daniélou's book on Hindu scales,[4] attacks these calculations for not being precise enough. The exact value of the *śruti*, therefore, is still debated. It would seem, however, that, so far as the Indian opinion of ancient times is concerned, *śruti* is a generic name for any interval smaller than a semitone. No mathematical approach to the matter is found in India before the eighteenth century.[5]

Śrutis are important in practice in defining the character of parallel modes with similar intervals; a *śruti* smaller or larger in the one mode than in the other creates a different mood or atmosphere. They are also of practical importance in ornamentation when the voice, or the vibrating string pulled sideways, swings above and below the actual pitch of the intended note without deviating as much as a semitone. But it is quite wrong to suppose that these *śrutis* are ever used in succession, like our semitones in a chromatic scale.

Svaras

In theory the *śrutis* are important to define the notes (*svaras*) of the octave and to establish their consonance or otherwise. A note—or, rather tonal interval—is defined as 'an uninterrupted series of *śrutis*, belonging together in harmonic connection'.[6]

ṣaḍja or *sa*, consisting of four śrutis,
ṛṣabha or *ri*, consisting of three śrutis,
gândhâra or *ga*, consisting of two śrutis,
madhayma or *ma*, consisting of four śrutis,
pañcama or *pa*, consisting of four śrutis,
dhaivata or *dha*, consisting of three śrutis,
and *niṣâda* or *ni*, consisting of two śrutis.

[1] *Indian Antiquary*, 1912.
[2] Op. cit., p. 112.
[3] *Grundelemente der altindischen Musik* (Bonn, 1922).
[4] *Introduction to the Study of Musical Scales* (London, 1943).
[5] In the *Saṃgîta-pârijâta* (Paradise Tree of Music) of Ahobala.
[6] *SR*, i. 3. 26:

śrutyanantarabhâvî yaḥ snigdho'nuraṇanâtmakaḥ
svato rañjayati śrotṛcittam sa svara ucyate.

Bharata says that notes at a distance of nine or thirteen *śrutis* from one another (viz. fourths and fifths) are consonant. Those at a distance of twenty *śrutis* (viz. seconds or sevenths) are dissonant. The remaining intervals are assonant. The later texts give two *śrutis* distance as the definition of *vivâdî* notes.

Grâmas

The scale according to the ratio 4, 3, 2, 4, 4, 3, 2, given above, is only one of the two basic scales, or *grâmas*, in practical use. It is called the *sa-grâma*, because it starts from the *sa* of the middle register.[1] Parallel to this we find the *ma-grâma*, which is identical, except for the difference of one *śruti* in the *pa*, which in the *ma-grâma* consists of three *śrutis*, causing the *dha* to have four. It is expressly stated that the *ma-grâma* starts on the *ma* of the middle register.[2] The ratio of the *ma-grâma* thus is: 4, 3, 4, 2, 4, 3, 2.

The fourth *śruti* of *pa* which in the *ma-grâma* becomes the first *śruti* of *dha* is called *pramâṇa* (standard) *śruti*, probably because it was the only *śruti* readily demonstrable in practice. As both the *sa-* and the *ma-grâma* were living conceptions in Bharata's times, it was possible to set the middle of the *sa-grâma*, 4, 4, 3, 2, (*ma*, *pa*, *dha*, *ni*), against the beginning of the *ma-grâma*, 4, 3, 4, 2, (*ma*, *pa*, *dha*, *ni*) on two identical *vîṇâs*, the *pa* being played on the second open string in both cases. The difference in pitch between the two *pas* gave a demonstration *ad auras* of a *śruti* (*śru* = to hear) which then could serve as a measure—*pramâṇa*—for the determination of the other, purely theoretical tonal divisions.

Following the indications of the ancient texts, which—probably as a remnant of the original descending order of the scale in Vedic times—accept the axiom that a note is realized on the last of its component *śrutis*, the four *śrutis* of *sa* lie between *sa* and *ni* and not, as we would reckon, between *sa* and *ri*.

Consequently the *sa-grâma* roughly corresponds to a D mode, the *ma-grâma* to a G mode, the former beginning with a minor third, the latter with a major third. Bharata explains in book 28, in the prose following verse 32, that one can play the *ma-grâma* starting from *sa* by changing the initial minor third of the *sa-grâma* into a major third by giving the *ga* four *śrutis* instead of two.

A third basic scale, the *ga-grâma*, starting on the *ga* of the middle register, has no practical value and is not mentioned by Bharata, but

[1] *SD*, i. 79: *tatra madhyasthaṣaḍjena ṣaḍjagrâmasya mûrchanâḥ*. *SR*, i. 4. 12b.
[2] *SR*, i. 4. 13b. *SD*, i. 79. *Madhyamadhyamam ârabhya madhyamagrâmamûrchanâḥ*.

only by writers some centuries younger than he. It is said, even by the first writer who mentions it (Nârada), to exist only in heaven. This may refer to an arrangement of *śrutis* that once existed, but had fallen into disuse at the time when the theoretical treatises were written, or to the fact that it is a purely theoretical construction. Its ratio is 3, 3, 3, 4, 3, 2, 4, and consequently it seems to have no connexion either with the *sa*- or with the *ma-grâma*, except for the fact that the *pa* consists of three and the *dha* of four *śrutis*, as in the latter. Apart from mentioning it in passing, the texts take no further notice of this *ga-grâma* and base their subsequent calculations exclusively on the *sa*- and the *ma-grâma*.

Alterations

The difference in allocation of *śrutis* to the *pa* and the *dha* found in the two *grâmas* is a basic and unalterable one. Apart from this, one finds that the notes in each *grâma* can be subject to other alterations, some comparable to our Western accidental sharps and flats. Including the change of the *sa*- to the *ma-grâma* the *Saṃgîtaratnâkara* mentions twelve possible changes in *śruti* allocation, though, as some of them overlap, they work out to only seven in reality. Out of these seven only two (the *kâkalî ni* and the *antara ga*) are in general use and taken into consideration when making permutations and combinations.

As in the classical texts the names of the notes are attached to the last of the series of their constituent *śrutis*, the basic *sa-grâma* presents itself as follows:

1 2 3 4, 5 6 7, 8 9, 10 11 12 13, 14 15 16 17, 18 19 20, 21 22
sa, *ri*, *ga*, *ma*, *pa*, *dha*, *ni*

It is evident that, as the notes were understood to be at the end of their constituent *śrutis*, the loss of a *śruti* at the beginning of a note was perceptible only by the fact that the note below it was raised one *śruti* in pitch.

The alterations are:[1]

(i) *Sa*, having four *śrutis*, comes down from the fourth to the third *śruti*, at the same time giving its first *śruti* to *kaiśika-ni* (see the

[1] Joanny Grosset, 'Inde', in Lavignac, *Encyclopédie de la musique*, 1re partie, i (Paris, 1913), p. 289.
SR, i. 3. 41–47:

ta eva vikṛtâvasthâ dvâdaśa pratipâditâḥ (41)
cyuto'cyuto dvidhâ ṣaḍjo dviśrutivikṛto bhavet
sâdhâraṇe kâkalitve niṣâdasya ca dṛśyate (42)
sâdharaṇe śrutim sâdjîm ṛṣabhaḥ saṃśrito yadâ

eleventh alteration). *Sa* thus becomes a note of two *srutis*. This is the first audibly altered note, *cyuta* (fallen) *sa*.

(ii) *Sa* remains on its proper, fourth, *śruti*, but has its two initial *śrutis* annexed by *kâkalî-ni* (see twelfth alteration). This *sa* is called *acyuta* (not-fallen) *sa*, and is not audible as an actually different note, as the position of the name-*śruti* is not changed.

(iii) *Ri* remains on its proper, seventh, *śruti*, but annexes *sa*'s top-*śruti*. *Sa* thus becomes *cyuta-sa* (first alteration).

(iv) *Ga* shifts from its proper (ninth), to the tenth *śruti*, annexing the first *śruti* of *ma* and thus becoming a note of three *śrutis*. This is the second really new note, called *sâdhâraṇa* (common) *ga*.

(v) *Ga* annexes one more *śruti* of *ma*, thus becoming a note of four *śrutis*. This is the third really new note, *antara* (medium) *ga*.

(vi) *Ma* comes down from its original (thirteenth) *śruti* to the twelfth, giving at the same time its first *śruti* to *sâdhâraṇa-ga* and thus becoming a note of two *śrutis*. This is the fourth really new note, called *cyuta* (fallen) *ma*.

(vii) *Ma* remains on its original (thirteenth) *śruti*, but gives its first two *śrutis* to *antara-ga*. It is called *acyuta-ma*, analogous to *acyuta-sa*.

(viii) *Pa* cedes its upper *śruti* to *dha* (in the *ma-grâma*) and is called *triśruti* (*three śruti*) *pa*. This is the fifth really new note.

(ix) *Pa* gives its top *śruti* to *dha*, but annexes the top *śruti* of *ma*, which thereby becomes *cyuta-ma*. This *pa* is called *kaiśika* (fine as a hair) *pa*.

(x) *Dha* annexes the last *śruti* of *pa*, in the *madhyama grâma*, but remains on its original (twentieth) *śruti*. This is called *vikṛta* (altered) *dha*.

(xi) *Ni* annexes the first *śruti* of *sa*. This is the sixth really new note, called *kaiśika ni*.

(xii) *Ni* takes the first two *śrutis* of *sa*. This is the seventh really new note, called *kâkalî* (soft) *ni*.

It will be seen that the alterations follow strictly parallel lines in the two tetrachords of the octave.

catuḥśrutitvam âyâti tadaiko vikṛto bhaved (43)
sâdhâraṇe triśrutiḥ syâd antaratve catuḥśrutiḥ
gândhara iti tadbhedau dvau niḥśankena kîrtitau (44)
madhyamaḥ ṣaḍjavad dvedhâ 'ntarasâdhâraṇâśrayât
pañcamo madhyamagrâme triśrutiḥ kaiśike punaḥ (45)
madhyamasya śrutim prâpya catuḥśrutir iti dvidhâ
dhaivato madhyamagrâme vikṛtaḥ syâc catuḥśrutih (46)
kaiśike kâkalitve ca niṣâdas tricatuḥśrutiḥ
prâpnoti vikṛtau bhedau dvâv iti dvâdaśa smṛtâḥ (47)

Mûrcchanâs

The word *grâma* in its general sense means village or community. In its musical sense[1] it is defined as 'a collection of notes and the dwelling place of the *mûrcchanâs* and their derivations'. Weber suggests in his *Indische Streifen*[2] that the Greek word *gamma* in its musical sense of scale, is a derivation from the Sanskrit *grâma*, through some intermediate vernacular form. Certainly the modes in Greek music are derived from the basic scale very much as the *mûrcchanâs* are derived from the two *grâmas*. In the Indian theory each *grâma* gives rise to seven *mûrcchanâs* (extensions or gradations) by taking each successive note of the descending scale of the *grâma* in question as the basis of a new series of seven. Thus the first *mûrcchanâ* of the *sa-grâma* will be *sa-ni*, the second *ni-dha*, the third *dha-pa*, and so on, the seventh being *ri-sa*. It is expressly stated that the first *mûrcchanâ* of the *sa-grâma* starts on the middle *sa*, the first *mûrcchanâ* of the *ma-grâma* on the middle *ma*. It is clear that this procedure changes the relative position of tones and semitones within the octave in exactly the same way as does the Western method of building modes.

In each of the fourteen *mûrcchanâs* one can introduce either the *kâkalî-ni* or the *antara-ga* or both *kâkalî* and *antara*, which gives three possible variations to each basic pattern, adding up to fifty-six, i.e. four times fourteen, *mûrcchanâs* in all. Apart from these alterations, the Indian theory recognizes not only full, heptatonic (*saṃpûrṇa*) *mûrcchanâs*, but also hexatonic (*ṣâḍava*) and pentatonic (*auḍava*) varieties, each again with such alterations as the remaining notes allow. From this substratum the later modal system of *rāgas* and *râgiṇîs* could develop naturally.

Mûrcchanâs can be sung in their natural, diatonic order or in meandering sequences. In a detailed text like the *Saṃgîtaratnâkara* no possibility of combination or permutation is left unexplored. For the development of the modal system, however, only the basic heptatonic modes with their hexatonic and pentatonic varieties have to be considered, as it is from them that the classical system of *râgas* and *râgiṇîs* was finally born.

Jâtis

There was, however, an intermediate stage in the development from *mûrcchanâs* to *râgas*, namely, the *jâtis*. Out of the fourteen *mûrcchanâs*

[1] *SR*, i. 4. 1. *SD*, i. 68:
grâmaḥ svarasamûhaḥ syân mûrcchanâdeḥ samâśrayaḥ
tau dvau dharatale tatra syât ṣaḍjagrâma âdimaḥ.

[2] Albrecht Weber, *Indische Streifen* (Berlin, 1863), i. 3. 544.

of the two *grâmas* only seven assumed the status of *jâti* or basic mode. Four, those starting on *sa*, *dha*, *ni*, and *ri* were based on the corresponding *mûrcchanâs* of the *sa-grâma*; three, starting from *ma*, *ga*, and *pa*, belonged to the *magrâma*. Contrary to the custom followed with the *mûrcchanâs*, the sequence of the *jâtis* is always given in ascending order: *ṣâḍjî* is the first *jâti*, *ṛṣabhî*, not *niṣâdavatî*, the second.

In addition to the seven basic *jâtis*, Bharata enumerates the names of eleven more, combinations of two or more of the first seven. Each *jâti* has its own 'pillar notes', incipient, final, and melodic centre, and some additional individual features, which stamp them clearly as the ancestors of the subsequent *râgas*. In the *Bharatanâṭyaśâstra* the term *râga* in its technical sense is yet unknown, but the *râgas* incorporate all the melodic permutations and combinations of the older system to which numerous new characteristics have been added. For all its intricacies and delicate refinements, the classical system of *râgas* has nothing intrinsically different from the Western modal system of the Middle Ages.

Pitch

One difference of approach to melodic structure in India and the West seems to be due to the fact that at a very early stage the Western systems fixed a definite pitch for each note, whereas everything in the Indian theory points to the fact that pitch was strictly relative and had no connexion with the names of the notes separately. The tendency to identify *sa* with *c*, very general in our days, cannot be much more than fifty years old and dates especially from the introduction and virulent spread of the portable harmonium through towns and villages.

The only indication as to pitch in the classical texts is[1] in verses like the following, in which each successive note is identified with the cry of a bird or beast, not always the same creatures in each case.

> The peacock utters the note *sa*;
> the *câtaka*-bird *ri*;
> the goat the note *ga*;
> the *krauñca* bird *ma*;
> the woodpecker with its clear voice *pa*;
> the frog, excited by love, the note *dha*;
> the elephant, hit on the head with the driver's hook,
> utters the last note (*ni*) through its nose.

[1] *SR*, i. 3. 48. *SD*, i. 152, 153:
ṣaḍjam vadati mayûraḥ ṛṣabhâkhyam câtako brute
gândhârâkhyam châgo nigadati pakṣi to madhyamam krauñcaḥ
gadati pañcamam añcitavâkapiko ratati dhaivatam unmadadarduraḥ
śṛṇîsamâhatamastakakuñjaro gadati nâsikayâ svaram antimam.

Now, unless this has some, not immediately apparent, symbolical or mythological meaning, it has little meaning at all. For instance, the cry of the peacock consists of at least two notes which are certainly not even an octave apart; consequently it cannot stand for *sa* without further elucidation. In the same way anyone hearing the confusion of different noises emerging from a herd of goats would be sorely pressed if he had to determine the fixed pitch of *ga*.

The current practice—and there is no evidence that things were materially different in former days—is, that a singer chooses his *sa* according to his convenience, and keeps to it for the duration of the whole performance, irrespective of the number of *râgas* he presents. The same is the case with instrumentalists. A change of *sa* would entail a very laborious retuning of the accompanying drums, one of which usually gives the *sa*, the other the *ma* or *pa*. When more than one musician performs at the same function, each generally has his own drummer, or at least his own set of drums, which are tuned to the *sa* he has chosen.

Râgas

Clearly this is all that is required in a purely modal system. It is always this relative position of tones and semitones measured against a certain fixed point which determines the character of a mode, whether in the West or in the East, and the *râgas*—as the *jâtis* before them—have certain salient points of the scale which serve as a skeleton for their individual structure. These points bear the name of *graha*, *aṃśa*, and *nyâsa*:[1]

Graha is the incipient note, 'the note that is placed at the beginning of a song'.

Aṃśa is the melodic centre, 'the note that occurs often in the course of a performance'.

Nyâsa is the final, 'the note that finishes a song'.

In the performance of a mode, whether a *jâti* or a *râga*, the first thing necessary is to establish these three sufficiently clearly, and in the lists of *râgas* in the textbooks, the notes of the scale that have these functions are always clearly given. It not infrequently happens that one note assumes two or even all three functions, so that the same note is *graha*, *aṃśa*, and *nyâsa*.

[1] *SR*, i. 7. 30, 33, 38. *SD*, i. 146, 147:

gîtâdau sthâpito yas tu sa grahasvara ucyate
nyâsaḥ svaras tu vijñeyo yas tu gîtasamâpakaḥ (146)
bahulatvam prayogeṣu sa aṃśasvara ucyate (147)

It is customary to preface the performance of a *râga*—as it must have been with the *jâtis* before—with a prelude, called *âlâpa*, in which, against the note chosen for the function of *sa*, the salient points are established, as well as the secondary features, such as hexa- or pentatonality, frequency or paucity of certain notes or intervals, high, middle, or low tessitura, and so on.

It is the combination of all these secondary characteristics that makes a *râga* into something more than a simple mode, and gives it the quality expressed in the word *râga* as compared with *jâti*. The latter means simply genus, the former, however, from the root *rañj* (to colour), means everything which that root suggests: colour, emotion, and atmosphere. A *râga* is a mode which has developed such a special ethos that it cannot be mistaken for another combination of notes expressing a different emotion. Two *râgas* can be based on the same basic mode or *jâti*, and yet be entirely different in the mood that they convey. There can be several reasons for this effect; for instance, if the first has its *aṃśa*—the centre of musical gravity—near the drone, while in the second it soars far away from it, the first will create an atmosphere of sadness and depression, the second one of exuberance.

In this way the variations, permutations, and combinations are endless, especially when existing *râgas* are combined to form new, composite ones, partaking of the characteristics of two or even more components. In the classical *râga* system such a new creation usually bears the name of its parents, as, for instance, *Megh-Malhâr*, *Gauḍ-Sarang*, *Mâlava-Kauśika*, or *Sindhu-Bhairavi*. This tendency is traceable to the oldest times on record. Bharata mentions the phenomenon of *jâti-sâdhâraṇa* (community of *jâtis*) in which one *jâti* partakes of the notes of the other. One also can link up *râgas* by a process comparable to modulation, starting in one *râga* and skilfully introducing—after a suitable lapse of time—characteristics belonging to another, thus weaving what is called a *râgamâla* (garland of *râgas*). At a performance by a famous artist the listeners, that is to say those who have the intimate knowledge of the *râgas* performed, without which the refinements and variations of the presentation of the known features cannot be properly appreciated, will be startled and surprised the moment a foreign element is introduced and approve only when this leads towards the shape, feelings, and emotions of the next *râga*.

In the later stages of development of the classical system, that is to say, mainly after the influx of Muslim culture, which set the seal on the differentiation between the music of north and south India, we find a tendency in the north to carry the specialization so far that the musical shape gives rise to a physical shape. The Râgas are depicted as divine or human beings in surroundings that suggest the atmosphere they create. The gender, *râga* and *râgiṇî*, masculine and feminine, had been established at a fairly early date; connexions with times of day and night and seasons of the year are also enumerated in the older classical texts, both in north and south India, but the paintings, the last possible stage in personification, belong to the north. Thus, for instance, the *râga Megha* (cloud) is described as follows in the *Saṃgîtadarpaṇa*:[1]

Megha is heptatonic, having *dha* in the three functions of *graha, aṃśa,* and *nyâsa,* in the *mûrcchanâ uttarâyatâ* (the third of the *sa-grâma*), to be sung with the altered (*vikṛta*) *dha.* A gush of erotic sentiment.

Râga Megha, the Youth, having a body like the blue lotus, with garments like the moon, dressed in yellow, implored by thirsty *câtaka*-birds (who drink only raindrops), with a smile sweet as nectar, is resplendent among heroes, in the midst of clouds.

Only the north Indian system bases its classification on the gender of the *râgas.* Usually one finds six *râgas* with five wives—*râgiṇî*—making a total of thirty-six, with innumerable offshoots classified as children. It is a system that gives room to unbridled flights of fancy in which no measure of uniformity between the different local traditions has been achieved.

Side by side with it we find, however, the system of dividing the *râgas* and *râgiṇîs* into *thaṭs* or groups, more or less along the lines of the different original basic modes, the *jâtis* of the *Nâṭyaśâstra.* A *thaṭ* groups together those *râgas* and *râgiṇîs* which have a similar construction. The word[2] originally applied to the arrangement of the movable frets of a stringed instrument such as the *setar*, for the playing of one chosen mode, which of course included several *râgas.* One generally recognizes ten *thaṭs.*

This second and less universal north Indian system, which, however, has gained a much wider popularity with the spread of music-teaching in schools and colleges, is of a later date than the more

[1] *SD*, ii. 108, 109:
meghaḥ pûrṇo dhatrayaḥ syâd uttarâyatamûrchanâ vikṛtadhaivato geyaḥ śṛngârarasapûrakaḥ (108)
nîlotpalâbhavapur indusamânacailaḥ pîtâmbaras tṛṣitacâtakayâcyamânaḥ
pîyûṣamandahasito ghanamadhyavartî vireṣu râjati yuvâ kila megharâgaḥ (109)

[2] Fox Strangways, op. cit., p. 106.

fantastic male *râgas* with five wives each, as shown by its name (taken from the technique of an instrument imported from Persia). All the same it has striking affinities with the universal south Indian system, that of the *melakartas* which may be said to be a modified continuation of the ancient arrangement in *jâtis*.

Melakartas, of which there are seventy-two, are divided into two exactly parallel groups of thirty-six each, identical but for the circumstance that the first group uses natural fourths, the second augmented fourths from *sa*. The *râgas* follow one another according to their gradually increasing number of accidentals in the two tetrachords. The names are arranged according to a definite plan, so that anyone who knows the codeword can tell at once which notes have to be sung in a particular *râga* and also what place the *râga* occupies in the *melakarta* scheme.

North and south use different names.[1] The *thaṭ* based on notes corresponding to our major mode is called *Bilâval* in the north and is the *melakarta* '*Śankarâbharaṇa*' in the south. The north Indian *Bhairavî thaṭ* (our medieval Phrygian mode) is *Hanumantoḍi* in the south, and so on. On the other hand, one finds that identical names, such as *Hindola*, denote different *râgas* in north and south. All the same, there is no basic difference between the two systems; one may regard them as two dialects of the same language. Generally speaking, the classifications as well as the system of south India as a whole are more logical and bespeak a more mathematical intellect than the pronouncedly emotional northern traditions.

As mentioned above, accomplished musicians establish the ethos of the *râga* they are going to perform in the *âlâpa*. This unaccompanied prelude in free time may last for an hour or more. Each detail of the *râga* that is being presented is minutely illustrated from all possible angles. The accompanying drum comes in fully only when the actual composition begins. In general a complete composition consists of the following four divisions: *asthai* (the theme), *antara* (the second subject), *sañcâri* (development), and *âbhog* (coda) which may be replaced by a return to the *asthai*. The corresponding south Indian divisions are *pallavi*, *anupallavi*, *caraṇam*, and *pallavi*.

For teaching in schools, the *râgas* are somewhat simplified and instead of the improvised *âlâpa*, the children are taught a short song which incorporates all the characteristics of the *râga* in question, as, for instance, the following song, meant to illustrate the pentatonic (*auḍava*) *râga* called *Bhûp* or *Bhûpkaliân* (Ex. 293).

[1] Fox Strangways, op. cit., p. 139, footnote.

Ex. 293

Râga Bhûpkaliân
Sa - dhe su - ra sa dhe sa - dhe su - ra sa - dhe
su - ra su - ra - lo - ka de - na sa - dhe su - ra sa - dhe
au da - va ye - hi — râ - ga. sam - gî - ta ma - ta prâ - mâ - ṇa
sa re ga pa dha sa dha pa ga re sa u - la - ta -
po - la - ta su - ra - na - ki — sa - dhe su - ra sa - dhe sa - dhe

In this song *ga*, the third note of the scale, quite clearly has the functions of *graha*, *aṃśa*, and *nyâsa*. According to Fox Strangways[1] this represents the Poona tradition, as *Bhûpkaliân* when sung according to the tradition of Gwalior has *ri*, the second note of the scale, in these functions. *Ma*, the fourth note, and *ni*, the seventh note, are missing, but the former is touched on once in the first bar, which is permissible. The way in which phrases have to be constructed in this *râga* is exemplified as succinctly as possible. Such an example differs from an *âlâpa* in two aspects: it has time (*tâla*) and it has words. The words, in this case, are a reminder of the real function of music. They say:

Oh *Sâdhu* (wise man), notes open the realm of Heaven.
This *râga* is pentatonic according to the laws of music:
—*sa*, *re*, *ga*, *pa*, *dha*, *sa*, *dha*, *pa*, *ga*, *re*, *sa*—. The notes can be sung in a topsy-turvey way, can't they?

Tâlas

As for the time (*tâla*) of Ex. 293, this is one of the irregular time-divisions of Indian music, the time of ten, consisting of 4+2+4 beats, the strong beats being one, five, and seven. Consequently this is not a doubling of quintuple time, which also occurs and consists most commonly of 3+2 beats, though sometimes we find 2+3.

[1] Fox Strangways, op. cit., chart facing p. 151.

Ex. 294

Just as the time of ten is not composed of twice five, so the time of fourteen does not consist of twice seven. The time of seven is composed of 3+2+2, that of fourteen may be 4+4+2+4.

Ex. 295

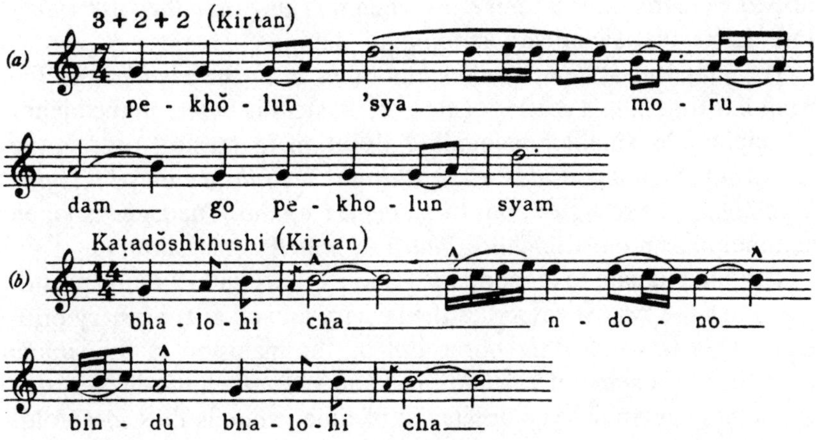

Both these examples are taken from the *Kirtan* music of Bengal, the devotional music of the Vaishnavas. This time of fourteen bears the name of *kaṭa-dŏshkhushi* (the small *dŏshkhushi*) and, as the name leads us to expect, we find also a *madhyam* (middle) and a *bŏṛŏ* (large) *dŏshkhushi*. The *madhyam-dŏshkhushi* consists of twice a *kaṭa-dŏshkhushi* and has twenty-eight units in a period. The accents in the second half are an exact replica of those in the *kaṭa-dŏshkhushi:* *1* 2 3 4, *5* 6 7 8, *9* 10, *11* 12 13 14, *15* 16 17 18, *19* 20 21 22, *23* 24, *25* 26 27 28. The *bŏṛŏdŏshkhushi* is again the *madhyam dŏshkhushi* taken twice and consists consequently of *fifty-six* units. Both derive the right to be called separate *tâlas* from the fact that their whole length is occupied by one musical phrase. The conception is the full period, not the component parts. Bar lines would give an entirely wrong emphasis.

Such long periods give an ideal scope for interplay between drum and solo instrument, each making its own variations on the underlying rhythmical scheme and both landing triumphantly together on the first beat of the next period which is therefore called *sam* (together). This contest is followed with breathless attention and suspense by a well-trained audience, who heave a sigh of satisfaction when the tension is over. This enjoyment presupposes an extraordinarily well-developed sense of rhythm and a passion for cross-rhythm which seem to be inborn. Even quite small children are observed beating intricate rhythmic patterns when they get hold of an empty tin or anything that gives sound when beaten. On the other hand, keeping time as we feel it, progressing from stressed beat to stressed beat, seems to be difficult for Indians; one often sees boy scouts being drilled to march in step, but even when marking time they invariably lose the regular swing very soon.

The classical system of *tâlas* embodies both the regular and the irregular times. As a matter of fact, the system is based on the binary principle. The smallest recognized duration in musical time is the *anu-druta*. Two *anu-drutas* make a *druta*. Two *drutas* make a *laghu*. Two *laghus* make a *guru*, but three *laghus* a *pluta*. The *laghu* is taken as time-unit and is also called *mâtra* or *mâtrika* (measure).

The *pluta*[1] is said to embody the Hindu Trinity with Brahma presiding. Thus the system embodies the ternary as well as the binary principle. This fact is further borne out by the inclusion of the *virâma* (rest) in the scheme of calculations. The *virâma* adds half the value to the note again. The complete list of time-values is thus sevenfold: the *anudruta*, the *druta*, the *druta* with *virâma* (three *anudrutas*), the *laghu*, the *laghu* with *virâma* (three *drutas*), the *guru* and the *pluta* (which is equal to the *guru* with *virâma* or three *laghus*).

This system has been preserved almost intact in south India, where it forms the mathematical basis of the current system of music. From the exposition given by Professor Sambamoorthy of the University of Madras,[2] it appears that the unit is the *anudruta* and no longer the *laghu*. This *anudruta* equals the time-duration of a hand-clap. The *druta* consists of a hand-clap and a sideward movement of the right hand. The *laghu* consists of a hand-clap and two or more finger counts (i.e. putting the thumb against the different fingers). The *laghu* varies in duration according to whether it consists of a clap and two or more than two finger-counts, but in one and the same *tâla* not more than

[1] *SR*, v. 258a. *SD*, vi. 50b: *dîpte trayo virincyâdyâ devatâḥ munibhiḥ smṛtâh.*
[2] P. Sambamoorthy, *The Musical Time Chart* (Madras, n.d.).

one species of *laghu* may occur. Five different kinds of *laghu* occur, equalling 3, 4, 5, 7, and 9 units, in other words, a clap with two, three, four, six, or eight finger-counts. It appears that the fifth category is not in very frequent use.

The terms *guru* and *pluta* seem to have fallen out of use. With the remaining *anudruta*, *druta*, and *laghu* seven principal *tâlas* are constructed:

1. *Eka*, consisting of one *laghu*.
2. *Rûpaka*, consisting of a *druta* and a *laghu*.
3. *Jampa*, consisting of a *laghu*, an *anudruta*, and a *druta*.
4. *Maṭya*, consisting of a *laghu*, a *druta*, and a *laghu*.
5. *Tripuṭa*, consisting of a *laghu* and two *drutas*.
6. *Aṭa*, consisting of two *laghus* and two *drutas*.
7. *Dhruva*, consisting of a *laghu*, a *druta*, and two *laghus*.

Owing to the five different values which a *laghu* can have, these seven basic *tâlas* immediately grow to a set of thirty-five principal *tâlas*. The basic *tâla*, called *Eka*, consisting of one *laghu* only, can thus represent the times of three, four, five, seven, and nine units to a bar. The first variety of the basic *tâla* called *Dhruva*, consisting of a *laghu*, a *druta*, and two *laghus*, gives a total of eleven units to the bar, 3+2+3+3. The second variety of the same basic *Dhruva* gives fourteen units, 4+2+4+4, a general scheme not very different from the above quoted *kaṭadŏshkhushi* of Bengal.

The time of ten of Ex. 293 would be defined as the second variety of *Maṭya*. As a matter of fact, the north and south Indian system of *tâlas* again differ not in kind but in degree, the southern system having drawn the logical consequences of the underlying principles in a much more consistent fashion.

It is clear that this system of musical time has its roots in prosody. None of the irregular times could have sprung up independently of the recitation of poetical metres. Seen in this connexion they present no difficulty. An instance is provided by the Buddhist metre *Buddhapriya* of nineteen syllables, in which, contrary to the strict classical Sanskrit rules for metres of this class, one long may be dissolved occasionally into two short syllables, and even one short syllable into two ultra shorts:

– ᴗ – ᴗ ᴗ / – ᴗ – ᴗ ᴗ / ᴗ ᴗ ᴗ – ᴗ ᴗ – ᴗ – /
– ᴗ – ᴗ ᴗ / ᴗ ᴗ ᴗ – ᴗ ᴗ / – ᴗ – ᴗ ᴗ – ᴗ – /

If this metre is recited with a short note to a short, and a long note to a long syllable, with a lengthening of the last syllable of the line in accordance with the general custom, we see that the time of seven emerges naturally.

Ex. 296

Considering the intimate connexion of the classical theory with the system of Vedic chanting, and the prevalent custom of never reciting but always chanting poetry, the influence of the metres on the formation of musical times is hardly surprising.

There is little doubt, however, that influences from popular customs, for instance ordinary dances and working songs which demand a strong and regular beat, have also contributed to the actual development of *tâlas*. Sometimes perhaps the musical tradition of invaders has made its contribution as well. Fox Strangways attributes the incidence of the lilting 6/8 time, called *dâdra*, in the north of India, to Muslim influences.[1]

In any case it would be surprising, in a country like India where drumming is so ancient and has reached such an astonishing degree of perfection, if there had not been a strong contribution from the purely instrumental side to the system of musical times, quite independently of, and side by side with, the pronounced vocal and literary bias expressed in the official formulation of the system in the classical texts.

CLASSICAL INSTRUMENTS

That instrumental music as a whole retains its character of a secondary art—at least in theory—in spite of the flowering of a very distinct and elaborate solo instrumental style, is proved by the defini-

[1] Fox Strangways, op. cit., p. 300.

tion given as late as the seventeenth century in *Saṃgîtadarpaṇa*:[1] 'lending charm to both vocal music and dance.' At that time instrumental technique was actually at its zenith, and already for centuries before that the voice must have been striving to imitate the intricacy and speed of ornaments devised for solo instruments like the *vîṇâ*. The treatment of the voice in modern days is first and foremost a purely instrumental one. In several of the most applauded styles the agelong connexion between word and melody has been greatly weakened and replaced by a show of instrumental agility in which words have no importance, or hardly any, but which for perfection of speed, neatness, and precision of intonation has perhaps no equal anywhere in the world.

The Indian texts divide the instruments into four classes: *ghana*, *avanaddha*, *suṣira*, and *tata*.

Idiophones (*Ghana*)

Under the first heading fall the percussion instruments which we call idiophones: vibrating pieces of metal, like cymbals, which are beaten together to produce sound. *Ghana* means body, according to the texts,[2] but it also can mean iron and pewter and anything compact. Its mental association with the root *han* (to strike) probably plays its part in the denomination of this class, but it is not mentioned by way of explanation.

These instruments must have existed in a variety of shapes and forms at a very early date. Even nowadays they have a strong connexion with religion, being employed at religious ceremonies and during processions on account of their spiritually purifying properties. Purely musically, they have no great value although they can have a very important rhythmical function in supporting and accentuating the development of figurations on the drum, whether played solo or as an accompanying instrument. In Kathiawar the playing of cymbals has developed into a separate art requiring great technical skill.

Drums (*Avanaddha*)

The drums are grouped together under the heading *avanaddha*: instruments which have their openings covered with stretched hides.[3] This class is also very old and comprises a very great number of

[1] *SD*, v. 1: *vâdyam nirûpyate gîtanṛtayor anurañjakam.*
[2] *SD*, v. 4b: *ghano mûrtiḥ.*
[3] *SD*, v. 3a, 4b: *carmâvanaddhamvadanam vâdyate paṭahâdikam avanaddham ca tat proktam.*

different forms. Anything in India may on occasion serve as a drum, from an earthenware pitcher to a carefully tuned pair of drums like the *tabla*, used for court-performances, or the large metal battle-drums placed on the back of an elephant or a camel to lead troops in battle or to head processions. The last mentioned kind is beaten with sticks, but drums in India are generally played with the fingers and parts of the palms of the hand with such delicacy and skill that it is a joy to listen to a solo performance. In all its refinement the technique takes years of strenuous practice to master. The different strokes of the right and left hand are defined and named, and the combinations and variations of the right- and left-hand strokes, together and separately, give an almost unlimited scope to the artist, especially within the long phrases which the more intricate *tâlas* present.

Prominent in our days are the *pakhawaj* and the *tabla*. The former is a descendant of the classical *mṛdanga*, still its present south Indian name, and has a clay body of irregular cylindrical shape, tapering slightly towards the left hand, with a large surface of parchment tuned to the note chosen as a drone for the performance. It tapers much more markedly towards the right hand, with a smaller stretch of parchment, tuned to the fourth or fifth above the drone. The tuning is very accurate and is effected by tightening or loosening the leather straps which hold the parchment in place.

Even more prominent perhaps is the *tabla*, a pair of drums, really the *pakhawaj* divided into two. The drum played by the left hand is made of metal (brass) and is semi-spherical. The drum for the right hand is made of wood and is cylindrical, only the top being open and covered with parchment. The tuning, regulated by blocks between the leather straps that keep the parchment in place, is the same as that of the *pakhawaj* and carefully and painstakingly adhered to. In this way the drums provide not only the rhythmical backbone of the performance, but also a firm basis on which the singer can rely for his pitch, and against which he can build his contrasts.

Considering the variety of indigenous drums, one would not suppose that there was any need for importation; nevertheless names like *naqqârah* and even *tabla* point in that direction, as they are of Arabic origin.

Wind Instruments (Suṣira)

Among the *suṣira* (wind instruments), too, we find autochthonous as well as foreign species. The different kinds of bamboo flutes certainly belong to India from time immemorial and also the snake-charmers' pipes, based on the principle of the bagpipes and, most probably, some kinds of real bagpipes such as are found in Kashmir. The conch also, which plays an important part in the majority of religious ceremonies and on all auspicious occasions as well, very likely belongs to the country and travelled from there into Buddhist lands such as Tibet, where it serves the same important religious ends.

Among the imported wind-instruments we may count the different varieties of the oboe class, such as the *shannai* (*surnahi*) which spread from the Near East across continents and to the far islands of the Indonesian archipelago. In this class only the flute—apart from the conch—has definite religious associations, being the beloved instrument of Krishna. There are numerous varieties of metal horns and trumpets, such as the *sringa* (horn) and *sarpa* (snake).

In modern times the clarinet has been introduced and is played happily in Indian style, to which it lends itself extremely well.

Stringed Instruments (*Tata*)

The fourth class, *tata* (stringed instruments) from the root *tan* (to stretch), again provides a great variety of indigenous and imported species. The most revered of all is the *vîṇâ*, a fretted plucked instrument. In its most primitive form the *vîṇâ* consists of a hollow bamboo stave with a gourd attached to the underside at both ends. The strings run parallel to the body on the upper side, passing across very high frets fixed to the body with wax. They are attached to the tuning pegs at one end and to a fixed tailpiece at the other. It is played either resting on the ground on its gourds, or held upright against the body, the upper gourd resting on the left shoulder. In another form of *vîṇâ*, popular in south India, the lower gourd has coalesced with the bamboo stave, which now rises out of it; the second gourd is loosely attached to the top near the tuning pegs. The frets are fixed in this form, too. The playing is usually done with a triangular plectrum of silver or steel wire slipped over the nail of the index finger of the right hand. The melody is played on the four chief strings. Three more strings run along the right side, tuned to the drone, the fifth (or fourth) and the octave respectively, and are struck intermittently with the other fingers of the right hand to provide the accompaniment. This instrument is capable of giving a wide variety of tone-colour, but its quality is extremely delicate and intimate, so that it is best enjoyed in a small room in which the finely spun ornamentation does not get lost in space. One way of creating these ornaments is to pull the string sideways with the fingers of the left hand after it has been vigorously struck, and thus to vary the tension, producing various *śrutis* as long as the vibration lasts.

The *vîṇâ* is one of the constant attributes of the Goddess of Learning, Sarasvatî, and in olden times it was one of the indispensable objects in a decent home for the welcome of a guest.[1] In the course of history the *vîṇâ* has had many forms, and it is not at all certain that the *vîṇâ* of the centuries B.C. looked like the *vîṇâ* of our days. It seems probable that *vîṇâ* was originally a generic name for stringed instruments; from ancient sculptures it is certain that a form existed with a boat-shaped body from which an arched neck stuck out, looking very much like the Egyptian harp. That form has now completely disappeared, but kindred forms had until recently survived in Burma. In the texts we find mention of *vîṇâs* with one, two, three, seven, nine, and twenty-one strings. (See pl. 7 (*a*).)

The *kinnarî* has three gourds, one in the middle, fixed sideways. The *tambura* has only one gourd, incorporated in the body, and has four strings but no frets. It is always played with open strings as an accompaniment, either by the singer himself or by one or two assistants immediately behind him. The tuning is the drone, the fifth (or fourth) and twice the octave, and the strings are sounded uninterruptedly to create an unchanging background for the chosen *râga*.

Another favourite plucked instrument is the *setar*, of Persian origin. It has movable frets which can be adjusted to the varying arrangements of notes within the octave according to *thâṭ*. It has a layer of sympathetic strings tuned to the notes of the octave, vibrating in consonance with the notes struck on the main strings, which gives a pleasant diffuse echo-effect. The technique of the *setar* has great affinity with that of the *vînâ*.

The *sarod*, played with a plectrum held between the fingers, has no frets. It has a balalaika-like tone-quality and a greater carrying power than most Indian instruments.

A bowed instrument is the *sarangi*, an instrument with a most pleasing tone-quality and good carrying power, but not in great social favour on account of its association with dancing-girls, in our days not a socially acceptable class. A peculiar legato quality is achieved on this instrument by pressing the nails of the left hand against the

[1] *Mahâbhârata Udyogyaparvan*, 40, 10–11:

ajokṣâ candanam vîṇâ adarśo madhusarpiṣî
viṣam audumbaram śankhaḥ svarṇanabho gorocanâ (10)
gṛhe sthâpayitavyâni dhanyâni manur abravît
devabrâhmaṇapûjârtham atithînâm ca Bhārata. (11)

melody string—not the tip of the finger on it—and sliding them along the string to the next note. The *dilruba* and the *esraj*—almost identical in appearance and technique—are two more bowed instruments, each with a layer of sympathetic strings. Both are socially acceptable, and both are of Persian origin.

In the villages there is a kind of very primitive small violin, made of half a coconut-shell with a bamboo neck attached to it, and played with a very arched bow. Skilled players extract a plaintive, but not at all unpleasant, sound from this toy. The European violin has been adopted with enthusiasm and serves its new masters very well, since it has a much more powerful tone than any of the indigenous instruments and is capable of producing all the refined shades of intonation essential to proper Indian music. It is so much at home in India now that it is counted as their own by many Indian musicians, especially in the south.

Unfortunately the Hawaiian guitar has also made its appearance and makes a powerful appeal, probably through its excessive slurring power, a continuous tone always being sought after in Indian music. Unmitigated harm has been done to Indian music by the introduction, probably through missionaries, of a miniature form of portable harmonium which, by its fixed keyboard and haphazard tuning—earnest but not altogether successful attempts at the European tempered scale—plays havoc with the delicate tonal differences essential to the system of *râgas* and *râginîs* and with the accurate aural perception of the Indian musician. The cheapness and the ease with which one can master its technique—up to a point—have added to its dissemination. It can be found in the most isolated and otherwise unspoiled villages. It is mass-produced in India itself, and it seems unlikely now that the evil can ever be eradicated.

MODERN DEVELOPMENTS

Indian music is passing through a critical period. The impact of the West has shaken its foundations more drastically than foreign influences have ever done before. Mistaken attempts to foist the finished Western system of harmony on to the perfect modal system of Indian monophony have been made for the last hundred years, not only by missionaries but also by enthusiastic Indian admirers of European culture. In this process the delicate structure of Indian music is crushed out of existence. Lately the music of the films, and jazz with its coarse appeal, have not beckoned in vain.

In this unfortunate development the radio plays an important part, but it also gives the champions of the severe classical style an opportunity to reach the ears of a great many more people than would have had the opportunity to hear this music in olden days. The medieval attitude of a master teaching only a few chosen pupils and not divulging his best to the uninitiated is still strong. Music for the masses is a very recent trend, and music teaching now tends to move away from the intimate teacher-pupil connexion towards class-teaching in schools and colleges. A certain amount of standardization has been unavoidable in the course of this development. Eminent men such as the late Pandit Bhatkhande—a Mahratta by birth but with enormous influence over the whole of north India, and founder of the Marris College of Music of the University of Lucknow—have striven to find a common denominator of the different current traditions of *râgas* and *râginîs* and fix them by means of notation, which had not been done systematically in the past. Yet the basis of the present system of notation is very ancient. It is a tonic sol-fa system in which the names of the notes, *sa* and so on, are used to indicate the melodic line with its time divisions.

This is a very strongly supported movement strengthened also by the growth of nationalistic feeling. But new developments, breaking away from the traditional system, are not lacking. The very perfection of that system precluded further development, and adventurous spirits have had to look for new avenues for their creative impulses. They have but rarely understood that the new developments must have their roots in Indian music itself to be viable, yet there are indications that that understanding is dawning. After a period of Western influence, Rabindranath Tagore turned to the folk-melodies of Bengal for inspiration, and all over India isolated poets and musicians are drawing their strength from the music of the people, often with very felicitous results. For Indian folk-music, which ranges from the primitive two-note sing-song of the Chencus of the jungles of Hyderabad to the stirring war-ballads of the bards of Rajputana and the mystical longing of the princess-saint Mirabai, is an expression of the whole life of the people, with their joys and sorrows. It is the depository of their traditional wisdom and their religious yearnings as well as of the pleasures and pastimes of everyday life. Side by side with this hopeful trend of a group of poet-musicians to get their inspiration from folk-music, classical musicians are feeling their way to a widening of tonal expression along polyphonic lines, but starting from Indian premises. There is nothing in the Indian system which would prevent a natural development in that direction, provided that the impulses spring not from intellectual curiosity, but from inner necessity.

V

THE MUSIC OF ANCIENT MESOPOTAMIA

By Henry George Farmer

INTRODUCTION

So far as our present knowledge goes, the earliest civilization was that of Mesopotamia, where an amazingly advanced stage of society existed in the fourth millennium B.C. at the very latest. The centre of this cultural elevation was in southern Mesopotamia, a land often called Babylonia, between 30° and 34° north latitude. In the upper part of this land, later called Akkad, was a linguistically Semitic group, while in the lower part there may have been other Semites. Before 4000 B.C. the latter were supplanted by a people called Sumerians, who spoke a non-Semitic tongue so strange that we cannot even say from whence they came. Their land was known as Sumer. The culture of the newcomers is generally considered to have been far in advance of that of the land of their adoption, so much so that it soon influenced both Akkad in the north and contiguous territories. In spite of this, it seems unwise to refer to the people of either Sumer or Akkad, *per se*, as the creators or stabilizers of this culture, since we know little or nothing of the earlier history of either.

If we view the movement of history in the light of the conditions which increase men's knowledge, it seems that the most potent results are to be found where the greatest number of culture-contacts meet. For this reason, it is of Mesopotamian civilization that we speak, rather than of Sumerian or Akkadian. Thus we are compelled to look beyond strictly geographical limits in our survey of Mesopotamian music of the distant past, for indeed all peoples on what Breasted calls 'the fertile crescent' and its periphery must come within this purview, because it was by reason of admixture of stock, contrasts in habits, diversities in religion, and even friction of interests, that cross-fertilizations of ideas were produced, which made the supreme greatness and vitality of Mesopotamian civilization possible.

Nowadays, when scarcely a month passes without some fresh archaeological discovery, or a new philological deduction being registered, it is difficult to speak with any chronological certainty. That being so, many of the early dates that will be posited in what follows must be considered simply as helpful stepping-stones, placed temporarily to accommodate the eye and mind in their stride across the stream of history, until a more durable bridge has been erected. The readjustments so ably determined and summarized by Albright[1] have persuaded us, with some latitude, to draw up the following table which enables the reader to appreciate why certain dates do not synchronize with those of Dr. Curt Sachs and the late Canon F. W. Galpin who have contributed so much to our knowledge of the music of the peoples of the Mesopotamian past.

FIFTH MILLENNIUM B.C.

The Sumerians in Babylonia . . .

FOURTH MILLENNIUM B.C.

Al-ʿUbaid, Warka, and Jamdat Nasr periods

THIRD MILLENNIUM B.C.

Early Dynasty I	Twenty-eighth century
Royal Tombs of Ur	Twenty-fifth century
Akkad Dynasty	*c.* 2360–2180
Guti Dynasty	*c.* 2190–2065
Ur Dynasty III	*c.* 2070–1960

SECOND MILLENNIUM B.C.

Babylonian Dynasty I	*c.* 1830
Babylonian Dynasty II (Sea Kings)	*c.* 1675
Babylonian Dynasty III (Kassites)	*c.* 1600
Assyrian Hegemony (Shalmaneser I)	*c.* 1270–606

FIRST MILLENNIUM B.C.

Chaldaean Dynasty	626
Achaemenid Dynasty	538–331
Seleucid Dynasty	312–65

THE PRIMITIVE ELEMENT IN MUSIC

What first presents itself in early Mesopotamia is a well-established culture already far advanced, the more glittering features of which have the appearance of an origin elsewhere. Although the older literature of Sumer, such as the Gilgamesh Epic, offers vague hints

[1] *Bulletin of the American Schools of Oriental Research*, nos. 77, 78 (1940), 88 (1942).

of what an earlier culture may have been, we are not able to experience so interesting a panorama as the gradual passage from that community of reed huts at Ur to the *civitas*. There is, however, abundant evidence of the survival of primitive culture in Mesopotamian civilization, not merely at the dawn of history in this land at the turn of the fifth millennium B.C., but even down to the Christian era.

When we observe that Assyrian bells are embossed with symbols of Ea, the divine Patron of Music, it may be assumed that it is a relic of the animistic past.[1] The skin head of the Babylonian drum (*balag*) was made from the hide of a bull, and as late as the Seleucid era (312 B.C.) the Temple of Ea (Lumḫa) was the place of an elaborate ritual at the fixing of the skin head on this sacred instrument.[2] The image of a bull was also a prominent feature on the sound-chest of the grand kithara (? *algar*),[3] so that its resonance would be amplified in mind if not in ears. Like those animals who play instruments in Mesopotamian art remains,[4] and those gods, kings, priests, and mummers, dressed in animal or fish-like garb, they recall earlier totemistic conceits.[5] Yet we must not interpret these semeio-lineaments wholly by this cause, since there must have existed a purely naturalistic *raison d'être* sometimes. There are two or three well-known art remains which show animals listening to, or in the presence of, music, in what might readily be considered bucolic scenes.[6] The Mesopotamian psalms and lamentations continually voice complaint against the gods for searing and flooding the land, for the thoughts of the people were ever with their herds and harvests,[7] and they considered the bull in the animal world and the reed in the vegetable world as antithetical. Their psalms tell of strength in the 'gigantic steer' and weakness in the 'crouching reed'. This symbolism of puissance and docility, force and persuasion, was reflected in the deafening roar of the drum (i.e. the bull) and in the plaintive sigh of the pipe (i.e. the reed), for they were the 'outward visible sign' of an 'inward spiritual grace'. Being a highly imaginative people they resorted to symbolism in many ways, but none is more intriguing than their use

[1] M. Jastrow, *Bildermappe zur Religion Babyloniens und Assyriens* (Giessen, 1912), fig. 70.

[2] *Revue d'Assyriologie*, xvi (1919), pp. 145 ff.

[3] F. W. Galpin, *The Music of the Sumerians and their immediate successors the Babylonians and Assyrians* (Cambridge, 1937), pl. vii.

[4] Ibid., pls. iv, v, vii, viii.

[5] C. J. Gadd, *History and Monuments of Ur* (London, 1929), pp. 36 ff.

[6] Galpin, op. cit., pls. ii, 2; iv, 1; viii, 6, 7.

[7] S. Langdon, *Babylonian Liturgies* (Paris, 1913), pp. 1 ff.

of sound for this purpose, as Heuzey,[1] King,[2] and Thureau-Dangin[3] have observed.

A close connexion between gods and music in Mesopotamia is significant. One of the most ancient of the gods, Ea, the ruler of the deep, had his name written with a sign which stood for drum (*balag*),[4] the dread sound of which was the personification of his essence. Then there was Ramman, who commanded the thunder and the winds. He was conceived as the 'spirit of sonorous voice',[5] which was in keeping with the ancestor of Thor, although it was probably because of its wind-like tone that the reed-pipe (*ḫalḫallatu*) was likened to his breath.[6] One of the names of the goddess Ishtar, the virgin mother, was 'the soft reed-pipe', and her partner, Tammuz, was the 'god of the tender voice',[7] while the name 'singer' (*zammēru*) was given to another of the immortals.[8] It is such fantasies, 'nothing but vain' perhaps, in which sound, as the *anima* of all phenomena, was used to adjure and conjure benevolent and malevolent nature, that were the foundation upon which the later elaborate temple services of Mesopotamia were built.

THE MUSIC OF THE TEMPLES

All the cities of the Mesopotamian plains had their temples in the fourth millennium B.C. Within their sacred precincts were worshipped the many gods of their pantheons. Here, priests and liturgists, mathematicians and astrologers, passed their lives in quiet seclusion,[9] for the temple was the centre of the intellectual and cultural life of the day.[10] First among the liturgists was the precentor, known in Sumerian as the *gala* (Akkadian *kalū*). Unlike the priest, he was not a consecrated functionary, although it was his duty to intone the liturgic cantillation.[11] There seem to have been three classes of precentor in the Sumerian period, the higher, intermediate, and lower, the last being counted in a menial grade. That many a *kalū* was only a part-time official is borne out by several contracts, but the existence of the

[1] *Revue d'Assyriologie*, ix (1912), pp. 85 ff.
[2] *A History of Sumer and Akkad* (London, 1910), pp. 74 ff.
[3] *Sumerische und Akkadische Königsinschriften* (1907), pp. 118 ff.
[4] Hastings' *Encyclopaedia of Religion and Ethics*, ix (Edinburgh, 1917), p. 14.
[5] Langdon, *Sumerian and Babylonian Psalms* (Paris, 1909), pp. 26 ff.
[6] C. Virolleaud, *Astrologie chaldéenne* (Paris, 1908), Adad. xi.
[7] Langdon, op. cit., p. 301.
[8] C. Virolleaud et F. Pélagaud, in Lavignac and La Laurencie, *Encyclopédie de la musique*, 1re partie, i (Paris, 1913), p. 45.
[9] Langdon, *Tammuz and Ishtar* (Oxford, 1914), p. 184.
[10] M. Jastrow, *Aspects of Religious Belief and Practice in Babylonia and Assyria* (New York, 1911), p. 273.
[11] Langdon, *Babylonian Liturgies*, pp. x ff.

Sumerian *galamaḫ* (Akkadian *kalamaḫḫu*) or chief precentor, who held the highest position in the city, reveals the sacred significance of his office.

These precentors were formed into guilds and they were housed, seemingly, in the temple college,[1] just as were vicars-choral in Christian Europe.[2] Here they were taught the mysteries of their sacred office, including a precise knowledge of the cantillation (*kalūtu*) which, like the *prae-cantus* of the Christian Church, was an art requiring a long training. The Sumerian language, like the Latin in the Roman Church, was the language of the liturgies although, later, an interlinear Akkadian version existed. As in Christian lands, these precentors of Mesopotamia were well versed in the sciences, and we have an astrological report signed by a precentor. Yet their most important work in this respect was as copyists and editors of the temple liturgies, so many of which have been preserved together with the names of the copyists.

The ordinary temple musician was called in Sumerian the *nar* (Akkadian *nāru*), the Semitic word being also used, probably, for 'musician' in the generic sense.[3] We cannot be sure of the *nāru*'s actual duties, but he was possibly a chorister who, with others, made the responses in the liturgies. That the 'chorister' also played upon an instrument is well attested. Langdon says that his frequent connexion with private penitential services, especially those connected with magic, led to his ultimate dissociation from public services. At burial services it was the *nāru* and not the *kalū* who contributed to the penitential psalming and wailing.[4] It is certain that the *nāru* was later seen quite frequently in the secular sphere. Equally important was the Sumerian *ilukaka* (Akkadian, *zammēru*), whose specific function is not easy to determine since the term often equates with *nāru*. Virolleaud and Pélagaud opine that while *nāru* signifies the generic term for 'musician', *zammēru* stands for 'instrumentalist'.[5] Yet he was definitely a singer also, and took part in the liturgies. Even Langdon does not help us except to say that the *zammēru* sang to an instrument and that he was distinct from the *nāru*.[6]

[1] Langdon, *Babylonian Liturgies*, p. xii.

[2] H. G. Farmer, *A History of Music in Scotland* (London, 1947), p. 55.

[3] Langdon looks upon the *nāru* as one who 'leads the congregation' in public worship, just as the Presbyterian 'uptaker of psalms' did in the Scottish kirk; the same authority identifies 'the familiar figure on seals, who leads a penitent to his god' as the *nāru*. See Langdon, *Babylonian Penitential Psalms* (Paris, 1927), p. v.

[4] Langdon, *Babylonian Liturgies*, pp. xxvii ff.

[5] Op cit., p. 44.

[6] Langdon, *Babylonian Liturgies*, p. xxvi.

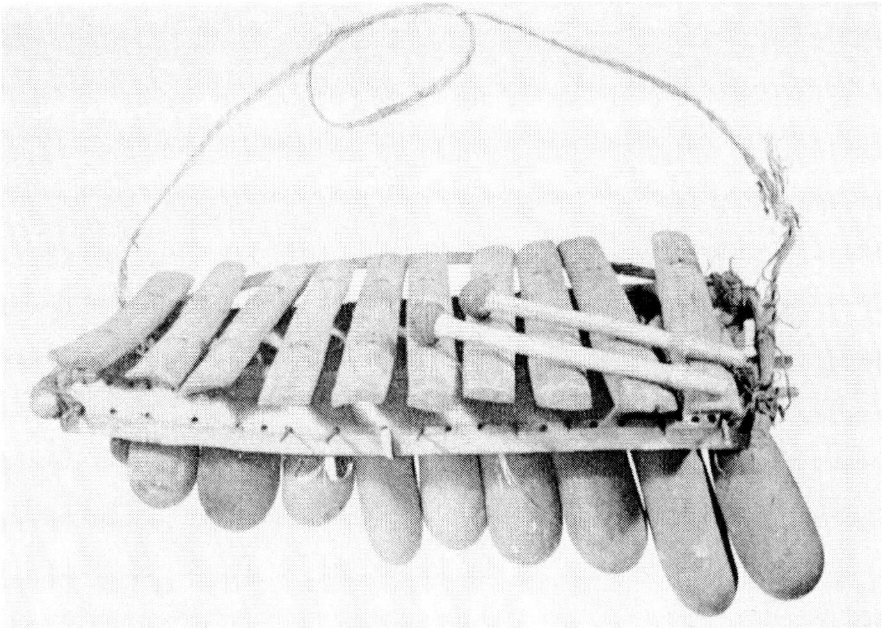

(*a*)

(*b*)

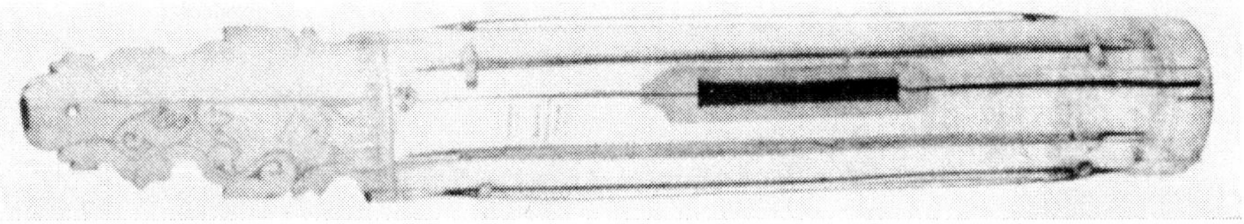

(*c*)

(*d*)

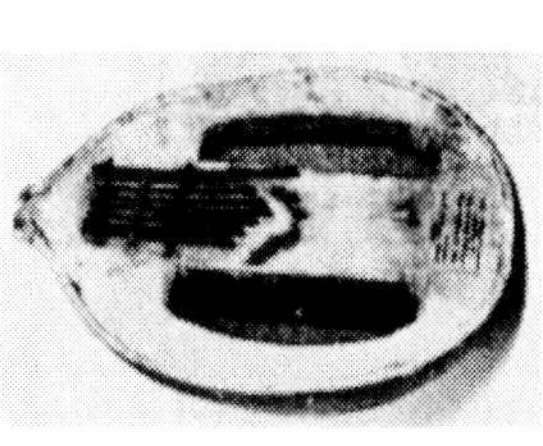

(*e*)

PRIMITIVE INSTRUMENTS

(*a*) Xylophone ($\times \frac{1}{7}$); (*b*) Slit drum ($\times \frac{1}{6}$); (*c*) Zither ($\times \frac{1}{8}$); (*d*) Rattle ($\times \frac{1}{6}$); (*e*) Zansa ($\times \frac{1}{7}$)

For further details see page xiii

PLATE II

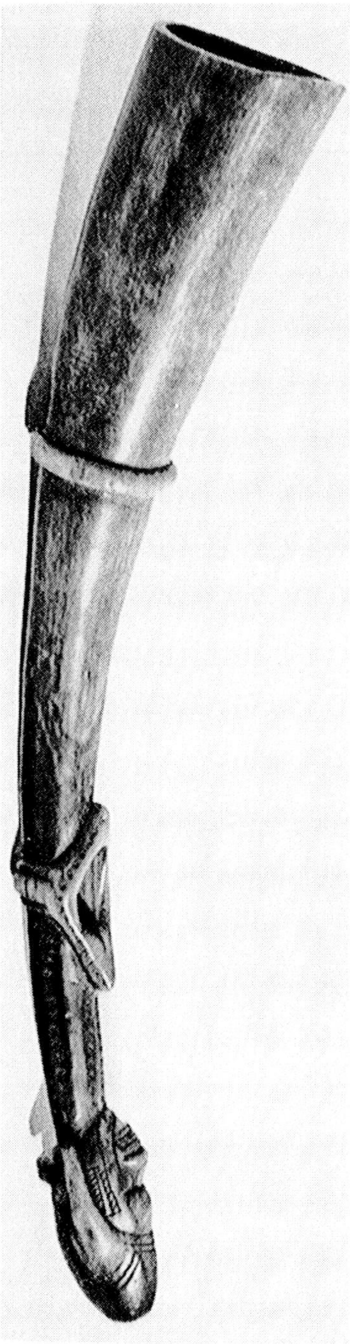

(*a*)

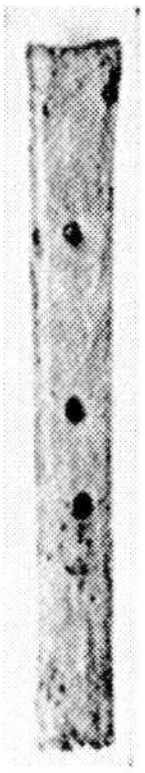

(*b*)

(*c*)

(*d*)

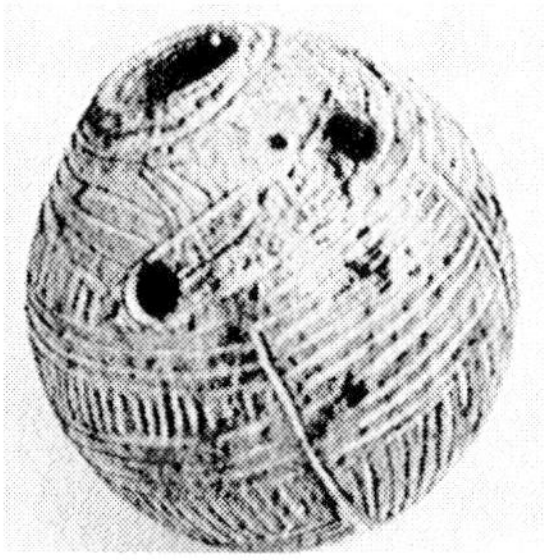

(*e*)

PRIMITIVE WIND INSTRUMENTS

(*a*) Side-blown trumpet ($\times \frac{1}{3}$); (*b*) Vertical flute ($\times \frac{1}{3}$); (*c*) Conch-shell trumpet ($\times \frac{1}{3}$); (*d*) Palaeolithic whistle ($\times \frac{2}{3}$); (*e*) Globular flute ($\times \frac{2}{3}$)

For further details see page xii

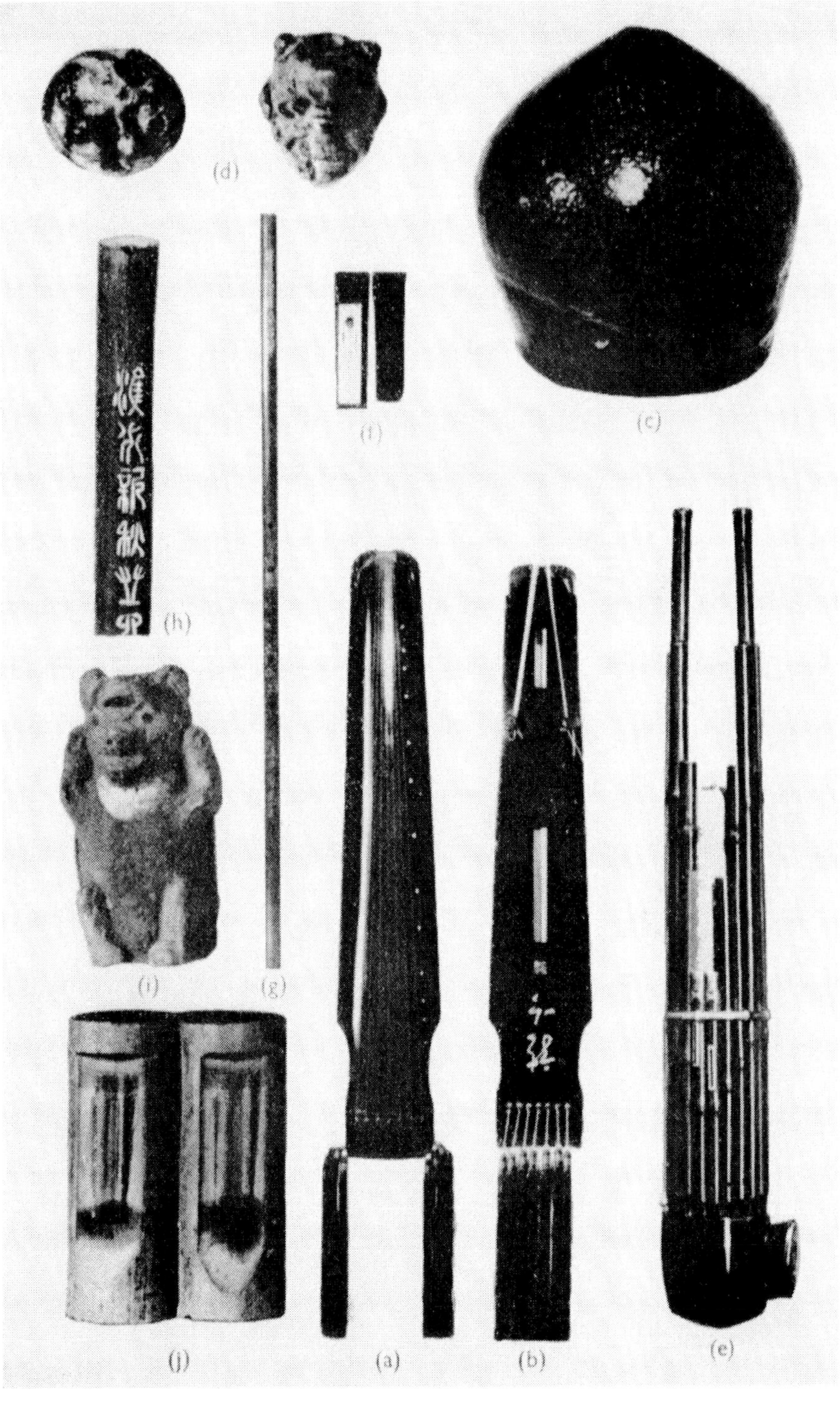

CHINESE INSTRUMENTS

(*a*) Zither ($\times \frac{1}{16}$); (*b*) The same ($\times \frac{1}{16}$); (*c*) Globular flute ($\times \frac{1}{2}$); (*d*) Two globular flutes ($\times \frac{1}{4}$); (*e*) Mouth organ ($\times \frac{1}{16}$); (*f*) Detail of the same ($\times \frac{1}{2}$); (*g*) Vertical flute ($\times \frac{1}{12}$); (*h*) Detail of the same ($\times \frac{1}{2}$); (*i*) Whistle flute ($\times \frac{1}{2}$); (*j*) Whistle ($\times \frac{1}{2}$)

For further details see page xiii

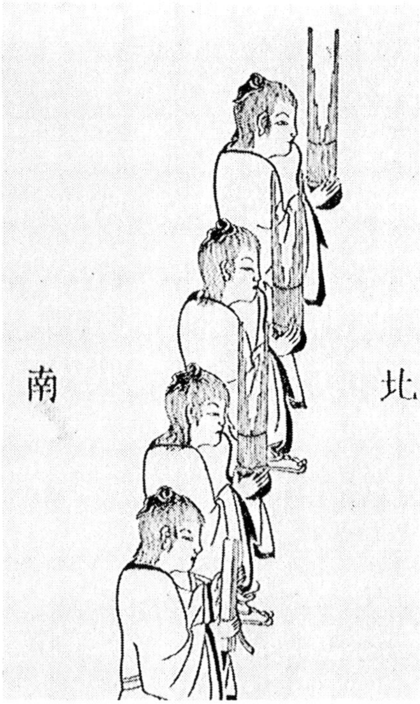

(*a*)

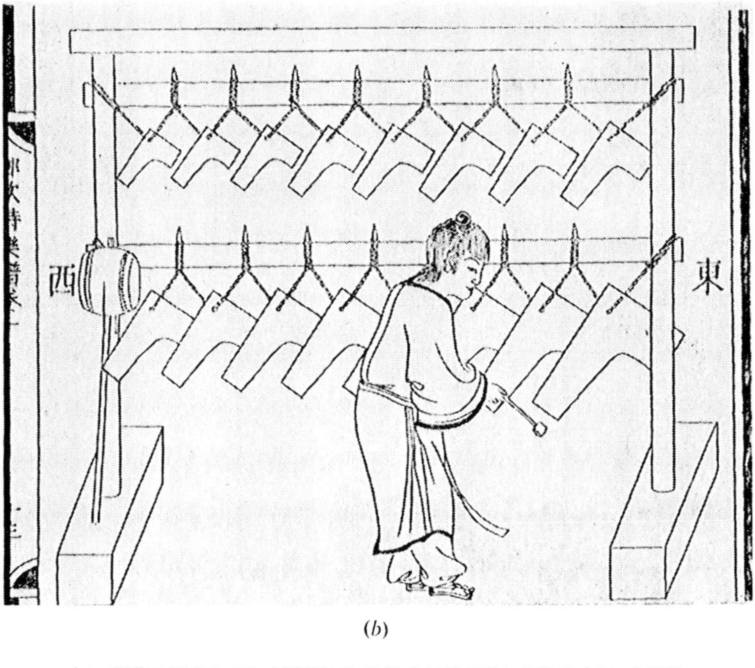

(*b*)

(*a*) CHINESE PLAYERS OF MOUTH-ORGAN AND PERCUSSION-CLAPPER
(*b*) CHINESE SONOROUS STONES AND HAND-DRUM
From Prince Ju Tzayyuh, *The Handbook of Music* (1596)

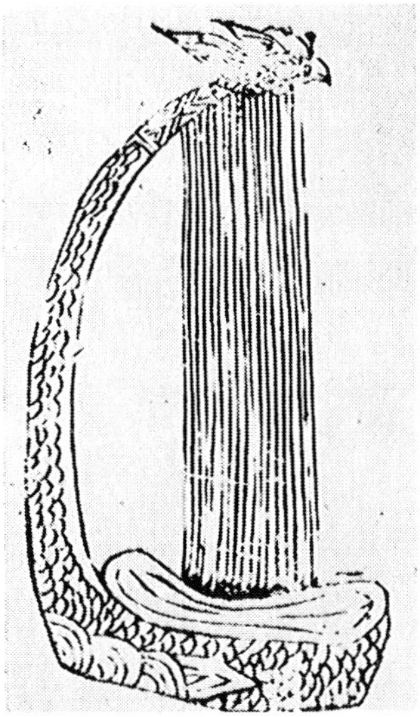

(*a*)

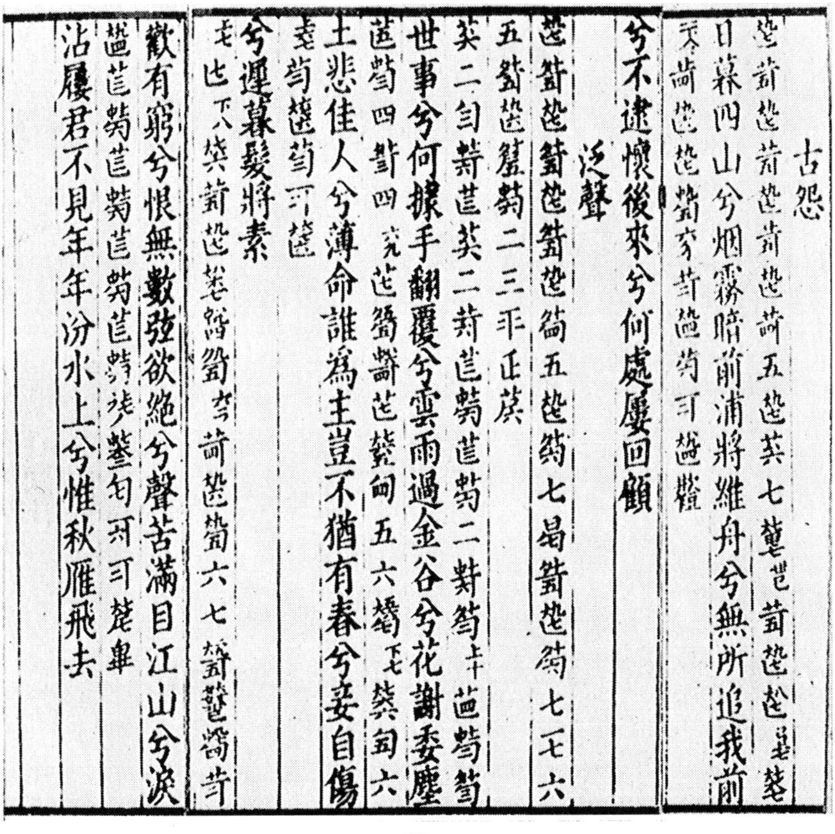

(*b*)

(*a*) CHINESE ROC-HEADED VERTICAL HARP WITH 18 STRINGS
From Chern Yang, *Yueh Shu* (13th–14th century)

(*b*) CHINESE 7-STRINGED ZITHER TABLATURE
From the end of the 12th century

For fuller details see pages xiv *and* 99

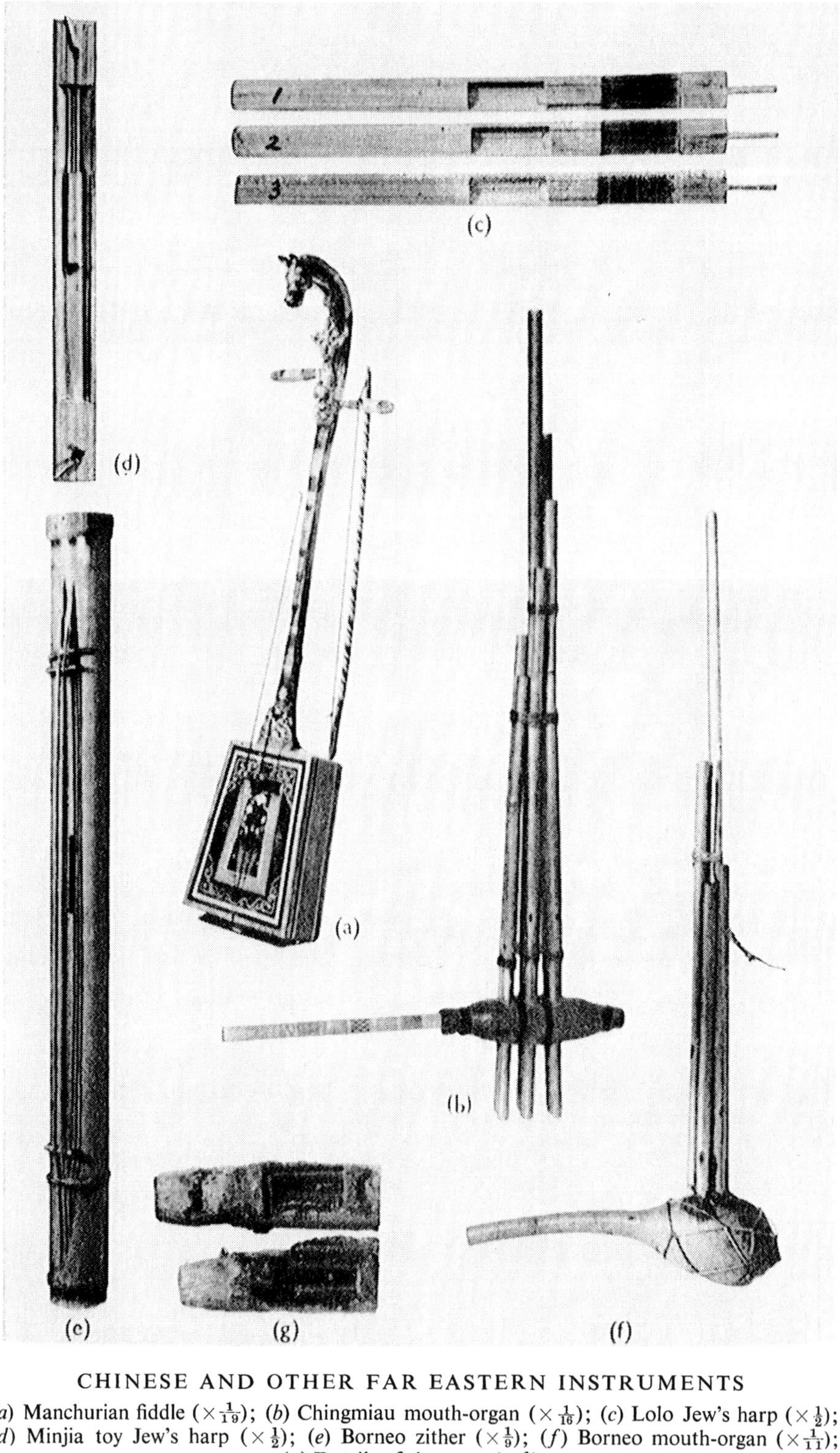

CHINESE AND OTHER FAR EASTERN INSTRUMENTS

(*a*) Manchurian fiddle (× $\frac{1}{19}$); (*b*) Chingmiau mouth-organ (× $\frac{1}{16}$); (*c*) Lolo Jew's harp (× $\frac{1}{2}$); (*d*) Minjia toy Jew's harp (× $\frac{1}{2}$); (*e*) Borneo zither (× $\frac{1}{9}$); (*f*) Borneo mouth-organ (× $\frac{1}{11}$); (*g*) Details of the same (× $\frac{1}{2}$)

For further details see page xiv

(*a*)

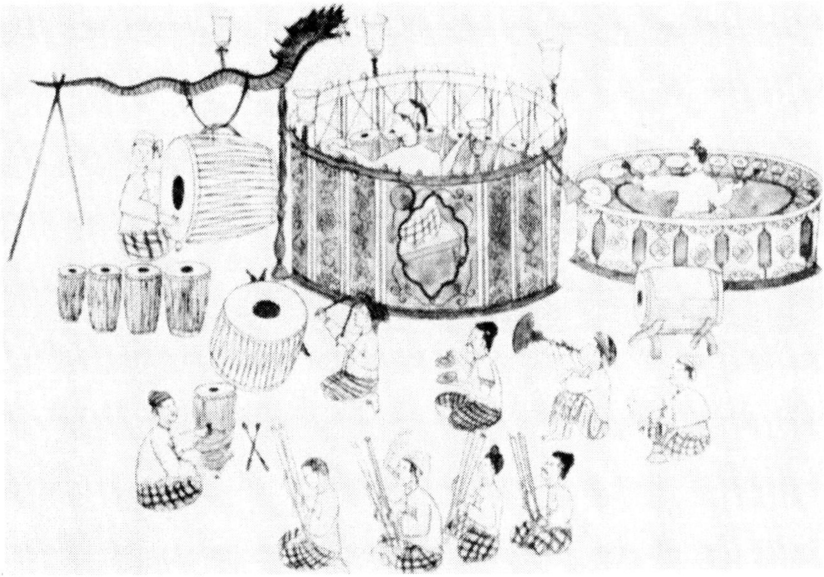

(*b*)

(*a*) INDIAN *VÎNÂ* PLAYER

For further details see page xv

(*b*) A BURMESE ORCHESTRA, *SAING* TYPE

For details of instruments see page xv

(a)

(b)

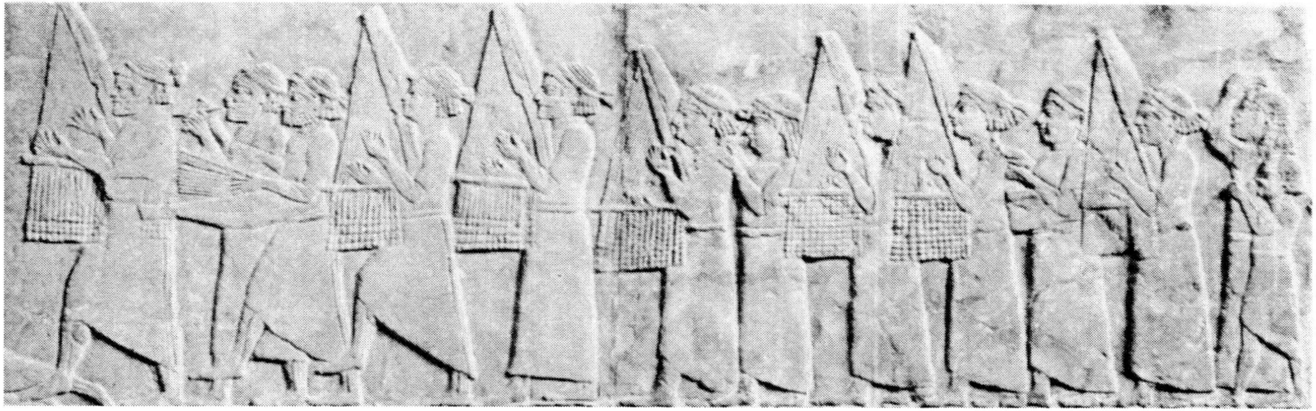
(c)

MESOPOTAMIAN INSTRUMENTS

(*a*) Assyrians playing lower-chested harps (883–859 B.C.)
(*b*) Harp from Ur (25th century B.C.)
(*c*) The royal Elamite orchestra, showing upper and lower-chested harps, double reed-pipes, and drum (668–626 B.C.)

See pages 237–8

(*a*)

(*b*)

EGYPTIAN INSTRUMENTS

(*a*) Lower-chested harp and flute (18th Dynasty, 1570–1310 B.C.)

(*b*) Harp, lute, and double reed-pipe (*c.* 1475 B.C.)

(*a*)

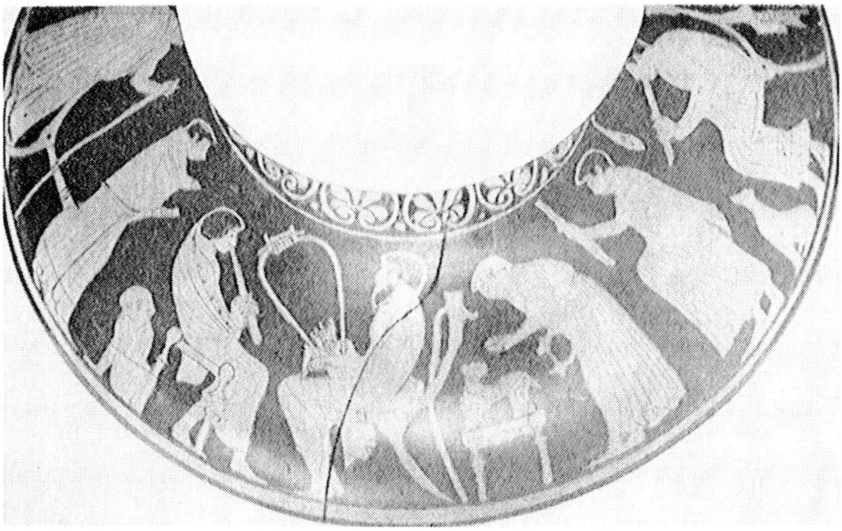

(*b*)

GREEK INSTRUMENTS

(*a*) A kithara player singing (*c*. 480 B.C.)
(*b*) A Greek music school showing lyres and double *auloi* (early 5th century B.C.)

(*a*)

(*b*)

ROMAN INSTRUMENTS

(*a*) A priest of Cybele. Relief showing cymbals, tympanum, and twin Phrygian pipes (*c*. A.D. 150). *See page* 405

(*b*) Roman musicians at the circus. Mosaic showing the *tuba*, *hydraulus* with female player, and *cornu* (late 1st century A.D.)

A ROMAN CONCERT

Showing twin pipes and kithara. From a fresco at Herculaneum

See page 413

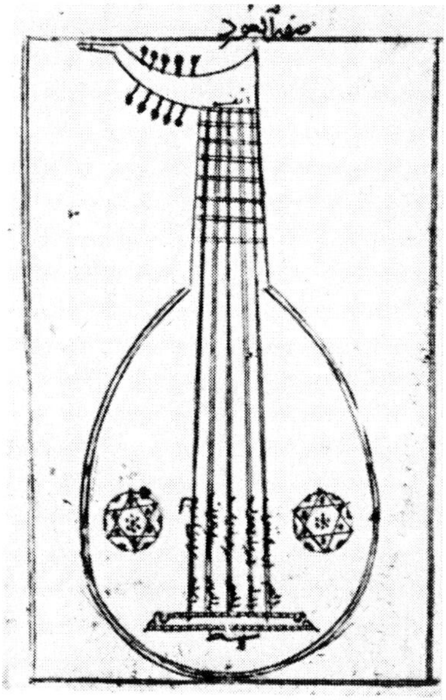

(*a*)

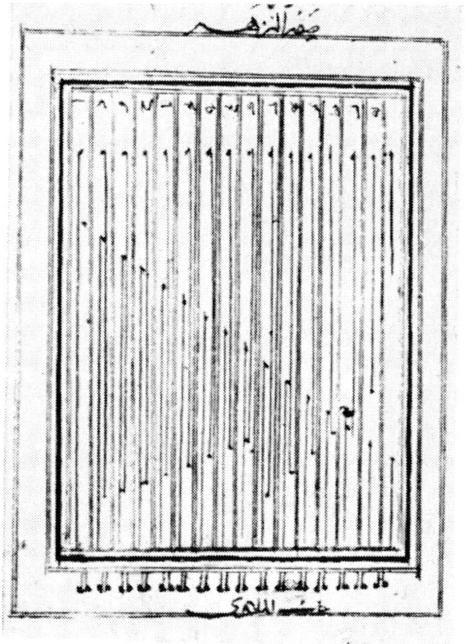

(*b*)

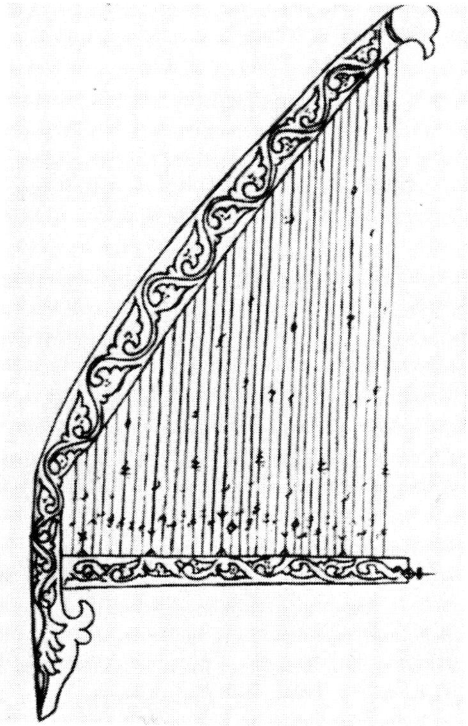

(*c*)

ARABIC INSTRUMENTS

(*a*) Lute of 5 double strings (A.D. 1333–4)
(*b*) Psaltery of 32 strings (A.D. 1333–4)
(*c*) Harp of 34 strings (A.D. 1326–7)

See also pages xvi *and* 462–3

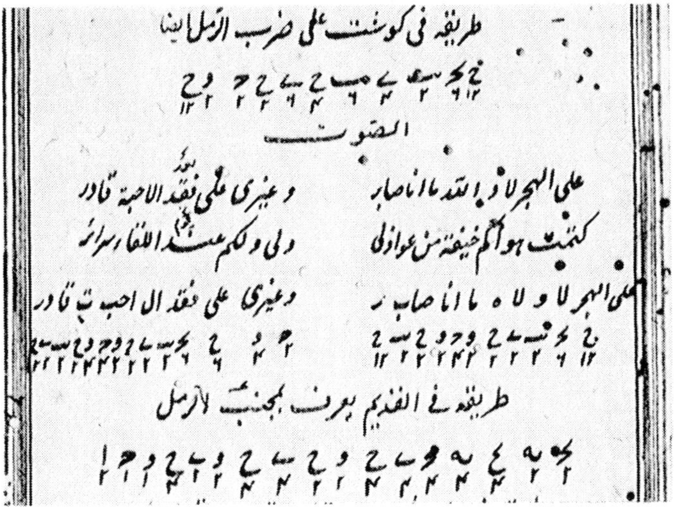

(*a*)

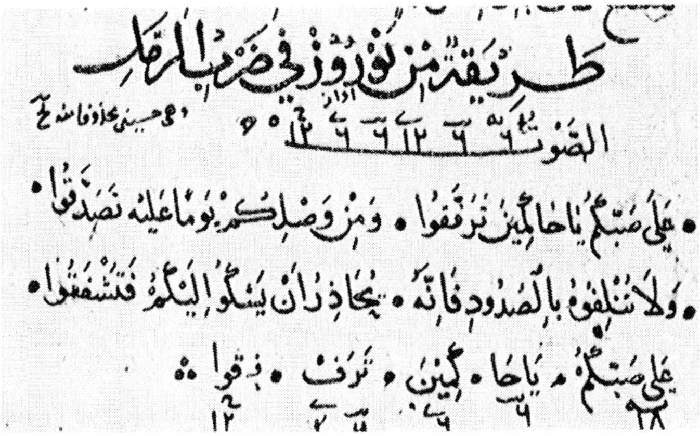

(*b*)

ARABIC MUSIC MANUSCRIPTS

(*a*) Upper half: Song in the *Kuwāsht* mode
Lower half: Melody in the *Mujannab al-ramal* mode

(*b*) Melody in the *Naurūz* mode. Late 13th century

For transcriptions see pages 454–5

The place in the temple and the duties in general of all these temple and extra-mural musical functionaries are nowhere definitely described. One imagines that the precentor specialized in the cantillation (*kalūtu*) and sometimes, if not generally, accompanied himself on an instrument. It is prescribed in some texts when 'he shall sing' (*izamur*) and when 'he [the patient] shall recite' (*imannū*). The chorister's business, whether he was a *nāru* or *zammēru*, was the chant called in Sumerian *sir* (Akkadian *ṣirḫu*). Deimel (447*b*),[1] however, cites the Akkadian *šēru* as 'a section of a song', a word cognate with the Hebrew *šīr*. Then there was the penitential psalm (Akkadian *zamāru*), which has a derived name in the Hebrew *mizmōr*, and it is possible that the Akkadian *zamar tušgi* (√*šigū*) and the *zamar šēri* can be matched in the Hebrew *mizmōr šiggaiōn* and the *mizmōr šīr* (Psalms, vii, lxvii, lxviii).[2] Lamentation proper in Akkadian was *inḫu*, and its character is preserved in the *nehī* of Micah (ii, 4) and the *nauḥ* of the Arabs. The cult wail may have been known as *alālu*, although Deimel says 'shouts of joy'. If correct it may have given rise to the name of the sixth month (*elūl*), which was the time of wailing for Tammuz,[3] still kept by the Jews.

Of the actual music of the Mesopotamian temples or elsewhere we know but little, although the vehicle by which it was expressed has come down to us in vast treasures by way of liturgies, breviaries, psalms, and songs, edited by Langdon, Reisner, Ebeling, and others. Indeed Langdon has said that a full index of this musical material 'would rival that of the Roman or Anglican books of devotion'.[4] These public services date back to Sumerian days, at which date they consisted of but a single psalm or hymn, generally a lamentation, termed in Sumerian an *eršemma*, which strictly meant a psalm or hymn set to a reed-pipe. Yet other instruments were also used to accompany the psalm—the flute (*tig*), drum (*balag*), kettledrum (*lilis*), and tambourine (*adapa*)—and in the course of time the music came to be known by the name of the complementary instrument.[5] This one-psalm service passed away before the time of the first Babylonian dynasty (1830 B.C.), when the *eršemma* was supplanted by a complete liturgical service called a *kišub*. These new services had been compiled by the schools of liturgists who had combined several of the

[1] *Akkadisch-Sumerisches Glossar* (Rome, 1937).

[2] *Journal of the Royal Asiatic Society*, (1921), pp. 175 ff. Cf. *Revue d'Assyriologie*, xviii (1921), p. 41. Deimel (479*b*) gives *tešqū* and *teškū*.

[3] Hastings' *Encyclopaedia of Religion and Ethics*, ix (Edinburgh, 1917), p. 14. A. Deimel, op. cit., p. 13. Cf. the Greek ἀλαλά.

[4] *Sumerian and Babylonian Psalms*, p. x.

[5] Ibid., p. ix.

eršemma type of psalms or hymns which had a common appeal. 'Here', to quote Langdon, 'we have extremely long services composed of a succession of melodies characterized by changing refrains and musical motifs.'

Each liturgy was now called a 'series' (*iškāru*), and it is found with as few as five psalms or hymns and as many as twenty-seven. At a later period the term *eršemma* was revived as an intercessional hymn at the end of a *kišub*.[1] According to Langdon, our foremost authority on the subject, when the public services began to develop in this way, the music, which had hitherto been confined to a single instrument, now became based on what seems to be a wider instrumental conception.[2] We read for example, in an addendum to the series called *Exalted Heaven*:[3]

> The precentors a chant to the drum (*balaggu*) shall sing.
> To the sacred kettledrums (*uppu* and *lilissu*) shall sing.
> To the reed-pipe (*ḫalḫallatu*) and tambourine (*manzū*) shall sing.

Liturgies now came to be known by their first lines,[4] and so perhaps their melodies also. Many of the latter are frequently mentioned, and Langdon says 'that a certain tune was associated with all passages characterized by this refrain'.[5] One might be reading an early English psalter when we see a rubric which says: 'A song to the tune "Thou wilt not cast me down".' That the *kišub* was attended by processional movements on the part of the choir is also stressed by Langdon, who suggests that a 'choral march'—'a real recessional'—came at the end of the litany.[6] Interludes are also found in lengthy litanies, and one may perhaps see in these an explanation of the much discussed *selah* of the Old Testament.

That the antiphon (*gišgigal*) was fairly common seems to be accepted by Langdon,[7] Cumming,[8] and Galpin,[9] and it may be mentioned that in later days the Akkadian word *enū* meant 'answer', 'repeat'. It may have been derived from the Sumerian *en* (Akkadian *šiptu*).[10] There is a Babylonian antiphonal lamentation in Akkadian

[1] Langdon, *Babylonian Liturgies*, p. xli. Cf. his statement in *Babylonian Penitential Psalms*, p. v.

[2] Ibid., p. xlii.

[3] Langdon, *Sumerian and Babylonian Psalms*, pp. 70–71; *Babylonian Liturgies*, pp. viii ff.

[4] Langdon, *Sumerian Liturgies and Psalms* (Philadelphia, 1919), p. 325.

[5] Langdon, *Babylonian Liturgies*, p. xxxv.

[6] Ibid., p. xlviii.

[7] *Babylonian Liturgies* (Paris, 1913), p. 1.

[8] *The Assyrian and Hebrew Hymns of Praise* (New York, 1934) pp. 72 ff.

[9] Op. cit., p. 62.

[10] Langdon, *Babylonian Penitential Psalms*, pp. vii, 48–52.

of a late period.[1] which is a copy of a Sumerian original of the time of Narām-Sin (*c.* 2280 B.C.). In this the women of various towns participated. Sidney Smith suggests that they were divided into two groups and that 'each half-chorus sang alternately' the lines which were appropriate to themselves in the destruction of their lands by the Guti.[2] Perhaps a more moving example of an antiphon is the *Liturgy and Prayer to the Moon God*, which dates from the time of Dungi (twenty-first century B.C.). It is an appeal to the god Sin to care for flocks and harvests, with twin recurring refrains, seemingly responsory.[3]

In addition to the instruments mentioned as being used in the *kišub* services, the harp (*zagsal*) also had a recognized place.[4] Further, those epical productions known as the *zagsal* compositions may very well have been accompanied by this harp.[5] Galpin says that it was used during the oracles of the high-priest.[6] Before closing this section it may be advisable to mention that while Langdon generally refers to the *kišub* as being a 'choral service',[7] and frequently speaks of 'melodies',[8] we must always understand that these terms merely relate to what was set to music, since not a solitary note has come down to us save what may be divined from the so-called 'notation' which will be dealt with later. In any case, Mesopotamian temple music was *cantus* in its primitive significance, for the simple reason that the liturgy demanded a fixed and immutable *chant*, any variation from which by precentor or chorister would be unthinkable, since its whole efficacy depended on a rigid interpretation. That a particular chant had a certain ethos in a theurgic sense is frequently mentioned in Mesopotamian documents, and we read of the *kalū* and *nāru* who 'know the melodies' and are 'masters of the musical movements', meaning the appropriate liturgic and ethoidal chants. This was an absolute desideratum, since the gods were equally skilled, as we know from the epithet of the goddess Ishtar, the patroness of litanies, as the one 'who understands the measures' of the psalming.[9] As for the verbal form and content of the Mesopotamian liturgy Langdon has

[1] Cf. Galpin, op. cit., p. 62. Langdon, *Babylonian Liturgies*, xix; *Sumerian and Babylonian Psalms*, p. 176.

[2] *Journal of the Royal Asiatic Society*, (1932), pp. 303 ff.

[3] Langdon, *Babylonian Liturgies*, p. 1. The refrain was quite common (pp. 70–71).

[4] F. Martin, *Textes religieux assyriens et babyloniens* (Paris, 1903), p. 196.

[5] Langdon, *Sumerian Liturgies and Psalms*, p. 233. Cf. his *Sumerian Liturgical Texts* (Philadelphia, 1917), pp. 130 ff.

[6] Op. cit., p. 53.

[7] *Sumerian Liturgies and Psalms*, p. 245.

[8] *Journal of the Royal Asiatic Society*, (1921), p. 170.

[9] Langdon, *Sumerian Liturgies and Psalms*, p. 237.

rightly praised it as 'the greatest system of musical ritual in any ancient religion'.[1]

SECULAR MUSIC

Words alone are sometimes graciously eloquent of purpose, and at the very threshold stands the generic Akkadian word for 'music', *nigūtu* or *ningūtu*, which also has the connotation of 'joy', 'merry-making'. *Alālu*, which also meant 'singing', had a similar import. This is admirably illustrated on an archaic seal in the Louvre which displays a bucolic scene, seemingly of a peasant playing a flute to one of his flock or herd.[2] Such scenes are not uncommon in the art remains, and whilst they may be mere cameos, we can descry in them the part played by music in the lives of the people. Indeed in some instances it was considered as part of education.[3] It has been said that 'the old danced whilst the young made music'.[4] One imagines that there were toil songs among the ancient Semites, as we know in the 'well song' of Numbers xxi. 17. Singers and drummers, in a picture of Assyrians felling palm-trees, certainly appear to be facilitating labour. Indeed an Assyrian annalist gives a picture of the Arabs who, as prisoners of war, were working as slaves at Nineveh, where they sang their native songs to relieve their sorrows. Their exotic music fascinated the idle Assyrians who begged for more.[5]

One of the oldest Sumerian art remains, the Standard of Ur (twenty-fifth century B.C.), depicts a singer and a performer on the grand kithara (? *algar*) at a royal banquet, which was planned to 'dispel gloom'.[6] Several seals from the same period also suggest that the instruments shown accompany festive scenes, even with dancing.[7] Here, not only the grand kithara, but the harp (*zagsal*), sistrum, and clappers, play their part. Then there are the many representations of animals, or mummers dressed as such, playing instruments of music—kitharas, harps, pandores, tambourines, drums, and the like—which scarcely represent religious scenes.[8] All these bear testimony that from early Sumerian to late Assyrian days, music was part and parcel of social life in Mesopotamia.[9]

[1] Langdon, *Babylonian Liturgies*, p. xxxiv.

[2] F. Lajard, *Introduction à l'étude du culte public et des mystères de Mithra* (Paris, 1847), pl. xxix, 7.

[3] B. Meissner, *Babylonien und Assyrien*, ii (Heidelberg, 1925), pp. 320, 328.

[4] Ibid. ii, p. 331.

[5] E. Schrader, *Keilinschriftliche Bibliothek*, ii (Berlin, 1889 et seq.), p. 234.

[6] *Antiquaries Journal*, viii (1928), pl. lix.

[7] Galpin, op. cit., pl. ii.

[8] Ibid., pls. v, viii.

[9] P. Dhorme, *Textes religieux assyro-babyloniens* (Paris, 1903), p. 375.

Assyria, from quite an early period, was certainly very fond of secular as well as religious music. In the martial moments of Tiglath-pileser I (*c.* 1113 B.C.) we read of a grand personage in the royal palace named the *rab zammēre* ('chief musician'), and we are informed that the royal musicians gave public performances 'to gladden the hearts of the people of Ashur'.[1] It is worth noting that when the victorious Assyrian generals put a city to the sword, they generally spared the musicians, who were sent to Nineveh with the valuable booty. To the very last days, music played a wholesome part in Assyrian social life, even though most of our testimony comes from regal sources.

From the time of Ashur-naṣir-pal II (*c.* 883–859 B.C.) we get ample lithographic material of music and musical instruments. First we have the sculptured slabs in the British Museum showing two players on the lower-chested harp (*zagsal*) (pl. 8 (*a*)). Sargon (*c.* 722–705 B.C.) also employed the joyous art in the celebrations consequent on his widely trumpeted victories.[2] A probable sidelight on alien influence on Assyrian music is furnished about the year 701 B.C. when Sennacherib invaded Syria, sending one of his generals to lay siege to Jerusalem. To soften the wrath of the conqueror, the king of Judah sent 'his wives and his daughters, his musicians both male and female' as a gift, hoping that he himself might be spared.[3] From this period dates a fine bas-relief in the British Museum showing playe on the upper-chested harp and the diagonal kithara. It was the two court functionaries facing them with batons of office in their hands which led Rawlinson to suppose that they were time-beaters.[4]

In the year of the ascent of Esar-ḥaddon (680–669 B.C.) to the throne, we read that when he re-entered Nineveh it was 'with musicians playing the lower-chested harp (*zagsal*)'.[5] The British Museum bas-reliefs also illustrate the artistic interests of Ashur-bāni-pal (668–626 B.C.). When Teumman, the Elamite king, invaded Assyrian territory, Ashur-bāni-pal sought the goddess Ishtar for counsel. She quietened his fears and bade him turn to music and feasting.[6] He obeyed, and in the midst of these pleasures came the news of the defeat and death of Teumman. The joyous scenes of the victory celebrations, with which music went hand in hand, have been recorded

[1] Schrader, op. cit. i, p. 46.
[2] Hastings' *Encyclopaedia of Religion and Ethics*, ix, p. 14.
[3] Schrader, op. cit. ii, pp. 96–97.
[4] G. Rawlinson, *The Five Great Monarchies*, ii (London, 1854), pp. 167 f; Kinsky, op. cit., p. 3.
[5] Schrader, op. cit. ii, pp. 126–7.
[6] Ibid. ii, p. 252.

in stone.[1] The great orchestra and choir of the vanquished king are delineated on another British Museum sculpture (pl. 8 (*c*)). The former consists of seven performers on the upper-chested harp, one on the lower-chested harp, two on the double reed-pipe, and one on a drum. The choir was made up of six women and nine children,[2] and one of the former indulges in the favourite Eastern vocal practice of squeezing the larynx by the hand, to effect the high notes.

The Old Testament story in the book of Daniel (iii), written in the second century B.C., has an abiding interest, if only because of the instrumentation of that much-discussed orchestra of the Chaldaean king Nebuchadnezzar (604–562 B.C.). It comprised the '*qarnā* (horn), *mašrōqīthā* (pipe), *qīthros* (kithara), *sabbekā* (? trigonal lower-chested harp), and *pṣantrīn ṣūmfonyāh* (upper-chested 'concord harp').[3] Although these were for the dedication of 'an image of gold', they were, no doubt, for secular purposes also, if not primarily. Another musical scene of Nebuchadnezzar's time, although not Mesopotamian, is pictured in Judith (iii. 8–10). It represents the Assyrian general Holophernes in his murderous descent upon Syria, where the petty kings and their people, to appease the invader, receive him with 'crowns, illuminations, and dancing to drums (*tympana*) and reed-pipes (*tibiae*)'.

Mesopotamian court minstrelsy, even in later Achaemenid days, was usually conceived on a grandiose scale. With the Assyrians the position of the court minstrel was a high one, as his apparel and situation often denote. His place was among the *seniores priores*, taking precedence of the savants, coming immediately after gods and kings.[4] It may be recalled that it was a court minstrel who warned the Median king Astyages (d. 550 B.C.) of the aims of Cyrus (d. 528 B.C.).[5] Crowds of singing-girls usually graced the palaces at this period, as Xenophon testifies.[6] Yet 'Darius the Mede' (*c*. 521–485), when he had cast Daniel into the den of lions, was sore distressed and passed the night badly, 'neither were instruments of musick brought before him' (Daniel, vi. 18). The singing-girls were the later Arabian *qaināt*, a term used to denote both female musicians and attendants, and the cognate Akkadian word, *kināti* (female attendants), had probably the other meaning also. The Greek historian Ctesias, who was physician

[1] M. Jastrow, *Aspects of Religious Belief and Practice in Babylonia and Assyria* (New York, 1911), pl. 13.

[2] Kinsky, op. cit., p. 3.

[3] See infra, pp. 245–6.

[4] Schrader, op. cit. vi, pp. 72–73, 386.

[5] Athenaeus, *Deipnosophistae*, xiv. 633.

[6] *Cyropaedia*, iv. 6, 11; v. i, 1; v. 5, 2, and 39.

to Artaxerxes II (404–358 B.C.), tells us that one of the Babylonian king's lieutenants had 150 of these female singers at his table,[1] and we know that when Parmenio, the Greek general, reduced Damascus, he took 329 of these singing-girls from the court of Darius III (d. 330 B.C.).[2] Quintus Curtius (v. 1) has described the triumphal entry of Alexander the Great into Babylon, where he was met by a procession of priests (*magi*) chanting hymns, followed by Chaldaean diviners and astrologers, and musicians with string instruments, 'whose office it was to sing to their king'.

What secular music sounded like in Mesopotamia in those days we know no more than we do of the actual music of the temples. As with the latter, we only know of the media. Langdon has given some remarkable lists of song titles of purely secular import, although some may have been used in the temples.[3] Among these are workers' and shepherds' songs, youth songs and love ballads, the initial words of which reveal lofty thoughts and passages deeply moving.

INSTRUMENTS OF MUSIC

Of the instruments of music in ancient Mesopotamia we possess a fair store of knowledge through the existence of actual specimens and a multitude of delineations, although much perplexity lies in their names, of which both the Sumerian and Akkadian languages offer quite an assemblage. Among idiophones we possess actual specimens of clappers from Ur (twenty-fifth century B.C.).[4] These consist of a pair of copper blades. Other specimens were found at Kish.[5] We also have them depicted in the art remains,[6] although we do not know their names. Sistra were also discovered at Ur, but all that remains are the jingling plates.[7] Yet we know the complete form from art sources.[8] At a late period (*c.* 600 B.C.) we have a bell from Assyria,[9] and sonnettes from the same place and period.[10] Cymbals occur in two kinds: the plate type, pictured on a Babylonian plaque (? *c.* 1100 B.C.),[11] and a cup type of late Assyrian times (eighth–seventh centuries B.C.).[12]

[1] Athenaeus, xii. 530.
[2] Ibid. xiii. 608.
[3] *Journal of the Royal Asiatic Society* (1921), pp. 169 ff.
[4] Leonard Woolley, *Ur Excavations*, ii (London, 1934), pp. 126 ff.
[5] Langdon, *Excavations at Kish* (London, 1925), pls. vi, xxxviii.
[6] Woolley, op. cit., figs. 21 ff.
[7] Ibid., pp. 260 ff.
[8] W. H. Ward, *Seal Cylinders of Western Asia*, v (Washington, 1910), p. 5.
[9] Jastrow, *Bildermappe zur Religion Babyloniens und Assyriens* (Gießen, 1912), fig. 70.
[10] A. H. Layard, *Discoveries in the Ruins of Nineveh and Babylon* (London, 1853), p. 177; G. Loud and C. B. Altman, *Khorsabad*, ii (Chicago, 1938), pl. 60.
[11] Galpin, op. cit., pl. iii, fig. 2.
[12] C. Engel, *The Music of the Most Ancient Nations* (London, 1870), p. 73.

During the Greek, i.e. the Seleucid, period, we also find cymbalists in figurines.[1] Their name has not been revealed, but the Akkadian verb *sanāqu* (to push, press together) reminds us of the Arabic *sanj*, pl. *ṣunūj* (cymbals).[2]

Both the texts and the art remains furnish names and delineations of membranophones. The Sumerian *lilis* (Akkadian *lilissu*) was definitely a kettledrum, and we have a precious description of its composite parts.[3] Evidence of a smaller type is quite positive in the Sumerian *ub* (Akkadian *uppu*) which equates with *lilis*.[4] What one may picture from the ideogram to be an hour-glass shaped drum was the Sumerian *balag* (Akkadian *balaggu*).[5] The temple instrument must have been reasonably large, but there were smaller types as such names as *balag-tur* (small *balag*) may indicate. Such an instrument exists in Susian art.[6] A grand-daughter of Narām-Sin (*c.* 2280 B.C.) played on a *balag-di*,[7] which equates in Akkadian with *timbūtu* and corresponds with *ṭabālu*.[8] The former possibly survives in the Persian *dunbaq*, and the latter, certainly, in the Arabic *ṭabl*; whilst *balaggu* was handed down in the Aramaic *palgah* and the Syriac *pelāggā*. Two unidentified drums, held vertically and played at the waist, occur in late Assyrian art (eighth–seventh centuries B.C.).[9]

Frame drums, ordinarily called tambourines, existed in many sizes. A monster frame drum is delineated on the stele of Ur-Nammu (*c.* 2070 B.C.), now at Philadelphia.[10] Slightly smaller examples exist in the art remains. One of the time of Gudea (*c.* 2200 B.C.) is at Paris,[11] whilst another, a Carchemish relief (*c.* 1050 B.C.), is in the British Museum.[12] It is believed to be the Sumerian *alal* (Akkadian *alū*).[13] A portable tambourine figures in a relief from Tell Halaf (third millennium B.C.),[14] and in other examples.[15] This may have been the

[1] Statuette: British Museum (no. 91794).

[2] H. G. Farmer, *Journal of the Royal Asiatic Society* (1939), p. 626. Langdon's unidentified *šiqatu* (ibid. 1921, p. 180) may be a rattle (= Arabic, *shaqshaq*). Cf. Egyptian *šeq* = to strike.

[3] Galpin, op. cit., pl. iii, fig. 5, p. 65; *Revue d'Assyriologie*, xvi (1919), p. 145.

[4] *Beiträge zur Assyriologie*, v (1906), p. 582; *Revue d'Assyriologie*, xxi (1924), p. 80; Farmer, *Oriental Studies* (London, 1953), p. 18.

[5] *Beiträge zur Assyriologie*, v (1906), p. 581; *Revue d'Assyriologie*, xxv (1928), p. 155.

[6] *Revue d'Assyriologie*, xvii (1920), p. 49.

[7] F. Thureau-Dangin, *Les Inscriptions de Sumer et d'Akkad* (Paris, 1905), p. 237.

[8] F. Thureau-Dangin, . . . *La Huitième Campagne de Sargon* (Paris, 1912), p. 26, line 159. Galpin suggests that the *timbūtu* may have been a friction drum.

[9] C. Engel, op. cit., pp. 63 ff.

[10] Galpin, op. cit., pl. iii, fig. 6.

[11] Kinsky, op. cit., p. 1, fig. 1.

[12] Galpin, op. cit., pl. iii, fig. 1.

[13] Ibid., p. 6. Langdon (*Babylonian Liturgies*, p. xxii) says 'Kettledrum?'

[14] M. F. von Oppenheim, *Tell Halaf* (London, 1933), pl. xxxviii.

[15] Galpin, op. cit., pl. iii, figs. 3, 5.

Sumerian *meṣi* (Akkadian *mazū, manzū*),[1] a term linked by Langdon with the Sumerian *adapa* (Akkadian? *aṭapu*)[2] which Galpin considers to have been a rectangular instrument[3] having in mind, probably, the Hebrew *toph* and the Arabic *duff*.

Woodwind instruments were the most important of the aerophones in Mesopotamia. In the Sumerian *tig, tigi* (Akkadian *tīgū*) we have the vertical flute, the longer instrument being the *gigid*[4] (Akkadian *malīlu*). We also read of the Akkadian *kanzabu*,[5] a name phonetically reminiscent of the Arabic *qaṣaba*.[6] A flute of archaic times is featured on a Sumerian seal at the Louvre, Paris,[7] whilst there is also a bone instrument, a small whistle, from Tepe Gawra.[8] There once existed a bone whistle from Nimrod which gave three notes, but it has disappeared.[9]

Among reed-pipes and oboes[10] there existed the Sumerian *šem* (Akkadian *ḫalḫallatu*)[11] which may have been an ordinary reed-pipe. How far it differed from the *malīlu*[12] which, on one special occasion, was made of lapis lazuli, we do not know, although this latter equates with the Akkadian *imbubu*, a word common to all Semitic tongues. Perhaps the instrument is figured in the conical-tubed oboe in Engel.[13] A double cylindrical reed-pipe in metal is preserved at Philadelphia from the Ur tombs (*c.* 2500 B.C.),[14] but only one of the pipes is playable, giving four notes of the diatonic scale. The art remains also display examples of the double reed-pipe.[15] We are without evidence of its name but the *ṣinnitu*[16] may refer to such an instrument, if it alludes to an accompanying drone-pipe (Arabic *ṭann, ṭanīn*).[17] A Susian figurine (*c.* 750 B.C.) seems to show a crooked double reed-pipe,[18] and

[1] Langdon, *Babylonian Liturgies*, p. xxxii.
[2] Neither in Deimel nor in Muss-Arnolt is *aṭapu* given as a musical instrument.
[3] Op. cit., p. 8. See also *Journal asiatique*, Jan.–Fév., 1909, p. 85.
[4] Langdon, *Babylonian Liturgies*, p. xxxiii.
[5] F. Martin, *Textes religieux* (Paris, 1903), p. 196.
[6] Farmer, *A History of Arabian Music* (London, 1929), p. 47.
[7] F. Lajard, *Introduction à l'étude du culte public et des mystères de Mithra* (Paris, 1847), pl. xli, 5.
[8] *Bulletin of the American Schools of Oriental Research*, lxiv (1936), p. 8.
[9] C. Engel, op. cit., p. 76; *Journal of the Royal Asiatic Society* (1921), p. 180.
[10] Galpin, op. cit., p. 16.
[11] Ibid., loc. cit. Cf. Langdon, *Babylonian Liturgies*, p. xxxii.
[12] *Beiträge zur Assyriologie*, v (1906), p. 566.
[13] Op. cit., p. 77.
[14] L. Woolley, *Ur Excavations*, i, pp. 258 ff.
[15] Kinsky, op. cit., p. 3, figs. 1, 4.
[16] F. Martin, op. cit., p. 196. Another instrument mentioned in this place is the *arkā[tu]* which is not known.
[17] Galpin suggests that the *ṣinnitu* is a two-stringed lute (= pandore). Op. cit., pp. 35, 54.
[18] J. de Morgan, *Délégation en Perse* (Paris, 1901), i, pl. viii, figs. 10, 14.

Galpin suggests[1] that this is the *pītu* or *pitū* mentioned by Langdon.[2] It is doubtful.

So far as horns and trumpets are concerned, we have but few references and illustrations. An archaic Sumerian tablet found at Ur (second millennium B.C.) seemingly describes a wooden horn called in Akkadian *pukku* (Sumerian *ellag*).[3] The Sumerian *karan* mentioned by Galpin is not registered by Deimel who, by the way, says that the *pukku* was a drum. Yet we know that several instruments of the *pukku* and *mikkū* types were presented (*c.* 1380 B.C.) by the Mitanni ruler under Dushratta to Amen-ḥotep III of Egypt.[4] We observe a very short trumpet in a religious scene on a Hittite relief from Carchemish (*c.* 1050 B.C.).[5] The long metal trumpet may possibly be identified in the hands of the kneeling figure on the stele of Narām-Sin (*c.* 2280 B.C.),[6] but a shorter type occurs on a Hittite relief (first millennium B.C.).[7] In late Assyrian days a long type is clearly depicted in two examples (eighth–seventh centuries B.C.), whilst an actual fragment of one has been preserved.[8]

The chordophone group of Mesopotamian instruments reveals types of the highest interest to musicologists. Perhaps the most remarkable are of the harp and kithara family; the evolutionary stages of the harp are particularly fascinating. In the lower-chested harp, the generic name for which Galpin has supposed to be *zagsal*,[9] we see three distinct forms. In the first, found on a slab from Khafāja (*c.* 2700 B.C.), now at Chicago, we have an upright portable instrument, with a neck and sound-chest in one graduated piece.[10] Similar examples (*c.* 2600 and 2500 B.C.) are at Philadelphia.[11] In all these we can discern that this harp is of the progeny of the warrior's bow. In Sumerian the instrument was possibly called the *ban* or *pan* (bow),[12] a name associated in this way, maybe, from time immemorial.[13] We do not know its later Semitic name in Mesopotamia, although its last

[1] Op. cit., p. 19.
[2] *Journal of the Royal Asiatic Society* (1921), pp. 174, 191.
[3] *Revue d'Assyriologie*, xxx (1933), pp. 138, 153. The word endured for millennia in the Syriac *pūqā'ā* (fragor, crepitus).
[4] J. A. Knudtzon, *Die El-Amarna Tafeln* (Leipzig, 1908 et seq.), pp. 155 ff.
[5] Galpin, op. cit., pl. iii, fig. 1.
[6] Jastrow, *Aspects of Religious Belief* (New York, 1911), pl. 8.
[7] Kinsky, op. cit., p. 1, fig. 4.
[8] Engel, op. cit., pp. 61 ff.
[9] Op cit., pp. 26 ff.
[10] H. Frankfort, *Sculptures of the Third Millennium B.C from Tell Asmar and Khafājah* (Chicago, 1939), pl. 107.
[11] Galpin, pls. ii, fig. 4; v, fig. 5. Galpin's name for it is *mirītu*.
[12] Ibid., p. 28.
[13] J. F. Rowbotham, *A History of Music*, i (London, 1885–7), p. 154.

descendants were the Pahlavi *vōn* and the Arabic *wann*.[1] The second form, with a separate bow-shaped neck fixed to a horizontal sound-chest, was not unlike the Burmese *saun*. It is delineated on a vase from Bismaya (*c.* 3000 B.C.) at Stamboul,[2] although there is an actual specimen from Ur (twenty-fifth century B.C.) at the British Museum (pl. 8 (*b*)).[3] The instrument of the foremost player on the Bismaya vase has only seven strings whilst the Ur instrument has eleven. The former may relate to the *šibītu* (seven [stringed] harp),[4] but no name has come down for the latter instrument, although we seem to have *šiššatu* (six [stringed]) and *eširtu* (ten [stringed]) as names of instruments according to Langdon.[5] The third form, with a separate vertical neck in the horizontal sound-chest, shows itself on a Nippur plaque (*c.* 1800 B.C.), now at Philadelphia.[6] It is also recognizable in the hands of one of the Elamite musicians on the Kūl-i Fir'aun sculptures.[7] In later Assyrian days (eighth–seventh centuries B.C.) we have several examples in art remains.[8] Owing to the reconstruction of a fracture on the British Museum sculpture, where a joint cut through one of the designs of this instrument, the newly imposed position of the strings misled some musicographers to imagine a dulcimer[9] or a psaltery,[10] instead of a harp.

The last-mentioned type of lower-chested harp gave rise to the upper-chested harp, which was, to all intent, the previously described instrument turned sideways. It has been identified with the Akkadian *zaggal*, a doubtful name which Galpin thought was the parent of the Persian *chang*.[11] This latter had an acutely angled upper sound-chest with a distinct hump, and when we first espy it on a bronze vessel from Nihāwand (*c.* 2000 B.C.) this sound-chest is almost vertical but with a sudden bend at the peak.[12] We notice it also on a figurine from

[1] Farmer, *Studies in Oriental Musical Instruments*, ii (Glasgow, 1939), p. 74.

[2] E. J. Banks, *Bismaya* (New York, 1912), p. 267.

[3] L. Woolley, *Ur Excavations*, i, pp. 74 ff., ii, pls. 108–10. The British Museum's reconstruction of its sound-chest was definitely wrong. Even Galpin, with his encyclopaedic knowledge of the morphology of instruments, did not object to this faultily conceived modelling when he reproduced the design in 1929 (*Music and Letters*, x, pp. 108 ff.). In view of this the present writer made his own reconstruction in 1931, to which Galpin agreed, and in 1933 both Galpin and Curt Sachs made representations to the British Museum for the necessary alteration. However, Galpin remedied the design in his monumental work of 1937.

[4] F. Martin, *Textes religieux* (Paris, 1903), p. 196.

[5] *Journal of the Royal Asiatic Society* (1921), pp. 180, 183–4. The Hebrew *nebel 'āsōr* as its name tells us, had ten strings.

[6] Galpin, op. cit., pl. vi, fig. 4.

[7] J. de Morgan, op. cit. iii, pl. 23.

[8] Engel, op. cit., p. 49.

[9] Ibid., pp. 44 ff.; Rowbotham, op. cit. i, p. 335.

[10] Virolleaud et Pélagaud, op. cit., p. 46.

[11] Op. cit., pp. 29, 56.

[12] E. Herzfeld, *Archaeological History of Iran* (London, 1935), p. 7. See also *Revue d'Assyriologie*, xxv (1928), pp. 169, 175, fig. 1.

Sippar (*c.* 1700 B.C.) now at Philadelphia.[1] In later Assyrian scenes the chest has a graduated curve throughout its length.[2] The same is to be seen in Elamite designs.[3]

The kithara family reveals some unique specimens. In late Assyrian times (eighth–seventh century B.C.), one delineated example is a folk instrument.[4] It is of asymmetrical construction, an outline which is maintained in the instruments of professionals.[5] A rectangular type occurs on the Tell Halaf relief (third millennium B.C.),[6] and in Assyrian art remains (eighth–seventh centuries B.C.).[7] Its name is not as yet known to us. The most outstanding instrument of this class was the grand kithara, seemingly known in Sumerian as *algar*.[8] Langdon said that *algar* was merely a longer form of the mythical instrument called *al*, which is the subject of an Enlil psalm,[9] but Galpin insisted that it is the *al* and the *zagsal* that are identical. This grand kithara is depicted on the standard of Ur (twenty-fifth century B.C.),[10] and on seals of the same period.[11] A slightly larger example is limned on the Tello relief (*c.* 2200 B.C.),[12] whilst the plaque from Ur (twenty-fifth century B.C.) is almost the height of a man.[13] Even these representations, expressive though they may be, are not comparable with the actual instruments from Ur (twenty-fifth century B.C.) which are preserved in splendid examples at the British Museum, Baghdad, and Philadelphia.[14]

Our final section concerns the pandore. The Sumerian word *pan* or *ban* stood for 'bow', and later perhaps for 'harp' also. If the curved neck of the lower-chested harp were straightened, quite a different

[1] V. Scheil, *Une Saison de fouilles à Sippar* (Cairo, 1902), p. 90, fig. 2; Galpin, op. cit., pl. vi, fig. 6.

[2] Kinsky, op. cit., p. 3, figs. 1, 3.

[3] J. de Morgan, op. cit., iii, pl. 23. The Arabs of the East and the Moors of Spain appear to have been the last to use this harp (*jank*, Persian *chang*). See Farmer, *The Minstrelsy of the Arabian Nights* (Bearsden, 1945), pls. 4, 5; J. F. Riaño, *Notes on Early Spanish Music* (London, 1887), p. 122.

[4] Engel, op. cit., p. 39, fig. 7.

[5] Kinsky, op. cit., p. 2, fig. 3; p. 3, figs. 2, 3.

[6] M. F. von Oppenheim, op. cit., pl. xxxviii.

[7] Engel, op. cit., p. 38, fig. 5.

[8] Galpin, op. cit., pp. 31 ff. In April 1937 I suggested to the late Dr. Langdon that the Akkadian *qaṭāru* (to strike) or *kaṣāru* (to gather together, tie, hence *kiṣru*, something tied) might have produced the name of such an instrument, hence κιθάρα. In reply he informed me that the former word was now known to mean only 'to smoke', but gave no opinion about the latter. Cf. *kassar* and *kasrā*, the lyre in modern Upper Egypt.

[9] *Sumerian Liturgical Texts* (Philadelphia, 1917), p. 187.

[10] Galpin, op. cit., frontispiece, p. 31.

[11] Ibid., pl. ii, figs. 1, 3, 5.

[12] Heuzey and de Sarzec, *Découvertes en Chaldée* (Paris, 1884), pl. 23.

[13] Woolley, op. cit. ii, pl. 105, 111–14, 118–21.

[14] Galpin, op. cit., pl. vii.

instrument would be created, as I have shown elsewhere.[1] This change would produce the Sumerian *pantur* (small *pan*), as both Galpin and Sachs suggest,[2] a name which easily could have been the parent of the Greek *pandoura*. Julius Pollux said that while the Arabs invented the one-stringed instrument, the Assyrians were responsible for the *pandoura* of three strings.[3] We see an early pandore on a plaque from Nippur (*c.* 1700 B.C.),[4] as well as in later designs.[5] In Assyrian times (eighth–seventh centuries B.C.) it is also featured.[6] Was this the *nebel* which Isaiah wished to silence in his denunciation of Babylon (Isaiah xiv. 11)?

There is still that list of instruments of the 'Golden City' of Babylon as recorded in Daniel (iii. 5, 7, 10, 15) to be discussed. With one exception—the last-named—they are Semitic by name and origin. The Aramaic *qarnā* (horn) needs no comment, since we have seen its Akkadian parent. The root of the Syriac *mašrōqīthā* (pipe), which is *šāraq*, is as old as Judges (v. 16), where it more properly refers to the sounds of the shepherd's pipe, an instrument called *šarqōqīthā* in Talmudic times. The Syriac lexicographers tells us that the *mašruqitho* is the Arabic *ṣaffāra* (recorder), *shabbāba* (flute), or *ṣūr* (horn). Of the *qīthros* (kithara) we have already spoken. The *sabbekā* (lower-chested harp) owes its name, in all probability, to the fact that multiplicity [of strings] was confused with multiflexity, as we see in the root *sābaq* (to intertwine, interweave), hence *sebāq* (lattice-work) and *sebāqā* (net-work), whose kindred still thrive in Arabic. The *pṣantrīn ṣūmfonyāh* (concord harp), reopens an old controversy about the *ṣūmfonyāh* being a separate instrument, to wit, a bagpipe or some other instrument, in spite of St. Jerome's early rejection of such a notion[7] as pointed out by Pusey.[8] Since the time of the latter there has been a change of heart, and several attempts have been made to solve the problem, notably in the more recent interpretation by

[1] *Transactions: Glasgow University Oriental Society*, v (1930), p. 26.

[2] Galpin, op. cit., p. 35; Sachs, *The History of Musical Instruments* (New York, 1940), p. 82.

[3] *Onomasticon*, iv. 60.

[4] Galpin, op. cit., pl. viii, fig. 6.

[5] Ibid., pl. viii, fig. 7; Kinsky, op. cit., p. 2, fig. 1; J. Garstang, *The Hittite Empire* (London, 1929), pl. xxx. In this last, a Hittite example, we see incurvatures in the waist of the sound-chest, the parent of the modern guitar.

[6] Engel, op. cit., pp. 54 ff., figs. 12, 23. See A. W. Pope, *A Survey of Persian Art*, iv (London, 1938) for pandores from Luristan, p. 72, and Susa, p. 74; M. Ebert, *Reallexikon der Vorgeschichte* (Berlin, 1926), vi, p. 216; Farmer, *Oriental Studies: Mainly Musical* (London, 1953,) pp. 61 ff.

[7] The *ṣūmfonyāh* is also omitted from the list of Daniel iii in the pseudo-graphic Letter to Dardanus: *Patrologiae Latinae*, xxx, p. 221.

[8] *The Book of Daniel* (London, 1864), pp. 24 ff. In two verses *ṣūmfonyāh* and *ṣīfonyā* occur as separate instruments since they are preceded by the conjunctive *vav* ('and').

Galpin.[1] In the above, however, a different solution is offered. The *pṣantrīn* (= psalterion) was, according to St. Augustine, an upper-chested harp. Its wide gamut, twenty strings, perhaps, may have led to it being termed symphonious, in the sense that it could be played in octaves. Because of that the word *ṣūmfonyāh* is used as a noun in apposition to *pṣantrīn*, just as in *nebel ʿāsōr* (decacord harp) in Psalms (xxxiii, xcii).

Thus we see that for 3,000 years before the Christian era at least, ancient Mesopotamia had instruments of music, not only of a most varied character, but of a very high and advanced degree of construction, as the harps and kitharas of Sumerian days alone eloquently testify. Yet although we have so many instruments, and even more names of instruments than we can identify by form or even class, we must ever be cautious in accepting identification except with the greatest latitude.

THE THEORY AND PRACTICE OF MUSIC

With the growth of the temple organization, the earlier animistic beliefs in the potency of music had given way to more scientific ideas. The marvels of the heavens became a greater source of wonderment, and this led to the deification of the planets as man's protectors. Astrology induced mathematics, and since we find that the very gods were subjected to the exact sciences, we can be fairly certain that music also fell under their dominion. Of the attainments of the Mesopotamian peoples in astronomy and mathematics we have ample knowledge from indigenous sources. Of the theory of music, however, nothing on the subject has been unearthed, save what we know from Greek writers. From the latter we learn that the fame of Babylon for mathematical and occult accomplishments had spread to the western world, an esteem which was the means of attracting scholars to the Mesopotamian centres of learning. According to Iamblichus[2] and Diogenes Laertius,[3] one of those so allured was Pythagoras. From Valerius Maximus[4] we know that he also learned there the motion of the stars, their intrinsic properties, and their effect and influence on mankind. These beliefs seem to have had their origin in Mesopotamia.

Quite early we find the peoples of the 'fertile crescent' in the possession of an elaborate cosmic system in which there existed a

[1] Op. cit., pp. 67 ff.; Sachs, *The History of Musical Instruments* (New York, 1940), pp. 83 ff.

[2] *De vita Pythagorae*, iv, p. 3.

[3] *Lives of Eminent Philosophers*, viii (London, 1925), p. 3.

[4] *Facta et dicta*, vii, p. 7.

spiritual inter-relation between the entire macrocosm and microcosm, a belief which gave birth to tenets which were known later as the 'harmony of the spheres', the 'doctrine of the ethos', and the 'theory of numbers'. Censorinus says that Pythagoras taught that the universe was constructed according to musical ratio, and that the seven planets, revolving in the heavens, emitted sounds so consonant as to produce the most exquisite music.[1] One wonders whether the Mesopotamian *kalū* or precentor petitioned those 'Lords of the Heavens', as they called the planets, through their appropriate musical ratios.[2] The teachings of Pythagoras concerning the principles of the ethos have almost a Mesopotamian flavour, in that music, being a cosmic ingredient, possessed qualities and sensibilities which could evoke the like if the appropriate and related kind of music were used. Thus one species would banish depression, another would assuage grief, a third would check passion, while yet another would dispel fear. Although both the above beliefs were connected with the theory of music in a vague way, trust in the efficacy of the 'theory of numbers' was an integral part of the theory of music. In Mesopotamia, number was something more than a mathematical unit; it was believed that number in itself possessed an active force, having properties that were sacred attributes.[3] Philo Judaeus writes that 'the law of the Chaldaeans, taken symbolically, is mathematical speculation',[4] and he saw that these people, by availing themselves of the principles of music, had imagined the most perfect harmony existing throughout the universe.[5] In this cosmic scheme some numbers had greater efficacy than others, and the numbers *seven* and *four* were among these.[6] Nature herself had made both sacrosanct. The potency of seven could be seen in the planetary system, while its sum was apparent in the quadrangle plus the triangle, both of which were used in the auguries. Philo Judaeus appreciated that seven had four boundaries and three interval ratios, i.e. 1:2, 2:3, and 3:4.[7] Is it any wonder that the heptatonic scale was formulated, linked as it was with the planetary system which interpreted the will of the gods?[8]

On the practical side of music our knowledge is equally sparse. Both the late Francis W. Galpin and Curt Sachs have provided

[1] *De Dei nat.*, p. xiii.

[2] Cf. J. Burnet, *Early Greek Philosophy* (London, 1930), pp. 87 ff. and Chap. IX p. 341.

[3] F. Cumont, *Astrology and Religion among the Greeks and Romans* (New York, 1912), pp. 29 ff.

[4] *Works*, iv (London, 1854), p. 404.

[5] Ibid. ii, p. 82.

[6] L. W. King, *A History of Babylon* (London, 1915), p. 307.

[7] Op. cit. i, p. 30.

[8] Diodorus Siculus, ii, 30.

lengthy discussions on the subject, although much of the probing must necessarily be in the land of conjecture. The great enticement to all investigators has been the existence of instruments, either actual or delineated, from ancient days, which have acted as lodestones to the inquisitive. Yet no matter how sedulously we count the cords of stringed instruments, the answer to the computation is always a number, not a gamut. It is true that we possess a real Mesopotamian wind instrument or two, but they are palpably insufficient for our purpose.

On the other hand, both Galpin and Sachs have contrived to elucidate the Mesopotamian scale by other means. The former, under the impulsion of Landsberger,[1] imagined a scale of three octaves, being urged to these dimensions by an endeavour to embrace a supposed 'ordered arrangement' of the Semitic alphabet of twenty-one letters into a scale which is said to have been used at the 'opening centuries of the second millennium B.C.'.[2] It must be pointed out that there is neither an instrument, nor a delineation of an instrument, from this region and period, which carries so great a number of strings. Incidentally, in this worthy attempt to solve the so-called musical notation on certain cuneiform tablets, to be dealt with presently, Galpin registers his conviction that he could find 'no trace of harmony' in this sole exemplar of Mesopotamian music, although such an opinion is obviously conditioned by his own interpretation of the cuneiform signs. It may be stated that others have held opposite views, notably Langdon whose argument was that since there were female as well as male choristers in the temples they must have chanted in four parts, a quite unwarranted assumption.[3]

Curt Sachs has also stated that harmony was used in Mesopotamian music. He bases his deductions on a series of studies which began in 1923,[4] were continued in 1929,[5] and were reaffirmed in 1933,[6] 1940,[7] and 1943.[8] From these he concluded that 'consonant chords' were used, i.e. harmony in the accepted sense of the word. Taking the Elamo-Assyrian harpers depicted on the British Museum bas-reliefs, and examining their technique in plucking the individual strings, he

[1] *Festschrift Max von Oppenheim, Archiv für Orientforschung*, i (Berlin, 1933).
[2] Galpin, op. cit., pp. 38 ff., 99 ff.
[3] *Babylonian Liturgies*, p. xi.
[4] *Sitzungsberichte der preußischen Akademie der Wissenschaften*, xviii (1924), pp. 120–3; *Archiv für Musikwissenschaft*, vii (1925), p. 1.
[5] *Festschrift für Johannes Wolf* (Berlin, 1929), pp. 168 ff.
[6] *Zeitschrift für ägyptische Sprache*, lxix (1933), pp. 68 ff.
[7] *The History of Musical Instruments* (New York, 1940), p. 82.
[8] *The Rise of Music in the Ancient World* (New York, 1943), pp. 99–101.

pursued quite an ingenious line of inquiry. From this he believed that the position of the hands and fingers of the harpers showed that 'chords' were played. To the present writer it seems that any attempt to determine, from this bas-relief, which strings are plucked, can be no more than a gratuitous assumption. Sachs supposes that 'each harper plucks two strings' simultaneously. Yet might not one just as readily assume that each harper is plucking *one* string with one hand, and is preparing to pluck another string with the other hand? Sachs also touches upon scalar theories, and states categorically that there existed in Mesopotamia 'almost certainly a pentatonic tuning', although 'singing', he says, 'at least in the last one thousand years B.C., was heptatonic without any trace of pentatonism'. These theses are palpably dependent upon his own interpretation of the harpers' technique and on his reading of the cuneiform scale. Eighty years earlier the musicologist Carl Engel also held to the pentatonic scale theory,[1] and Langdon, admittedly a non-musician, followed suit.[2]

NOTATION

Did Mesopotamia possess a musical notation? When texts and translations of certain cuneiform tablets at Berlin were published by George Reisner in 1896,[3] they were claimed to reveal a musical notation, a pronouncement which created considerable stir in both the archaeological and musicological worlds. These finds dated from about 800 B.C., although others were discovered later from the sixteenth century B.C. The claims for a notation were based on certain vocalic characters, as well as ideograms, contained in the texts, and Theophilus G. Pinches thought that since the former occurred at the beginning, in the middle (the caesura), and at the end of a line, rather than over words, they represented 'tonalities' rather than 'notes', a judgement which was quite sound.[4] In 1919, when Erich Ebeling published such texts,[5] fresh interest accrued, and in 1923 Curt Sachs worked at a musical transcription of the 'notation'.[6] Benno Landsberger repudiated Sachs's transcription,[7] and the latter has since admitted that his initial attempt was a failure.[8] In 1937 Galpin published

[1] Op. cit., p. 122.
[2] *Babylonian Liturgies*, p. lii.
[3] *Sumerisch-babylonische Hymnen* (Leipzig, 1896).
[4] Hastings' *Encyclopaedia of Religion and Ethics*, ix (Edinburgh, 1917), p. 14.
[5] *Keilschrifttexte aus Assur religiösen Inhalts*, i (Leipzig, 1919), p. 4.
[6] *Sitzungsberichte der preußischen Akademie der Wissenschaften*, xviii (1924), pp. 120 ff.
[7] *Festschrift für Max von Oppenheim: Archiv für Orientforschung* (Berlin, 1933), p. 170.
[8] *The Rise of Music in the Ancient World*, p. 86.

his noteworthy study of Sumerian music, in which he rebuffed Landsberger's pessimism regarding a solution, but he too rejected Sachs's transcription.[1] We have already dealt with Galpin's proposed scale of twenty-one notes.[2] Sachs, in turn, declined acceptance of Galpin's scheme, and again set out, but with fresh premises, to solve anew the cryptic signs. The results were published in an article entitled 'The Mystery of the Babylonian Notation' which appeared in 1941.[3]

THE HERITAGE

The influence exerted by Mesopotamian culture on the western world was far reaching.[4] Unfortunately the glories of the intellectual and artistic conquests of Greece have dazzled the view of our cultural debts to others. Not that the Greeks are responsible for this obscurity. On the contrary, both they and the Romans acknowledged their indebtedness to the Orient. Strabo says that 'the cultivators of ancient music are said to be Thracians', and that 'from its melody, rhythm, and instruments, all Thracian music is supposed to be Asiatic'.[5] The legend of Orpheus, the 'Father of Songs', is pre-eminently a Thracian one. It is admitted that it was through Asia Minor that Thrace received these Oriental refinements. The two semi-mythical originators of flutes and reed-pipes, Hyagnis and Marsyas, were both Phrygians.[6] Terpander, the accredited systematizer of Greek music in the introduction of *nomoi* for the lyre, and Olympus, the founder of the Phrygian school of music, who introduced *nomoi* for the woodwind (*auloi*), were also from these parts. What was the *nomos*? Could it have been a survival of the old Semitic *neum* or '[intoned] utterance of soothsayer and prophet'? Indeed the shades of Babylon, 'learned and wise', may be discerned over the shoulders of many of these reputed founders of the arts and sciences in Greece, mythical though they may be. Pseudo-Euclid, i.e. Cleonides, makes Terpander say that the lyre had four strings until he made them seven,[7] which Strabo seems to confirm.[8] Whence did this inspiration come? Could it have been Babylon? If we can trust pseudo-Plutarch[9] it would appear that the Greeks at this time were most conservative in musical matters. Boëthius says that it was the seven planets which suggested

[1] *The Music of the Sumerians* (Cambridge, 1937), pp. 38 ff.

[2] See supra, p. 248.

[3] *The Musical Quarterly*, xxvii (1941), pp. 62 ff.

[4] L. W. King, *A History of Sumer and Akkad* (London, 1910), pp. 321 ff.; *A History of Babylon* (London, 1915), pp. 289 ff.

[5] *The Geography*, x. iii. 17.

[6] ps.-Plutarch, *De musica*, v–viii.

[7] iii. 67.

[8] XIII. ii. 4.

[9] *De musica*, III. xviii.

this number of strings to Terpander,[1] a statement which agrees with a Mesopotamian origin.

Diodorus Siculus tells us that it was Linus who gave verse and music to the Greeks,[2] and the Linus myth in Greece, which represents this god as a musician and the creator of the Linus song, is simply the older Mesopotamian legend of Tammuz. Euripides judged the cry αἴλινος in the mournful Linus songs to be a Phrygian custom, and indeed we see its fellow in the Hebrew *ai lānū*, the like of which we find at the close of some of the psalms. Frazer identifies Linus with Adonis,[3] as did Pausanias,[4] and the Phoenicians called the latter Gingras, a name which was actually given to the wailing reed-pipe, as Xenophon and Aristoxenus relate.[5] Curiously enough, Adonis was worshipped in Asia Minor under the name of Abobas,[6] a word strikingly reminiscent of the Syriac *abūba*, which was the Akkadian *imbubu*.

Instruments of music found their way into Greece from the Orient in great numbers. Strabo says: 'And those writers who have consecrated the whole of Asia, as far as India,[7] to Dionysus, derive the greater part of music from there. One writer says: "striking the *asias kithara*"; another calls pipes "Berecyntian" and "Phrygian", and some of the instruments have been called by barbarian names, *nablas*, *sambykē*, *barbitos*, *magadis*, and several others.'[8] Some of these others are quoted by Athenaeus, and among them the *pectis* and *phenix* (*phoinix*).[9] The word *kithara* may not be Greek.[10] That it was sometimes called *asias*,[11] rather than *asias kithara*, is worthy of notice. It is more than strange that 'to play' upon the *kithara* is conveyed by the word κρέκω, and practically the same word, *ḥaraka*, has been used in Arabic from time immemorial in connexion with playing the lute (*'ūd*),[12] a term which, in its pristine form, means 'to hasten', as does the cognate Akkadian *araḫu*.

[1] *De musica*, i. 20. See *Bibliothèque archéologique et historique*, XXX (1939), pp. 161 ff.
[2] *Bibliotheca Historica*, III. 67. See also p. 378.
[3] *The Golden Bough*, ii (London, 1900), pp. 224, 253.
[4] ix. 29.
[5] Athenaeus, op. cit. iv, pp. 174 ff., who said that the *gingras* was Phoenician.
[6] Hesychius, s.v.
[7] Strabo, op. cit., x. iii. 17.
[8] That the term 'India' meant eastern countries much nearer, see the *Cosmographia Ethici* (p. 28) with the additions by Julius Honorius (p. 7). Even the ecclesiastical historians call the Arabs 'Indians'.
[9] iv. 175–85.
[10] ps.-Plutarch, op. cit. 6. Euripides, *Cyclops*, v. 443. The Trojans used the *kithara* whereas the Greeks had the *phorminx*.
[11] C. Daremberg et E. Saglio, *Dictionnaire des antiquités grecques et romaines* (Paris. 1877 et seq.), p. 1438.
[12] *Transactions: Glasgow University Oriental Society*, xi (1946), p. 29.

The *nabla*, as its name (Hebrew *nebel*) indicates, has a distinct Semitic physiognomy. Indeed it was called the Sidonian *nabla*, which particularly identifies it with Phoenicia. It was known quite early in Greece, since Sophocles (d. *c.* 406 B.C.) speaks of it, as does Ovid (d. A.D. *c.* 17 in Rome). For the *trigōnon* and/or *sambykē* a Syrian origin is claimed and in Rome it was the *sambuca* which was found in the hands of Syrians in the time of Hadrian (d. A.D. 38). Of course, we recognize this harp immediately in the Aramaic *ṣabbekā* which we read about in Daniel (iii). The *barbitos* (cf. the Persian *barbaṭ*) is attributed to Terpander, and both Sappho of Lesbos (7th cent. B.C.) and Ovid in Rome sang its praises. The *magadis* is acknowledged to be of Lydian origin, as also the *pectis*, while Lydian reed-pipes (*auloi* and *tibiae*) were lauded by both Pindar (d. 438 B.C.) and Horace (d. 8 B.C.). Indeed it is the latter who tells us about Oriental female reed-pipers in Rome. They were the Syrian *ambubaiae* mentioned by Papias, and their name reveals that they played the Akkadian reed-pipe *imbubu*, in spite of the Syriac equivalent being *abbūba*. As early as Terence (d. *c.* 159 B.C.) Roman orchestras had players on the *tibiae sarranae*, i.e. the Phoenician reed-pipes. One of the Phrygian *auloi* of the double reed-pipe group was the *elymos*, the drone-pipe of which was turned up with a horn 'bell', hence, probably, its name. This was the type of Akkadian pipe which Galpin wanted to identify in the *pītu*. Yet whether it was Phoenicia or Syria, Lydia or Phrygia, that were dubbed the 'inventors' of these instruments, the *fons et origo* was Mesopotamia.

Perhaps the most marked impinging of Mesopotamian musical culture on Greece is discernible in Pythagorean traditions. Pythagoras himself is claimed by both Greek[1] and Persian[2] writers to have been a Syrian born, one making Tyre, and the other Sidon his birthplace. Instructed at first by Sidonian and Phoenician hierophants, he was initiated into the mysteries of Tyre and Byblos. Later he passed into Egypt, where he remained twenty-one years. Taken captive by Cambyses, he was carried to Babylon where, says Iamblichus, he was instructed by the priests 'in their venerable knowledge, and learned from them the most perfect worship of the gods. Through their assistance likewise, he arrived at the summit of arithmetic, [the theory of] music, and other disciplines.'[3] After twelve years at Babylon he settled at Samos, where, because of his learning, he was immediately dubbed a *sophos* (Akkadian *āšipu*).

[1] Porphyry, *De vita Pythagorae*, i.
[2] Mīr Khāwand, *Rauḍat al-Ṣafa'*, i. ii (London, 1891–4), p. 268.
[3] Iamblichus, *De vita Pythagorae*, iv.

It was through Pythagoras and his disciples that Greece became acquainted with such doctrines as the 'harmony of the spheres', the 'principles of the ethos', and that alluring theory of the 'efficacy of numbers', which have already been described. It is true that he has been credited as the first to determine the consonances of the fourth, fifth, and octave, but the inherently false accounts of this so-called 'discovery', as preserved by Nicomachus,[1] Gaudentius,[2] and Boethius,[3] reveal the improbability of this.[4] There is no reason why the peoples of Mesopotamia who made so creditable an advance in arithmetical and geometrical progressions, and who possessed rules for finding the areas of squares, rectangles, right triangles, and trapezoids, could not have had as complete a knowledge of the speculative theory of music as the earliest of the Greek theorists, Pythagoras.

Plutarch, in his commentary on the *Timaeus* of Plato, informs us that the Chaldaeans connected musical intervals with the seasons, i.e. the fourth (3:4) = Autumn, the fifth (2:3) = Winter, the octave (1:2) = Summer, whilst the tonic (1:1) = Spring.[5] This was a cornerstone in the doctrine of the ethos. Actually, it is the most useful reference by the Greeks to the Mesopotamian theory of music that we possess apart from the Pythagorean passages, although we must not forget the statement of Nicomachus, that Iamblichus had testified that it was the people of Babylonia who discovered the harmonic proportion which Pythagoras introduced into Greece.[6] It seems therefore not unlikely that Mesopotamia possessed a theory of music which was actually the starting-point of our present system.

That the peoples of the Mesopotamian plains were the pioneers of civilization, and that they contributed remarkably to the progress of music, must be allowed them. The mere comparison between the advanced structure of Mesopotamian instruments of music, especially in their harps and citharas, with what the Greeks had accomplished, at once proclaims the immense superiority of the former. Although the peoples of Mesopotamia never exerted a permanent hegemony over the lands of the western Mediterranean, their culture dominated Syrian, Phoenician, and Hittite lands, from whence it infiltrated into Greece and Egypt, to become the seed for the intellectual development of the West.

[1] Meibom, *Antiquae musicae auctores septem* (Amsterdam, 1652), pp. 10 ff.
[2] Ibid., p. 13.
[3] *De musica*, i. 10.
[4] Farmer, *Historical Facts for the Arabian Musical Influence* (London, 1930), p. 292.
[5] *De animae procr.* 31.
[6] *Intro. Arith.* xxvi, xxix.

In the sphere of religion we can dimly recognize the germ of our own religious practices, not merely in the liturgy, the penitential psalm, the antiphon, the precentor, the incense, and the rest, but in the *mater dolorosa.* As Langdon says, one cannot doubt the great influence of the Mesopotamian temples upon the late Jewish Church and upon Christianity.[1] One recalls that the Mesopotamian *kalū* or temple precentor had to be skilled in an eight-day liturgy,[2] each day of which would have had its appropriate 'trope' or 'tone'. Does not the Hebrew *shemīnīth* in the captions of the psalms refer to an eighth mode, as Isaac ben Abraham ibn Latif (13th cent.) avers? Could that practice have been the reason for the Syriac *ikhadias* of the Jacobite Church, the *octoēchos* of the Byzantine Church, and the eight Gregorian tones of the Roman Church? Although the Prophet cries 'Babylon is fallen, fallen', the plainchant of the Roman Church today carries the titles *Primus gravis*, *Secundus tristis*, and *Tertius mysticus*, which are but ethoidal relics from the ancient Mesopotamian past of probably 6,000 years ago.

[1] *Sumerian Liturgies and Psalms*, p. 238.

[2] Langdon, *Journal: American Oriental Society*, xlii (1925–6), p. 112.

VI

THE MUSIC OF ANCIENT EGYPT

By HENRY GEORGE FARMER

INTRODUCTION

WHEN we approach the history of ancient Egypt we are confronted with a highly developed social and cultural melioration which is already a *fait accompli.* The previous chapter has described a similar circumstance in Mesopotamia. Yet, as in that land of the 'two rivers', we do not know why, how, or when this surpassing achievement came about. Modern research has revealed abundant proof of the impingement of a 'new culture' in Egypt during the early dynasties—that is, from about the twenty-ninth century B.C.—not unlike that of Mesopotamia and Iran. How far this affected instruments of music is not at present as discernible as it is in other spheres, for the cultural impact must have taken place long before the twenty-fifth century B.C., the date of the Royal Tombs of Ur. Indeed the harps of the 4th dynasty (twenty-sixth century B.C.) delineated at Gizeh reveal a stage of instrumental construction earlier than that of Sumer and Akkad in the twenty-fifth century B.C. This seems to show that whatever initial promptings may have come through Mesopotamian or Iranian migrations, or subsequent influences from these sources, the cultural contacts with the East must have ceased meanwhile.

As in Mesopotamia, we are denied precise dates in the earlier periods; those used in this chapter, like those in the previous one, are based on the readjustments of Professor W. F. Albright,[1] which have brought us very near to what Sir John G. Wilkinson had guessed more than a century before.[2]

FIFTH MILLENNIUM B.C.
Prehistoric period

FOURTH MILLENNIUM B.C.
Predynastic period

[1] *Bulletin of the American Schools or Oriental Research,* nos. 77, 78 (1940), and 88 (1942).

[2] J. G. Wilkinson, *The Manners and Customs of the Ancient Egyptians,* i (London, 1837), pp. 41 ff.

THIRD MILLENNIUM B.C.

Dynasty I	Twenty-ninth century
Dynasty IV	Twenty-sixth century
Dynasty VII	Twenty-second century

SECOND MILLENNIUM B.C.

Dynasty XII	*c.* 1989
Dynasty XIII	*c.* 1776
Dynasty XVIII	*c.* 1570
Dynasty XX	*c.* 1200

FIRST MILLENNIUM B.C.

Dynasty XXI (Tanis)	*c.* 1090
Dynasty XXII (Libyan)	*c.* 945
Dynasty XXVI (Saite)	*c.* 664
Dynasty XXVII (Persian invasion)	*c.* 525
Greek period	332
Roman period	30

PRIMITIVE MUSICAL SURVIVALS[1]

It is not improbable that music, or at least sound, stood at the cradle of all religion. Animism certainly had its origin in sound, for when primitive man struck a piece of wood, stone, or skin, or blew into a tube or cavity, and contemplated the resultant sound, he naturally concluded that what he heard was the 'voice' of the object struck, or of that into which he blew. He therefore assumed that by awakening their 'voices' he could propitiate unseen nature of which they were all a part. We see this in our first glimpse of Egyptian instruments of music.

Man's earliest instruments were idiophones, and we find them in ancient Egypt. These were clappers, and they are figured in pairs on predynastic pottery (fourth millennium B.C.).[2] Clappers also occur on monuments of the 5th dynasty (twenty-fourth century B.C.) where they were used for animistic purposes. In one instance we seem to see the god of the harvest, Min, being conjured by means of clappers to make fruitful the toil of vintagers.[3] In another example, harvesters

[1] In transliterating Egyptian words the conventional system has been adopted with the following exceptions: ꜣ = a': ꜥ = 'a: ỉ = i. The use of the vowel *e* between the consonants is quite arbitrary, and has been introduced, together with the above modifications, solely for the convenience of the general reader.

[2] D. Randall-MacIver and C. Mace, *El Amra and Abydos* (London, 1902), pl. xiv.

[3] R. Lepsius, *Denkmäler: Ergänzungsband* (Leipzig, 1913), pl. xxi.

perform a dance of appeasement to Ia'ru the god of the reeds, or to Nepri the corn spirit, perhaps, to the accompaniment of clashing sticks.[1] The application of like to like in this fashion is patent magic, rhythmical application still more so, for man saw measured motion in nature itself. This is precisely what Plutarch detected in the four jingling metal bars on the sistrum, presumably linked with the four elements, which immediately became active forces because, he says, 'all things are subject to motion'.[2]

Plutarch has also handed down a pretty conceit of Egypt's archaic musical past. Before the days of Menes, its first king, Egypt was ruled by gods, and one of these, Osiris, was responsible for teaching the world the arts of civilization. What enabled him to accomplish this was his 'persuasive discourse, combined with song, and all manner of music'.[3] (That gods were ever musically inclined is, of course, a universal tale.) Osiris was the 'Lord of the sistrum', an instrument specially dedicated to the goddess Ḥatḥor, the later Isis. The dwarf god Bes was supposed to be the 'god of music and dancing', and in art remains he is delineated with either the harp or kithara in hand,[4] while 'singing gods' and 'dancing gods' were innumerable in the Duat or land of the dead. Indeed there were 'choirs of angels' in the latter abode. Thoth was presumed to be the 'god of knowledge and wisdom', but as Hermes Trismegistus he was the 'inventor of music'[5] and the author of books of chants to the gods.[6] Indeed there is no end to the legends of the harmonious attributes of Egypt's deities.

That many of the gods were of totemistic origin is generally conceded.[7] When we discern birds, animals, and reptiles figured on instruments of music, or playing them, let us not attribute the circumstance to aesthetic fancy alone; it was due to a much more hallowed incitement. In the *Book of the Dead* the animal world, with man, laud god together, and Maspero has referred to predynastic chants or songs to animals.[8] As in Mesopotamia mummers, probably for secular as well as sacred purposes, assumed masks or other disguises as animals in ancient Egypt. Sacred masking, so as to represent deities, was hinted at by Maspero in 1899, but M. A. Murray developed the

[1] Lepsius, *Denkmäler aus Ägypten*, ii (Berlin, 1859), pl. 56*a*.
[2] *Isis and Osiris*, 376.
[3] Ibid. 356.
[4] C. Sachs, *Die Musikinstrumente des alten Ägyptens* (Berlin, 1921), figs. 59, 60, 104.
[5] Plutarch, *Isis and Osiris*, 352.
[6] Clement of Alexandria, *Stromateis*, vi. 4.
[7] *The Cambridge Ancient History*, i (Cambridge, 1924), pp. 328 ff.
[8] *Études de mythologie et d'archéologie égyptiennes*, i (Paris, 1894), p. 153; A. Erman, *Life in Ancient Egypt* (London, 1894), pp. 9, 60.

theme in 1934.[1] We have several examples of animals performing on instruments of music,[2] but equally important is their occurrence as figures on these instruments. All nature was one by the banks of the Nile, and this is patent in the sphere of religion. Goddesses were generally symbolized by the serpent and the latter was connected with the sistrum down to the Roman period (30 B.C. onward).[3] Ḥatḥor (Isis) and Nephthys are delineated on sistra,[4] in which the very jingling bars are fashioned as serpents.[5] A similar interpretation may be placed on the falcon's head and the goose's head on the scrolls of harps and citharas, since they symbolized the gods Month and Amen respectively.[6] Then there was the cat on sistra typifying Ba'stt, the goddess of fire, while the jackal on kitharas was emblematic of Anubis.[7] These features were of far deeper significance than mere emblems or symbols. They were a constant reminder that the voice of deity was ever present in their tones; it was not only ears in tonal appreciation that listened, but rather minds in transcendental anagogue that understood.

Music therefore had a twofold influence on man in ancient Egypt; one brought about by a purely physical sensation, and another created or sustained by a power known as *ḥeka'* or *ḥike*, which was something like, and yet different from, what we understand by 'spell'. It may be difficult to appreciate this hyperbole, and yet we still say 'enchanting' (√*cantus*) and 'charming' (√*carmen*) in our praise of music today without ever thinking that we are speaking in precisely the same way as did the ancient Egyptians, although they meant what they said.

RELIGIOUS MUSIC

All through the history of music in ancient Egypt, modulated sound itself was an arcanum. The name for sound was *ḫerw* (lit. 'voice'), and the word had an esoteric import in the cults.[8] One recalls its omnipotence in Mesopotamia where Ramman, for instance, was the 'spirit of sonorous voice'. We read of the Egyptian god Thoth who made Osiris 'true of voice'. The amulet which Isis hung about her neck was interpreted as 'a true voice'. One of the special parts of the temple liturgy was 'the going forth of the voice', but, as Alan H. Gardiner has shown, it is not easy to apprehend what was actually performed

[1] *Mélanges Maspero: Orient ancien*, i (Cairo, 1935), pp. 251 ff.

[2] Erman, op. cit., p. 369; W. Chappell, *The History of Music* (London, 1874), p. 399; Sachs, *Die Musikinstrumente*, pp. 57, 74.

[3] Sachs, *Die Musikinstrumente*, fig. 22.

[4] Plutarch, *Isis and Osiris*, 376.

[5] Wilkinson, op. cit. ii, p. 323.

[6] Ibid. ii, pp. 275, 280, 287, 291.

[7] Ibid. ii, pp. 293, 326.

[8] See Plutarch, *Isis and Osiris*, 355.

in this symbolic act. Certain it is that 'such ceremonial utterance had magical power'.[1] Here is what Maspero has said of its conjurative potency in the Egyptian temple:[2]

> The human voice is the instrument *par excellence* of the priest and enchanter. It is the voice that seeks afar the Invisibles summoned, and makes the necessary objects into reality. Every one of the sounds it emits has a peculiar power which escapes the notice of the common run of mortals, but which is known to and made use of by the adepts. . . . But as every one [of the notes] has its peculiar force, great care must be taken not to change their order or substitute one for the other.

Herodotus says that there was a college of priests in each temple,[3] and although there was an 'hour priesthood' of laymen, who may have been something like the secular priests of the Christian west, the temple ecclesiastics were few in number, generally about five, including a high-priest and a lector-priest or precentor (*hery-ḥeb*). Like the Mesopotamian *kalū* ('precentor'), some of these priests were 'scribes of divine books', and Clement of Alexandria has described, at a very late period, some of these writings. Speaking of the service he says: 'First comes the Singer, bearing one of the symbols of music, for they say that he must learn two of the books of Hermes, the one comprising the hymns of the gods, the second the regulation for the king's life.' There were also ten books devoted to hymns, prayers, processions, festivals, first fruits, and other constituent parts of temple worship.[4] It was a part of the regular duties of the priests to extol the god in songs in the daily ceremonial as well as at the great festivals, but Erman remarks that we do not know whether these songs were merely recited or whether they were sung.[5] This incertitude is of little import because, in these early days, whatever was recited was done so in a chant. Philology often confirms this, and the Arabic equivalent to the Egyptian *šedi* ('to recite') is *shadā* ('to sing').

Many of the rituals, liturgies, hymns, and lamentations have been translated for us, and in these we are able to grasp the abiding significance of the solemn temple services. Among the above translations are two by Raymond O. Faulkner, the 'Songs of Isis and Nephthys' in *The Papyrus Bremner-Rhind*, and the 'Lamentations of Isis and Nephthys' in *Mélanges Maspero*, which have passing interest because the first was part of a ritual spread over five days, while the second was what one might term a breviary for one day, and the two were

[1] *Proceedings of the Society of Biblical Archaeology*, xviii, p. 108; *Egyptian Grammar* (Oxford, 1927), p. 172. [2] *Études de mythologie*, i, p. 106.
[3] ii. 37. A. H. Sayce, *The Religion of Ancient Egypt* (London, 1913), p. 32.
[4] Op. cit. vi. 4. [5] *Life in Ancient Egypt* (London, 1894), p. 47.

musically distinct. Of the 'Songs' Faulkner says: 'Apart from a hymn to Osiris sung by the lector-priest in the middle of the ceremony, the songs consist of alternate duets by the two priestesses and solos on the part of her who represented Isis.' In this, Osiris is invoked as 'the fair sistrum player', and the priestesses carry tambourines. In the 'Lamentations' we do not find any of these things, and in the place of tambourines other sacred tokens are carried.

When the New Kingdom arose (*c.* 1570 B.C.), the female temple musician began to make her appearance. She was the *šem'ayt* who was already a feature in secular life. Many of these were wives and daughters of the priests, although other classes were also represented. They were looked upon as inmates of the harem of the god, in which they held nominally the same position they would have held in real life. For this reason the highest ladies of the land took these sacred offices in the cults, being known as the 'wife of the god', 'chief of the singers of the table of Amen', or 'songstress of Amen'.[1] These came to be a powerful corporation, and their lady superior, the 'divine adorer of Amen', shared sovereignty with the kings during the Saite period (*c.* 664–525 B.C.).[2] Their instrument of sacerdotal potency and ecclesiastical authority was the sistrum, or sistra rather, since we more frequently see one of each kind, the *śeḫem* and *seššet*, being used, one in each hand.[3] The word *śeḫem* itself meant ['divine] power', but its metallic 'voice', i.e. its jingling apparatus, was made mute since its form was sufficiently symbolic of its potent sound. Precisely the same metamorphosis came to the clapper called *menyt* which, after the rise of the New Kingdom, is generally found folded in the hands of the priestesses or divine singers.[4]

Under the Old and Middle Kingdoms, the court musicians held high positions, and were considered as 'near relations' of the king. Under the New Kingdom their significance was just as weighty, and the actual names of several have been preserved who held the position of 'chief of the singers of Pharaoh'. He was the nominal head of all musicians since he is designated 'chief of the singers of all the gods'. When we get glimpses of the royal family at worship, sistra predominate,[5] and these are often in the hands of princesses.[6] Occasionally

[1] Wilkinson, op. cit. i, p. 260; G. Fouchart, *Tombes thébaines* (Cairo, 1932), p. 35.

[2] G. Maspero, *Histoire d'orient*, iii (Paris, 1896–9), pp. 164, 173, 490.

[3] Lepsius, op. cit. vii, pls. 175, 186, 193; viii, pls. 247–50.

[4] V. Loret, 'Égypte', in Lavignac and La Laurencie, *Encyclopédie de la musique*, 1re partie, i (Paris, 1913), figs. 20–24.

[5] N. de G. Davies, *The Rock Tombs of El Amarna* (London, 1903–8), iv pls. xv, xxxi, xliv; v, pls. iii, xxvi.

[6] Ibid. vi, pls. xxviii, xxxvi.

clappers[1] and tambourines[2] found a hallowed place in adoration or supplication in the temples, possible because, like the sistra, their 'voices' were in monotone, a something nearer to the womb of things.

Yet temple music consisted of much more than chanting, jingling, rattling, and drumming. From early times quite a variety of other instruments found acceptance in worship, except perhaps in that devoted to Osiris at Abydos where, says Strabo, neither singer, piper, nor kitharist was allowed.[3] We see a royal family in adoration of deity [i.e. the sun's disk] with a harpist and three singers,[4] and in one of the art remains at Leiden, there are delineated a harpist, pandorist, and two flautists accompanying the chanting of an incense-sprinkling priest.[5] Indeed in every representation of religious life and practice in ancient Egypt, music and musical instruments play a prominent part. Even in the funerary proceedings we not only hear the gruesome lamentation (*neẖwt* = Arabic *niyaḥat*) of more primitive animistic times, but also the joyous sounds of singing, harping, fluting, and dancing, not merely delineated on the tomb walls but in actual practice.

Music in the temples continued to be of the utmost importance even throughout the Greek and Roman periods. Among the numerous art remains revealed in the Greek city of Naukratis is a figure of Apollo with a harp,[6] and at Armant of Roman times, the sistrum still found a place in the hands of goddess and priestess.[7] The flute or reed-pipe was certainly still attached to the service of Amen, and Apuleius and Claudian both testify to its presence in the temple.[8] Of course it was the emblem of fertility, and indeed the 'field of reeds' was one of the promised scenes in Elyseum.[9] The common people were certainly attached to it when they entered into the spirit of open-air worship. Once a year they 'joined their priests in a melancholy procession through the streets, singing a doleful ditty called the *Manerōs*',[10] and Herodotus also affirms that at the festival of Osiris they had processions, the women carrying images preceded by an *aulos* player (reed-piper).[11] In his account of the crowd of 700,000 [*sic*]

[1] A. M. Blackman, *The Rock Tombs of Meir* (London, 1914), pl. xviii.

[2] E. Naville, *The Festival-Hall of Osorkon II* (London, 1892), pp. 14, 24, 26; pls. xi, xvi.

[3] Strabo, *Geographus*, XVII. i. 43.

[4] N. de G. Davies, op. cit. i, p. 33; pl. xxxiii.

[5] Wilkinson, op. cit. ii, p. 316; G. Steindorff, *Die Kunst der Ägypter* (Leipzig, 1928), p. 244.

[6] W. M. Flinders Petrie, *Naukratis*, ii (London, 1888), p. 57; pls. xiv, 14; xvii. 4.

[7] R. Mond, *Temples of Armant* (London, 1940), p. 180; pl. xcii, 16.

[8] *Metamorphosis*, xi.

[9] A. Erman, op. cit., p. 306.

[10] S. Sharpe, *Egyptian Mythology* (London, 1863), p. 10.

[11] ii. 48.

pilgrims who journeyed to the Bubastis festival, we see the flute or reed-pipe players leading the semi-hysterical multitude. Some of the women jingled their sistra in frenzied excitement, while others, in greater abandon, exposed themselves;[1] as Curt Sachs has shown in his *Geist und Werden der Musikinstrumente*, the flute has ever been considered the sexual instrument *par excellence*. Strabo tells of similar scenes among the visitors to the temple of Serapis at Canobus, where there was fluting or reed-piping with dancing and 'extreme licentiousness'.[2] It is no wonder that Aristotle considered that the *aulos* did not improve morals.

SECULAR MUSIC

All music, whether in the temple, the palace, or the street, was called *hy*, which meant primarily 'joy', 'gladness'. It was sometimes written with a hieroglyph which represented a fragrant lotus in bloom. A musician was known by a genuine Semitic word *šemʻa* (Hebrew *šamāʻ*, Arabic *samāʻ* = 'music'), as well as by other names. The word for 'praise' was *henw*, and it probably meant 'song' also (cf. *ʻaānn* 'to sing'), in which case we would have cognates in the Hebrew *ʻānāh* and the Arabic *ghanna* ('to sing'). The Hebrew word (cf. the Egyptian *ʻan*) came to mean 'to answer', and we have seen that the Akkadian word *enū* implied this also.[3] Perhaps *henw* was only used when the strophe and antistrophe were employed, and we have seen that the antiphon existed in the Egyptian temple liturgy. On the instrumental side we also find a few provoking technical terms, e.g. *teḫ* or *teḫen* ('to beat', 'to play'), of which the Hebrew *tāqaʻ* and the Abyssinian *takeʻ* may be kindred.

The male musician is a familiar figure in the art remains from the 4th dynasty (twenty-sixth century B.C.).[4] Here he is to be seen in all phases of professional activity: singer, instrumentalist, and dancer. Erman held the view that the singers waved their arms when performing,[5] which is also the opinion of Blackman.[6] On the other hand, Curt Sachs avers that the delineations do not merely indicate arm waving. He thinks the positions of the hands and fingers of the singers reveal certain manual and digital movements by which definite indications were communicated to the accompanists.[7] Yet it is not improbable

[1] ii. 60.
[2] Op. cit., XVII. i. 17.
[3] Chap. V., p. 234.
[4] Wilkinson, op. cit. ii, pp. 232, 239, 257, 316, 335–7; Lepsius, op. cit. iii, figs. 35–36, 52–53, 61, 74; iv. 109.
[5] Op. cit., p. 251.
[6] Op. cit., p. 12.
[7] *The Rise of Music in the Ancient World* (New York, 1941), p. 78.

that the conjunction of the finger and thumb in the so-called 'hand-signs' may be no more than the physical prelude to the 'tick-tack' or finger snap.[1] It is likely, however, that Sachs rightly interprets the position of the hand of the singer which is placed at the side of the head[2] as the Eastern custom of compressing the larynx so as to force the high notes,[3] as we have seen in Mesopotamia,[4] and the shrill high-pitched voice (*ḥy*) was much admired in the East.[5]

In 1949 and 1952 Hans Hickmann developed this chironomic theory. In his first paper, *Sur les survivances de la chironomie égyptienne dans le chant liturgique copte*, he shows that a system of chironomy exists today in this church, but no evidence is produced of its earlier usage by this church. In the second paper, *La Musique polyphonique dans l'Égypte ancienne*, the author demonstrates the probability of 'accords'—the octave and dominant—on the harp by other means than those mentioned by Sachs. Further, he shows that the chironomic conjunction of the thumb and forefinger by the singer conveyed to the accompanist on the flute or harp that he was to play the tonic, whilst the vertical open hand signified the dominant. Why a singer should have to convey such signs to an accompanist to obtain such elementary musical accomplishments is not explained.[6]

Besides these performers there were the female musicians who swarmed into social life soon after the rise of the 18th dynasty (*c.* 1570 B.C.). The court of the king and the palaces of the nobility were replete with these newcomers from Syrian and other Semitic lands; they belonged to the harem. Under the Old Kingdom we read of the 'chief of the singers' who was also 'chief of the harem', and we even know their names, but under the new dispensation their responsibilities must have been far greater in this control of what was known as the 'beautiful pleasures of the king'.[7] A most intimate scene is revealed during the 18th dynasty in a bird's-eye view of a palatial academy of music, with harps, kitharas, and pandores crowding out the furniture of the apartments. Here we espy these 'singing-girls' being instructed in the vocal and instrumental art.[8] There were

[1] L. Borchardt, *Denkmäler des alten Reiches*, i (Berlin, 1927), pl. 47.
[2] M. E. Grébaut, *Le Musée égyptien* (Cairo, 1890–1900), p. 25, pl. xxvi.
[3] Sachs, *The Rise of Music*, p. 78.
[4] See Chap. V, p. 238.
[5] *Revue égyptologique*, xii, p. 8.
[6] *Annales du Service des Antiquités de l'Égypte*, xlix (1949); *Bulletin de l'Institut d'Égypte*, xxxiv (1952).
[7] A. Mariette, *Les Mastabas de l'ancien empire* (Paris, 1881).
[8] N. de G. Davies, op. cit. vi, p. 20; pls. xxviii, xxxvi.

even independent academies of music, since we are told that the finest of these was at Memphis.[1]

What it was that these damsels of the 'beautiful face' sang we know in one respect, for thanks to the labours of Maspero, Max Müller, and Baillet, we are at least able to scan the lines of the verses, though not a note of music is vouchsafed to us. If the music were comparable to the verse, then it was most praiseworthy, since almost every human chord is touched in these beautiful songs, and with an artistry of expression that is superb. The 'Song of the Harper', first crooned at the funerary rites of the priest Nefer-ḥetep millennia ago, is known the world over. Who can forget the lines:[2]

> Let there be music and singing before thee,
> Cast behind thee all cares, and mind thee of joy,
> Till there cometh that day,
> When we journey to that land that loveth silence.

There were instruments in abundance to accompany singers and dancers. Every conceivable type known in the ancient world found its place in ancient Egypt. Kitharas and harps of all shapes and sizes, with flutes and reed-pipes of equal diversity, and manifold drums, tambourines, and crotala. When the world was young, under the Old Kingdom (third millennium B.C.), a harp, a flute, and a reed-pipe, handled by males, were deemed sufficient with singers,[3] but with the bevies of Oriental singing-girls that had been brought into Egypt, the male performer seems to have been overshadowed. Still, the latter remained, it would seem, the mainstay of the music of the people, as the picture of the blind harper and his seven blind singers seems to prove.[4] From the time of the Saite period, the male musician probably regained his prestige.

Herodotus visited Egypt about 440 B.C. The Egyptians, he says, like the Spartans, followed the trades and professions of their fathers, so that a musician would naturally be the son of a musician.[5] Another statement concerns a national song called the *Manerōs* which, he said, had been known to the Egyptians from time immemorial. 'It was the first and only song that they used at that early period of their

[1] S. Birch, *The Anastasi Papyri in the British Museum* (London, 1843). For music as a profession see H. Hickmann, 'Le Métier de musicien au temps des Pharaons', in *Cahiers d'histoire égyptienne*, sér. iv. (Le Caire, 1952), pp. 79 ff.

[2] Erman, op. cit., pp. 385 ff. See also *The Cambridge Ancient History*, i, pp. 324 ff., and *Journal of Near Eastern Studies*, iv, pp. 178–212.

[3] Lepsius, op. cit. iii, figs. 35–36.

[4] Wilkinson, op. cit. ii, p. 239; fig. 193.

[5] vi, 60.

history.' It was identical with the Linus song which he had heard in Phoenicia, Cyprus, and elsewhere, and he was surprised to find it in Egypt.[1] Of supreme importance is the testimony of his later contemporary, Plato, who is said to have studied in Egypt. It will be recalled that the Athenian guest in Plato's *Laws*, in laying down plans for the education of youth, pointed out that in Egypt only the highest art and the best music were permitted, and that such were approved by the temple. No deviation, it was said, was permitted from the established forms in art and music, to which principle Plato heartily subscribed.[2] The statement reveals that in spite of its political troubles, Egypt still maintained a musical standard that was marvelled at by others.

However far-fetched the lengthy panegyric of Callixenus of Rhodes may be, as retailed by Athenaeus at a later period, one cannot forbear to cite that 'choral band of six hundred men', among whom were 300 harpers performing together on gilded harps. That was in the days of Ptolemy Philadelphus (285–246 B.C.).[3] Nor was the flair for music to be found only in courtly and patrician circles, since one of the interlocutors in the dialogues of Athenaeus remarks:

> I would have you know . . . that there is no record in the history of other people more musical than the Alexandrians, and I am not speaking merely of singing to the harp, for even the humblest layman among us . . . can immediately detect the mistakes which occur in striking the notes.

He then goes on to dilate on the number of flutes and reed-pipes, four at least, with which the Alexandrians were familiar.[4] One of Egypt's later rulers, Ptolemy Auletes (81–52 B.C.), the reputed father of the great Cleopatra, was addicted to piping, hence his name.[5] In the palace concerts he contested with the professional musicians for supremacy.[6]

Diodorus Siculus, writing a few years later, avers that music was not, in those days, a part of normal education, since it was thought not only useless but morally injurious, in that it created effeminacy.[7] Whether this is strictly true of the classes as a whole is doubtful. Yet that such a puritanical view existed in Egypt at this time is not improbable. Indeed the word *šenı*ʻ ('to sing') came to mean something unrighteous ('to be perverse', 'to corrupt').[8] Such protests, probably by the few, would have had little sway with the people at large.

[1] ii. 79. Strabo says (XVII. i. 52) that Herodotus talked 'much nonsense'. Cf. Plutarch, *Isis and Osiris*, 379.

[2] *Laws*, 657.

[3] Athenaeus, v. 201–2.

[4] Ibid. iv. 176.

[5] J. P. Mahaffy, *The Empire of the Ptolemies* (London, 1895), pp. 429 ff.

[6] Strabo, op. cit. VII, i. 11.

[7] i. 81.

[8] *Journal asiatique* (Mars-Avril, 1908), pp. 263, 266. Cf. the Coptic *tchoome*.

Whether it was taught or not, music was the heritage of all, and social life, from the cradle to the grave, called for it. Between those two events, almost every phase of life demanded music of some sort, and we still possess the papyrus contract of a musician who was engaged in Egypt, nearly 2,000 years ago, to play with his fellows for the delight of those who cried: 'Let there be music and singing!'[1]

If we turn to military music, we see the trumpeter and drummer at their duties, summoning the troops, sounding them past the saluting point, or inciting them to battle.[2] If we look at the toilers, we have the opportunity of reading the words at least of a shepherd's song of the twenty-fifth century B.C., a thresher's song of the sixteenth century B.C.,[3] as well as the sedan-chair bearer's song,[4] and others.[5] We probably see what sufficed for the crowd on a papyrus in the British Museum which depicts a 'march of the animals' to the droning of a double reed-pipe,[6] whilst one of the Tell al-Amarna scenes shows us what joy emerged in country dancing,[7] all of which may be seen today by the banks of the Nile. Not a note of the actual music that was played or sung has come down to us.

Under the Old Kingdom, perhaps the days of a more indigenous art, dances were possessed of a gravity and seriousness that does not appear in those of the New Kingdom, which had been spiced with Oriental fashions. One of the most expressive dance scenes in Egyptian art remains is that reproduced by Champollion,[8] Rosellini,[9] and Wilkinson,[10] in which the graceful attitudinizing shows an unmistakably spacious solemn rhythm. How different is the tempo on the Saqqara bas-relief, now at Cairo. Here the pace of the dancers is fast and furious.[11] The larger deep-toned tambourine of rectangular shape has been cast aside, and its place has been taken by a smaller circular instrument, of which the higher-pitched 'tap' is more in accord with the sharper click of the accompanying clappers.

INSTRUMENTS OF MUSIC

Idiophones occur in the earliest Egyptian art remains. On archaic pottery (fourth millennium B.C.) are delineated clappers with curved

[1] *Journal of Egyptian Archaeology*, x (1924), p. 145.
[2] Wilkinson, op. cit., pp. 260–9; Champollion, op. cit. iii, pls. ccix, ccxviii.
[3] Erman, op. cit., pp. 385 ff.
[4] N. de G. Davies, *The Rock Tombs of Deir el Gebrâwi*, 2 vols. (London, 1902), i, p. 11.
[5] *Mélanges Maspero: Orient ancien* i (Paris, 1934), pp. 133 ff.
[6] Erman, op. cit., p. 369.
[7] Lepsius, op. cit., vi, pl. 104.
[8] Op. cit. ii, pl. clxxv.
[9] *I Monumenti dell' Egitto* (Pisa, 1832–4), pl. xcviii.
[10] Op. cit. ii, fig. 236.
[11] L. Borchardt, *Kunstwerke aus dem Ägyptischen Museum zu Cairo* (Cairo, n.d.), pl. 28; Erman, op. cit., p. 249.

blades,[1] and these persist as late as the 18th dynasty (*c.* 1570 B.C.) at least.[2] The wand type of clapper is observed in the 5th dynasty (twenty-fourth century B.C.).[3] What we nowadays call the 'bones' are to be seen under the New Kingdom (*c.* 1570 B.C.).[4] Another kind, clashing maces, were popular during the 6th dynasty (*c.* 2300 B.C.) and later.[5] These concussive instruments may have been called *iḥy* and *na'ṯaḫi*, the latter word being possibly cognate with the Hebrew *nāṣach.* In addition to these were artificial hands and feet in bone, wood, or ivory, which were beaten together in the same way as hand-clapping, a practice known in Egyptian as *ma'ḥ*,[6] a word identical with the Hebrew *mācha.* Innumerable specimens of these artificial hand and feet clappers are to be found in museums.[7]

Sistra of various kinds were known, and in these particular types we may have indigenous productions. One kind, the *śeḫem*, had a body of pottery or wood with jingling plates inserted.[8] We see it in the 6th dynasty (*c.* 2300 B.C.).[9] A more sonorous kind was the *šeš*, *seš*, or *sešše t*, which had a metal body with jingling metal bars inserted.[10] Both types are to be seen in museums,[11] and in art remains,[12] down to Roman times. Cymbals of the plate type were of late intrusion, although the cup type is probably to be recognized on a figurine of the Greek period (332–30 B.C.).[13] Clapper cymbals also occur in actual specimens of the Graeco-Roman period.[14] Bells of all kinds are plentiful.[15]

Membranophones are well represented in actual specimens and art remains. Cylindrical,[16] as well as squat and elongated barrel-shaped

[1] D. Randall-MacIver and C. Mace, *El Amra and Abydos* (London, 1902), pl. xiv.

[2] J. J. Tylor and F. L. Griffith, *The Tomb of Paheri at El Kab* (London, 1894).

[3] Lepsius, op. cit. ii, pl. 56*a*.

[4] Borchardt, op. cit., pl. 28.

[5] W. M. Flinders Petrie, *Dedasheh* (London, 1898), p. 8; pl. xii; N. de G. Davies, *The Tomb of Antefoḳer* (London, 1920), p. xxiii.

[6] J. de Morgan, *Fouilles à Dachour en 1894–95* (Vienna, 1903), pl. xxv.

[7] Loret, op. cit., p. 5, figs. 10–12.; Sachs, *Die Musikinstrumente*, pl. i.

[8] E. A. W. Budge, *An Egyptian Hieroglyphic Dictionary* (London, 1920), pp. 616, 754. Cf. Sachs, *Die Musikinstrumente*, pp. 28 ff., and *History of Musical Instruments* (New York, 1940), pp. 89 ff. Cf. Hickmann, *Catalogue*, pp. 76–77, for classification.

[9] Flinders Petrie, *Dendereh* (London, 1900), pl. x.

[10] Champollion, op. cit. iii, pl. cclxxxi.

[11] Wilkinson, op. cit. ii, pp. 325 ff.; Sachs, *Die Musikinstrumente*, pls. 3–5.

[12] Lepsius, op. cit. vii, pls. 175, 186, 193; viii, pl. 247.

[13] C. Engel, *Music of the Most Ancient Nations* (London, 1870), p. 227.

[14] Loret, op. cit., p. 7; Sachs, *Die Musikinstrumente*, pl. i.

[15] Sachs, *Die Musikinstrumente*, pp. 23 ff., pl. i. Cf. Hickmann, *Catalogue général des instruments de musique du Musée du Caire* (Cairo, 1949), pp. 1–103 for all idiophones. This author has also made a separate study of bells in an article entitled 'Zur Geschichte der altägyptischen Glocken' in *Musik und Kirche* (Kassel, 1951), Heft 2.

[16] J. Garstang, *Burial Customs of Egypt* (London, 1907), fig. 155.

drums,[1] are preserved at Cairo and Paris, the former dating from the 12th dynasty (*c.* 1989 B.C.). The elongated form persisted up to the Saite period (*c.* 664–525 B.C.), if not later.[2] There was also a hand kettledrum, so well known from Champollion's design,[3] which dates from the 18th dynasty, as well as the vase-shaped *darabukka* type, and the cylindrical body form, often found in the hands of the god Bes, which was probably the drum called *qemqem*.[4] The generic name for the drum was *teben* (Akkad. *ṭabālu*). Budge thought that *a'seh* stood for the squat barrel-shaped drum. The tambourine or frame drum was known as the *ser* or *śer*, a large example of which, not unlike the supposed *alal* of Mesopotamia, was used in Egypt at the Temple of the Sun at Abusir (twenty-sixth century B.C.). Even later, at the time of Osorkon II (*c.* 800 B.C.), we see a tambourine over 2 feet in diameter being used,[5] although Borchardt, who devoted an article to the tambourine, suggested—wrongly—that this was a gong.[6] A more portable instrument of the 18th dynasty is shown by Champollion in the picture just mentioned, while an even smaller specimen found favour during the Greek period.[7] Under the New Kingdom (*c.* 1570 B.C.) a large rectangular tambourine, with concave sides, appeared.[8] It is also seen in a bronze figure of the time of Amenḥetep IV (*c.* 1377 B.C.).[9] Specimens are conserved in museums.

Among the woodwind, the earliest example of the upright, end-blown flute is figured on a predynastic (fourth millennium B.C.) palette.[10] In spite of opinions to the contrary, the flute may have been known as the *seba'* or *seby*, in which case we recognize its progeny in the Coptic *sêbe* and *sêbi*.[11] Normally *seb* or *seba'* means 'to play [a flute or reed-pipe]'. This instrument is often found during the Old

[1] Wilkinson, op. cit. ii, pp. 264–70; figs. 202–4.

[2] G. Maspero, *Le Musée égyptien* (Cairo, 1907), pls. xl, xli.

[3] Champollion, op. cit. ii, pl. clxxxvi.

[4] See Hickmann, 'La Daraboukkah', in the *Bulletin de l'Institut d'Égypte*, xxxiii (Cairo, 1952), pp. 229 ff., for this and similar drums.

[5] E. Naville, *The Festival-Hall of Osorkon II* (London, 1892), pp. 14, 24, 26; pls. xi, xiv, xvi.

[6] Borchardt, *Mélanges Maspero, Orient ancien*, i (Cairo, 1934), pp. 1–6.

[7] W. Weber, *Mitteilungen aus der ägyptischen Abteilung der Königl. Museen zu Berlin* (Berlin, 1914), pl. 24.

[8] Champollion, op. cit. ii, pl. clxxxvi; Kinsky, *Geschichte der Musik in Bildern* (Leipzig, 1929), p. 5.

[9] A. Weigall, *Ancient Egyptian Works of Art* (London, 1924), p. 152. The instrument has been fully described by Hans Hickmann in 'Miscellanea Musicologica', x, 'Le Tambourin rectangulaire du Nouvel Empire' (*Annales du Service des Antiquités de l'Égypte*, li (Cairo, 1951), pp. 317 ff.).

[10] J. E. Quibell and F. W. Green, *Hierakonpolis*, ii (London, 1903), pl. 28.

[11] See Loret, op. cit., pp. 14 ff. and *Journal asiatique* (juil.–août, 1889), pp. 121–33, but cf. Sachs, *The History of Musical Instruments*, p. 90.

and Middle Kingdoms (third–second millennia B.C.).[1] Some of these flutes were from 4 to 5 feet in length. Two other types of flutes, doubtless of Semitic origin,[2] were the *wa'yr* and the *wa'di*, mentioned in connexion with Ptolemy Auletes (81–52 B.C.).[3] The *wa'yr*, *wa'ra'*, or *wa'r*, is possibly cognate with the Arabic *yarā'*, which was a recorder.[4] The *wa'di*, *wa'd'ai*, or *wa'deni* is likely to have been the instrument called by the Greeks the *photinx*.[5]

The reed-pipe seems to have been known as the *ma'* (Old Kingdom), *met* or *ma'*, although the term was applied to any woodwind instrument.[6] This reed-pipe may be discerned as early as the 4th dynasty (twenty-sixth century B.C.).[7] The double reed-pipe is shown in both the parallel and the angular forms. Loret once hinted,[8] that this instrument may have been the *is* or *isit* (lit. 'reed'), but he later abandoned this identification.[9] E. Brunner-Traut has now given the name *a'a't* to this type. Under the New Kingdom the parallel form was superseded by the angular, most likely under Oriental prompting.[10] It frequently appears in the art remains,[11] and on a wall painting in the British Museum one can plainly distinguish the embouchure reeds.[12] Actual specimens are fairly plentiful in museums, and their scales have been made the subject of special studies by several musicologists.[13] Statuettes demonstrate the popularity of the instrument down to the Christian era.[14]

The animal horn was the *'ab*, *'abw*, and *deb*, but there is no evidence of its use under these names as a wind-instrument, although we have seen wooden horns or trumpets being presented to Amen-ḥetep III by the Mitanni ruler Dushratta (*c.* 1380 B.C.).[15] On the other hand,

[1] Lepsius, op. cit. ii, pls. 36, 52, 61, 74; A. M. Blackman, *The Royal Tombs of Meir* (London, 1915), p. 12; pl. xxi, 2. See pl. 9 (*a*).

[2] Erman, op. cit., p. 516.

[3] S. Birch, *The Anatasi Papyri in the British Museum*, iv (London, 1843), pl. xii. See also A. H. Gardiner, *Egyptian Hieratic Texts* (Leipzig, 1909).

[4] H. G. Farmer, *Studies in Oriental Musical Instruments* (London, 1931), i, p. 64; A. Chottin, *Tableau de la musique marocaine* (Paris, 1939), pl. xvi. *Līra = al-yarā'*.

[5] Athenaeus, *Deipnosophistes*, iv. 175, 182; *Journal asiatique* (juil.–août, 1889), p. 133; K. Sethe, *Zeitschrift für ägyptische Sprache*, xlv (1908), p. 85.

[6] Cf. A. H. Gardiner, *Egyptian Grammar* (Oxford, 1927), p. 525; E. Brunner-Traut, *Der Tanz im alten Ägypten* (Gluckstadt, 1938), p. 17.

[7] Lepsius, op. cit. iii, pl. 36.

[8] *Journal asiatique* (juil.–août, 1889), p. 133.

[9] *Encyclopédie de la musique*, 1re partie, i, p. 15.

[10] Ibid., p. 16.

[11] Wilkinson, op. cit. ii, pp. 232, 234–5, 312. See pl. 9 (*b*).

[12] Erman, op. cit., facing p. 250.

[13] See Bibliography.

[14] Sachs, *Die Musikinstrumente*, p. 80. See Hickmann, 'Classement et classification des flûtes, clarinettes et hautbois de l'Égypte ancienne' in *La Chronique d'Égypte*, xxvie année (Bruxelles, 1951), pp. 17 ff.

[15] J. A. Knudtzon, *Die El-Amarna Tafeln* (Leipzig, 1908), pp. 155 ff.

the straight metal trumpet is well represented in military and processional scenes during the New Kingdom and earlier.[1] It was also used in the cults; Eustathius (*Ad Iliadem*) attributes its invention to Osiris, and it was used in his worship as late as the third century A.D.[2] We cannot be sure of its Egyptian name but Eustathius says that the Greek *chnoue* was sounded to gather the congregation for the sacrifice, and this may well be the Greek pronunciation of the Egyptian *šneb*. It has been assumed that the Egyptians 'were not very successful' in making trumpets, the apparent authority being Plutarch;[3] yet the author of *De Iside et Osiride* merely states that the inhabitants of Busiris and Lycopolis did not permit the use of the trumpet because its sound resembled the braying of an ass.[4] This veto had nothing to do with any supposed Egyptian imperfection in the trumpet as such; it was because the evil god Typhon was considered to have all the attributes of the ass. Cairo possesses among its museum treasures a silver and a copper trumpet, both with gold mountings, from the tomb of Tut-anḫ-amen,[5] which have been played in modern times and sound quite brilliant.

The *hydraulus*, the so-called water organ, was invented by Ctesibius of Alexandria (*fl.* 246–221 B.C.),[6] the son of a barber who lived in the quarter of the Aspendia. Clément Loret's researches on the *hydraulus* are summarized in his son's study of the musical instruments of ancient Egypt in Lavignac's *Encyclopédie de la musique*,[7] but the instrument is usually allocated to colonial Greece, which also claims another Egyptian writer on the hydraulus, Hero of Alexandria (*fl.* A.D. 150).[8]

The chordophones of ancient Egypt are even more interesting than those of ancient Mesopotamia, because their morphological development can be discerned with greater clarity over several millennia. The upright lower-chested harp goes back iconographically to the 4th dynasty (twenty-sixth century B.C.) at the very least. At Gizeh we

[1] Lepsius, op. cit. ii, pl. cxii; iii, pls. ccix, ccxviii.
[2] Sachs, *Die Musikinstrumente*, p. 89.
[3] Reese, *Music in the Middle Ages* (New York, 1940), p. 7.
[4] *Isis and Osiris*, 362.
[5] H. Carter, *The Tomb of Tut-ankh-Amen*, ii (London, 1927), pp. 19, 30; pl. 2.
[6] Paul Tannery in *Revue des études grecques*, ix (1896), pp. 23 ff., xxi (1908), pp. 326 ff.
[7] 1re partie, i, pp. 30–34.
[8] For the most complete description, see H. G. Farmer's *The Organ of the Ancient* (London, 1931).

espy the identical bow-harp predicated in Mesopotamia as the *ban* or *pan*, but in a form much nearer its days of puberty. At this early date, when it was known in Egypt as the *ben*, *bent*, or *bin*, *bint* (cf. Coptic *boini*, *oyoini*), it had a narrow and perfectly cylindrical crescent-shaped body with six strings (but seemingly seven pegs).[1] By the 5th dynasty, the lower end of this narrow cylindrical body had developed a definite hemispherical sound-chest.[2] From the 6th dynasty (*c.* 2300 B.C.) onwards, these forms seem to continue with but slight deviation, until we perceive the gradual widening of the body and sound-chest, from top to bottom, which became the recognized structure about the 12th dynasty (*c.* 1989 B.C.),[3] although earlier forms still appear from time to time even until the seventh century.[4] With the rise of the 18th dynasty a melioration and refinement of structure and purpose are clearly revealed, until by the time of Rameses III (*c.* 1200 B.C.), we have the superb so-called Bruce's harps.[5] In these two instruments, which stood over 6 feet high, furnished with ten (? eleven) and twelve (? thirteen) strings respectively, handsomely ornamented, we reach the apogee of harp construction in ancient Egypt,[6] although even taller instruments (7 feet high) had existed earlier.[7]

Meanwhile (*c.* 1989 B.C.), the ordinary smaller harps had changed their outline from the crescent to the semicircular,[8] a contour which lasted until the Christian era.[9] All the foregoing were played in the conventional way, i.e. standing on the ground, although in a few instances we find stands being used to raise the sound-chest from the floor.[10] The portable shoulder harp appeared very much later,[11] although its seemingly novel raised sound-chest dated back to early days.[12]

[1] Lepsius, op. cit. iii, pl. 36. In the art remains, strings and pegs often disagree.

[2] Flinders Petrie, *Dedasheh*, p. 8; pl. xii; Kinsky, *Geschichte der Musik in Bildern*, p. 4.

[3] Wilkinson, op. cit. ii, pp. 234 ff. See pl. 9 (*a*) and (*b*).

[4] N. de G. Davies, *The Rock Tombs of Deir el-Gebrâwi*, i, p. 15; pl. viii.

[5] J. Bruce, *Travels to Discover the Source of the Nile*, i (London, 1790), p. 127. He fancifully depicts them with thirteen and eighteen strings.

[6] Wilkinson, op. cit. ii, frontispiece. Cf. Rosellini, op. cit. ii, pl. xcvii, and Champollion, op. cit. iii, pl. cclxi, for the number of strings. Cf. Hickmann, 'Les harpes de la tombe de Ramsès II' in *Annales du Service des Antiquités de l'Égypte*, l (Cairo, 1950), pp. 523 ff.

[7] Champollion, op. cit. iv, pl. ccccix.

[8] Wilkinson, op. cit., pp. 238–9; P. E. Newberry, *Beni Hasan* (London, 1893), pl. xii.

[9] Sachs, *Die Musikinstrumente des alten Ägyptens*, p. 66; figs. 95*a*, 96.

[10] Wilkinson, op. cit. ii, figs. 185–6; Rosellini, ii, pl. lxxix.

[11] Wilkinson, op. cit. ii, figs. 209, 215; Champollion, op. cit., ii, pl. cxlii.

[12] Champollion, op. cit. iv, pl. ccccì.

Among other Oriental borrowings under the 18th dynasty was the upper-chested harp.[1] This, as we have seen in Mesopotamia, was simply the horizontal lower-chested harp turned sideways and with the angle made semi-acute.[2] We cannot be sure of its name, but it may have been the instrument called the *d̲a'd̲a't*, with a possible variant *d̲a'd̲a'newt*.[3] Delineations also date from this period,[4] and it continued to enjoy popularity right through the Greek period (332–30 B.C.).[5] Like the lower-chested harp, the face of the hollow sound-chest was covered with leather or parchment, a feature which may be noted in actual specimens or reproductions at Paris, Cairo, and New York,[6] on the first of which are twenty-two strings,[7] while a small wooden figurine in the British Museum carries but six strings on the instrument. By the time of Euergetes II (second century B.C.) the sound-chest had become an acute angle.[8]

Older still was the kithara, which was also of exotic origin.[9] We first discern it in the 12th dynasty about the year 1890 B.C., in the famous Beni Hasan pictures. These represent Bedouin called the 'Aa'mu (Arabic *'amm* = 'men of a tribe') who, under their shaikh, Abšai, i.e. Abū Shahī, go to Egypt to pay tribute to a certain Prince Henem-ḥetep.[10] Among the shaikh's retainers is a kitharist, and perhaps the shaikh himself was called Abū Shahī ('Father of Pleasantry') because of his esteem for music, since the Arabs give this nickname to the lute itself.[11] This scene shows a plain, rectangular folk kithara which is played with a plectrum.[12] It is held with the strings lying horizontally, a custom which continued for centuries, even when an

[1] Erman, op. cit., p. 253.

[2] See Chap. V, p. 243.

[3] A. H. Gardiner, *The Admonition of an Egyptian Sage* (Leipzig, 1909), pp. 7, 13; H. Brugsch, *Thesaurus Inscriptionum Aegyptiacarum* (Leipzig, 1881–91), p. 524. Cf. East-African *ze-ze*, and Hickmann, *Bulletin de l'Institut d'Égypte*, xxxv, pp. 361 ff.

[4] N. de G. Davies, *The Rock Tombs of El Amarna* (London, 1903–8), vi, pls. 6, 28.

[5] C. M. Kaufmann, *Graeco-ägyptische Koroplastik* (Leipzig, 1915), pls. 5, 58.

[6] Loret, op. cit., p. 29; *Catalogue of the Crosby Brown Collection of Musical Instruments*, iii (New York, 1906), p. 3.

[7] Wilkinson, Engel, and Chappell show the instrument with twenty-one strings, but with twenty-two tassel string ends.

[8] Champollion, op. cit. i, pl. li. Wilkinson's picture of this harp is given upside down, obviously the way in which it was displayed at Paris (cf. the tassels). This was copied by musicologists, including Engel and Chappell, for three-quarters of a century. Further currency was given to the blunder when Sir Laurence Alma-Tadema represented it thus in his well-known painting 'Pastime in Ancient Egypt'.

[9] Erman, op. cit., p. 253.

[10] The derivation of '*Aa'mu* is not settled.

[11] Ibn Ma'rūf, *Kanz al-lugha*, s.v. *shahī*.

[12] Lepsius, op. cit. iv, pl. 133; Wilkinson, op. cit. ii, pl. xiv; Rosellini, op. cit. i, p. xxviii.

asymmetrically shaped kithara had been adopted in the 18th dynasty (*c.* 1570 B.C.).[1] After a while, larger and more imposing instruments came into use, some with as many as fifteen strings, as in the satirical Turin papyrus (20th dynasty)[2] and other delineations.[3] Some were standing types as large as those of Mesopotamia.[4] A few portable specimens exist in museums at Leiden, Cairo, and Berlin.[5] Being a harp-like instrument, it was probably counted generically as a *ben* or *bent*, yet about 1200 B.C. it seems to have been given a distinctive name in *kena'na'wr*, a word strongly suggestive of the Hebrew *kinnōr* and the Arabic *kinnāra*, which possibly survived in the Coptic *qinêra*. There is no evidence of lyres, as distinct from kitharas, being adopted during the Greek period.[6]

Lastly comes the pandore or long-necked lute, whose Egyptian name has been the subject of so much pother (see pl. 9 (*b*)). Tempted by the ideogram *nefer* (good), which resembled the form of the pandore, and by the fact that 'f' and 'b', and 'r' and 'l' were interchangeable, some authorities considered the Egyptian *nefer* and the term *nebel* (instrument) of the Old Testament to be identical; ergo, the *nefer* was the pandore.[7] Although much has still to be said for the claim of identity, the theory has been abandoned.[8] The pandore may be of Oriental origin, since it does not occur prior to the New Kingdom (*c.* 1570 B.C.).[9] The sound-chests show the short oviform,[10] the long oviform,[11] and the periform,[12] with a belly of skin or parchment perforated with one large and several smaller sound-holes. The strings were not attached to pegs as in the harps, but to tasselled tuning thongs. The pandore continued to be favoured until the Graeco-Roman periods, and the old Egyptian types are still popular in North

[1] Wilkinson, op. cit. ii, pp. 235, 291; Kinsky, op. cit., p. 5.

[2] Chappell, *The History of Music* (London, 1874), p. 399.

[3] Sachs, *Die Musikinstrumente*, figs. 53, 63.

[4] J. G. Wilkinson, op. cit. ii, p. 281; N. de G. Davies, *The Rock Tombs of El Amarna*, ii, pls. v, xxxiii; vi, pls. xxviii, xxxvi.

[5] *Revue musicale* (1907), p. 337; Wilkinson, op. cit. ii, p. 293; Sachs, *Die Musikinstrumente*, pls. 6–8. Hickmann, *Catalogue*, pls. xciii, ff.

[6] Cf. Reese, op. cit., p. 7, and the terminology of Hickmann, *Catalogue*, p. 153.

[7] This was Burney's premise, which was accepted everywhere after Champollion (*Dictionnaire égyptien*, 1841) had laid it down that *nefer* was 'une sorte de Théorbe'.

[8] Scepticism began with Petrie (*Medum*, 1892, p. 29); he was followed by F. Ll. Griffith, N. de G. Davies, and Loret, until Petrie (*The Wisdom of the Egyptians*, London, 1940, pp. 59 ff.) himself gave the *coup de grâce*.

[9] Cf. C. Sachs, *History of Musical Instruments*, p. 102.

[10] Wilkinson, op. cit. ii, pl. xii; figs. 187–8, 191, 205, 222–3.

[11] Wilkinson, ii, figs. 221, 229; N. E. Scott, 'The Lute of the Singer Ḥar-Mosĕ' in *Bulletin: Metropolitan Museum of Art*, ii (New York, 1944), pp. 159–63).

[12] Wilkinson, op. cit. ii, p. 303; J. Capart, *Documents pour servir à l'étude de l'art égyptien*, ii (Paris, 1927–31), pl. 91.

Africa today under the name *ganābir* (sing. *gunbrī*),[1] with two or three strings[2] as in ancient Egypt.[3]

Looking back over nearly three millennia of iconographic material, in which instruments of music have been delineated so profusely with such great care, one cannot help being amazed by the diverse structures, the neatness of design, the clearness of detail, and the almost methodical portrayal of instrumental technique in ancient Egypt. In the wider use of these instruments, Egypt surpassed Mesopotamia a hundredfold and it is no wonder that Greece sang its praises.

THE PRACTICE AND THEORY OF MUSIC

As we saw at the outset, what was envisaged by the Egyptians when they listened to music was affected by, or was subject to, the influence of *ḥeka*' or *ḥike* ('spell'). Like the *ṣūfī* of medieval Islam, or the Maulawiyya dervish fraternity at Cairo today, the Egyptians of old did not hear 'music', but only 'sounds', and the latter were but a symbol of something else. One imagines that this interpretation obtained generally, even under purely festive conditions. Music, as we understand it, was simply one of the concomitant joys of life inseparable from floriage, feasting, and fragrance. A sidelight on this collateral appreciation is thrown by the sound-chest of the harp, which is sometimes fashioned to represent a lotus in bloom. Thus, before a note was struck, the instrument spelt 'joy'. Yet in spite of these esoteric doctrines, the practice and technique of music seems to have been quite exoteric, seemingly very little different from our conceptions.

A few instrumental features deserve notice. The large plectrum for the cithara in use by the *badāwī* 'Aa'mu must be compared with the delicate implement between the finger and thumb of the graceful pandorist on a tomb picture,[4] or the even smaller one, no larger than that of the modern mandoline, at another tomb.[5] These plectra are attached to a cord lest they be lost. Observe also the seeming affectation of the pandorists who occasionally strike the strings above the

[1] Ibn Baṭṭūta, *Tuḥfat al-nuẓẓār*, iv (Paris, 1853–9), p. 406. See also Farmer, 'Ṭunbūr' in the *Encyclopaedia of Islām* and paper in the *Transactions: Glasgow University Oriental Society*, v (1930), pp. 26 ff.

[2] Farmer, *Studies in Oriental Musical Instruments*, i (London, 1931), pp. 39–49.

[3] The Egyptians used up to four strings. See Champollion, op. cit. ii, pl. clix, and Wilkinson, op. cit. ii, pl. xii. For the 'accordage' of Egyptian stringed instruments see Hickmann, 'Miscellanea musicologica' in *Annales du Service des Antiquités de l'Égypte*, xlviii (Cairo, 1947), pp. 646 ff.

[4] Erman, *Life in Ancient Egypt*, p. 214.

[5] N. de G. Davies, *The Tomb of Nakht at Thebes* (New York, 1917), frontispiece and pp. 57 ff.

sound-chest instead of at the bridge, in order to obtain a subdued effect, a custom still practised in the Occident. Tricks or dexterities were also indulged in, and a wall-painting in the British Museum shows a female reed-piper fingering the *dextra* pipe with the left hand and the *sinistra* pipe with the right.

The gradual development of the sound-chest in the harp shows early recognition of the principle that loudness equates with amplitude. The adoption of a taut skin, later parchment, as the belly of the sound-chest of the harp and pandore, reveals the taste of the Egyptians for what we should term a 'banjo timbre'. The strings of different lengths on their harps were the natural outcome of the adoption in primitive times of the bow-harp, which we know existed in Mesopotamia and Egypt in the third millennium B.C. Obviously these people must have recognized that the length of a string, other things being equal, determined the pitch of the sound, a principle which Pythagoras is said to have introduced into Greece. Yet Helmholtz once remarked that 'if, as is possible, his [Pythagoras's] knowledge was partly derived from Egyptian priests, it is impossible to conjecture in what remote antiquity this law was first known'.[1] We have seen, however, from the above dates, that this principle was recognized by both Mesopotamia and Egypt at least two millennia before the dawn of Greek civilization, and it was in these lands that Pythagoras had studied both mathematics and musical theory.[2]

How much of this knowledge of the theory of sound, and its application to vibrating string lengths and a column of air in tube lengths was indigenous? Carl Engel once said: 'There can scarcely be any doubt that the Egyptians, like the Greeks, possessed written dissertations on the theory of music.'[3] In the absence of documents this attitude is quite inadmissible. Yet it is pardonable for several reasons. That there existed a Greek or Syriac version of a treatise on the theory of music attributed to Hermes, which was known in an Arabic translation during the Middle Ages, is hinted by Arabic and Persian authorities;[4] and while 'Hermetic' works were not necessarily from the hand of Hermes, or the person to whom this name was given—the label was attached to any anonymous Pythagorean, Neo-Platonic, or similar writing—still, Hermes was a name with which to conjure in the realm of music, since he was claimed as the 'inventor

[1] *Sensations of Tone* (London, 1895), p. 1.
[2] Iamblichus, *De vita Pythagorae*, iv.
[3] Op cit., p. 237.
[4] Farmer, *The Sources of Arabian Music* (Bearsden, 1940), p. 29 (= *Records of the Glasgow Bibliographical Society* (1939), vi.)

of music'[1] and the 'first to observe the orderly arrangement of the stars and the harmony of musical sounds and their natures',[2] which was the very pivot of the religious conceptions of the ancient Egyptians. However, no such books on the theory of music have come down to us from ancient Egypt. Whether those 'Egyptian books' which were among the original Alexandrian libraries of Ptolemy Philadelphus (309–246 B.C.) and Ptolemy Euergetes I (246–221 B.C.) contained treatises on music, we have no knowledge. However, it is clear enough that Egyptians had such knowledge of musical theory, as we shall see presently.

Just as in ancient Mesopotamia apparently, music was thought to belong to things that were anterior to experience. As a result of this belief, each note of music not only had a particular cosmic value,[3] but a magic potency,[4] a circumstance which almost implies the existence of modal formulas. It will be recalled that Plato's Athenian guest said when commenting on the educational system of the Egyptians:[5]

> What they ordained about music is right; and it deserves consideration that they were able to make laws about things of this kind, firmly establishing such melody as was fitted to rectify the perverseness of nature.

From the whole passage one may readily conclude that a modal system was in vogue in Egypt which was approved by the temples and so became a fixed and immutable law. We know that certain modes or modal motives of a fixed character called *nomoi* (lit. 'laws') were current in Greece, the strict use and interpretation of which were rigorously enforced. By Plato's time, the 'pleasure-seeking' crowd were setting these at naught, and that was why Plato praised the Egyptian practice of strict adherence to what was 'lawful' in music. It must be admitted, however, that the tenets of Plato and the Egyptians were prejudicial to the progress of art but, as the former says, they were beneficial to the State, since where there was licence in music there was likely to be laxity in morality.

What these modalities or modal motives were in ancient Egypt there is no record, no more than there is of the *nomoi* of Greece. One is inclined to believe that if music was regularized by the priests there must have been a norm, since no canonical standard could have

[1] Plutarch, *Isis and Osiris*, 352.

[2] Diodorus Siculus, i. 16.

[3] Maspero, *Études de mythologie*, i, p. 106.

[4] Cumont, *Astrology and Religion among the Greeks and Romans* (New York, 1912), p. 30.

[5] *Laws*, 657.

existed without rule. Yet rules can be observed without being written. On the other hand, the rather late testimony of Clement of Alexandria (second century A.D.) may not come amiss, for his authorities may have been early.[1] He says that among the innumerable books of the 'thrice greatest Hermes' were two for the 'Chanter' in the Egyptian temple which dealt with hymns of the gods and the regulation of the king's life.[2] These may have contained modal directions, seeing that such were obvious desiderata in temple chanting, and some of the art remains show the lector-priest ('precentor') with such a book in his hand.[3]

In recalling the view of Maspero that each note of music possessed an inherent character,[4] one is reminded of the assertion of pseudo-Demetrius Phalerius (first century A.D.) which almost confirms the above. He says: 'In Egypt, the priests hymn the gods through the seven sounds [lit. "vowels"] in direct succession.'[5] The perpetual iconographical incidence in the early period of seven-stringed harps, and the occasional occurrence of seven harpists and seven flautists may have significance as cosmic affinity.[6] Indeed the earliest hint of music theory *per se* in ancient Egypt, which occurs in Dio Cassius (*c.* A.D. 150–235), most certainly has an astrological bearing. He tells us, in his usual credulous way, that it was the tetrachord which gave birth to the names of the days of the week. A series of fourths, he says, were taken from Saturn thus: *E* [Saturn] to *A* gave the Sun; *A* to *d* gave the Moon; *d* to *g* gave Mars; *g* to *c'* gave Mercury; *c'* to *f'* gave Jupiter; *f'* to *b''* gave Venus; and thus it was that the names of the days of the week, Saturday, Sunday, Monday, and so on, came to us. This recital, of what Dio Cassius calls the 'musical connection with the arrangements of the heavens', would be hardly worth the telling did he not state that the idea originated in Egypt, 'but is now found among all mankind, though its adoption has been comparatively recent; at any rate the ancient Greeks never understood it, so far as I am aware'.[7] In any case, this proceeding is just what one would expect from the Egyptian priests who, as Diodorus Siculus affirms, were the first to make a scientific observation of the stars.[8] Indeed, if the origin of the mathematical arts,[9] especially geometry,[10] is to be allowed to Egypt, and if a high skill in arithmetic[11]

[1] Much of his other material can be traced to older sources.
[2] *Stromateis*, vi. 4.
[3] Erman, op. cit., pl. between pp. 320–1; Rosellini, op. cit., pl. cxxxii.
[4] Op. cit. i, p. 106.
[5] *De Elocutione*, 7.
[6] Loret, *Encyclopédie*, I. i, p. 25.
[7] xxxvii. 18.
[8] i. 50.
[9] Aristotle, *Metaphysics*, 981.
[10] Proclus, *Commentary on Euclid*, bk. i.
[11] Plato, *Laws*, 819.

is also to be counted to her credit, it would certainly be passing strange that the fourth group of the *quadrivium* should not have thriven as vigorously there also, as one is tempted to believe from the remarks of Philo Judaeus.[1]

From Dio Cassius it is clear that Egypt was conversant with the so-called Pythagorean system in the second century A.D., and there is no reason why it should not be assumed that it was practised there before the time of Pythagoras who was *in statu pupillari* possibly when he studied in this land *c.* 547–525 B.C. That Josephus says that the Egyptian temple harpists were using a *trigōnon enarmonion* in his day (first century A.D.) is no argument against this assumption.[2]

Musicologists have tried to decide this question by appeal to the actual instruments that have come down to us, and much patient research has been made in this territory. Victor Loret investigated the string lengths on harps, though these by themselves (as he recognized) are insufficient data;[3] on the other hand, his contribution to the study of the digit holes on the woodwind is useful,[4] as are the researches of his confrères in this field.[5] Yet so far as one can see, the results lead us only into generalizations. Out of thirty-six instruments examined, dating from the 12th to the 22nd dynasty, only one could be classified as a 'many-toned' flute or reed-pipe, which the *Onomasticon* tells us the Egyptians possessed.[6] Erich von Hornbostel took pains to measure the frets on a pandore which had been delineated with such, but again the results were practically negative.[7]

Though we cannot solve the problem of the theory of music in ancient Egypt, we may still be able to answer the vexed question: 'Did harmony exist in ancient Egypt?' Many writers have answered in the affirmative. James Baikie says that 'it seems out of question to suppose that these aggregates of instruments were designed only to multiply the melody', and so concludes that the existence of harmony is proved.[8] To this one can only reply that we see the same 'aggregates of instruments' which are 'multiplying the melody' in every Arabic-speaking land from the Pillars of Hercules to the Tigris without a vestige of harmony, as we understand the term, discernible.

[1] *Moses*, i. 23.
[2] Cf. Nicomachus, in Meibom, ii, pp. 36, 38.
[3] Loret, *Encyclopédie*, I. i, p. 24.
[4] Ibid., pp. 17–20.
[5] Hickmann, 'Fabrikationsmarken an altägyptischen Blasinstrumenten', *Die Musikforschung*, iii, pp. 241 ff.
[6] Pollux, *Onomasticon*, iv, 10.
[7] *Handbuch der Physik*, viii (Berlin, 1927), p. 435.
[8] *Encyclopaedia of Religion and Ethics*, ix (Edinburgh, 1917), pp. 33–34.

To more purpose are the studies made by Curt Sachs who, in furtherance of his thesis of the pentatonic tuning of Mesopotamian harps, has adopted similar criteria in his study of the technique of Egyptian harpists. Taking seventeen representations of these harpists, he found that 'seven are striking a fourth chord, five a fifth chord, and five an octave chord; that is, taking for granted that the accordatura was pentatonic'.[1] From this it is argued that 'simultaneous consonances' and a 'pentatonic accordance' are indicated.

It has already been demonstrated:[2] (1) that simultaneity cannot be accepted as a criterion from the mere position of the digits on the strings; and (2) that arguments for a pentatonic tuning based on the assumptions of (1) are invalid. It is true that in many delineations of Egyptian harpists we are confronted with hands stretched far apart over the strings, a circumstance which prompts one to conclude that the notes played, whether simultaneously or otherwise, must be far apart in the intervallic sense. But what inferences are we to draw from those pictures in which the hands are shown to be close together, with digits on adjacent strings? To draw positive conclusions from either of these facts, especially when based on preconceived notions of tuning, is extremely hazardous if not fallacious.

In conclusion it may be said that, while harpists in Egypt may have sounded fourths, fifths, or octaves in playing, the practice was probably merely a heterophonic device, just as it is today in Islamic lands where it has been practised since the time of Al-Kindī (d. *c.* A.D. 874) if not earlier; but heterophony does not constitute harmony in the accepted connotation of the term.[3] The pentatonic system was pre-Pythagorean. That the former persisted after the latter had been established in Greece is quite understandable, but the heptatonic principle must have prevailed in Egypt long before it was accepted in Greece; at least that is what the Greeks themselves would lead us to believe. In any case, in historic (post-Pythagorean) times there is not the slightest indication in literature that there was any dissimilarity in this respect between the music of Egypt, Syria, and Greece.

THE LEGACY

Egyptians had a wide reputation as educators. Menecles, the historian of Barca (third century B.C.), recorded that 'the Alexandrians were the teachers of all the Greeks and barbarians at a time when the

[1] *The History of Musical Instruments* (New York, 1940), pp. 82, 94.
[2] See Chap. V, pp. 248–9, and Galpin, op. cit., p. 96.
[3] Farmer, *Historical Facts for the Arabian Musical Influence* (London, 1930), pp. 327–32; *The Legacy of Islām* (Oxford, 1931), p. 374.

entire system of education had broken down by reason of the continually recurring disturbances which took place in the period of Alexander's successors [post 323 B.C.]'.[1] Herodotus (*ca.* 484–425 B.C.) states that 'the Egyptians were the first to introduce solemn assemblies, processions, and litanies to the gods, all of which the Greeks were taught by them'.[2] Indeed, Diodorus Siculus would have us believe in even greater borrowings when he says that 'in general, . . . the Greeks appropriated to themselves the most renowned of both Egyptian heroes and gods'.[3] By the third century B.C. the spread of the cults of Isis and Serapis in Greece was vast.[4] The craze was extended to Rome where Tibullus the poet (*fl.* 54–19 B.C.) questioned the efficacy of the 'brazen sistra'. Yet Isis worship found votaries by the Rhine, the Danube, and the Seine, while even the Anglo-Saxons recognized the 'Egyptian days'. With these Egyptian cults went the liturgy, hymns, chanting, and above all the 'grief-compelling' sistra of which Lucan writes,[5] and it is from the western use of the latter that so many specimens have been preserved. Indeed the Isis temples in Europe continued a liturgy which was just as elaborate as in Egypt,[6] since both sistra and *tibiae* were still in use, although Clement of Alexandria adds harps (*psalteria*), cymbals, and drums.[7]

When the Greeks borrowed the Egyptian *seššět* they called it the *seistron* which, in turn, became the Latin *sistrum*. Among the woodwind of Egypt, one or two found acceptance in Greece. Julius Pollux says that the Greek *giglaros* was an Egyptian kind of *aulos*.[8] Athenaeus tells us much about Egyptian flutes and pipes and says, on the authority of Juba, that 'the Egyptians call the *monaulos* an invention of Osiris, just as they do the *plagiaulos* which is named the *photinx* . . . which is peculiar to our country' [it is an Alexandrian who is speaking].[9] Later we are told that the 'lotus pipes' are what the Alexandrians call 'photinxes'; 'they are made of lotus, as it is called, which is a wood that grows in Libya'.[10] Yet Euripides, several centuries earlier, reveals that the 'sweet-sounding lotus [flute]' was a sacred instrument even in those days.[11]

There is also a slight suspicion that the 'foreign' harp used by the Greeks under the name of *phoinix* may have been the Greek vocaliza-

[1] Athenaeus, iv. 184. [2] ii. 58. [3] i. 23.
[4] W. H. Roscher, *Ausführliches Lexikon der griechischen und römischen Mythologie* (Leipzig, 1884–1901), s.v.
[5] *Pharsal.* viii. 832.
[6] Erman, *A Handbook of Egyptian Religion* (London, 1907), pp. 239–55.
[7] *Stromateis*, ii. 4.
[8] *Onomasticon*, iv. 10. [9] iv. 175.
[10] Ibid. 182. [11] *Bacchae*, line 160.

tion of the Egyptian *bainit* (= *bint*), rather than the accepted meaning of Phoenician [harp].[1] In Athenaeus, after the mention of several 'foreign' stringed instruments catalogued by Aristoxenus, the interlocutor referred to above boasts that 'the Alexandrians are well acquainted with all these instruments', and says that a fellow citizen of his, Alexander of Alexandria, 'gave a public recital with the instrument called the *trigon*, and sent all Rome into such a state of music-madness that most Romans can repeat his tunes'.[2] That Egyptian musicians, like the Syrian, were to be found in both Greece and Rome, is well evidenced. In later years this was partly due to the persecution of the Alexandrians by Ptolemy VII, when 'not a few' of them were sent into exile: philosophers, mathematicians, musicians, and other men of skill in their professions, who 'instructed many distinguished men' in the lands of their refuge, where they were the means of bringing about a rejuvenation of culture which had fallen to a low ebb.[3]

Indeed we must not forget that some of the greatest names in the history of ancient music belong to Alexandrians and other Egyptians: Ctesibius of Alexandria (*fl.* 246–221 B.C.) the presumed inventor of the hydraulus, Claudius Ptolemy of Canopus (*fl.* A.D. 127–51) the famous mathematician and musical theorist who wrote the weighty *Harmonica*, Hero of Alexandria (*fl.* A.D. 150) who presented a later account of the hydraulus in his *Pneumatica*, and Athenaeus of Naucratis (*fl.* A.D. 180–230) whose chatty *Deipnosophistes* tells so much about instruments of music and other neglected musical lore.

All this may be but a scant indication of the musical heritage of Egypt to the rest of the world, and it may come from even comparatively late sources; for when history strides over millennia, the earlier footprints are not easily discernible. So, ultimately, one is compelled, in the earlier period, to fall back on the general cultural impingement of Egypt on Aegean civilization. As Breasted has shown, the Aegean world was influenced by the Orient from two directions.[4] Just as Asia Minor was the cultural bridge connecting Greece with Mesopotamia, so Crete, the centre of the Aegean, was the half-way house which passed on Egyptian civilization to the Hellenic mainland. Of the reality of the latter inducement we have ample evidence, and in the sphere of music there is that archaic Cretan stoneware vase which shows a harvest thanksgiving procession headed by a head-shaven

[1] Victor Loret, *Journal asiatique* (juil.–août, 1889), p. 133.
[2] Athenaeus, iv. 184.
[3] Ibid., loc. cit.
[4] J. H. Breasted, *Ancient Times* (New York, 1935), p. 287.

priest with sistrum in hand;[1] the motive and craftsmanship tell their own story. Alan J. B. Wace has said that it was from this impulse to Cretan culture that sprang the Minoan and Mycenaean civilization, 'from the ashes of which there rose Phoenix-like in the first millennium B.C. the brilliance of Hellas, which was in its turn the forerunner of European culture'.[2]

[1] Breasted, *Ancient Times*, p. 285.
[2] *The Cambridge Ancient History*, i (Cambridge, 1924), p. 591.

VII

MUSIC IN THE BIBLE

By CARL H. KRAELING and LUCETTA MOWRY

AMONG the world's books few can lay claim to greater importance for the history of music than the Bible. Its religious lyrics have not ceased to be sung in divine worship throughout the many centuries since they were written. The words of some of these lyrics, like many of the stories of the Bible, have been a source of inspiration for generations of composers, particularly in western Europe, down to modern times, and have found an echo also in the folk-songs of many lands. In the more recent past the book and its lyrics have come to be recognized by scholars as a treasure-house of information about the history of music in antiquity. Through the Old Testament it provides a partial record of the music of the Hebrew nation during the many centuries of its existence. Through the New Testament it gives at least a rudimentary acquaintance with the music of a nascent religious community, the early Christian Church, in the crucial formative years of its life.

LIMITATIONS OF BIBLICAL INFORMATION

As a source for the history of Hebrew music the Bible has certain limitations and presents certain problems. Being a sacred book, it provides only incidental witness to the range and character of Hebrew secular music. Being a collection of ancient literary documents, it gives the words of many ancient Hebrew religious lyrics—together with scattered references to the occasions on which they were performed, the instruments employed in accompaniment and even the names of some of the tunes used—but not the actual melodies to which the songs were sung. Since the Bible draws its materials from the entire range of Hebrew religious literature, and since in any such literature the use of the lyric form is by no means limited to the song proper, it is sometimes impossible to say whether a given composition was or was not intended to be sung. Lastly, since the documents are arranged according to categories—Law, Prophets, and Writings—and, what is more troublesome, are often either pseudonymous or composite or both, it is not always immediately evident to what particular period of Hebrew history the songs contained in them and the historical information conveyed by them actually belong. Of the limitations mentioned, some are today being surmounted with the help of a growing body of information about the music of the ancient Orient generally, while others are yielding to a fuller understanding of the music of the later Synagogue. What is known about the music of ancient Egypt, Babylon, and Persia—their lyrics, their instruments, and even their melodies—has already been summarized (Chaps. V and VI). The music of the Synagogue is discussed in the next chapter. As to the problems mentioned, these may be said to have been brought nearer to solution, at least in broadest outline, by the literary criticism which in the last century has applied itself successively to the historical, the prophetic, and the lyric elements of the Biblical record, clarifying the stratification of the materials and determining the basic forms and categories of Hebrew poetry. The most immediately pertinent of the critical works produced in the course of these labours, together with those treating the music of the Bible directly, are listed in the Bibliography (pp. 493–4).

THE NOMADIC PERIOD

Reconstructed with the help of literary criticism and comparative materials, the history of Hebrew music develops in several stages, beginning with the earliest days of Hebrew tribal life and extending through the periods of the occupation of Palestine, the monarchy, the exile, and the post-exilic community respectively. Throughout the many centuries embraced in this development, music, and especially song, played an important part both in the secular and in the religious life of the Hebrew people, testifying to the high order of the nation's intellectual gifts and to its emotional and aesthetic sensitivity. In the earliest known phase of their history the Hebrews were apparently nomads. To interpret correctly the nature and range of their music in this period recourse must be had to the information supplied by our knowledge of primitive migratory groups. What European travellers in the Near East have reported about the music of the Bedouins and what early Islamic authors tell us about the music of the Arabs in the 'period of ignorance', is particularly helpful in this connexion.[1] The chants which the nomadic Hebrews, like their successors, undoubtedly sang to while away the monotony of the long desert

[1] See R. F. Burton, *Pilgrimage to el-Medina and Meccah* (London, 1856), especially iii; A. Musil, *Kusejr 'Amra* (Vienna, 1907); H. St. John B. Philby, *The Empty Quarter* (London, 1933); Bertram Thomas, *Arabia Felix* (New York, 1932); H. G. Farmer, *A History of Arabian Music* (London, 1929), pp. 1–9.

marches, the songs they once had for special occasions in the life of the individual and his family, were not remembered in the days of the Biblical writers. But of the songs that are associated with the life of the tribes and reflect the nomad's bitter struggle against the forces of nature and the claims of rival groups a few snatches have been preserved. One of these, connected with the desert travellers' eternal quest for the means of survival, is the Song of the Well:

Spring up, O well;
Sing ye unto it:
The princes digged the well,
The nobles of the people digged it,
By the direction of the lawgiver,
With their staves. (Num. xxi. 17–18.)

Probably sung in response to the invitation of the precentor by the members of the clan as they approach a tribal watering-place, the theme and refrain of the song has its counterpart in the repertory of the Bedouins even today.[1]

Characteristic of the group movements of desert tribes are the shouts associated with the Hebrew banner ('The hand upon the throne [read: the banner] of the Lord', &c., Exod. xvii. 16), with the Ark ('Rise up, O Lord, and let thine enemies be scattered. . . .' Num. x. 35–36), and in a later period with individual leaders ('For the Lord and for Gideon!', Jud. vii. 20). Such shouts are still used by Bedouin groups, their set tonal forms making it possible to identify the tribe to which the group belongs.[2] More distinctly lyric in character are the songs of vengeance and triumph preserved in the early historical books of the Bible. It is the thirst for blood revenge that echoes in the Song of Lamech:

Hear my voice,
Ye wives of Lamech;
Hearken unto my speech:
For I have slain a man to my wounding
And a young man to my hurt

If Cain shall be avenged sevenfold,
Truly Lamech seventy and sevenfold. (Gen. iv. 23–24.)

It is deliverance from the hand of the enemy that comes to expression in the tumultuous refrain and invitation of the song of triumph that

[1] Musil, op. cit., p. 9, quotes three examples, of which the simplest is the brief couplet:

Spring, O water,
Flow in plenty.

[2] See Musil, *Arabia Petraea* iii (Vienna, 1908), pp. 386 ff.

Miriam sang and the women of the Hebrew camp repeated at the shore of the Red Sea:

Sing ye to the Lord,
  For he hath triumphed gloriously;
The horse and his rider
  Hath he thrown into the sea. (Exod. xv. 21.)

Other lyrics of this type from the same period of Hebrew history were contained in the lost 'Book of the Wars of the Lord' mentioned in Num. xxi. 14, where a few lines are quoted.[1] With Bedouin music in its simplest forms these remains of early Hebrew song share certain formal traits. They are marked by conciseness and simplicity and by strong accentual rhythm, implying that the tonal patterns in which they were rendered were brief and that the rendering was strident and staccato. At least in the case of Miriam's song of triumph we hear that the singing was accompanied by the beating of percussion instruments (timbrels) and by rhythmic motions of the body.[2]

EARLY PALESTINIAN PERIOD

When in the course of the second millennium B.C. the Hebrew tribes made their way into Palestine, this was in all probability a matter of great consequence for the nature and development of their music. Here they began a new sedentary phase of their national history, entered upon a new agricultural form of life, and came into close contact with peoples of different racial stocks and varied social and cultural antecedents. Their first effort was naturally to make a place for themselves in the new land by conquest. In the circumstances they naturally perpetuated some of the musical forms belonging to their earlier repertory, especially the war songs. A particularly brilliant song of triumph from the period of the conquest of Canaan is the Song of Deborah (Judges v) containing the familiar lines:

The kings came and fought,
  Then fought the kings of Canaan
In Taanach by the waters of Megiddo;
  They took no gain of money.
They fought from heaven;
  The stars in their courses fought against Sisera.
The river Kishon swept them away,
  That ancient river, the river Kishon.
O my soul, thou hast trodden down strength.
(Judges v. 19–21.)

[1] For the poetic material in the Pentateuch see J. A. Bewer, *The Literature of the Old Testament* (2nd ed., New York, 1933), pp. 1–20, and R. H. Pfeiffer, *Introduction to the Old Testament* (New York, 1941), pp. 271–81.

[2] For Bedouin analogies see Bertram Thomas, op. cit., pp. 381–4.

Its length and scope reveal an advance in the powers of sustained composition, while the statement with which the prose writer introduces the song suggests that different sections of it may have been sung by singers of opposite sex (historically Deborah and Barak: Judges v. 1), no doubt with the use of a large variety of tonal patterns. Two verses quoted from the 'Book of Yashar' is all that remains of an analogous song about the battle at Gibeon in the prose narrative that has replaced it (Joshua x. 12–13).[1]

Echoes of the shorter, simpler lyrics celebrating the deeds of individual heroes appear in the texts dealing with the period of the Judges and the early monarchy—for instance, in the familiar couplet celebrating Samson's victory over the Philistines:

> With the jawbone of an ass, heaps upon heaps,
> With the jaw of an ass have I slain a thousand men.
>
> (Judges xv. 16.)

and in the song with which Saul was welcomed at his homecoming in 1 Sam. xviii. 7:

> Saul hath slain his thousands
> And David his ten thousands.

It will be noted in the last passage that the song welcoming the triumphant hero was sung by the women with the accompaniment of the dance and the use of various instruments.[2]

To the songs of war belong also those mourning the death of the fallen hero, the dirges. As a literary form the dirge appears in many parts of the Old Testament, but the first examples are from the period of the early monarchy. The earliest, quoted from the 'Book of Yashar' (perhaps to be translated, 'Book of Songs'), is the lament of David for Saul and Jonathan, beginning with the words:

> The beauty of Israel is slain upon thy high places

and containing the familiar refrain:

> How are the mighty fallen. (2 Sam. i. 19–27).

The second is the brief lament of David over Abner found in 2 Sam. iii. 33–34. The typical dirge, particularly in its later form, is marked by a peculiar 'limping rhythm', which must have been reflected also in the melodic phrases to which such songs were sung.[3] Originally the singers were probably the battle companions of the

[1] For a related taunt song, perhaps from the period of the early monarchy, see Num. xxi. 27–30.

[2] Cf. Exod. xv. 20 and Judges xi. 34, where only percussion instruments are mentioned.

[3] See infra, p. 295.

deceased, the women accompanying the singing by sounds of wailing and weeping (2 Sam. i. 24), but 2 Chron. xxxv. 25 suggests that in later times lyrics lamenting the death of kings were performed publicly by male and female singers.

With their entry into Canaan the Hebrews undoubtedly added to their musical repertory the songs normally associated with the labours and joys of agricultural life. How large was the variety of such songs in the ancient Orient we learn from a cuneiform text giving an inventory of the titles (or first lines) of songs, listing them under various headings, including the songs of the workman, of the shepherd, songs of love, of youth, &c., and specifying the instrument to which they were sung, in the manner of the Biblical Psalter.[1] Presumably the Babylonian lyrics were not fundamentally different from the songs of the shepherd and of the thresher, the texts of which are recorded in ancient Egyptian inscriptions. Those that the Hebrews sang once they had settled in Palestine were probably analogous to both. The joyous celebration of the harvest in field and vineyard was proverbial for the later writers of Hebrew religious literature (Isa. ix. 3; Jer. xxv. 30; Ps. iv. 7, cxxvi. 6), and of sufficient importance for Isaiah in one of his oracles against Moab to say:

> And gladness is taken away,
>   And joy out of the plentiful field;
> And in the vineyards there shall be no singing,
>   Neither shall there be shouting:
> The treaders shall tread out no wine in their presses;
>   I have made their vintage shouting to cease. (Isa. xvi. 10.)

But the songs of the Hebrew vintner and of those treading the grapes have long since disappeared, unless Isaiah has quoted or parodied a harvest song in the familiar parable beginning with the words:

> Now will I sing to my well-beloved
>   A song of my beloved touching his vineyard.
> My well-beloved hath a vineyard
>   In a very fruitful hill. (Isa. v. 1.)

The 'shouts' of those who trod the grapes (Jer. xxv. 30) may well have been single words repeated *ad infinitum* with the use of a simple melodic phrase, like the *ḥādandelli ḥādandōl* still used by the Arabs of Palestine.[2]

[1] E. Ebeling, *Keilschrifttexte aus Assur religiösen Inhalts*, i (Leipzig, 1919), no. 158, pp. 267–276; cf. S. Langdon, 'Babylonian and Hebrew Musical Terms', *Journal of the Royal Asiatic Society*, l (1921), pp. 169–91; and Chap. V, p. 239.

[2] G. Dalman, *Palästinischer Diwan* (Leipzig, 1901), p. 28.

In Palestine the Hebrew tribes found also well-established shrines sacred to diverse Canaanite and Egyptian deities. How extensive was the use of music and particularly of song in such temples and how varied the repertory we learn from the hymns inscribed on the walls of Egyptian sanctuaries and from the lyric prayers, the liturgies, litanies, processionals, offertories, hymns, and penitential psalms preserved in the cuneiform texts of Babylonia. Very shortly after their entry into the land the Hebrews also created for themselves local shrines—for instance, at Shechem and Shiloh. It had long seemed probable that the practices of contemporary oriental cults gave a strong impetus to the development and use of the religious lyric among the Hebrews in Palestine. The suggestion was verified by the discovery at Ras Shamra in Syria of a body of epic texts reflecting a form of religious belief and observance allied to the Canaanite worship of Baal.[1] The poems, including at least one hymn, are closely related to the Psalms of the Old Testament in vocabulary, phrases and even thought patterns, a relationship illustrated by the analogy between the Ugaritic

> Behold thy enemies, O Baal;
> Behold thy enemies thou shalt smite,
> Behold thou shalt destroy thy foes.

and Psalm xcii. 9:

> For, lo, thine enemies, O Lord,
> For, lo, thine enemies shall perish;
> All the workers of iniquity shall be scattered.[2]

The fact that such analogies appear in lyrics of quite different periods—the earliest of the extant Hebrew Psalms being a good deal later in date—makes the inference confirmed by them the more significant.

Upon their entry into Palestine the Hebrew tribes probably came to know and use also a larger variety of musical instruments, their types being essentially those portrayed in the art of Egypt and Babylonia. The passage in Gen. iv. 21 speaking of Jubal as the father of those who 'handle the harp (*kinnôr*) and the pipe (*'ûgābh*)', is among the earliest to mention such instruments and, what is more important, suggests the appearance of families or guilds of professional musicians among the Hebrews at this time.[3]

[1] See in general J. Obermann, *Ugaritic Mythology* (New Haven, 1948).

[2] For the Ugaritic text see *Syria*, xvi (Paris, 1935), p. 32; the translation is that of J. H. Patton, in *Canaanite Parallels in the Book of Psalms* (Baltimore, 1944), p. 29, where a detailed comparison of the two bodies of material is made.

[3] H. Gunkel, *Genesis* (3rd ed. Göttingen, 1910) ad loc., and others associate the passage with the nomadic phase of early Hebrew history.

MONARCHIC PERIOD

With the period of the monarchy, that is, from the beginning of the first millennium B.C., the Hebrew nation takes its place among the established peoples of the ancient Near East, the general pattern of its life for upward of three centuries being approximately that of the many lesser states lying between the great empires of Egypt and Assyria. As the foci of its national life the court, the Temple, and the large urban communities of the land are henceforth of outstanding importance. Trade, the crafts, and the fine arts thrive, historical literature begins and music can scarcely have lagged far behind, though our knowledge of its development remains very defective.

At the court, music played a well-defined and familiar role. Already in the days of Saul we find the young David serving as musician to the king, playing 'with his hand' and soothing the ruler's violent temper (1 Sam. xix. 9).[1] Tradition has it that he not only performed and composed music—the entire Psalter being subsequently credited to him—but that he also invented musical instruments (Amos vi. 5). What we read in the Bible about instrumental music at the Hebrew court, and what we learn incidentally about the vocal music performed there by male and female singers (cf. 1 Kings x. 12; Amos viii. 3, reading 'songstresses' for 'songs', and for the later period Sirach ix. 4), serves only to reflect the palace usage of the Orient as a whole. That this usage should have spread from the court to the houses of the wealthy, so that Amos (vi. 1–5) could speak of those 'that are at ease in Zion' singing 'idle songs to the sound of the viol' (*nebhel*, 'instrument', probably a harp) is but natural.

Special events in the life of the court required and produced special music. The accession of a new monarch was celebrated with ceremonies involving the blowing of trumpets and the shouting of formulas of acclamation (1 Kings i. 34). The analogy of the enthronement ritual found in Babylonian texts suggests that songs were sung by the rejoicing populace and by choirs of professional singers at the occasion.[2] The Biblical Psalter contains a whole category of lyrics, the 'royal psalms' so-called, that scholars have associated directly or indirectly with events in the life of the court, with the enthronement of the king

[1] On music in the life of oriental monarchy generally see B. Meissner, *Babylonien und Assyrien*, i (Heidelberg, 1920), p. 331 and H. Frankfort, *Kingship and the Gods* (Chicago, 1948), pp. 79–88. On the magical and curative power of music in the Biblical sphere see H. Gressmann, *Musik und Musikinstrumente im Alten Testament religionsgeschichtliche Versuche und Vorarbeiten* ii, 1 (Giesen, 1903), pp. 5–19.

[2] Conveniently accessible in H. Gressmann, *Altorientalische Texte und Bilder zum alten Testament* (2nd ed., Berlin, 1926), pp. 295–303.

or the anniversary of this event (Ps. xxi, lxxii, cx), with the marriage of the king (Ps. xlv), with his departure for and victorious return from war (Ps. xviii, xx, cliv. 1–11), and with his consecration (Ps. ci). So noteworthy were the singers of the Hebrew court that Sennacherib specifically mentions their removal to Nineveh in recording the booty taken from King Hezekiah.[1]

MUSIC IN THE TEMPLE

Alongside the court, the Temple was all-important in the monarchic period as a centre of Hebrew music. Familiar in this connexion are the stories of how David brought the Ark to Jerusalem with dancing, with shouting, and with the sound of the trumpet (2 Sam. vi. 14–15), and how Solomon dedicated the sanctuary in which it was housed (1 Kings viii and 2 Chron. v. 11–14). The music of the Temple ceremonial was undoubtedly not as elaborate in Solomonic times as the Chronicler later imagined, but it probably followed the general lines he develops, and was associated with both the regular morning and evening sacrifice and with the important festivals of the religious year. Apart from the blowing of trumpets (Num. x. 1–10, cf. Ps. xcviii. 6) it consisted largely of the singing of religious lyrics and the accompaniment of them with stringed instruments (cf. the protest of Amos v. 23). As in the later period the musical part of the service probably followed the performance of the sacrifices.[2]

Literary criticism having shown that most of the Psalter belongs to a later period, individual psalms can no longer be used with absolute confidence as sources for the knowledge of temple music in the monarchic period. But types of lyrics tend to perpetuate themselves, and recent typological studies of the Psalms make it possible at least to say what kinds of lyrics were sung in the Solomonic Temple, and with what occasions they can legitimately be associated.[3]

Biblical psalms connected with public rather than private devotions give evidence of the continuous existence in later times of three important types, namely, songs of praise (e.g. Ps. cxlv, cxlvii, cxlviii, cl), songs of petition (e.g. Ps. xliv, lxxiv, lxxix, lxxx, lxxxiii) and songs of thanksgiving (e.g. Ps. xxx, lxvi, cxvi, cxviii, cxxxviii). These types the music of the Solomonic sanctuary can scarcely have lacked. Those of the first type are properly hymns celebrating the majesty of the deity, for instance, as the Lord of creation, have at least partial

[1] Cf. D. D. Luckenbill, *The Annals of Sennacherib* (Chicago, 1924), p. 34.

[2] Cf. in general W. O. E. Oesterley, *Sacrifices in Ancient Israel* (New York, 1937), pp. 193–4, and I. Benzinger, *Hebräische Archäologie* (3rd ed., Leipzig, 1927), pp. 245–52.

[3] See especially H. Gunkel, *Einleitung in die Psalmen* (Göttingen, 1933).

analogies in the temple lyrics of the ancient Orient generally, and associate themselves naturally with the performance of the regular cult acts.[1] The penitential psalms of petition, to which there are counterparts at present only in Babylonia, seem particularly adapted to the ritual of stated or especially instituted fast days of national calamity and repentance. The songs of thanksgiving have been connected with the performance of the thankoffering (cf. Jer. xxxiii. 11) and thus with the annual observance of one of the great Hebrew festivals, the Feast of Tabernacles, at which such offerings were commonly made.

Still other classes of the Biblical psalms give indications of their one-time use. The royal psalms, sung at occasions when special honour was done to the king, have already been mentioned. To these may be added a well-defined category of processional psalms (e.g. Ps. xxiv, xlviii, lxxxvii, xcv, c), also connected no doubt with festival usage. Still other songs (especially Ps. xlvii, xciii, xcvi–xcix) are believed to be associated with a festival supposed to have been celebrated annually at Jerusalem in the period of the First Temple, namely, that of the enthronement of the Lord upon his holy hill.[2]

In the period under discussion here the lyrics used in the Temple were probably sung largely by the priests themselves. Some may have had instrumental interludes, if that is what the enigmatic 'Selah' frequently found in the text of the Biblical psalms (cf., for example, Ps. iii. 2, 4, 8) really means, as the Greek translation *diapsalma* suggests. In others the congregation may have participated, but this was probably limited at first to the singing of a simple Amen or a Hallelujah, there being a goodly number of psalms beginning or ending with the latter formula (Ps. civ–cvi, cxi–cxiii, cxv–cxvii, cxxv, cxlvi-cl). Songs connected with religious pilgrimage (e.g. Ps. lxxxiv, cxxii) were naturally sung by the pilgrim bands, but at least one processional psalm (Ps. xxiv) seems to have been rendered antiphonally. The ritual enacted with the use of this lyric involves the presence of a choir outside the Temple seeking entrance to the sacred precincts and being required by another to identify the object of its faith before being admitted. Twice repeated, the familiar exchange between the two groups runs as follows:

I Choir: Lift up your heads O ye gates;
Even lift them up, ye everlasting doors;
And the King of glory shall come in.

[1] See S. Langdon, *Sumerian and Babylonian Psalms* (New York, 1909), and H. Zimmern, *Babylonische Hymnen und Gebete* (Leipzig, 1905).

[2] See particularly S. Mowinckel. *Psalmenstudien II* (Christiania, 1922).

II Choir: Who is this King of glory?

I Choir: The Lord of Hosts,
He is the King of glory. (Ps. xxiv. 9–10.)

So well established is the relation of Temple worship and music that the psalmists naturally associate the act of coming into the divine presence with that of 'making a joyful noise to him [the Lord] with psalms' (Ps. xcv. 2) and of singing 'praises unto Him with the timbrel (*tōph*) and harp (*kinnôr*)' (Ps. cxlix. 3).

THE PROPHETS AND MUSIC

Prophecy and the prophetic movement throw interesting sidelights on the association of religion and music in the period of the early Hebrew monarchy. Originally, it would seem, instrumental music was used to further prophetic inspiration and ecstasy. The prophets of whom Samuel spoke to David when telling him where to find his father's asses are described as having 'a psaltery (*nebhel*) and a tabret (*tōph*), and a pipe (*ḥālîl*), and a harp (*kinnôr*), before them' (1 Sam. x. 5). Similarly Elisha, on being required to give an oracle to Jehoshaphat, demands of the king a minstrel, and we hear that when the minstrel played 'the hand of the Lord came upon Elisha and he prophesied' (2 Kings iii. 15). In the later period the relation between prophecy and music changes. Of the prophets whose oracles are recorded in the Bible none is known to have used instrumental music for inspirational purposes, and some like Amos reacted violently against even the use of song in the Temple (Amos v. 23). Yet many of the greatest among them used lyric forms in their pronouncements. This was not because the words were to be sung but because the forms were congenial to the thought to be conveyed.

Prophetic poems that can only be regarded as psalms and are sometimes explicitly described as such are to be found, for example, in Isa. xii. 1–3, 4–6; xxv. 1–5; xxvi. 1–6; xxvii. 2–11; xlviii. 20–21; lii. 7–10; Mic. vii. 8–10, 14–17, 18–20; Nah. i. 2–10 (acrostic). Hymns in praise of the deity appear, e.g. in Isa. xlii. 10–13; xliv. 23; one and the same pilgrimage lyric can be read in both Isa. ii. 2–4 and Mic. iv. 1–3, and a penitential psalm in Jer. xiv. 19–22. For those who in later times collected and codified the prophetic writings, the association of prophecy and the religious lyric was apparently so close that they incorporated in the prophetic books still other, later psalms, for example, those found in Hab. iii; Jonah ii. 3–10, and Isa. lxiii. 7–14. Another type of lyric that appears frequently in prophetic writings is the dirge or lamentation. Examples are to be found everywhere, for instance, in Amos v. 2–3; Isa. xiv. 4–21; Mic. i. 8–16; Jer. viii. 18–ix. 3; and of the later period in Isa. lvii. 1–6; Ezek. xix. 1–14. Of the Book of Lamentations in the Biblical canon at least chapters two and four are dirges belonging to the period under discussion. The lyric form has in these instances undergone a literary development, for the verses are so arranged as to form an alphabetic acrostic. For our knowledge of the contemporary religious lyric of the Hebrews the study of its echo in prophecy is of the utmost importance, providing a check on the inferences drawn from the Psalter.

SECULAR MUSIC

What we know about the secular music of the urban and rural communities of Palestine at this time is pitifully meagre. No doubt it was analogous in type to that in use elsewhere and continued the patterns of the previous period though on a richer scale. Amos's allusion to the association of feasts and song has already been mentioned (Amos viii. 10). Isaiah says of the inhabitants of Jerusalem that 'the harp (*kinnôr*) and the lute (*nebhel*) and the tabaret (*tōph*) and the pipe (*ḥālîl*) and wine are in their feasts, but they regard not the work of the Lord' (Isa. v. 11–12). He counsels Tyre to follow the example of the harlot, and to 'take an harp (*kinnôr*), go about the city, ... make sweet melody, sing many songs' (Isa. xxiii. 16). Songs of the bridegroom and the bride are mentioned repeatedly, for instance in Jer. vii. 34. Funerals had their own proper type of music. As in the Orient generally, professional mourners, particularly women, expressed in wailing and in songs of lament the emotions of the bereaved (e.g. Amos v. 16 and Jer. ix. 17–18, the latter apparently parodying a song of lamentation). For all else, evidence is wanting save where it can be conjectured that the prophets have on occasion parodied secular songs, as in Isa. xxi. 11–12 and xxii. 13.

LYRICAL METRES

From the character and form of the lyric material preserved in the Hebrew Bible as a whole it is possible to draw limited inferences about the nature of the music used to accompany it. Hebrew poetry throughout its earliest history is accentual. Its form is determined not by the number of the syllables or the quantity of the vowels in a given structural unit, but by the number of accented words the unit contains. As for the basic structural unit, this may be regarded either as a couplet of two lines or as a single poetic line divided into two halves by a weak or a strong caesura. The number of accents to the half-couplet or half-line varies from two to four, with three the most common. Normally the number of accents or beats is the same in both halves of a couplet or line, the exception being the so-called *qināh* 'metre' used in dirges, where a combination of three and two beats is commonly used, giving the structural unit its typical 'limping' or elegiac character. Halves of structural units commonly correspond to each other also in sense, exhibiting what is known as 'parallelism of members', a parallelism that may be synonymous, antithetical or progressive (step-parallelism). The accentual pattern (3:3) of a single structural unit whose halves exhibit synonymous parallelism may be illustrated by the passage:

> O cóme, let us síng unto the Lórd:
> Let us make a joyful noíse to the róck of our salvátion
> (Ps. xcv. 1.)

Most lyrics are made up of an unspecified number of such units, but whether groups of these units may be said to form strophes is not clear save in the case of the more stylized acrostic compositions.[1]

Using the information collected by those who have studied Oriental and particularly Oriental Jewish music in its later phases, it is possible to conjecture how lyrics constructed in this fashion were actually performed. The basic elements were apparently not the single note and the melodic phrase but a number of short patterns or motives each developing a musical interval. More than one pattern was required to sing a single line or couplet of a song, and all patterns must have been subject to variation to allow for the changing number of unstressed syllables in each structural unit. In successive lines or couplets the patterns could be repeated or changed, depending upon established usage, changes in the subject matter of the lyric, and the extent of the singer's repertory.[2]

INSTRUMENTS

At least in Biblical times Hebrew song was normally accompanied by instrumental music (1 Kings x. 12; 1 Chron. xvi. 42 *et al.*). Of the instruments themselves not a single example has as yet come to light, and from the pre-Hellenistic period no native representation of a Palestinian instrument survives.[3] For our knowledge of the types used we are therefore thrown back largely upon the names applied to them

[1] For the structure of Hebrew poetry see, for example, S. R. Driver, *An Introduction to the Literature of the Old Testament* (2nd ed., New York, 1913), pp. 366–7.

[2] Cf. on this subject Curt Sachs, *The Rise of Music in the Ancient World* (New York, 1943), esp. pp. 71–102.

[3] Asiatics bearing instruments of the type probably in use in Palestine are portrayed in the art of the ancient Orient. See, for example, Meissner, op. cit., p. 332.

in the Bible, upon the rendering of these names in the ancient versions of the Biblical text, and upon probable analogies in the literature and on the monuments of contemporary Oriental cultures. That there should be a measure of uncertainty about the identity of some of them is quite intelligible under the circumstances. In general it can be said that the three basic types of instruments, string, wind, and percussion, were each represented by one or more examples. Among the stringed instruments the *kinnôr*, a lyre of the kind known to the Greeks as the *kithara*, and the *nebhel*, probably a harp with as many as ten strings, were the oldest and most important. (The fact that the latter was commonly rendered 'psaltery' in the ancient versions has led to the confusing translation of the Hebrew *nebhel* and *kinnôr* by 'psaltery and harp' in the King James Version, for example, in Ps. cl. 3). Except for the *shôphar*, a ram's or goat's horn, and the *ḥăṣôṣerāh*, a metal trumpet, both of which were blown rather than played and that apparently only on special occasions, the important wind instrument is the *ḥālîl*, probably a double oboe. Less frequently mentioned is the *'ugābh*, apparently a vertical flute or pipe used mainly in connexion with secular music. Percussion instruments include the *tōph*, a tambourine or hand-drum, the *ṣelṣĕlîm* or *mĕṣiltayîm*, that is cymbals, and the *mĕna'ăn'îm*, probably a sistrum.[1]

AFTER THE CAPTIVITY

The destruction of the Temple and downfall of the Jewish state in the sixth century B.C. marks a significant break in certain aspects at least of the life of the Hebrew people. We cannot follow the exiles themselves into Mesopotamia or reconstruct with any measure of assurance that part of their life that would be of importance in the present context. A gifted singer of the later period has described the effect of the exile upon the musical life of the people in the immortal words:

By the rivers of Babylon, there we sat down,
  Yea, we wept, when we remembered Zion.
We hanged our harps upon the willows in the midst thereof.
  For there they that carried us away captive required of us a song;
And they that wasted us required of us mirth, saying,
  Sing us one of the songs of Zion.
How shall we sing the Lord's song in a strange land?

(Ps. cxxxvii. 1–4.)

[1] See in general Sachs, *The History of Musical Instruments* (New York, 1940), pp. 105–27; S. B. Finesinger, 'Musical Instruments in the Old Testament', *Hebrew Union College Annual*, iii (Cincinnati, 1926), pp. 21–76; Max Wegner, *Die Musikinstrumente des alten Orients* (Münster, 1950), pp. 38–44.

With the return of some of the exiles to Palestine in the Persian period, the corporate life of the Jewish community was resumed, albeit on a greatly reduced scale. The royal court, once the centre of so much of the nation's cultural life, was no more. Jerusalem, inhabited by but a small handful of folk, no longer boasted its urban luxury. Economic and political difficulties beset the community on every hand. Yet in Jerusalem a modest successor to the Temple of Solomon was erected, and with the High Priest assuming administrative responsibility for the direction of the community the Temple and the Law became the foci of Jewish religion and corporate life. It is natural, therefore, that the worship at the Temple and the effort of the individual to live in accordance with the demands of the Law serve as the occasion for the best known of the later developments in the history of Biblical and Jewish music. For the knowledge of these developments the work of the Chronicler and the Psalter are the outstanding sources.

Using the Chronicler's historical narrative as a source of information for conditions in his own day, it would appear that in the fourth century music played an even greater part in the worship at the Temple than in the earlier period. The vocal and the instrumental music at the shrine was now performed by families or guilds of professional musicians who associated themselves by descent with Heman, Asaph, and Jeduthun (and Korah), and thus ultimately with Levi, and claimed that they had been commissioned by none other than David (1 Chron. vi. 16–32; xv. 16–24; xvi. 41–42; 2 Chron. xx. 19). One of the Chronicler's sources gives their number as 4,000 (1 Chron. xxiii. 5), while another divides them into twelve courses of twenty-four persons each (1 Chron. xxv), the courses presumably taking turns at the services.[1] That they were under the direction of a 'chief musician', as the traditional translation of the titles of certain Psalms (e.g. Ps. iv; see also the LXX of 1 Chron. xv. 22) would suggest, is extremely doubtful.[2] About the 'psalteries (*nĕbhālîm*), harps (*kinnōrôth*) and cymbals (*mĕẓiltāyîm*)' that are commonly mentioned in Chronicles as the instruments accompanying their songs (e.g. 1 Chron. xv. 16), it is recalled in Mishnaic times that they were used in large numbers, but they can scarcely be said to have formed an 'orchestra'.[3]

Undoubtedly vocal and instrumental music had by this time been given a fixed place in the order of worship, but the descriptions of

[1] For the point of view and the sources of the Chronicler's work cf. especially A. C. Welch, *The Work of the Chronicler*, Schweich Lectures for 1938 (London, 1939).

[2] Cf. W. O. E. Oesterley, *A Fresh Approach to the Psalms* (New York, 1937), pp. 76–78.

[3] Cf. *Mishnah*, 'Arakhîn ii. 3, 5; Sukkah v. 4.

services to be found in 2 Chron. xxix. 20–30 and Sirach i. 11–21 indicate only that the musical part followed the sacrificial, a fact which the fuller Mishnaic description bears out (Tamid v. 6).[1] Once the place of music in the order of worship had been established, the development of musical *propria* for the daily and the festival services was inevitable. The Psalter itself reflects the beginning of this development, the titles of Ps. xcii and xxx indicating that they were used on the Sabbath and at the Feast of the Dedication of the Temple respectively. Titles in the Greek Psalter associate still other Psalms each with a day of the week.[2] Mishnaic and Talmudic traditions embodying the recollections of men who had participated in the worship at the Second Temple and inferences drawn from the study of the liturgy of the Synagogue suggest a much fuller development of lyric *propria* than these scattered references demonstrate.[3] That other prose elements of Scripture found a place even in the worship of the Temple and that eventually they were rendered in musical form, seems entirely likely.[4] As for the psalms, the congregation probably participated by joining in refrains such as 'For his mercy endureth for ever' (Jer. xxxiii. 11; 2 Chron. vii. 3; Ps. cxviii, cxxxvi), and in doxologies such as those now appended to the several 'books' of the Psalter (Ps. xli. 13, lxxii. 18–19, lxxxix. 52, cvi. 48; see 1 Chron. xvi. 36).[5]

The establishment of the musicians' guilds was of great importance not only for the rendering but also for the composition of Jewish music, the post-exilic period being that in which the largest proportion of the lyrics contained in the Biblical Psalter was produced. Various collections of psalms seem to have sprung up at this time, each representing the repertoire of a different guild. These were eventually merged to produce the Biblical Psalter, leaving only the

[1] See further A. Z. Idelsohn, *Jewish Music* (New York, 1929), pp. 18–19.

[2] In the order of their Hebrew numbering Ps. xxxviii and xcii are assigned in the LXX to the Sabbath, and Ps. xxiv, xlviii, xciii and xciv to the first, second, fourth and sixth days of the week. The full list for the entire week beginning with the first day is given in the *Mishnah* (Tamid vii. 4) as follows: Ps. xxiv, xlviii, lxxxii, xciv, lxxxi, xciii, xcii.

[3] See, for example, the various Mishnaic tractates of the Seder Mo'ed, the extra-canonical tractate Sopherim of the *Babylonian Talmud*, and for the regular and festival usage of the Synagogue I. Elbogen, *Der jüdische Gottesdienst in seiner geschichtlichen Entwicklung* (Leipzig, 1913). Among the lyrics associated with festival usage, the Hallel (Ps. cxiii–cxviii) was perhaps the first to be used regularly. Cf. the allusion to its use in the home at Passover in Mark xiv. 26. The evidence is conveniently summarized by Oesterley, op. cit., pp. 133–45.

[4] See particularly H. St. J. Thackeray, *The Septuagint and Jewish Worship*, Schweich Lectures of 1920 (2nd ed., London, 1923) and F. L. Cohen in the *Jewish Encyclopedia* s.v. Cantillation.

[5] For differences of usage in the responsive rendering of the Hallel (Ps. cxiii–cxviii) see *Mishnah*, Soṭah v. 4.

divisions of the book and the titles 'A Psalm of David', 'A Psalm of Korah', &c., to testify to their existence.[1]

The titles of the Biblical Psalms yield yet further information about the music of the post-exilic Temple, though many of the expressions used in them are still quite obscure. Some of the titles appear to indicate what the song was used for: namely, for pilgrimage (e.g. Ps. cxx ff., A.V.: 'Song of Degrees'), for instruction (?) (e.g. Ps. xxxii, A.V. 'Maschil'), for atonement (?) (e.g. Ps. xvi, A.V.: 'Michtam') and for sickness (?) (e.g. Ps. v, A.V.: 'upon Nehiloth'). Others suggest that the lyric was to be accompanied by one or more stringed instruments, so the expression *binĕgînôth* (e.g. Ps. iv, A.V.: 'on Neginoth') and the word *mizmôr* (e.g. Ps. iii, which, being translated *psalmos* in the Septuagint, has given rise to the name 'Psalm' applied to the lyrics of the Psalter generally). Still others give the names of the 'tunes' to which the lyrics were sung, as, for instance, 'The Hind of the Morning' (Ps. xxii, A.V.: *Aijeleth Shahar*), 'Lilies' (Ps. xlv, A.V.: 'Shoshannim'), 'The Dove of the Distant Terebinths (?)' (Ps. lvi, A.V.: 'Jonath-elem-rechokim'), and 'Destroy not' (Ps. lvii, A.V.: 'Al-taschith').[2]

Among the lyrics produced in the post-exilic period and included in the Biblical Psalter are many that answer to the religious needs of the individual rather than the congregation (e.g. Ps. xvi, xxiii, xxiv, xlii–xliii, cxvi). Appealing to God for succour from affliction and from the malice of the wicked 'enemy', these psalms express the individual's abiding faith in God and in the moral order and indicate how deeply the prophetic spirit and the zeal for the Law had entered into the religious life of the common people. In the present context they are important because they show the religious lyric in transition from the sacrificial cult and its personnel to the private devotions of individuals and smaller groups, paving the way for important later developments.

What we know about the secular music of the Jewish community in the post-exilic period is at once more limited and more precise than in the preceding period. It is said that the returning exiles brought back household singers with them, both male and female (Ezra ii. 65; Neh. vii. 67), and of the services of such persons at festive occasions evidence is naturally not wanting in the later period (Sirach xxxii. 4–6; xlix. 1). Allusions to the songs of workers, such as the ploughman

[1] On this see, for example, Oesterley, op. cit., pp. 58–67.

[2] See, in general and on the obscure expressions not treated here, Oesterley, op. cit., pp. 75–115.

(Sirach xxxviii. 25, 𝔖 mg.) and the builder (Job xxxviii. 6–7), appear on occasion, but suggestions about the nature of any of these songs are lacking, in large measure because later prophecy and the apocalyptic that followed it abandoned increasingly the use of genre-forms taken from contemporary folk-song. At the same time the Bible supplies us with one whole book that is nothing more or less than a collection of secular lyrics, namely, the Song of Songs. Admitted to the canon on the strength of an allegorical interpretation of its material, it is in fact a compilation of love lyrics of the third century B.C., comparable in their passionate character and their flowery language to the love songs of ancient Egypt and contemporary Arabia.[1]

GRAECO-ROMAN PERIOD

In the Greek period, after the conquest of Alexander, new influences made themselves felt in Palestine. The Jews become familiar for the first time with the music of the Greek world and with the instruments in use in that area. Instructive in this connexion are the lists of instruments associated by Daniel with the performance of pagan acts of worship (iii. 5, 7, 10, 15). They not only provide new names for instruments of Oriental origin but list in addition at least three that are Greek, the *qithārôs* (Greek *kitharis*, a lyre), the *pĕsanṭērîn* (Greek *psaltērion*, a harp [?]), and the *sûmpōnyāh* (Greek *symphonia*: possibly a bagpipe). Josephus reports that Herod the Great, in instituting quinquennial games in honour of Augustus, caused Greek choral singers (*Thymelici*) to enter the competition (*Antiquities* xv. 8, 1 = § 270), following the example of the Hellenized monarchs and cities of the Orient generally.[2]

Yet the impact of these foreign instruments and modes upon Jewish music was anything but profound, at least in Palestine. Josephus himself describes the hostility with which Herod's innovations were received, and Talmud and Midrash echo the opposition to Greek song, which intensified itself after the destruction of the Second Temple, when all instrumental music even for religious purposes was prohibited by the sages as a sign of national mourning.[3] More important in this connexion is the reverence in which the writers of the Biblical lyrics were held (Sirach xliv. 5) and the fact that during the Greek and

[1] On the Song of Songs see, for example, M. Jastrow, *The Song of Songs* (Philadelphia, 1921), and such general compends as that of R. H. Pfeiffer, op. cit., pp. 708–16.

[2] Representations of Jewish instruments of the Roman period appear on Jewish coins. See, for example, G. F. Hill, *British Museum: Catalogue of the Greek Coins of Palestine* (London, 1914), pls. 33–38. Josephus' remarks on Jewish musical instruments are given full consideration in the article by Finesinger cited on p. 296, n. 1.

[3] See Idelsohn, op. cit., pp. 92–93; but cf. Chap. VIII, p. 315.

the Roman periods of Jewish history the production of religious lyrics continued, the vein being largely that of the older compositions. Examples of these later lyrics are to be found scattered about in the prophetic books of the Biblical canon, into which they were introducted by zealous editors, and in the Apocrypha and Pseudepigrapha, e.g. Sirach 51, Judith 16, Tobit 13, The Song of the Three Children in the supplements to the Greek Daniel, and the Prayer of Manasses, written by a Greek Jew and preserved among the Canticles that were added to the Greek Psalter in later times.[1] More important than any of these is the collection of Psalms produced in the middle of the first century B.C. and known as the Psalms of Solomon. In them the fervour of the post-exilic psalmists lives on, applying itself to the comfort and inspiration of pious folk who saw in the more secularized and pro-Roman elements of the community a threat to Jewish religious ideals and traditions.[2] Recent manuscript discoveries in caves by the Dead Sea have provided elements of further collections of Psalms—Psalms of Thanksgiving—and other liturgical materials. They imitate the poetic writings of the Old Testament but represent part of the religious literature of a separate Jewish (Essene?) sect of the first century A.D.[3] From them we should eventually learn more about the music and liturgy of Jewish groups looking toward the fulfilment of the eschatological hope.

SERVICES OF THE SYNAGOGUE

For the later history of Jewish music no one institution was of greater importance than the Synagogue. Whenever and wherever it began, it was already a regular feature of the scene both in Palestine and in the Dispersion in the first century of our era. By this time, too, the basic elements of its regular services of worship, comprising particularly the confessional *shĕma'*, the scripture lessons, and the Prayer (*tĕphillāh*), had undoubtedly been fixed.[4] How music came to play a part in these communal services of worship is not entirely clear, though the natural presumption is that it was carried over

[1] See Pfeiffer, op. cit., p. 632; on the apocryphal Baruch and its liturgical use, see the interesting suggestions of Thackeray, op. cit., pp. 80–111.

[2] For the texts of the extra-canonical documents see R. H. Charles, *Apocrypha and Pseudepigrapha of the Old Testament*, 2 vols. (Oxford, 1913).

[3] See particularly E. L. Sukenik, *Megillôth Genûzôth*, i (Jerusalem, 1948) in Hebrew; A. Dupont-Sommer, *The Dead Sea Scrolls* (Oxford, 1952), pp. 69–78, and H. L. Ginsberg, 'The Hebrew University Scrolls from the Sectarian Cache', in *Bulletin of the American Schools of Oriental Research*, No. 112 (Dec. 1948), pp. 19–23. Much of the material is as yet unpublished.

[4] See in general Elbogen, op. cit., and W. O. E. Oesterley and G. H. Box, *The Religion and Worship of the Synagogue* (2nd ed. London, 1911).

directly or indirectly from the worship of the Temple. Tradition has it that Levites going in groups from the Temple services to those of the Synagogue were the link between the music of the two institutions (*Babylonian Talmud*, 'Arakhîn 11*b*). Scholars have suggested that the custom of groups of laymen in the several parts of Palestine to gather for local worship synchronously with the performance of Temple sacrifice may have contributed to the development.[1] Of some importance, it would seem, is the further fact that in the post-exilic period the singing of psalms had become a part of the natural self-expression of the devout people, whose institution the Synagogue was. Paul singing hymns to God at midnight in Philippi (Acts xvi. 25), and the Jews of Alexandria spending the night after the arrest of their enemy Flaccus in the singing of hymns and songs of triumph (Philo, *In Flaccum* 14, §§ 121–2), is a part of this larger picture. Precisely at what points and in what form music entered into the worship of the early Synagogue is quite uncertain. The religious individualism of which the Synagogue was an expression undoubtedly led to the development of varieties of usage in this matter, particularly in the earliest period. Within the framework of the regular service it is the doxological elements and the benedictions that would have lent themselves most readily to musical rendering, perhaps with melismatic embellishments.[2] To the essential nucleus of this type of service there may often have been added the singing of stated or desired psalms, festival usage being known to have involved such practice, above all in the responsive singing of the Hallel (Ps. cxiii–cxviii).[3] How the Jewish communities of the Dispersion that used the Greek version of the Scriptures sang their 'hymns and songs', whether according to the old 'tunes', supposing that they could be adapted to a translated text, or with the use of Greek modes, is, unfortunately, not known.[4] Both at home and abroad, the music of the early Synagogue was exclusively vocal, whether because of opposition to pagan custom or as a sign of mourning for the destruction of the Temple.

[1] See, for example, Elbogen, op. cit., pp. 237–9. The reference is to the institution known as that of the *ma'ămādhôth*, described in the *Mishnah*, Ta'anîth iv. 2.

[2] On the doxologies of Synagogue and Church cf. the article of E. Werner, 'The Doxology in Synagogue and Church, a liturgico-musical Study', *Hebrew Union College Annual*, xix (1945–6), pp. 276–351.

[3] See in the *Babylonian Talmud* 'Arakhîn 10*a* and Ta'anîth 28*b*, where the difference between the number of times the Hallel is used each year in Palestine and Babylonia is reported. The differences and the extent of the usage suggest ancient practice.

[4] In a familiar statement Clement of Alexandria compares the chanting of Hebrew psalms as he had heard them to that of the Greek drinking song called *Skolion* (*Paedagogos* ii. 4). Cf. on this see Werner, op. cit., pp. 333–5.

MUSIC IN THE NEW TESTAMENT

As a source for our knowledge of the music of the early Christian Church the New Testament has its own limitations and problems. Far smaller in compass than the Old and lacking anything comparable to the Psalter, its documents are so closely associated with the practical purposes of the Christian missionary enterprise and so sharply delimited in their historical interest that they contain but little material bearing directly upon the question at issue here. Yet critical scholarship, applying itself to the study of the incidental information that does emerge, and keeping in mind both the background out of which Christianity came and the development of hymnody and liturgy in the later Church, has been able to reconstruct tentatively at least certain of the broader outlines of the use of music in the crucial formative years of the Christian movement. So far as we can tell the music of the early Church was almost entirely vocal, Christian usage following in this particular the practice of the Synagogue, in part for the same reasons.[1]

Like that of John the Baptist who preceded him and those of others who followed, the movement initiated by Jesus was rooted in the traditional piety of the Jewish people, bringing the search for individual acceptability before God to renewed expression within the framework of the conviction that the religious hopes of the Prophets, so intensely meaningful to the people of his day, were about to come to fulfilment. From the outset, therefore, both movements were pitched at that high level of spiritual exaltation for which the use of lyric material and form was both natural and traditional. Jesus's predecessor John, being of priestly descent, came of circles well acquainted with the music of the Temple. Jesus reflected more nearly the piety and worship of the Synagogue, and addressed himself commonly to the circles whose prayers for personal deliverance had been embodied in so many of the latest of the Biblical psalms, and who in the Psalter as in the New Testament are called 'the poor' (cf. Ps. lxxxvi. 1 and Matt. v. 3). It is not strange, in the circumstances, that echoes of the psalms appear in the sayings ascribed to him.

Both movements tended to create circles of faithful adherents in whose religious life certain of the elements of Jewish observance and the hope of an imminent deliverance were kept continually alive. To

[1] On the Christian opposition to instrumental music and the exceptions to its disuse see J. Quasten, 'Musik und Gesang in den Kulten der heidnischen Antike und der christlichen Frühzeit', *Liturgiegeschichtliche Quellen und Forschungen 25* (Münster, 1930), pp. 81–83, 103–10.

what extent vocal music, particularly psalmody, played a part in this during the lifetime of the two founders is quite unknown, save for the incidental mention of the use of the Hallel (Ps. cxiii–cxviii) by Jesus and His disciples at Passover (Mark xiv. 26). From the period after the death of John the Baptist we possess a hymn of praise probably sung at one time by his disciples and later placed in the mouth of John's father Zacharias in the Baptist nativity story. The hymn is the canticle familiar to all as the *Benedictus* (Luke i. 68–79), beginning with the words so familiar also from the language of the Psalter:

> Blessed be the Lord God of Israel;
> For he hath visited and redeemed his people.[1]

Among the groups of disciples who in ever-increasing numbers perpetuated and proclaimed the faith in Jesus, the use of psalmody was from the outset of no small importance. The background for this is provided by what we hear in Acts of their constant participation in the worship of the Temple (e.g. Acts ii. 46; v. 12, 42) and of their attendance upon the services of the Synagogue (e.g. Acts vi. 9; ix. 2; xiii. 5, 14). When the Christian believers established themselves as independent groups, they frequently organized themselves after the Synagogue pattern (see e.g. Acts xiv. 23), and, judging by the structure of the later services of worship (see Justin Martyr, *Apology*, i. 65–67) that eventually produced the proanaphora of the Mass, they commonly followed the outline of Synagogue observance in at least one part of their worship.[2] That psalmody played a part in Synagogue observance we have already seen. How important it was in the worship of the Christian communities throughout the ancient world can be judged from the statement of Paul, addressed to the Corinthians, 'when ye come together, every one of you hath a psalm' (1 Cor. xiv. 26). In large part the psalms used in the churches must have been the lyrics of the Biblical Psalter, for among the books of the Old Testament quoted in the New none occurs more frequently than the Psalter itself.[3] Yet there is good reason to believe that the exaltation associated with the belief in the coming deliverance, the imminent

[1] See H. Gunkel, 'Die Lieder in der Kindheitsgeschichte Jesus bei Lukas', *Festgabe von Fachgenossen und Freunden A. von Harnack zum 70. Geburtstag dargebracht* (Tübingen, 1921), esp. pp. 56–59. The assumption is that the hymn was composed in Aramaic.

[2] See in general L. Duchesne, *Christian Worship: its Origin and Evolution* (5th ed., London, 1923), W. O. E. Oesterley, *The Jewish Background of the Christian Liturgy* (Oxford, 1925), and more recently C. W. Dugmore, *The Influence of the Synagogue upon the Divine Office* (London, 1944), pp. 71–89.

[3] See H. B. Swete, *An Introduction to the Old Testament in Greek* (2nd ed., Cambridge, 1914), pp. 383–4.

return of Christ and the gift of the Spirit, produced from the outset new Christian lyrics analogous to those of the Biblical Psalter and the Psalms of Solomon and rendered no doubt in the same fashion. Two early examples translated out of the original Aramaic are sometimes said to be preserved in the Magnificat and the Nunc Dimittis of the Nativity story of Luke (i. 46–55; ii. 29–32), where they are placed in the mouth of the Virgin Mary and the aged Simeon respectively.[1] Both express in traditional language the confident assurance that salvation has come to the distressed. The same confidence is reflected in the 'song' of thanksgiving that the writer of the Book of Revelation has apparently translated and put into the mouth of those who have overcome 'the beast'.

> Great and marvellous are thy works,
> Lord God Almighty;
> Just and true are thy ways,
> Thou King of Saints.
> Who shall not fear thee, (O Lord) and glorify thy name?
> For thou only art holy:
> For all nations shall come
> And worship before thee;
> For thy judgments are made manifest. (Rev. xv. 3–4.)[2]

A peculiar feature of Gospel record may be of importance in this connexion. It is the fact that many of the sayings of Jesus reported in the Synoptic Gospels, when turned back into the Aramaic in which they were spoken, give indication of possessing the accentual rhythm typical of Hebrew poetry.[3] Some of them, particularly those of a Sapiential character, may have been uttered in poetic form, others, however, may have received their rhythmic form in the period before the existence of written Gospels, when they were recited in Christian assemblies whether as 'oracles' or as parts of a new Law.

It is important even in this context to realize that the earliest places of specifically Christian worship were the 'house-churches' (Philemon 2) as the earlier synagogues were 'house-synagogues'.[4] In this

[1] See the article of Gunkel in the *Festgabe . . . A. von Harnack* previously cited. Harnack himself has suggested that the Magnificat was originally assigned to Elisabeth, which might imply that it was a Baptist rather than a Christian lyric. See his article 'Das Magnificat der Elisabet nebst einigen Bemerkungen zu Lk. 1. u. 2', *Sitzungsberichte der kgl. preuß. Akademie der Wissenschaften zu Berlin*, 1910 (Berlin, 1910), pp. 538–56.

[2] On this and other 'songs' of Revelation see C. C. Torrey, *Documents of the Primitive Church* (New York, 1941), pp. 210–12.

[3] See C. F. Burney, *The Poetry of Our Lord* (Oxford, 1925).

[4] See the Christian Chapel and the earlier of the two synagogues at Dura-Europos (*The Excavations at Dura-Europos*, ed. M. I. Rostovtzef et al. *Preliminary Report V* (New Haven, 1934), pp. 238–85, and *Preliminary Report VI* (New Haven, 1936), pp. 332–7 and pl. ix).

type of setting there were brought into close connexion not only the devotional practices of the family and the local religious community but also the observances which the Church shared with the Synagogue and those which it had in excess of the Synagogue, particularly Baptism and the Eucharist. That psalmody had come to play a part in the private life of the pious Jews of the post-exilic period has already been indicated, and this together with the use of prayers and blessings in the home was not without meaning for the development both of Christian usage and of Christian music.[1] That it played a part also in the baptismal and eucharistic rites at very early times can be seen from the collection of Paul's letters, particularly in the familiar passages Col. iii. 16 and Eph. v. 19, where the Apostle encourages the faithful in the use of 'psalms, hymns and spiritual songs'. The immediate context of each of these passages is full of sacramental allusions, the one to Baptism, the other to the Eucharist.[2]

Of the part that music played in the baptismal practise of the early Palestinian Church we have no further evidence in the New Testament. For the Eucharist there may be information in Rev. v. 8–14 and xix. 1–7, where the Seer is describing acts of adoration in Heaven and seems to be paraphrasing and adapting forms actually in use in Christian circles.[3] The worship in Rev. xix. 1–7 turns about the use of Alleluia hymns in which God is praised by the assembly of the saints and to which there are responses of 'Alleluia' and 'Amen'. The first begins with the words:

Alleluia!
Salvation and glory and honour and power unto the Lord our God:
For true and righteous are his judgments. (Rev. xix. 1.)

The second celebrates the imminent marriage of the Lamb:

Alleluia!
For the Lord God omnipotent reigneth.
Let us be glad and rejoice,
And give honour to him.
For the marriage of the Lamb is come,
And his wife hath made herself ready. (Rev. xix. 6–7.)

[1] Cf. on this Clement of Alexandria, *Paedagogos* 2, 4, and Tertullian, *ad uxorem* ii. 9, and Quasten, op. cit., pp. 158–79.

[2] The categories 'psalms, hymns and spiritual songs (literally, odes)' are not to be distinguished too sharply from each other. 'Spiritual' as applied to odes may mean 'religious' in contra-distinction to 'secular', though it is the opinion of Paul that all the lyrics mentioned are 'inspired'. See, however, Vol II, Chap. I, p. 2.

[3] See W. Bousset, *Kyrios Christos* (2nd ed., Göttingen, 1921), p. 235, F. J. Dölger, *Sol Salutis* 2nd ed. (Münster, 1925), p. 127, and G. B. Gray, *Sacrifice in the Old Testament* (Oxford, 1925), pp. 164–78. On liturgy in Rev. see Lucetta Mowry, 'Revelation 4–5 and Early Christian Liturgical Usage' in *Journal of Biblical Literature*, lxxi (1952), pp. 75–84.

What seems to be parodied or quoted here is a Christian Hallel sung in responsive form, as Ps. cxiii–cxviii were sung in Jewish usage. The hymn follows the traditional pattern, praising God for his deliverance, but substitutes for the association with the Passover meal that with the marriage supper of the Lamb, thus adapting it to a eucharistic context. With the type of eucharistic observance reflected in these hymns we should perhaps connect also the Trisagion (Rev. iv. 8) and the invocations 'Hosannah to the God of David' and 'Maranatha' that are reported in the *Teaching of the Twelve Apostles* (x. 6) and 1 Cor. xvi. 22, assuming that the exclamations were rendered melismatically.

The order of worship in Rev. v. 8–14 begins and ends with acts of prostration by the Elders, and includes 'songs' sung by the Elders and by the angelic host respectively, a doxology said by the multitude of created beings, and a concluding Amen by the four beasts. The general analogy to the order described in Sirach i. 16–21 is evident, but the songs are of a new type, echoing the praise of the Lamb as in the words:

Worthy art thou to take the book
  And to open the seals thereof;
For thou wast slain and hast redeemed us to God
  By thy blood
Out of every kindred and tongue
  And people and nation
And hast made us unto our God
  Kings and priests,
And we shall reign on the earth. (Rev. v. 9–10.)

The form of the song, a declarative statement introduced by the word 'Worthy' (Greek: *axios*; Latin: *dignus*), is that of the acclamations that formed part of the ceremonial of oriental courts and pagan temples.[1]

THE CHURCH OUTSIDE PALESTINE

Except for the last item, the material discussed up to this point illustrates the use of music by the Jewish-Christian churches that existed in the earliest period of Church history, particularly in Palestine. In these congregations we must assume there were in use not only lyrics of the type familiar from the Old Testament and the post-canonical literature of Judaism, but also the modes of performance traditional in the Oriental, and particularly in the Jewish, environment.

[1] See E. Peterson, *'ΕΙΣ ΘΕΟΣ* (Göttingen, 1926), pp. 176–80.

Perhaps the only departure from Jewish standards in these circles was added importance given to the inherited melismatic forms in which the Alleluias and other liturgical exclamations may have been sung. The spiritual exaltation characterizing the beginnings of the Christian movement makes such departures entirely intelligible. Once the Church had expanded beyond the Palestinian scene and particularly when it struck new roots in the Greek world, it inevitably developed musical forms of expression in keeping with other musical traditions. Precisely when this happened it is no longer possible to say. At present the earliest example of a Christian hymn using the quantitative metrical form of the Greeks is the hymn to Christ attached to the end of the *Paedagogos* of Clement of Alexandria, and the earliest known to have been sung according to the Greek tonal system is the Oxyrhynchos hymn, recorded in a script of the third century A.D.[1] Such hymns may have existed even in earlier days, but in the New Testament no trace of them exists and in general the development of Christian hymnody and liturgy follows other lines than those of specifically Greek music.

More important for the interpretation of early Christian music as reflected in the Bible are the mixed forms that developed from the fusion of oriental and Hellenistic elements. Of such fusions the hymns from Rev. v that use the acclamation form are one example. Since they can be translated without difficulty into Aramaic, they may have originated in Jewish-Christian communities of the Near East and have been rendered in the traditional way in spite of the slight departure from Jewish tradition that their form implies. An analogous departure in another direction is to be seen in the fragment of a confessional hymn preserved in 1 Tim. iii. 16:

[Who] was manifest in the flesh,
Justified in the Spirit,
Seen of angels,
Preached unto the Gentiles,
Believed on in the world,
Received up into glory.

Here the structure is still oriental, and the music to it must have been oriental, but the parallelism is that of Hellenistic rhetorical construction.[2]

[1] *Oxyrhynchus Papyri*, ed. B. Grenfell and A. S. Hunt, xv (London, 1922), no. 1786. See Vol. II, p. 4.

[2] On the passage cf. the commentary of M. Dibelius on 1 Timothy in H. Lietzmann, *Handbuch zum Neuen Testament*, ed. 2 (Tübingen, 1931), and E. Norden, *Agnostos Theos* (Berlin, 1923), pp. 254–63.

Another type of departure is to be found in the hymn quoted by Paul in Phil. ii. 6–11. As read in the original Greek the lyric celebrating him who 'emptied himself' and took upon himself 'the form of a servant' has a regularity of construction hardly to be imitated in translation, and consists apparently of five stanzas of three lines each.[1] The absence of parallelism, the brevity and equality of the lines and the stanza-form shows that we are dealing here with a composition even more remote from Jewish psalmody. The lyric is in fact a hymn to Christ as *Kyrios* or Lord, and hence quite out of keeping with Jewish tradition. Yet the rhythm is not quantitative but accentual, with three beats to the line, which suggests that it must have been sung in oriental fashion and not in one of the Greek modes. Similar mixed types also arising from the early Christian use of music in the regular Lord's Day services are perhaps to be found in the Prologue of the Gospel of John and in a passage in Ignatius of Antioch. That the Prologue of the Gospel of John particularly John i. 1–18 embodies a hymn to the divine Logos constructed in the same way as Phil. ii. 6–11, has long been evident.[2] Less familiar, perhaps, is the hymn that seems to be quoted by Ignatius in his Epistle to the Ephesians vii. 2:

> One is the Physician,
> Both flesh and spirit,
> Born yet not born,
> God in man,
> True life in death,
> Both of Mary and of God,
> First passible and then impassible,
> Jesus Christ our Lord.[3]

Here again rhetorical parallelism and a hieratic style are to be noted, but the rhythm continues in the accentual pattern of oriental lyric.

For the antecedents of the song represented by this type of lyric it is useless to go either to native Greek or to Hebrew musical tradition. The former could supply only the language and some associations with the rhetorical structure, the other chiefly the accentual rhythm. Even what is known about the music of the official state cults and the

[1] See the commentary of E. Lohmeyer on Philippians in Meyer's *Kritisch-exegetischer Kommentar über das Neue Testament* (Göttingen, 1928).

[2] See now the commentary of R. Bultmann on John in Meyer's *Kritisch-exegetischer Kommentar über das Neue Testament* (Göttingen, 1937) ad loc. and originally C. F. Burney, *The Aramaic Origin of the Fourth Gospel* (Oxford, 1922), pp. 28–48.

[3] See in particular W. Bousset, op. cit., pp. 254–5, and in general J. Kroll, 'Die christliche Hymnodik bis zu Klemens von Alexandrien', *Braunschweiger Vorlesungsverzeichnis 1921–1922* (Königsberg, 1921).

mystery religions of Roman times, their hymns, their use of congregational responses and acclamations, does not supply complete parallels at the present time.[1] Two facts should be noted in this connexion: first, that the accentual rhythm is not exclusively Hebrew or Jewish but common in all forms of early Semitic lyric poetry; and second, that, so far as our evidence goes, the theology of the mixed types of Christian hymns is to be associated less with Jewish-Christianity than with that of Churches in the Eastern provinces of the Roman empire. In all probability the antecedents of these hymns are to be found in the hellenized pagan cults of the Orient, particularly those of Syria. The importance of *Kyrios*, Lord, as the designation of Christ in many of them suggests the environment of the traditional ruler cults of the Orient in the form in which they and their liturgy were adapted to the services of the Hellenistic Diadochoi.[2] The Ignatian hymn to Christ as the Physician suggests environment of the cult of Asclepius.[3] Which, if any, of the peculiar features of such Oriental cult music had already come to play a part in the life of the Greek synagogues of the Dispersion at an earlier date, it is difficult to say, but certainly the Jews in the world at large must have modified their traditional music somewhat in order to sing their psalms in Greek, and may even have used acclamation formulas such as have been noted above in connexion with Rev. v.[4] Whatever be true of the origin of these Christian hymns from the period of the New Testament writings, they already contain the germs for the development of certain types of Byzantine hymns, particularly of the *kontakion*,[5] where, if Wellesz is right, tonic rhythm is still normative for the development of the melody and where groups of short sense lines arranged in strophes set forth the thought.[6] In fact what has been said above about the use and rendering of acclamations and about cantillation suggests that all three of the major types of melodic formulation known in the cultural centres of the Orient had already come to expression in the

[1] See in general, Quasten, op. cit., pp. 3–68, and the important article by Werner, 'The Conflict between Hellenism and Judaism in the Music of the early Christian Church', *Hebrew Union College Annual*, xx (1947), pp. 407–70, where the whole question is considered in its broadest outlines.

[2] See above all W. Bousset, op. cit., and its sequel *Jesus der Herr* (Göttingen, 1916).

[3] See E. J. and L. Edelstein, *Asclepius*, 2 vols. (Baltimore, 1945), where the use of hymns is amply documented.

[4] Especially in the 'doxa' form cf. Peterson, op. cit., pp. 224–7, and Werner, 'The Doxology in Synagogue and Church: a liturgico-musical Study'.

[5] But see also Vol. II, p. 2 i.

[6] See particularly Wellesz, 'Aufgaben und Probleme auf dem Gebiet der byzantinischen und orientalischen Kirchenmusik', *Liturgiegeschichtliche Forschungen*, Heft 6 (Münster, 1923), esp. pp. 39–60, and *A History of Byzantine Music and Hymnography* (Oxford, 1949), p. 154.

life of the early Christian communities of the Near East before they can be documented in the liturgical literature of the established Church.[1]

EARLY CHRISTIAN ANTIPHONY

Certain aspects of the early Christian use of music can be understood only if brief consideration is given also to the immediately post-Biblical period in the life of the Church. Relatively unimportant in this connexion are the statements of Pliny the Younger, that 'on a stated day they [the Christians] were accustomed to gather before daybreak and to utter responsively a song (?) to Christ as to a god' (*Epistulae* x. 96: 'quod essent soliti stato die ante lucem convenire carmenque Christo quasi deo dicere secum invicem'), and that of the Church historian Socrates (b. about A.D. 380) suggesting that Ignatius, the bishop of Antioch in Syria, introduced antiphonal singing into the Church as the result of a vision (*Historia Ecclesiastica*, vi. 8).[2] The former may be less significant than is often imagined because it must be interpreted in the light of the terminology of a Roman official and need not say more than that a formula (be it prayer, invocation or song) was used.[3] The latter ascribes to a specific person at a late time a practice so common in both Judaism and in the responses of pagan cults that no special revelation is needed for its inauguration in Christian usage.

GNOSTIC HYMNS

Far more important in this connexion is the evidence for the existence of large collections of lyrics produced in the second and third centuries of our era by the Christians and Gnostics of Syria and the Near East. Of these collections two have in recent years become directly available, namely, the Odes of Solomon and the Manichean Psalter.[3] Other collections known largely or entirely from hearsay include those of Valentinus, Bardesanes, and Marcion, the two last mentioned representing attempts to create a substitute for the Biblical Psalter.[4] Individual lyrics by unknown authors are

[1] See Wellesz, 'Aufgaben und Probleme', p. 15, and Vol. II, pp. 2–3.

[2] Cf. Dölger, op. cit., pp. 103–36.

[3] For the former see R. Harris and A. Mingana, *The Odes and Psalms of Solomon*, 2 vols. (Manchester, 1920), for the latter C. R. C. Allberry, *A Manichean Psalm Book* (Stuttgart, 1938), representing the Psalter of the Coptic Manichean Church. The bibliographical information about the extensive body of Manichean hymns from Turkestan published largely by the Prussian Academy will be found in C. F. Burkitt, *The Religion of the Manichees* (Cambridge, 1925), and in the article of H. J. Polotsky s.v. Manichäismus in Pauly-Wissowa, *Real-Encyclopädie*, Supplementband vi (Stuttgart, 1935).

[4] The sources of information are listed in A. v. Harnack, *Geschichte der altchristlichen Litteratur bis Eusebius* (Leipzig, 1893), esp. pp. 171, 183, 185–6, 197.

scattered about in the apocryphal acts (e.g. the Syriac *Acts of Thomas*) or quoted in the writings of the anti-heretical Fathers (e.g. Hippolytus).[1] The material is important in this connexion for various reasons. It shows how extensive was the production of Christian hymns in the early days, particularly in the regions of Syria, Egypt, and Mesopotamia, and thus shows in proper perspective the scattered fragments surviving from the period of the New Testament writings, when the fires of inspiration burned even brighter. It indicates that in addition to the groups producing hymns of the mixed types already examined, there were those for which the traditional forms of Hebrew and Jewish psalmody continued to be largely normative (for instance, the authors of the Odes of Solomon). Finally, it exhibits for the period before Ephraem and Narsai the use of the isosyllabic form of verse construction, a form that subsequently became of the utmost importance for Byzantine hymnody.[2] This form, in which the traditional accentual rhythm is adapted to the use of homogeneous melodic patterns by a principle of line construction that demands an equal number of syllables (seven or eight) in each line, appears in the extra-Biblical material for the first time in the poems of Bardesanes (A.D. 222). It should be noted, however, that this principle of construction is not necessarily a late feature of oriental poetry, but possibly indigenous in the tradition of Aramaic literature, as an inscription of the fifth century B.C. has been taken to imply. Indeed, it has been suggested that the Lord's Prayer, in its Lukan form, was arranged in accordance with the principle in question.[3]

In both its parts, therefore, the Bible is a treasure-house of information for the knowledge of ancient music. The limitation that it shares with so much ancient literature, namely, the absence of specific information about the musical patterns used by singers and instrumentalists, is offset by the strategic nature of the lyric material it has preserved. This material in its developing form and character provides the bridge that connects the music of the ancient Orient with that of the Middle Ages and thus with that of the western world.

[1] For the former see *Apocryphal Acts of the Apostles*, ed. W. Wright, ii (Edinburgh, 1871), pp. 150–1, 238–45 (Hymn of the Soul), 245–51; for the latter see Hippolytus, *Philosophoumena* v. 5 (Naasene Hymn).

[2] See also Vol. II, pp. 19–32.

[3] C. C. Torrey, 'A possible metrical Original of the Lord's Prayer', *Zeitschrift für Assyriologie* xxviii (Straßburg, 1913), pp. 312–17. The Aramaic inscription referred to is that of the Carpentras Stele, an epitaph of four double lines, each half line containing seven syllables, after the manner of the later lyrics. For the text cf. G. A. Cooke, *A Text-Book of North-Semitic Inscriptions* (Oxford, 1903), pp. 205–6.

VIII

THE MUSIC OF POST-BIBLICAL JUDAISM

By ERIC WERNER

INTRODUCTION

THREE facts have to be taken into account in attempting to give a survey of the music of post-Biblical Judaism. In the first place the subject is connected with the religious and political history of a wandering people whose migrations brought it into contact with all the nations of Europe and most of the nations of Asia. Secondly, the liturgical music of Judaism, from the destruction of the Temple (A.D. 70) onward, had to take a place between genuine folk-lore and art music, yet—until the nineteenth century—belonged to neither of these categories. The Jewish centres of the Orient, however, underwent a decline to a kind of standardized folk-lore, a change from a genuine flexibility to an almost petrified musical system. In this respect the Oriental Jews are in no way different from their Christian and Moslem neighbours since they, too, show no signs of musical development since the ninth century (Christian) and the fourteenth century (Moslem) respectively. It remained the particular excellence of European culture that its churches were always and everywhere capable of stimulating, assimilating, and integrating new attitudes of thought, and this is equally true of European Jewry. Since such living development is completely absent in the Near East, we shall have to distinguish between the history of Oriental and European Synagogue music from the tenth century onward. Finally, the growth of Synagogal music is intrinsically connected with the development and gradual change of Jewish liturgy. Therefore it will be necessary to refer to the field of liturgy.

We must bear in mind that the natural heritage of the Temple's levitical psalmody constituted the nucleus around which the new synagogal chant evolved. Here it is important to decide whether the original performance of the psalms was metrical. This question, however, can be answered only if we know for certain that parts of the Scriptures, e.g. the psalms or certain hymnical passages of the Pentateuch, were understood or performed metrically. Unfortunately, we are far from any definite answer to the problem. E. Sievers, D. H.

Müller, and many other scholars have most carefully investigated the possibility of a metrical structure in the Scriptures; but their results are vague, controversial, and by no means conclusive. Only two facts stand out as established principles: (1) the parallelism of Scriptural poetry, sometimes called 'dichotomical structure', which divides almost every poetical sentence into two parts, similar or antithetic in thought; (2) strophic structure, especially in certain prophetic 'songs', e.g. Isa. v; Jer. xxxii; Ezek. xxxvii, to name only three of the most famous instances. Nevertheless, quite a few famous historians such as Josephus, Jerome, and other Church Fathers insist that certain passages of Scripture were written in strictly metrical form. Again, since there is no positive evidence for metrical performance of Scripture, we have to assume that the music of the Temple was non-metrical, i.e. polyrhythmic, and that its rhythm was entirely dependent upon the accentuation of the text. The principle of parallelism has to be considered the origin of all dichotomic systems of performance, such as the *responsorium*, the strict *antiphona* and the responsorial psalmody, both in Judaism and in Christianity. The strophic or refrain structure may have played a part in the 'Songs of Ascent' (Pss. 120–34), although modern scholars have replaced the old Christian concept of these *psalmi graduum* by either the Talmudic interpretation of 'Songs of Pilgrimage' or by a reference to a rhetorical device of these psalms, the so-called anadiplosis (chain-figure).

CONTINUITY OF JEWISH TRADITION

It is of paramount importance to the study of Jewish music to determine whether its tradition was continuous in general, or interrupted by the frequent disasters and migrations that have been the lot of the Jewish people. If we search for an answer to this question in other fields of Jewish civilization—philosophy, theology, literature—the continuity of its development is assured beyond doubt. Yet some writers have drawn a sharp line across the musical tradition of Judaism, separating the culture of 'the Bible from that of the Ghetto'.[1] Only if there had been a danger of a radical rupture at any time after the fall of the Temple, should we have reason to assume a new untraditional beginning. The historical facts, however, speak unequivocally. The Temple services were regularly attended by divi-

[1] Notably L. Saminsky in *The Music of the Bible and of the Ghetto* (New York, 1937), which is a collection of more or less aphoristic and apodictic statements, most of them without historical foundation.

sions of 'standing-men' from the various provinces of Palestine. These men had a synagogue in the Temple area at their disposal—the so-called 'Hall of Stones' (Luc. ii. 46; Acts iii. 11; v. 12)—and the priests were entitled to conduct the services there, thus linking the rural communities with the tradition of the central sanctuary. One of the numerous personalities who endeavoured to transmit the priestly music to the representatives of the synagogue was R. Joshua ben Hananya who regularly taught the 'stand-up men' the institutions and the customs of the Temple. He was a famous singer and used to go from the orchestra of the Temple to the 'Hall of Stones' in order to conduct the daily service.[1] As a disciple of Johannan ben Zakkai, he assisted him in saving as much as possible of the Temple ritual that it might be rendered in the academy of Jamnia.[2] He and his contemporaries formed a strong link in the chain of tradition at a most critical time. Apart from these historical facts there are sufficient data to warrant the integrity of the musical tradition of Judaism. Comparisons with the music of the early Church will presently confirm our conclusions.

Rabbinic sources explain the strict prohibition of any instrumental music in the Synagogue as an expression of mourning for the loss of the Temple and land, but the present writer has been able to show that a certain animosity against all instrumental music existed well before the fall of the Temple. It seems that this enmity towards instrumental music was a defence against the musical and orgiastic mystery cults in which Syrian and Mesopotamian Jews not infrequently participated.[3] Similar utterances came from Philo and one of the Judaeo-Christian Sybilles, to name only two chief witnesses. The primitive Christian community held the same view, as we know from apostolic and post-apostolic literature: instrumental music was thought unfit for religious services; the Christian sources are quite outspoken in their condemnation of instrumental performances. Originally, only song was considered worthy of direct approach to the Divinity.[4]

In the two centres of Jewry, Palestine and Babylonia, the liturgy of the Synagogue was gradually developed, and—with it—its music.

[1] *Talmud*, 'Arakhîn 11b.

[2] *Talmud*, Succa 53a.

[3] Cf. Eric Werner, 'The Conflict between Hellenism and Judaism in the Music of the Early Church', in *Hebrew Union College Annual* (1947), pp. 416–20.

[4] Clement of Alexandria, *Paedagogus* ii. 4; Arnobius, *Adversus Nationes* in *Corp. Script. Eccl. Lat.* 4, 270; also Gregory Nazianzen, *Oratio* 5, 25, in *Patrologia Graeca* xxxv, col. 708/9.

If we compare the constituents of early Synagogue and early Church music, we arrive at the following parallelisms:

Synagogue	*Church*
Cantillation of Scriptures	Cantillation of Scriptures
Psalmody	Psalmody
Post-Biblical Prayers	Christian Prayers (chanted)
Melismatic Songs	Hymns
	Melismatic Songs

These elements, however, which at first seem to be identical, diverged considerably as regards musical performance as early as the late second or early third century. Not only did the hymn attain a predominant position in the Church, especially in Eastern Christianity, contrary to the rite of the Synagogue where the hymn-forms were not introduced until the sixth century, but even the Christian performance of psalmody differed to a certain degree from the Jewish.

Whereas in the Synagogue the precentor was the sole musical functionary until the sixth or seventh century the churches early developed choral singing, especially with the development of monasticism. On the other hand, a good deal of the musical tradition of the Synagogue was taken over and preserved by the Church.

CANTILLATION OF SCRIPTURE

The attitude of the early Synagogue is clearly expressed in the Talmudic statement: 'Whosoever reads Scripture without chant . . . to him the Scriptural word is applicable "I gave them laws and they heeded them not".'[1] The term 'cantillation of Scripture' is very complex, however, inasmuch as there is more than one system of Scriptural chant in existence. Not only do the various parts of the Bible employ different cantillation, according to their liturgical function, but considerable divergences of regional traditions play a certain part. Thus, the Yemenite Jews, whose tradition is by far the oldest, use a cantillation much at variance with the central and west European Jews (Ashkenazim), and these again differ from the former Spanish Israelites (Sephardim).[2]

Notwithstanding these variants, a common source is clearly discernible, the more so since the cantillation was to a certain extent regulated by three successive systems of Jewish ecphonetic notation.

[1] Megilla 32a.

[2] Cf. A. Z. Idelsohn, *Thesaurus of Hebrew Oriental Melodies*, i (Leipzig, 1914), preface; also R. Lachmann, *The Cantillation of the Jews of Djerba* (Jerusalem, 1940).

The first system (Proto-Palestinian) arose in the fifth century A.D. in Palestine; it was closely akin to the ancient Syrian system of notation consisting only of dots and a few strokes.[1] The second system emerged in Babylon during the late seventh and eighth centuries and used an intricate method of indicating the respective accents by the first letters of their names. The third, which finally proved best, was the system of the Tiberian Masorites which came into being during the ninth and tenth centuries; it shows a remarkable similarity to that of the early Byzantine ecphonetic signs.[2] A few illustrations may be cited:

Byzantine signs	Hebrew signs
＼ Bareia	＼ Legarmeh
～ Kathiste	～ Zarqa
✓ Kremaste	✓ Shofar munach
ℰ Hypokrisis	⅃ Shalshelet

Since the rabbinic sources of the early fifth century already show familiarity with the existence of primitive accents, we may assume that the ecphonetic systems arose in a country equally accessible to Byzantines, Palestinians, and Syrians: possibly north-west Syria. It should be noted in passing that the primary purpose of these accents was not the fixation of Scriptural cantillation but the minutely perfect punctuation and syntactic division of the Biblical text. Then the newly created accents were adjusted to the older cantillation. That such a cantillation existed in the early Christian liturgies of Jerusalem and Antioch, we know from various sources, chiefly from the Western Church Fathers. Thus we can explain why certain phrases of the Roman *tonus lectionis*, which is based upon Western neums, bear a remarkable resemblance to Jewish motives of cantillation such as:

Ex. 297

The Half Close

Levante   Italy   Yemenites

Climacus resupinus   Benedi - - cti - o - ne per - petua.

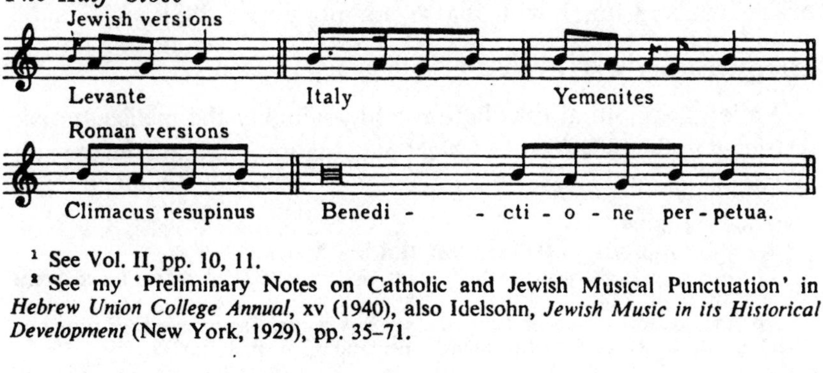

[1] See Vol. II, pp. 10, 11.
[2] See my 'Preliminary Notes on Catholic and Jewish Musical Punctuation' in *Hebrew Union College Annual*, xv (1940), also Idelsohn, *Jewish Music in its Historical Development* (New York, 1929), pp. 35–71.

The Full Stop

Jewish versions

Central European Yemenites Syrian

Roman versions

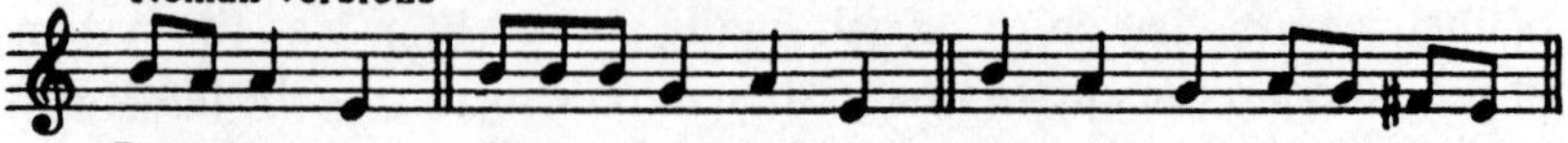

Punctus versus Tonus antiquus Close of First Psalm Tone

PSALM TONES

The same resemblance exists between the psalm tones; yet here a distinction must be made. Formerly, some scholars thought the Jewish and Gregorian psalm tones to be remnants of the Temple liturgy. This cannot be so, since, hardly 150 years after the fall of the Temple, the Rabbis disagreed concerning the Temple's singing of the Hallel (Ps. 113–18), the most solemn and revered collection of psalms.[1] All possible forms of responsorial and antiphonal performance are mentioned in those passages of the Talmud where the Hallel is discussed. The close kinship between Oriental Jewish psalmody, on the one hand, and Gregorian, Armenian, and Syrian psalm tones, on the other, impels us to assume that it was not the Temple, but the early Synagogue which served as a common source. The strict parallelism, the fundamental principle of Hebrew poetry, was carefully preserved in all the translations of the Bible. This dichotomic structure led to the establishment of such typically psalmodic practices as responses, antiphons, refrain-psalms, &c., all of which were taken over by the Churches. The claims of the Church Fathers that Basilius, or Flavian and Diodorus invented antiphonal singing, must be understood to mean that these men introduced such forms in the Gentile Church,[2] for in Judaism they were well known for centuries before the rise of Christianity.[3] It is instructive to compare a few psalm tones of the Roman Church with Jewish psalmody[4] (Ex. 298).

AUTONOMOUS MELODY

While in Scriptural cantillation and psalmody the melismata are restricted to the function of musical punctuation, marking the caesura

[1] *Talmud*, Sota 30b.

[2] See also Chap. VII, p. 311, and Vol. II, Chap. I, p. 6.

[3] Cf. *Tosefta*, ed. Zuckermandel (Halberstadt, 1881), pp. 303 f.; also *Mekhilta*, ed. Weiss (Vienna, 1865), pp. 42 ff.

[4] For the ancient version of Tonus IV see P. Wagner, *Gregorianische Formenlehre* (1921), p. 90; for the example from the Lamentations, see ibid., p. 239.

Ex. 298

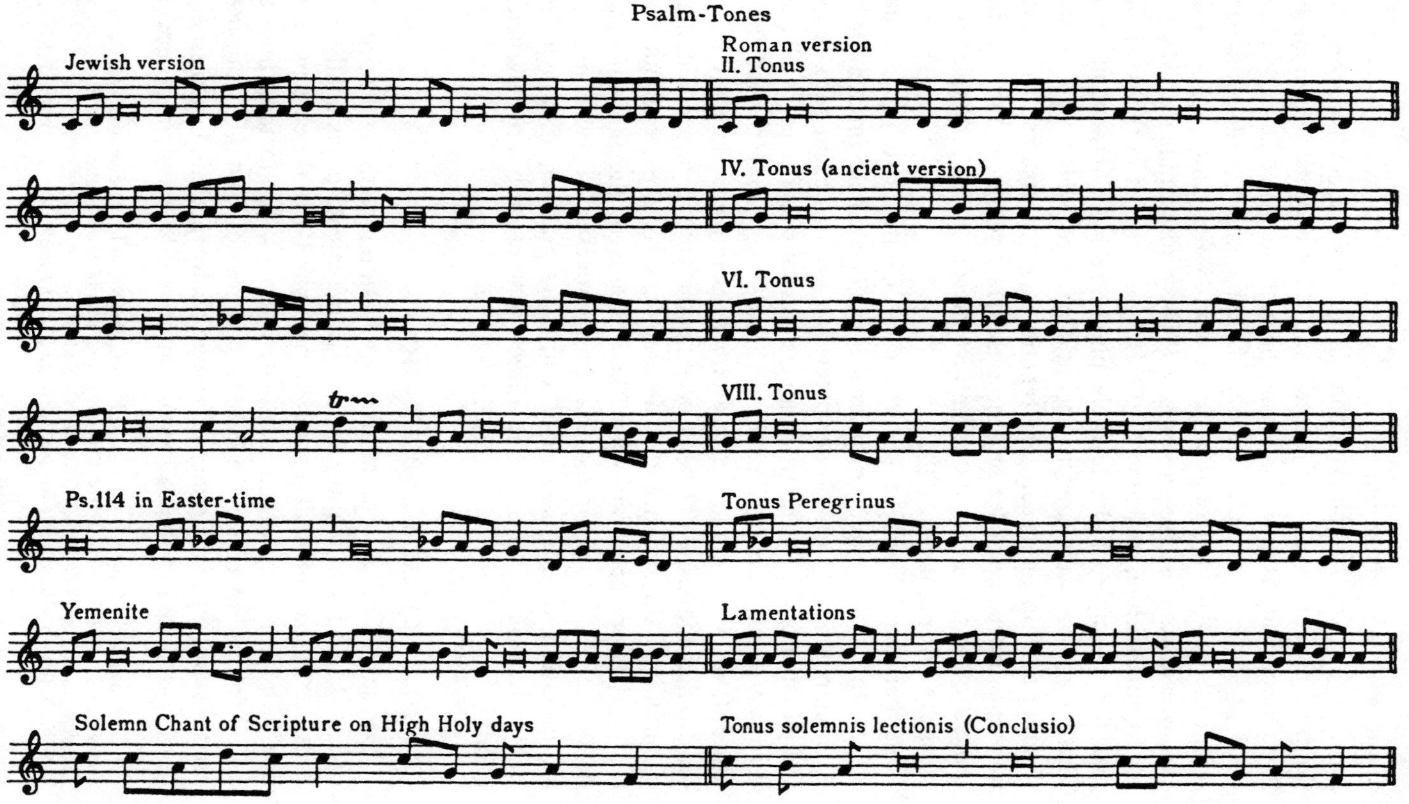
Psalm-Tones
Jewish version
Roman version
II. Tonus
IV. Tonus (ancient version)
VI. Tonus
VIII. Tonus
tr
Ps.114 in Easter-time
Tonus Peregrinus
Yemenite
Lamentations
Solemn Chant of Scripture on High Holy days
Tonus solemnis lectionis (Conclusio)

in the middle, and the punctus at the end of the verse, in another form the melisma assumes full domination. As distinct from cantillation and psalmody, where syntactic and tonic accents determine the flow, the melody is autonomous in the ecstatic 'Alleluias' and independent of the word. Even Isidore of Seville knew of the synagogal origin of the Alleluia songs when he said 'Laudes, hoc est Alleluia canere canticum est Hebraeorum'.[1] ('The praises, that is to say the singing of Alleluia, is a song of the Hebrews.') It is in the Alleluias that the principle of the formula plays the most important part. These formulas were ancient melodic patterns which were linked together and, through constant repetition, often assumed the function and character of leading-motives. They represent the first instances of absolute or 'autonomous' music. A few examples will illustrate this point (Ex. 299).

Neither the Synagogue nor the early Church had professional choirs. In the first three centuries the *sheliach tsibbur* (messenger of the congregation), an honorary precentor, performed all parts of the liturgy, supported by the worshippers' responses. The early Church used the terms *psalmista*, *lector*, *anagnostes*, or *cantor* for the same office. Only when monasticism attained its influence in the Church did trained monastic choruses become the rule in larger Christian communities. In Judaism this development took place about two centuries later—650–700—when the students of the talmudic academies of Babylon formed standing choruses.[2] It was perhaps an imitation of the successful Christian practice, although the Babylonian Jews were not in direct contact with any Christian Church.

THE MODES OF SYNAGOGUE MUSIC

No use of chordal or harmonic construction is made by the peoples of the Near East. Unison melody is prevalent, occasionally embellished by instrumental accompaniment parallel to the chief melodic line with improvised ornaments (heterophony). The melodic lines of all Near Eastern music are based upon modes. Judaism, too, uses certain stereotyped melodic patterns which, by repetition and association, crystallized in the course of centuries into a system of modes.

[1] Isidorus Hisp. *De offic.* i. 13, in *Patrologia Latina* 83, col. 750. See also Vol. II, p. 5, and Werner, 'The Attitude of the Church Fathers to Hebrew Psalmody', in *Review of Religion* (1943), pp. 339–52.

[2] Cf. Nathan ha-Babli in Neubauer, *Medieval Jewish Chroniclers*, ii (Oxford, 1887–95), pp. 83–88; also my study 'The Doxology in Synagogue and Church', *Hebrew Union College Annual*, xix (1946), p. 307, where a full translation is given.

Ex. 299

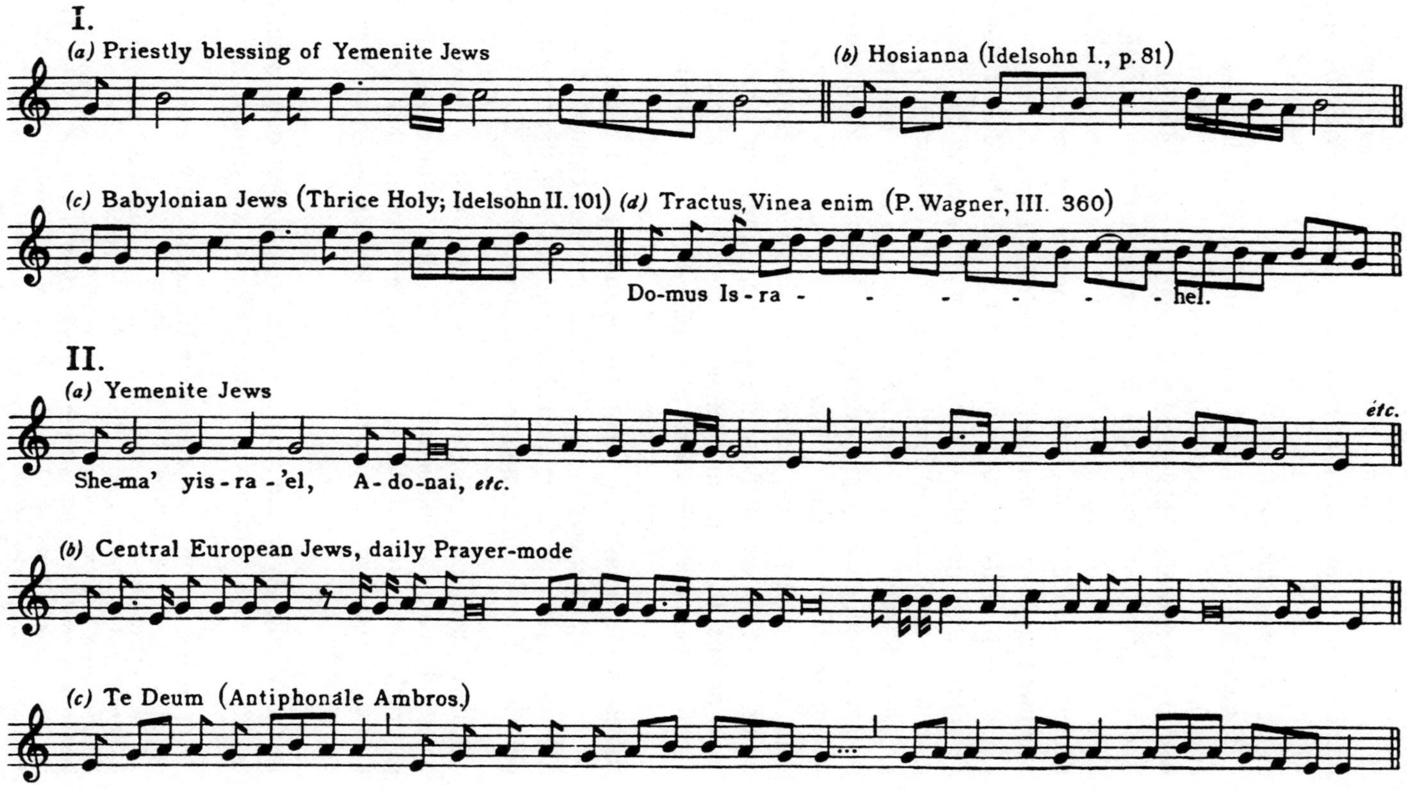
I.
(a) Priestly blessing of Yemenite Jews
(b) Hosianna (Idelsohn I., p. 81)
(c) Babylonian Jews (Thrice Holy; Idelsohn II. 101)
(d) Tractus, Vinea enim (P. Wagner, III. 360)
Do-mus Is - ra - - - - - - hel.
II.
(a) Yemenite Jews
etc.
She-ma' yis - ra - 'el, A - do-nai, etc.
(b) Central European Jews, daily Prayer-mode
(c) Te Deum (Antiphonale Ambros.)

Why eight modes seem to have constituted the generally accepted number is not quite clear; indeed, this question is so obscure that it will be useful to explore the origin of modality as much or as little as the scope of this chapter will permit.

The eight modes, which we know from Christian theorists (*Oktoechos*), in spite of their octave-like arrangement, have nothing to do with the system of a scale reaching through the interval of an octave. The earliest accessible sources demonstrate that the conception of eight modes originated with the calendar. Hittite and Babylonian documents allude to this,[1] but the connexion becomes quite clear when we bear in mind that the Syro-Byzantine *Oktoechos* was originally a group of hymns to be sung on the eight Sundays following Pentecost. This reminds one strongly of the ancient Pentacontade calendar of the Near East in which eight holidays were inserted into a period of fifty days (seven weeks plus one day). This calendar system is still, to a certain extent, linked to the *Oktoechos* of the Nestorian and Armenian Churches.

In Judaism the musical modes have undergone numerous developments. First, as we see from the superscriptions and structures of some psalms, they were an esoteric secret of the priestly cast. Thus Psalm vi bears the inscription '*'al ha-sheminit*'; the usual interpretation of *sheminit*, meaning 'the eighth', has led to translations such as 'tunes in the octave' or 'upon an instrument with eight strings'. Neither of these explanations is satisfactory when compared with an old rabbinic interpretation quoted by Saadya Gaon, the great Jewish philosopher of the ninth and tenth centuries. He writes:

> This is a hymn . . . in which the regular singers of the Temple were ordered to praise God in the eighth *laḥan* [Arabic for 'mode' or 'melodic pattern']. The expression '*'al ha-sheminit*' demonstrates that the Levites used eight modes, so that each time one of their regular groups executed one mode.[2]

In the Middle Ages, the Jewish modes were understood as hermeneutic devices to attune the human soul to the various emotions

[1] Cf. my study on 'The oldest sources of Octave and Octoechos', *Acta Musicologica*, xx (1948), p. 1, where all pertinent documents are quoted.

[2] Saadya Gaon's psalm-translation, ed. S. H. Margulies (Breslau, 1884), pp. 11, 13, 30 (Arabic and German); also H. Ewald, *Über die Arabisch geschriebenen Werke jüdischer Sprachgelehrten* (Stuttgart, 1844), pp. 14 ff. The entire question is comprehensively treated by H. G. Farmer in *Saadya Gaon and Music* (London, 1943), pp. 78 ff, and by E. Werner and I. Sonne, 'Philosophy and Theory of Music in Judaeo-Arabic Literature', *Hebrew Union College Annual*, xvi (1941 and 1943), pp. 295 ff. and E. Werner, 'The Origin of the 8 Modes', ibid. (1948), pp. 220 ff.

expressed in the Scriptural and post-Biblical poetry of Judaism. Then they deteriorated to musical habits, especially when they became imitations of Arab modes or melodies (*laḥanim*). In the eighteenth century they were all but forgotten, but in the middle of the nineteenth century they were rediscovered and reconsidered. In these circumstances their tradition is by no means free from corruption, and authenticity can be claimed for only a few. Owing to constant repetition and association with certain liturgical types, the Jewish modes have today a strong hermeneutic function, linking special prayer-types with special modes. This practice is, of course, one of the numerous instances of the 'ethos doctrine' of music, common to all ancient nations.

Ex. 300

Structure of Jewish Prayer-Modes

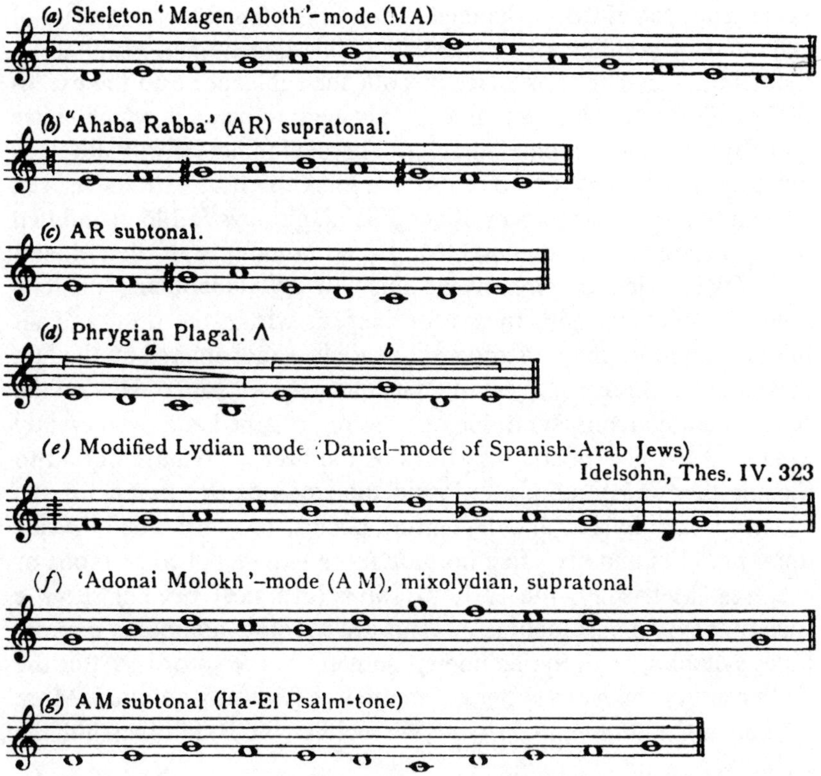

These modes are not of the scale character that was imposed upon the modes of the Church by medieval theorists; they are rather models of melodic types. In addition to these chief modes, we find, especially among the Oriental Jews, a number of other patterns that do not easily submit to systematization.[1]

One of these modes, the main strain of Hellenistic psalmody, was especially singled out by the Church Father Clement of Alexandria in the beginning of the third century. Clement praises the majestic psalmody of the Alexandrian Jews, which was chanted in the *Tropos Spondeiakos*.[2] We have exact descriptions of this ancient mode by Plutarch and other writers; and it can still be traced in the oldest strata of Jewish, Byzantine, and Roman Catholic chant.[3]

THE INFLUENCE OF POETRY ON THE DEVELOPMENT OF SYNAGOGUE MUSIC

So long as Biblical diction, and its more or less conscious imitation, dominated the language of the Jewish liturgy, the musical forms and expressions remained unchanged—even in the first bitter centuries of exile and of conflict with conquering Christianity. But gradually a momentous change took place in both the substance and the execution of the liturgy. A new poetic style came into being in which metre and rhyme played important roles. The beginnings of this development reach back to the fifth century. It was caused by external as well as by internal circumstances. Since Justinian's *novella* 146 prohibited the *Deuterosis* (Bible exegesis, Midrashic homily) in the Jewish service, Jewry tried to circumvent this law by introducing didactic homiletic poetry as substitutes for exegesis within the liturgy. That this was no more than an apparent cause is demonstrated by the fact that after the Arab conquest of Palestine and Babylonia (636–50) the Jews, liberated from Byzantine oppression, retained and even greatly expanded the new poetic insertions of the liturgy. We are bound to assume that Jewry simply followed the trend of the times, for the contemporary Syrian and Byzantine poems, too, are chiefly based upon homilies and are often nothing more than versified sermons or exegeses. Metrically, the early *piyyutim* (liturgical poems) show a variety of systems; sometimes accents are counted (homotony), sometimes syllables, as in Syriac poetry, sometimes even words. After the tenth century the Arab system of metre was generally adopted. More difficult is the problem of rhyme, for neither the Byzantines nor the

[1] Cf. especially the motives cited in Lachmann, op. cit., pp. 98 ff.; also R. Lach's remarks in 'Die vergleichende Musikwissenschaft', *Sitzungsberichte der Akademie der Wissenschaften* (Vienna, *c.* 1924), pp. 35 ff., 89.

[2] Clement of Alexandria, *Paedagogus*, ii, ch. iv (P.G. 8, col. 445).

[3] Cf. my study 'The Attitude of the Church Fathers to Hebrew Psalmody', *Review of Religion* (1943), esp. pp. 349–52.

Syrians ever cultivated it very much except for some forms of rhymed prose; perhaps Jewry adopted pre-Islamic or even Mandaic patterns of rhyme, although they were rather primitive.

The introduction of metre and rhyme brought with it a new type of music, not necessarily a periodic symmetrical one like the occidental music of the eighteenth century, but a kind of chant which could no longer disregard the principles of metre and strophic structure. The first pioneer to take cognizance of these changes seems to have been Rabbi Jehudai Gaon (*c.* 720), of whom it is said that 'the early *Ḥazanim* (cantors) learned musical tradition from him as he had learned it from his teachers for many generations'.[1] He championed the cause of new poetry and even ruled that a blind cantor might be appointed if his other qualifications recommended him. He also advocated the ternary form a–b–a in liturgical rubrics where the prayer opens and closes with a eulogy. They should be chanted to the same tune, 'but the middle should be sung differently, yet not too differently'. Jehudai Gaon, therefore, must be considered as the father of Jewish musical tradition. Shortly before his time, the great Palestinian poets Jannai and Jose ben Jose show, both in form and content, remarkable resemblance to contemporary Byzantine hymnody, especially to the form of the *kontakion*.[2]

After the Arab conquest of Babylonia, Palestine, and Spain (711), the Jews of the Iberian Peninsula established themselves in a close symbiosis with the ruling Arab class. The centuries between 800 and 1400 witnessed the rise of a magnificent Jewish culture in Spain which furthered religion, philosophy, literature, and music. The famous poet and philosopher of the Spanish epoch, Jehudah Halevi (1085–1141), discusses unfavourably the aspects of metrical music in his philosophical work *The Kuzari*, still preferring the old psalmodic improvising chant. Others, however, felt differently. A number of Spanish-Jewish writers, mostly writing in Arabic, showed considerably more understanding of the musical demands of metrical poetry; they even stressed the value of musical theory and championed its study. Their attitude represented a mixture of Arabic, Biblical, and Greek ideas.[3] Few musical documents, however, have been preserved.

[1] Cf. my study on Doxology in *Hebrew Union College Annual*, xix (1946), pp. 303 ff.

[2] The greatest Byzantine *melodos*, Romanus, was of Jewish parentage, and his famous hymn upon the reappearance of Christ and the Day of Judgement is based upon various rabbinic homilies. Cf. Vol. II, p. 21, and E. Wellesz, 'Melito's Homily' in *Journal of Theological Studies*, Oxford (1943), pp. 46 ff.

[3] Cf. Werner and Sonne 'Philosophy and Theory of Music in Judaeo-Arabic literature', *Hebrew Union College Annual*, xvi (1941 and 1943), pp. 262 ff; also Curt Sachs, *The Rise of Music in the Ancient World*, pp. 277 ff.

In contrast with the conservative Arab-inspired philosophy of the writers are the sources which have come down to us either by oral tradition or through documents. From the fourteenth century on, Judaeo-Spanish folk-songs, as well as artistic accomplishments, show a distinct inclination to follow Western and not Arab leadership, all efforts of the music department of the Baghdad *Bait-ḥikma* (Academy) notwithstanding.

The oldest known manuscript of Hebrew music[1] is a 'Eulogy on the Death of Moses', written in Lombardic neums on a four-line stave. Its text, and probably also its music, was composed by an otherwise unknown Amr ibn Saḥ'l who lived in the eleventh century; it is very much akin to the more elaborate types of Gregorian chant.[1]

Ex. 301

It seems to have originated at Ravenna, or thereabouts, although it was found in Cairo; the neums are Italian in type, while the Hebrew script shows Byzantine influence. Shortly after the thirteenth century the Italian Jews became the recognized leaders in poetry and music; their position was strengthened by the catastrophe that befell Spanish Jewry at the end of the fifteenth century.

THE MUSIC OF ITALIAN JEWRY

Generally speaking, the chant of the Synagogue had remained on

[1] The manuscript is in possession of the Jewish Theological Seminary in New York; (E. Adler Collection No. 4096). Cf. my paper, 'The Oldest Sources of Synagogal Chant', *Proceedings of the American Academy for Jewish Research*, xvi (1947), pp. 225–32.

the level of stylized folk-song for many centuries. The transition from this position to the sphere of genuine art music began with the early Renaissance and was nowhere so well developed as in Italy. There we find composers of Jewish extraction as early as the end of the fifteenth century. The papal court of Leo X (1513–21) employed two Jewish musicians, Jacobo Sansecondo, probably the model of Raphael's 'Apollo on Mount Parnassus', and Giovanni Maria, who, in honour of the Pope, surnamed himself 'De Medicis'.[1] The sixteenth century produced a score of outstanding Jewish musicians in Italy, of whom we need mention only those who were employed at the court of the Dukes of Mantua, the very liberal Gonzagas: Abramo dall' Arpa Ebreo, Isacchino Massarano, David da Civita and Allegro Porto.

Something must be said here about the institution of the ghetto and its influence upon the music of the Jews within its boundaries. The Fourth Lateran Council, under Pope Innocent III (1215), decided to segregate the Jews as radically as possible from their Christian fellow-citizens, placing them in ghetti that were closed at nightfall; social or professional intercourse with the Christian community was virtually made impossible. It took about two generations before these decrees were fully implemented, but from about 1270 until the end of the fifteenth century these stern rules were faithfully carried out, and the Franciscan and Dominican monks did everything in their power to excite the Christians against Jewry.[2] Under these circumstances, while every tradition was loyally preserved in the ghetti, there was no opportunity for development. The ghetto did not kill Judaism and its institutions, but it condemned them to stagnation and gradual deterioration. No wonder, then, that we hear practically nothing of music from Jewish sources. Italian archives, however, especially those of Venice, Leghorn, and Ferrara contain a number of decrees against Jewish music-teachers.[3]

At the end of the sixteenth century two remarkable persons appeared who at one stroke raised synagogal music to the high standard of contemporary music in general. They were Rabbi Leon da Modena and his protégé Solomone de' Rossi il Ebreo. The initiative came from the Rabbi, one of the most colourful personalities of Jewish history. Brilliant and profound scholar, anonymous pamphleteer against himself, composer and conductor, prolific writer, gambler, alchemist: in short, a jack of twenty-six trades (which he carefully enumerated), he

[1] Cf. E. Birnbaum, *Jüdische Musiker am Hof von Mantua* (Vienna, 1893).
[2] Cf. Cecil Roth, *The History of the Jews in Italy* (Philadelphia, 1946), pp. 177 ff.
[3] A. F. Rio, *Les Quatre martyrs* (Paris, 1856), p. 34.

founded a musical society in the ghetto of Venice. One of his (converted) disciples Giulio Morosini has given us a good description of Modena's *Accademia musicale*.[1] The practice of having double choirs, then popular in Venice, was introduced to the ghetto by Rabbi da Modena, and he himself composed a series of such choral pieces in the style of the Gabrielis.[2] But his chief merit is that he induced Salamone Rossi to compose a book of synagogal music. This work, *The Songs of Solomon*, published by Bragadin (Venice, 1620), contains thirty-odd choral pieces ranging from three to eight parts. The style of his music resembles that of Monteverdi, with whom Rossi collaborated in the composition of the sacred drama *Maddalena* (*Sacra rappresentazione di Giov. Batt. Andreini Fiorentino*) in 1617. Rossi's synagogue compositions contain few, if any, traces of Jewish tradition. While they are of enchanting beauty and religious spirit, they remained alien to the customary vein of synagogue song, which was the main reason why they fell rapidly into oblivion after Modena's death.[3]

The merit of having preserved portions of old Jewish music belongs not to a Jew but to the Christian Benedetto Marcello (1686–1739), a Venetian noble. He collected twelve traditional chants of Venetian Jewry and used them as *canti fermi* in his composition of the first fifty Psalms, the famous *Estro poetico-armonico*, published in 1724–7. This attempt to revive ancient psalm tunes must be considered a late aftermath of former humanistic efforts to explore scientifically the fields of Scripture, Hebrew history, and literature. It has been shown independently by Idelsohn and myself that a number of Marcello's Jewish tunes originate in the twelfth to the fourteenth centuries both in Spain and in central Europe. Here only three of the most interesting examples will be quoted, showing Arabic as well as Gregorian influences.[4]

Ex. 302

[1] A translation is given in my study 'Manuscripts of the Birnbaum Collection', *Hebrew Union College Annual*, xvii (1944), pp. 414–16.

[2] Ibid. The manuscripts are in the Library of the Hebrew Union College.

[3] A selected edition of Salamone Rossi's vocal compositions has been edited by Samuel Naumbourg and Vincent d'Indy, 2 vols. (Paris, 1876).

[4] Marcello's Hebrew tunes are published and analysed in my study 'Die hebräischen Intonationen B. Marcellos', *Monatsschrift für Geschichte und Wissenschaft des*

(b) Intonazione degli Ebrei tedeschi sopra *Maos Zur*

(c) Intonazione degli Ebrei spagnuoli su'l Salmo: *Shiru ladonai*

THE MUSIC OF CENTRAL EUROPEAN JEWRY

The music of Central European Jewry is of particular interest to the musicologist because of its amazing capacity for development and for active assimilation of foreign elements without loss of identity.

The finest musical monument erected by Central European Jewry is a group of solemn chants for the festivals and High Holidays which in the fifteenth century were already known as '*Missinai* tunes' (melodies from Mt. Sinai). They represent the highest musical accomplishment of German Jewry up to the nineteenth century and reflect, in every phrase of music and text, the eschatological and mystical longings of a persecuted people. While quite a few motives of the '*Missinai* tunes' originated in the Burgundian art music of the out-going thirteenth and early fourteenth centuries and show certain resemblances to pieces by Guillaume de Machaut, these borrowed elements are by no means clearly discernible; they are completely integrated into the traditional style of European Synagogue music. This style was replete with 'wandering motives' which soon became associated with certain Hebrew phrases or ideas, and thus in course of time became veritable leitmotives. Two examples will illustrate this point (Ex. 303).

Judentums (Breslau, 1937), pp. 393–416. Cf. also Idelsohn's 'The Traditional Songs of the German Jews in Italy', *Hebrew Union College Annual*, xiii (1938), pp. 569–91.

Ex. 303

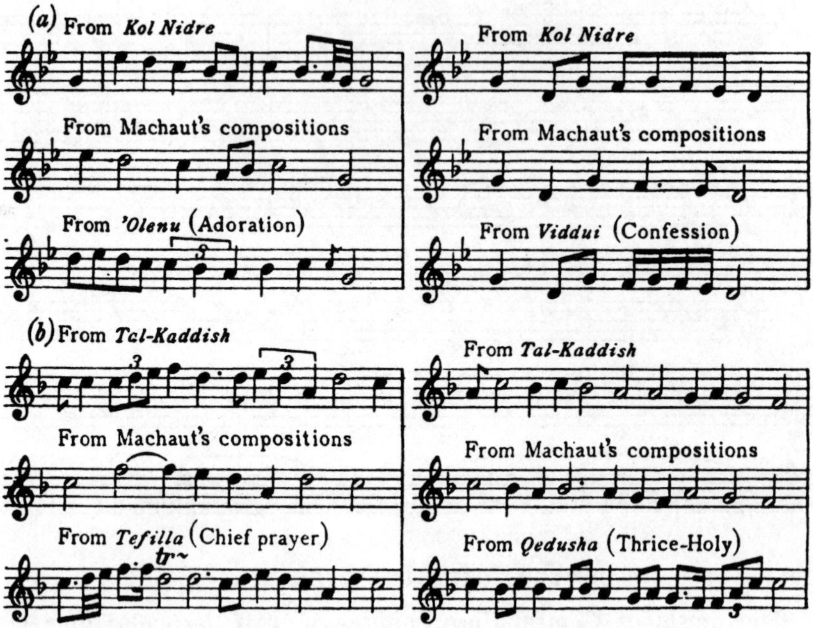

The region in which this assimilation with Burgundian music took place was that which surrounded the old Jewish communities of the Rhineland, especially the cities of Worms, Mainz, Speyer, Treves, and Strasbourg. There we encounter a surprisingly strong familiarity with western German and eastern French folk-songs, many of which were integrated and adjusted to the older style of Jewish chants. Songs like 'Wenn ich des Morgen's früh aufsteh', 'Der Lindenschmied', 'Der Bruder-Veit's Ton', &c., became—with altered rhythm and tonality (changed from the original second and eighth to modified first and fifth mode)—part and parcel of Central European Synagogue music. This kind of adaptation of German folk-music came to an end about 1600 when the constant persecutions, peasant and other wars had all but annihilated the Jewish communities so that many were forced to emigrate either to Poland and Russia or to Italy. With the end of the sixteenth century began the rapid deterioration of West and Central European Synagogue music.

As distinct from Jewry in the Arab orbit, European Jewry showed very little interest in musical theory. One interesting exception should be noted, however; in the year 1342 Leo Hebraeus (Rabbi Levi ben Gerson, also known as Gersonides) was requested by Philippe de Vitry to 'demonstrate a certain presupposition in musical science'. In fulfilling this request, Leo Hebraeus wrote his treatise *De Numeris Harmonicis* in which he placed Philip's principle of *prolationes* upon a secure mathematical basis which proved to be most appropriate for the further development of the notation of the *ars nova* and subsequent systems.[1]

THE MUSIC OF EAST-EUROPEAN JEWRY

The Jews who emigrated to Poland and Russia from the fourteenth century onward to 1600 found already established Jewish communities in their new homeland, chiefly in the south-eastern portions. Most of these earlier settlers had at one time or another escaped the turmoil in Persia, the Caucasus, or the persecution of the Byzantine government. They spoke Old-Slavonic or Tatar. It was only when the German immigrants came, with their superior Jewish culture and education, that these languages yielded to the Judaeo-German of the newcomers which in later centuries developed into a new language, the Yiddish idiom of all Eastern European Jewry. Together with their Middle-German language, the native Jews also learned their traditional songs. After a period of uncritical acceptance, a certain aversion to the German-Jewish songs set in and this led to a reshaping of the Synagogue chant of the eastern European Jews about the year 1620. During this revision the cantor (*Ḥazan*) attained a position of paramount importance. Keen to hear new music as the Eastern European Jews always were, but restricted to the synagogue as their main institution of learning and art, they naturally urged the cantor to satisfy this longing. He was forever called upon to provide new tunes for the weekly service on Friday evening and the Sabbath and to interpret and arrange them in a manner that would satisfy the artistic longings of the congregations. Says Idelsohn: 'The Jew demanded that the *Ḥazan*, through his music, make him forget his actual life and elevate him upon the wings of his tunes into a fantastic paradisiacal world, affording him a foretaste of Messianic times in the heavenly Jerusalem.'[2] The requirements of a good *Ḥazan* were: he had to possess a sweet voice, in the Oriental sense, meaning a lyric tenor of nasal quality (called by the Byzantians ἐνδόφωνον); he had to be well trained in brilliant coloratura-singing, since the Eastern European

[1] Neither Coussemaker, *Script. Med. Aevi*, iii. 10, nor Riemann, *Geschichte der Musiktheorie* (Berlin, 2nd ed., 1920), pp. 235 ff. understood the real intent of Leo Hebraeus's treatise, which I demonstrated in 'Theory and Philosophy of Music in Judaeo-Arabic Literature', *Hebrew Union College Annual*, xvii (1943), appendix ii, pp. 564–72.

[2] Cf. Idelsohn's study 'The Features of the Jewish Sacred Folk Song in Eastern Europe', *Acta musicologica*, iv (1932), pp. 19–21.

style is replete with virtuoso passages of dazzling fantasy and finesse; he had to be a versatile and original improviser upon certain traditional modes, exactly as the Arabic or Turkish recital singers improvise upon certain *maqāmāt*.[1] East European Jewry called these modes *Gust* (from the Italian *gusto*) or *Steiger*. The improvisations were strictly modal and polyrhythmic, rarely influenced by the West-European systems of beat or metre. The favourite modes were:

1. The *Ahaba Rabba* mode (Great Love): E–F–G♯–A–B–C–D–E, with a tendency to build the tune around the tenor D or A. The Greek Orthodox Church knows this mode, too, as its *Echos* ii and iv.[2] As in Jewish practice, it is used there mainly for supplicatory texts. It seems probable that the eastern Jews borrowed this mode from the Byzantine Church since it was unknown to Central European Jewry. Other elements of Greco-Slavonic church music have penetrated into eastern Jewish chant, as a comparison between the Russian Synodal hymn books and the Jewish folk-songs clearly shows. Cf. Ex. 300 (*b*), (*c*).
2. The *Tefilla* mode (Prayer): the melodic pattern strongly resembles the fifth Gregorian psalm-tone; its scale is mixolydian. Cf. Ex. 300 (*f*).
3. The *Magen Aboth* mode (Shield of the Fathers): this corresponds to a Dorian scale with a minor sixth and is characterized by its melodic pattern. It moves towards the fifth, leaps to the octave, and then rapidly descends to the *finalis*. Cf. Ex. 300 (*a*).

The emphasis on the vocal soloist, who at the same time had to perform a priestly function, led inevitably to the idolization of certain outstanding singers, improvisation led to anarchy, brilliance to empty showmanship; profound religiosity became, in the course of this development, a matter of routine or habit for the cantor. Still, by virtue of his experience, he was able to stir his audience to the depth of religious emotion. But by the end of the eighteenth century this style had lost its genuineness.

DISINTEGRATION OF SYNAGOGUE MUSIC BEFORE THE ERA OF EMANCIPATION

The beginning of the disintegration of Central and East European Synagogue music was arrested for almost a full century by a new movement whose roots lay deep in the realm of mysticism. Hasidism, which—in some respects—may be compared to the pietism of the seventeenth and early eighteenth centuries, came into being in eastern Europe. It was originally a reaction against rigid rabbinism, but in

[1] See pp. 449–50.

[2] J. B. Rebours, *Traité de Psaltique* (Paris, 1906), pp. 47, 90, 111. It seems that the mode is of Turko-Tatar origin, since neither classic Jewish nor Arab musicians up to the fourteenth century make any mention of it.

the course of time it developed an independent philosophy of its own. One of its main goals was the attainment of supreme bliss through a mystic approach to God. Music became a chief device of this esoteric philosophy. It was agreed by all adherents of Hasidism that song (without words) was capable of transforming the soul of the singing worshipper to such an extent that definite stages of a mystic approach to God could be reached, stages which otherwise were most difficult to attain.[1] The ideas that song is the soul of the universe, that the realm of heaven sings, and similar notions are amazingly like those of the early Christian mystics; even Augustine's description of the wordless *Jubili* is born out of the same feeling that mystical music reaches a realm near to God. (It would be a worthy task to compare the ideas of early Christianity concerning music with those of Hasidism; striking parallels would certainly emerge.) Since the Rabbi of the Hasidic community was always the guiding spirit in mystic lore, it became a common practice for the Rabbi to compose his own 'God-hymns'. Many of them have come down to us in full notation. They invariably start slowly and majestically, but increase in intensity and speed until they reach a fast dance-like rhythm that leads into either an ecstatic jubilation or a lament. These pieces were called *niggunim* (plural of *niggun*, tune). In the development of Hasidism they became something like musical symbols of the various schools and ideologies which the respective Rabbi-composers had conceived.

When the economic and political situation of eastern European Jewry became less and less tolerable, large waves of emigrants flooded central and then western Europe. A large number of the emigrants were singers and cantors; their route was usually via Silesia or Moravia to Bavaria. These eastern singers carried the traditions of Hasidic music with them; thus we frequently encounter Hasidic tunes in central Europe from about 1750 on. The central European cantors, fascinated by the beauty of Austrian and German art music as well as of Hasidic tunes, frequently tried to reconcile these two strange worlds of music. This was occasionally attempted by simple juxtaposition, often producing deplorable results, sometimes by a more refined technique, whereby occasionally fine pieces emerged. One of this latter category, a duet for soprano and alto, by Abraham di Caceres of Amsterdam (1740) is given here. The general style resembles that of Handel's or Jommelli's chamber duets, but the melodic

[1] Rabbi Shneor Zalman said: 'For the song of the souls—at the time they are swaying in the high regions to drink from the well of the Almighty King—consists of tones only, free and dismantled of burdensome words.'

line is strongly influenced by eastern Jewish chant (┌ ‡ marks such passages).[1]

Ex. 304

Through the influx of heterogeneous elements such as Slav and German folk-songs, Russian church music, Hasidic tunes, and, above all, art music of central Europe, the Jews who had lost much of their positive assimilating power since 1600 were faced with a task far beyond their ability. They were no longer capable of integrating the various elements into the body of their traditional music; they could no longer even preserve that treasure. Ignorant cantors, being exploited singers, urged by the cravings of the congregations for ever-new music, made a theatre or music-hall out of the Synagogue. Its songs were secularized: contaminated with poor imitations of Italian bravura arias, miserable vocal arrangements of Gluck's or Haydn's instrumental pieces. This development was all but inevitable since the ghetti could no longer completely segregate the Jews from their cultural environments. They hungered for new music but were, under the

[1] MS. in the Library of the Hebrew Union College, Cincinnati.

rabbinical and secular laws, permitted to hear music solely in the Synagogue where it was performed vocally, and usually by untrained singers. Small wonder, then, that the emancipation caught the Jews in a condition where they cared very little for traditional music; it was their primary desire to absorb the fascinating trends of contemporary European music. Typical of this is the enthusiasm with which certain Jewish laymen—and women—followed the course of two famous sons of Johann Sebastian Bach. Sara Levy, daughter of the Berlin 'Hofjude' Daniel Itzig, the financier of Frederick the Great, and her circle, were among the favourite disciples of Wilhelm Friedemann Bach and she was highly praised as a fine harpsichordist by C. P. E. Bach. She performed many of their works at the early performances of the Berlin Singakademie.[1] Only when a certain point of saturation was reached did they remind themselves of their abandoned treasure. By then, about 1840, a good deal of that tradition had been lost or irrevocably forgotten. Under the auspices of modern Liberal Judaism and the science of Judaism a rejuvenation of Synagogue music has taken place. But this *ars nova* had originally only a loose connexion with the ancient tradition; it took almost a century for the new style to become so firmly linked with tradition that it could be considered an integral part of Jewish musical history. This development will be discussed elsewhere (Vol. X). Let it suffice to say here that despite all changes, both internal and external, Judaism has succeeded in establishing, expanding, and preserving its own musical style and tradition. Notwithstanding many foreign elements absorbed in Jewish chant, and certain distinct similarities with the music of the Near East, Byzantium, and Eastern Europe, it can be said that the Jews have created a musical style *sui generis*, which satisfies all the criteria of an autonomous cultural entity.

[1] Cf. G. Schünemann, 'Die Bachpflege der Berliner Singakademie,' *Bach-Jahrbuch*, 1928, p. 144; also Ernst F. Schmid, *Carl Philipp Emanuel Bach und seine Kammermusik* (Kassel, 1931), pp. 14 ff, and *Jahrbuch der Sammlung Kippenberg* viii, pp. 167–9. Madame Levy was the great-aunt of Felix Mendelssohn, and conveyed the Bach tradition to his family.

IX

ANCIENT GREEK MUSIC

By Isobel Henderson

THE MUSICAL TRADITION IN ANTIQUITY[1]

In the nineteenth century it seemed not incredible that the music of the medieval churches might derive from some trickle of Hellenic tradition. Medieval studies have now dispelled such conjectures: even in antiquity we cannot assume the continuous evolution of one species of 'Greek music'. The main instrumental types and the main theoretical terms persist. But instruments are inadequate clues to a music predominantly vocal; and the terms of theory seldom referred to musical facts. With the notable exception of Aristoxenus, the purpose of Greek theorists was not to analyse the art of music but to expound the independent science of harmonics; and ultimately the transmission of this harmonic science had no more to do with the history of musical art than the transmission of Greek astronomy or medicine.[2]

History must start from the great and obvious divergence between the fates of language and of music among Greeks who could quote their Homer for two millennia, but who ceased, after a certain point, to know their musical past except as they knew names of dead athletes. Since the point of divergence vitally affects our interpretation of the ancient sources, it will be convenient to begin with a rough provisional summary of the stages in this history.

(1) Archaic and classical music was transmitted orally with its words. We shall find, flourishing in Athens of the fifth century B.C., a genuine classical tradition—that is, the perpetual competition of new music with recollected models and standards. The supreme document of this tradition is *The Frogs* of Aristophanes, produced in 405 B.C. Next year Athens fell in defeat and revolution. During the fourth century the reservoirs of musical knowledge in school and theatre were breached. Plato—who had been educated in the classic style brought to its early maturity by Pindar, and had conversed with

[1] In all citations of Greek authors, the figures refer to the numbered sections given in the margin of standard editions.

[2] Cf. Marrou, *Histoire de l'éducation dans l'antiquité*[2] (Paris, 1950), p. 190; *Saint Augustin et la fin de la culture antique*[2] (Paris, 1949), pp. 197 ff.

Aristophanes—was the profound and sensitive critic of new developments in the music of his times. By about 320 B.C., as the great teacher Aristoxenus noted, memory of the classic styles was almost obliterated. (2) Meanwhile a modernistic movement, starting from the later fifth century, had produced 'popular classics', which were upheld above a flood of transient stuff by the Hellenistic creation of repertory until, after the Roman conquest, they petered out in the backwoods of Arcadia. The music of the innovators, Philoxenus and Timotheus, was virtually dead by the later second century B.C., when two paeans from the derelict metropolis of Delphi sustain the literary façade, at least, of an obsolescent style. (3) Later antiquity retails a music of entertainment and artifice. Except under a brief spell of Grecian intoxication at Hadrian's court, which bestowed high patronage on Mesomedes, the composer never again aspires to classic rank. The musician is now an executant, staging his own impersonations of set literary themes or, more humbly, purveying background noises for social and ceremonial occasions. A favourite ballet or mime has its vogue and passes. Writers no longer discussed present music, for there was no renaissance; nor, as in other arts, could they study the past, for there was no conservatory. The situation can be seen in the state of our musical documents, and explained by the history of education.

(*a*) *The documents*. Out of the vast manufacture of music in antiquity we have less than twenty written pieces, mostly stray finds of papyrus and stone. Music was not transmitted in the great ancient editions from which the main body of Greek literature descends, and the insatiable scholarship of Alexandria shows no awareness of musical palaeography. Greek writers constantly quote literary texts, but in all their extant works there is only one specific reference to a musical text. This reference has some intrinsic interest. Dionysius of Halicarnassus, in Augustan times, observes that in the *Orestes* of Euripides the music did not rise and fall with the speech-accents, and further adds that in two paired verses, strophe and antistrophe, the melody must be identical.[1] Now we have a papyrus written about 250–150 B.C., containing some lines with music from an antistrophe of this very play. It has a variant of a textual error also present in the Alexandrian edition—but in different order—by which a line of verse is displaced. Such a displacement, if it had occurred after the extant music was composed, must almost certainly have broken the melodic correspondence with the strophe, noted by Dionysius

[1] *De compositione verborum*, 11 and 19. See also below, p. 374.

himself. Therefore this music was presumably composed after the textual corruption began to set in. Dionysius was in no position to know whether a later text had the music of the original production of 408 B.C., if he had seen a copy at all.

From other considerations, too, it seems unlikely that a written record of classical music would be preserved unless by a freak. Some archaic letter-forms in Greek notation may indeed indicate that professional musicians used their ciphers from an early date. But since, down to the fourth century B.C., no considerable work was composed for more than one public performance, there was no reason to preserve these memoranda. We have no evidence that written music was circulated before the times of the Hellenistic repertory.[1] Nor is it likely that many citizens could read music. In the later fourth century notation was taught for harmonic theory, but this habit seems to have been short-lived.[2] Practical training in music, which was an independent discipline, was oral both in school and in the citizen chorus. Musical settings were certainly not incorporated in texts made for reading—which meant recitation, as opposed to acting with gesture and song. Except, possibly, from the fourth to the second century B.C., musical literacy was rare among educated men. The spread of books may even be thought to have pushed music out of education, for the mutual *aide-mémoire* of verse and melody was no longer indispensable when the words were easily available in written copies.

(*b*) *Musical education*. Plato, attempting in the fourth century B.C. to save something of the classical education, gives the following advice to teachers:[3]

. . . The lyre should be used together with the voices, for the clearness of its strings, the player and the pupil producing note for note in unison. Heterophony and embroidery by the lyre—the strings throwing out melodic lines different to the *melodia* which the poet composed; crowded notes where his are sparse, quick time to his slow, high pitch to his low, whether in concert or antiphony, and similarly all sorts of rhythmic complications of the lyre against the voices—none of this should be imposed upon pupils who have to snatch out a working knowledge of music rapidly in three years.

[1] The first extant piece is a papyrus of *c.* 250 B.C. The early papyrus of Timotheus' musically famous *Persae* gives the words only. Players are never portrayed reading music. On a vase of *c.* 425 B.C. (Fitzwilliam G73) a singer reads from a scroll, but there is no evidence that it contained notation besides words. Nor can it be seriously argued that Alexandrian performances of 'kitharisms' from Euripides reproduced the original settings.

[2] Aristoxenus, *Harmonics*, 39-40; but see Marrou, '*ΜΕΛΟΓΡΑΦΙΑ*' in *L'antiquité classique*, xv (1946), pp. 289 ff.

[3] *Laws*, 812d. See pl. 10 (*a*) and (*b*).

Such accompaniments were heterophonic, not polyphonic or contrapuntal. Plato, speaking of elementary education, is not denying that classical accompaniments could be heterophonic, though they were almost certainly simpler or less obtrusive. What he does make clear is that the composer's legacy was simply the sung poem: the instrumental part is conceived as a free accompaniment at the executant's pleasure (too complex, Plato thinks, for elementary lessons). An archaic *crusis* (accompaniment) might occasionally be transmitted in set form; but the orchestration of a classical work—from the single *aulos* supporting a tragic chorus to the strings, wind, and dancers producing a Pindaric ode—was part of a unique spectacle which perished. Some fifth-century Athenians did learn to play not only the domestic lyre but the *kithara* (a big concert-lyre) and the *aulos* (a sort of oboe), but in public performance these instruments were normally left to professionals. The citizen's part on the stage was the choric voice; and the classics, repeated by the citizen's voice and his lyre in school and on domestic or social occasions, consisted in a body of song. Early in the fifth century the classical music had reasserted the leadership of the vocal part over the instrumental; from its close, the classicists complain that this priority is being reversed. The nature of the musical change will be more fully discussed below. But from Plato's advice we can already see how, in a music made to show off the professional instrumentalist, the decorative and ephemeral part might overbear the durable melodic structure, which alone passed into the store of remembered classics. When the classical language and its literature began to grow unintelligible, they were saved by the labour of ancient scholars. No such labour was undertaken for music; and the classical *melopoeia* in fact perished from ear and understanding. Its *ethos* or character was distorted, as Aristoxenus says—explaining more precisely that when modern musicians attempted the best classical styles at all, they hit wrong notes.[1]

For the history of music the decisive event was the fall of Athens in 404 B.C., and the revolt against the ideals of her former intellectual *élite*. In most other matters the post-war education was strongly conservative. But musical incompetence, once the mark of the cad, became a plume of the new snobbery. It was asked whether the citizen should practise music at all, or merely listen—as in Sparta and Macedon, the victorious powers of the fourth century. As Aristotle put it:[2] Could music, like cookery, be judged by the consumer, or was

[1] *Harmonics* 23 (cited below, pp. 387 ff.). [2] *Politics* 1339a–1342b.

practical knowledge needed? He argued that practice was desirable, and need not be pernicious or vulgarizing unless the citizen, indulging in the pre-war excesses of Athenian spiritual pride, learned the 'professional instruments'. Here began a divorce between the citizen and the professional, between theory and practice, from which Europe still suffers. The three years to which Plato, reluctantly, had reduced musical education were soon cut down to two; and in Hellenistic times we hear of schools founded with only one music-master or with none.[1] Choral singing was still taught to boys, but the adult citizen's musicianship so declined that professionals were already being imported into the fourth-century chorus; and the professional, on his side, was no longer a cultivated man. Genuine musical criticism ceases. The classic Athenian comedy had been made for a society which talked music as it talked politics or war. But in Aristophanes' post-war plays, a shrunken chorus gives us only a last flash or two of his musical parody; and his successors substituted *entr'actes* by variety artists. The Alexandrian era still has excellent stage gossip on performers, but a first-hand judgement on the style or quality of music is hardly to be found after the fourth century. Aristotle already prefers received opinions. His master Plato and his pupil Aristoxenus are the last who speak to us with the authority of musical understanding. Yet their overwhelming influence on later writers was due less to their understanding than to the authority which they carried into two subjects still respected in higher education: philosophy and harmonics. While practical music lost the intellectual prestige which it had enjoyed since Homer, these two independent sciences reigned on, using the language of music for their own ends, and finally usurping its name.[2] *Mousikê*, or *musica*, which had once included both music and words, is not always to be translated as 'music' in post-classical authors. Consequently, the evidence of any Greek theorist must be interpreted with due regard to his date and place in the history of Greek ideas: musical, mathematical, or metaphysical.

TRADITIONS OF HARMONIC SCIENCE

Harmonics meant *tuning*, or acoustic theory. Greek postulates were melodic and heterophonic, and ignored 'harmony' in our sense.[3] The central problem of harmonic theory was the proper

[1] Marrou, *Histoire de l'éducation dans l'antiquité* (Paris, 1950), pp. 197 ff.

[2] περὶ μουσικῆς is cited as the title of a work by Heraclides Ponticus (fourth century B.C.) on harmonic theory and psychology, which are regularly called μουσική in late antiquity.

[3] The term 'consonant' (σύμφωνος) refers to *melodic* progressions. Music had nothing

division of musical space. Music, though practically ruled by the voice, was theoretically analysed in terms of the stretched string, which yields the words *syntonos* (taut) for high pitch and *aneimenos* (slack) for low, the nomenclature of notes from the plucking fingers, and some basic features of the notations. The static tuning of the strings was irreconcilably pitted against the free-wheel of the voice plotting its own consonances along its undivided continuum; and this musical antinomy audibly illustrated the Greek theory of numbers as delimiting points on an infinitely divisible ground (*apeiron*). The earliest harmonic theory used an academic monochord for mathematical or physical demonstration by the concept of measurable sound. Academic controversy later divided theorists under various labels; but the true distinctions are between the high mathematical method, the empirical, and the inductive.

(*a*) The term 'Pythagorean' is loosely used to cover a long tradition of mixed doctrine. Pythagoras of Samos, in the sixth century B.C., is said to have bequeathed to his disciples the principle of expressing divisions of the monochord by ratios, which founded the original and typical tradition of harmonics. It must be taken at its own valuation, as a self-propelled science, inspired not by a special interest in the musical art but by a general interest in the nature of the universe, seen under the strongly mathematical bias of Greek thought. Its aim was to reach a theoretically satisfying scale, which was conceived as a structural element of the *cosmos*. The astronomical firmament was pictured in the Music of the Spheres, from whose revolutions was emitted a scale of tetrachords, each divided by two 9:8 tones with the *leimma*, or 'remnant', of the perfect fourth.[1] The Pythagorean ditone was really used in classical music,[2] but long after it was obsolete the austere scale of the Spheres played on—not to the sensual ear, but in manuals which recorded it by sheer force of theoretical tradition. Astronomy remained a regular branch of harmonics. The attempt to express the universe in numbers admitting of an irrational element was not absurd in itself, though it lacked experimental method and finally descended into morasses of Neopythagorean mysticism. It served as a hypothesis to stimulate much first-class

nearer to 'harmony' than choirs doubling at the octave (μαγαδίζοντες), which are attested from the fourth century B.C.

[1] Plato, *Timaeus* 35b (cf. A. E. Taylor's *Commentary*, pp. 136 ff.); T. Reinach, 'La Musique des sphères', in *Revue des études grecques*, xiii (1900), pp. 432 ff, and 'L'Harmonie des sphères', *Congrès international d'histoire de la musique* (Paris, 1900), pp. 60 ff.

[2] Aristoxenus, *Harmonics*, 23; R. P. Winnington-Ingram, 'Aristoxenus and the intervals of Greek music', *Classical Quarterly*, xxvi (1932), pp. 195 ff.

mathematical work, which was carried on not only by so-called 'Pythagoreans', but also by such scientists as Ptolemy.

(*b*) 'Harmonists' means simply 'harmonic theorists', but the term was applied by Aristoxenus to his immediate predecessors. The 9:8 tone is not equally divisible by ratios, and other mathematical difficulties were soon noticed. Lasos of Hermione, in the sixth century, had smothered such dilemmas with the crude if sensible suggestion that notes had *breadth*, but the less robust fourth-century minds were shocked by the discovery that musical space was irrational. They attempted an empirical solution by splitting up the musical continuum into the smallest intervals audible, represented in diagrams of what they called *pycnomata* (the meaning is of microtones crowding along a melodic register). There was no question of realizing equal temperament on physical instruments. The intention was to reduce all intervals to common numerical terms on a theoretical gamut of atomic microtones. Plato glanced ironically at the contemporary professors, with their ears to the kithara, each fancying he heard a still smaller tonal unit.[1] Aristoxenus had to explain to his raw students that the *pycnomata* (besides being logically absurd) were practically inept, since nobody could sing more than two consecutive microtones.[2]

The 'Harmonist' theory persisted in the form of a linear measurement of units, which have been compared with modern cents. The comparison is superficial. When ancient theorists measured intervals —whether by ratios or by units—they did so for no practical purpose, but because numerical formulation was expected of an exact science. Textbooks were infested with tables of all possible scales, which never coexisted in musical history; and while some of the measured intervals might coincide with some current tunings, they were not direct descriptions of music.[3] The unitary measurement of intervals, by a historical irony, was later attributed to Aristoxenus himself, who had exploded it. Harmonic doctrines known to Ptolemy in the second century A.D. as 'Aristoxenian' were largely derived from a school of empiricists and hack teachers of theory. There was no authorized canon of Aristoxenus' works, and of the 453 books ascribed to him, not all were from his pen.[4] On technical subjects ancient manuals were often issued—

[1] *Republic* 531a–c.

[2] *Harmonics* 28.

[3] The opinion that the equations represent intervals really heard in music, and that Aristoxenus heard less exactly, lacks concrete evidence: the nature of these works is not aesthetic but theoretical.

[4] See Düring, *Porphyrios und Ptolemaios* (Göteborg, 1934), p. 183. F. Wehrli's edition

whether for piety or fraud—under the pseudonym of an appropriate authority (e.g. 'Galen' for a medical treatise); and the Aristotelian school, to which Aristoxenus belongs, was much overlaid with such fakes. The so-called 'Aristoxenians' used the authentic and the spurious without discrimination. Their reversion to 'Harmonist' principles of measurement is incompatible with all that we know of Aristoxenus' authentic theory.

(*c*) Whereas Plato had embodied the musical civilization of a past Athenian nobility, Aristoxenus was the son of a professional musician from the western colony of Tarentum, where old fashions lingered. At Athens he learned the new inductive logic from Aristotle; and under the impulse of this scientific method—later to collapse into a mere terminology—he attempted a true descriptive anatomy of music from his unique knowledge of fourth-century practice and of the earlier classics. Besides excerpts of varying authenticity, we possess an important but incomplete text arranged in three books, but actually compiled from at least four sources, overlapping in subject-matter, and presumably put together from pupils' notes of his lectures in Athens soon after 322 B.C.[1] In substance it has no parallel among extant Greek theorists. Whereas mathematical harmonics (including the empiricist school) necessarily postulated a series of notes as fixed points on a hypothetical gamut—or, in effect, a diagram—an inductive theory of music had to start from the voice in action. As Aristoxenus recognized, real melody presupposed not a fixed scale or tuning, but a line on which the voice's potentially infinite stations could be determined only by ear and understanding (ἀκοὴ καὶ διάνοια). Given a good ear to hear intervals, the mind must define them by their melodic functions. The only sane division of musical space was by 'consonances' (i.e. the melodic progressions to the fourth, fifth, and octave): these the ear could judge exactly, or within a hair's breadth, whereas it found other intervals 'dissonant' and variable in size. For melodic purposes, any basic note-series must be so conceived that each note lay a perfect fourth from the fourth in succession or a perfect fifth from the fifth. That this principle excluded numerical expressions of intervals was obvious to any educated Greek. It was substituted for the numerical method as a practical assumption of the ear in a music which did not pose the

(Basle, 1945) undertakes no historical criticism of the excerpts, and brackets the anachronism of frag. 124 without comment.

[1] *Harmonics* 30; Düring, op. cit., p. 183.

acoustic problems of modern instrumental harmony over large registers. The less precisely heard variations of intervals were then defined, so far as the ear demanded, not by equations but by recognized shades (χρόαι).[1]

To the real meaning of ordinary musical terms in his day, Aristoxenus will be our clearest guide.

GRAMMAR AND SYNTAX

(*a*) *The Notes.* The basic figure of analysis was the tetrachord. It was coupled with another tetrachord, either disjunct or conjunct (*diezeugmenon* or *synemmenon*: genitive plurals with long ō). The skeleton is here represented in our natural key:

Ex. 305

(i) *Disjunct* (ii) *Conjunct*

(*a*) ***Diezeugmenon*** (*b*) ***Synemmenon***

This is the elementary grammar of fourths and fifths pivoting on the 'fixed notes' from which the melody takes its bearings. The fixed notes are called, in descending order: (i) *nete*, *paramese*, *mese*, *hypate* or (ii) *nete*, *mese*, *hypate*.

Each tetrachordal skeleton is filled in by two 'movable notes'. The possible ranges of their motion were classified in three *genera*, roughly represented as follows:

Ex. 306

(*a*) ***Enharmonic*** (*b*) ***Chromatic*** (*c*) ***Diatonic***

In each case, the higher of the two movable points is called *lichanos*, the lower *parypate*—or, in the upper of two tetrachords, the higher point is *paranete*, the lower *trite*. In the enharmonic and chromatic *genera*, the segment *lichanos-hypate* is collectively called the *pyknon*, and must be less than the interval mese-lichanos.

The names of the notes do not refer to pitch, for they may be differently placed in different *genera*, and *nete* varies with the conjunct

[1] e.g. Aristoxenus recognizes two 'shades' of each of the three 'generic' positions of *lichanos* (see Ex. 306 above).

and disjunct systems. They are mostly adjectives of the implied noun *chorde*—a string or, simply, a note. They are probably not names of actual strings, for some notes may have been played by stopping one string. They refer primarily to the action of the hand playing: e.g. *lichanos* means 'forefinger'; *hypate* means 'highest' to the hand on the tilted kithara; *nete* 'lowest' to the hand—although in pitch *hypate* is the lowest note and *nete* the top.[1]

The double tetrachord, thus filled with movable notes, is still only a melodic skeleton. It give the typical minimum of notes: our written pieces show that others could be inserted besides. Greek music must never be conceived in terms of any continuous scale—least of all the harmonic series of our 'just intonation'. Its essential character lies in the logical priority of the fixed notes, which hold the melody between the iron girders of consonant progressions, over the contrasting flexible effects of the mobile notes, which bound various and irregular intervals, some hair-split, some widely gapped (and are no less mutable in the more evenly spread diatonic *genus*). Only the fixed notes can be exactly translated on our schematic staff. The concept of uniform octave-scales is especially inept, since a pair of tetrachords could be of different *genera*. The unit of the later solmization, as of the earliest analysis, is still not the octave but the tetrachord.[2]

(*b*) *The Systems.* It was for purposes of nomenclature only that theorists, during the fourth century B.C., worked out an extended note-system. The 'Perfect System' was compiled of two pairs of conjunct tetrachords separated by a tone of disjunction (*diazeuxis*)—the double octave being completed by a bottom note, whose name *proslambanomenos* (implying the masculine noun *tonos*) indicates an 'addition' from theory, not from music. The 'Lesser Perfect System', by omitting *paramese*, drops the disjunctive tone, substituting a conjoined tetrachord (*synemmenon*) for the purpose of illustrating the transitory effect of a modulation to the fourth. The two Systems (which Ptolemy combined in one diagram) are given overleaf separately. Positions of movable notes will of course vary with the *genus*.

Each note was called by its name with that of its tetrachord: e.g. in (i) the note marked *e* is '*nete* of the tetrachord *diezeugmenon*', *E* is '*hypate meson*', &c.

[1] Greeks did *not*, as Curt Sachs conjectures, call high pitch 'low' and vice versa: cf. Plutarch, *Quaestiones Platonicae* IX. 2. i; ps.-Aristotle, *Problems*, xix. 3.

[2] Greek solmization (known only from late theory) rendered a tetrachord of the form *la sol fa mi* by *ta tê to tĕ*.

(i) *Greater Perfect System*

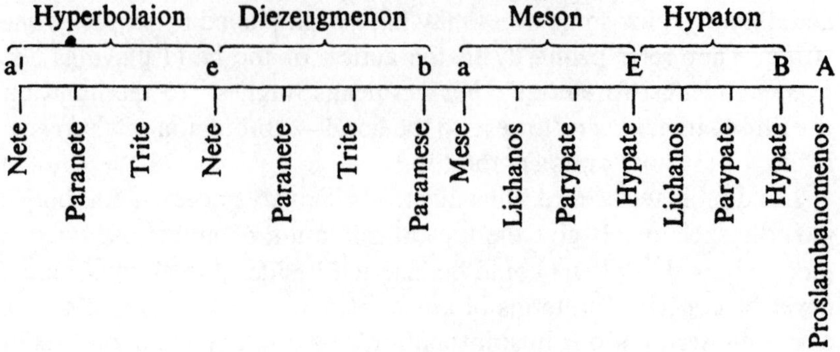

(ii) *Lesser Perfect System*

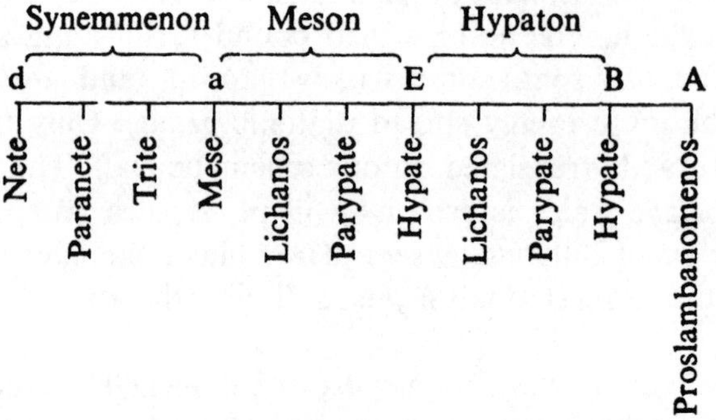

The pitch of these Systems is relative or, rather, abstract. They are themselves abstractions. Certainly a salient feature of the fourth-century musical revolution was the use of *metabolae* or modulations of various types. It raised—as does all modulation on instruments with fixed tuning—the problem of establishing a basic note-series sufficiently regular to minimize false melodic relations when two tunings are exchanged. But the working out of this problem in real music must be clearly separated from its elaboration in theory. The player modulating did not hitch on a spare tetrachord *synemmenon*. Though the hypothesis of a fixed pentatonic tuning is not proven, it remains most probable that he tuned his kithara not to a continuous scale, but by a gapped *accordatura* suiting the requirements of his music, and supplemented or adapted it by stopping his strings. (The *aulos* could be similarly adapted by devices of fingering and blowing.)[1]

[1] Düring, 'Studies in Musical Terminology in Fifth-century Literature', in *Eranos*, xliii (1945), pp. 176 ff. Only so can the attested complexity of much Greek instrumentalism be explained. Against the pentatonic hypothesis first proposed by Sachs in *Zeitschrift für Musikwissenschaft*, vi (1924), pp. 289 ff., and further developed by himself and Otto

The continuous scale was a purely academic apparatus. Its name—*systema*—is a term not of music but of harmonic theory; and the dual System was intended only to exemplify on the blackboard (as it were) the mechanism of a simple modulation.

Greek musical history is still bedevilled by confusions, ancient and modern, of the terms *systema, harmonia, tonos, eidos* (= *species*), *genos* (= *genus*), *tropos* (= *modus*). They can be clarified only by chronological and critical distinction between the Greek sources. To anticipate conclusions, we shall find that *harmonia*, in the classical composers and in musically intelligent prose-writers, means a musical idiom together with the tuning which it postulates—whereas in musically ignorant theorists it is confused with an *eidos* or *species* of the octave, which, like *systema*, is a term of theory, not of music. Again, to Aristoxenus the terms *genos* and *tropos* connote both a tuning and a musical style—whereas to inferior theorists both are mere scales. Above all, it is necessary to reach a true definition of *tonos*. It means, literally, 'a stretching'. It first occurs in harmonic theory in the fourth century B.C. From Homeric times the verb 'to stretch' was used of the preliminary stringing and tuning of the instrument; but the noun *tonos* is never used by a composer, never connotes a melodic style or operation.[1] In Greek theorists *tonoi* are continuous double-octave scales, in all three *genera*, set up on successive degrees of a basic note-series or System, with a superficial likeness to the scales of pitch-keys on a pianoforte. These *tonoi* were originally suggested by the musical fact of modulation in the fourth century; and the prevalent opinion of modern writers is that they represent real pitch-keys used in music. The view here set forth will be found to differ. It is, briefly, that the *tonoi* were theoretical concepts employed to define and name the relative *loci* of the topography of harmonic space. For nineteenth-century scholars, preoccupied with the search for continuity between ancient and modern, it was particularly hard to get away from the underlying notion of the octave with one supreme tonic; and efforts were made to ascribe such a tonic function to the Greek *mese*.[2] But, on the contrary, the

Gombosi, convincing arguments are marshalled by R. P. Winnington-Ingram in an article in *Classical Quarterly*, new series, vi (1956).

[1] Except by mere confusion with *harmonia*. ἐντείνω (-ομαι) does not, as a scholiast on Aristophanes *Clouds* 968 says, mean to pitch high: see Rogers's editorial note. In compounds -τονος means a tone or tension of the voice, with no pitch-connotation (e.g. ὑπέρτονος = loud). In late theory *tonoi* are miscalled *tropoi*.

[2] The one reference to musical usage is in ps.-Aristotle, *Problems*, xix. 20 (undated), saying that good tunes recur often to *mese*, like good prose to the word 'and'—a remark notable only for its stupidity.

Aristoxenian analysis shows us a music of tetrachords oscillating on plural pivot-notes between the disjunct scheme, which covers an octave, and the conjunct, in which *nete* comes down to the seventh from *hypate* (or the fourth from *mese*). These scholars persistently, if unconsciously, tended to treat the Greek Perfect System as though it corresponded to the tuning of a musical instrument, upon which key-scales could have some real meaning. It seemed to them incredible that Greek theorists played with harmonic concepts for their own sake and for no musical purpose. Here Aristoxenus was the exception. But he has left us no direct treatment of the *tonoi*, and we depend on other theorists, for whom harmonic science was superior to musical art precisely because it had no practical use.[1] A historical account of the *tonoi*, while recognizing their initial derivation from musical experience, must remember the unbounded capacity of fourth-century thought (outside the Aristotelian school) for generating abstract entities from words without facts.

THE TONOI

Pitch

The assumption that absolute pitch-values were recognized in Greek music is not warranted by any decisive ancient evidence. It rests on modern equations of *harmoniae* or *tonoi* with pitch-keys.

(i) In its original form, Monro's theory that the classical *harmoniae* were pitch-keys no longer needs refuting; and recent modifications of this theory—to the effect that the *harmoniae* had specific pitches as well as individual tunings—are no better founded.[2] Plato, indeed, tells us that some *harmoniae*, used for men's drinking-songs, were 'low', and others, used for women's keening-songs, 'high'. But since he adds that the latter are morally unfit for either sex, it is clear that they might be sung in a male register too. Their pitch-connotations are purely relative and general, meaning no more than what Greek authors call them—viz. 'high', 'low', or 'middle'.[3]

In the fourth century B.C. the new *tonoi* were at first described vaguely as *harmoniae*, and the Academician known as Heraclides Ponticus rightly protested that a *harmonia* was not defined by its

[1] In late antiquity it was compared for speculative purity to the science of generation of birds, which (unlike the best harmonic science) was pure nonsense (Berthelot-Ruelle, *Collection des anciens alchimistes grecs*, v. 15, 52, 436, lines 7–11).

[2] Gombosi's ingenious *Tonarten und Stimmungen der antiken Musik* (Copenhagen, 1939) does not refute major arguments brought against D. B. Monro, *Modes of Ancient Greek Music* (Oxford, 1894), nor adequately criticize sources of uneven value.

[3] Plato, *Republic* 398e (cf. Denniston in *Classical Quarterly*, vii (1913), p. 99).

pitch.[1] His own definition, however, only serves to show the confusion of these terms in a period of change, when the old *harmoniae* were forgotten and the old education disrupted. A *harmonia*, he declares, must have 'a peculiar *eidos* of *ethos* and *pathos*'. *Eidos* technically meant a *species* or segment of the octave; *ethos* and *pathos* (musical character and feeling) he can only connote with irrelevant nonsense about the racial psychology of Dorians, Aeolians, and Ionians, whose names had been attached to some of the old *harmoniae*. These names suggest to his witless fancy that there are three *harmoniae*, because there are three Greek races. Other speculators of the time were busy reducing all *harmoniae* to two—and all winds to north and south.[2] Late antiquity believed that Lamprocles and Damon, in the fifth century B.C., had already analysed *harmoniae* as octave-species—whereas the *species* had barely been enumerated before Aristoxenus.[3] The late Neoplatonist Aristides Quintilianus actually produced six irregular *species* of the enharmonic scale purporting to be the *harmoniae* named in Plato's *Republic*, but he cites no authority.[4]

Against such confusions of idioms with scales we must appeal to Aristoxenus. He briefly dismisses the preoccupation of his predecessors with 'the seven octachords which they called *harmoniae*'.[5] To avoid this misnomer he refers to the old Phrygian *harmonia* as 'the Phrygian *melos*' (*canto*)—with the significant remark that one would not understand it merely by transcribing it. Few musicians of his day, he tells us, still knew the classical idioms (*tropoi*).[6] Few theorists of his day had been educated in music at all. The confusion was merely verbal. When the old *harmoniae* were obsolescent, some of their names had been applied or adapted to the new *tonoi* with their attendant *species*. But *species* and *tonoi* together, as we shall see, formed a coherent theoretical structure postulating a basic scale which was drawn up in the fourth century. They can have borne no relation, except in name, to the *harmoniae* of the earlier music.

(ii) The *tonoi* certainly had 'pitch' in the sense of relative position. But Aristoxenus, *c.* 320 B.C., finds them still in the chaos of novelty,

[1] Cited by Athenaeus, 324e–325c. 'The man from Heraclea Pontica', writing *c.* 365–310 B.C., was given to miscellaneous speculation without experience (cf. Cicero, *Ad Quintum fratrem*, III. 5, 1).

[2] Criticized by Aristotle, *Politics* 1290a.

[3] By Eratocles only (Aristoxenus, *Harmonics* 6). On Lamprocles and Damon, ps.-Plutarch, *De musica* 16. In Plato, *Philebus* 17 c-d, note *systema* (not *eidos*).

[4] Mountford, 'The musical scales of Plato's Republic', in *Classical Quarterly*, xlvii (1923), accepts Aristides' authority, but see Monro, op. cit., pp. 94–100. Aristides' source was presumably some commentary on Plato.

[5] *Harmonics* 36 (Westphal's reading).

[6] Ibid. 39 and 23.

without agreement as to their relative position or the order of their names. He gives two lists from contemporary theory, in ascending relative order, as follows:[1]

I	Interval	II	Interval
Hypophrygian	?	Hypophrygian	
			$\frac{3}{4}$ tone
Hypodorian		Hypodorian	
	$\frac{1}{2}$ tone		$\frac{3}{4}$ tone
Mixolydian		Dorian	
	$\frac{1}{2}$ tone		1 tone
Dorian		Phrygian	
	1 tone		$\frac{3}{4}$ tone
Phrygian		Lydian	
	1 tone		$\frac{3}{4}$ tone
Lydian		Mixolydian	

The second school took their three-quarter-tone intervals from the borings of *auloi*. In rebuking their illogicality, Aristoxenus emphasizes the inaccuracy of manufacture and intonation for which the *aulos* was notorious, but says nothing of any absolute pitch. Manufacturers of *auloi* did preserve some pitch-standard by general reference to other *auloi*; but this very fact shows that the Greek idea of pitch was relative. Absolute pitch, on the contrary, would have determined the manufacture of instruments. Some passages from late theory, assigning different *tonoi* to different instruments or ranges of the voice, have been taken to imply real pitch-keys: yet the same theorists postulate a pure relativity of pitch, in which the limits of musical sound are definable only by the limits of instruments or hearing.[2] These vague and contradictory assumptions are outweighed by clearer inferences. The anomalies of the two lists of *tonoi* cited above are incompatible with any idea of absolute pitch. Absolute pitch is nothing if not a practical convention, and it cannot exist in convention or in practice without some consistent terms of reference to the notes or keys indicated by such a pitch-standard. But Greek writers never had consistent terms of reference to pitch. Both the nomenclature and the number of *tonoi* were in endless fluctuation and dispute. Seven *tonoi* represented the diatonic degrees of the octave—or the Seven Spheres (a book *On the Seven Tonoi* was written by Thrasyllus, astrologer to the emperor Tiberius). In imperial Roman times a baker's dozen—one on each semitone and a superfluous thirteenth at the octave—was imputed (incredibly) to Aristox-

[1] Ibid. 37. In List I no interval is given for the Hypophrygian, which was sometimes omitted.

[2] Bellermann's *Anonymus* 28 (but cf. 13); Aristides 16 J (but cf. 15 J). Note Gaudentius 20–21 and Aristoxenus, *Harmonics* 13–15.

enus.[1] A set of fifteen was begotten by a passion for verbal triads (e.g. Hypodorian—Dorian—Hyperdorian).[2] The various sets co-existed, with alternative and often anomalous names: no need for practical agreement was felt.

(iii) None of these nomenclatures agrees with the names given to kitharists' tunings in Ptolemy's day. Theorists used an academic fifteen-stringed apparatus, of no fixed register, to represent the Perfect System; and Ptolemy, after tabulating his own scientific results, shows which sections of his gamut will also yield tunings in current use. But these tunings, whatever they may signify, are variously tempered sequences of intervals, not pitch-keys; and their names show no relation between the practical and the theoretical uses of terminology.[3] Once, in Aristoxenus, the name of a *tonos* is associated with a low *aulos*; but the same passage proves that the attempt to define tonal relations by *auloi* was an ignorant mistake.[4]

(iv) In late antiquity *tonos*-scales are sometimes transcribed with musical notation. Since the notation may be merely an alternative means of expressing their relative positions, these *tonoi* are not thereby proved to be pitch-keys for practical reference. But if Greek notation were applicable at any pitch required, we should, *a priori*, expect to find all musical pieces transcribed in the same central nucleus of notational signs, with the least possible use of 'sharps'. Now this expectation is not falsified by the Delphic paeans of the second century B.C.—our earliest fragments of sufficient length to provide a valid test. But of the later pieces, one (the 'Ajax' fragment) is written with the dashes which, in the *tonoi*, raise a note by an octave; and, while the rest fall within a central nucleus spanning a twelfth, they do not all use the same basic notational sequence of 'naturals' and 'sharps'. The use of variant sequences is generally taken to denote differences of real pitch; and it must be clearly stated that this hypothesis has not been disproved. Yet other explanations, though unconfirmed, are conceivable. In late antiquity at least, variant notational sequences might have indicated different temperaments of intervals (as on the several sections of Ptolemy's abstract gamut), or different *loci*

[1] 'Cleonides', *Isagoge* 12. Both the number and the names are too illogical for Aristotle's pupil. The work on *tonoi* ascribed to him, if genuine, may have been about 'tones' (so Düring).

[2] Cf. Winnington-Ingram, *Mode in Ancient Greek Music* (Cambridge, 1936), pp. 15–21.

[3] See further below, p. 357.

[4] Aristoxenus, *Harmonics* 37–43, if the text is sound. In Athenaeus 634 f., citing Aristoxenus, names of *aulos*-registers are not related to *tonoi*.

upon a standard tuning of instruments or theoretical apparatus, or different conventions of musical transcription. Those who prefer the hypothesis of fixed pitch-keys have to explain the absence, in Greek writers, of reference to absolute standards of pitch, and, in Greek music, of the conditions which would plausibly account for the development of such standards. They freely admit that, on this hypothesis, a radical distinction must be drawn between the *tonoi* on consecutive semitones, as indicating pitch, and the Ptolemaic system of seven *tonoi*, which is pitchless: yet Ptolemy's polemics against the former would be inept if the distinction existed. In sum, difficulties arise on either view. In the present writer's provisional judgement, the arguments for attributing fixed pitch-values to some *tonoi* (but not to all) are outweighed by the improbabilities.[1]

It is agreed that Ptolemy's *tonoi* have no real pitch. Here at least, *tonoi* and *species* were together devised for a purpose independent of musical practice: to name points, both fixed and movable, upon an ideal diagrammatic structure of no real pitch-value, but of unquestioned importance for ancient scientific thought.

Nomenclature by Tonoi and Species

The *tonoi* transpose the scale-form of the Perfect System to other degrees of the System's own tonal series.[2]

Ex. 307

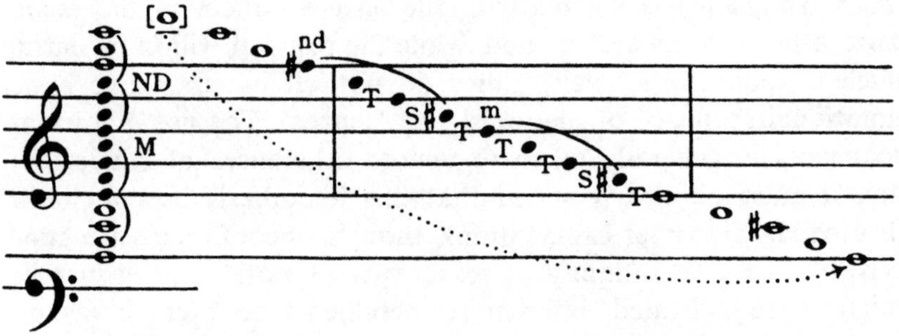

Here the Perfect System (cf. p. 340 above), filled out in the diatonic *genus* and in a handy key, is set up on the staff vertically, while a *tonos*-scale in transverse descent transposes the same tonal

[1] See, however, Winnington-Ingram's careful discussion, op. cit., pp. 49–53.

[2] No real pitch is here implied. Logically, *sol-fa* should be used (as by Düring, op. cit.), but the modern notation gives a clearer picture.

sequence one degree higher.[1] The double tetrachord which is the scale-form's central core (= *mi*¹–*mi*) is marked in black notes, and its 'natural' *locus* on the System's register is set between bars. The System is here treated as a static register around which the typical scale-form is borne by the revolving *tonoi*. As this scale-form moves one degree higher, one top note of the *tonos* is cut off and one bottom note is added within the System's register.

The System's nomenclature was used in a double sense: (1) as a term of reference to notes by their serial order of position (*thesis*) on the basic System; and (2) like a *sol-fa*, to describe notes by their function (*dynamis*) in the melodic scale-form (= *mi*¹–*mi*) without regard to its position. In Ex. 307, *M* remains *mese* by *thesis* on the System; *m* becomes *mese* by *dynamis* in the scale-form (here transposed by the *tonos*).

Our staff, with its assumptions of equal temperament and real pitch, might tempt us to identify the dynamic *m* with the thetic *paramese* as the same pitch-note (here written as middle B). But Greek theory could neither refer to external pitch-standards, nor ignore the fact that the scale-form's fixed and movable notes must shift their positions in different *tonoi*. *Nete diezeugmenon*, dynamically defined as a fixed fifth from *mese*, cannot be precisely described by *thesis*; and this is doubly evident in the present example, where dynamic *nd* takes a sharpened position with no place nor name on the diatonic System. It can only be described as '*nete diezeugmenon* in this *tonos*'. Therefore the *tonoi* themselves had to be named and fixed in a relative order of intervals one from the other. Our keys are serially numbered A, B, C, &c., by the sequence of their tonics in a note-series established by musical usage. But, although C always stands at the same interval above or below A, it is not true that the *key* of C is higher or lower than the *key* of A, since two melodies in A and C may use the same register. Greek theory logically defined *tonoi* by reference not to any single note like our tonic in an arbitrarily chosen series, but to the whole central register of the System where the *tonoi* meet and are comparable—viz. the octave set between bars. Within this octave each of the seven *tonos*-scales casts a different segment or *species* of the octave. In Ex. 307 the segment of the *tonos* between the bars has the sequence of tones and semitones T S T T T S T. This sequence was named the Phrygian octave-*species*, and the *tonos* was accordingly called the Phrygian. The names

[1] *Tonos*-scales were read downwards at first, later upwards. The change confused the notation, but is otherwise irrelevant. A uniform method is here adopted.

were given artificially, and the sole purpose of the *species* was to locate each *tonos* by its position relatively to the other six *tonoi*, without using arbitrary or practical criteria. The whole set may for provisional purposes be presented as follows:[1]

Ex. 308

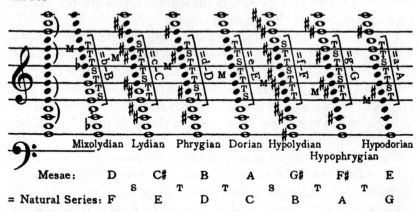

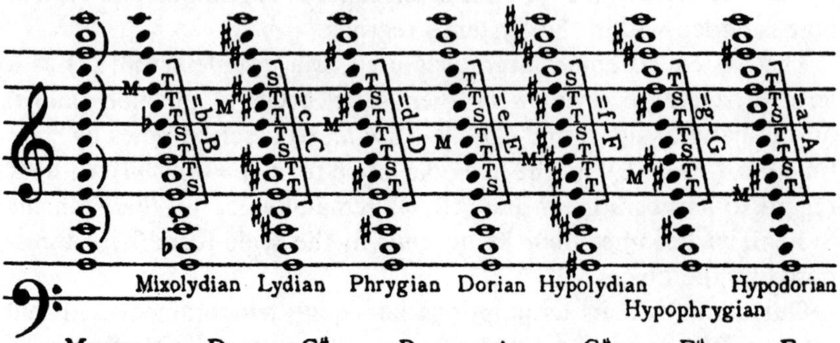

Mesae: D C♯ B A G♯ F♯ E

S T T S T T

= Natural Series: F E D C B A G

The typical scale-form *mi*ˡ–*mi*—always in black notes—is carried down the System's register by each tonos successively; the white notes at either end represent the space through which this scale-form moves. The System's central octave-register (here = e–E, marked not between bars but in square brackets on each *tonos*) is successively filled by seven different *species* of the revolving scale. These *species* have no melodic meaning: they exist only as thetic terms of reference to the relative positions of the *tonoi*. It will be noted that the System's central octave-register is the only octave whose terminals all the *tonoi* have in common. If, like the feebler Greek theorists, we insert extra *tonoi* at the inter-diatonic semitones, these *tonoi* will fail by a semitone to touch the two terminals of the central octave where the *species* meet. Since there are only seven *species* of the octave, the logical number of *tonoi* is seven. These must be projected on the System at a relative pitch-position one-and-a-half degrees below their 'natural' sequence (i.e. the *mesae* D C♯ B A G♯ F♯ E correspond to a sequence F E D C B A G).

It is, however, only for the limited purpose of showing the relative locations of the *tonoi* that they are projected on the System. For this purpose the unequal temperament of the dynamic scale is ignored, and all the thetic degrees of the System are treated as equal tones or

[1] This figure, serving only to correlate *tonoi* by *thesis*, appears to hypostatize the System as a keyboard; but see below, pp. 355 ff.

semitones. But both *tonoi* and *species* are purely thetic concepts—the *thesis* of a *tonos* being expressed by its *species*. Greek harmonic thought could also compass the abstract idea of modulation as a purely dynamic act. Ptolemy, after discussing the modulation expressed by the Conjunct System (cf. p. 340), proceeds to explain the general idea of modulatory dynamics, as follows:[1]

> The construction of *tonos*-modulation does not occur for the purpose of adapting a melody to higher or lower voices: for a change of that kind it is enough to tune the whole instrument up or down, since no variation is produced within a melody when it is sung right through as a whole, the same by higher voices as by lower. Modulation occurs in order that the identical melody, in the same voice, starting now from the higher registers, now from the lower, should produce a certain alteration of *ethos* (mood), through the fact that the two extremes of the melody, as it modulates, no longer coincide with the two extremes of the voice, but at the one end the voice's limit always terminates before the melody's, and at the other end the melody's before the voice's. Thus a melody originally fitted to the compass of the voice, by falling short at the one end and gaining ground at the other as it modulates, gives to the ear the impression of an altered *ethos*.

Ptolemy's point will be easily seen in diagrammatic form.

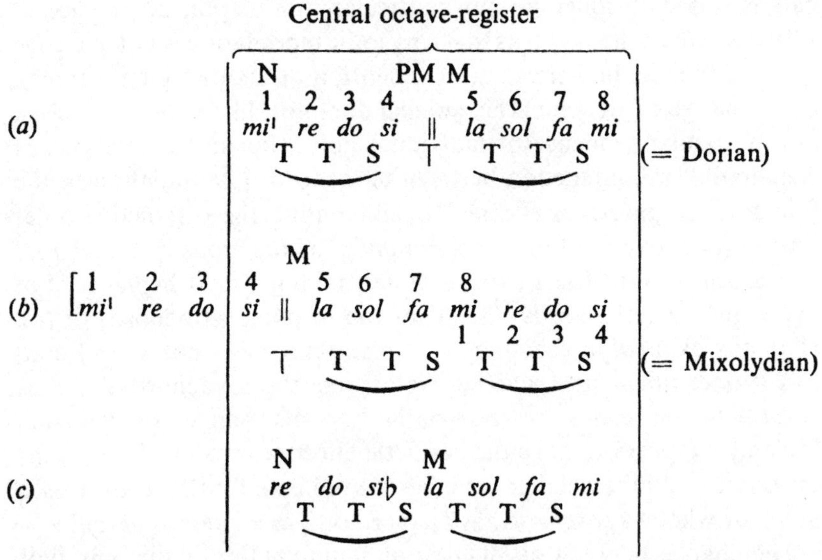

The melodic scale-form is unchanged by modulation: i.e. there is no change of 'mode'. Ptolemy conceives the central octave-register as the vocal space, always and completely filled by the melody, which is symbolized by the constant scale-form *mi–mi*. This melodic

[1] *Harmonics* ii. 7.

scale may lie within the vocal register in its continuous form T T S T T T S (numbered 1 2 3 4 5 6 7 8 in (*a*), above). If a modulation to the fourth occurs (*b*) we may imagine the continuous scale bodily shifted up a fourth; but then its upper notes would fall outside the register's top limit. They can, however, be picked up again an octave below, in the empty space left at the bottom of the register. As Ptolemy puts it, the melody falls off the register at one end and gains ground at the other. The register is still completely filled with the same melodic scale-form *mi*^{1}–*mi*, but in a differently distributed sequence (numbered 4 5 6 7 8 [= 1] 2 3 4). So, in our music, modulation may shift the tonic without changing the tessitura.

Viewed as a continuous scale, the note-series within the register has changed from T T S T T T S (the Dorian *species*) to T T T S T T S (the Mixolydian). But this has nothing to do with the melodic movement, in which the scale-form does not change. The *species* merely indicates the *tonos* or thetic degree of the modulation, which does not here concern Ptolemy. He is conceiving the register not as a basic scale (as in Ex. 308) but as an empty space which the voice can fill as it chooses: there is no question of specifying the sharps or flats required to illustrate any particular modulation in practice.

Elsewhere Ptolemy insists that a melodic modulation is not a change of *tonos* (i.e., as he here says, of repetition at another pitch-degree), but a change of *systema*. The *systema* does not, like a *species*, consist in a particular sequence of individual notes, but in the relations of disjunction or conjunction between tetrachords.[1] Modulation to the fourth (he explains) is effected by eliminating the disjunctive tone: thus in (*c*) above the functional *paramese* of (*a*) drops out, and *nete* comes down to the fourth above *mese*, making a total heptachord of two conjunct tetrachords instead of the disjunct tetrachords of (*a*). Here our own *sol-fa* becomes inept: the octave was not a rigid unit, and it does not matter whether we express the tetrachord T T S as *la sol fa mi*, *mi re do si*, or *re do si♭ la*. It is this change of *system* that Ptolemy supposes to have the aesthetic effect of an altered *ethos*: the ear is left in doubt whether *mese* has moved up a fourth, as expressed in (*b*), or whether *paramese* has dropped out, as expressed in (*c*).[2]

The change between disjunction and conjunction is the only type of modulation that Ptolemy will call *melodic*, although any permutation of *tonoi* or *genera* could be admitted theoretically and on paper.

[1] *Harmonics* ii. 6. This is the only significant distinction between *systemata*, though some theorists enumerate them by size, *genus*, &c., as any ordered note-series.

[2] Ptolemy is, however, hazy and abstract on the aesthetic effect: it may be merely his own intellectual inference.

In theory, also, the idea of other tetrachordal forms besides T T S was entertained; but only T T S was used in regular harmonic structures—with its corresponding enharmonic and chromatic *genera*, which are attested in real musical use from the fourth to second centuries B.C. Whether, or when, other forms were realized in musical practice we have not sufficient evidence to say. Ptolemy, after his theoretical demonstrations of his own temperament of intervals, turns to the empirical data of kitharistic tunings in current use, to find them at various segments of his academic gamut. These tunings consist of tetrachords and octachords, both diatonic and chromatic, in several forms or shades of tonal sequence, which are named *sterea* and *malaka* on the lyre, *tritae*, *hypertropae*, *parypatae*, *tropoi*, *iasti-aeolia*, and *lydia* on the kithara. This nomenclature is a *pot-pourri* of technical jargon, and cannot be connoted with Ptolemy's *tonos*-names. If, as some maintain,[1] the tunings are melodic scales of variant modal idioms, they are remoter than ever from Ptolemy's concept of a uniform melodic scale. But Ptolemy's words do not imply so much;[2] and since the terms differ from the lyre to the kithara, they would seem to refer to some more mechanical aspect—e.g. to professional operations of preliminary tuning of the instruments, like the conventional tuner's chords in testing a pianoforte. This would fit the context. Ptolemy adduces these tunings as phenomena independent of his own harmonic system, to show that his academic calculations of tuning are not incompatible with common acoustic experience. With this confirmation, he can proceed to his purpose—the harmonics of astronomy.

Whatever these tunings may represent, their names show how far musical practice had diverged from harmonic theory. To imagine that Ptolemy of Alexandria did, or could, reflect contemporary forms of music in his main doctrine is to mistake his position and aims. He lived nearly five centuries away from the inductive method by which Aristoxenus had analysed music as he knew it 'by ear and understanding'. In all his many works, his great achievement was to recapture the high Alexandrian tradition of mathematical sciences after an age of collapse and decline. He did not change the terms of the problems: it was hard enough to recover them—and, on occasion, to improve their expression. In the harmonic field (a small part of his activity) the decline can be seen from his own criticisms of recent pretenders to the names of 'Pythagorean' or 'Aristoxenian'.[3] He was

[1] Düring, op. cit., pp. 201–15: the first serious analysis of Ptolemy, *Harmonics* i. 16, ii. 1 and 16, but the solutions are inevitably speculative.

[2] τὰ μελῳδούμενα (ii. 16, chapter-heading) does not in theoretical contexts refer only to melopoeic use.

[3] Cf. Düring, op. cit., p. 83.

perhaps the one man alive who had the logical insight and the experience of astronomical diagrams to assimilate the harmonic system of early Alexandrian thought; and in harmonics, as elsewhere, it is early Alexandrian thought that he interprets to us.

Some account of Greek harmonic theory has been necessary for a negative purpose: to prevent unprofitable searching for musical significance in mathematical concepts. There is also a positive reason. Greek notation, though also used for transcribing musical compositions, was developed largely by theorists for their own purposes, and cannot be properly understood without reference to the theoretical *tonoi*. Not that the better minds—Aristoxenus or Ptolemy—had recourse to notation. It could neither define the functions of notes, like the verbal nomenclature, nor measure the exact size of intervals, like the arithmetical cipher. It was used among a lower class of harmonic professors, known only from late antiquity. Since they too claimed to be 'theoretical', prestige obliged them to include the Perfect System in their doctrine; but their heads were too weak to relate it correctly to the *tonoi*—nor, indeed, could it be correctly related to their irrational sets of thirteen or fifteen *tonoi* on consecutive semitones. Some merely gave lists of *tonos*-names with relative intervals. Others set out their *tonoi* with notational signs; and the anomalies of Greek notation, as we know it, may owe something to their hands.

THE NOTATIONS

The Greek notations are explained to us only by a few minor theorists of the third or fourth centuries A.D.—in particular, one Alypius, who gives a set of *tonos*-scales with reproductions and verbal descriptions of the corresponding signs in two notations. A central nucleus of the signs of both occurs in extant musical fragments going back to *c.* 250 B.C. The final series of the Alypian signs is here given in continuous sequence with the relative diatonic note-series in our staff (no absolute pitch):

Ex. 309

The second notation, which is the earlier, shows a nucleus of fifteen signs—some alphabetic, but in no regular alphabetic order—evidently put together to fit the Perfect System a^1–A in the fourth century B.C. This is extended upwards, by signs repeated with a dash, to the top g^1. Below A two extra bottom notes G_1 and F_1 have been added, with signs later borrowed from the first notation. Each sign of row no. 1 (which is the diatonic note-series) is triplicated with its own sharp and double-sharp: for example, in the triad E Ш Ǝ horizontal Ш is the sharp and reversed Ǝ the double-sharp of E erect. The triads doubtless originated in the enharmonic and chromatic *dieses*; but only theorists distinguish the chromatic (by a cross-stroke) from the enharmonic; and the same signs are also used for other sharps. It is possible that a triad could be played on one string, but the hypothesis that the notations were tablatures will not bear examination.[1]

The first notation, avoiding archaic signs, makes a central octave of the Ionic alphabet *A B Γ*, &c., in continuous descent, *A* being the double-sharp and *B* the sharp of *Γ* (so that row no. 1 is the diatonic note-series). Alypius calls the first notation 'vocal', the second 'instrumental'; but, although these names are too well established in modern usage to be abandoned now, the distinction is pointless and was adopted only in late antiquity.[2] The 'vocal notation' is obviously a translation of the 'instrumental', with its obsolete cipher, into the familiar and consecutive series of the Ionic alphabet, which was gradually spreading into common use from the end of the fifth century B.C.

The nucleus of the 'instrumental' signs stands logically enough on the System's series a^1–A, which is just as we should have expected, and we may hope that the alphabetic disorder of the other signs dates back without change to the fourth century. The 'vocal' notation, however, has been much reshuffled.[3] Its most important segment is the erect Ionic alphabet, with the two or three triads adjacent, which together supply all signs found in our 'vocal' texts. Its serial order is certainly correct, but the question is whether the group has been bodily shifted from its original segment on the diatonic note-series. The erect nuclear alphabet is irrationally set on the meaningless

[1] See above, pp. 346 f., n. 1.

[2] e.g., in the Berlin papyrus (after A.D. 156): not in the Delphic Hymns (second century B.C.).

[3] In ex. 309 above, the nucleus of the System's note-series is marked by continuous bars, additions or displacements by dotted bars. Bits of five alphabetic sequences have been patched together where three would have sufficed.

octave f'–f; and where we should expect a translation of the 'instrumental' nucleus a'–A, we find displaced signs at either end of this note-series. On a' and g' are two signs torn from their proper sequence (in the lower register), like a rubble filling between a' and f'. At G and F, below A, that sequence is prolonged by two additional letter-forms (which also appear as additions to the 'instrumental' notation). On its top g'' the notation abruptly decants a solitary *omega*. From these and other anomalies we are bound to suspect that the erect central alphabet, with its neighbours, may have suffered a shift of tonal sequence—that it was not originally set on the f'–f octave. On the assumption that past music was commonly written and read, such a shift might seem impossible. But notation was known to few, as the laborious verbal descriptions of Alypius show; and it was used by theorists as a mere numerical cipher for *tonoi* of no real pitch-value. Certain theoretical aberrations of late authors do, in fact, strengthen the suspicion of a shift of the erect alphabet to f'–f:

(1) Alypius and his kind do not present *tonoi* as scales revolving about the System (as in Ex. 308), but simply as continuous double-octave scales at semitonal intervals. We may imagine them on the pianoforte, if we exclude all idea of real pitch. The Alypian note-series extends over fifteen of such *tonoi*. As Ptolemy argues, *tonoi* set at or beyond the octave are logically superfluous. Of the three extra *tonoi* of Alypius, one was added to round off the octave, and the other two merely to complete a set of *tonos*-names in triplicate (with the prefixes *hypo-* and *hyper-*). The logical note-series would run from top g' to bottom A. The extra bottom notes G and F can only be the additions to that note-series which were made to accommodate the three superfluous *tonoi*.[1] Since the *tonoi* were mere names and the signs mere ciphers, it did not matter at which end either were added. In fact, the new *tonos*-names were put at the top of the list and the new signs at the bottom. Consequently the old *tonos*-names, in their conventional order, were shunted two diatonic degrees down the notational series: i.e. the bottom *tonos* called Hypodorian, to make room for the new *tonoi* at the top, was pushed from the old terminal A down to the new terminal F.[2]

(2) Since the *tonoi* are A-scales, the *tonos* that begins from A of the notational series, whatever its name, will be the 'natural' tonos (i.e.

[1] Alypius' Hyperlydian, Hyperaeolian, Hyperphrygian. The fourth so accommodated (Hyperionian, *mese* = g♯') was placed top of twelve semitonal *tonoi* (from A), but the notation has no corresponding top g♯': it was extended at the bottom instead.

[2] See Ex. 310 below.

that in which the signs keep their unsharpened forms). In the shifted Alypian *tonos*-list, the *tonos* that falls on the A is called 'Hypolydian'. Now in both the Alypian notations, the Hypolydian *tonos* has the 'natural' signs. It has been supposed that there was a real and musical change from a 'Dorian' to a 'Hypolydian' tuning. But this view is based on the modern assumption of absolute pitch. If it is not accepted the change can be simply interpreted as a diagrammatic shift of *tonos*-names; and this is perhaps confirmed by a reference in late antiquity to 'the *tonos now called Hypolydian*'.[1]

(3) But this was not all. Ptolemy, in arguing against the habit of interposing *tonoi* on the semitones between the diatonic series, pointed out that there was a risk of transposing the whole System—since the central octave of the System does not coincide with the terminals of any octave of these interposed *tonoi*. In the correct projection of Ex. 308 the 'natural' *tonos* was the Dorian, which shared the System's own central register at the thetic *mi*[1]–*mi*. But if we take the seven primary *tonoi*, to which the names of the *species* belong, and reproduce them with the sharps and flats assigned to them by Alypius, they appear as follows:

Ex. 310

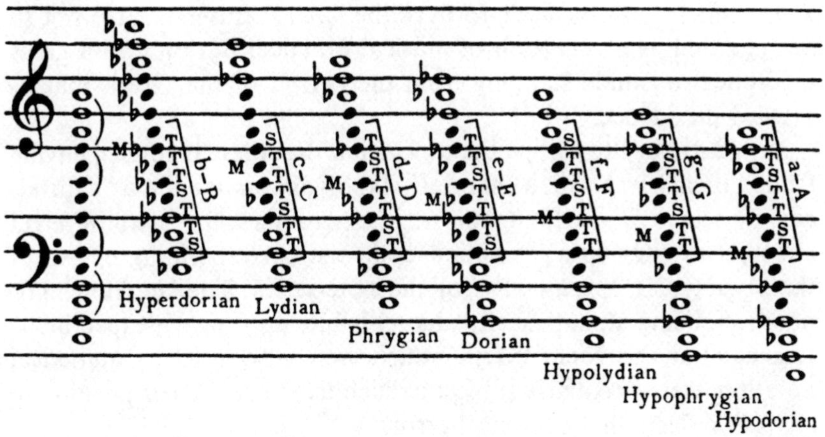

Mesae:	E♭	S	D	T	C	T	B♭	S	A	T	G	T	F
=Natural Series:	F		E		D		C		B		A		G

These *tonoi*, while preserving the same natural sequence (= FEDCBAG) are projected at E♭DCB♭AGF instead of the correct DC♯BAG♯F♯E of Ex. 308 above. In other words, these theorists

[1] ps.-Plutarch, *De musica* 39, 1.

have not contained their *tonoi* within the System's basic scale a'–A.[1] They have simply started their bottom Hypodorian *tonos* on an extra-Systematic bottom F, and proceeded accordingly. If they were to extend the basic scale at all, they should have started their Hypodorian on a low D. As it was, the Lydian was pushed up from its old C♯ to the old Mixolydian position of higher d. In the confusion the Mixolydian name drops out of the later list, and the Lydian is often treated as 'the first of the *tonoi*'.[2] From the false projection it follows inevitably that the Hypolydian *tonos*, from its place in the list, falls on the System's thetic a'–A previously occupied by the Dorian.

So far, it might be more accurate to say that they were not relating their *tonoi* to the System at all, but merely ignoring it. But when they had to find the *species* known as synonymous with these primary *tonoi*, they got into trouble with their central octave. On their projection the one octave common to these *tonoi*—the octave in which the *species* lie—is not, as before, the central *mi'–mi*, but *fa'–fa*. This is a real error of construction. The scale-form of the Alypian *tonoi* is still the *la'–mi'–mi–la* of the System's proper scale, which corresponds to the Dorian *species mi'–mi*, and should fall on the central octave *mi'–mi*. But Alypius' primary seven *tonoi* are placed to fall on the central octave *fa'–fa*, which corresponds to the Hypolydian *species* and conflicts with the scale-form of the *tonoi* themselves. It is not to be regarded as a reflection of musical practice, but only as a gross theoretical misunderstanding from the period of the Greek mathematical decadence.

Now it is hard to escape the conclusion that these theorists, having landed themselves with a 'natural' Hypolydian *tonos* and a 'natural' central octave *fa'–fa*, thought it necessary to place the 'natural' erect alphabet of the 'vocal' notation upon the corresponding octave of the Hypolydian *species*—f'–f of the note-series. The 'instrumental' notation, being alphabetically unintelligible, may have escaped interference; but the Ionic letters, which were also used as numerical notation, were peculiarly subject to such treatment. Their position in Alypius reflects the theoretical error.

Once the Alypian notation was established in theory, it will also have been used for transcribing real music. But it is not so certain

[1] They actually read scales upwards, and counted them from the bottom terminals. In Ex. 308 above, one *tonos* (Hypolydian) is inevitably extra-systematic at its terminals, but there *tonoi* are properly counted from the *Mesae*, and the common central octave is the logically important feature.

[2] Among others, Alypius 3: ὧν ἐστὶ πρῶτος ὁ λύδιος. Some echo of controversy as to whether the Mixolydian should be on high or low D may be preserved in the scholium on Aristophanes, *Clouds* 967–8.

to apply to our earliest documents in 'vocal' notation. The mistake postulates the addition of the bottom G and F for new *tonoi*, and the set of fifteen was believed to be comparatively late. The notation known to Aristoxenus cannot have been consistently related to the embryonic and divergent *tonos*-lists that he describes; and we have no means of knowing when it was adapted, as we find it in late antiquity, to the purpose of writing out *tonos*-scales. What is evident is that, apart from the modern hypothesis of absolute pitch-keys, the extended Alypian series in its two notations absurdly exceeds any conceivable requirements of musical practice. All that was needed to transcribe a melody was a convenient nucleus of signs (with their triadic sharps) in a sequence which could be used at any desired register. There is a strong *a priori* probability that, as in the 'instrumental' notation, so in the 'vocal' version of it, the fourth-century nucleus was the fifteen-note System a^{1}–A. This would require a reversed alphabet above the erect alphabet. But otherwise we can only try to pick out fixed notes, in Greek musical documents, by reference not to theoretical *tonoi* but to indications (if any) of melodic structure and function. A suggestion, here to be put forward with all reservations, must be taken only as a lead towards further study.

THE EXTANT MUSICAL DOCUMENTS

(1) The 'First Delphic Hymn' or paean to Apollo (our most extensive piece) was composed almost certainly in the later second century B.C., and written in the 'vocal' notation on stone at Delphi, where it must have won a prize in the Pythian festival. From the ceremony of its occasion and from the clichés of its literary style, it seems to be highly academic and archaistic stuff; and where academic rules were observed at all, they were unlikely to have changed much since Aristoxenus. On this assumption, Aristoxenian principles may be applied, first, to the schematic note-series of the Hymn (below, I is the transcription according to the Alypian signs, II a hypothetical new version):[1]

Ex. 311

[1] The notational sharps are here set above the 'natural' signs, and are transcribed by black notes.

There are two *pykna* on ʊ and M, which, therefore, are fixed notes, and, being a fifth apart, should be *paramese* and *hypate* (i.e. in the mere abstract *schema*, for in melody modulation could vary their functions). *Mese* would then be Γ, which must lie a whole tone below *paramese* ʊ. In Aristoxenus' extant treatment the tonal location for such a *schema* would equate *hypate* with our *mi*; and this brings the first alphabetic triad A B Γ to our *la*, where the nucleus of signs a'–A also starts in the 'instrumental' notation. Against the usual transcription (I) it may be pointed out that (i) the key-signature of E♭, not here reproduced, but commonly inserted from modernized *tonos*-scales, is spurious, for in this version of the score itself the B is always natural; and (ii) by this transcription the composer is twice made to break an Aristoxenian rule of melodic grammar which forbids a progression from a *pyknon* to an interval less than a tone (Ex. 312 below, §§ 45–48, 60–61). The new transcription (II) avoids this error. As to the *pykna*, the sharp-sign × here implies no choice between enharmonic *dieses* and chromatic; but at this date the chromatic *genus* is to be presumed. If so, the *lichanos* will be nearer *fa*♯ than *fa*, but in any case a movable note cannot be transcribed exactly.[1] The continuous parts of the paean are here transcribed both in the Alypian reading (I) and in the version here suggested (II):[2]

Ex. 312

[1] Aristoxenus, *Harmonics* 23: the 'shades' of *lichanos* could not have been indicated by notation.

[2] Restorations are omitted. The repeated notes and time-values of the usual transcriptions may be plausible, but are inferential.

15 I
Μ Υ Μ Υ Μ F Φ Υ F
Φοιοῖ - βον ᾠι - δαεῖ - σι μέλ - ψη - τε χρυ - σε - ο - κό - μαν·
II
19 I
Θ Ʊ ⋔ Ʊ Θ Ʊ Θ Μ Θ Ι
ὃς ἀ - νὰ δι - κό - ρυν - βα Παρ - νασ - σί - δος ταᾶς δὲ πε - τέ - ρας
II
23 I
Μ Υ Υ Μ Υ Μ Ι Θ Ι Θ Γ Ʊ ⋔ Γ
ἕ - δραν ἅμ' ἀγα - κλυ - ταῖεις Δεελ - φί - σιιν Κα - στα - λί - δος
II
27 I
Ʊ ⋔ Ʊ Θ Γ Λ Μ Υ
εού - ύ - δρου νά - ματ' ἐπ - ι - νίσ - σε - ται, Δελ - φὸν ἀ - νὰ πρωῶ - να
II
31 I
Μ Ι Θ Ι Μ Φ Γ Ʊ ⋔ Ʊ
μααν - τεῖει - ον ἐφ - έ - πων πά - γον . . . . κλυτὰ με - γα - λό - πο - λις
II
36 I
Κ Λ Μ Ο Κ Λ Κ Γ
Ἀθ - θὶς εὐ - χαιεῖ - σι φε - ρό - πλοι - ο ναί - ου - σα Τρι -
II
40 I
Ʊ ⋔ Ʊ Θ Γ Μ Γ Β Γ Λ Κ Γ Ο Μ
τωω - νί - δος δάπε - δον ἄ - θραυσ - τον· ἁ - γί - οις δὲ βω - μοιοῖ - σιν
II
44 I
Γ Κ Μ Λ Κ Λ Μ Λ Μ Ο Κ Λ
Ἅ - φαι - στος αἰεί - θει νέ - ων μῆ - ρα ταού - ρων, ὁμ - ουοῦ
II

47 I
Γ Μ Ʊ Θ Ι Θ Γ Θ Υ Ο Μ Λ Μ Ο
δέ νιν Ἄ - ραψ ἀ - τμὸς ἐς Ὄλ - υμ - πον ἀν - α - κί - δνα - ται,
II
53 I
Υ Ο Μ Λ Μ Λ Κ Λ Μ Μ Υ Ο Μ
λι - γὺ δὲ λω - τοός βρέ - μων αεὶ - ό - λοιοις μέ - λε - σιν ὠι - δαὰν
II
57 I
Λ Μ Γ Λ Κ Λ Μ Κ Λ Μ Ο Υ
κρέ - κει, χρυ - σέ - α δ' ἁδ - ύ - θρους κίθα - ρις ὕ - μνοι - σιν
II
61 I
Ο Μ Λ Μ Ο Φ Ʊ ⋀ Γ Ʊ Θ Γ
ἀ - να - μέλ - πε - ται. ὁ δὲ τεχνι - τωῶν πρό - πας ἑ - σμὸς
II
65 I
⋀ Ʊ Θ Γ ⋀ Ʊ ⋀ Ι
Ἀθ - θί - δα λαχὼν . . . - σει κλυ - τὸν παῖ - δα με - γά - λου . . .
II
72 I
Ι Θ Γ Ʊ ⋀ Ʊ ⋀ Γ ⋀ Ʊ ⋀ Γ
ἀ - κρο - νι - φῆ τόν - δε πά - γον . . . πᾶ - σι θνα - τοιοῖς·
II
77 I
Ʊ Γ Μ Υ Μ Ι Μ Ι Θ Γ Θ
προ - φαί - νει - . . . τρί - πο - δα μαν - τειεῖ - ον ὡς εἷειλες . . .
II
82 I
⋀ Γ Ʊ ⋀ Ʊ Φ Ʊ Ι Ο Γ ⋀
ἐφρουού - ρειει δρά - κων ὅ - τε τεοῖσι . . . . ἔτρηη - σας αἰ - ό - λον
II

Whatever be the true reading of the signs, our schematic staff is singularly ill adapted to this music. Greek notation was also schematic; but contemporary Greeks had the advantage of understanding the music. For us it would be better rendered on a differently constructed staff, reserving black lines for the fixed notes, giving dotted (hypothetical) lines to the chief movable notes, and leaving the rest indeterminate in the spaces—as in the following sample from the Hymn (notation II), admittedly a conjectural version:[1]

Ex. 313

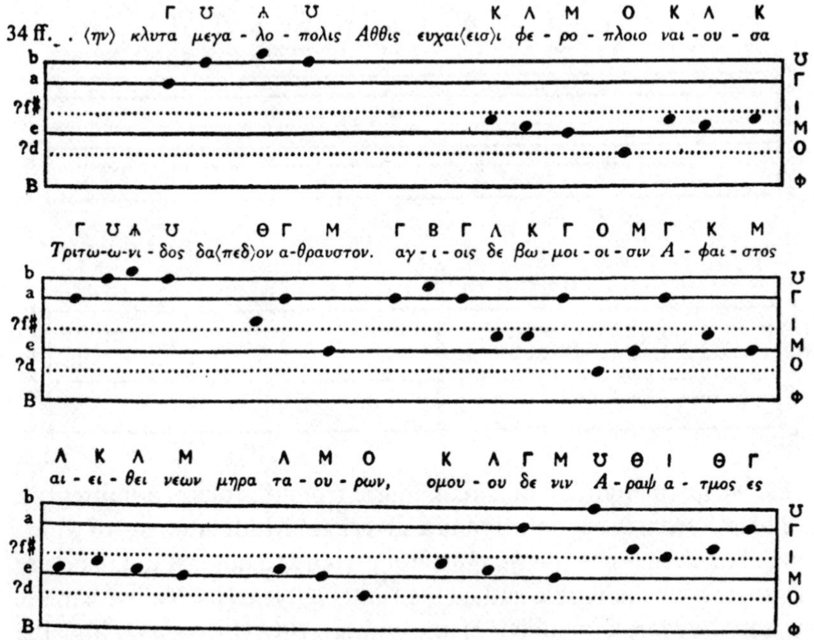

[1] Here, and in examples below, speech-accents are omitted, as their application to different dialects and periods is very uncertain. See, however, the new and careful discussion by R. P. Winnington-Ingram in *Symbolae Osloenses*, xxxi (1955), pp. 64–73.

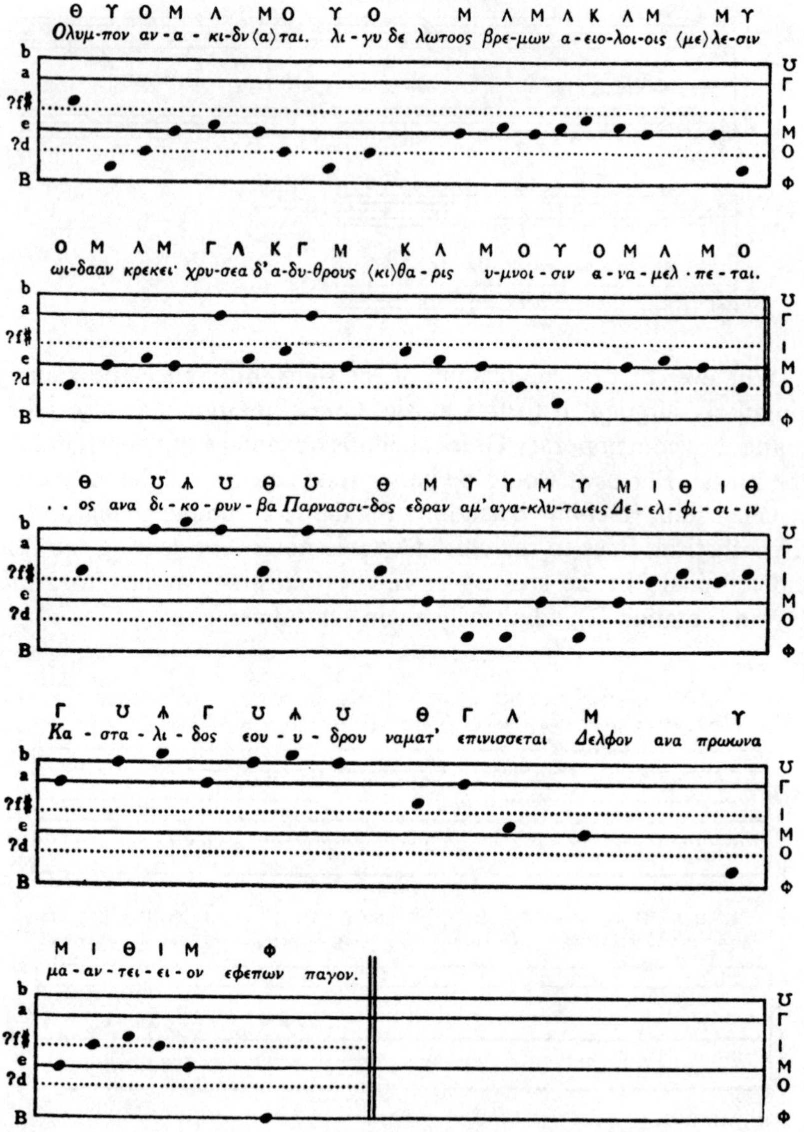

Do we learn anything of Greek music from this piece, admittedly a last breath from the dissolution of a silver age? Modulations—of which much has been written—we must not pretend to understand. The use of progressions is visible rather than intelligible to us. Yet we can see the rapid decorative effects of the *pykna* at ΚΛΜ or ⋇⩚Ʊ, and the *tremolo* or variation of notes on one syllable—once parodied by Aristophanes as a new trick of Euripides and the modern dithyrambists, but now become a cliché. In the fourth century, 'programme music' had been popularized by Timotheus, whose lyric nome *The Persae* featured sound-effects of the battle of Salamis. In this Hymn, at §§ 45 and 55, the words *αἰείθει* and *αἰειόλοισι* are set to imitate the flickering of flames and the *tremolo* of an *aulos*. We may reasonably believe that the style preserved some echo of the tradition of Timotheus, which was just dying.

(2) The 'Second Delphic Hymn'—a long but battered inscription in the 'instrumental' notation—was composed by an unknown Limenius of Athens in 128–127 B.C. Although the setting seems even sparser, this paean is to us, at least, stylistically indistinguishable from the other; and their likeness encourages the belief that the notations are not hopelessly corrupt. The second Hymn shows no signs of any such shift of tonal sequence as must be suspected in the 'vocal' notation of the first. It will be sufficiently illustrated by two extracts: Apollo's advent at Delphi, and a final prayer for the Roman empire:

Ex. 314

(3) Our only other engraved musical document is the 'Epitaph of Seikilos'—an inscription beginning with an elegiac couplet, on a tombstone found at Aidin in Turkey, near Tralles. The Greek script might date from the second century B.C., but is probably much later. The convention of musicography differs sharply from that of the Delphic pieces, and approximates to that of papyri of the first, second, or later centuries A.D., in which every syllable is

set and rhythmic signs are introduced. It is possible, therefore, that the song was transcribed according to the Alypian values of the notation, although its diatonic banality in this transcription is disconcerting. It has commonly been assigned to the 'Ionian *tonos*', whose note-series in Alypian theory overlaps its own:

Ex. 315

But in the song (Ex. 316 below), the opening fifth CZ, if it is intelligible at all, must surely be a main progression between fixed notes—whereas in the *tonos* C and Z are movable notes. There is no musical relation between the two. The usual solution is to postulate a 'Phrygian mode' for the song, and thus to combine the hypothesis of absolute pitch-value with the hypothesis that the octave-species of harmonic theory represented a multimodality of music. But even if the transcription is correct, enough has been said to suggest that the interpretation of Greek music in terms of theoretical octave-structures may be unhistorical. A particular range of signs may have been chosen to indicate, not an absolute pitch, but a special temperament of intervals, or by force of musicographical habit.

Ex. 316

Σεικιλος Ευτερ(πηι)

In our uncertainty about the notation, the chief interest of the piece must lie in its rhythmography. Of the rhythmic signs the dot or *stigme* (marking the strong beat of the metric foot) and the bracket (linking groups of notes) have no time-value. The unit of time (*protos chronos*) is left unmarked; the *diseme* — is equivalent to two time-units, and the triseme ⌴ to three. Now, whereas the four lines of the verse have respectively 9, 11, 11, and 11 metric units (in 5, 7, 8, and 9 syllables), each line of the music has twelve rhythmic units.[1] In ordinary Greek melopoeia, although a long metric syllable sometimes counted for more than two short ones, the length of musical lines was determined simply by the words of the verse, and a piece was commonly written out like prose, not in lines. In the Seikilos song, on the contrary, a uniform time-scheme is imposed on irregular verses by the music. It is a warning that breeds of music alien to the orthodox tradition might exist among the mixed populations of a superficially Hellenized world—and nobody can guess what sort of music a well-to-do Asiatic Greek might have chosen for the grave-stone of a female relative.

Although we have no other examples of verses prolonged and determined by the musical line, we know from a scholium (probably of late antiquity) that 'the verse is not completed by the metric line alone: it puts a full stop to its movement only when the lyre stops sounding'.[2] We also have what sounds like a description of Seikilos' metric scheme—but strangely misapplied to an incompatible verse-form—in the Byzantine annotation to some musical setting of a Greek poem on a sundial, known from the thirteenth-century Ottoboni Codex 59:[3] 'The *tropos* is the Lydian; the rhythm is of twelve beats (δωδεκάσημος). . . . Taking the line as a whole, the rhythm is of twelve beats, for the verse has eleven syllables, but (since the line is for twelve syllables, and there is one beat missing) the last syllable of each verse counts for three time-beats.' A rhythmic time-scheme of twelve-beat lines with three beats on the final syllables corresponds to Seikilos' song, and might possibly be taken from some ancient treatise on rhythm; but the Byzantine annotator, who scanned verse by syllables not quantities, has attempted to relate it to a regular hendecasyllabic poem which will not fit it, and has counted wrong.

(4) This Byzantine annotation, whatever it means, is directly

[1] For a recent transcription and analysis see E. Martin, *Trois documents de musique grecque* (Paris, 1953). He divides each line into four sections of three beats.

[2] Scholium to Dionysius Thrax (Bekker, *Anecdota Graeca*, ii, p. 751).

[3] See Wilamowitz-Moellendorff, *Griechische Verskunst* (Leipzig, 1921), pp. 595 ff.; 599–600 (no. 4).

connected with the problem of the famous musical documents first published by Vincenzo Galilei in 1581: the Hymns to the Muse (two poems run together), to the Sun, and to Nemesis. They were transmitted among ancient and Byzantine treatises of musical theory: so, too, were the metrically similar poems which are copied in the Ottoboni Codex without the music itself, but with Byzantine annotations on musical settings of the poems to Nature, to Isis, and on a Sundial. The two groups therefore had a common source. As to the words, modern scholars accept the Byzantine attribution of the poems on Nemesis and on the Sun, at least, to Hadrian's celebrated court musician Mesomedes (second century A.D.).[1] But the music is another question. It certainly existed by the thirteenth century: the question whether it was ancient in origin or a Byzantine reconstruction, undertaken as an exercise in ancient notation, may be stated as follows:

(i) Mesomedes—as Byzantine scholars knew—published a collection of his 'kitharoedic nomes'.[2] But since these poems are choral hymns, not nomes, the hypothesis that they were transmitted from that collection is unfounded.

(ii) The Galilei pieces are preceded in both our two archetypal codices by a tenth-century theoretical treatise addressed to Constantine Porphyrogenitus by one Dionysius, who was editing or emulating the ancient treatise of Bacchius—a work containing Greek notation.[3]

(iii) The extreme rarity of rhythmic signs in these pieces is in striking contrast with all known pieces so late as Mesomedes.

(iv) The Byzantine annotation cited above from the Ottoboni Codex certainly cannot refer to an ancient setting of the poem to which it is attached. Firstly, it is metrically impossible. Secondly, whereas the other poems might well have been written for singing, this is an epigrammatic conceit upon a sundial, of a literary genre quite alien to music. The idea that it could have been intended as a song is absurd. Therefore (unless the annotation has been somehow displaced) in this case at least the music was a subsequent and artificial addition. In the other cases, taken singly, an ancient origin cannot be disproved; but since the six pieces were evidently transmitted together, it is doubtful.

(v) Mesomedes was a famous figure in Byzantine minds, and Byzantine theorists understood the Alypian notation. In four cases

[1] G. Martellotti, *Mesomede* (Rome, 1929).

[2] Dio Cassius LXXVII 12 (transmitted by the Byzantine excerptor Xiphilinus).

[3] For the date of Dionysius' iambics see P. Maas in *Byzantinische Zeitschrift*, xii (1903). p. 273.

the annotator has interpreted the *tropos* of the settings as Lydian or Hypolydian by reference to the notational signs of late Greek theoretical *tonoi* (called by Alypius *tropoi*). Therefore Dionysius or his successors had the knowledge to attempt such settings in ancient notation for poems attributed to Mesomedes. A subsidiary point is that red ink is used, as it was for Byzantine notation.

(vi) The correspondence of speech-accents with melodic rise and fall is hardly consistent enough to prove an ancient origin.

The probability, then, perhaps seems to favour an erudite Byzantine reconstruction. On the most cautious estimate, we must refrain from basing any idea of the composer Mesomedes of Crete upon these curious emissions. We can be sure only that he was a kitharoede of extraordinary virtuosity. In that period of sentimental Hellenic revivals he got a public salary; he was docked of it by Hadrian's successor, on the ground that a musician was a useless member of society; but the amateur strummer Caracalla afterwards built him a mausoleum. His immortality may have been fraudulently perpetuated by the Galilei pieces: yet, since these pieces (whatever their origin) have excited the interest of European scholars for centuries, a sample from the Hymn to Nemesis is here given in the usual transcription.

Ex. 317

(5) Of papyrus fragments in Greek notation, the most considerable so far published is a Christian hymn from Oxyrhynchus, transcribed

in the third century A.D.; but since its melody is now recognized to belong to the oriental tradition of the Early Church, it lies beyond the scope of this chapter.[1]

From other papyri we have the following fragments:[2] (i) a Zenon papyrus (Cairo), *c.* 250 B.C.: a few words (? from a tragedy); (ii) a Rainer papyrus (Vienna), 250–150 B.C.: lines 339–45 from Euripides' *Orestes*; (iii) a papyrus (Berlin) inscribed after A.D. 156 with parts of (*a*) twelve lines of a paean, (*b*) a brief example without words, (*c*) four lines of verse (? tragic) addressing Ajax, (*d*) a brief example without words, (*e*) half a lyric line. These are cited only as fragments, and are best explained as examples composed to illustrate musical declamation, rhythm, &c., from some theoretical treatise,[3] (iv) *P. Osloensis* 1413. It contains two separate pieces in nineteen lines of text (all incomplete, some very fragmentary) with 'vocal' notation and profuse rhythmical signs. The script may be of the late first or early second century A.D. Published by Amundsen and Winnington-Ingram in *Symbolae Osloenses*, 1955.

(6) Two considerable fragments await publication:

(i) *P. Michiganensis Inv.* 2958. The papyrus, of the second century A.D., contains twenty-five fragmentary lines, of which 1–8 and 10–25 consist of Greek text with notation above, while line 9 is of notation without words.[4]

(ii) An Oxyrhynchus papyrus from Oxford.[5]

The papyri hitherto published are problems of palaeography rather than objects of musical history. All are too brief or too broken for assured analysis; and not all their rhythmic signs are fully understood. What is more certain is that music in Roman imperial times was distinguished from Alexandrian music by explicit rhythmical marking, which in all but our earliest pieces (the Zenon papyrus and the Delphic stones) replaces unaided interpretation of rhythm by the verse-metre.[6] In the first century B.C., as Dionysius of Halicarnassus

[1] Egon Wellesz, 'The earliest example of Christian hymnody', in *Classical Quarterly* xxxix (1945), pp. 34–45 ff. See vol. ii, p. 4.

[2] Jan, *Musici Scriptores Graeci*, supplement (Leipzig, 1899); Reinach, *La Musique greçque* (Paris, 1926), appendix; Mountford, 'Greek Music in the Papyri and Inscriptions', in Powell and Barber, *New Chapters in Greek Literature*, ii (Oxford, 1933), and 'A New Fragment of Greek Music in Cairo' in *Journal of Hellenic Studies*, li (1931). pp. 91 ff. E. G. Turner has re-dated the *Orestes* papyrus.

[3] Mountford, however, regards the papyrus as part of an anthology.

[4] Information courteously supplied by Prof. Youtie and Dr. Pearl of Michigan.

[5] Information courteously supplied by Mr. Winnington-Ingram.

[6] On Greek metric (too complex a subject for discussion here) see works cited in Bibliography, II. (i).

implies, music normally followed the rise and fall of speech. This was impossible in the classical music, where a strophe was melodically repeated by an antistrophe. How far it occurred in late antiquity we can seldom be sure, since the accent of words is too imperfectly represented by the Alexandrian signs which we use, and the pitch-accent was in any case being replaced by stress. But we know that in the second century A.D., when crowds would flock to hear a sophist speak Greek correctly and beautifully, these rhetorical performances were accompanied by academic study of rhythm.[1] So passionate an interest in declamation must have influenced music generally, and may account for the attention paid to rhythm in late antiquity. A school of rhythmic theorists grew up beside the classical metricists, working on other principles. In a philosophical treatise—strangely compounded of neoplatonic speculation, notational lore, and garbled musical antiquarianism—the otherwise unknown writer Aristides Quintilianus speaks of rhythmical matters with some realism, which may reflect the art of his own age, and at some length, which certainly reflects the contemporary interest.

Such writers, however, cannot help us towards an understanding of contemporary music, as Aristoxenus does for an earlier epoch. In their textbooks nothing is more depressing than the fossilization of the doctrine of *melopoeia*—musical composition—as a mere branch of theoretical terminology. The writer dubiously named 'Cleonides', professing the doctrine then claimed as 'Aristoxenian', first defines *metabole* as change from one *tonos* or *systema* or *genus* to another; then he adds that 'in *melopoeia*', *metabole* is something different—a change from an expansive mood (*ethos*) to a mood of contraction or of calm, &c.[2] But his second definition has no more to do with real music than his first. It is only 'ethical' speculation overlaid with the academic terms of the professional rhetoricians. He illustrates it with a list of examples of the 'calm *ethos*': hymns, paeans, encomia, and *symbulae*. Now the *symbule* or deliberation was not a musical form at all, but a regular exercise of the rhetorical schools. It has crept into a purely conventional list of musical forms under influence of the habit of applying musical terms to oratory, which may, indeed, have been the most serious use of music for an educated mind in this age. These later sources preserve little more from the musical past than a few

[1] Plutarch (*Ti. Gracchus* 2) reflects academic rhetorical practice of his own day in the absurd legend that C. Gracchus' speeches were accompanied by a wind-instrument.

[2] *Isagoge* 13–14.

technical terms which have lost such meaning as they may ever have had. 'Cleonides' produces *agoge* for conjunct motion, *ploke* for disjunct, *tone* for a sustained note, *petteia* for a note struck repeatedly. *Petteia* was apparently a metaphor from the repeated click-click of pieces on a draughts-board. But Aristides Quintilianus, who also knows the word, misinterprets the metaphor as a reference to the draughts-player's strategy, and defines *petteia* as the choice of notes in composition.[1] It has no musical context for either writer: the one repeats what he has read, the other makes a wrong etymological guess. None of these theorists think of describing current principles by which we might analyse our later musical documents.

For the most part, however, written documents of music had never existed. It is not from fragments nor from harmonic theorists that we can hope to gain an idea of its historical character. The best sources are the earliest—poets who were also composers and critics who were also musicians. They cannot reveal what Greek music might have meant to us, but on the question what it meant to the Greeks their evidence is the clearest that we have.

THE HISTORY OF GREEK MUSIC

(i) *Music in Homer's Greece.* By the end of the eighth century B.C. Greece was a land where 'beggar bears spite to beggar, and bard to bard'.[2] Such jealous professionals sang epics like the Iliad to their own lyre—*phorminx* or *kitharis*—freely adapting a conventional recitative style, with an initial appeal to the divine muse who possessed them to sing.[3] They came, as Homer shows, of a society whose twin-born music and poetry were already mature, consciously removed from the primitive, barbaric, or rustic. Not all Greek music was skilled art, but we know nothing of a period before a skilled art existed.

Music was early practised as an ingredient of magical medicine; its festival occasions and its formal conventions were often religious; but the line between the religious and the secular was differently drawn in antiquity. In the Iliad music already has the status of an art over and above a mere ritual; and the Greek tradition remained humanistic, anti-liturgical, swiftly sensitive to social or mental change. Gods as well as men daily demanded new music. The old was remembered in the classical period as a model and as a possession for ever, but not as a rite to be reiterated. There is no adequate foundation for

[1] II. 17 J. Some scholars, however, prefer Aristides' definition.

[2] Hesiod, *Works and Days*, 25–26.

[3] Cf. the pose of Phemius (*Od.* xxii. 345 f.): 'I am self-taught and God has planted in me all kinds of song.'

recent interpretations of Greek musical 'modes' as groups of melodic *formulae*, on Indian, Jewish, or Byzantine analogies: Byzantine composers could never have been personally parodied as Athenian composers were. In competitive individualism, at least, classical Greek music was nearer to modern Europe. It was an accomplishment open to all talents. The gods of Agamemnon's army not only receive music from mortals but make it at their own banquets, to Apollo's *phorminx*; and on earth, not only the paid professional but the lord Achilles sings epics of the renowns of warriors to his own *phorminx* for his pleasure.[1] This ideal of a music respected among an aristocracy by practice, as well as by patronage, reached its fullest expression in fifth-century Athens. There were, however, higher and lower classes of music. On a sleepless night Agamemnon, looking across from his tent to Troy, heard the skirling of oboes and pipes in the besieged Phrygian city.[2] The *aulos* and the *syrinx*, though common to Greece, were later thought to be Asiatic imports beside the pure Hellenic *lyra*, *kithara* or *phorminx*; and two rival musics were symbolized in the legend of the Greek Apollo flaying the Phrygian satyr-aulete Marsyas. But in the Iliad the wind-instruments are rustic and popular rather than alien. Paris, being a prince of Troy, plays the aristocratic *kitharis*.[3] Common folk may also use the *aulos*, and shepherds the *syrinx*—the pipes of the satyr Pan. Dionysus, to whom the *aulos* later became what the lyre was to Apollo, is not yet among the Olympian *élite* of Homer's gods; and Homer's heroes sing the Apolline paeans, not the Dionysian dithyrambs.

It is in the Odyssey that we find the apotheosis of the professional kitharoedic bard. Semi-divine beings like the Sirens, the nightingale, or Circe are allowed to sing; but music is otherwise monopolized by the resident minstrel. He has become a self-conscious ornament of noble households, and claims, although a servant, that recognition of genius which Pindar could still demand of a later aristocracy. The bard in the story—Phemius in Odysseus' manor or Demodocus in Alcinous' palace—is deliberately dramatized as a secondary hero, and incidentally used to introduce compliments to the musical profession as an indispensable asset of good dining.[4] He sings epics of warriors or love-stories of gods; he advertises his forthcoming works; he also performs for dancers in athletic contests. In Homeric and classical times *music* included not only poetry but often dancing as

[1] *Il.* i. 472 and 601 ff.; xxii. 391; ix. 186 ff.
[2] *Il.* x. 13.
[3] *Il.* iii. 54. The precise difference between *kitharis* and *phorminx* at this date is unknown. The terms *kithara* and *lyra* are later.
[4] Cf. *Od.* viii. 73 and 261 ff.; i. 337 ff.; xxiv. 197; &c.

well. As the sung word expressed the intonation, so the beat of the dancing foot (sometimes marked by castanets) expressed the rhythm.[1] The bard advances into a dancing-ground (*chorus* or *orchestra*) and the youths dance time to his song. If a dance is performed without song—as was the famous Phaeacian ball-throwing dance—there is no music either: the rhythm is conducted by the hand-claps of the spectators, or by the arms of Nausicaa dancing among her maids.[2]

For the music of the archaic community as a whole we must return to the earlier, less self-assertive Homer of the Iliad. He describes, for instance, the form of the dirge sung over Hector's body. Professional bards begin the lamentation, after which a chorus of women keens; then Hector's widow Andromache, his mother Hecuba, and his sister-in-law Helen take up their laments in turn, with a keening of women after each.[3] Improvisations set within a formal sequence may still have been the structure of the dirges known to Plato. Almost every social occasion also had its song—often a more or less traditional elaboration of some simple cry like the *Ailinon* ('alas for Linus!') in an ancient and celebrated harvesting-shanty, or the *Hymen O Hymenaee* of the wedding-hymns.[4] Some of this music is set into scenes on the Shield of Achilles. Here girls with garlands and boys with knives, holding hands, dance in rings or in rows to the song of a bard with a lyre, while two acrobats turn somersaults at the beginning of each verse or strain.[5] In other scenes, a boy with a lyre sings the 'Linus' at the vintage; two shepherds play the pastoral *syrinx* to their flocks; and a wedding-feast is celebrated with the chant *Hymenaeus* and the dancing of boys to *auloi* and lyres.[6]

These scenes, though drawn from real experience, are as artfully idealized as Gongora's poetic pictures of country life. They give us the context of the archaic lyrical music which went on beside the grand style of the epic with its tales of the gods and heroes.

(ii) *The Music of the Early Lyrics.* Down to the mid-fifth century B.C., sophisticated poets composed songs of skilled art but of popular inspiration—songs for such daily doings as dances of young girls or fighting men, weddings, funerals, processions, wars, drinking-bouts; love-songs and songs of political or private hate. This lyric move-

[1] A metric *foot* is a term borrowed from dancing. For castanets see Hom. *Hymn.* iii. 162.

[2] *Od.* viii. 261 ff.; ibid. 370 ff.; vi. 100 ff.

[3] *Il.* xxiv. 720 ff.

[4] On the Linus-song (which did not explain who Linus was nor why he was mourned) see Frazer, *Golden Bough*, vii. 216. See also above, p. 251.

[5] *Il.* xviii. 590 ff. Acrobats also in *Od.* iv. 17 ff.

[6] *Il.* xviii. 491 ff., 525 ff., 561 ff.

ment sprang from Ionian Greece, and found its first great metropolis in Sparta, whose aristocracy was still Homeric enough to love good music next to good fighting. Its early stages are extremely hard to trace. The attribution of extant poems is often in doubt, the dates of composers in confusion. Musical history was first reconstructed in the fourth century B.C. by Glaucus of Rhegium, whose work is known chiefly through an unintelligent source of late antiquity, the pseudo-Plutarchian *De musica*.[1] No subject is more confused by legend and invention. The main sources were local histories compiled from the later fifth century onwards; and these records, to judge from the many ancient doubts and divergences on the dates of archaic poets, must have been either unreliable or sketchy. The musical victories of early poets in local or Panhellenic festivals may have been interpolated into the annals by the competing vanities of Greek cities. It was claimed that a Pythian festival of music was held at Delphi long before the official Pythian era (582 B.C.), and a high though hazy antiquity was also ascribed to musical contests at the Spartan Carnea. None were included in the indubitably ancient Olympian Games, and Homer knows no more than musical accompaniments to athletics or dances. Even if musicians began so early to compete for their own prizes, no firm chronology was transmitted from these events.

Festival music consisted of epic declamation and poetic forms dedicated to particular deities. The 'Pythian Nome' for Apollo was a composition or genre on the set theme of Apollo and the Dragon (or Python), which still recurs in the extant Delphic paeans of the second century B.C., and which was revived by sixteenth-century pioneers of Italian opera.[2] The Delphic contest of auletes originated, according to Pindar, in an archaic 'Many-headed Nome' on the theme of Perseus slaying the Gorgon. The dithyramb probably began in the sixth century B.C. as a recital of the Birth of Dionysus, not acted, but danced and sung to the *aulos* by a circular chorus of fifty men or boys. It was brought to maturity, in a strophic form, by the early classic composers, and broke away from the limits of the set subject. No special themes were prescribed for tragedy and comedy as we know them in the fifth century, but they may originally, like the dithyramb, have had some particular reference to their patron Dionysus.[3] Of all these festival genres, however, no clear example

[1] Ascribed to Plutarch by Weil and Reinach (ed. 1900), but no longer accepted as his. See the edition of F. Lasserre (Paris, 1954).

[2] The opinion of later authors that the original Pythian Nome was an *aulos*-piece without words is hardly credible.

[3] See further A. W. Pickard-Cambridge, *Dithyramb, Tragedy, and Comedy* (Oxford,

has come down to us from the archaic period. Early lyric poets, while they may also produce hymns to gods, are more concerned with the musical occasions of ordinary private and social life than with the set ritual narrative or drama. Even the more formal choric works of Stesichorus, which do narrate mythological stories, were probably designed (like Pindar's) for the personal occasions of a patron's court. Most of the lyric genres are less grandiose. From Alcman, for instance, we have a piece, possibly composed for two choirs, in which the poet bandies compliments to pretty girls as they sing and dance, calling them by their names.[1] To Tyrtaeus were attributed the patriotic marching-songs (*embateria*) of the Spartans, who had the unusual habit of keeping step, and took auletes with them into battle.[2] Archilochus of Paros, the most famous figure of all, composed colloquial songs—gnomic, satirical, autobiographical, and above all, convivial. Songs called *scolia*, often on political subjects, were sung to an *aulos* by gentlemen after dinner over their wine, each delivering one line in turn.[3] But of Archilochus' music the fifth century seems to remember only the triple *tenella kallinike*—three cheers for an Olympic victor. Pindar thought it crude stuff beside his own regal victory odes.[4]

What was recorded of these poets' lives was mainly inference or romance. They were dated to the seventh century (or, in the case of Stesichorus, variously to *c.* 600 and *c.* 485 B.C.). This patch of history was much confused by the later Greek passion for deriving every musical form or instrument from a First Inventor, to whom extant works would then be apportioned.

The founder of auletic music was said to be Olympus, who was a myth, but was credited with real archaic compositions still known in the fourth century B.C.: e.g. a ritual libation-song (*spondeion*) which used some ascending three-quarter-tone intervals—presumably related to the irrational borings of the *aulos* which Aristoxenus noted.[5] The early *aulos*, of which the Argive Sacadas was the first known virtuoso, was improved in the later fifth century by Pronomus of Thebes or his school.[6] Besides common devices for modifying notes,

1927), and *The Dramatic Festivals of Athens* (Oxford, 1953): the origins of these forms is obscure.

[1] Diehl, *Anthologia Lyrica Graeca* (Leipzig, 1942), ii., p. 7, n. 1. The interpretation is difficult and uncertain.

[2] Cf. Thuc. v. 20. Later stories that Tyrtaeus was (*a*) a general, (*b*) a music-teacher, need not be credited.

[3] Examples in Diehl, op. cit. ii, pp. 181 ff. Singers either repeated known *scolia* or composed as they went.

[4] *Ol.* ix. 1 (cf. *Pyth.* ii. 55).

[5] See above, p. 350. On the '*spondeion* scale' of ps.-Plut. *De musica*, see Winnington-Ingram in *Classical Quarterly*, xxii (1928), pp. 83 ff.

[6] No full account of Greek instruments can here be attempted. See Reinach, articles

metal rings were used to close or half-close holes, and the number of holes (sometimes as few as six) was raised to fifteen. *Auloi* were made in five registers covering three octaves between them. They were of wood, bone, or ivory, with a double (or less probably, a single) reed in the bulb of the mouthpiece. The player wore a leather halter to hold in his puffing lips. Often he used a pair of *auloi*, modifying the note by drawing them apart or together.[1] The *aulos* might accompany any choral singing, down to drinking-parties after dinner; but a soloist accompanied himself on strings, and strings were naturally used by the composers themselves.

Bigger and better stringed instruments may have come in about Pindar's times. The classical *kithara* had a body of wood, and a sound-box made of, or shaped like, a tortoise's shell, with oxhide stretched over the face and two curved horns rising from it, joined by a cross-bar carrying the pegs, to which strings of gut were stretched over a bridge. For plucking, an ivory plectrum was generally used in one hand, and in the other the fingers alone. From the seventh century onwards, archaeological evidence shows varying numbers of strings (from four to eleven or twelve) in concurrent use. This simultaneously attested variety is enough to suggest that the exact number had less practical significance than was attached to it in apocryphal anecdotes of the fourth century B.C. Terpander—a shadowy figure assigned to variant seventh-century dates and suspiciously coupled with the mythical Olympus—was inflated into a Founder of kitharistic music, and was supposed to have increased the strings of the *phorminx* from four to the symbolic number of seven, also imputed to Orpheus.[2] He was made responsible for poems of uncertain origin and traditional kitharistic nomes (e.g. the *nomos orthios* or 'shrill nome', still familiar in the fifth century). According to Pindar, however, his instrument was not the *phorminx* but the *barbitos*, which he invented in antiphonal answer to the Lydian *pectis*.[3] Exactly how these instruments differed from others was disputed. The *barbitos*, which was a lyre with long strings, was certainly used by the two great Aeolian

'Lyra' and 'Tibia' in Daremberg-Saglio, *Dictionnaire d'antiquités* (Paris, 1877–1919); Sachs, *History of Musical Instruments* (New York, 1940), and article in *Reallexikon der Musikinstrumente* (Berlin, 1913); Schlesinger, *The Greek Aulos* (London, 1938; inacceptable on musical theory). Illustrations (undated) in Wegner, *Musikleben der Griechen* (Berlin, 1949).

[1] Aristox. *Harm.* 42. The left *aulos* might also answer the right: Varro *R R* i. 2, 15–16, *may* also mean that the *tibia succentiva* (left) was held lower than the *incentiva* (right), but certainly implies that its part was a subsequent response (cf. *succino* in Hor. *Ep.* i. 7, 48).

[2] The poem on the subject ascribed to Terpander is spurious.

[3] *Frag.* 125 (*ap.* Athen. 635d, discussing the instruments).

composers of the early sixth century, Alcaeus and Sappho. Both were of Lesbos, which was also the reputed home of Terpander. It is not necessary to decide whether 'Terpander'—a title meaning Rejoicer of Man—was a historical personage or merely a πρῶτος εὑρετής: the equivalent of a patron saint. In either case his quasi-legendary fame is best interpreted as a symbol of the musical influence of the Aeolian school which followed in the sixth century.

(iii) *Aeolian Music.* Of Sappho's life little but legend is preserved. Alcaeus, on the other hand, is the first tangible figure in the history of European music. He was a nobleman of Lesbos with a colourful record of war, exile, and political opposition to the local Tyrants. He is said to have sung in exquisite dress, and his own songs were especially popular in classical Athens at those fashionable drinking-parties where the aristocracy made music.[1] Both Alcaeus and Sappho were brilliant metrical innovators; both wrote in their native Aeolian dialect. Their art was personal, and their lyric forms usually monodic. In literary genre there is little to relate them to the first classical composers at the end of the sixth century. But these composers have a special predilection for a style which they call 'Aeolian', although they themselves came from Boeotia or the Peloponnese; and while no influence can be traced from Alcaeus and Sappho in particular, it is possible that a general influence was exercised by the school of Lesbos.

At Athens the pioneer of the classical movement was Lasos of Hermione, the powerful dithyrambist who caught a creature of the Pisistratid Tyrants forging oracles. Lasos refers to his own music 'in the deep-sounding Aeolian *harmonia*'; and Pratinas, another Peloponnesian, not much later exhorts musicians to 'follow neither the high nor the low Ionian muse, but plough the middle course and *Aeolize* in your song'.[2] The verb means 'to speak the Aeolian (musical) language'. *Harmonia* in its melodic sense denotes not only a tuning but a *tropos* or idiom. That the Aeolian idiom was 'deep' to Lasos but 'middle' to Pratinas only shows that its pitch was a relative matter: at any rate, it was something opposed to the shrill archaic styles. Evidently they were proud to practise and advertise this music.

Pindar, though he also has a Lydian manner, more often describes his *tropos* as Aeolian. For his Lydian he can employ a *phorminx* as

[1] Aristoph. *Thesm.* 160; *Lys.* 1236 f., &c.

[2] Both cited by 'Heraclides Ponticus' (*ap.* Athen. 624e–625f), who ignorantly equates the Aeolian *harmonia* with the Hypodorian octave-species.

well as wind, and for his Aeolian *auloi* as well as strings, or he can combine both with dancers in a full-dress epinikian ode: the difference is not in the instruments, but simply in the styles. A problem, however, arises when Pindar seems to call the same music both Aeolian and Dorian. For King Hieron's Olympian victory on his horse Pherenicus, Pindar writes: 'Take from its peg my *Dorian phorminx*. . . . Him I must crown with a horseman's strain of *Aeolian* song.'[1] Elsewhere he speaks of 'an *Aeolian* walking the *Dorian* road of hymns,' and of some new *tropos* (unnamed) which he is tuning to his 'Dorian sandal'.[2] Later scholiasts, noticing the difficulty but knowing nothing of his music, conjectured that in the former case the rhythm was Aeolian, in the latter Dorian. But these are not metric terms, and the idea that a 'Dorian' rhythm could simply be clapped on to an 'Aeolian' *tropos* (or vice versa) seems purely academic. Pindar's language suggests rather that he was somehow adapting an Aeolian melopoeia to principles of rhythm and string-tuning which were called Dorian. That the term Dorian in fact referred to tuning as well as rhythm is shown by the following passage of Pratinas:[3]

> What is this uproar, what these dancings? What outrage has attacked the trampled altar of Dionysus? . . . It is the voice that is queen, by order of the Muse: the *aulos* must dance behind, being indeed a servant. Only in the rout and fisticuffs of young mummers banging at the door let him act the General and be thankful. Beat that bad breath of a coloratura-mottled toad! Burn that varlet of a low-crooning babbling reed that wastes spittle and spoils time and tune as he steps along, with his body all gimlet-holes! Now look at me, O God of the ivied hair, Dionysus triumphant in dithyrambs: this is the right fling of hand and foot. Hear my own performance—the Dorian!

Here Pratinas, notwithstanding his other manifesto in favour of the Aeolian style, is calling his own music Dorian. Taken together with Pindar's evidence, it tends to strengthen the suspicion that in this early classical period the terms Dorian and Aeolian might be applied to the same music; and it is notable that in the later fifth century, although Pindar was by no means obsolete, the Aeolian name dropped out of musical use, while the Dorian remained. But we cannot pretend to understand such terms too exactly in a period of rapid musical development, when the main styles were certainly losing any real association with the local schools and dialects from

[1] *Ol.* i. 17 and 101 f.

[2] *Frag.* 19; *Ol.* iii. 5. Aeolian *tropos* also in *Pyth.* ii. 69 ff., *Nem.* iii. 79.

[3] *Frag.* 1 (*ap.* Athen. 617e, where the musical point is misunderstood). Text and meaning are often dubious, but the general sense is clear.

which they may originally have been named. What emerges clearly is that to Pratinas the Dorian stands for true rhythm and tuning led by the voice, as against the rhythmical and tonal errors of an uncontrollable *aulos*. By the end of the century our sources distinguish, above all, two major types of tuning and idiom: the one clean and sustained (*entonos*), typified by the high classical Dorian, the other chromatic and quivering (*aiolos*), often assorted with the style then known as Phrygian and with the *aulos* or its tonal effects. Other distinct brands of music still existed, but they were falling away into the popular background of the more mature fifth-century movement. To illustrate this point, it will be necessary to clarify the terms in which Plato surveys the range of *harmoniae* known during the later classical period.

(iv) *The Harmoniae of Plato's Republic*. We know from Aristophanes that fifth-century schoolboys were taught to tune their lyres to more than one *harmonia* or *accordatura*. But these tunings need not be interpreted as mechanical scale-forms. The stylistic connotations of the word emerge clearly in the classical Greek preference for an adverbial form, *Doristi, Lydisti, Phrygisti*—used of speaking 'in a certain idiom'—rather than an adjectival phrase, 'Dorian, Lydian, or Phrygian *harmonia*'. Plato's own usage can best be studied in a famous passage, here summarized as follows:[1]

> The *harmonia* and the rhythm must follow the sense of the words; and in words (as we were saying) we have no use for dirges and lamentations. Which, then, are the *harmoniae* of dirges? That in the Mixolydian, the High Lydian, and suchlike *harmoniae*. Then these must surely be abolished, for they are unprofitable even for decent women, let alone men. Now, in the men who defend the City drunkenness, softness, and laxity are most unbecoming. Which are the soft wine-bibber's *harmoniae*? That in the Ionian; and some in the Lydian are also called low and lax. These can be of no good to fighting men. So you seem to be left with two *harmoniae*, in the Dorian and in the Phrygian.

The term *harmonia* here has two connotations. (*a*) Since there can be more than one *harmonia* in the low Lydian, Plato at this point equates *harmonia* with a single *melodia*, or at least a sub-type; and this usage is confirmed by Euripides, who speaks of the nightingale 'weaving her fine-spun *harmonia* in the trees'.[2] (*b*) Otherwise Plato

[1] *Rep.* 398d–399a (abbreviated). The word *chalaros* is punningly used for both 'low-pitched' and 'morally lax'. The reading αὖ τινες is here accepted.
[2] *Frag*. 773.

gives to *harmonia* the more general sense of a whole melodic idiom (e.g. what Aristoxenus calls 'the Phrygian *melos*').

Some, though not all, of the *harmoniae* named are associated with (relatively) high or low pitches. But their more fundamental associations are with special forms or occasions of music—for instance, the hysterical shrieking of dirges or the sensual crooning of wine-songs. Plato elsewhere tells us that at the end of the classical era these and other associations broke down, and the various forms and idioms were confused.[1] Later Greeks, no longer knowing the old forms of musical expression, imagined that Plato was attaching abstract ethical effects to the various *harmoniae*: a superstition which Aristoxenus briefly repudiates.[2] It is true that to classical Greek minds music was like a second language, capable of expressing almost all that could be said in words, and of bringing out the moods or passions latent in them. Such bilingualism of speech and music is perhaps unparalleled in Europe: certainly it is the antithesis of the idea of music as a closed world existing for its own sake in its own terms. Like all Greek art, music was *mimetic* or representative—a direct photography (as it were) of mental objects formed by the *ethos* and *pathos* of the soul. This psychological theory was carried to absurdity by later Greeks who (as an ancient writer says) fell into ecstasies and compared tunes with natural objects.[3] But Plato's own meaning is quite straightforward and sensible. Music in the classical tradition expressed the words and was indivisible from their substance, which was not always edifying. Aristophanes has given us a decisive example of the Ionian style which Plato regards as unfit for boys' education. It is, in fact, an outrageously indecent duet between two prostitutes.[4] The polite Hellenistic society of a later age had forgotten that music could be barbarous and orgiastic. The famous oriental dirge for Adonis was civilized into a conventional piece of Alexandrian recitative, which Theocritus could cast into charming verse; but this was not the real *Adoniasm*, with its dinning drums, known to fifth-century Athens. The excruciating 'Ai-ai Adonin!', screamed from the housetops by a frenzied female, falling on the ear like an evil omen, had been almost enough to break off the Assembly's debate on the invasion of Sicily.[5]

The 'high and low *harmoniae*' (like the archaic 'shrill nome')

[1] *Laws* 700a ff. (cited below, p. 395). [2] *Harm.* 31.

[3] *Papyr.* Hibeh i. 13.

[4] *Eccl.* 893 ff. (in 918–19, 'Ionic *tropos*' is used punningly, alluding to the musical sense in l. 883).

[5] Theocr. *Buc.* xv; Aristoph. *Lys.* 393 ff.

may represent a lingering ancient stratum of popular music. We cannot define them precisely. The Mixolydian aroused endless curiosity in late antiquity owing to the problems of placing a seventh theoretical *tonos* of that name, and speculations on its archaic nature were then quite unhistorical. The archaic Lydian and Ionian date from the period when Ionia was in the Lydian empire, and the two terms may have meant much the same. The 'high Lydian' and 'low Lydian and Ionian', which Plato banishes from education, can scarcely have differed very much from the 'high and low Ionian' which Pratinas banished from music. Both were of the primitive or popular stuff against which the first classical composers were asserting the modern refinement of their Aeolian or Dorian manner.[1] In the later fifth century respectable composers ceased to write in the old popular genres, which early poets had refined and adorned. These genres fell back into a musical underworld, which could still inspire the genius of Euripides, but was generally regarded as vulgar.[2] The Dorian and Phrygian were the main styles now practised in serious music. They represented two indispensable but sharply contrasted modes of expression. The Lydian name is still occasionally used, but is virtually identified with the Phrygian. Telestes, at the end of the century, speaks of 'that *Phrygian* king of the holy *aulos* . . . who first tuned the quivering (*aiolos*) *Lydian* strain, rival of the Dorian muse'.[3]

Telestes' adjective *aiolos* exactly reflects that quivering, flexible melodic line which Aristophanes parodies in the new dithyrambists. The dithyrambic *tropos* of the day was the Phrygian, which was closely associated with the *aulos*, though the new composers imitated its effects on strings as well. The *aulos* (as Pratinas complained) drowned both rhythm and tuning with its incontinent wobbles unless it was subordinated to the voice, and a music dominated by its noise can have had little regard for rational laws of consonance. Its attraction was emotional excitement. Phrygian music was not always exaggerated or intemperate: Plato admits it as a necessity for the softer moods of persuasion or appeal. But its antithesis to the Dorian tuning went far deeper than any alleged difference of 'modal' species. Greek writers, in contrasting the Dorian music's measured firmness with the pliant ecstasy of the Phrygian, are not merely word-painting. When Philoxenus tried to compose a dithyramb in the Dorian he found it a stylistic impossibility.[4] The Dorian was *entonos*, a music

[1] Pindar's Lydian (whether related to archaic Lydian music or not) belongs to a different musical level. Plato implies that there were several 'Lydian' *harmoniae*.

[2] Aristoph. *Frogs* 1301–4.

[3] Diehl, op. cit. ii, p. 126; cf. ibid., p. 156.

[4] Aristotle, *Pol.* 1342b.

of notes firmly tuned and sustained without quavering or *kampai*, incapable of the *enthusiasmos* demanded by the Dionysiac dithyramb.[1]

Plato and Aristoxenus are at one in their preference for the high classical school of the earlier fifth century. But they refer to their ideal in different terms. For Plato, it is represented by the Dorian *harmonia*; for Aristoxenus, by the enharmonic *genus*. There is some reason to believe that the Dorian *harmonia* and the enharmonic *genus* were intimately related.

(v) *The 'enharmonic' music.* It is not till the fourth century that we hear of the classification of the tetrachord into three *genera*. Ex. 306 is here set out on a less rigid staff, with continuous lines for the fixed *mese* and *hypate*, a dotted line for the movable *lichanos*, and movable *parypate* in the space:

Ex. 318

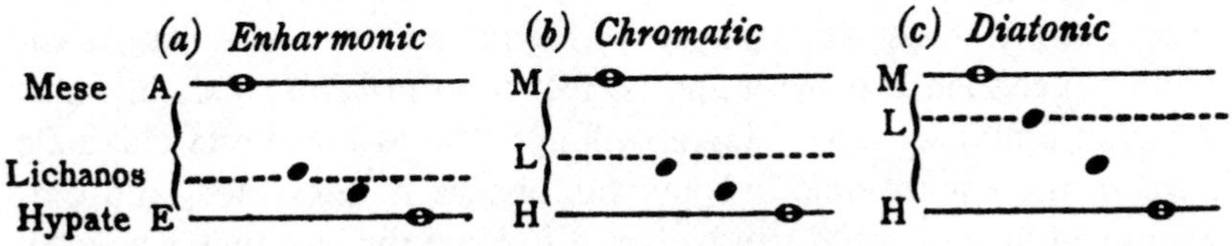

These are still only schematic figures or skeletons of melodic styles. According to Aristoxenus the diatonic (which dominates post-Alexandrian music) was the oldest. The chromatic was a novelty in 411 B.C., when Aristophanes parodied its fashionable exponent Agathon, with the comment: 'Ant-crawls—or what's this warbling?'[2] *Chroma* means the minor shades of the movable notes, and the chromatic developed as a moist relentment of the sharp enharmonic outlines. It connoted a very different style, attuned to the poetic prettiness of the fourth century.

Analytically, the *genera* were defined by the tuning of *lichanos*. Aristoxenus contrasts the classical enharmonic with the fourth-century cult of chromaticism in an illuminating passage:[3]

That there is a melodic style which demands a ditonal *lichanos* [i.e. two whole tones below *mese*]—and no mean style, but about the finest of all—is far from evident to most musicians nowadays, although it could be shown to them by induction from examples. But what I say will be clear enough to those familiar with the first and second of the old *tropoi*. Those used only to the present style of composition will of course reject the ditonal *lichanos*, since the great majority nowadays use a higher tuning.

[1] See further below, pp. 389, 393 ff. [2] *Thesm.* 100. [3] *Harm.* 23.

The reason is a hankering for more and more sweetness: that this is their aim is shown by the fact that they practise chiefly and almost always the chromatic—or if they ever do touch the enharmonic, they approximate its tuning to the chromatic, wherewith its stylistic character (*ethos*) is distorted to ruin.

The numbering of 'first and second *tropoi*' can only be pedagogic. It refers, not to the archaic beginnings of music, but to the melopoeic styles taught in the classical curriculum of schools, beginning from Simonides and Pindar, or the first period of what was recognized by the classicists as 'the finest style of all'.[1]

In this 'finest style', Aristoxenus treats the ditonal progression from *mese* to *lichanos* not as a mere option of the ear, but as a demonstrable necessity of musical syntax. The term *induction* is taken from the logic of his master Aristotle.[2] The exact effects are of course irrecoverable, but we can imagine how a music built upon the contrast between fixed and movable notes, consonant and dissonant progressions, might be deranged by the introduction of a new quasi-consonance such as a sweet and perfect 5:4 third from *mese* down to a higher tuning of *lichanos*. According to the pseudo-Plutarchian *De musica*, the enharmonic *pyknon* was originally undivided, and old-fashioned auletes could still be heard to keep the semitone whole 'in the tetrachord *meson* as well'.[3] The implication is that the *dieses* were used chiefly or solely in the tetrachord *meson*, and that, even there, they were regarded as a later decorative addition. These so-called 'quarter-tones' often strike modern minds as the salient feature of the enharmonic *genus*. In fact, they were incidental to it. The enharmonic style was basically defined by the progressions resulting from the ditonal *lichanos* of the classical period.

The pseudo-Plutarch somewhat unconvincingly derives enharmonic music from the archaic *spondeion* of Olympus, but adds that the irregular three-quarter-tone interval of the *spondeion* is alien to the real enharmonic (and to all the *genera*). This account at least serves to emphasize the purity of the enharmonic tuning by contrast with archaic *aulos*-music. Now it is a striking fact that the term 'enharmonic' is not found till the fourth century, when the three *genera* were first classified. The traditional name of the *genus*—still used by Plato, and often by Aristoxenus—was simply 'The *Harmonia*': i.e. 'the tuning', or music *in tune*. The opposite term, *exharmonic*, means

[1] When the 'second *tropos*' began is uncertain, but not here relevant.

[2] ἐπάγεσθαι.

[3] *De mus.* 11, 6. The source of this datum can hardly be later than the fourth century, when the enharmonic music was dying out.

'out of tune'. The false notes produced by violent modulation in the new anti-classical styles are called *exharmonic*: i.e. transgressions of 'The (enharmonic) Tuning'.[1] Before Aristoxenus, no theorist had ever analysed any *genus* except the enharmonic;[2] and Aristoxenus himself uses it as the typical figure for general demonstration. It is clear that, until the fourth century, 'The *Harmonia*' was in some sense unique—the only note-series which was considered to be truly 'in tune' and worth logical analysis. Historically, it may be supposed to represent the principles of rational consonance worked out in music by the first classical composers, and in mathematics by their contemporaries, the first harmonic scientists. This is not to say that the archaic idioms necessarily lacked all acoustic logic; but the classical music represented some more conscious achievement of a well-tuned tonality, which first superseded the archaic styles, then broke down under the chromaticism of the modernists.

The double enharmonic tetrachord (with the ditonal *lichanos*) is to Aristoxenus the pure theoretical figure of the great classical styles which he remembered. In fourth-century terms, it corresponds to the octave-species called Dorian (in the enharmonic *genus*). Without the melopoeic progressions, the scale conveys little to us; but it may reasonably be regarded as an abstract *schema* of the old classic Dorian tuning. In other words, 'The *Harmonia*' may probably be identified as both 'enharmonic' and 'Dorian'. The idea that a composer took a mode called Dorian and then chose between its three alternative *genera* is an unhistorical impression from later analytical textbooks. In classical melopoeia, *harmonia* and *genus* were not so dissociable.

The other fourth-century scale-forms were only artificial segments, with artificial names, cut out of this rationalized note-series for theoretical purposes. The old Phrygian *harmonia* or *melos*, which called for the tonal uncertainties of the *aulos* or emulated them on the *kithara*, may have been stylized to some degree, but it cannot be explained as a sub-type of the same note-series.

Thus far a tentative discussion of this fifth-century terminology may be justifiable; but it is hampered by our ignorance of contemporary teaching. Of the mysteriously influential Damon, the musical friend of Pericles and Socrates, we know little for certain, though much was conjectured by later Platonists.[3] He is said to have standardized the nomenclature of some *harmoniae*. In any case, the

[1] 'Pherecrates' *ap.* ps.-Plutarch, *De mus.* 30, 3.

[2] *Harm.* 2.

[3] All references to extant writings by Damon are suspicious or late. Few will accept as authentic his alleged speech before the Areopagites.

poet-composers who were absorbing local dialects into a literary language must also have universalized the chief musical idioms. A common and conscious Hellenism was the tendency, if not the achievement, of the age. The Greek belief that Dorian music was more 'Hellenic' than Phrygian was true only in the sense that the Dorian was a typical creation of the classical spirit.[1] For oriental influences in music of this date there can be no concrete evidence. The names and natures of *harmoniae* have evoked both ancient and modern speculation, but it is doubtful whether they could ever define more than the broader differences of musical character. Between the Lydian of Pindar and the Lydian or Phrygian of Telestes much had changed. The classical music did not develop through musically autonomous forms; it was more aptly classified (as Plato also knew) by the literary forms which it served.[2] These forms, too, were in rapid growth and change. Within them, contemporaries were sharply aware of differences in the dates and styles of individual composers.

(vi) *Aristophanes and Athens*. Pindar, though he may have boasted of noble lineage, speaks and behaves as a professional musician.[3] His patrons were the aristocracies of Greece and the kings or lords of Sicily, where Stesichorus had brought choral performances into fashion. The distinctive contribution of Athens to music was the tragic and comic theatre, still financed by wealthy persons but effectively patronized by the whole City: a drama in which the simple movements and plain accompaniment of a citizen chorus required no professional training in choreography and instrumentation, as did the dithyramb or the Pindaric ode. Whereas gentlemen like Alcaeus had touched only the smaller forms of lyric song, free-born Athenians could now compose big works. A set of three tragedies with a comedy had to be presented for a prize at the Great Dionysia or other yearly festivals. The tragedians, being financially independent and bound to a dramatic theme, tell us far less of their own music than the professional Pindar, who is continually aware of his art, his lyre, and his orchestration, his patrons and rivals, and his purse. But it was a prime function of the classic comedy to criticize music as well as politics and persons. The greatest of comedians was himself probably the greatest of Athenian composers,[4] and certainly the greatest of

[1] Cf. Plat. *Lach.* 188 d. 'Heraclides Ponticus' on racial origins of music is anachronistic fantasy.

[2] *Laws* 700a.

[3] *Pyth.* v. 72 ff; but professional status is proved by his references to fees.

[4] So Plato's epigram: the Graces (goddesses especially of music) chose Aristophanes' soul as their home.

Greek musical critics. Aristophanes and his audience—or its upper layer—could catch musical allusions back to Archilochus or Alcman, and could enjoy parodies ranging from the first classics to the latest dithyrambic novelty. His plays are the epitome of the Athenian musical education of his time.

Boys of the upper classes went to a music-master, and in company they were expected to intone their piece of epic or to sing the classics at meals.[1] 'Musical hoggishness' was a social and political insult.[2] For advanced students there were professors of composition, caricatured in Aristophanes' hack Poet with his stock in trade of model styles—Homer, Simonides, Pindar, the maiden-song, the dithyramb.[3] Choruses were also trained by professionals, unless the composer (like Aristophanes) could do it for himself. But music was much more than an academic discipline and a fine art. At every drinking-party an *aulos* was there to accompany *scolia* and favourite numbers from musical comedy. The first man to drain his vase of wine during the breath of a trumpet-blast got a prize; the drinker who sang the night through 'took the cake' as a reward.[4] At a smart party, as staged by Aristophanes, the guests first pour the libation of wine on the floor (the social rite at which libation-songs were sung); then the *aulos*-girl tunes up, and the *scolia* go on until the eldest guest makes off with the *aulos*-girl.[5] Auletes were also employed by gymnasts for rhythmical exercises, and by magistrates for public proclamations in the City.

The forms of rural music were afterwards collected by Alexandrian scholars, more from literary references than from life. They catalogued over fifty generic or regional types of dance, with innumerable songs of shepherd loves or of rustic labours—the 'practical songs' sung at work by spinners, millers, reapers, and water-drawers.[6] Fifth-century composers had drawn upon the melodic fund of popular music for their own work. Aristophanes often uses the popular metric forms, polishing them into sophisticated art and mixing them on occasion with the grand styles.[7] It had been done before, as he tells us, by Phrynichus and other early classical composers. 'I reveal' (sing his Birds) 'the nomes sacred to Pan, the dances to the Great Mother of the mountains, from which Phrynichus ever drew his sweet melody,

[1] Aristoph. *Peace* 1267 ff.; *Clouds* 1355 ff.

[2] *Knights* 985 ff.

[3] *Birds* 904–58.

[4] *Ach.* 1000; *Knights* 277.

[5] *Wasps* 1212 ff.

[6] Athen. 618e–620a, with some examples. (But the 'Nile Chantey' of Powell, *Collectanea Alexandrina* (Oxford, 1925), p. 185, no. 7, is scarcely an Egyptian bargee song.)

[7] e.g. Aristoph. *Clouds* 563–74.

sucking like a bee that ambrosial fruit of song.'[1] The 'old honey-sweet songs from Phrynichus' *Phoenissae*' were inspired by hymns from country liturgies. Modernists dismissed the choruses of his contemporary Lamprocles as 'prehistoric maypole-stuff full of grass-hoppers'—to which the classicists retorted that this was the music that bred the men who fought at Marathon.[2] In the *Frogs*, Euripides is made to accuse Aeschylus of stealing from this antiquated folk-song: 'Did you get those water-drawer's ditties from Marathon, or where?' —'From Beauty I drew them to Beauty', replies Aeschylus impressively, adding, 'that I might not be seen to have reaped the self-same holy meadow of music as Phrynichus.'[3] The point is that Aeschylus did, in fact, draw upon the same rustic hymnal. Its influence appears in the rhythmical refrains used at the end of strophic movements in some of his choruses.[4] Echoes of a more primitive music are audible too. In a chorus of Persian elders bewailing the destruction of Xerxes' army, his mind goes back to the dirge-cry for Bormus sung by serfs as they reaped the cornfields by the Black Sea; at the end of two choric strophae of the *Agamemnon* he recalls the *Ailinon* of the Linus-song sung by peasants since Homeric times.[5] Aristophanes himself, at the end of a play, will often use the old wedding-cry *Hymenaeus*, or the *tenella kallinike* of Archilochus, or some country dance. Popular melody was still an ingredient in the subtle and modern music of Euripides, though he drew it (so Aristophanes alleges) not from pure and solemn rural chants, but from the dregs of vulgar song —dirges, drinking-catches, dances fit for castanets: in fact, the *harmoniae* of low life which Plato rejected.[6]

The *Frogs* is Aristophanes' last tribute to the composer whom he had parodied so often that he could not leave the subject when, in 406 B.C., Euripides died. In the play of 405 the god Dionysus, sick of the bad poets left swarming on earth, goes to Hades to hear Euripides once more. The souls of dead frogs in the Stygian marshes are initiates of the Orphic mysteries (which claimed communication with the after-life). Against the contrasting chorus of their simple chants, sung to the Elysian *aulos*, Aristophanes stages the competition between the two

[1] *Birds* 745 ff. (misunderstood by Wilamowitz, *Griechische Verskunst* (Berlin, 1921), p. 436, n. 2).

[2] *Wasps* 220; *Clouds* 984 ff. (The aboriginal country-folk of Attica were believed to have worn gold grasshoppers in their hair.)

[3] *Frogs* 1298 ff. (cf. 910).

[4] Aesch. *Agam.* 381–5 (cf. E. Fraenkel's commentary, vol. ii, p. 186).

[5] Aesch. *Pers.* 935–40; *Agam.* 121 (with Fraenkel, vol. ii, p. 74 on refrains, &c., at end of movements).

[6] *Frogs* 1301–4.

great tragic composers. Aeschylus wins by superior weight. The clattering pomp of his oracular lines, between the monotonous thrumming of the *kithara—tophlattothrat tophlattothrat*—is calculated to make the modern lyrical sophistries of Euripides sound insubstantial and wispy.[1] In his later plays Euripides had withdrawn the chorus somewhat from the action, using it often for interludes of evocative poetry in which musical sound (so critics thought) counted more than dramatic sense. His chief innovation, however, was the lyric monody sung by an actor on the stage. Instead of observing the strophic correspondence of classical tradition, these monodies were *durchkomponiert*. Aristophanes himself had adopted this form to his own style in his brilliantly new Hoopoe Song, where he strings together a series of brief passages (*anabolae*) in variant and contrasting metres.[2] But it was originally and especially associated with the musical manner of the school of Phrynis and Cinesias, who were working out modern ideas in the dithyramb and the kitharoedic nome.

In the last quarter of the fifth century[3] the dithyrambist Melanippides and his successors began to exploit or emphasize the quivering intonation suggested by the *aulos*, and to copy it in their kitharoedic nomes. Although Aristophanes' musical parodies are lost, his verbal metaphors are vivid and illuminating. He defines the style by contrast with the early classics. The new music was no longer virile, taut, *entonos*—well tuned and unwavering: it was marked by flamboyant *kampai* ('bends') and by a formless flexibility of melodic line.[4] It is not clear whether *kampai* were in fact modulations or decorative shakes, but Aristophanes certainly insists upon the tonal instability of this music. The modernist tragedian Agathon appears on the Aristophanic stage spreading out his *strophae* to melt in the sun: if cold, they will not *bend*. When he sings, his song is like the zigzagging of ants.[5] The new dithyrambists, ecstatic and effeminate creatures, are so easily bent that they have to wear stays. Their bodies are willowy; their souls after death go fluttering among the clouds in search of brand-new *anabolae*; their music is made of snowflakes and feathers eddying in the sky; they long to be birds.[6] Aristophanes is obviously alluding to the same new, sky-borne, fluttering manner

[1] *Frogs* 1264–1363.

[2] *Birds* 227 ff.; cf. Fraenkel in *Eranos*, xlviii (1950). The form occurs in Euripides' *Orestes*.

[3] For this Melanippides the date usually accepted (*c.* 480–450 B.C.) makes nonsense of musical history, and is unproved: we know only that he died before 413 B.C.

[4] Aristoph. *Clouds* 967 ff.

[5] *Thesm.* 66–192.

[6] *Peace* 830 ff.; *Clouds* 332 ff.; *Birds* 1372–1409.

when, in the *Frogs*, he burlesques Euripides' coloratura on the first syllable of the word for 'twirling': *εἰ-ει-ει-ειλίσσουσα*.[1]

In the light of subsequent evidence we can see that what Aristophanes was describing was the breakdown of the classical tonality, which came about chiefly through modulation and chromatic tuning. A little later, a comedian stages a personal protest by the Muse against the tortures she has suffered from Melanippides, Phrynis, Cinesias, and their successors Philoxenus and Timotheus, who twist her on the rack with their 'exharmonic' notes as they modulate, knocking a dozen different *harmoniae* out of five strings, regardless of the false melodic relations produced.[2] We are further told that Agathon was the first tragedian to use the chromatic *genus*, which Aristoxenus noted as a prime factor in the breakdown of the classical *melopoeia*. *Metabolae* and *chromata* are expressly cited as features of the style of Philoxenus, the next leader of the new movement. In its experimental stages, when Aristophanes wrote, these technical terms cannot yet have been invented to describe its innovations. But it must not be supposed that, because we now possess only Aristophanes' word-pictures, his musical criticism was any the less precise or mature. The reason why classical Greeks invented few technical terms was that they did not depend on the imperfect medium of words alone; they criticized music by caricaturing it in music, so long as a musically educated public existed.

The *Frogs* was not only a foreboding of musical disruption. It was an appeal for the whole tradition of Athenian citizens 'bred in athletics, the chorus, and the arts of music', against uncultured or alien ideas.[3] The chorus had already been cut down under the financial stress of the war. At the end of the play the demagogue Cleophon is requested to hang himself, and the spirit of Aeschylus is sent up to counsel Athens, 'that the City may be saved and have her chorus still'. From Aristophanes' later plays we know what happened. Such music as he could still provide, with a much reduced chorus, had to conform to a level of popular taste which can be judged by the vulgarity of the genres and the crudity of the metres.[4] The dithyramb survived the war because its wide popular appeal induced the rich—and eventually the City—to go on paying its high costs of production. The comedy could not maintain its choric tradition, and the best

[1] *Frogs* 1348 (cf. 1314).

[2] 'Pherecrates' *ap*. ps.-Plutarch, *De mus*. 30, 3; cf. Düring in *Eranos*, xliii (1945). The number of strings has been emended through editorial misunderstanding.

[3] Aristoph. *Frogs* 729; ibid. 1419 (*cf*. 1504).

[4] *Ecclesiazusae* and *Plutus*.

school of public musical education in Athens virtually closed down with the Spartan *auloi* chortling over the destruction of the city walls.

(vii) *Plato and the revolution.* Plato's brief history of the musical revolution in Athens, written in the mid-fourth century B.C., is worth summarizing at some length:[1]

Our music was once divided into its proper forms. Prayers were one form of ode, surnamed 'hymns'; opposed to this was another form, 'dirges'; another called 'paeans', and another 'dithyrambs'. . . . 'Nomes' were a distinct kind, surnamed 'kitharoedic'. It was not permitted to exchange the melodic styles of these established forms and others. Knowledge and informed judgment penalized disobedience. There were no whistles, unmusical mob-noises, or clapping for applause. The rule was to listen silently and learn; boys, teachers, and the crowd were kept in order by threat of the stick. . . . But later, an unmusical anarchy was led by poets who had natural talent, but were ignorant of the laws of music. Over-intoxicated with love of pleasure, they mixed their drinks—dirges with hymns, paeans with dithyrambs—and imitated *aulos*-music in their kitharoedic song. Through foolishness they deceived themselves into thinking that there was no right or wrong way in music—that it was to be judged good or bad by the pleasure it gave. By their works and their theories they infected the masses with the presumption to think themselves adequate judges. So our theatres, once silent, grew vocal, and aristocracy of music gave way to a pernicious theatrocracy—for had it been a free democracy, it would have been nothing to fear. As it was, the criterion was not music, but a reputation for promiscuous cleverness and a spirit of law-breaking.

If classical drama without applause sounds austere, it must be remembered that the theatre was the only school of the poorer citizens. Seats were free, and under the Periclean system of State education the poor were paid two obols' maintenance whenever they attended. That they had to be kept quiet with sticks is only one instance of the well-known fact that Periclean ideals of enlightenment failed to penetrate the lower strata of society. Plato's charge against the new dithyrambists is not lack of musical genius: it is that they used high musical talents, showmanship, and virtuosity in the pursuit of sensationalism, consciously rejecting educated standards of judgment, and proclaiming that their end was immediate pleasure. The proof of this charge is that the new middle classes of the fourth century, while they no longer knew the past classics, turned away from the music of their own time as from a vulgarizing influence, enjoyable indeed, but no matter for serious practice or thought. Hence the

[1] *Laws* 700a–701a (abbreviated).

reduction of musical schooling to an elementary level and the disappearance of critical judgments on compositions.[1] The perpetual disparagement of new music in later philosophers has given the impression of a mere general prejudice against modernism, but these writers are not expressing opinions on any actual music: they are mechanically repeating Plato.[2]

From another passage we know that Plato was thinking particularly of the school of Cinesias the dithyrambist, which had since produced the ultra-modernists Philoxenus and Timotheus. Aristophanes in his last play had parodied the solo of the Cyclops, sung to the '*threttanelo*!' of the strumming *kithara*, which Philoxenus flung into one of his dithyrambs—a concrete case of the mixing of musical genres, for a dithyramb had never contained a kitharoedic piece.[3] Philoxenus, it was told, was sent to the quarries for laughing at the old-fashioned compositions of Dionysius the tyrant of Syracuse, who treasured Euripides' pen. Phrynis, as well as Euripides, was now thought out of date. Timotheus of Miletus repudiated the entire past tradition in a famous manifesto:[4]

I do not sing the old things,
Because the new are the winners.
Zeus the young is king today:
Once it was Cronos ruling.
Get out, old dame Music.

A deliberate blatancy and toughness distinguishes the post-war rebels from their precursors, who had affected to be aesthetes. The bombastic libretto of Timotheus' *Persae* was written for programme-music of the sort which attempted (Plato says) to make the noises of thunder, wind, hail, cats, dogs, cattle, bird-song, and all kinds of instruments, with frequent and startling modulations.[5] The dithyrambist and the kitharoede were professional musicians, normally aliens; and music of this kind depended on the virtuosity of performers, especially of instrumentalists. The problem of modulation produced many instrumental experiments. Plato mentions a 'panharmonium', strung for all tunings at once. A certain Pythagoras of Zacynthus is said to have invented a pyramid of three *kitharae*, tuned to the Dorian, Phrygian, and Lydian *harmoniae*, on a revolving stool which he kicked round with his foot as he played—but, as the source

[1] See above, pp. 339–40.

[2] On such repetition of Plato down to medieval times, see Egon Wellesz, *A History of Byzantine Music* (Oxford, 1949), pp 38–55.

[3] Plat. *Gorg.* 501e; Aristoph. *Plut.* 290 ff.

[4] Diehl, op. cit. ii, p. 150, no. 7.

[5] Plat. *Rep.* 397a–b.

confesses, this contraption may be apocryphal.[1] Certainly apocryphal are the stories that Timotheus himself added new strings to his *kithara*, was ordered by the conservative Spartans to cut them out, and appealed to the archaeological evidence of a many-stringed lyre in a statuette of Apollo. A contemporary fragment of comedy suggests that Timotheus and his school got their modulations upon a small number of strings, and that new devices were introduced for stopping.[2] Though eleven-stringed instruments probably came into use in this period, the additions were exaggerated by theorists ignorant of real kitharistic technique, familiar only with the kitharoid apparatus of harmonic science, which had a string to each note. In practice we know only that rapid changes from one idiom to another dissolved the characteristic tunings and progressions of each. The 'exharmonic' effects were soon enjoyed for their own sake. 'How well,' said an admirer of Philoxenus, 'his melodies are concocted with modulations and *chromata*.' How inferior, he adds, is the insipid prettiness of more recent music—all ivy and flowers and water, a string of unrelated tunes.[3]

(viii) *Music after the revolution.* The iconoclasts soon became the idols: Timotheus and Philoxenus eclipsed both their predecessors and their posterity. Aristoxenus is quoted for the story of a contemporary musician, Telesias of Thebes, who, after being educated on the classics, grew enamoured of modern music and learned the works of Philoxenus by heart, but could never, in his own composition, break himself of the classical idiom.[4] It shows how decisive was the break between the old and the new. While the immediate precursors of Philoxenus and Timotheus seem to have been scarcely better remembered than the classics, their successors lacked their vitality, and could not rival their appeal to the wider public of an enlarged Hellenistic world. They had created a large pool of enthusiastic listeners who liked nothing better than to hear the old favourites again; and prizes were won by musicians repeating the works of Timotheus, instead of producing their own according to the classical rule. By Aristoxenus' day the new style had become conventional: contemporary music, to him, is not shocking but sugary. This was partly, no doubt, because the new tonality no longer surprised the ear; but another reason may be that the Alexandrian age did not (so far as we know)

[1] Artemon *ap.* Athen. 637e–f.

[2] Düring in *Eranos*, xliii (1945) (but the 'Pherecrates' fragment is far from clear).

[3] Antiphanes, in Athen. 643d.

[4] ps.-Plut. *De mus.* 31.

pursue the more bizarre instrumental experiments of the revolutionary period—the noises which (as Aristotle says) could excite babies or beasts. Among the instruments which Plato associates with these effects is the *pectis*: yet a century later, when Philoxenus and Timotheus were still widely performed, the *pectis* seems to be obsolete, for Alexandrian scholars begin disputing what it was.[1] Their original orchestration cannot have been reproduced: as in the classical period, only the vocal part in music was permanent. Although Alexandria, for its part, invented the hydraulic organ, we hear little of its use before the days of the Roman arena.[2] In Hellenistic times, more fashionable types of performance were the massed choirs, sometimes doubling at the octave, which filled the big new theatres; solo kitharisms without words; duets of *auloi* playing now in unison, now antiphonally (but only the philistinism of a Roman general could order a band of auletes to play all at once). Nor did the duets lead to any ventures in polyphony. The question whether harmony and counterpoint were practised by the Greeks, which intrigued eighteenth-century scholars, can be briefly disposed of. A heterophonic accompaniment was common, as we know from Plato;[3] but the instrumental parts could not have been left to improvisation if they had been solid elements in a truly polyphonic structure. Choral unison and monody, in their post-classical forms, remained the staple genres of music; the astrophic dithyramb, now using wind or strings indifferently, persisted down to the second century B.C. and straggled on afterwards; the kitharoedic nome flourished into late antiquity.

A century and a half after Timotheus was dead, when Philopoemen came into the theatre victorious from Mantinea, the kitharist could still bring the house down with the opening line of the *Persae*:[4]

He who fashioned for Hellas the glorious adornment of Freedom.

Two generations later, when Greek freedom was gone, it was known as a curiosity of folklore that Philoxenus and Timotheus were till lately performed as a part of boys' education in Arcadia.[5] The leaders of revolution had ended as school classics of a rustic and inaccessible countryside. Our knowledge of music now becomes so dim that we do not even know when or how the chromatic manner was superseded by the common diatonic; but it is probable that by the time of the Delphic Hymns the chromatic was used only by force of tradition

[1] Plat. *Rep.* 399 c-d; Athen. 635–636.
[2] On the *hydraulis* (*-us*) see pp. 270 and 408.
[3] *Laws* 812d (cited above, p. 338).
[4] Plut. *Philopoemen* 11.
[5] Polyb. iv. 20–21.

for rare and ceremonial occasions. All our later pieces are based on a diatonic note-series. About 193 B.C., in a vote of thanks from Cnossos in Crete, a visiting musician had been praised for performing not only Timotheus and his disciple Polyidus, but also old Cretan songs, 'as befits an educated man'.[1] His programme was primarily a compliment to the Cretans, whose folk-songs were famous, but it may also indicate a growing taste for something simpler and more popular than the grand metropolitan style which Timotheus now represented.

The typical popular genre of Hellenistic times (though it dated back much earlier) was the pantomime. Mummers called by various generic or local names—*hilarodists*, *magodists*, *deikelists*, *autokabdali*—gave mixed shows of ballet and acrobatics, indecent jokes, comic scenes about drunkards or foreign doctors, escapes, romances, success stories, parodies of themes from mythology. On a more pretentious level, the story of Andromache or Antiope might be performed as a sort of sung ballet. Cicero remarks with surprise that there were people who could recognize a piece of this sort from the opening instrumental notes.[2] We must infer that such music could attain at least the relative permanence of a popular vogue. But the example of the pantomime tended to break up set forms of drama. A chorus of Euripides might be rendered as a separate concert-piece or kitharism, though not with the original music. One actor would sometimes give his own selected part from a tragedy, or sometimes sing a personal interpretation of a tragic role or theme. Nero, who took lessons from the Greek kitharoede Terpnus, improvised an interminable piece about Niobe, and also executed tragic parts—Canace bearing her incestuous child, Orestes killing his mother, Oedipus blind, Hercules mad. He seems to have sung these parts as solos, in his 'thin husky voice', with other figures on the stage merely to supply the action.[3] Roman drama was by then extinct, and such performances were more like recitals with music and costumes. Another of Nero's enterprises was a choir called *Augustiani* to lead his own audience's chants of applause. The rhythmical chanting of praises to the Emperor on public occasions was a direct precedent for the acclamations of the Byzantine Church.[4] Together with Quintilian's outburst against orators who liked to sing their speeches, it shows how closely, in this period, formal or ceremonial speech approximated to a musical recitative.

[1] *Corpus Inscriptionum Graecarum*, 3053.

[2] *Ac.* ii. 20.

[3] Suet. *Nero* 21; see also p. 418.

[4] Cf. M. P. Charlesworth in *Journal of Roman Studies* xxxiii (1943), pp. 4–6.

From the fourth century B.C. onwards the musician thought of himself as actor rather than creator or 'discoverer' (as Greeks preferred to put it). His patrons no longer wanted new music for themselves and their children to sing, but exhibitions to applaud from the hands of a maestro, lavishly staged and subsidized. Technical standards were high: it was the age of the virtuoso. A star kitharist might get for one concert a fee that would maintain a Greek trireme for a year, or more than the cost of a first-class dithyrambic chorus.[1] Extravagant verses were written on the tomb of the aulete Telephanes, whom Demosthenes employed for a chorus in 347 B.C.; and the inscriptions that commemorate a winning performance soon begin to name the aulete before the poet. The division of labour between words and music may have begun already in the fourth century, when new settings had to be provided for Euripides and other revived classical drama, but poet and musician are still one in the Delphic Hymns, and there was perhaps no sudden or universal change.[2] Certainly, however, sophisticated poets were growing incapable of making music, and musicians of writing sophisticated verse. When the classical unity of Music was broken, the 'music' (in our narrow sense of the term) was supplied by a professional engaged in the performance. The modern figure of the pure composer, who is neither poet nor player, was unknown to antiquity.

It would not be true to say that post-classical music was altogether monopolized by the professional. Singing was still taught to children in most Greek schools, and encouraged in some cities by prizes both for song and for the lyre. Boys' choirs represented their cities in festival competitions. In one city thirty noble boys were trained to sing a hymn to Hecate once a month in the town hall. A city had to keep a choir for festivals and religious occasions, and those who found professional singers too expensive sometimes economized by training the ephebes, lads of eighteen to twenty conscribed for military and public service. But even these elementary duties were largely taken over by unions of hired musicians. One of the Delphic Hymns advertises the performers as *technitae* of the famous musicians' union of Athens, which served half of mainland Greece and included composers with other professional players. These bodies soon became

[1] Athen. 623d; Demosth. *In Meid.* 155; Lysias xxi. 1–2.

[2] A new post-Hadrianic inscription (*Hesperia*, xxii, 1953, pp. 125 ff.), apparently discarded for the cutter's mistake, commemorates a musician with an unintelligible phrase, of which Dr. P. Maas kindly offers his still unpublished emendation: . . . *μόνον καὶ πρῶτον ⟨μετ'⟩ Εὐρειπίδην Σοφοκλέα καὶ Τιμόθεον ἑαυτῷ μελοποιήσαντα* . . ., interpreting: 'the first and only since Euripides, Sophocles, and Timotheus to compose the music to his own words.' I cannot construe K. Latte's rendering in *Eranos*, lii (1954), pp. 125 ff.

universal. In Augustan times a 'collegium symphoniacorum', engaged for public religious services in Rome, was recognized by a special decree of the Senate as a legitimate association. The local unions finally amalgamated into one 'holy oecumenical synod of artists in the service of Dionysus'.[1] In spite of the majestic title—and high rates of pay—musicians stood much lower in the social scale than doctors or teachers of grammar and rhetoric. The public recognition of Mesomedes was an exception and a scandal. In archaic and classical times the professional composer as well as the citizen had been honoured for musical excellence. In Alexandrian sources music is reduced to a topic for anecdotes of low life or oddments of curious information, which were later collected by Athenaeus in the form of table-talk, suitably sandwiched between similar talk on famous courtesans and gastronomic delicacies.

'Unheard music is better than heard' was a Greek proverb in late antiquity. Against it Nero used to quote another: 'Unheard music is unregarded.'[2] Contemporary opinion was not on his side. No reputable woman would play an instrument too well, no gentleman would dance unless in his cups, and a musical emperor was a disgrace:[3] these views were held no less by upper-class Greeks than by Romans. But both had inherited from Alexandria a profound reverence for the classical past; and classical authors had spoken respectfully of music. The music that Plato had admired was lost: what remained was Plato's admiration. He could never (so these later minds assumed) have set such a value upon mere audible music, which they knew as a stimulant laid on at theatrical shows or at banquets where girls from Cadiz did their celebrated hip-wobbling dances.[4] It was impossible, by now, to realize that music had been or could be a higher form of artistic expression: Plato must have meant some mysterious ethical alchemy which music could work upon the motions of the soul, or else the harmonic science of 'number conceptual and immaterial' which enshrined truths of astronomy. This was the 'unheard music' of the proverb. Through its own traditional prestige it was persistently cultivated, without relation to any heard music, in the harmonic theory and philosophy of the later ancient world. The idea of music—so much holier than music itself—

[1] A. H. M. Jones, *The Greek City from Alexander to Justinian* (Oxford, 1940), pp. 229 ff.; A. W. Pickard-Cambridge, *The Dramatic Festivals of Athens* (Oxford, 1953), chap. vii; Dessau, *Inscriptiones Latinae Selectae* 4966.

[2] Plut. *De an. procr. in Tim.* 26 (cf. Keats, *Ode to a Grecian Urn* 11–12); Suet. Nero 20.

[3] Sall. *Cat.* 25; Cic. *Pro Mur.* 13; Tac. *Ann.* xiv. 14–15.

[4] Martial, xiv. 203.

embraced not only cosmological doctrine but moral and medical belief. Staunching-songs, to be sung over a bleeding wound, were already known to Homer and Pindar. Sciatica, according to Theophrastus, was treated by playing the *aulos* over the part affected; musical healing was important in psychiatry, and incantation in the magical rites of Gnostic sects.[1] The more intelligent valued harmonic theory for its mathematical beauty. But no specific motive, after all, is necessary to explain the pious transmission of an inherited and venerated branch of learning. *Musica* was established as the seventh of Varro's 'liberal arts', but it was not an art in the modern sense: it belonged to the *quadrivium* of mathematical subjects. The transference of the term *musica* to harmonic science in itself implies that for the liberal education music did not exist.

Our present difficulty in studying Greek music is, in the main, a consequence of this contempt of educated post-classical Greeks for the practical art, together with the obstinate survival of the mathematical subject miscalled *musica* in the ancient and medieval curriculum. Earlier Greeks had found in music an art which was seldom independent of verse, but was capable of co-operation in the highest poetic enterprises; then, at a critical moment, before music had adequate means of surviving memory, the standards of judgement were changed or shaken and the legacy of the past dissipated. From Alexandrian times, when the old oral schooling grew insufficient, education was based on books, and the unwritten had not the prestige of the unheard. If the classical music had still been extant and intelligible in writing, it could not have been neglected by so many curious and diligent generations.[2] The post-classical music, if written, was seldom methodically stored, because it was not considered worth methodical study. Musical illiteracy in an age of book-learning is a sure index of the decline in the status and quality of the art. Isidore of Seville, whose erudition covered a great bulk of ancient writings, had never heard of the existence of notation. His words are an epitaph on the music of antiquity: 'Unless the sounds are retained by the memory of man, they perish, for they cannot be written.'[3] Fifty years ago we hoped to recover indefinite quantities of music from papyri: now, on the contrary, papyrology has shown by cumulative evidence that the preservation of music in writing was casual and sporadic. Failing some lucky chance, our knowledge of Greek melo-

[1] Hom. *Od.* xix. 457; Pind. *Pyth.* iii. 51; Theophr. *fr.* 87 and 88 (cf. Athen. 624a–b); Wellesz in *Ambix* iv (1951), pp. 145 ff.

[2] The hypothesis that its loss is due to medieval scribes is no longer accepted.

[3] *Etym.* III. 15, ii (early seventh century A.D.).

poeia is likely to remain, for the most part, indirect. Nor can we now look for any considerable help in the post-Aristoxenian harmonic theorists, since we must reject the assumption that the *musica* of the schools was directly concerned with heard melodic structures.

This is not to say that historical study of Greek music is impossible, but only that certain kinds of evidence have yielded less than was once expected. The subject therefore needs some reorientation towards other problems. Work remains to be done on the deciphering of such written pieces as we have or may find, but the central task is still the better dating and interpretation of the large ancient literature from which we can reconstruct the history of poetic forms and rhythms, of musical criticism and ideas, of the social and intellectual environment. This, though difficult, is not beyond reach. To recover the music itself might have been preferable. But it was to Greek music that a good scholar applied the wise motto: *Quod vides perisse, perditum ducas.*[1]

[1] G. Pasquali, 'Ulrico di Wilamowitz-Moellendorff', reprinted in *Pagine Stravaganti*[2] (Florence, 1952), p. 95.

X

ROMAN MUSIC

By J. E. SCOTT

INTRODUCTION

THERE is no lack of material for the study of music in the Roman world, but the greater part of it is concerned with the instruments rather than the music itself. What little is known about the music proper is evidence of unequal value and often open to more than one interpretation. We should further bear in mind that in the Graeco-Roman world we cannot without danger apply evidence from one part or period to the whole, and the dividing line between what is to be called Greek and what Roman in any of the arts is never quite certain.

Three main influences affected the Romans; the first was from the Etruscans, the second from the Greeks, and the third from the East. But Rome did not only borrow instruments and music; she adapted, blended, and developed what other nations had to offer. Certain aspects of ancient music may fairly be regarded as Roman, though other influences may have been present. Music of some kind was specially composed for the Latin comedy. The songs and instrumental calls of the Roman army were presumably of native origin; popular 'lays of ancient Rome', according to the elder Cato, had once been sung to the *tibia* at banquets, though they were extinct by Cicero's time; and the colourful popular music of the Empire, with its emphasis on rhythm and percussion, was probably, in the main, an Italian growth separable from Greek traditions.

Some believed that foreign ostentation in music was effeminate and was leading to a lowering of moral standards. The archaic Law of the Twelve Tablès, published in the middle of the fifth century B.C., forbade more than ten pipers at a funeral.[1] A number of anti-luxury laws were passed to restrict ostentatious performances and banquets; one, for example, in 115 B.C. allowed only the Latin piper in Rome.[2] But Roman expansion opened the way for new music and foreign influences. We can only mention here the great number of

[1] Cicero, *De leg*. ii. 59.

[2] Cassiodorus, *Chron*. A. U. 639.

Greeks who came to Rome in professional though humble capacities. In the capital there existed numbers of foreign groups who kept their entity and brought their own forms of worship.[1] Trade expanded enormously and brought in new fashions and new demands for luxury. New religions were first banned, then tolerated, and then often actively encouraged at different times by various emperors. During the second Punic war the cult of the Great Mother, Cybele, which centred in Phrygia, was brought to Rome in 204 B.C. It never became completely Roman and citizens were not allowed to take part in the ceremonies or wear the peculiar dress. However, the priests brought with them their musical instruments and these—pipes, cymbals, and tambourines—soon gained great popularity. So we see portrayed, and read of, the Berecynthian pipe with bent horn (*inflexo Berecyntia tibia cornu*), the mad pipe (*furiosa tibia*), the hollow drums (*inania tympana*) and the din made by the attendants of the goddess as they thump the brass and the rumbling leather (*aera deae comitas raucaque terga movent*).[2] Pl. 11 (*a*)[3] shows one of the chief priests and some of the instruments. The twin Phrygian pipes and a tambourine hanging above are to be seen on the right, while a pair of cymbals are suspended on the left. (The other things do not concern us here.) These pipes were much more powerful than the twin straight ones; they could be rivalled only by the *tuba*. They tended to drive out the older kind, though they never completely succeeded in doing so. It is not possible here to discuss the spread of oriental cults in the west during the Empire, but they should not be forgotten in considering the spread of new ideas in music and the changes in musical instruments.[4]

It must not be thought, however, that Rome absorbed so much without difficulty. Polybius relates a story of Greek musicians who came to Rome in 167 B.C. to give a performance during victory games; their style of playing not being understood, they were laughed off the stage and compelled to stop their concert and improvise a kind

[1] G. La Piana, 'Foreign groups in Rome during the first centuries of the Empire', in *Harvard Theological Review*, xx (1927), pp. 183 ff.; R. Paribeni, 'Cantores Graeci nell' ultimo secolo della repubblica in Roma', in *Raccolta di scritti in onore di Giacomo Lumbroso* (Milan, 1925), p. 287.

[2] Dionysius Halicarnassensis, *Antiq. Rom.* ii. 19. Ovid, *Fasti* iv. 181 f. Horace, *A.P.* 202.

[3] Strong, *La Scultura romana*, ii (Florence, 1926), fig. 248; Jones, *Catalogue of the Ancient Sculptures preserved in the Municipal Collections of Rome: Palazzo dei Conservatori* (Oxford, 1926), pl. 100. There is an excellent detailed representation of the Phrygian pipes in Jones, ibid.: *Museo Capitolino* (Oxford, 1912), pl. 34A.

[4] Cumont, *Les Religions orientales dans le paganisme romain* (Paris, 4th ed., 1929), is the standard work of reference.

of burlesque.[1] Writers long continued to protest at the new styles. Juvenal was bitter at the Syrian Orontes pouring into the Tiber with its language, manners, and music.[2]

Roman authors sometimes write about music with a patronizing air and with the notion that there existed nothing but a pale glimmer of the past greatness of Greek music.[3] This was fundamentally wrong; music, though not to everyone's taste, was very much alive. There was nothing amateurish about either instruments or performers. Not only in Hellenistic times, but also during the Roman empire, instruments became more complicated, capable of greater sonority; new and improved experimental types were introduced. The evidence of instruments has limitations. It is, for instance, quite unsafe to take a particular instrument and say that because it could be played in such and such a way and with such a technique, it must therefore have been so played by its original owner. Nevertheless, the various instruments used are in themselves typical of Roman musical occasions, in which their part was often more prominent than in classical Greece, although in most music the voice still retained its leading position.

INSTRUMENTS[4]

Aerophones

The *tuba* was long and straight and made usually of bronze, though it is known to have been made also of wood and leather, or iron; it was constructed in sections which fitted into each other and the usual length was about 1·3 metres. The instrument was cylindrical in shape almost to the very bell end where it rather abruptly swelled out. The mouthpiece—conical rather than cup-shaped—was detachable and determined the quality of the note produced just as its length determined its pitch. There was frequently a strap to hold the instrument tight against the mouth when playing; this was attached to a small loop near the bell end. Perhaps about eleven harmonics could be obtained from the instrument, which was not, one might imagine, a very easy one to handle. It was essentially an army instrument and, like so much Roman military equipment, borrowed from the Etruscans. The Greeks had a similar instrument, the *salpinx*, perhaps rather shorter in length and with a more prominent bell end

[1] Polybius, xxx. 22.
[2] Juvenal, iii. 62. Nor did he think much of the raised status of the *cornicines*: iii. 34.
[3] Cf. pp. 337 and 401.
[4] For further information see the books and articles listed in the Bibliography.

which in addition to its use in the army was a popular solo instrument in the musical contests.

The *cornu*, also of bronze but originally of horn, was conical in section and curved into rather more than half a circle. A supporting cross-bar allowed it to be played carried over the shoulder with the bell end aloft over the player's head and facing in the same direction as the player. Like the tuba, it had a detachable mouth-piece, apparently rather longer than the tuba's. The *cornu* was Etruscan in origin and at first used mostly for military purposes.

The *bucina* is often confused with the *cornu*, and was so confused in Roman times, but there is no doubt that it was a separate instrument; right to the end the *bucinator* (as the player on this instrument was called) was sharply distinguished from the *cornicen*. There is no certain representation of it in the Roman world. Tombstones of *cornicines* sometimes show the *cornu*, but the *bucinator*'s never his *bucina*. Descriptions of the instrument are contradictory[1] but probably it was originally the animal's horn made into an instrument. Certainly it was intimately connected with the countryman and it became in the army the instrument for giving non-tactical signals. It was less powerful than the *tuba* or *cornu* and could not be used by itself in the heat of battle.

The *lituus* was of bronze and Etruscan in origin.[2] It was J-shaped with a long extension to the straight part, generically a natural horn with a greatly enlarged mouth-piece. The *lituus* found at Caere and now in the Vatican is 160 cm. long. The instrument is in *g* and produces six notes; another *lituus*, found in the Rhine near Düsseldorf is in *a*. Its sound is that of a soft trumpet. This was also an army instrument though it was used on state occasions.[3]

The *aulos* or *tibia* was a reed instrument known to the East Mediterranean world generally.[4] It was nearly always played in pairs with the help of a φορβειά (Lat. *capistrum*; Eng. *mouth band*) to steady the twin instruments in the mouth and to help to maintain a constant pressure of wind (see pl. 12). The short pipes with perhaps three or four holes were known in very early Roman times. There were several Greek types used for different purposes. In the late Republic and early Empire, pipes grew longer, perhaps 2 feet or more in length. The

[1] For instance, see the descriptions in the works of reference listed in the Bibliography.

[2] The Caere *lituus* is from an Etruscan grave. In general see McCartney, 'Military indebtedness of early Rome to Etruria', *Memoirs of the American Academy in Rome* (Bergamo, 1915), p. 121.

[3] Cf. F. Behn, *Musikleben im Altertum u. frühen Mittelalter* (Stuttgart, 1954), pp. 137–8.

[4] See pp. 269, 280, and 380–1.

musical range was extended by increasing the number of holes to as many as fifteen. Mechanical devices were used, when required, to cover certain of the holes.[1] The single cross-flute is known to have existed[2] but it is rare. Phrygian pipes were probably brought to Rome when the worship of Magna Mater was introduced in the year 204 B.C.; these powerful instruments were used in the ritual but appear to have become popular everywhere; one pipe was straight, the other ended in a large curved bell.[3]

The *utricularius* or *ascaules*, in English 'bagpipe', came from the East. (It is necessary to be careful in identifying the instrument, for *utricularius* usually meant wine trader, and not the performer.) One or two genuine representations in art are known;[4] many, including one from Richborough, are false.

The organ, said to have been invented in Alexandria in the third century B.C.,[5] became a most important instrument in imperial times. The evidence from literature is extensive but by itself insufficient to explain the instrument completely. Archaeology supplies more evidence: there are two portable organs from Pompeii, and two terracotta models,[6] while the instrument is shown on a number of mosaics and *contorniates*. At Aquincum the remains of an organ were found among the debris of a cellar into which it had fallen from a clubhouse above during a fire. The date is fixed at A.D. 228 by an inscription[7] attached to the instrument. There are four ranks of pipes, thirteen in each, the remains of levers, sliders, and a sounding board. Organs were worked usually by water pressure, hence the name *hydraulis*, though the pneumatic action was also in use, especially in later times.

The *syrinx* (panpipes) was more the instrument of the shepherd and the instrument of mythology than a serious musical instrument.

[1] There is a convenient summary in the *Oxford Classical Dictionary* (Oxford, 1949), p. 589.

[2] e.g. Giglioli, *L'Arte Etrusca* (Milan, 1935), pl. ccccvii, from Perugia.

[3] This was the *tibia Berecynthia* mentioned by Horace, *Odes*, iii. 19, 18.

[4] See the dictionaries listed in the Bibliography. The poem *Copa*, sometimes attributed to Vergil, contains a description of what can only be the bagpipes.

[5] By Ctesibius, *Athenaeus*, iv. p. 174. See, however, the important article by Apel, 'Early History of the Organ', in *Speculum*, xxiii (1948), p. 191, where the literary evidence is considered in detail.

[6] A photograph of the bronze portable organs is in Anderson 25880. There is a convenient illustration in the *Catalogue of the Mostra Augustea della Romanita* (Rome, 1938), plate cxlii, of some reconstructions made for the exhibition.

[7] Nagy, *Die Orgel von Aquincum* (Budapest, 1934), was the the original work. See also Hyde, 'An Inscribed Water Organ', *Transactions of the American Philological Association* lxix (1938), p. 394. Most of the reproductions of the water organ have been collected and studied by Mercurelli in *Rivista di Archeologia cristiana* xv (1938), p. 73.

Reeds, in number up to a dozen or so, were joined together like a raft and stopped with wax at one end. The lengths were graded and the player blew across the open mouths, moving the instrument as he desired.

Chordophones

The Greek lyre (λύρα) and *kithara* were distinct instruments. In Roman times the lyre tended to die out and the *kithara* acquired more strings; the sounding-board became larger and more unwieldy. The instrument was now often played sitting down.[1] It remained to the end the king of instruments for the soloist.

Harps with large numbers of strings were, of course, well known to the Greeks. In the Roman world they become more popular.[2] They were played sitting down with the instrument resting on the knees. Other stringed instruments came into use, the most interesting of which was the pandura or pandore with long thin neck and finger-board.[3]

Idiophones

There were several instruments of percussion which can only be mentioned here. The *scabellum* was a hinged flapping board of wood or metal worked by the foot and used for beating time.[4] The *sistrum* was an Egyptian rattle used in the worship of Isis,[5] and there were several kinds of cymbals and tambourines, bells and whistles.[6]

Literary Description

It is interesting to notice in both literature and in art how music and musical instruments are portrayed by writers or artists who do not possess the musical knowledge required for a precise description. For example, in the poem *Aetna* (lines 297 ff.) the author wishes to describe the organ being played; his observant eye has perceived the essential features, though he is unable or unwilling to use the technical terms.

[1] These statements are based on a survey of the surviving illustrations, especially in Pompeii.

[2] e.g. Juvenal, *Satires*, iii. 64 tells of the *chordae obliquae* brought to Rome from the East.

[3] See p. 273.

[4] For references see the works listed in the Bibliography. See also below, p. 414, for the terra-cotta from Alexandria.

[5] See p. 267.

[6] Cf. the well-known mosaic of street musicians, now in the Naples Museum, from Pompeii, made by Dioscorides of Samos.

carmineque irriguo magnis cortina theatris
imparibus numerosa modis canit arte regentis,
quae tenuem impellens animam subremigat unda.

(Just as in some vast theatre, a water organ whose musical modes harmonise through their unequal pipes, sounds its water-worked music thanks to the organist's skill, which starts a small draught of air while causing a rowing movement in the water below.)[1]

Here we have in a few words what an intelligent onlooker sees: the caldron-shaped body, the row of different-sized pipes, the organist controlling the instrument, and the rowing-like action of the blowers. Sometimes, of course, the writer has the accurate knowledge and expresses it in the form of an enigma. Thus Julian describes the organ, with pneumatic action and not worked by water.[2]

I see reeds, or pipes, of a different kind: I ween that from another, a metallic soil, they have perchance rather sprung up. They are agitated wildly, and not by our breath; but a blast, rushing from within the hollow of a bull's hide, passes underneath, below the foundation of the well-pierced pipes, and a skilled artist, possessed of nimble fingers, regulates by his wandering touch the connecting rods of the pipes, and these rods, softly springing to his touch, express (squeeze out) the song.

Perhaps the neatest description is of the double pipes:

εἷς ἄνεμος· δύο νῆες· ἐρέττουσιν δέκα ναῦται·
εἷς δὲ κυβερνήτης ἀμφοτέρας ἐλάει.

(One wind, two ships, ten sailors rowing, and one steersman directs both.)[3]

SOCIAL STATUS OF MUSICIANS

In the Roman world musicians held a place of honour from the earliest times. In the list of trade guilds into which the people of Rome were traditionally divided by Numa, successor to Romulus the first king of Rome, pipers come first.[4] If the sacred pipers went on strike, as they once did, the work of the State was held up; the pipers were recalled to duty by a trick and a bribe.[5] A boy piper was usually present near the altar at a sacrifice, but he played not for the music's own sake but to cover up any sound that might be accidentally heard

[1] *Minor Latin Poets* (Loeb Classical Library), p. 386. Duff's translation.

[2] Julian, Epig. ii. W. Chappell's translation in his *History of Music* vol. i (London, 1874).

[3] *Anth. Pal.* xiv. 14. Loeb Classical Library.

[4] Plutarch, *Numa* 17. For some of the duties of the State pipers see Ovid, *Fasti* vi. 657. A number of inscriptions attest to the guild organization. A piper is included among the list of magistrates' officials at Urso (Spain) in 44 B.C. Riccobono, *Fontes Iuris Romani Antejustiniani. Leges* (Florence, 1941), p. 177. On the guilds, see also p. 401.

[5] Livy, ix. 30. Plutarch, *Qu. Rom.* 55.

in the vicinity and thereby spoil the ceremony.[1] This scene is portrayed many times in Roman art, always with the short *auloi*. On festal occasions, or when the emperor was welcomed on his return home, there was always music to greet him.[2] A *tuba* player is normally seen near the emperor at his triumph.[3] There is no doubt that the way in which music could stimulate or calm a crowd was well known in the ancient world and that much use was made of this knowledge.[4]

In the army from the days of the Servian reforms, usually regarded as military in character, when in the sixth century B.C. *tuba* and *cornu* players (but not *bucina* players) were named as an official class in the Roman list of citizens, musicians had a well-defined status.[5] From inscriptions we learn that the order of seniority was *tuba* player, *cornu* player, and lastly *bucina* player.[6] Like other professional groups, they would at times organize themselves into clubs with elaborate rules and conditions of entry. Thus, for example, when a member joined he paid into the common chest 750 denarii, and when he died or got his discharge, or if he were reduced in rank, or promoted inside the legion, or if he had to make an unwelcome voyage overseas, he or his heir received stated sums. This was in the early years of the third century A.D.[7]

MILITARY MUSIC

In the army orders were given on different instruments. The *tuba* sounded the attack or retreat, and the time for the posting of sentries. The *bucina*, which could scarcely be heard outside the camp if there was much noise, sounded the watches; it was superseded later for this duty by the *cornu* which was also responsible for the sounding of the relief for the sentries.[8] There were well-known calls. Pollux tells of

[1] Brendel has collected a number of examples in his article, 'Immolatio Boum', *Römische Mitteilungen*, xlv (Munich, 1930), p. 196.

[2] Alföldi, 'Die Ausgestaltung des monarchischen Zeremoniells am römischen Kaiserhofe', *Römische Mitteilungen*, xlix (1934), p. 79.

[3] See the Triumph of Marcus Aurelius in Strong, op. cit., fig. 162.

[4] Quintilian, *Inst. orat.* ix. 4 i. 10.

[5] H. Last, 'The Servian Reforms', in *Journal of Roman Studies*, xxxv (1945), p. 34, where the sources are discussed.

[6] e.g. *C.I.L.* viii. 2564. There is a list of musicians in the army in *Ephemeris Epigraphica*, iv (Rome, 1881), p. 374, but it needs to be brought up to date.

[7] Tubicines, *I.L.S.* 9096 (A.D. 202–5); Cornicines, *C.I.L.* viii. 2557+18050 = *I.L.S.* 2354 (A.D. 203). They have been discussed several times. A good account is by Carcopino in *Rendiconti della Pontif. Acad. Rom. di Archeol.* series 3, iv (1926), p. 217.

[8] This is a simplified account applicable to the Republican period; there were changes in procedure in later time. A convenient method of approach is to work through the articles on the separate instruments, so far as they are published, in the *Thesaurus Linguae Latinae* (Leipzig, 1900). Note also the different attempts to describe the sounds, e.g. Ennius on the *tuba* (taratantara), frag. 143.

four for the trumpet: the setting off or attack, the call of encouragement during battle, the retreat, and the sign to halt or encamp.[1] In the sixth century A.D. Procopius says that the Roman army in the old days had two calls: the charge and the retreat. Sometimes they must have been misunderstood, coming as they did from the same instrument. He therefore suggested to Belisarius that the cavalry trumpet, lighter in weight, being made of leather and thin wood, should sound the charge; while the bronze trumpet of the infantry, which would be of a different sound, should sound the retreat when a more distinctive call was necessary in the noise of battle.[2]

Several stories are told of Roman generals who kept musicians in empty camps after the army had moved on; they remained sounding the regular calls to deceive the enemy. At other times a trumpet player would be sent by himself away from the main body so that the enemy would get a wrong impression of the position of the army.[3] These were well-worn tricks and they show how the various calls were identified with army life. Frequently in literature, battle or camp life was described in terms of one or other of the instruments; thus *in medias tubas* would mean 'into the midst of the battle', and *post lituos* could be translated 'after the battle was over'.[4] In camp and on the march the *cornu* players stayed near the standards, giving the sign to move off and with the *tuba* encouraging the men in battle. Thus when the Temple of the Sun at Palmyra was pillaged by the *aquiliferi*, *vexilliferi*, and the *draconarius* (different kinds of standard bearers) in A.D. 272, under Aurelian, the players of the *cornu* and the *lituus* of the legion also took part.[5] In art the *cornu* players are usually placed hard by the standards.[6]

Twice a year, on 23 March and 23 May, the sacred trumpets were symbolically purified at a ceremony called *Tubilustrium*.[7] There is reason to believe that this originally had to do with the opening of the new campaigning season. It shows the intimate connexion that existed between the instrument and military life. In the navy, a comparatively late development with Rome, the need for call signs was not so great, though there is some evidence for the use of music to keep oarsmen

[1] Pollux, iv. 85. [2] Procopius, *Bell. Goth.* vi. 23.

[3] e.g. Frontinus, *Strat.* i. 5; Livy, ii. 64.

[4] Claudian, *de con. Stil.* iii, pref. 12, 13. [5] *Historia Augusta. Vita Aurel.* xxxi. 7.

[6] e.g. Trajan's army marching over the bridge of boats across the Danube in Strong, op. cit., figs. 97/98. There is a novel view of this scene in *La Colonna Traiana* (Rome, 1942), pl. 15.

[7] *C.I.L.* i², I, p. 313. Quasten, *Musik und Gesang in den Kulten der heidnischen Antike und christlichen Frühzeit* (Münster, 1930), esp. pp. 16–25, gives an account of Roman state music, including the *Tubilustrium* and the College of Pipers.

in time.[1] Even though the *tuba* was to become a popular solo instrument and often heard with other instruments in the shows, this connexion with war was never forgotten. When L. Norbanus Flaccus, a keen player of the *tuba*, was heard practising on this instrument on the day he entered into his consulate in A.D. 19, it was taken as a bad omen that the consul should be heard playing on an instrument associated with war.[2]

MUSIC IN EVERYDAY LIFE

Interest in music increased during the Empire. In private life, whether it was a little light music after supper at Pliny's villa or a noisy trumpet playing at Trimalchio's dinner party, music was in universal demand.[3] The best entertainment, Martial believes, is where there is no piper to drown the conversation, implying that a man is fortunate if he finds that when he goes out to dinner.[4] Petronius tells of a man of fashion who possessed a clock in his dining room with a uniformed *bucina* player to tell him how much of his life was lost and gone.[5] Music was employed at funerals from earliest Roman times; later no funeral was complete without wailing pipes and trumpets playing a last call to the dead. Trimalchio, very drunk, orders a mock funeral and the trumpeters break into a loud funeral march (*consonuere cornicines funebri strepitu*).[6] The phrase, 'You may send for the trumpeters' (*ad tubicines mittas*) signifies 'prepare for the funeral'.[7] So, too, at other ceremonies and on state occasions, music played an increasingly important part.[8] Large choirs sang and more ensemble playing was demanded.[9]

Indoor concerts took place in the houses of the rich. Pl. 12, a fresco found at Herculaneum, now in the Naples Museum, shows a duet between a piper and a *kithara* player. Before an attentive audience the piper vigorously plays her two very long straight pipes; she wears the usual mouth band, and her bulging cheeks and eyes

[1] Starr, *The Roman Imperial Navy* (Cornell, 1941), pp. 56 and 59.

[2] Cassius Dio, lvii. 18.

[3] Pliny, *Ep.* ix. 36. Petronius, *Satiricon* (*Cena Trimalchionis*), e.g. c. 26. Coleman-Norton has made a study of musical terms and expressions from literature which were known or could have been known to Cicero in 'Cicero Musicus', *Journal of the American Musicological Society*, i (1948), pp. 3–22.

[4] Martial, ix. 77.

[5] Petronius, *Sat.* 26.

[6] Ibid. 78.

[7] Ibid. 129.

[8] For the *carmen saeculare* see Gagé, 'Recherches sur les Jeux séculaires', *Les Belles Lettres*, Paris (1934), pp. 45 f.

[9] There is a charming painting from Ostia of a small group of boys singing in honour of Diana. This is reproduced in Strong, *Art in Ancient Rome*, ii (London, 1929), p. 28.

indicate the intensity of her performance. The *kithara* player uses the developed form of the instrument; not so graceful and finely balanced as the classical Greek version, it is of more solid construction and capable of hard wear and tear. The arms are straight and there is a strong cross-bar to hold the tuning pegs, seven of which are shown, though the painter has indicated at least a dozen strings. The instrument is held by an arm-strap, though this is not clear in the painting; it is played with a plectrum in the right hand, the left hand plucking or damping the strings as required. It will be noticed that the performers do not play from notated music.

Small bands of street musicians paraded in the streets playing pipe, cymbal, and tambourine. Jugglers and acrobats entertained the crowds. The one-man band showed how feet, arms, hands, and voice could be used at the same time. There is an interesting terra-cotta from Alexandria, recently misunderstood, which is worth considering in greater detail;[1] it is 16·7 centimetres high and represents an old man playing a large *syrinx* with his left hand. Under his left arm he presses against his side a bag with a single pipe attached; he holds this pipe with his right hand, playing a simple tune or drone; his right foot plays a *scabellum*. There is no connexion between the bag and the *syrinx*; this is not an early form of portable organ as has been suggested; it is the bagpipe played with other instruments. A young assistant claps a pair of miniature cymbals as his master plays.

MUSIC IN THE THEATRE

In 389 B.C. performances of simple stage plays with musical accompaniment (*saturae modis impletae*) took place, with Etruscan actors brought to Rome to dance to music played on the pipes.[2] This native drama was driven off the stage by innovations from Greece and took on a literary form. More music, with more than one kind of pipe, came into use in Latin versions of Greek comedies. The prefaces to Terence's plays tell of four kinds besides giving the name of the composer.[3] Music was played also during the intervals. *Atellana* and mimes were broad farces, which tended to drive out comedy. Played by a very few actors, male and female, they were vulgar and often obscene but attracted great popularity.[4]

[1] Weber, *Die Ägyptisch-griechischen Terrakotten* (Berlin, 1914), pl. 30, no. 324; Sachs, *History of Musical Instruments* (New York, 1940), pl. viiic.

[2] Livy, vii. 2.

[3] e.g. *Didascalia* to Terence's *Phormio*: 'Modos fecit Flaccus Claudi tibiis inparibus.'

[4] Duff, *Literary History of Rome* (London, 1909), p. 221.

A most interesting papyrus gives a number of cues for the music.[1] It dates from the second century or end of the first century A.D. The identification of the marks is far from certain, but they include cues for the drums, singly, five times or many times, for the striking of some instrument (perhaps cymbals or *scabellum*), and two others which cannot be explained with any degree of certainty, possibly for castanets and pipe. It must be explained that these are only cues; no fragments of the music, if indeed it ever consisted of more than percussion effects, exist.

The pantomime[2] (*pantomimus* means the single actor who takes part) was quite different from the mime. Its themes were from mythology and it was essentially a dramatic dance for a single performer, accompanied by chorus and orchestra. The actors were male until very late times. Predominantly, though not exclusively, Roman, by the time of Augustus it was established in the capital. The orchestra included pipes, panpipes, cymbals, and stringed instruments; time was kept by the *scabellum*.[3] In some respects the pantomime may be regarded as the successor to tragedy on the Roman stage. It made certain demands of the audience: the facts of the story must be known, the different steps of the dance had to be recognized; it required a cultivated taste and never became entertainment for the masses. The music took second place to the dancing. 'There reigns the art of dancing', says Plutarch, 'to which music is almost entirely subordinated.'[4]

In the amphitheatre a show began with a procession. Led by trumpet and horn players, the principal performers with decorated helmets marched into the arena. The start of the performance was announced by the *tuba* and a small orchestra played in the background. Pl. 11 (*b*) shows part of a mosaic from Zliten in North Africa,[5] with different kinds of gladiators. The orchestra consists of a water organ, a *tuba* player, and two *cornu* players. The organ is on a low stand; the reservoirs for the water are on either side. A number of surviving illustrations of similar scenes bear witness to the enormous popularity of the amphitheatre shows.

At times the desire for noise and large numbers of performers led

[1] *Greek Literary Papyri, Poetry*, i, no. 76. Loeb Classical Library, ed. D. L. Page.

[2] Robert, 'Pantomimen im griechischen Orient', *Hermes*, lxv (1930), p. 106. Lucian, *De Salt.*, *passim*.

[3] The players of the *scabellum* (*scabellarii*) had their own guild.

[4] Plutarch, *Quaest. conviv.* ix. 15.

[5] Aurigemma, 'I mosaici di Zliten' (*Africa Italiana*, ii, Rome, 1926). For the *pompa* and other scenes in the amphitheatre, see the long article 'Il rilievo gladiatorio di Chieti' by Ghislanzoni in *Monumenti Antichi* (Rome), xix. 1908, col. 541.

to incredible extravagance. Ammianus Marcellinus tells of *kitharas* as large as carriages.[1] In A.D. 284 Carinus gave a series of games to the Romans at which one hundred trumpets played together; others taking part included a hundred horn blowers and two hundred pipers of different kinds. It was the most-talked-of event of the year.[2] The mania for novelty and large-scale entertainment was encouraged by those in authority, who saw in this a means of distracting the attention of the masses from action in the political field.

RECITALS AND VIRTUOSI

Authors 'published' by big public readings and there are numerous references to clients dutifully listening to their patron's dull books. Under the Empire dramatic recitals became popular, even of works which had never been intended for declamation to music. The Greek practice of singing and accompanying oneself on the *kithara* was known in the Greek cities of the south and to a lesser degree in Rome and the western provinces, but it was a foreign intrusion and, though actively sponsored by different emperors and despite hero-worship of the star performers, did not succeed in becoming Romanized. The principal performers and the best teachers, so far as we can tell, were Greek. This was the form of art that Nero wished to excel in.[3]

Despite the amount of ensemble playing known to have existed, it was the soloist and, above all, the brilliant virtuoso who caught the fancy of the Romans. Successful individual players were mobbed by the crowd, paid fantastic engagement fees, and allowed to indulge in any amount of artistic temperament off stage or on stage. Such artists rarely settled in any place for long; they had full time-tables of bookings, and in any event it is doubtful whether there was enough popular demand for a man to remain very long in one place. These artists, too, banded themselves into professional groups not unlike trade unions, and by the second century A.D. had a practical monopoly.[4] The artist, when he became well known, would be honoured by his native city and perhaps given honorary citizenships of other cities; statues would be set up to him.

[1] Ammianus Marcellinus, xiv. 6, 18.

[2] *Vita Carini*, xix.

[3] See p. 399.

[4] Dionysiac artists: see Pauly–Wissowa, art. 'technitai' in *Real-Encyclopädie*. For the spreading of professionalism in the Hellenistic world, and the peripatetic life, see Rostovtzeff, *Social and Economic History of the Hellenistic World* (Oxford, 1941), pp. 1077 f. and 1113.

On special occasions a star performer might receive a very large fee, in money or otherwise. Vespasian, for all his covetousness, rewarded his artists well. When the theatre of Marcellus was reopened he hired performers, paying no less than 400,000 sesterces to the tragic actor Apollinaris, 200,000 sesterces to Terpnus and Diodorus the *citharoedi*, as well as other lesser amounts to others who took part.[1] (For very rough calculation the *sestertius* was worth about 2*d*.) The amount of prize money a successful musician might win was considerable. Two inscriptions from Aphrodisias in Asia Minor[2] give lists of prize money for different contests; the highest prize was 3,250 *denarii* for the first *citharoedus*. It would not be safe to build much on so little evidence, but so far as they go, they are of importance at least for one part of the world.

Unfortunately we know practically nothing about the style of playing or what the music was like. Sometimes it was only a question of how loud and how long a note could be played, a test of physique and power of lung.[3] There is little doubt, however, that the standard of performance was high and the technique elaborate. Competition was keen, and audiences were critical.[4] Not even the hired claque, so commonly employed, would cover up poor playing or indifferent singing. Many of the pieces played were intimately known by the crowd and favourite tunes were hummed in the street.[5]

IMPERIAL AMATEURS

The amateur vied with the professional though there was always a social gap between the two. Society was shocked by Nero not because of his appearing as a musician, but because he posed as a professional artist. Many men and women of society became distinguished amateurs. The Augustan histories tell of many emperors who were good players. Hadrian[6] boasted openly of his knowledge of *kithara* playing and singing; Verus[7] travelled about through Corinth and Athens with instrumentalists and singers, and on his return from the Parthian war brought from Syria players of stringed instruments and pipers; Commodus[8] is described as adept in certain arts not becoming to an emperor, one of which was singing; Elagabalus[9] sang, danced,

[1] Suetonius, *Vesp.* 19.

[2] C.I.G. 2758 and 2759. There is a convenient translation in Tenney Frank, *Economic Survey of Rome*, iv (Baltimore, 1938), p. 856.

[3] Galen, viii. 287.

[4] In general, see the chapters in Friedländer, *Darstellungen aus der Sittengeschichte Roms*, ii (Leipzig, 9th–10th ed., 1921–3), pp. 161 ff.

[5] Ibid., p. 175.

[6] *Vita Had.* xiv. 9.

[7] *Vita Veri*, vi. 9; viii. 11.

[8] *Vita Comm.* i. 8.

[9] *Vita Elagab.* xxxii. 8.

declaimed to the pipes, played on the trumpet, the *pandura*, and the organ; Severus Alexander[1] had a taste for music and could play on the lyre, pipe, organ, and trumpet, though he never played the last when he became Emperor.

Others, from the first century, had been interested in the art, but none like Nero. He wished to be taken seriously as a musician and there is every reason to believe that he had considerable, though not exceptional, natural ability. Music was only one of his many interests, but he trained hard and practised diligently. The services of Terpnus, a well-known singer to the *kithara*, were obtained when he became Emperor and lessons went on late into the night. He endured bodily discomfort, lying on his back with a metal weight on his chest, taking purges, refraining from various fruits and meat that were supposed to injure the voice, indeed trying all the tricks of the profession to develop his voice. At one time he refused to address his soldiers in person so as to rest his voice, and he would have a singing teacher present to see that he never strained it. Before appearing in public he made detailed plans for his claque who, more than 5,000 strong, were divided into groups and taught the various kinds of applause that would ensure their master the success he so earnestly longed for. We are told of three kinds of applause; *bombi* (probably like the buzzing of bees), *imbrices* (like rain or hail on the roof), and *testae* (like the crashing of pots together). The whole account given by Suetonius in his life of Nero is most amusing. Extremely jealous of possible rivals, the Emperor was highly sensitive about his reputation as a musician. During the rebellion of Vindex nothing excited him so much as the low opinion Vindex expressed about him as a *kithara* player. To the very end of his life he was interested in new kinds of instruments and promised to appear in person at the victory games, playing on different instruments, among which were different kinds of organ and the bagpipe.[2]

Nero made his first public appearance in his own palace at Rome in A.D. 59, at the age of twenty-two. In 64 he took part in the contests at Naples, and in 65 appeared as a *citharoedus* (i.e. sang and played on the *kithara*) in the theatre of Pompey in Rome. Towards the end of 66 he went on a professional tour of Greece, returning publicly in the beginning of 68. No doubt the judges at the different contests in which he took part would hesitate before refusing a prize; his successes, therefore, need not be taken too seriously. Yet we know that

[1] *Vita Alex.* xxvii. 5, 9.
[2] Suetonius, *Nero*, xli, liv.

he kept to the rules, adopted a humble attitude, and on at least one occasion was very nervous lest a mistake he had just made should be noticed and lose him points.

MUSIC TEACHING

Details of what pay music teachers in schools received are not numerous, though there is a little information from Teos, in Asia Minor, in the late third or early second century B.C.[1] Three teachers of reading and writing in an elementary school were paid sums from 600 to 500 drachmas, the two teachers of gymnastics received 500, and the music teacher 700. His duties were to give instruction in music (i.e. theory) and in playing the *kithara* with the plectrum and with the fingers; no mention of instruction on the pipes or any other musical instrument; some of the boys were taught theory only; not all the boys in the school received music lessons. There was an examination in music at the end of the year to see how the pupils had benefited by the instruction. The salary mentioned was comparatively generous and indicates the importance attached to adequate musical training. (The salary of a skilled workman was about one drachma a day at this time; the highest recorded salary from the Hellenistic world is that of a doctor who received 1,000 drachmas a year.)[2]

From Alexandria comes a papyrus of unique interest[3] of the year 13 B.C., in the form of an apprenticeship contract between the owner of a slave and a music teacher. The papyrus is not in good condition and there are several technical terms which are not yet fully understood. However, the boy was to be taught to play various tunes on specified instruments and also to be able to accompany other performers; he was to be tested by an independent body of three, suitably qualified. The payment of one hundred drachmas was to be made in two parts, and the period of the contract was a year. A lot had to be learnt in that time and it is likely the slave had some knowledge before he started.

There is reason to believe that music was learned not from a written text but by ear.[4] This conclusion must be treated with reserve, but in art remains musicians are always represented as playing by ear or

[1] Dittenberger, *Sylloge* (3rd. ed., Leipzig, 1915–24), 578. Hansen, *Attalids of Pergamon* (Ithaca N.Y., 1947), p. 354.

[2] Tarn, *Hellenistic Civilization* (London, 2nd ed. 1930), p. 100; A. Wilhelm, *Neue Beiträge zur griechischen Inschriftenkunde* (Vienna, 1915), p. 54.

[3] *Aegyptische Urkunden aus den königlischen Museen zu Berlin*, 1125. Westermann in *Journal of Egyptian Archaeology*, x (1924), p. 143.

[4] H.-I. Marrou, '*ΜΕΛΟΓΡΑΦΙΑ*', *L'Antiquité classique* (Brussels), xv (1946), p .289.

memory. A number of paintings show scenes from mythology of master teaching pupil to play on the pipes or the lyre; the master explains, shows how the instrument should be held, then lets the pupil try for himself, gently controlling an awkward position by guiding the pupil's arms and hands. Other scenes depict the pupil imitating the master as he plays, carrying out with his fingers the action as he sees it. Although these are scenes from mythology, it is reasonable to suppose that the painters incorporated in their work scenes from everyday life.[1]

There are many such gaps in our knowledge of Roman music, and we can only hope that new material will come to light. At present there is enough to see the main picture, though it be blurred in places and may always remain unfinished.

[1] e.g. paintings of Marsyas teaching Olympus to play the pipes.

XI

THE MUSIC OF ISLAM

By HENRY GEORGE FARMER

ISLAMIC CIVILIZATION

IN the history of civilization, Islam stands as the chief animating idea culturally between the Dark Ages and the Renaissance. Yet when one speaks of Islamic civilization a purely sociological connotation is implied, since in spite of its religious basis and its pristine insularity, it spread over and conditioned a quarter of the then known world, giving rise to a mode of life which became a cynosure for all eyes beyond its boundaries. The explanation of this is simple enough. When the revelations of Muḥammad flashed on the world in the seventh century of the Christian era, a message was delivered which could not be confined to the Hijaz, the cradle of Islam. As a result, within three-quarters of a century, the banner of the Prophet was planted eastward at the extremities of Transoxiana, southward by the banks of the Indus, northward to the shores of the Black Sea, and westward on the slopes of the Pyrenees.

Out of this newly won empire arose a civilization which dwindled that of much of the rest of the world into insignificance. From Samarcand in the east to Cordova in the west, the grandeur of courts, the fame of colleges, and the wealth of bazaars became a byword. Not since the days of Grecian splendour had art, science, and literature shone with such radiance, nor had inventions, discoveries, and improvements excited so much wonderment. It was Islam in its sociological trend which produced this sublimation, although it was its religious basis that was the *causa causans*,[1] since it preached a universal brotherhood which knew no racial or national distinctions, and saw no geographical boundaries. Similarly, while it was an Arabian polity which made this cultural elevation possible, and while the medium of most of its dissemination was Arabic, many other peoples of the Near and Middle East, and even of the European West, were producers and partakers of this culture.

In such wide dominions it was inevitable that alien notions should impose themselves on the culture of the Arab conquerors and, in

[1] See the remarks of the editor of *The Legacy of Islam* (Oxford, 1931), p. v.

consequence, what was once purely Arabian became considerably modified, tempered, and even replaced by other cultures, yet it was this fusion of ideas that gave greater mobility to the new civilization which was to have so vital an influence on the western world. Many peoples of the Near and Middle East, and of western Europe also, contributed to this Islamic civilization: Arab, Turk, Kurd, Persian, Aramaean, Syrian, Egyptian, Greek, and Goth. In the East, two lands especially played a prominent part in the music of this new cultural uprising, Persia and Syria; and in the West, Spain. The role of Greece was more in the theoretical sphere, through the influence of the works of authors centuries dead.

Mesopotamia and Persia	*Syria and Egypt*	*Spain and North Africa*	
Orthodox Caliphs			632
	Conquest of Syria		638
Conquest of Persia			642
	Conquest of Egypt		647
Umayyad Caliphs	Umayyad Caliphs		661
		Conquest of N. Africa	708
		Conquest of Spain	713
'Abbāsid Caliphs	'Abbāsid Caliphs	Umayyad Caliphs (Spain)	750
	Fāṭimid Caliphs		909
Buwaihids			932
		Petty Kings (Spain)	1016
Saljūqs			1037
Khwārizmī Shāhs			1077
		Almoravides (Spain & Africa)	1086
	Saljūqs (Syria)		1094
		Almohades (Spain & Africa)	1130
	Ayyūbids		1169
		Naṣrids (Granada)	1232
	Mamlūk Turks		1250
Mughals. Fall of Baghdad			1256
Tīmūrids			1369
	Mamlūk Circassians		1382
		Fall of Granada	1492
Ṣafawids			1502
Ottoman Turks	Ottoman Turks		1517

THE CULTURAL BACKGROUND

The idea that Arabia has ever been a land of nomads and barbarism has long disappeared. Archaeological remains have revealed traces of a high stage of civilization in the ancient Arabian past, and we now know that this land was once a trading centre of the world which had a profound influence on the destinies of the East.[1] This could scarcely have been otherwise, since not only Syria and Phoenicia, but much of Arabia, was under the irresistible influence of Mesopotamian culture

[1] *Encyclopaedia of Islam*, i (Leiden, 1913–38), pp. 377–80.

as far back as the third millennium B.C. While political and commercial ties between these lands, where practically the same tongue prevailed, must have contributed to a certain level of melioration, there was also a fundamental reason for the persistence of cultural conformity, in that the urban population of both the Mesopotamian and Syrian plains was being continually reinforced by nomadic and country elements from the peninsula itself, a flux which secured the maintenance and revitalizing of the pristine Semitic features of their culture.[1] What we know of the outward visible signs of music and religion in ancient Arabia, partly confirms the view that the Arabs of the peninsula were the inheritors and conservators of much of the great Mesopotamian culture of the past.

Music, as found in the towns and oases of pre-Islamic Arabia, was mainly practised by the women-folk, and especially by a class of singing-girls (*qaināt*) attached to households of the upper classes or employed at places of entertainment. The male musician (*mughannī*) and instrumentalist (*ālātī*) were not so common, although one writer, Ibn Mūsā al-Naṣībī (d. *c.* 860), wrote about them in a *Book of Songs* (*Kitāb al-aghānī*).[2] We know little of the nature of music in those days but, as in ancient Mesopotamia, the art was associated with joy and brightness, as etymology reveals. The word *zahara* meant 'to shine brightly', hence that which produced 'brightness', a tambourine, was called *mizhar*. The origin of musical instruments among the Arabs is not unlike the story of Genesis iv. 21. According to Ibn Khurdādhbih, Tūbal b. Lamak is to be credited with the invention of the tambourine (*duff*) and the drum (*ṭabl*), whilst his sister Ḍilāl is claimed to have originated the lyre or *kithara* (*mi'zaf*). Lamak himself was responsible for the lute (*'ūd*), and Lot's people are given the credit of the pandore (*ṭunbūr*). Likewise, the Kurds were thought to be the first to use the recorder (? *ṣaffāra*) type of instrument, while upon the Persians was conferred the honour of devising the reed-pipe (*nāy*), the double-pipe (*dūnāy*), the shawm (*surnāy*), and the upper-chested harp (*jank*).[3]

In 'Stony Arabia', the *ka'ba* as a place of pilgrimage, and 'Ukāẓ as the home of the fair, were centres where musicians and poets congregated to contest for supremacy in their arts, for even those 'treasured poems', the *Mu'allaqāt*, were sung as well as recited, just

[1] L. W. King, *Legends of Babylonia and Egypt in Relation to Hebrew Tradition* (London, 1918), p. 8. Cf. A. T. Clay, *The Empire of the Amorites* (New Haven, 1919), *passim*.

[2] Farmer, *Sources of Arabian Music* (Bearsden, 1940), p. 18. Reprint from the *Records of the Glasgow Bibliographical Society*, xiii (1939).

[3] Al-Mas'ūdī, *Prairies d'or*, viii (Paris, 1861–77), pp. 89–90.

as entire odes (*qaṣā'id*) were sung in the desert in modern times.[1] Tradition avers that singing (*ghinā'*) arose from the caravan song (*ḥudā'*). Out of this were developed the lament (*biqā'*) and the elegy (*nauḥ*), until there was fashioned the secular song (*naṣb*).[2] In 'Happy Arabia' we are told that two species of song were practised, the *ḥimyārī* and the *ḥanafī*.[3] What distinction existed between them we are not told, but the former was evidently that of the Ḥimyarites, whilst the latter, of more recent origin perhaps, may have been religious music.[4] It is in 'Desert Arabia', thanks to the poets, that we get a fuller and more colourful picture of music. They tell of the joy when listening to the tavern singing-girl (*dājina*, *qarīna*), of the fascinating high trill (*tudhrī*), the swinging refrain (*tarjī'*), and the antiphon (*jawāb*). The instruments were the lyre or *kithara* (*mi'zaf*), certain kinds of lutes or pandores (*muwattar*, *kirān*), probably with skin 'bellies', the flute (*quṣṣāba*), the reed-pipe (*mizmār*), the percussion wand (*qaḍīb*), and tambourines (*duff*, *mizhar*).[5]

Judging by technical musical nomenclature, little alien influence had come to Arabia since the fall of the great Mesopotamian civilization. Where foreign influence did assert itself was at the perimeter, especially in those lands reached through two gaps in the desert to the north-west and north-east which, in the early years of the Christian era, were inhabited by two Arab peoples, the Nabaṭaeans and the Lakhmids, whose culture bore a fairly clear impress of Syria and Persia respectively. The former was a land which had, in the past, seduced Greece by the sounds of the *sidonios nablas* (Hebrew *nebel*), the *kinyra* (Hebrew *kinnōr*), and the *sambykē* (Aramaic *ṣabbekā*), as well as the *phoinix*.[6] If we can believe the Syrian Bar Ṣalībi (d. 1171), 'musical tunes and melodies, with canons, stichera, and the rest came to the Greeks from outsiders'.[7] Even Rome was caught by the Syrian *anbūba* and the *tibiae sarranae*.[8] The persistence of the more ancient Mesopotamian culture in Syria certainly shows itself in musical instruments, as in the Syriac *abbūba*, *ṭablā*, *pelāggā*, *qarnā*, and *zemmōra*.

If Syria could influence Greece and Rome in music, peoples nearer home would certainly be affected more easily. The Nabaṭaean Arabs

[1] J. L. Burckhardt, *Notes on Bedouins and Wahābys*, i (London, 1830), pp. 75, 253.

[2] *Encyclopaedia of Islam*, v, pp. 81–82.

[3] Al-Mas'ūdī, op. cit. viii, p. 93.

[4] Farmer, *History of Arabian Music* (London, 1929), pp. 2–3.

[5] Ibid., chap. i, *passim*.

[6] E. Pélagaud, 'Syriens et Phrygiens' in Lavignac and La Laurencie, *Encyclopédie de la musique*, 1re partie, i (Paris, 1913), pp. 54–58.

[7] A. Mingana, 'Woodbrooke Studies', *Bulletin of the John Rylands Library*, xi (1927), p. 145.

[8] Pélagaud, loc. cit.

at Petra, and later farther north as far as Palmyra, were a people of some political and commercial standing in the early years of the Christian era. That they used the Aramaic script is well testified. An inscription at Palmyra tells of the *kennārā* (*kinōrā*),[1] and Strabo mentions the joy of music at their festivals.[2] Their successors, the Arab Ghassanids (fifth–sixth centuries), who were phylarchs of the Byzantines, were passionately fond of music. The Arab poets have praised the Ghassanid courts, where singing-girls from Mecca, al-Ḥīra, and Byzantium sang to the accompaniment of the *barbaṭ* or lute.[3] It was from this region, possibly, that the Arabs borrowed the reed-pipe called *zanbaq*, whose very name reveals its origin, in that it was made of *sambucus* wood.[4] Indeed the Arabic harp-like instrument known as the *wannaj* may have been a phonetic borrowing from the Syro-Greek *phoinix*.[5]

The other gap in the desert to the north-east, the land of the Arab Lakhmids of Mesopotamia, had been under Persian domination for centuries, yet Persia, like other lands, had felt the pressure of ancient Mesopotamian culture, as we have already seen.[6] However, Persia was now the fount of culture, although with her grotesque fable was as persistent as with others on the origin of music which, according to the *Dabistān*, began in the misty Mahābād days at the beginning of time.[7] Firdausī in his great epic, the *Shāhnāma*, dresses up the old stories of the mythical kings and their prodigious exploits, although much was claimed to have come from Pahlavī sources. The brilliant courts of the kings are made resplendent with music (*rūd*) and singing (*sarwad*), whilst the strings of the harp (*chang*), the pandore (*tanbūr*), and lutes (*barbat*, *rubāb*), and the breath of pipe and reed (*rūyin nāy*, *nāy*) murmured their delightful notes. Of martial and processional sounds were the strident blasts of horns and trumpets (*karranāy*, *shaipūr*, *būq*), the thundering of drums and kettledrums (*tabīra*, *kūs*), and the noise of a tintinnabulating throng (*hindī darāy*, *zang*, *ṣinj*).[8]

From Pahlavī sources we get safer news, in that we read of the upper-chested harp (*chang*), the lower-chested one (*vōn*), the lute (*barbūt*), the pandore (*tambūr*), the *kannār*, the *shīshak*, probably a

[1] Farmer, *History of Arabian Music*, p. 5.
[2] xvi, iv. 27.
[3] Farmer, *History of Arabian Music*, p. 12.
[4] J. Robson, *Ancient Arabian Musical Instruments* (Glasgow, 1938), pp. 16–17.
[5] Al-Fīrūzābādī, *Al-Qāmūs*, s.v. Al-Mas'ūdī, op. cit. viii, p. 91 (for *zannaj* read *wannaj*).
[6] See above, pp. 250 ff.
[7] *The Dabistān*. Translated by D. Shea and A. Troyer (Paris, 1843), p. 32.
[8] For page references to the *Shāhnāma* see my chapter in A. U. Pope, *A Survey of Persian Art* (London, 1938), p. 2786.

near cousin of the Sanskrit *ghoshaka*, and the drums (*tumbak*, *dumbalak*), all of which can be recognized by Persian equivalents.[1] Pahlavī contains many Semitic words, although *kannār* is the only one in the preceding list of instruments, yet the *tabīra*, *karranāy*, and *shaipūr* of Firdausī reveal a genuine Mesopotamian lineage. Many of these instruments are delineated on the Tāq-i Bustān reliefs (A.D. 590–628)[2] and elsewhere.[3]

This was the flourishing period of the Sāsānid dynasty (224–642). It was Shāpūr I (d. 272) who is said to have introduced the lute into his land.[4] Bahrām Gūr (d. 438) was famed for his musical talents, and his famous singing-girl, Āzāda, with her harp, is one of the commonest themes with the old Persian painters.[5] Another king who was fond of music was Khusrau Parviz (d. 628), whose favoured singing-girl, Shīrīn, is extolled by Nidhāmī in his *Khusrau va Shīrīn*,[6] and portrayed by the painters.[7] Among the famed musicians of this time was Bārbad of Fars, whose melodies were being played in Merv in the tenth century.[8] Another was Angisiyyā (cf. Nigisā), who submitted melodies to measure.[9]

As for the scientific theory of music in Persia in those days nothing is known. The claims for the existence of treatises on music in pre-Islamic time,[10] have been shown to be myths;[11] there were no such books until long after Islam was established. Of practical theory there is some evidence, e.g. the *dastānāt* of Bārbad.[12] We read of seven modes before the time of Bārbad,[13] and of twelve and thirty during his time,[14] as well as 360 melodies of his,[15] all of which were possibly linked up with siderial conceits (cf. the numbers), as in Mesopotamia of old.[16]

It was through al-Ḥīra, the capital of the Lakhmids, that Persian musical practices filtered into Arab lands. These people, like their

[1] J. N. Unvalla, *King Husrav and his Boy* (Paris, 1921), pp. 27–29.
[2] Farmer, *Studies in Oriental Musical Instruments*, ii (Glasgow, 1939) pp. 69–85.
[3] A. U. Pope, op. cit., pls. 208A, 230B, 233B.
[4] Abu'l-Fidā, *Historia anteislamica* (Leipzig, 1831), pp. 82–83.
[5] A. U. Pope, op. cit., pls. 664, 672, 679.
[6] E. G. Browne, *A Literary History of Persia*, i (London, 1908), p. 17.
[7] A. U. Pope, op. cit., pls. 898, 1042, 1476C.
[8] W. Ouseley, *The Oriental Geography of Ibn Haukal* (London, 1800), p. 216.
[9] R. d'Erlanger, *La Musique arabe*, iii (Paris, 1938), p. 548.
[10] Albert de Lasalle, 'La Musique des Persans', *La Chronique musicale* (1864), p. 81.
[11] Farmer, 'Ghosts: An Excursus on Arabic Musical Bibliographies' in *Isis*, xxxvi (1946), p. 125.
[12] Al-Khwārizmī, *Mafātiḥ al-'ulūm* (Leiden, 1895), p. 238.
[13] *Asiatick Researches*, iii (5th ed., London, 1807), p. 63.
[14] *Burhān-i qāṭi'* (Calcutta, 1818), s.v. 'laḥn'.
[15] A. de Biberstein Kazimirskī, *Menoutchehri*, xl (Paris, 1886), pp. 13-14.
[16] See p. 247.

suzerains, were great lovers of music, and earned some fame in this respect. Bahrām Gūr, as a prince, was sent to al-Ḥīra to be educated, probably with this latter accomplishment in mind. It was certainly the most important centre of Arabian culture in pre-Islamic times, and it was from al-Ḥīra that Al-Naḍr b. al-Ḥārith (d. 624) introduced the lute (*'ūd*) and the more artistic song (*ghinā'*) into Mecca.[1] Through this corridor also came the Persian harp (*chang*, Arab. *jank*) and pandore (*tanbūr*, Arab. *ṭunbūr*), as well as the shawm (*surnāy*).

The part played by music in the peninsula as a whole during the so-called 'Days of Ignorance', meaning ignorance of Islam, was little different from its role in the earlier Semitic civilizations. If the Arabs toiled for the Assyrians to the lilt of a song, they did likewise in digging the fosse at Al-Medīna at the dawn of Islam.[2] If the temples of Ishtar and Yahveh had their chants, so possibly had the shrines of the Arabs.[3] If the Hebrews likened music at a banquet to 'a carbuncle set in gold', so could the pagan Arabs refer to it as 'painters' work set off with gold'.[4]

THE RISE OF ISLAMIC MUSIC

At the birth of Islam in the Hijaz, in the first year of the *Hijra* or 'Flight', which we know as A.D. 622, a new spiritual world dawned in which naught else mattered but Islam. At first all was austerity. When Muḥammad had passed to greater glory (632), his 'Companions' sought, like the Prophet, to keep the mind of man away from what was termed the *malāhī* or 'forbidden pleasures' which, as of old, included 'wine, woman, and song'. The *Qur'ān* had not contained a word against music, but the purists of Islam began to collect *ḥadīth* or 'sayings' of Muḥammad which were supposed to condemn listening to music, and these were used with considerable effect by the legists (*fuqahā*) to forbid any kind of music save that which was known to have been tolerated by the Prophet. Eventually, the four great legal schools of Islam, the Ḥanafī, the Mālikī, the Shāfi'ī, and the Ḥanbalī, decided, more or less, against 'listening to music' and a most interesting controversial literature on its permissibility or otherwise grew up.[5]

[1] Al-Mas'ūdī, op. cit. viii, pp. 93–94.
[2] Farmer, *History of Arabian Music*, p. 17.
[3] R. A. Nicholson, *A Literary History of the Arabs* (London, 1914), p. 73.
[4] C. J. Lyall, *The Mufaḍḍaliyyāt*, ii (Oxford, 1918–21), p. 101.
[5] Farmer, *The Sources of Arabian Music = Records of the Glasgow Bibliographical Society*, xiii (1939), pp. 92–93; *History of Arabian Music*, pp. 20–36; *Music: The Priceless Jewel* (Bearsden, 1942), pp. 1–27; J. Robson, *Tracts on Listening to Music* (London, 1938).

As we have seen, music was in the hands of matrons and singing-girls, although a few of the latter were suppressed under the earlier of the Orthodox Caliphs (632–61). By the close of the reign of ʿUthmān (d. 646) the male musician and instrumentalist came to the fore in the person of Ṭuwais (d. 710), who is claimed as the first male musician under Islam.[1] He made his name by imitating the Persian melodies which could be heard on every hand from captives who had been brought to the Hijaz as slaves. Indeed, so popular had this music become, that Arab musicians found it necessary to become better acquainted with this Iranian art in order to satisfy their clients. At the same time, the Persian musicians, such as Nashīṭ, were compelled to include Arabian melodies in their repertory so as to please their patrons.[2] Precisely the same thing happened in Persian lands, to which thousands of Arabs had migrated at the conquest. Here, Arabian music seems to have been as well known as the native art, and a century later, when Ibrāhīm al-Mauṣilī went to Persia, he was able to study both Persian and Arabian music there.[3] The influence of Persian music on the Arabian practical art was considerable.[4]

Under the Umayyad Caliphs (661–750) the capital was removed from al-Medina to Damascus in Syria, where their courts, unlike those of their predecessors, almost became conservatories of music. Yazīd I (d. 683) was the earliest to have court minstrels, much to the horror of the pious.[5] He was 'appassioned of music'.[6] Al-Walīd I (d. 715) was another music-lover and the patron of the famous singers and composers Ibn Suraij (d. *c.* 726) and Maʿbad (d. 743). The former was the first to introduce the Persian lute into Mecca (*c.* 685), which was an important event since its accordatura (*taswiyya*) and frets (*dasātīn*) were the means of widening the gamut and generally consolidating Arabian music.[7] Another great musician was Ibn Misjaḥ (d. *c.* 715) of al-Medina. He travelled in Syria, Persia, and elsewhere, and picked up much that was new in these lands.[8] His contemporary, Ibn Muḥriz (d. *c.* 715), did very much the same.[9] Other great artists of the period were Al-Gharīḍ (d. 716),[10] Ibn ʿĀ'isha (d. *c.* 743),[11] and Mālik al-Ṭā'ī (d. *c.* 754).[12]

[1] Farmer, *History of Arabian Music*, pp. 52–53; *Encyclopaedia of Islam*, iv, p. 283.
[2] Farmer, *History*, p. 55.
[3] Ibid., p. 116.
[4] Ibid., pp. 48–49; *Encyclopaedia of Islam*, iii, p. 750.
[5] W. Muir, *The Caliphate* (Edinburgh, 1915), p. 314.
[6] Al-Masʿūdī, op. cit. v. 156.
[7] Farmer, *An Old Moorish Lute Tutor* (Glasgow, 1933), pp. 26-27.
[8] Farmer, *History of Arabian Music*, pp. 69–70; *Encyclopaedia of Islam*, v, p. 94.
[9] Farmer, *History*, p. 70.
[10] Ibid., p. 80.
[11] Ibid., pp. 82–83.
[12] *Encyclopaedia of Islam*, iii, p. 211.

The early 'Abbāsid period (750–847) has well been called the 'Golden Age', and in music, as in art and letters, it certainly deserved this estimation. Although court demeanour reflected Persian custom on every side, in music, the old Arabian art, as established under the Umayyads, held complete sway. The greatest musician of his day, Ibrāhīm al-Mauṣilī (d. 804) was a protagonist of the indigenous music,[1] as was his son Isḥāq al-Mauṣilī, perhaps the most famed musician in Islam.[2] At the court of Al-Mahdī (d. 785), 'music refined the age',[3] and 'no man had a finer voice than he'.[4] As for Hārun al-Rashīd (d. 809), the pages of *The Arabian Nights* reveal the wide horizon of his musical interests.[5] Besides those mentioned, such great minstrels as Ibn Jāmi', Zalzal, 'Allawaya, and Yaḥyā al-Makkī were among those patronized.[6] Under Ma'mūn (d. 833) there flourished the famous Prince Ibrāhīm b. al-Mahdī (d. 839), with a wondrous voice of three octaves.[7] It was this prince who led the Persian romantic school in music in opposition to the Arabian classical school of Isḥāq al-Mauṣilī.[8] The craze lasted for a century, but when its course was run, much of the older music, which was only preserved viva voce had disappeared.[9] In Spain the Umayyad courts at Cordova vied with Baghdad in their patronage of art and science.[10] 'Alūn and Zarqūn were the favoured minstrels under Al-Ḥakam I (d. 822). Others were 'Abbās b. al-Nasā'ī and Manṣūr al-Yahūdī.[11] When the great Ziryāb appeared at the court of 'Abd al-Raḥmān II (d. 852) all who had preceded sank into oblivion, for 'there never was, either before or after him, a man . . . more admired'.[12] Here the old Arabian school flourished in the form which Ibn Misjaḥ had created it, and Isḥāq al-Mauṣilī had confirmed it.

The second Baghdad period (847–945) saw the beginning of the decline of the Caliphate, and as the years crept on the great political empire of Islam gradually slipped away.[13] The decay showed itself in music. Most of the caliphs still kept up huge musical establishments,

[1] Farmer, *History of Arabian Music*, pp. 116-18.

[2] Ibid., pp. 124–6.

[3] W. Muir, op. cit., p. 467.

[4] Ibn Khallikan, *Biographical Dictionary*, iii (Paris, London, 1843–71), p. 464.

[5] Farmer, *History of Arabian Music*, p. 94; *The Minstrelsy of the Arabian Nights* (Bearsden, 1945), p. 19.

[6] Farmer, *History*, pp. 113–23.

[7] Ibid., pp. 120–1.

[8] Ibid., pp. 124–6.

[9] Ibid., pp. 147–9. Barbier de Meynard, 'Ibrahim, fils de Mehdi', in *Journal asiatique*, [? vol.] (1869), pp. 201–342.

[10] Farmer, *History*, p. 97.

[11] Ibid., p. 131.

[12] Ibn Khaldūn, *Notices et extraits des manuscrits de la Bibliothèque du Roi*, xx (Paris, 1865), pp. 421–2; Al-Maqqarī, *The History of the Mohammedan Dynasties in Spain*, ii (London, 1840–3), pp. 116–21.

[13] Farmer, *History of Arabian Music*, p. 138.

and some, Al-Muntaṣir (d. 862) and Al-Mu'tazz (d. 869), were gifted musicians,[1] yet the brilliance was but reflected glory of the past. The minstrels, Ibn Bāna, Abū Ḥashīsha, and others, were second-rate.[2]

The last period of the 'Abbāsid Caliphate (945–1258) heralds the rapid decay and the fall of Baghdad and all its greatness. It opens with the political control of the caliphs by the Buwaihids (945) from Dailam. Music still flourished, since the Dailamī amirs, together with the caliphs, were as much addicted to all forms of the art and its concomitants as ever.[3] With the coming of the Saljūqs (1037) from Turkestan, who became virtual masters of the Caliphate, a fresh cultural impingement began to show itself in Persia, Syria, and Mesopotamia which, as we shall see, developed elsewhere. In Egypt the Fāṭimid anti-Caliphate had been set up (909–1171), and its rulers, with but one exception, patronized music, literature, and science unstintedly.[4] Al-Mustanṣir (d. 1094) even dared to say that his court music was 'pleasanter' than listening to the cantillation of the caller (*mu'adhdhin*) to prayer, while pictures of his dancing-girls, contrary to Islamic custom, adorned his palaces.[5] Then came the Ayyūbid sultans (1169), bringing with them a Turkomanian influence which made itself felt in the arts in general.[6] This alien influence displayed itself in music even more strongly under their successors, the Mamlūks (1252–1517), who were of Kurdish and Circassian breed, and delighted in Turkomanian instruments such as the *qūpūz* (mandore).[7]

In North Africa, the Berber Almoravides became a political force in 1056, and it is not unlikely that their dominion brought an indigenous music to the fore in Africa, and certainly we find that Spain was manufacturing special Berber instruments.[8] Yet although the Berber Almoravides (1086) and Almohades (1130) became masters of Arab Spain, it is unlikely that their musical preferences had much sway over the accepted Arabian practice in the Iberian peninsula. If any extraneous inducements were likely in this respect, it would be from Christian Spain, and indeed this did show itself in Arab Andalusia in one or two instruments, the *kaitāra* (guitarra) and *bandair* (pandero). In the last Arab stronghold in Granada, the Naṣrid rulers (1232–1492) attempted to maintain the grandeur of the past, 'and for a time revived the splendour and distinction of Moorish Spain'.[9] We

[1] Farmer, *History*, p. 140.
[2] Ibid., pp. 157–9.
[3] Ibid., pp. 179–80.
[4] Ibid., pp. 189–92.
[5] Ibid., p. 191.
[6] *Encyclopaedia of Islam*, i, p. 223.
[7] Al-Maqrīzī, *Histoire des sultans Mamlouks*, i/i (Paris, 1837), p. 36.
[8] Al-Maqqarī, op. cit. i, p. 59.
[9] S. Lane-Poole, *The Mohammadan Dynasties* (London, 1894), p. 27.

know from Ibn al-Khaṭīb (d. 1374) what an important position the court singers held in his day. The end of Moorish Spain came in 1492 when Ferdinand and Isabella of Castile captured Granada.

In the east, where we last saw the Saljūqs in power, the situation of the Caliphate was rapidly deteriorating. Chafing at the Saljūq bit, the Caliph Al-Nāṣir (d. 1225) begged the Khwārizmī Shāh to ease his condition, and in 1194 this was done. However, music was still one of the glories of the palaces of the last of the caliphs, Al-Musta-'ṣim (d. 1258); and the author of *Al-Fakhrī* tells us that this ruler would spend many of his leisure hours in its enjoyment. His chief court minstrel was the greatest musician of his age, Ṣafī al-Dīn 'Abd al-Mu'min (d. 1294).[1] In the year 1258 the Mughal hordes under Hūlāgū put Baghdad to the sword, 'while the treasures, material, literary, and scientific, accumulated during the centuries while Baghdad was the metropolis of the vast empire of the 'Abbāsid Caliphs were plundered or destroyed'.[2] Thus closed one of the great and splendid civilizations of history. It is true that Egypt and Syria became, by virtue of the Arabic language, the pivot of the intellectual life of Islam, but here it was but a shadow of the past. The Mamlūk sultans maintained elaborate court music and splendid military bands, but all this came to an end when the Ottoman Turks conquered Egypt in the year 1517.[3]

After the fall of Baghdad, the axis of culture moved to the east, when Persian, instead of Arabic, became the *lingua franca*. Here the Mughal rulers, softened by Islam and Iran, became ardent and open-handed patrons of the arts. The great musician, Ṣafī al-Dīn 'Abd al-Mu'min, whose theoretical works on music dominated the Near and Middle East for over 300 years, was patronized by the Juwainī family in the service of Hūlāgū.[4] Ibn Taghribardī tells us that the Il-Khān Abū Sa'īd (d. 1335) himself 'cultivated music, played well on the lute, and composed songs'.[5] At the court of the Muẓaffarid ruler Shāh Shujā' of Shīrāz (d. 1384) was the famed minstrel Yūsuf Shāh and the great scholar and music theorist Al-Jurjānī (d. 1413).[6] With the Jalairids of Mesopotamia, Ḥusain (d. 1382) and Aḥmad (d. 1410), music seems to have been of as much import as politics.[7] Here,

[1] *Encyclopaedia of Islam*, v, pp. 191-2.
[2] E. G. Browne, *A Literary History of Persia*, ii (London, 1920), p. 463.
[3] S. Lane-Poole, *A History of Egypt: The Middle Ages* (London, 1901), vi, pp. 248–9, 318, 327–8; W. Muir, *The Mameluke or Slave Dynasty of Egypt* (London, 1896), pp. 58, 82, 88.
[4] Farmer, in 'Preface' to R. d'Erlanger, *La Musique arabe*, iii, pp. v–xiv.
[5] A. U. Pope, *A Survey of Persian Art* (Oxford, 1938), p. 2796.
[6] Ibid., p. 2797; R. d'Erlanger, op. cit. iii, pp. xii–xiii.
[7] *Journal asiatique*, ser. iv (1845), v, p. 448.

Riḍwān Shāh and 'Abd al-Qādir b. Ghaibī, the most famed musicians of the day, flourished.[1] When the conquering Tīmūr (d. 1405) appeared on the horizon, the Persian minor dynasties vanished. Samarcand, farther east, became the new cultural centre, and here 'Abd al-Qādir b. Ghaibī (d. 1435) found shelter.[2] Yūsuf-i Andakānī, who 'had no equal in the seven climes', was court minstrel to Shāh Rukh (d. 1408).[3] Amīr Shāhi was favoured by Bāysungur (d. 1433) because of his threefold accomplishments as musician, poet, and painter.[4] Even with the last of the Tīmūrids, Ḥusain Mīrzā Bāyqarā (d. 1506), music was patronized without stint,[5] and some of its exponents, such as Qul-i Muḥammad, won celebrity far and wide.[6] Under the Mughal Il-Khāns and the Tīmūrids, several new features appeared in eastern Islamic music. Among them were such Chinese instruments as the *shidirghū*, a long-necked lute, the *yātūghān*, possibly a type of psaltery, the *pīpa* or lute, and other instruments.[7] These probably infused fresh sound effects, something which may find a parallel in painting; indeed the decorative feature in music, called the *naqsh*, may also be traced in the rhetorical prose of the period, and both may have been due to the same alien promptings.

Meanwhile the Ottoman Turks in Asia Minor had become the rising Islamic power in the Near East, and their conquests in eastern Europe, culminating in the capture of Constantinople (1453), gave them a terrific prestige which was soon to carry them to the walls of Vienna. Like other Islamic potentates, their sultans indulged in music and song to their fullest measure, and musicians found their courts a cornucopia. Here a son 'Abd al-'Azīz, and a grandson Maḥmūd, of the great Persian musician 'Abd al-Qādir b. Ghaibī, received the bounties of Muḥammad II (d. 1481) and Bāyazīd II (d. 1512) respectively, whilst many Arabic and Persian works on the theory of music were rendered into Turkish.[8] Turkish influence on the instrumental music of the Near East and Balkans was considerable, but that is outside our purview.

Islamic music was born and cradled in Arabia, yet, under Persian,

[1] *Encyclopaedia of Islam*, v, pp. 4–5. [2] Ibid., loc. cit.

[3] *Notices et extraits des manuscrits. . . .* xiv (Paris, 1843), p. 137.

[4] Pope, op. cit., p. 2798.

[5] *The Bābur-nāma* (London, 1921), pp. 272, 291–2.

[6] E. G. Browne, *Persian Literature under Tartar Domination* (Cambridge, 1920), p. 505.

[7] Farmer, *Studies in Oriental Musical Instruments*, ii (Glasgow, 1939), pp. 15–17, pl. 10; Pope, op. cit. 633A, 778A.

[8] *Encyclopaedia of Islam*, v, p. 5; R. d'Erlanger, op. cit. iv, pp. 3, 261; Raouf Yekta Bey, 'La Musique turque', in Lavignac and La Laurencie, *Encyclopédie de la musique*, 1re partie, v (Paris, 1922), pp. 2978–9.

Syrian, and Greek tutelage, it became a universal art. Its extrinsic character was changed when Ṣafī al-Dīn (d. 1294) introduced the Khurasānī scale. Then, under Mughal and Turkoman pressure, came other alien influences. These were followed, in the fourteenth century, by a reversion to the plain Pythagorean scale in Persia, to be spread elsewhere later. Finally came the adoption of the modern quarter-tone (*rub*ʿ) scale in the seventeenth century, which made the final break with the old Arabian-Persian-Syrian system of the 'Golden Age' of Islam. Only in al-Andalus of the West was this latter preserved, and today in Morocco one may still hear sometimes, perhaps, an echo of that music about which Shahrazad, although a Persian, whispers so enchantingly in *The Arabian Nights*.

SECULAR MUSIC

We read in one of those delightful nocturnes in *The Arabian Nights*: 'To some people music is like *food*; to others like *medicine*; to others like a *fan*.'[1] This mention of music as 'food' has an esoteric significance, as will be shown later. The remark 'like medicine' is also strange, because the Oriental attitude towards music did not admit of the 'appreciation' of music as we understand the term. Aesthetics, the science of the beautiful, did not exist in Islamic conceptions. The chief reason for this was that the Orient, as we have seen in ancient Mesopotamia and Egypt, put great trust in the doctrine of *tāʾthīr* (influence) in music, a dogma called by the Greeks the *ethos*. This belief, together with the accretion of anthropomorphism, reigned supreme, and one has but to read *The Arabian Nights* to appreciate its far-reaching effect. The delightful imagery in the 'Song of the Lute',[2] is not mere metaphor but anthropopathy. Music was part of the macrocosmic system, and was accepted as such by many Islamic philosophers, astronomers, mathematicians, and physicians.[3] For that reason the melodic modes (*maqāmāt*) and rhythmic modes (*īqāʿāt*) were closely linked up with the universe.[4] It was because of this that the lute had 'four strings, four sides, four parts, and four tied places (frets)',[5] and that the dimensions of instruments —which, incidentally, were given almost human attributes[6]—were

[1] *Arabian Nights* (Lady Burton's edition), ii (London, 1886–7), p. 463.

[2] Ibid., v, p. 294.

[3] Farmer, 'The Influence of Music' in *Proceedings of the Musical Association*, lii (1929), pp. 89–124.

[4] Farmer, *An Old Moorish Lute Tutor*, pp. 9–15.

[5] Farmer, 'An Anonymous English-Arabic Fragment', in *Islamic Culture*, xviii (Hyderabad, 1944), p. 202.

[6] Farmer, *The Minstrelsy of the Arabian Nights* (Bearsden, 1945), p. 13.

subject to mathematical formulas.[1] In addition, all was related to, and conditioned by, cosmic things: the humours, the elements, the seasons, the winds, the planets, the zodiac, and so on.[2] The hearing of special kinds of music at particular times of the day and month, under certain other conditions, became a part of therapeutics. It was used in hospitals, not so much for its soothing effect, but because of its geometrical proportion together with its astrological significance.[3] Within such principles there could have been no room for aesthetics.

What is of greater interest is the more universal approval of music as the story-teller in *The Arabian Nights* puts it, likening the art to 'a fan [on a sultry day]'. When a child was born into Islam the opening lines of the call to prayer (*adhdhān*) was chanted in its ear, whilst the neighbouring matrons assembled with their tambourines (*dufūf*) to herald joy. At the celebrations of circumcision there was further music and entertainment. Marriage occasioned an even greater display, since the procession had its shawms (*zumūr*) and drums (*ṭubūl*) in noisy service, while hired female musicians (*mughanniyāt*) performed less strident music in the courtyard. Even at the bier, the wailing (*wilwāl*) of the mourning women (*naddābāt*) and the thud of their tambourines, was followed by the chanting of the Qur'ān. Thus, between the cradle and the grave, music was ever present in Islam. All the great religious festivals encouraged public music, for the cry was 'Gladden thine heart, drum thine drum, and pipe thine pipe'.[4] Military and processional music was cultivated on a grandiose scale in the shape of trumpets (*anfār*), horns (*būqāt*), shawms (*zumūr*), drums (*ṭubūl*), kettledrums (*naqqārāt*), and cymbals (*kasāt*).[5] Its performance of a divertimento (*nauba*) at certain prescribed hours of the day must have beckoned the crowd. In addition there was the attraction of the singing-girls (*qaināt*) in the taverns, against which the pious raved in wrath, and the less scandalous story-teller (*rāwī*) and violist (*rabābī*) in the coffee-houses. The household in general found the matrons indulging in singing to the rhythm of the tambourine.

The music of the Islamic folk was little different then from what it is today. The toil song, a relic from the cradle of humanity, was practised by the boatman, the sailor, the porter, the weaver, the gleaner, and the rest,[6] for its lilt and measure not only softened the

[1] Farmer, *Studies in Oriental Musical Instruments*, ii, pp. 90–98.

[2] F. Dieterici, *Die Propaedeutik der Araber* (Berlin, 1865), pp. 141–6.

[3] Farmer, *Sa'adyah Gaon on the Influence of Music* (London, 1943), p. 6; E. Werner and I. Sonne, 'The Philosophy and Theory of Music in Judaeo-Arabic Literature', *Hebrew Union College Annual*, xvi (1941), pp. 292–88.

[4] *Arabian Nights*, ii, p. 413.

[5] *Encyclopaedia of Islam*, v, pp. 217–22.

[6] Dieterici, op. cit., p. 103.

sweat of toil but ordered it rhythmically. Then there was domestic music: the lullaby, the children's ditties, the bridal song, and the elegy.[1] Nor was this simple homely art confined to the folk. The Caliph Hārūn delighted in listening to his minstrels repeating the songs of the people, as we know from the reception he gave Ibn Jāmi' when he sang the song of the Yemenite negress, and Abū Ṣadaqa when he chanted the ditties of sailors and masons.[2]

With the middle and upper classes, music assumed a far different character, much of it being determined by the modes and tastes set by courtly procedure. The caliphs, nobility, and rich merchants kept musical establishments in which highly skilled singing-girls were part of the household.[3] They usually came from music schools established specially for their training, and fabulous sums were sometimes paid for them,[4] the price being determined by both physical and musical charms, although the Persian poet Sa'dī said 'a sweet voice is better than a beautiful face'.[5] They were usually given an excellent education.[6] The male musicians and those who were specifically instrumentalists, were usually freedmen (*mawālī*) of foreign extraction, mainly Persian, and the demand for them at the court and elsewhere was inordinate, while the gold and other gifts showered on them almost passes credence.[7] Certainly the concerts given at court, which were staged with great lavishness, dwarfs anything else in the history of music.[8] In Umayyad days these musicians, both male and female, were quite unrestrained in their public performances at court or elsewhere,[9] but later a curtain shut them off from the audience, this provision satisfying the consciences of the auditors somewhat, in that if they heard this 'forbidden pleasure' (*milhā*, pl. *malāhī*), at least they did not see it.[10] The truth was that in spite of all the condemnation of music by the puritans, ways and means were found, sometimes with the most delightful casuistry, to escape censure.[11]

At concerts in Umayyad days (661–750) 'the utmost propriety was observed', and the slightest breach of decorum was reproved by the stroke of a stick.[12] The earliest minstrel, Ṭuwais, used to walk back-

[1] See Bibliography.

[2] Al-Iṣfahānī, *Kitāb al-aghānī* (Bulaq, 1869), vi, p. 86; xxi, p. 104; J. Ribera, *Music in Ancient Arabia and Spain* (London, 1929), p. 61.

[3] Farmer, *History of Arabian Music*, p. 67.

[4] Ibid., pp. 86–87, 102, 132–6.

[5] *Gulistan*, iii. 28.

[6] Farmer, *The Minstrelsy of the Arabian Nights*, pp. 18–22.

[7] Farmer, *History of Arabian Music*, pp. 81, 100, 112–17, 124–6.

[8] Ibid., pp. 65–77, 99–112, 145–56, 194–211.

[9] Ibid., pp. 67–68.

[10] Ibid., pp. 102–4.

[11] Farmer, *Music: The Priceless Jewel* (Bearsden, 1942), p. 13.

[12] Farmer, *History of Arabian Music*, p. 55.

wards and forwards along the lines of his audience.[1] Al-Gharīḍ, before he gave a recital, would explain to his audience the type of music he was about to perform, adding some little history of the composer and author, together with something about its first performance and performers. The mannerisms of these musicians are not without interest. Yazīd Ḥaurā' was given to attitudinizing and gesticulating while performing, which may have had an emotional or rhythmical effect; these affectations impressed the great Ibrāhīm al-Mauṣilī, who made his singing-girls copy every movement of this artist.[2] The famous Isḥāq al-Mauṣilī usually began his own songs on a high note with a terrific *sforzando*, hence his nickname *al-malsū'* ('stung by a scorpion').[3] Ziryāb, in Muslim Spain, practised some novel methods in teaching; for instance, bad articulation was remedied by the insertion of a piece of wood in the pupil's mouth so as to keep the jaws apart; it was kept there night and day until cure was effected.[4]

Methods of composition seem to us just as odd. Some composers, when in an inventive mood, took a rhythmic wand (*qaḍīb*) to beat out a known rhythm, and then gave utterance to what was called an 'improvised song' (*ghinā' murtajal*).[5] Ma'bad, the spirit moving him to compose, would leap into a saddle and beat on the pommel with his wand in his chosen rhythm until his melody took definite shape.[6] Ibn Suraij would put on a robe garnished with jingling grelots which, when he swayed in rhythm, helped him to fashion a new melody.[7] When Ibrāhīm al-Mauṣilī was asked how he composed he said that the first thing he did was to banish all thoughts of mundane affairs. This enabled him to lift his thoughts to the requisite emotional plane; his creative self emerged only when he could no longer see or hear anything external. When this sensation or transcendence was reached, he visualized his rhythm, and within its framework, his tonal images took shape.[8] Ibrāhīm al-Mauṣilī, his son Ishāq, and Ziryāb claimed to have been taught melodies by the devil and genii.[9] The latter, when the *jinn* had been prompting him in his sleep, would jump out of bed, call his singing-girls, and get them to memorize the music while it was still fresh in his mind.[10]

In early days, the more solemn rhythms (*thaqāl*) were preferred to

[1] Farmer, 'The Minstrels of the Golden Age of Islam', *Islamic Culture*, xvii (1943), p. 272.

[2] Al-Iṣfahānī, op. cit. iii, p. 70.

[3] Al-Iṣfahānī, op. cit. v, p. 70.

[4] Al-Maqqarī, op. cit. ii, p. 121.

[5] Farmer, *History of Arabian Music*, p. 47.

[6] Al-Iṣfahānī, op. cit. i, p. 21.

[7] R. d'Erlanger, *La Musique arabe*, i, p. 10.

[8] Al-Iṣfahānī, op. cit. v, p. 34.

[9] Farmer, *The Minstrelsy of the Arabian Nights*, p. 20.

[10] Al-Maqqarī, op. cit. ii, pp. 116–21.

the festive rhythms (*ramal, hazaj, mākhūrī*). Under the later 'Abbāsid régime, the latter became very popular. Ḥakam al-Wādī, censured for pandering to the public taste by composing and singing in the lighter vein, said: 'For thirty years I have sung in the *thaqīl* rhythm and have hardly gained a living, yet in three years of singing in the *hazaj* rhythm I have earned more money than thou hast ever seen.'[1] That melodies and rhythms should be in conformity with the sentiment of the words was stressed by Ibn 'Abd Rabbihi (d. 940), the Ikhwān al-Ṣafā' (*c.* 961), and Ibn Sīda (d. 1066), and it is this which accounted for preferences in lighter music. We are told, however, that there were kinds of music designed for joy and sorrow, music for the tavern and flowing bowl, music for lovers and for mourners, music for the description of scenes as widely asunder as the hushed scented garden and the moving chase. Indeed, Isḥāq al-Mauṣilī spoke of a composition of his in which he portrayed a game of ball with a stick, complete with the getting of a goal at the end.[2] That is real programme music. Only those who have heard music in the Near and Middle East can possibly appreciate the wide dissimilarity of reaction to music between the Orient and the Occident.[3] The rending of garments, and similar sudden, unpremeditated, and often violent acts, under music's influence, are commonplaces in Arabic literature. Swooning is the general result of the 'killing charm' of music, as we read in *The Arabian Nights*,[4] although death itself has been recorded several times.[5]

The sums awarded to musicians, as recorded in the annals, are absurdly large if judged by our standards. The same may be said of the numbers of compositions said to be theirs or in their repertories. Badhl, a famous songstress, is alleged to have known 30,000 songs,[6] and yet, prodigious as this may seem, there are still people who know the Qur'ān by heart. More modest was the accomplishment of 'Uraib, another songstress, who claimed 21,000, while Ziryāb in Spain knew only 10,000.[7] The compositions of individual musicians do not 'hit' so high a mark, to use an Arabism, although Ibrāhīm al-Mauṣilī boasted of 900 works.[8] As with us in the West, certain songs became famous, such as the *Seven Fortresses* of Ma'bad,[9] the *Seven Songs* of Ibn Suraij,[10] the *Hundred Chosen Songs* edited by Ibn Jāmi',[11] the song called 'Three Maidens', the words being attributed to

[1] Farmer, *History of Arabian Music*, p. 111. [2] Al-Iṣfahānī, op. cit. v, p. 97.
[3] Farmer, *The Minstrelsy of the Arabian Nights*, pp. 11–12.
[4] Ibid., loc. cit. [5] *Arabian Nights*, ii, 439. [6] Farmer, *History*, p. 134.
[7] Ibid., pp. 130, 133. [8] Ibid., p. 117. [9] Ibid., p. 82. [10] Ibid., p. 80.
[11] Farmer, *Sources*, p. 15.

the Caliph Hārūn,[1] and the 'Zayānib' of Yūnus al-Kātib.[2] Complete song collections existed in profusion,[3] as well as biographies of singers, instrumentalists, and composers,[4] together with popular story-books about music.[5] It is humbling to scan the pages of the *Great Book of Songs* (*Kitāb al-aghānī al-kabīr*) by Al-Iṣfahānī (d. 967), which took fifty years to compile, consisting of twenty-one volumes, containing nearly 2,000,000 words, dealing with the history of Arabian music and song up to the tenth century, and to compare it with similar Occidental achievement during the same period.

RELIGIOUS MUSIC

That music played its part in religious ceremonial in ancient Arabia seems clear enough. St. Nilus speaks of the pagan Arabs chanting when encircling a stone.[6] Noeldeke suggested that this was similar to the Islamic *tahlīl*, a musical utterance which belonged to moon worship; it was used with the *talbiyya*, which is claimed to have been indulged in by Adam and Noah.[7] Epiphanius avers that Dhu' l-Shāra, a god of the Nabaṭaeans, was worshipped on his birthday 'with hymns'. Indeed Hisham b. al-Kalbī tells us in his *Book of Idols* that 'the melodies of mankind' were due to the god named Al-'Uqayṣir. When Islam came to Arabia, Muḥammad cried anathema upon much of this, but from the Atlantic to the Oxus music and magic were closely connected. What was turned directly into Islamic practice were the *tahlīl* and *talbiyya*. Similarly, the pagan songs during the pilgrimage (*ḥajj*) were given a new character and even allowed to be accompanied by fife (*shāhīn*) and drum (*ṭabl*).[8] Islam strove to discredit the dance (*raqṣ*), and the literature in its condemnation is not inconsiderable.[9] Ibn Taimiyya (d. 1328) scorned it as 'proud walking upon the earth',[10] yet it was never eradicated. Today, among those Arabs who are far distant from the Occidentalized towns, one may still hear and see the choral dance which, while outwardly secular, still retains its religious mien. As we shall see later, the religious dance still exists.

Strictly speaking, however, Islam has no religious music in our

[1] Ibn al-'Arabī, *Al-futūḥāt*, ii (Cairo, A.H. 1329), p. 612.
[2] Farmer, *History*, p. 80.
[3] Farmer, *Sources*, pp. 89–90.
[4] Ibid., pp. 88–89.
[5] Ibid., pp. 90–93.
[6] Migne, *Patrologia latina*, lxxi, p. 612.
[7] *Encyclopaedia of Islam*, i, p. 965; iv, p. 640. Al-Kalbī, *The Book of Idols* (Princetown, 1952), p. 33.
[8] *Journal of the Royal Asiatic Society*, (1901), pp. 220–1.
[9] Farmer, *Sources of Arabian Music*, p. 90.
[10] Sirajul Haq, 'Samā' and Raqṣ', in *Islamic Culture*, xviii (1944), pp. 111–30.

normal sense of the term, since there is no service in the Muslim mosque comparable to that in the Christian church. Yet music in praise of Allāh has always found a place both inside and outside the Muslim places of worship, e.g. in the 'reading' (*qirā'a*) of the Qur'ān, the cantillation (*talḥīn*) of the call to prayer (*adhdhān*), the 'listening to music' (*al-samā'*) of the Ṣūfī and Darwīsh fraternities, and the simple religious chants of the folk. The Qur'ān lent itself to cantillation because of its prosodic structure; much of it consists of rhymed prose (*saj'*), the assonance of which tempted the voice to use modulated sound in 'reading'. Further, there was the *hadīth* which said, 'Allāh listens more intently to a man with a beautiful voice reading the Qur'ān than does the owner of a singing-girl to her voice'.[1] In this wise the cantillation of the Qur'ān became a necessity, and Ibn Qutaiba (d. 889) tells us that the earliest of these chanters who used melodies (*alḥān*) was 'Ubaidallāh b. Abī Bakr (*fl.* 669), though he informs us that this early cantillation was dirge-like and quite different from ordinary melody (*laḥn*) in singing (*ghinā'*).[2] This distinction seems to have been a fiction created by the legists who, in their opposition to music, looked upon this singing as improper (*makrūh*),[3] and so discriminated between 'cantillation' (*taghbīr* = 'raising [the voice]')[4] and singing (*ghinā'*).[5] By the ninth century, however, even the melodies of popular ballads were being used in the cantillation of the Qur'ān.[6] Despite the violent opposition of the purists to all music, the cantillation of the Qur'ān became one of its supreme religious and cultural accomplishments. While the prosodic vocalization and punctuation are strictly governed by rules laid down later by Ibn al-Jazarī (d. 1429),[7] the cantillation itself was not confined to any fixed melodic contour, and so, from the shores of Morocco to the Oxus, one may hear this cantillation today in almost as many patterns as there are mosques.[8]

The 'call to prayer' (*adhdhān* = 'announcement') was instituted in the first or second year of the Hijra (622–4) as a means of summoning the faithful to their religious duties. At first it was but a simple announcement in the streets,[9] and it was thus that Bilāl, the first

[1] Al-Ghazālī, *Iḥyā 'ulūm al-dīn*, ii (Cairo, A.H. 1326), p. 185.
[2] *Ibn Coteiba's Handbuch der Geschichte* (Göttingen, 1850), p. 265.
[3] Farmer, *History of Arabian Music*, pp. 22–23.
[4] Or *ta'bīr* = 'narration'.
[5] *Notices et extraits des manuscrits*, xx (Paris, 1865), p. 419.
[6] *Ibn Coteiba's Handbuch der Geschichte*, loc. cit.
[7] Al-Suyūtī, *Itqān*, i (Cairo, A.H. 1278), p. 96.
[8] For a modern plain example see E. W. Lane, *Modern Egyptians* (London, 1860), p. 376.
[9] *Encyclopaedia of Islam*, iii, p. 373.

'caller' or muezzin (*mu'adhdhin*), performed it.[1] Shortly after this we find it being called from the minaret of the mosque in a similar way to the cantillation of the Qur'ān as a dirge-like chant, a character which persisted until the tenth century in Egypt, as Al-Muqaddasī (d. 946) tells us.[2] Then, as with the 'reading' of the Qur'ān, melody proper, indistinguishable from ordinary singing (*ghinā'*), came into general use; the performance of this was known by the purely secular term *taṭrīb*,[3] although we read at Fars in Persia that the 'call' was made without *taṭrīb*.[4] In the Ḥijāz the office of muezzin was at first hereditary,[5] but before long the duties became so onerous that several muezzins were to be found in each mosque, and by the ninth and tenth centuries, these were taking it in turns to make the 'call',[6] while within the mosque itself they later joined in chorus when chanting the 'second call' (*iqāma*).[7] As with the cantillation of the Qur'ān, the 'call' is still to be heard in totally different styles, from the plain, ingenuous, unaffected chant,[8] to highly festooned coloratura.[9]

The Ṣūfī and Darwīsh conception of music as an aid or approach to religion is of the highest importance since they reveal how intimately their ideals are connected with ancient beliefs,[10] although on a higher and more rationalized plane. Ibn Zaila (d. 1048) says: 'Sound produces an influence in the soul in two ways: one on account of its musical structure [i.e. its physical structure], and the other because of its similarity to the soul [i.e. its spiritual structure].'[11] Ṣūfī disciples, such as the Persian Al-Hujwīrī (eleventh century) and Al-Ghazālī (d. 1111), divide people influenced by music into two classes—those who hear the material sound, and those who apprehend its spiritual meaning. The latter, in Ṣūfī doctrine, do not hear notes or beats, melodies or rhythms, but music *per se*. Al-Hujwīrī quotes the saying of the Prophet, 'O Allāh, let us see things as they *are*', and listening to music could alone accomplish that, since 'right audition consists

[1] Ibn Sa'd, *Biographien Muhammeds*, iii, i (Leiden, 1904), p. 165.
[2] *Bibliotheca geographorum arabicorum*, iii (Leiden, 1877), p. 205.
[3] Ibid. iii, p. 327.
[4] *Ibn Jubair* (*Gibb Memorial Series*), v (Leiden, 1907), p. 194. [5] Ibid. iii, p. 439.
[6] *Bibliotheca geographorum arabicorum*, vii (Leiden, 1892), p. 111.
[7] Ibid. iii, p. 327.
[8] E. W. Lane, op. cit., pp. 374-5; Jules Rouanet, 'La Musique arabe' in Lavignac and La Laurencie, *Encyclopédie*, 1re partie, v, pp. 2818–19; J. Parisot, *Rapport sur une mission scientifique en Turquie d'Asie* (Paris, 1889), p. 204.
[9] G. A. Villoteau, *La Description de l'Égypte: état moderne*, i (Paris, 1809–26), pp. 705–6; J. Parisot, op. cit., p. 103.
[10] See above, pp. 231, 258.
[11] British Museum MS. Or. 2361, f. 220v.

of hearing everything as it is in quality and predicament'.[1] Thus Sufī teaching reveals to us the meaning of music in almost the Schopenhauerian sense that it is the eternal will itself.[2] The Arab mystic, Abū Sa'īd b. al-'Arabī (d. 952), believed that ultimate truth could be apprehended only through divine ecstasy, and 'ecstasy is lifting the curtain and witnessing the Watcher [Allāh]'. The most potent means to the attainment of ecstasy is 'listening to music', for as Dhu' l-Nūn, the Egyptian mystic has said, we have in this 'listening' a power that 'creates a divine influence which stirs the heart to seek Allāh', and leads one 'to find the existence of the Truth beside the Veil', as Abu' l-Ḥusain al-Darrāj has testified.[3]

It was from such beliefs and practices, although far less spiritual, that sprang the numerous Darwīsh orders, the Mevlevi (*Maulawiyya*), the Aïssaoua (*'Isawiyya*), and others, with whom music and dancing are used to create an hypnosis for the attainment of religious sublimation. The Mevlevi order, founded at Konia by Jalāl al-Dīn al-Rūmī (d. 1273), better known as the 'dancing dervishes', has a most interesting ceremonial dance of thirteen sections which have been described by Helmut Ritter.[4] A somewhat analogous rite from Upper Egypt, consisting of seven sections, has been recorded by Victor Loret.[5] The Aïssaoua fraternity was founded in Morocco by Muḥammad b. 'Īsā (d. 1524), hence its name, but since then it has spread to other parts of the Maghrib and Egypt.[6] It still exists.[7]

Yet the religious music of Islam does not begin and end in pious edifices or institutions, since in every Muslim land the religious chant has been an integral part of social life. Just as the Calvinists were wont to indulge in psalm-singing as a secular pleasure, so the Muslims in their festivals found social pleasure in the religious chant. Wherever one looks in Islamic lands, the universality of hymns (*nashā'id*) and cantillation (*talḥīn*) is apparent. Indeed, in some instances, they have been a part of education, and this has prevailed in spite of the fact that there has always been a powerful group of

[1] Al-Hujwīrī, *Kashf al-humūm* (London, 1911), p. 403.

[2] Farmer, *The Influence of Music: From Arabic Sources*, p. 91.

[3] D. B. Macdonald, 'Emotional Religion in Islam', *Journal of the Royal Asiatic Society* (1901), p. 719.

[4] *Zeitschrift für vergleichende Musikwissenschaft*, i (Berlin, 1933), pp. 28-40, pls. 5–23; Dorothy Walker, 'Akhar al-darāwīsh al-maulawiyya', in *Al-mustami' al-'arabī*, viii/21 (*Arabic Listener*), pp. 18–19.

[5] *Mémoires . . . de la mission archéologique française au Caire*, i (Paris, 1889), pp. 329–63.

[6] *Encyclopaedia of Islam*, ii, pp. 527–8.

[7] E. W. Lane, op. cit., pp. 460–63; Rouanet, op. cit., pp. 2830–1; R. d'Erlanger, *Méloaies tunisiennes* (Paris, 1937), pp. 18–20.

legists who strenuously opposed music in any form, if not always as something sinful (*ḥaram*), at least as a diversion which was considered unpraiseworthy (*makrūk*).[1]

INSTRUMENTS OF MUSIC

The Arabs admitted that 'with the exception of the Persians and Byzantines, no people had a greater liking for musical instruments' than themselves.[2] Certainly no other people ever wrote so enthusiastically about them. Many of the Arabic and Persian writers on music from Al-Fārābī (d. *c.* 950) to 'Abd al-Qādir b. Ghaibī (d. 1435), fully describe the instruments of their day. In Muslim Spain, where Seville was the centre of the instrument-making trade, there were 'works on the art of making instruments common amongst us', says Ibn Sa'īd al-Maghribī (d. *c.* 1286).[3]

One of the earliest of the instruments of the Arabs was the *qaḍīb* or rhythmic wand, whose tick-tick (*ṭaqṭaqa*) the Prophet disliked.[4] Hand-clapping was called *taṣfīq*, hence *muṣāfiq* or clappers,[5] which to the Syrian Arabs were the *shuqaifāt*;[6] the Persians called them the *chārpāra* or *chālpāra*. Small finger cymbals were the Arabic *kāsāt*, which the Syrians termed *ṣajjāt*. Cymbals proper, when plate-shaped, were the *ṣunūj*, but if bowl-shaped were the *ku'ūs* or *kāsāt*.[7] Musical glasses (harmonica) called *ṭusūt*, were known to Ibn Khaldūn (d. 1406), but the instrument was played with sticks.[8] The Persian 'Abd al-Qādir b. Ghaibī speaks of *saz-i ṭāsāt* (musical cups) and *sāz-i kāsāt* (musical bowls), as well as the *sāz-i alwāḥ-i fūlad* (instrument of slabs of steel), i.e. the glockenspiel.[9] We first read of a metallophone in Ibn Sīnā and Ibn Zaila in the eleventh century, who term it the *ṣanj ṣīnī* (Chinese *ṣanj*).[10]

The generic name for a drum was the Arabic *ṭabl*, which equated with the Persian *duhul*, and the Turkish *dāwūl*. In the specific sense it was a cylindrical drum with two heads. A waisted drum was the *kūba*.[11] Among single-headed drums was the small vase-shaped

[1] *Arabian Nights*, vi, p. 59.
[2] Al-Mas'ūdī, op. cit. viii, p. 93.
[3] Al-Maqqarī, op. cit. i pp. 42, 58–59, 197.
[4] Madrid MS. 603 (Arabic), fo. 79.
[5] Farmer, *Studies in Oriental Musical Instruments*, ii, pp. 28–29.
[6] *Encyclopaedia of Islam*, v, p. 196; Farmer, *Sources*, frontispiece; A. Lane, *Early Islamic Pottery* (London, 1948), pl. 49A.
[7] T. Arnold and A. Guillaume, op. cit., fig. 91.
[8] *Notices et extraits des manuscrits*, xvii (1858), p. 354; xx (1865), p. 412.
[9] Bodleian MS. Marsh 282, ff. 78, 81.
[10] R. d'Erlanger, *La Musique arabe*, ii, p. 234.
[11] Farmer, *Studies*, ii, fig. 13; A. Pavlovskij, 'Décoration des plafonds de la Chapelle Palatine', *Byzantinische Zeitschrift*, ii (1893), p. 384; Pope, op. cit., pl. 603.

durraij,[1] while a larger type was the Berber *agwal*, and the Arabian *darbakka* or *darbūka*, which was identical with the Persian *tunbūk*.[2] Kettledrums ranged from tiny *nuqairāt*, through medium-sized *naqqārāt* equating with the Turkish *quddūm*, to the larger *kūsāt*, and the monster Mughal *kuwargā* or *kūrgā*. Single kettledrums were the *ṭabl shāmī*, *qaṣʿa*, and *ṭabli bāz*.[3] Tambourines were plentiful. *Duff* was the generic term for both the circular and rectangular kind; among the former was the *mizhar*, while with 'snares' across the skin it was the *ghirbāl* because of its likeness to a 'sieve'. In Muslim Spain the Christian *pandero* (*bandair*) was borrowed. It was somewhat like the preceding but when rings and sonnettes were added it was called the *dāʾira*, or with jingling metal plates the *ṭarr*.[4]

Among horns and trumpets the Arabic *būq* was generic for both, although the word was used particularly for the conical tube types, while the cylindrical tube was called *nafīr*. The Persian *karnā* was extremely long and had the 'bell' turned back into an 'S' shape.[5] Turks and Turkomans had the *būrū* and *būrghū*. The woodwind were covered by the term *mizmār* in Arabic and *nai* in Persian, but the latter distinguished the flute and reedpipe as the *nay-i safīd* (white *nai*) and the *nay-i siyāh* (black *nai*). The Arabs used *mizmār* or *zamr* specifically for the reedpipe, while they called the flute the *quṣṣāba*. Smaller flutes were the Arabic *shabbāba*, the Persian *pīsha*, and the Berber *juwāq*, the latter being the puzzling instrument written *ḥumāqī* by a careless copyist of Al-Maqqarī. The panpipes had the name *shuʿaibiyya* in Egypt, but elsewhere the more classical term *mūsīqāl* was used, hence the Turkish *mithqāl*.[6] The *balāban* of the Persian and Turkoman was a cylindrical reed-pipe, while the conical shawm was the Persian *surnā*, the Arabic *surnāy*, and the Turkish *zurnā*.[7] Other varieties were the *ghaiṭa*, *nāy zunāmī* (vulg. *zullāmī*), and the *būq* [*zamrī*]. Double reedpipes, such as the Persian *dūnāy*, the 'Iraqian *zammāra*, the Maghriban *maqrūn*, and the Turkī *qōshnāy*, belonged to the folk, as did the 'drone' type of the *tibiae pares*, as exemplified in the *arghūl*.[8] An instrument of Chinese provenance

[1] J. Robson, op. cit., pp. 14–15.

[2] Farmer, *Minstrelsy of the Arabian Nights*, p. 36.

[3] *Encyclopaedia of Islam*, v, pp. 215–17; Pope, op. cit., pl. 706; Farmer, *Minstrelsy*, pl. 11.

[4] *Encyclopaedia of Islam*, v, pp. 73–75; Farmer, *Minstrelsy*, pls. 1, 9.

[5] *Encyclopaedia of Islam*, v, pp. 42–44; Farmer, *Turkish Instruments of Music in the Seventeenth Century* (Glasgow, 1937), pp. 28–31, 47; Kinsky, op. cit., p. 43, figs, 1, 3; T. Arnold and A. Guillaume, op. cit., fig. 91; *Ars Asiatica*, xiii (Paris, 1929), pl. lv.

[6] *Encyclopaedia of Islam*, iii, pp. 541–2; Farmer, *Studies*, i, pp. 65–67; *Minstrelsy*, pls. 7, 8, 12.

[7] Farmer, *Turkish Instruments*, pp. 23–27.

[8] *Encyclopaedia of Islam*, iii, pp. 539–41.

was the mouth-organ of free reeds called the *mushtak* in Sāsānid days, and it was still thriving under the Mughals as the *chubchīq*.[1] That the Arabs knew of and constructed pneumatic and hydraulic organs we know from the Mūrisṭus treatises, but both the former and the hydraulus were early types. Their hydraulic organs were masterpieces of mechanism, based mainly on the appliances of Philo, Hero, and Archimedes. Their hydraulus was certainly of a type anterior to Hero and Vitruvius.[2] The portative was known in Persia in the fifteenth century.[3]

It is in chordophones that Islamic peoples gained world-wide fame. The upper-chested harp or *chang* was the more favoured in Persia; it was the Arabic *jank*, sometimes called *ṣanj*. Al-Fārābi (d. *c.* 950) mentions various methods of stringing and accordatura, one with fifteen strings tuned diatonically from *G* to *g*ꞌ, while another with twenty-five strings was tuned chromatically from *G* to *g*ꞌ.[4] The Persian *Kanz al-tuḥaf* (fourteenth century) gives twenty-four strings tuned diatonically from *c* to *c*ꞌꞌ, while the *Jāmiʿ al-alḥān* (1435) describes the *chang* with thirty-five strings tuned enharmonically for two octaves.[5] It appears in both Arabian and Persian art.[6] Persia had another harp which had a wooden face to the sound-chest, instead of a parchment face as in the *chang*; it was called the *agrī*, but was tuned similarly to the *chang*.[7] In Egypt was produced another type called the *jank miṣrī* which had a wooden sound-board placed on one side of the strings for greater resonance.[8] Off the beaten track, in the Yemen and the Hijaz, the more primitive lyre or kithara (?) known as the *miʿzaf* was still favoured in the tenth century. In Baghdad it was laughed at as a 'rat trap',[9] although Al-Fārābī recognized it.[10]

The psaltery was attributed to Al-Fārābī,[11] but the instrument is not mentioned by him under its millennium-old name of *qānūn*. Nor do Ibn Sīnā (d. 1037) or Ibn Zaila (d. 1048) mention it, yet it is figured in its trapezoidal form in the tenth-century Syriac lexicons.[12]

[1] Farmer, *Studies*, ii, pp. 9–10.
[2] Farmer, *The Organ of the Ancients: From Eastern Sources* (London, 1931), *passim*.
[3] Bodleian MS. Marsh 282, fo. 80.
[4] R. d'Erlanger, *La Musique arabe*, i (Paris, 1930), pp. 286–94.
[5] King's College (Cambridge) Persian MS. 211, ff. 21ᵛ–22.
[6] A. U. Pope, op. cit., pls. 646A, 652, 727B, 1300A–B, 1808, 1330A, 1353B; see pl. 13 (*c*).
[7] Bodleian MS. Marsh 282, fo. 78.
[8] Glasgow University MS. Bi 22-z. 18, fo. 145.
[9] *Encyclopaedia of Islam*, iii, pp. 528–30.
[10] R. d'Erlanger, *La Musique arabe*, i, p. 286.
[11] Ibn Khallikān, op. cit. iii, p. 309.
[12] R. Payne Smith, *Thesaurus Syriacus* (Oxford, 1891), p. 3613.

As the *qānūn* it was known in Muslim Spain in the eleventh century,[1] and in the fourteenth century it was mounted with sixty-four strings, tuned tricordally, in Persia,[2] the latter being of twisted copper.[3] Ṣafī al-Dīn 'Abd al-Mu'min (d. 1294) invented a rectangular psaltery of sixty-four strings called the *nuzha*.[4] The names *ṣantūr*, *sinṭīr*, and such like variants, were given the dulcimer, possibly from the Aramaic.[5] Ibn Khaldūn (d. 1406) mentions it in the Maghrib,[6] but it fell into disuse generally among the Arabs, although much favoured in Persia. See pl. 13 (*b*).

Bowed instruments can only be definitely traced to the tenth century, when Al-Fārābī clearly mentions a *rabāb* being bowed.[7] The rebec of Islamic peoples had many forms. The pear-shaped instrument was possibly the one which Al-Fārābī described, showing it to be mounted with from one to four strings.[8] The boat-shaped type was a survival of the sound-chest of the old barbiton,[9] and this may have been the *rabāb* of Muslim Spain praised by Yaḥyā b. Hudhail (d. 995) and Ibn Ḥazm (d. 1064).[10] For centuries it had but two strings tuned a fifth apart, as was the *rubèba* of Jerome of Moravia (thirteenth century).[11] The hemispherical-chested viol, with a long iron foot, has been more favoured in the Middle East; it is generally called the *kamāncha* (Ar. *kamānja*), and may have been the type to which Ibn al-Faqīḥ referred in 902–3 when speaking of its use by the Copts of Egypt and the people of Sind;[12] it was usually found with two strings, tuned a fourth apart. A more elaborate instrument was the *ghichak* of Persia and beyond; it had a larger sound-chest than the *kamāncha*, and had eight sympathetic strings in addition.[13] The shallow, rectangular sound-chest type, has long been a folk instrument; it is the one which the ancient poets may have used to accompany

[1] Shihāb al-Dīn, *Safīnat al-mulk* (Cairo, 1891), p. 473.

[2] Kings College (Cambridge) Persian MS. 211, ff. 23r–23v.

[3] Bodleian MS. Marsh 282, fo. 78; Farmer, *Studies*, pp. 12–15.

[4] *Encyclopaedia of Islam*, iii, pp. 529–30; Farmer, *Arabic Musical Manuscripts in the Bodleian Library* (London, 1925), frontispiece, *Oriental Studies: Mainly Musical* (London, 1953), facing p. 66, and *Minstrelsy*, pls. 6, 12. The name—*nāqūr*—given the instrument in d'Erlanger, *La Musique arabe*, iii, p. 220, is incorrect.

[5] Cf. *Pṣantrīn* in Chap. V, p. 245.

[6] *Notices et extraits des manuscrits*, xx (1865), p. 412.

[7] Farmer, *Studies*, i, pp. 101–3.

[8] R. d'Erlanger, *La Musique arabe*, i, pp. 277–86; A. Pavlovskij, op. cit., in *Byzantinische Zeitschrift*, ii (1893), p. 383; J. F. Riaño, *Notes on Early Spanish Music* (London, 1887), figs. 44/4–5.

[9] Kinsky, op. cit., p. 18, fig. 2.

[10] Farmer, *Studies*, i, p. 106.

[11] E. de Coussemaker, *Scriptores de musica medii aevi*, i (Paris 1864–76), p. 152.

[12] *Bibliotheca geographorum arabicorum*, v (Leiden, 1885), p. 59; King's College (Cambridge) Persian MS. 211, fo. 19v.

[13] Bodleian MS. Marsh 282, fo. 78v.

their verses,[1] and we know of its shape from the time of 'Abd al-Qādir b. Ghaibī (d. 1435), although it may be seen in the frescoes of Quṣair 'Amra (eighth century), but here it is a plucked instrument.

The greatest of all the instruments of Islamic peoples was the *'ūd* or lute. Its precursor was the Persian *barbaṭ*, although there existed earlier lute types with parchment bellies. It was when the wooden-bellied lute was adopted that the instrument was named the *'ūd* ('wood').[2] Before the Persian lute was adopted, the Arabs tuned their lute *B*♭ˡ–*c*ˡ–*f*ˡ–*g*ˡ, but the new Persian accordatura gave it *G*–*c*–*f*–*b*♭. By the ninth century a fifth string, *e*♭ˡ, was added (see pl. 13 (*a*)).[3] A lute of six strings, the *shashtār*, was introduced later, one species of which had sympathetic strings.[4] From the tenth century the *kaitāra* was used in Muslim Spain, perhaps a borrowing from the Mozárabes.[5] A diminutive of this name, *kuwaitira* (vulg. *kuwītira*: Span. *guitarra*), is still used in the Maghrib for a small lute. The *shāhrūd* was an archlute invented in the tenth century; it originally had a compass of three octaves.[6] Another class of lute was the curiously shaped *rubāb* (not to be confused with the bowed *rabāb* as in a misprint in the *Legacy of Islam*, fig. 90), the lower part of the belly being of skin; it was mounted with three to five strings tuned in fourths and was most popular in Persia.[7] The *qūpūz* was a Turko-Greek mandore, hollow throughout, including the neck, and had five double strings.[8] The *shidurghū*, *yātūghān*, and *pīpa* have already been described.

Among pandores the types were innumerable. Al-Fārābī mentions two, the *ṭunbūr baghdādī* (Baghdad pandore) or *ṭunbūr mīzānī* ('measured pandore'),[9] and the *ṭunbūr khurasānī* (Khorasanian pandore). The former had two strings, variously tuned, with a fretted

[1] Farmer, 'An Anonymous English-Arabic Fragment', in *Islamic Culture*, xviii (1944), p. 204; *Kashf al-humūm*, Glasgow University MS. Bi 22-z. 18, fo. 263.

[2] R. d'Erlanger (*La Musique arabe*, i, p. 323) thought that *'ūd* was a translation of the Greek *chelys* which, he said, was a 'tortoise', but the Arabic lexica do not support this. Curt Sachs (*History of Musical Instruments*, p. 253) has attempted to connect the word *'ūd* morphologically with the 'musical bow' of the primitives by making the word equate with 'flexible stick'. This reading is also denied us by the lexicographers.

[3] Farmer, *Studies*, ii, pp. 45–57. Farmer, *Minstrelsy*, pls. 1, 2, 9; R. Lachmann, *Musik des Orients*, pl. 11; T. Arnold and A. Guillaume, fig. 89; A. U. Pope, op. cit., pls. 832C, 850B, 900, 909, 1308, 1316, 1330A, 1353.

[4] Bodleian MS. Marsh 282, fo. 77; Cairo MS. fo. j. 539, *bab* 4, *maq*. 2. Farmer, *Turkish Instruments*, p. 43.

[5] Madrid MS. (Arabic), 603, fo. 15ʳ.

[6] R. d'Erlanger, *La Musique arabe*, i, p. 42–43. Farmer, *History*, frontispiece.

[7] Kings' College (Cambridge) Persian MS., 211, fo. 20; Bodleian MS. Marsh, 282, fo. 78; T. Arnold and A. Guillaume, op. cit., fig. 9; *Encyclopaedia of Islam*, iv, p. 987.

[8] *Encyclopaedia of Islam*, iv, p. 986; Farmer, *Turkish Instruments*, pp. 36–37, and *Studies*, i, pp. 72–75, fig. 25; Bodleian MS. Marsh, 282, f. 77ᵛ.

[9] Al-Khwārizmī, *Mafātīḥ al-'ulūm* (Leiden, 1895), p. 237.

neck which gave a 'pagan scale' of quartertones.[1] The latter also had two strings, the frets being arranged in the order of *limma*, *limma*, and *comma*.[2] In the fourteenth–fifteenth centuries there were innumerable pandores in use, and three may be mentioned. The *ṭunbūr-i shirvīnān* (Shirvanian pandore) had a deep, pear-shaped sound-chest, with a long neck, its two strings being tuned a tone (204 cents) apart; the *ṭunbūra-yi turkī* (Turkish pandore), with a smaller sound-chest but a longer neck, was mounted with two or three strings tuned a fourth (498 cents) apart; both of these were played with the fingers. The *nāy ṭunbūr*, however, was played with a plectrum (*miḍrāb*) like the lute (*'ūd*), and had two strings a fourth apart.[3] The *yūnqār* was a Turkish three-stringed pandore invented by Shamsī Chelebī, a son of the author (d. 1509) of *Yūsuf va zulaika*.[4]

The names, forms, and varieties of instruments in the Islamic east and west of the past are legion, and several volumes would be required to enumerate and describe them fully. How much they were treasured by all, and how rapturously their music was appreciated, can be justly evaluated only by a perusal of the countless lines of poetry alone which have been devoted to their praises.[5]

THE PRACTICAL ART

The chief characteristics of Islamic music were, and are, modal homophony, *fioritura*, and rhythm. From its earliest history this art had been modal, and its systemization with the Arabs seems to have been accomplished by Ibn Misjaḥ (d. *c*. 715). In Syria we are told that he 'took hold' of the ideas of its lute players (*barbaṭiyya*) and theorists (*usṭūkhūsiyya* = στοιχειαταί), while in Iranian lands he learned some of their singing (*ghinā'*) and their rhythmic accompaniment (*ḍarb*). When he returned to the Hijaz he adopted some of these things which he had learned abroad into a new system of music which he founded, although he 'rejected what was disagreeable' in the notes or melodic modes (*nagham*) of Syria and Persia which he considered were 'alien to Arabian music'. We are told that the system formulated by him was thereafter accepted by the people.[6] Yet we see that in spite of these accretions to Arabian music there was still a characteristic indigenous basis.[7]

[1] R. d'Erlanger, *La Musique arabe*, i, pp. 218–42.
[2] Ibid. i, pp. 242–62.
[3] Bodleian MS. Marsh 282, fo. 77v.
[4] *Encyclopaedia of Islam*, v, pp. 251–3; Farmer, *Turkish Instruments*, pp. 34–35.
[5] Al-Nuwairī, *Nihāyāt al-arab* (Cairo, 1923–37), v, pp. 113–22; Shihāb al-Dīn Muḥammad b. Ismā'īl, *Safīnat al-mulk* (Cairo, A.H. 1309), pp. 464 ff.
[6] Farmer, *History*, pp. 71–72.
[7] J. P. N. Land, *Transactions of the Ninth Congress of Orientalists* (London, 1893), p. 156.

This modal system, which Ibn Misjaḥ seems to have consolidated, consisted of eight 'finger modes' (*aṣābiʿ*), as we read in the earliest period of the *Great Book of Songs* (*Kitāb al-aghānī al-kabīr*) of Al-Iṣfahānī (d. 969), and each of these modes was classified according to its 'course' (*majrā*) either with the middle finger (*wusṭā*) on the lute, giving the minor third, or with the third finger (*binṣir*), giving the major third. That these modes may have been suggested by the Syrian *ikhadias* is most likely, but that they were not quite identical may be assumed from Al-Kindī,[1] although the last word has not yet been said on this problem.[2] These 'finger modes' dominated Arabian practical theory until the eleventh century when Persian ideas took a firmer hold on Islamic culture. They have been fully described by Ibn al-Munajjim (d. 912) in his *Risāla fi'l-mūsīqī* (*Treatise about Music*). With one exception (No. 7) all of these modes were identical with the Greek and church modes. They are given here with the fourth string taken as base (*ʿimād*):

1. *Muṭlaq fī majrā al-wusṭā*	G. A. B♭. c. d. e. f. g.
2. *Muṭlaq fī majrā al-binṣir*	G. A. B. c. d. e. f. g.
3. *Sabbāba fī majrā al-wusṭā*	A. B♭. c. d. e. f. g. a.
4. *Sabbāba fī majrā al-binṣir*	A. B. c. d. e. f. g. a.
5. *Wusṭā fī majrāhā*	B♭. c. d. e. f. g. a. b♭.
6. *Binṣir fī majrāhā*	B. c. d. e. f. g. a. b.
7. *Khinṣir fī majrā al-wusṭā*	c. d. e♭. f. g. a. b. c^{1}.
8. *Khinṣir fī majrā al-binṣir*	c. d. e. f. g. a. b. c^{1}.

The rhythmic modes (*īqāʿāt*), and there were eight of these also, are described by Al-Kindī (d. *c.* 874) as follows:

1. *Al-thaqīl al-awwal*
2. *Al-thaqīl al-thānī*
3. *Al-makhūrī*
4. *Khafīf al-thaqīl*
5. *Al-ramal*
6. *Khafīf al-ramal*
7. *Khafīf al-khafīf*
8. *Al-hazaj*

[1] Farmer, *History*, p. 151, and *Historical Facts for the Arabian Musical Influence* (London, 1930), pp. 240–6.

[2] X. M. Collangettes, *Journal Asiatique* (1906), pp. 167–8. The present writer has dealt with the question fully in his *Music in the Kitāb al-aghānī*, still unpublished. Meanwhile consult Farmer, 'The Song Captions in the Kitāb al-aghānī', *Transactions: Glasgow University Oriental Society*, xv (1955).

Each of these modes is given above in its cycle (*daur*) or theme, which is repeated *ad libitum.* It could be varied in its character, as there were several species (*anwāʿ*), just as the order of the notes (*naghamāt*) in the melodic modes (*aṣābiʿ*) did not keep to their scale-like order in performance.

In Persia, as we shall see,[1] the melodic modes were known by fanciful names rather than by descriptive ones, and by the time of Ibn Sīnā (d. 1037) and Ibn Zaila (d. 1048) there were twelve in use.[2] Before long we find these Persian titles being adopted by the Arabs, although one may assume from their names that some agreed with the older 'finger modes' in structure. By the thirteenth century these twelve modes were called *maqāmāt*, and in addition there were six secondary modes called in Persian *avāzāt.*[3] With Turkoman and Mughal sway came branch modes or modal formulas called *shuʿab*,[4] and by the fifteenth century there was a total of forty-eight modes, now entitled *shudūd.*[5] In Muslim Spain it had also become customary to give fanciful names to their twenty-four *ṭubūʿ* or melodic modes, a title which discloses their cosmic affiliation with the four elements (*ṭubūʿ*). As in eastern practice,[6] these western modes, in submission to the doctrine of the *ethos*, were allotted specific times of the day for their performance,[7] a conceit which still prevails.[8] Here are the twelve primary modes (*maqāmāt*) used in Eastern Islamic lands from the thirteenth to the sixteenth century, seven of which have Persian names. They are based on the oldest known manuscript (dated 1276) of the *Sharafiyya* of Ṣafī al-Dīn ʿAbd al-Muʾmin preserved at Berlin. The enharmonic form of these modes is due to the adoption of the scale of the Systematists which proceeded by *limma, limma, comma.* For a clearer apprehension of these new modes a common tonic has been chosen, while the notes have been transcribed into their nearest Occidental equivalent, although the fretting of the lute on p. 463 should be consulted.

ʿUshshāq	c. d. e. f. g. a. b♭. c¹.
Nawā	c. d. e♭. f. g. a♭. b♭. c¹.
Būsalīk	c. d♭. e♭. f. g♭. a♭. b♭. c¹.
Rāst	c d. f♭. f. g. b♭♭. b♭. c¹.

[1] See below.
[2] Farmer, *History*, p. 197.
[3] R. d'Erlanger, op. cit. iii, pp. 135–6.
[4] British Museum MS. Or. 2361, ff. 26–26ᵛ.
[5] R. d'Erlanger, op. cit., pp. 397–401.
[6] Farmer, *History*, p. 204, and *An Old Moorish Lute Tutor*, pp. 38–40.
[7] Farmer, *The Influence of Music: From Arabic Sources, passim.*
[8] A. Chottin, *Tableau de la musique marocaine* (Paris, 1939), p. 123.

'Irāq	c. e♭♭. f♭. f. a♭♭. b♭♭. b♭. d♭♭. c′.
Iṣfahān	c. d. f♭. f. g. b♭♭. b♭. d♭♭. c′.
Zīrāfkand	c. e♭♭. e♭. f. a♭♭. a♭. b♭♭. c♭. c′.
Buzurk	c. e♭♭. f♭. f. a♭♭. g. a. c♭. c′.
Zankūla	c. d. f♭. f. a♭♭. b♭♭. b♭. d♭♭. c′.
Rahāwī	c. e♭♭. f♭. f. a♭♭. a♭. b♭. c′.
Ḥusainī	c. e♭♭. e♭. f. a♭♭. a♭. b♭. c′.
Ḥijāzī	c. e♭♭. f♭. f. a♭♭. b♭♭. b♭. c′.

By the sixteenth century, under Persian influence, the old Pythagorean scale—already flourishing in Persia since the fourteenth century—found acceptance in the Near East. This meant that not only the notes of the *maqāmāt*, *avāzāt*, and *shu'ab* were changed, but their forms also. They were now no longer 'modes' in the commonly understood sense of the term (i.e. scales within the gamut of which melodies were composed) but melodic patterns which became matrices for composition, as one may see from the examples given by Laborde, Villoteau, and Kiesewetter.[1] It may be thought that these patterns restricted originality in composition, but actually they meant no more than the Occidental practice of fixed diatonic sequences.

The second element in Islamic music, *fioriture* (*zawā'id*, *taḥāsīn*, *zuwwāq*), consisted of shakes, grace notes, the drawled scale, *appoggiatura*, and the *tarkīb*. This last device was the occasional decoration of the melody, by striking certain notes simultaneously with their fourth, fifth, or octave. All of this arabesque or festooning gave great licence to performers to display their artistry. Special syllables were set apart for the vocal decoration, such as *lā* and *yā*, although the more conventional *yā lailī* would be just as often used. In the instrumental sphere, one form of decoration was the above-mentioned *tarkīb*. Ibn Sīnā (d. 1035) gave this name *tarkib* (lit. *organum*) to doubling simultaneously with the fifth, fourth, or other interval except the octave which was naturally termed the *taḍ'īf*. The interval of the third is not mentioned specifically, but its use is obviously implied among those 'other' intervals. Many of these are given in a lute exercise by Al-Kindī (d. *c.* 874) which is contained in a unique manuscript in the Staatsbibliothek at Berlin (Ahlwardt, *Verzeichniss*, 5530, fo. 25–31) which is probably a fragment of the work entitled *The Treatise on Music in Relation to the Corporeal Natures* (*Risāla fī . . . al-naghm . . . 'alā ṭabā'i' al-ashkhāṣ*). In it are described two kinds of movements by the plectrum hand and fingers: one which struck

[1] See Vol. II, pp. 42–43, for the parallel Byzantine practice.

two notes *simultaneously* 'with one movement', and another in which three notes were struck *successively* 'with three movements'. Here is this exercise. It opens with a phrase which shows these two movements. This is followed by three simultaneous unisons, obtained by the fourth finger on one string and the open string of another. (See pp. 446, 457.) The remaining phrases explain themselves. The exercise has been transposed.

Ex. 319

The third constituent was rhythm (*īqā'*). By the third quarter of the seventh century this had already been systematized, since we read of four rhythmic modes, and under the Umayyad régime (661–750) two more had been added.[1] By the ninth or tenth century there were seven or eight principal (*uṣūl*) rhythmic modes used by the Mesopotamian and Syrian Arabs as described by Al-Kindī[2] and Al-Fārābī.[3] By the days of Ṣafī al-Dīn 'Abd al-Mu'min (d. 1294), the Persians had added some modes of their own devising.[4] When Turkomanian and Turkish influence made itself felt in the Near and Middle East, new rhythms in galore were tapped out, and the craze for novelty grew apace. By the fifteenth century there were no fewer than twenty-one rhythmic modes,[5] while Al-Lādhiqī (*c.* 1481–1512) gives a total of thirty.[6]

In the eyes and ears of the Arabs, vocal music was superior to instrumental, and this preference lasted until the final scenes depicted in the monumental work of Al-Iṣfahānī (d. 967). After that, Persian, Turkomanian, Mughal, and Turkish tastes brought instrumental music more to the fore. How important was the vocal art may be gleaned from Al-Fārābī who devoted a section to 'production'—head notes, chest notes, nasalized notes, and so on; adverting to the glottal hiatus (*nabara*), and the whys and hows of the staccato notes (*shadharāt*) and long-vowel notes (*amālāt*), as well as the various

[1] Farmer, *History*, p. 71. To Al-Khalīl (d. *c.* 791) a 'Book of Rhythm' (*Kitāb al-īqā'*) has been attributed. See Farmer, *Sources*, p. 14.

[2] Farmer, *Sa'adyah Gaon*, pp. 78–99, which contains the notation of the rhythmic modes.

[3] R. d'Erlanger, op. cit. ii, pp. 40–48.

[4] Ibid. iii, pp. 172–8.

[5] Ibid. iii, pp. 183–232.

[6] Ibid. iv, pp. 470–98.

forms of songs.[1] Dynamics, as we understand the term, had no existence in Islamic music, which was essentially a quiescent art, and its instruments, whether for solo work or accompaniment were, of necessity, in accordance with this tranquility; indeed we must always think of this art in terms of chamber music.[2] It is true that we sometimes read of fifty or so lutenists playing together, but such occurrences were unusual.[3] Throughout the book of Al-Iṣfahānī it is generally the lute, flute, or reed-pipe that is displayed, and the well-known miniature which accompanies the story of Isḥāq al-Mauṣilī in the *Maqāmāt* of Al-Ḥarīrī (d. 1122) shows only a lute and reed-pipe.[4] In the later *Arabian Nights*[5] and in the subsequent miniatures of Persian art, more bounteous instrumental displays are granted: the lute, flute, psaltery, reed-pipe, viol, and harp in concert. Of course, these combinations invariably included the tambourine or drum, since these determined the rhythm, although not all music was submitted to this mensural discipline.

The forms of musical composition were various. The *nashīd*, originally a nasal psalming was, in the time of Al-Fārābī, unrhythmic,[6] but later it was submitted to rhythm.[7] The *basīt*, of light character, was a vocal piece with an instrumental prelude (*ṭarīqa*), although it was set later to more imposing rhythms.[8] The *ḍarb* was a composition in which two rhythmic modes were used simultaneously. Some lengthy compositions were to be found in the *kull al-ḍurūb* and the *kull al-nagham*, which implied, respectively, the use of all the rhythmic modes and all the melodic modes in sequence.

Among the Persians, Khorasanians, and Turkomans of the tenth century, instrumental pieces known as the *ṭarā'iq* and *rawāsīn* were immensely popular.[9] Later it was the *'amal*, *naqsh*, *ṣaut*, *hawā'ī*, and *muraṣṣa'* which were in demand. The first was of a composite nature and opened with a prelude. The second, as its name tells us, had 'decoration' as its characteristic. The last two had much in common by way of their fantasia-like construction. The most important of all was the 'suite' called the *nauba*. This seems to have originated at the 'Abbāsid court, where the performers who attended at special hours on particular days, played in succession (*nauba*), and since each minstrel usually excelled in some particular type of music, a combination of these features into one performance or piece was named a

[1] R. d'Erlanger, *La Musique arabe*, ii, pp. 79 ff.
[2] Farmer, *Oriental Studies: Mainly Musical* (London, 1953), p. 58.
[3] Farmer, *History*, pp. 72, 102.
[4] Farmer, *Minstrelsy*, pls. 1, 8.
[5] Ibid., p. 6.
[6] R. d'Erlanger, op. cit. ii, p. 94.
[7] Ibid. iv, p. 233.
[8] Ibid. iv, p. 235.
[9] Ibid. i, p. 17.

nauba.[1] Up to the fourteenth century the *nauba* comprised four movements, the *qaul*, *ghazal*, *tarāna*, and *furū-dāsht*, but in the year 1379, 'Abd al-Qādir b. Ghaibī introduced a fifth movement called the *mustazād.*[2] Each of these sections, which were vocal, was preceded by an instrumental prelude (*ṭarīqa*). Later still, the instrumental *chef d'œuvre* known as the *pishrev* (Ar. *bashrau*) was used as an overture to the *nauba*. In Muslim Spain the *nauba gharnaṭī*, as it is now called, was known in its twenty-four modes.[3] The eastern *nauba* was carried on by the Ottoman Turks and had constituent parts not unlike the 'suite' of Persia.[4]

What the Islamic music of these days was actually like is not easy to determine because of the mere scrap which has come down to us, and even this presents on paper less vitality than our transcription of the neumatically notated compositions of the early Christian Church. It has been stated that the *Great Book of Songs* of Isḥāq al-Mauṣilī contained music.[5] This is quite fallacious. At the same time it is equally erroneous to state that the 'Arabs never had a musical notation'.[6] In early days, neither the Arabs or Persians committed their compositions to paper as a general rule, although Ibn Sīnā tells us that a stenography was used by practitioners for this purpose.[7] Yet the theorists from the time of Al-Kindī used an alphabetic notation.[8] It is not until the thirteenth century, however, that we have examples of music recorded by this means, and the present writer has published two specimens,[9] while other examples exist in the works of 'Abd al-Qādir b. Ghaibī (d. 1435).[10] In these compositions the pitch of the notes is determined by an alphabetic notation and the mensural values by a numerical one. Meanwhile a semi-staff notation arose farther east in Khwārizm where, in the time of the Shāh 'Alā al-Dīn Muḥammad (d. 1220), an eighteen-line stave was used to carry a pitch and mensural notation.[11] It was not unlike the early attempts of western Europe.[12] In Syria we know from

[1] *Encyclopaedia of Islam*, iii, pp. 855–7.
[2] R. d'Erlanger, op. cit. iv, pp. 236–8.
[3] Farmer, *An Old Moorish Lute Tutor*, pp. 19–24; *Encyclopaedia of Islam*, iii, pp. 386–7.
[4] *Encyclopaedia of Islam*, iii, p. 386.
[5] Phyllis Ackerman, in A. U. Pope, *A Survey of Persian Art* (1939), p. 2812.
[6] *Grove's Dictionary of Music* (1940), i, p. 66.
[7] Farmer, *Historical Facts*, p. 91.
[8] Ibid., pp. 312 ff.
[9] Farmer, *History*, p. 202, and *Minstrelsy*, frontispiece.
[10] Bodleian MS. Marsh 282, ff. 93v–95.
[11] V. Belaiev, 'Khoresmian Notation', *The Sackbut*, iv (1924), p. 171, and 'Turkomanian Music', *Promusica*, v (1927), p. 4.
[12] M. Gerbert, *Scriptores* (St. Blaise, 1784), i, p. 157.

a treatise by Shams al-Dīn al-Saiḍawī al-Dhahabī (16th. cent.) that a more practical scheme had been evolved in which a stave of seven to nine coloured horizontal lines served for this purpose,[1] a device somewhat similar to that shown in eastern Europe by Vincenzo Galilei (1581) and Kircher (1650).[2]

At the period when the Arabs and Persians wrote music by means of an alphabetic (*abjadī*) and numeric (*ʿadadī*) notation, the former stood for the pitch of the note (*naghma*) whilst the latter represented its mensural (*mīzānī*) extent. Reference to the fretting of the lute (*ʿūd*) on p. 463, where the accordatura (*taswiyya*) is *G–c–f–b♭–e♭*ʹ, will explain the reason for introducing the special flat sign to indicate the minor tone of 180 cents which is a *comma* lower than the whole tone of 204 cents, reserving the ordinary flat ♭ to indicate a note which is a *limma* of 90 cents.

Here is one verse (*bait* = stanza) of a song (*ṣaut*) taken from the *Kitāb al-adwār*, said to have been written before 1236, but more probably twenty years later, by Ṣafī al-Dīn ʿAbd al-Muʾmin (d. 1294). It is in the melodic mode (*ṭarīqa*) of *kuwāsht*, set to the rhythmic mode (*ḍarb*) of the *ramal al-ḍiyyā*, better known as the *khafīf ramal*. The transcription is made from the British Museum Manuscript Or. 2361, fo. 32, but with the copyist's errors rectified by comparison with other manuscripts. This has meant changing the minims for the syllables *ba-ti* into crotchets. That was necessary on account of the measure. The melody has been transposed. (See upper part of pl. 14 (*a*).)

Ex. 320

('Desertion, by Allāh, I cannot abjure, Though some, the loss of a lover could endure!')

[1] Bodleian MS. Marsh 82, ff. 70–73; J. B. de la Borde, *Essai sur la musique* (Paris, 1780), i, pp. 183–90; J. P. N. Lard, 'Tonschriftversuche und Melodieproben aus dem muhammedanischen Mittelalter', *Vierteljahrsschrift für Musikwissenschaft*, ii (1886), pp. 348–50.

[2] Farmer, *Historical Facts*, pp. 323–6.

The rhythmic modes had changed considerably since the time of Al-Kindī (see p. 448) and those shown in these examples on a single stave line under the melody, would have been performed on a tambourine (*dā'ira*) with jingling metal plates (*ṣunūj*) or bells (*jalājil*) in the frame, a drum (*ṭabl*), or tiny kettledrums (*nuqairāt*). Two or more tones were obtained on these instruments, one of them low and strong and the other high and weak. In addition to these the plectrum (*miḍrāb*), by which the strings of the lute were pulsated, also obeyed this rhythm when it was convenient. Since the rhythmic phrase (*daur*) of the *ramal* mode comprised twelve beats it has enabled us to submit the music to the un-Oriental custom of using a time signature and bars. Here is a theme in the old mode known as the *mujannab al-ramal*. (See lower part of pl. 14(*a*).)

Ex. 321

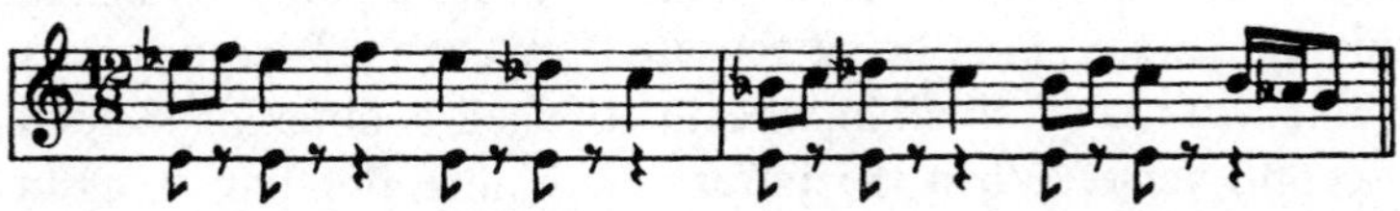

The last example is the melody of a hemistich (*miṣrā'*) of the first verse of a song called *'Alā ṣabbikum*. It is in the *naurūz* melodic mode and the *ramal* rhythmic mode. This is also from the *Kitāb al-adwār* of Ṣafī al-Dīn 'Abd al-Mu'min, although the transcription is made from a different manuscript in the British Museum, viz. Or. 136, fo. 38v. The contour of the melody, being plain and simple, may appear to be quite uninteresting in itself. In performance, however, when the singer and players introduced *fioriture*, a far more intriguing picture would have been presented. These ornaments were termed *taḥāsīn*, and since the cleverness of singer and instrumentalist was judged by their ingenuity in the use of *fioriture* it is no wonder that 'applause' and 'approbation' went by the name of *taḥsīn*. Here is this melody. (See pl. 14(*b*).)

Ex. 322.

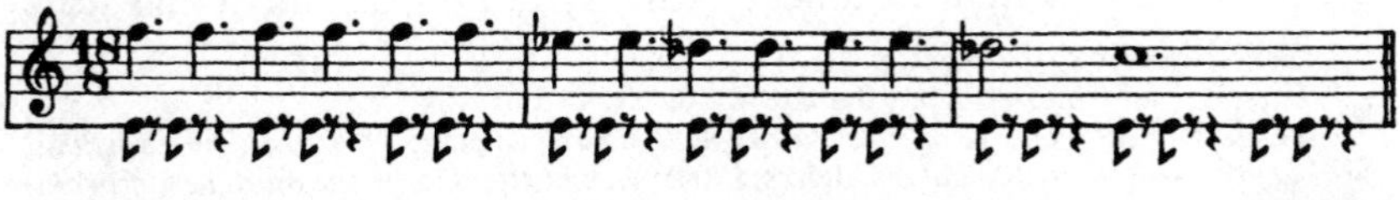

In view of the above it is evident that we possess no written Arabian music earlier than the thirteenth century, no Persian before the fourteenth century, and no similar example of Turkish music prior to the seventeenth. On the other hand, there is an enormous amount of music handed down orally and by rote. The Maulawiyya darwīsh fraternities claim to use music composed by Al-Fārābī.[1] One of the movements of the Turkish suite (*faṣl*) known as the *kiār* contains, in most of its modes, examples of the works of 'Abd al-Qādir b. Ghaibī (d. 1435), and although these, like what has preceded, have also been handed down orally, they may be more authentic since the composer's *Treasury of Melodies* (*Kanz al-alḥān*), which contained his compositions, existed until recent years.[2] Lastly, the *naubāt andalusiyya* or *gharnaṭiyya* (i.e. of 'Andalusia' or 'Granada'), still played in the Maghrib handed down by the refugees of the expulsions of the 'Moors' from Spain, exist in many specimens,[3] although those in the *sīka* and *jahārka* modes cannot be earlier than the sixteenth century and cannot be Andalusian.

Finally, there is the question of form. Since every verse in Arabic poetry contains a complete thought, a short melody was made to fit this alone, the same being repeated for each subsequent verse. It was Ibn Muḥriz (d. *c.* 715) who introduced a different melody for the second verse. When the refrain came into popularity, as in the *zajal* in Spain, this also necessitated a different melody. Yet although these short melodies were repeated times out of number, especially in a classical ode (*qaṣīda*), they were not always used in precisely the same form, since it was in its variation that the singer, in his handling of the 'gloss' or *fioritura*, was able to display his artistry and originality. It was much the same in instrumental music.

THE THEORY OF MUSIC

That Islamic savants were supremely gifted in the field of mathematics is universally acknowledged,[4] and they were especially so in the science of music (*'ilm al-mūsīqī*).[5] At the threshold we meet with what Al-Fārābī (d. *c.* 950) calls a 'pagan scale', i.e. a scale from pre-Islamic times.[6] It was to be found on a fretted instrument called the *ṭunbūr mīzānī* (measured pandore) or *ṭunbūr baghdādī* (Baghdad pandore). Its fingerboard was divided into forty equal parts, the frets giving a scale of quarter tones.[7] Although this instrument and scale

[1] *Encyclopaedia of Islam*, ii, p. 54.

[2] Personal information from the late Ra'ūf Yektā Bey.

[3] N. E. Yafil, *Répertoire de musique arabe et maure* (Algiers, 1904); *Majmū' al-aghānī wa'l-alḥān min kalām al-andalus* (Algiers, 1904); A. Chottin, *Corpus de musique marocaine* (Paris, 1931); Rouanet, op. cit., pp. 2845–77.

[4] *Encyclopaedia of Islam*, i, pp. 989–90; ii, pp. 257–8, 315–16; T. Arnold and A. Guillaume, *The Legacy of Islam*, pp. 376–97.

[5] *Encyclopaedia of Islam*, iii, pp. 749–55.

[6] R. d'Erlanger, *La Musique arabe*, i, p. 227.

[7] Ibid. i, p. 218. The interval was known to Eratosthenes. See Ptolemy, *Harmonicorum* (Oxford, 1682), ii, p. 14.

persisted in Islamic civilization until the fifteenth century, seemingly only for the performance of those 'pagan melodies' of which Al-Fārābī speaks, its place in the evolution of the Arabian scale is vague. What sort of scale obtained in the early days of Islam, when the system of Ibn Misjaḥ (d. *c.* 715) was established, we have no certain knowledge, but all evidence seems to show that it was the Pythagorean. It was not until the time of Isḥāq al-Mauṣilī (d. 850) that we get a complete view of the theory and scale of the Old Arabian School. Possibly two early works may have dealt with this system, the *Book of Melody* (*Kitāb al-naghm*) of Yūnus al-Kātib (d. *c.* 765) and the *Book of Melody* by the father of prosody Al-Khalīl b. Aḥmad (d. *c.* 791), but none of these has been spared for us.[1] In any case, these works would have been based on what I have frequently termed 'practical theory', in contradistinction from 'scientific theory'. Indeed, a later writer, Ibn al-Munajjim (d. 912), very aptly distinguished between these two schools of theorists as 'the masters of Arabian music (*ghinā'*)' and 'the masters of [Greek] music (*mūsīqī*)'.[2] In the Old Arabian School, all theory was made to conform to the lute, in the same way as the Greeks used the *kithara* for this purpose. According to Isḥāq al-Mauṣilī and his pupils Ibn al-Munajjim and Ibn Khurdādhbih, the scale of this school was Pythagorean, and here is the fretting of its lute in cents:[3]

	4th string (*bamm*)	3rd string (*mathlath*)	2nd string (*mathnā*)	1st string (*zīr*)
Open string (*muṭlaq*)	0	498	996	294
1st finger (*sabbāba*)	204	702	1200	498
2nd finger (*wusṭā*)	294	792	90	588
3rd finger (*binṣir*)	408	906	204	702
4th finger (*khinṣir*)	498	996	294	792
				[906]
				996

[1] *Isis*, xxxvi (1946), p. 128.

[2] Farmer, *Historical Facts*, p. 243.

[3] *Cents* are hundredths of an equal semitone. It has been stated that Isḥāq al-Mauṣilī's accordatura of the Arabian lute gave a fifth (702 cents) between the third and second strings. I have shown this to be completely erroneous; the tuning was by fourths (498 cents) throughout. See my *Historical Facts for the Arabian Musical Influence* (London, 1930), pp. 280–5, and cf. the persistent views of Kathleen Schlesinger in *The Greek*

Prior to this, certain alien elements had entered the scale. Persian practitioners had been using their own second finger fret (303 cents), and a certain instrumentalist at Baghdad, Zalzal (d. 791), had introduced a neutral third (355 cents). Confusion and embarrassment followed these innovations, and it was to rectify the position, it would seem, that Isḥāq al-Mauṣilī recast the theory of the old Arabian school into its original Pythagorean mould, which was accomplished, we are told, without recourse to the Greek theorists who were unknown in Arabic at that date.[1]

By the middle of the ninth century the famous treatises of the Greeks were translated, some through Syriac, into Arabic, and most of them had appeared before the close of the century. Aristotle's *De anima*, the *Problemata*, and other works of his were well known. The *Harmonica* of Aristoxenus which we possess today is known to have been constructed from two works, the *στοιχεῖα* and the *ἀρχαί*.[2] That the latter was a separate work existing in the ninth century is evidenced by the translated Arabic work, the *Kitāb al-ru'ūs*, as was demonstrated in 1928.[3] That his lost work on rhythm also existed in Arabic at this time is shown by his *Kitāb al-īqā'* (*Book of Rhythm*). Euclid was known by a *Kitāb al-naghm* called *al-mūsīqī*, which was obviously the *Introductio harmonica*, now attributed to Cleonides, and a *Kitāb al-qānūn* which was clearly the *Sectio canonis*. Nicomachus appeared in Arabic in more than one book. The present *Enchiridion* which we possess in Greek includes fragments from another treatise, unknown, but the Arabic book of Nicomachus, the *Kitāb al-mūsīqī al-kabīr* (*Opus Major on Music*) proves that he did write that 'larger work' which he had promised in the *Enchiridion*. That the *Harmonica* of Ptolemy was also translated into Arabic there is considerable evidence, and it is likely that Aristides Quintilianus was similarly represented. In addition there were commentaries on Aristotle's *De anima* by Themistius and Alexander of Aphrodisias, as well as other works, that were known in Arabic.[4]

The first-fruits of this epoch-making harvest by the *Bait al-ḥikma* or 'House of Wisdom', as this school of translators at Baghdad was called, was the interest taken in music by the 'philosopher of the Arabs', Al-Kindī, whose extant treatises on the theory of music

Aulos (London, 1939), pp. 274–90, 537–40, in spite of my protests.

[1] Al-Iṣfahānī, op. cit. v, p. 53; British Museum MS. Or. 2361, f. 237v.

[2] Cf. pp. 342–3.

[3] Farmer, 'Greek Theorists of Music in Arabic Translation', *Isis*, xiii (1930), p. 326. (A paper read before the 17th Congress of Orientalists, Oxford, 1928.)

[4] Farmer, *Sources*, pp. 23–30.

reveal his dependence on Greek theory.[1] Other leading scholars then crowded into the arena of music theory: Al-Sarakhsī (d. 899), Thābit b. Qurra (d. 901), Muḥammad b. Zakariyyā al-Rāzī (d. 932), Qusṭa b. Lūqā (d. 932), and the famous Al-Fārābī.[2] Only the works of the first and last have survived the holocausts of the past. Al-Kindī was well acquainted with Euclid, and probably with Ptolemy also. Indeed his *Book of the Division of the Canon* (*Kitāb fī qismat al-qānūn*) was most likely a commentary on Euclid's work. Ziryāb, in Muslim Spain, had already added a fifth string to the lute, and Al-Kindī did likewise in the east, so as to enable him to reach the *jamā'at al-tāmma* (σύστημα τέλειον). He then sought to introduce a semitonal fret called the 'anterior' (*mujannab*) between the nut and the first finger fret, but owing to the fixed fretting of the lute, his innovation presented a difficulty in that while the new fret, giving an interval called the *baqiyya* (90 cents), i.e. the Greek *limma*, fitted in admirably on the fourth, third, and second strings, it was flat by a *comma* of 24 cents on the first and the new 'extra' strings. To obviate this he added another fret of an interval called the *infiṣāl*, the Pythagorean *apotomē* (114 cents) which, although not used on the three lower strings, gave the desired notes on the two higher strings, thus:[3]

	4th string	3rd string	2nd string	1st string	Extra string (*zīr thānī*)
Open string (*muṭlaq*)	0	498	996	294	792
1st finger (*mujannab* 1)	90	—588	—1086	—[384]	—[882]
1st finger (*mujannab* 2)	[114]	—[612]	-[1110]	—408	—906
1st finger (*sabbāba*)	204	—702	—1200	—498	—996
2nd finger (*wusṭā*)	294	—792	—90	—588	—1086
3rd finger (*binṣir*)	408	—906	—204	—702	—1200
4th finger (*khinṣir*)	498	—996	—294	—792	——

[1] Farmer, *The Influence of Music: From Arabic Sources*, pp. 101–3; *History*, pp. 151–3; *Sa'adyah Gaon*, pp. 12–16; R. Lachmann and M·el-Hefnī, *Ja'qūb Ibn Isḥāq al-Kindī* (Leipzig, 1931), *passim*.

[2] Farmer, *Sources*, pp. 19–36.

[3] Farmer, *Studies*, ii, pp. 47–48. This, and the above fretting of the lute of Isḥāq al-Mauṣilī (d. 850), disposes of the gratuitous assumption of Willi Apel that 'Al-Fārābī [d. *c.* 950] introduced a new scale based on the interval of the fourth . . . 0–204–294–408–498', *Harvard Dictionary of Music* (Harvard, 1944), p. 45.

Al-Kindī's scale reveals that the Persian and Zalzalian accretions at 303 and 355 cents had lost recognition in Mesopotamia, and this inhibition partly continued, as we know from the *Risālat al-mūsiqī* of the Ikhwān al-Ṣafā (*c*. 980).[1] In Syria, however, these anomalies were at least acknowledged, together with their concomitant notes, as we see in Al-Fārābī:[2]

	4th string	3rd string	2nd string	1st string	Extreme string (*ḥadd*)
Open string (*muṭlaq*)	0	498	996	294	792
1st finger (old *mujannab*)	90	588	1086	384	882
1st finger (Persian *mujannab*)	145	643	1141	439	937
1st finger (Zalzal's *mujannab*)	168	666	1164	462	960
1st finger (*sabbāba*)	204	702	1200	498	996
2nd finger (old *wusṭā*)	294	792	90	588	1086
2nd finger (Persian *wusṭā*)	303	801	99	597	1095
2nd finger (Zalzal's *wusṭā*)	355	853	151	649	1147
3rd finger (*binṣir*)	408	906	204	702	1200
4th finger (*khinṣir*)	498	996	294	792	—

The above scheme represents all the intervals recognized in lute playing at this period, and does not necessarily imply that any one lute was so fretted. According to Muḥammad b. Aḥmad al-Khwārizmī (*fl.* 976–7), writing in Khorasan and Transoxiana, the Persian and Zalzalian thirds were being used in those lands, revealing how far afield they had been accepted.[3] Al-Fārābī was a good mathematician and physicist, and his *Grand Book of Music* (*Kitāb al-mūsīqī al-kabīr*) is not only 'the most important treatise on the theory of Oriental music',[4] but the greatest work on music which had been written up to his time. He was certainly in advance of the Greeks.[5] Later came the Ikhwān al-Ṣafā (*c*. 980), whose contribution

[1] F. Dieterici, op. cit., pp. 118–20.
[2] Farmer, *Studies*, ii, pp. 49–50.
[3] *Mafātīḥ al-'ulūm*, pp. 240–2; Farmer, *Studies*, ii, p. 50.
[4] *Encyclopaedia of Islam*, ii, p. 54.
[5] Baron Carra de Vaux, in R. d'Erlanger, *La Musique arabe*, i, pp. vii–xi.

to acoustics is noteworthy.[1] In Egypt a great physicist, the Alhazen of European fame, more properly Ibn al-Haitham (d. 1039), wrote a *Commentary on* [*Cleonides*'] *Harmonics* (*Maqāla fī sharḥ al-*[*a*]*rmūniqī*) and a *Commentary on Euclid's Canon* (*Kitāb sharḥ qānūn Uqlaidis*), both of which have unfortunately perished.[2]

In Persia there appeared the works of the famous Avicenna, i.e. Ibn Sīnā (d. 1037), *The Cure* (*al-Shifā*), and *The Deliverance* (*al-Najāt*), which contain full information on the state of musical theory in Iranian lands, as does the *Book of Sufficiency in Music* (*Kitāb al-kāfī fi'l-mūsīqī*) of Ibn Zaila (d. 1048). Ibn Sīnā does not appear to have accepted Al-Kindī's solution of the difficulty of the 'anterior' (*mujannab*) fret at 90 cents by duplicating it at 114 cents. Further, he assigns 343 cents for Zalzal's second finger (*wusṭā*) fret, with its 'anterior' fellow at 139 cents. Nor does he admit the 'anterior' fret at 90 cents, but furnishes the just semitone of 112 cents in its place. Yet he realized that the normal tuning of the lute in fourths would not produce Zalzal's second finger fret in the second octave, and to remedy this he suggested an alternative *accordatura* (*taswiyya*). By tuning the 1st string (*zīr*) a major third (408 cents) higher than the 2nd string (*mathnā*), instead of a fourth (498 cents), Zalzal's intractable notes were regularized as follows:[3]

	4th string	3rd string	2nd string	1st string	Extreme string
Open string (*muṭlaq*)	0	498	996	204	702
1st finger (*mujannab*)	112	610	1108	316	814
1st finger (Zalzal's *mujannab*)	139	637	1135	343	841
1st finger (*sabbāba*)	204	702	1200	408	906
2nd finger (Persian *wusṭā*)	294	792	90	498	996
2nd finger (Zalzal's *wusṭā*)	343	841	139	547	1045
3rd finger (*binṣir*)	408	906	204	612	1110
4th finger (*khinṣir*)	498	996	294	702	1200

[1] *Encyclopaedia of Islam*, iii, p. 752.

[2] Farmer, *Sources*, p. 42; 'Greek Theorists of Music', *Isis*, xiii (1930), p. 331.

[3] Farmer, *Studies*, ii, pp. 54–57; R. d'Erlanger, op. cit. ii, pp. 234–6; M. el-Hefnī, *Ibn Sina's Musiklehre* (Berlin, 1930), pp. 71–73.

In other parts of the Islamic East there were many more who were interested in music theory, and in Syria there flourished Ibn al-Naqqāsh (d. 1178), Abu'l-Ḥakam al-Bāhilī and his son Abu'l-Majd Muḥammad (d. 1180), as well as 'Alam al-Dīn Qaiṣar (d. 1251).[1] In Muslim Spain there was a long run of theorists beginning with Ibn Firnās (d. 888), 'the first who taught the science of music in al-Andalus'.[2] In the tenth century (?), 'Alī b. Sa'īd al-Andalusī compiled a book *On the Composition of Melodies* [*Risāla fī ta'līf al-alḥān*].[3] Greater still were the savants of the twelfth century, when Ibn Bājja or Avenpace (d. 1139) wrote a *Book of Music* (*Kitāb al-mūsīqī*), and the *Commentary on Aristotle's 'De anima'* (*Sharḥ fi'l-nafs li Arisṭūṭālis*) of Ibn Rushd or Averroës (d. 1198) was famous in its day, especially in Latin.[4] In the east both Fakhr al-Dīn al-Rāzī (d. 1209) and Naṣīr al-Dīn al-Ṭūsī (d. 1273) wrote on music,[5] the contribution of the former being found in his *Collector of the Sciences* (*Jāmi' al-'ulūm*).[6]

In Baghdad, in the service of the last of the 'Abbāsid caliphs, was the greatest musician of his day, Ṣafī al-Dīn 'Abd al-Mu'min (d. 1294), whose two works on theory, *The Sharafian Treatise on Harmonic Relations* (*Risālat al-sharafiyya fī nisab al-ta'līfiyya*) and the *Book of Modes* (*Kitāb al-adwār*), made history.[7] He was the founder, or organizer, of the Systematist school of music theory, a circumstance which has earned him the title of 'the Zarlino of the Orient',[8] while Helmholtz considered his theories to be 'noteworthy in the history of music'.[9] He derived his scale from the Khorasanian pandore, whose successive frets of *limma, limma, comma* have been detailed by Al-Fārābī.[10] How Ṣafī al-Dīn used it on the lute is shown on the opposite page.[11] One can see at a glance that this scale affords consonances purer than our tempered system,[12] and Sir Hubert Parry considered it 'the most perfect scale ever devised'.[13] It was this system that led so many writers to refer erroneously to the existence of 'thirds of a tone' in Arabian and Persian music.

[1] Farmer, *History*, pp. 223–5.
[2] Al-Maqqarī, op. cit. i, p. 148.
[3] Farmer, *Sources*, p. 39; and *History*, p. 177.
[4] Farmer, *Sources*, p. 44.
[5] Ibid., pp. 45, 47.
[6] British Museum MS. Or. 2972, ff. 151^{v}–155^{r}.
[7] *Encyclopaedia of Islam*, v, pp. 191–2; R. d'Erlanger, op. cit. iii, pp. v–xiv. See pl. 13.
[8] R. G. Kiesewetter, *Die Musik der Araber* (Leipzig, 1842), p. 13.
[9] *The Sensations of Tone* (London, 1895), p. 283.
[10] R. d'Erlanger, *La Musique arabe*, i, pp. 242–62.
[11] Ibid. iii, pp. 371, ff.; Carra de Vaux, *Le Traité des rapports musicaux* (Paris, 1891), pp. 52–58.
[12] Riemann, *Catechism of Musical History*, ii (London, 1892), p. 65.
[13] *The Art of Music* (London, 1896), p. 29.

	4th string	3rd string	2nd string	1st string	Extreme string
Open string (*muṭlaq*)	0	══498	══996	══294	══792
1st finger (*zaid*)	90	—588	—1086	—384	—882
1st finger (*mujannab*)	180	—678	—1176	—474	—972
1st finger (*sabbāba*)	204	—702	—1200	—498	—996
2nd finger (Persian *wusṭā*)	294	—792	—90	—588	—1086
2nd finger (Zalzal's *wusṭā*)	384	—882	—180	—678	—1176
3rd finger (*binṣir*)	408	—906	—204	—702	—1200
4th finger (*khinṣir*)	498	—996	—294	—792	——

This theory soon enveloped both the Near and Middle East, where we see it fully utilized by the Persian theorists Quṭb al-Dīn al-Shīrāzī (d. 1310) in his *Jewel of the Crown* (*Durrat al-tāj*)[1] and by Muḥammad b. Maḥmūd al-Āmulī (fourteenth century) in his *Precious Things of the Sciences* (*Nafā'is al-funūn*).[2] It was also the basis of the Persian *Treasure-house of Rarities* (*Kanz al-tuḥaf*) of the same century,[3] and the prompting of that masterly Arabic treatise entitled the *Maulānā Mubārak Shāh Commentary* by Al-Jurjānī (d. 1413).[4] It was the sheet-anchor of the Persian *Collector of Melodies* (*Jāmi' al-alḥān*) of 'Abd al-Qādir b. Ghaibī (d. 1435),[5] the Arabic *Muḥammad b. Murād Treatise*,[6] and the book called *The Conqueror* (*Al-Fatḥiyya*) by Al-Lādhiqī a few decades later.[7] The same dependence is traceable in the Turkish *Book of Modes* (*Kitāb al-adwār*) of Khiḍr b. 'Abdallāh,[8] and the treatise of Aḥmad Ughlū Shukrallāh.[9]

Side by side with this systematist theory there was still to be found the occasional expression in Persia of the less intricate teaching of the old Arabian school, the occurrence of which led Kiesewetter to

[1] British Museum MS. Add 7694.

[2] Ibid., Add. 16827.

[3] Ibid., Or. 2361.

[4] R. d'Erlanger, op. cit. iii, *passim*, especially the preface by the present writer.

[5] Bodleian MS. Marsh 282, *passim*.

[6] British Museum MS. Or. 2361, ff.

[7] R. d'Erlanger, op. cit., iv, *passim*.

[8] Berlin MS. See J. G. L. Kosegarten, *Alii Ispahanensis Liber Cantilenarum Magnus* (Greifswald, 1840), p. 36.

[9] Information from the late Ra'ūf Yektā Bey.

imagine that it was introduced by Christian missionaries.[1] Yet, as Helmholtz said of this suggestion: 'The Europeans of those days could teach the Orientals nothing that they did not know better themselves, except some rudiments of harmony which they did not want.'[2] The teachings of the systematist school lasted in the Near East until the sixteenth century when the old Arabian system, i.e. the Pythagorean, found acceptance once more. Yet the longing for the diverse chromaticisms of the past, especially such variants as the minor tone (180) and the Systematists Zalzalian third (384), which had coloured their music and charmed their ears in the past had not died, and it was that yearning which gave birth to the modern quarter-tone system.

THE INFLUENCE

Most historians have allowed that it was to the Arabs and Persians that 'the mediaeval world, from Samarcand to Seville, for a very long time, owed its highest literary and scientific culture'.[3] It would not be too much to add 'artistic culture'. That this great artistic urge, which included music, should have made itself felt in the neighbouring east is easily understood, because many of these lands had much in common culturally. It is true that the Arabs borrowed a few technical musical words from the Persians, as well as the accomplishments which these terms implied, but the Persians returned the compliment by adopting the entire Arabic musical nomenclature. That both India and Turkestan borrowed innumerable instruments and technical practices through Arab–Persian persuasion is evident to this day. One can also appreciate why peoples culturally inferior, overwhelmed by the impact of Islam, should also be unable to resist its musical influence. We find this with the Berbers of North Africa, the Negroes of the western Sudan, the Swahili on the East African coast, and the Malagasy, who have all been borrowers from this fount, while the names of musical instruments in distant Celebes, Borneo, Java, and even 'Far Cathay' carry evidence of their origin.

In Europe Islamic cultural influence took a different turn. Greece, at Europe's eastern outpost, had always been absorbent of Oriental ideas, and so was Byzantium.[4] Not a single Byzantine theoretical work

[1] *Die Musik der Araber*, pp. 14, 46–49. Through a misunderstanding of the Arabic term *mithl*, which Kiesewetter called *Messel*, a host of writers have given the unmeaning title of 'Messel system' to the theory standardized by Ṣafī al-Dīn 'Abd al-Mu'min, while prompting others to refer erroneously to the scale of the latter as comprising 'third tones' (*Dritteltöne*).

[2] Op. cit., p. 285.

[3] R. A. Nicholson, *A Literary History of the Arabs* (London, 1914), pp. 446–7.

[4] *Cambridge Mediaeval History*, iv (Cambridge, 1923), pp. 152, 773.

on music was put forward from the time of Anonymus II (fourth century) until Psellos (*fl.* 1050); it was only the Arabic authors who were producing works of speculative theory.[1] We know that it was the Greek Mūrisṭus manuscripts, translated into Arabic, which brought about the revival of the *hydraulus* in Byzantium and western Europe, when Muslim constructors began to build this instrument from the long-forgotten Mūrisṭus designs.[2] Byzantium continued to be the highway by which many other 'Saracen arts' came to the West.[3] As late as the Crusades Christian Europe, impressed by the use of the Saracen military band, made it a part of its own martial tactics.[4]

The more important impress of Islamic civilization on Europe was due to the presence of Muslims in the Iberian peninsula, Sicily, and elsewhere. Spain, which was in Muslim hands, more or less, from the eighth to the fifteenth century, became the centre from which this new culture radiated to the rest of Europe. Indeed it is to this land that we must turn for some of the influences which directly affected the Renaissance.[5] The poverty of Christian Europe in the sphere of music theory and its stagnation in the practical field are suggested by the fact that from the end of the sixth century to the mid-ninth century no work on theory appeared in western Europe.[6] While Europe only knew the Greek theorists through scraps interpreted by Martianus Capella, Boëthius, and Cassiodorus, the Muslims possessed complete Arabic translations of Aristotle, Aristoxenus, Nicomachus, Euclid, Cleonides, and probably Ptolemy and Aristides Quintilianus.[7] Muslim theorists themselves, from Al-Kindī (d. *c.* 874) to Al-Jurjānī (d. 1413), had produced important works on the theory of music.[8] What Al-Fārābī and the Ikhwān al-Ṣafā in the tenth century had to say on acoustics was undoubtedly in advance of the Greeks. They certainly acknowledged the Greeks as their teachers, but they were critical enough to specify or to ignore some blunders. The Arabic commentaries on Euclid's *Canon* and Aristotle's *De anima* must surely have led to some advance in the speculative art.[9] It is true that most of these treatises had remained in the Arabic

[1] Farmer, *Historical Facts for the Arabian Musical Influence*, pp. 290–4.
[2] Farmer, *The Organ of the Ancients*, chap. viii.
[3] *Cambridge Mediaeval History*, ii, p. 592.
[4] *Encyclopaedia of Islam*, v, pp. 217–21; Farmer 'Oriental Influences on Occidental Military Music', *Islamic Culture*, xv (1941), pp. 235–8.
[5] C. H. Haskins, *Studies in the History of Mediaeval Science* (Cambridge, U.S.A., 1924), p. 3.
[6] Excluding the unoriginal Isidore of Seville. See Farmer, *Historical Facts*, pp. 177–96, 208–28.
[7] See above, p. 458.
[8] Farmer, *Sources*, pp. 19–21, 56.
[9] See Farmer, *Historical Facts*, pp. 292–4.

script and could not therefore have been generally available, but others were translated into Latin and Hebrew, and one can still read Averroës' *Commentary on Aristotle's 'De anima'*, translated into Latin by Michael Scot, and benefit from what he tells us concerning the teachings of the Stagirite, including the theory of the spherical propagation of sound.

Two compendia of the arts and sciences, *De scientiis* by Alpharabius (Al-Fārābī) and *De ortu scientiarum*, both translated from the Arabic, became textbooks in European educational institutions, as did dozens of other Latin translations from the Arabic. We find quotations from, or references to, both these textbooks in the writings of Gundisalvus, Magister Lambert (Pseudo-Aristotle), Vincent de Beauvais, Roger Bacon, Jerome of Moravia, Walter Odington, and others.[1] Such works would probably urge scholars to seek the more extensive writings of Muslim authors for wider information; and even supposing that some of these were available only in Arabic, the mere fact that the Muslims and Mozárabes of Spain were using them must have produced some benefit, even though it came orally.

In the Islamic colleges in Spain, music was part of the 'science of mathematics', as in the Islamic East,[2] although the mysterious Virgilius Cordubensis would have us believe that it was a separate study at Toledo.[3] We know from Ibn al-Ḥijārī (d. 1194) that 'students from all parts of the world flocked . . . to learn the sciences of which Cordova was the most noble repository, and to derive knowledge from the doctors and *'ulamā* who swarmed in it'.[4] There was good reason for the fame of the Islamic schools. Anthony à Wood tells us that Roger Bacon, using faulty Latin translations from the Arabic in lecturing to students at Oxford, was ridiculed by those who came from Spain, evidently because they knew the originals.[5] Indeed both Bacon and Adelard of Bath recommended students to forsake the European schools for those of the Muslims. Yet, although the potentialities of Islamic influence on European musical theory were considerable, especially in view of the unmistakable proofs of influence in the other sciences of the *quadrivium*,[6] the fact is that, beyond the quotations made by European theorists from Alpharabius, and

[1] See Farmer, *Al-Fārābī's Arabic-Latin Writers on Music* (Glasgow, 1934), where the question is fully discussed.

[2] F. Dieterici, op. cit., pp. 1–2; E. Werner and I. Sonne, op. cit., pp. 269–72.

[3] Farmer, *Historical Facts*, p. 341.

[4] Al-Maqqarī, op. cit., i, p. 30.

[5] J. S. Brewer, *F. Rogeri Bacon: Opera quaedam hactenus inedita* (London, 1859), i, p. lxxxvii; J. B. Trend, *The Civilization of Spain* (London, 1944), pp. 45–46.

[6] T. Arnold and A. Guillaume, op. cit., pp. 344–54, 376–97.

the mere scraps on music and therapeutics from Alkindus, Haly, Avicenna, and Constantine the African,[1] we have little positive evidence.

We have already seen the universality of the practical art among Muslims everywhere, and under their domination in European lands the same inordinate love of music sprang up among the Christian population. Some Christian rulers adorned their courts with Oriental musicians.[2] It was the same with the people at large, who would gather at the *zambra* (Ar. *zumra*) or festival, where they took delight in the new-fangled *caña* (*ghaniyya*), *huda* (*ḥudā'*), *anaxir* (*nashīd*), and the *leile* (*laila*), to become delirious with rapture as they listened to an exotic *aravia* or *mourisca*, whose very names tell of their paternity. That some of this Oriental art had infiltrated quite early into the north is evident from iconography, as we see in the instruments delineated in the St. Médard *Evangeliarum* (eighth century), the *Psalterium Aureum* (ninth century), and elsewhere.[3] Much of this may have been due to emigrant Mozárabes,[4] although the real disseminators were the minstrel class, whose showy habiliments, painted faces, and long hair, which were the mark of the Oriental minstrel,[5] had already been borrowed. The Spanish word *mascara*, like the English 'masker' (play actor), was derived from the Arabic *maskhara* (buffoon). The hobby-horse and grelots were part of the impedimenta of the morris dancers, alias 'Moorish Dancers', who were still painting their faces like the 'Moors' in the time of Thoinot Arbeau (1589). The hobby-horse (*kurraj*) and its bells (*jalājil*) are mentioned by Jarīr (d. *c.* 728), and is described among the Moors of North Africa by Ibn Khaldūn (d. 1406), and its Basque descendant, the *zamalzain*, is simply the Arabic *zāmil al-zain* ('gala limping horse').

What were the new arts which these minstrels spread abroad? Firstly, there were some novel Arab–Persian instruments of Spain, the best verbal display of which, although rather late, occurs in the fourteenth-century *Libro de buen amor*,[6] while we have delineations of them a century earlier in the *Cantigas de Santa María*.[7] Among

[1] Farmer, *Al-Fārābī's Arabic-Latin Writings on Music*, pp. 32, 50.

[2] Farmer, *Historical Facts*, pp. 157–8. *Grove's Dictionary of Music*, v (London, 1954), p. 870.

[3] R. Mitjana, 'La Musique en Espagne', in Lavignac and La Laurencie, *Encyclopédie*, 1re partie, iv (1920), p. 1928; J. Riaño, op. cit., p. 109; Kinsky, *Geschichte der Musik in Bildern* (Leipzig, 1929), pp. 35, fig. 1; 39, fig. 3.

[4] G. T. Rivoira, *Moslem Architecture* (London, 1918), pp. 231, 284, 346.

[5] Al-Maqqarī, op. cit. ii, p. 108; Al-Iṣfahānī, op. cit. ii, p. 174; *Alf laila wa laila*, iv (Calcutta, 1839–42), p. 166.

[6] Juan Ruiz, *Il libro de buen amor* (Toulouse, 1901), ll. 1251–7.

[7] J. Riaño, *Critical and Bibliographical Notes on Early Spanish Music* (London, 1887), pp. 109–28; J. Ribera, *La Música de las Cantigas* (Madrid, 1922).

them were the *atambor* (*aṭ-ṭunbūr*), *guitarra morisca* (*kaitāra ʿarabiyya*), *laud* (*al-ʿūd*), *rabé* (*rabāb*), *canon* (*qānūn*), *sonajas de azofar* (*ṣunūj aṣ-ṣufr*), *axabeba* (*ash-shabbāba*), *annafil* (*an-nafīr*), *atambal* (*aṭ-ṭabl*), as well as the *albogon* (*al-būq*). Many of these, together with their names, spread throughout Europe, the lute, rybybe, canon, tabor, as well as the naker (*naqqāra*), finding acceptance in Britain. The Spanish *laud* and *atambor*, as well as the *guitarra morisca*, were among the novelties, as was the bowed *rabé*.[1] The first named were especially interesting since their necks were fitted with frets (*dasātīn*) discreetly measured so as to give the Pythagorean scale, which was common to both Muslim and Christian. Prior to this Europeans had only the rote and harp among stringed instruments, and had only their ears to guide them in tuning. All this was altered by the introduction of instruments with fretted necks. The existence of this Arab–Persian device of frets on the lute was once doubted,[2] but the objection has been completely disproved.[3]

It may have been from the Islamic lute that western Europe received an alphabetic notation for practical purposes,[4] as we see in Hucbald's *De harmonica institutione*,[5] although we get no definite proof of Muslim influence in this respect until later when, in a Latin work on the *Ars de pulsatione lambuti et aliorum similium instrumentorum*, dated 1496–7, it is admitted that the tablature mentioned was invented by 'a Moor of the Kingdom of Granada'.[6] Although the Conde de Morphy considered that the Spanish lute tablature was only 'probably of Oriental origin', his assessor, the more erudite Gevaert, had little doubt that the Castilians and Aragonese 'elaborated their tablature in imitation of that of the Muslims'.[7]

What else emerged out of Islamic practice or theory is not always patent. Odo of Cluny (d. 942), in his section on the eight tones, annexes to the *chordae* names which have a decidedly Semitic physiognomy, three of them being Arabic, *schembs* (Ar. *shams* = 'sun'), *caemar* (*qamar* = 'moon'), and *nar* (*nār* = 'fire'),[8] all of which appears to have a *raison d'être* in the doctrine of the *ethos*, as

[1] For all these instruments see *Grove's Dictionary of Music* (London, 1954), *s.v.*

[2] Karl Geiringer, 'Vorgeschichte und Geschichte der europäischen Laute', *Zeitschrift für Musikwissenschaft*, x (1928), p. 570; C. Sachs, *The History of Musical Instruments*, p. 254. The singular of *dasātīn* (frets) is *dastān*.

[3] Farmer, *Studies in Oriental Musical Instruments*, ii (1939), pp. 61–68.

[4] Farmer, *An Old Moorish Lute Tutor*, pp. 25–26.

[5] Gerbert, op. cit. i, p. 118.

[6] Jaime Villanueva, *Viage literario a las Iglesias de España* (Valencia, 1821), xi.

[7] Morphy, *Les Luthistes espagnols du XVIe siècle* (Leipzig, 1902), pp. xi, xvii.

[8] Gerbert, op. cit. i, pp. 249–50. Cf. P. Wagner, *Neumenkunde* Leipzig (1912), pp. 105, 225.

in the Islamic melodic modes and the Syrian *oktoechos*.[1] Of the parts played by Gerbert of Aurillac (d. 1003), Hermannus Contractus (d. 1054), Constantine the African (d. 1087), and Alfred the Englishman (thirteenth century),[2] all of whom were connected with music and had contact with Islamic culture, we know but little, and yet this little is extremely suggestive. Indeed one lights upon a number of allusive points. Is it not strange, for example, that such words as *conductus*, *estribillo*, and *stanza*, should be identical in their pristine significance as in their artistic meaning with the Arabic *majrā*, *maṭlaʿ* or *markaz*, and *bait*? The *conductus*[3] was a form which, in spite of its later ecclesiastical harbouring, had a secular upbringing as a song form, and Anglès has recognized specimens as early as the ninth century.[4] Yet outside the philological closeness of meaning we know of no musical identity between the Latin *conductus* and the Arabian *majrā*. Some of the *conducti* have the forms of the *rondeau* and *ballade*, which were within the ken of the troubadours, who may not have been the inventors of the *gaya ciencia*, since we have yet to discover where these people found this art,[5] although both their verse and their lives tell much of Spain.[6] J. B. Trend has suggested that they 'really derived much of their sense of form, and even their subject matter, from the Spanish Muslims',[7] and their name certainly reminds one of the Arabic *ṭarrāb* (minstrel),[8] a hint which has not passed unnoticed.[9]

It has long been speculated that when the Spaniards took the verse and rhyme in the songs of the Arabs, as they did in the *villancico*, they may also have adopted the music as well. This is quite understandable when we realize that it was often the stroke of the plectrum on the Islamic lute or pandore which enhanced the characteristic rhythm of the song. It was for that reason that the Arcipreste de Hita (fourteenth century) insisted that some instruments were inseparable from certain types of songs, and pointed out that the Spanish *vihuela de arco*, *cinfonie*, and the like, were alien to Arabian music, e.g. in the song called 'Caguil hallaco'.[10] Certainly one of the

[1] Farmer, *The Influence of Music*, pp. 97–101, 105–7, 111; J. Jeannin, 'Le chant liturgique syrien', *Journal asiatique*, Sér. X, 20 (1912), pp. 330–3.

[2] Farmer, *Historical Facts*, pp. 32–37, 177–186.

[3] See Vol. II, pp. 171–4.

[4] *El Còdex musical de las Huelgas* (*Música a veus dels segles XIII–XIV*), i (Barcelona, 1931), p. 25.

[5] Jean Beck, *La Musique des troubadours* (Paris, 1910), p. 67.

[6] J. Anglade, *Les Troubadours* (Paris, 1908), p. 252.

[7] *The Music of Spanish History* (New York, 1926), p. 30.

[8] Julian Ribera, *Historia de la música arabe* (Madrid, 1927), p. 335.

[9] T. Arnold and A. Guillaume, op. cit., pp. 17, 373.

[10] Juan Ruiz, op. cit., ll. 1516–17.

intrinsic features of Islamic music which affected Spain, and even countries beyond, was the melisma or 'gloss' (*zaida*), which J. B. Trend has graphically likened to arabesques in Mudéjar art. Indeed he suggests that 'the Moorish contribution to Spanish music . . . is the Mudéjar style, that is, a manner of performance rather than a type of musical construction',[1] an opinion with which most people will agree.[2]

At the same time there are strong reasons for believing that western Europe owes something to the Muslim theorists and practitioners in the sphere of rhythm. This was what Julian Ribera, the Spanish protagonist of Islamic influence, believed, although he built up his thesis on false premises. He amassed a splendid array of literary evidence on the Islamic influence in general which was fairly convincing,[3] but his testimony from musical sources, the *Cantigas de Santa Maria*, was less telling. It may be true that the Arabic *zajal* is the parent of the *virelai* and *ballade* (perhaps even of the *rondeau*), and that they may be found in the *Cantigas*, but it does not necessarily follow that the music is of the same origin.[4] It has been urged against Ribera's thesis that there are no confirmatory Arabic musical documents. That may be passably true, since it has been shown (p. 453) that these do not exist before the mid-thirteenth century, yet the *argumentum ex silentio* is proverbially inconclusive. The real case against Ribera is his erroneous transcription of the rhythmic modes of the classical Arabic authorities, which considerably invalidates his versions of the *Cantigas* and of the music of the troubadours.[5]

In 1925, independently of Ribera, certain other clues for possible Islamic influence on medieval European mensuralists were brought forward.[6] It was demonstrated that there were references in the Latin treatise by the so-called Anonymus IV (late thirteenth century) to new mensural note-values which bore such Arabic names as *elmuahym* and *elmuarifa*,[7] and that Johannes de Muris (*post* 1325) described another notated device called the *alentrade*, also of seemingly Arabic

[1] Op. cit., p. 36.

[2] Farmer, *Historical Facts*, p. 157.

[3] Ribera, *La Música de las Cantigas*, pp. 95 ff.; *Music in Ancient Arabia*, pp. 177 ff.

[4] Gustave Reese, *Music in the Middle Ages* (New York, 1940), pp. 245–7, where the pros and cons of 'Islamic influence' are fairly presented.

[5] Farmer, *Sa'adyah Gaon on the Influence of Music* (London, 1943), pp. 78–87.

[6] Farmer, 'Clues for the Arabian Musical Infiuence', *Journal of the Royal Asiatic Society*, 1925, pp. 61–80 = *The Arabian Influence on Musical Theory* (London, 1925) issued separately.

[7] E. de Coussemaker, *Scriptores de musica medii aevi*, (Paris, 1864), pp. 339–341.

origin.[1] The two former were counted among the *currentes* or 'running notes' to which Gustave Reese has drawn attention in the melodies of Léonin of Paris, that same *optimus organista* praised by Anonymus IV.[2] It was also suggested that the musical term *ochetus* (*hoquetus*) was derived from the Arabic *īqā'āt* (rhythms), just as Avicenna is made to speak in the Latin *Canon* of *Medicine* of *hash*, which is the Arabic *'ishq*. Muslim rhythm was one of the features of the Oriental art that was quite novel to Europe, which listened in wonderment to a singer in one rhythm while the accompanying instrumentalist played in another. So far, only two musicologists have recognized these hints of 1925.[3] Of course, it may be that these Arabisms crept in through some Mozárabian scribe; yet why should one have used Arabic if there had been a Latin term available? Anonymus IV was certainly well acquainted with Spanish and Pamplona manuscripts on musical theory.[4]

If so many things are hidden from us in this vexed question of Islamic influence, there are a few which are not. One can safely say, for instance, that the old notion that we owed our syllables of solfeggio to an Arabic source is quite unlikely, although even the more accepted origin may be very doubtful.[5] That the Muslims practised harmony, in our connotation of the term, as stated at length by Julian Ribera, is quite erroneous. That they permitted devices known as the *tarkībāt*, i.e. the simultaneous striking of the fourth, fifth, or octave with other notes, is true enough, but this was only an infrequent decoration (*zaida*) of the melody. 'In view of their practice of the *tarkībāt*', it may be asked, 'how was it that the Muslims did not develop harmony?' The answer is that, in our Middle Ages, the Muslims knew of the principles of harmony, in the Greek sense of *harmonia*,[6] better than Europe did, but they viewed the laws of 'harmonia' horizontally, and continued to do so, whereas Europe, since the tenth century, has apprehended a vertical harmony. The Muslims have advanced in their horizontal *harmonia* as much as the European west has developed in its vertical harmony, while in another sphere they have outstripped the Europeans, in the 'heart-beats of God', as the infinite, boundless, rhythms of the Muslims have been called.[7]

[1] Ibid., ii, p. 419. [2] Ibid., i, p. 342; Reese, op. cit., p. 298.

[3] J. B. Trend in *The Legacy of Islam*, p. 18; Reese, op. cit., p. 321. See G. Sarton, *Introduction to the History of Science*, ii (Washington, 1931), p. 25.

[4] E. de Coussemaker, op. cit. i, p. 345.

[5] Farmer, *Historical Facts*, pp. 72–82. [6] See pp. 340 ff.

[7] See Farmer, 'What is Arabian Music?' *Oriental Studies: Mainly Musical* (London, 1953), pp. 53–58.

On the other hand, some Islamic peoples have advanced beyond the use of simultaneous fourths, fifths, and octaves merely as occasional *fioriture*, as the present writer has shown elsewhere.[1] Uspensky and Belaiev, in their *Turkmenskaya Muzyka* (Moscow, 1928), have given innumerable examples of the normal music of Turkomanian peoples which reveal the widespread use of consecutive fourths and fifths, in a way identical with the organum of medieval Europe. Belaiev, in dealing with the folk-music of Georgia—where he found the same technique—would have us believe that this feature antedates the organum of Europe and says that 'Europe did not invent it but acquired it elsewhere in a ready-made form'.[2] The present writer had merely hinted at the probability that the 'rudimentary *tarkīb*' of Islamic peoples was the 'forerunner of the European organum', whereas Belaiev voices a certainty.[3] Laurence Picken[4] has made comparable studies in rural Turkey where he found similar features to those of Uspensky and Belaiev in Turkestan. Their occurrence in Asia Minor, says Picken, shows 'that . . . the practice of parallel fourths and fifths can exist side by side with more or less sophisticated homophony' which is the norm in most Islamic lands. Like Belaiev[5] Picken favours an indigenous origin for this early polyphony, i.e. organum, and suggests that since 'long-necked lutes', i.e. pandores, 'have great antiquity' in that area, we cannot rule out the possibility that 'the ancient Hittite lutes (first millennium B.C.) should not have been played polyphonically'. Yet the fact remains that we have no documentary evidence of organum among any peoples of Islam before comparatively modern times, and that the use of simultaneous fourths, fifths, and octaves, was not known to them earlier than the ninth century A.D., and even then only occasionally as *fioriture*.

On the question of Moorish influence in Spain the Spaniards themselves are not in complete accord.[6] If such authors as Menéndez y Pelayo[7] and Mitjana y Gordan[8] recognize that influence, some of the musicians, notably Pedrell and Falla, do not. Pedrell avers that Spanish music 'has absorbed *no* influence from the Arabs':

[1] 'Turkestani Music', *Grove's Dictionary of Music*, viii, 1954.

[2] 'The Folk-Music of Georgia', *Musical Quarterly*, ix (1933), p. 417.

[3] See Farmer, *Historical Facts*, p. 112

[4] 'Instrumental Polyphonic Folk-Music in Asia Minor', *Proceedings of the Royal Musical Association*, 1953–4, pp. 73 ff.

[5] *Christian Science Monitor*, 8 Sept. 1927.

[6] See Farmer, 'Moorish Music', especially the bibliography, *Grove's Dictionary of Music*, v (London, 1954), pp. 868–76.

[7] *Antología de poetas líricos*, ii (Madrid, 1903), p. 68.

[8] 'La Musique en Espagne', in Lavignac and La Laurencie, *Encyclopédie de la musique*, 1re partie, iv, p. 1925.

although on another page he expresses less certainty when he says that it 'owes nothing *essential* to the Arabs or Moors',[1] a statement which loses its conviction unless we know what he considered to be 'essential'. Pedrell would trace the orientalism in Spanish music to the Byzantine period, but does not produce that 'documentary evidence' which is always demanded from those who claim a Moorish influence. Falla, whilst admitting the oriental stratum in Spanish folk music, attributes some of it to the gipsies, seemingly because of the word *flamenco*, a term which, like *canto jondo*, is not a century old. Trend has dealt at considerable length with the views of Falla on this gipsy influence in his *Manuel de Falla and Spanish Music* (New York, 1929). Yet one is constrained to ask whether there is such a thing as gipsy music *per se*? The latter, like gipsy religion, is, to a considerable extent, determined by the culture and beliefs of the land in which the gipsy abides. If gipsy music exists, how is it that it has not influenced the music of Poland and Italy where there have been such large settlements of gipsies? Not that the *flamenco*, *canto jondo*, or *siguiriya gitana* reveal—in the contour of the melody or the swing of the rhythm—any clearly cut Moorish or Arabian features: since it is more the circumjacence, especially in the 'manner of performance', as Trend so acutely observes, which displays those elements.[2] In these latter, we must inevitably allow, as Raoul Laparra has said, that 'the origin of this *mentalité* of the *flamenco* goes back to the domination of the Moors in the Iberian peninsula'.[3]

During the past two decades there has been a marked change of view on the question of the Arabian or Moorish influence, although that modification has been mainly on the literary rather than the music claims. Yet a few are still adamant. While Isabel Pope thinks that the melodies of the *Cantigas de Santa María* 'display the influence of the Church combined with the influence of the folk song, both European and Oriental,'[4] Higini Anglès still holds an opposite view; he states that in the 423 melodies of the *Cantigas* he found not the slightest trace of Arabian influence.[5] Jeanroy, on the other hand, who in 1899 had said that the Arabian hypothesis was 'a pure legend', had been compelled to confess in 1934 that 'it is no longer

[1] *Cancionero musical popular español*, i (Valls, 1919), pp. 69, 84.

[2] J. B. Trend, *The Music of Spanish History* (Oxford, 1926), pp. 33–37.

[3] R. Laparra, 'La Musique et la danse populaires en Espagne', Lavignac and La Laurencie, op. cit. iv, pp. 2394 ff.

[4] *Annales musicologiques*, ii (Paris, 1954), p. 212.

[5] *Die Musik in Geschichte und Gegenwart*, ii (Kassel, 1952), col. 777.

possible to dismiss the hypothesis by a negation pure and simple'.[1] That admission had been forced on him by the researches of a new generation of scholars, many of whom were not only competent in Romance literature but in Arabic. The several works of Alois R. Nykl had placed the problem on 'a solid basis',[2] and those who had sneered at Ribera now found that later Spanish Arabists of the standing of A. González Palencia[3] and E. García Gómez were supporting some of the theses of the older Arabist. The tempo of acceptance was speeded after the appearance of R. Menéndez Pidal's *Poesía árabe y poesía europea* (1938–41)[4] and later works.[5] Then followed the troubadour studies of Gustave Cohen,[6] Nykl,[7] and Henri Pérès,[8] while the contributions of Samuel Stern,[9] Dámaso Alonso,[10] and Leo Spitzer[11] on the Mozarabic lyric—Arabic and Hebrew—shed further light on the subject.

The question of the Arabic *kharja*, i.e. the *coda* strophe in Oriental and Romance poetry, which had been raised by Stern, was emphasized by E. García Gómez,[12] and it still exists, as a musical feature, in the Moroccan *khurūj*.[13] One of the most interesting discoveries was that of Lévi-Provençal who, in 1954, demonstrated in a most positive way that Chanson V in Jeanroy's *Les Chansons de Guillaume IX* was not only wrongly transcribed but that it contained in its *coda* four lines of undiluted Arabic.[14]

[1] *Revue des Deux Mondes*, 151 (1899), p. 351. *La Poésie lyrique des troubadours*, ii (Toulouse, 1934), p. 368.

[2] *The Dove's Necklace* (Paris, 1931); *El cancionero de Aben Guzmán* (Madrid, 1933).

[3] 'La Poesía arábigo andaluza y su influencia', *Revista Hispánica Moderna*, i (New York, 1934).

[4] Published in *Bulletin hispanique*, xl (1938), and in 1941, with other studies, at Madrid.

[5] *Cantos románicos andalusíes* (Madrid, 1950), 'Les origines de las literaturas románicas', *Filologia romanza*, i (Turin, 1954).

[6] 'Le Problème des origines arabes de la poésie provençale medievale', *Bulletin de la classe des lettres . . . de l'Académie royal de Belgique*, 5e série, xxxii (1946).

[7] 'The latest in Troubadour studies', *Archivum Romanticum*, xix (Florence, 1935); L'influence arabe-andalouse sur les Troubadours', *Bulletin hispanique*, xli (Bordeaux, 1939); *Hispano-Arabic Poetry in its Relation with the Old Provençal Troubadours* (Baltimore, 1946); *Speculum*, xxvi (1951), pp. 179–84.

[8] 'La Poésie arabe d'Andalusie et ses relations possibles avec la poésie des troubadours', *L'Islam et l'Occident*, *Cahiers du Sud* (1947).

[9] 'Les Vers finaux en espagnol dans les muwaššahas hispano-hébraïques', *Al-Andalus*, xiii (1948); *Les Chansons mozarabes* (Palermo, 1953).

[10] 'Cancioncillos *De Amigo* Mozarabes', *Revista de Filologia Española*, xxxiii (1949).

[11] 'The Mozarabe lyric', *Contemporary Literature* (Oregon, 1952).

[12] 'Sobre un posible tercer tipo de poesía arábigo-andaluza', *Estudios dedicados a Menéndez Pidal* (Madrid, 1951); *Al-Andalus*, xvii (1952), pp. 57–127; ibid., xviii (1953), pp. 138–9; ibid., xix (1954), pp. 43–52.

[13] A. Chottin, *Corpus de musique marocaine*, i (Paris, 1931), p. 8.

[14] 'Les Vers arabes de la Chanson V de Guillaume IX d'Aquitaine', *Arabica*, i (Leiden, 1954).

From this we see that the oldest of the French troubadours not only came in touch with Eastern Oriental culture during the Crusades, but with the more potent civilization of Muslim Spain. How much the troubadours could have been influenced from the south is brilliantly revealed in an article entitled 'Concerning the Accessibility of Arabian Influence to the Earliest Provençal Troubadours' by A. J. Denomy.[1] For the latest opinions on the question of the Arabian influence see Pierre Le Gentil's *Le Virelai et le villancico: Le problème des origines arabes* (Paris, 1954), and Ettore Li Gotti's *La 'Tesa araba' sulle 'Origini' della lirica romanza* (Palermo, 1955).

On the terrain of actual examples of Arabian or Moorish music of the Middle Ages little has been revealed since the present writer called attention to existing examples in 1929,[2] although a recent writer, Isabel Pope, still believes that 'no examples . . . are known to survive'.[3] In 1929, however, a doubtful attempt was made by Clifton J. Furness to solve the identity of a piece of thirteenth-century music which was considered by Bourdillon to have been originally 'an Arabian or Moorish chant'.[4] The article by Furness was entitled 'The Interpretation and Probable Derivation of the Musical Notation in the *Aucassin et Nicolette* MS.'.[5] After having heard Tunisian music, in which a man and a boy performed a similar *chante-fable*, he concluded that it was no different from the type of performance which has been considered to have been practised in the *Aucassin et Nicolette* recital. His account was on all fours with that which Bourdillon,[6] Gaston Paris,[7] and Walter Pater[8] had pictured. He even went so far as to identify the scale of the thirteenth-century music with the Algerian *jahārka* mode which he found in the present writer's version of F. Salvador Daniel's *La Musique arabe* (1863).[9] The latter says that it was identical with the Aeolian mode, but his example in the song of the Banī ʿAbbās, notated in the book quoted, shows that it was the Mixolydian, which would equate with the *Muṭlaq fī majrā al-binṣir* mode of Baghdād and Cordoba of old. Unfortunately the

[1] *Mediaeval Studies*, xv (Toronto, 1953).
[2] *History of Arabian Music* (1929), p. 203 and pl. 3.
[3] *Annales Musicologiques*, ii, p. 212.
[4] F. W. Bourdillon, *Aucassin et Nicolette* (Manchester, 1919), p. xxxi.
[5] *The Modern Language Review*, xxiv (Cambridge, 1929). [6] Op. cit., p. xxxi.
[7] *Poèmes et légendes du Moyen Âge* (Paris, 1900), pp. 101–2.
[8] *The Renaissance*, i (of *Works*, London, 1900), p. 16.
[9] *The Music and Musical Instruments of the Arab* (London, 1915), pp. 99 (not 93), 210–12.

name *jahārka*—in relation to a mode—was unknown in the Maghrib before the opening of the sixteenth century, although it was used in the Near East from the fifteenth century.[1] There is no *jahārka* mode—by name—in Tunisia,[2] but in Egypt it is practically identical with our major mode.[3] On the other hand there is obviously nothing particularly Oriental about the mode itself, although the airs of *Aucassin and Nicolette* may have Oriental features. Strange as it may seem, an unusual—although only partial—confirmation of the latter appeared in that same year, 1929, when Arnold Dolmetsch undertook a musical pilgrimage to Morocco where he frequented native musical assemblies.[4] On one such occasion he was asked to play something on the lute from his own land. Among other items which he and his son Carl played in response to that invitation was the music of *Aucassin et Nicolette.* The old blind Moorish lutenist who led the native musicians hailed the music with delight saying, '*I know that tune,* only we would embroider it thus'. The item was then performed in the Moorish way, which was, as Mrs. Mabel Dolmetsch put it, 'what we would call *divisions on a ground*', although the latter did not suspect that the term 'divisions' (*taqāsim*) had been favoured by Arabic-speaking peoples for centuries before Simpson issued his *Division Violist* (1659), and the *taqsīm* is still the most favoured instrumental form in the Near East.[5]

More important was a discovery by the distinguished Arabist Louis Massignon in 1949.[6] This was reported by Isabel Pope to be 'a collection of Arabic music with notation'[7] found in two manuscripts of the Andalusian poet Al-Shushtarī (d. 1269) at Aleppo and Cairo. It would appear, however, that these latter, neither of them very old copies, simply show some of the songs rubricated with the names of the modes, i.e. the *talāḥin* (melodic modes or 'patterns') and the *ḍurūb* (rhythmic modes) to which they were sung. Among the former are some very old names, e.g. *ʿirāq*, *ḥijāz*, *ḥusainī*, and *ʿushshāq*, although others, such as *dūka*, *sīka*, and *jahārka*, were scarcely known in Al-Shushtarī's day. Yet we know, on the authority of Ibn ʿAbbād al-Nafzī (d. 1390), that music had been set to these verses.[8] Since by that time all of the above

[1] R. d'Erlanger, *La Musique arabe*, iv, pp. 133–4. [2] Ibid., v, figs. 144–7.
[3] A. Chottin, *Tableau de la musique marocaine* (Paris, 1939), p. 181.
[4] Letter from Mrs. Dolmetsch, 22 January 1930; *The Consort*, Dec. (1931), p. 13.
[5] *Recueil des travaux du Congrès de Musique arabe* (Cairo, 1934), pp. 112–13, 170.
[6] 'Investigaciones sobre Šuštarī', *Al-Andalus*, xiv (1949).
[7] *Annales musicologiques*, ii, p. 214.
[8] *Encyclopaedia of Islam* (Leiden, 1913–38), iv, 393.

modes had become melody 'patterns' we can form as general an idea of the contour of the melodies of Al-Shushtarī's *muwashshaḥāt* as of that of neum-written music of the early Christian Church.

Whatever may be our certainties and doubts concerning the extent of Islamic influence on European culture, we must remember that for 700 years at least it was the Muslims and Mozárabes of Spain who, in the earlier centuries undoubtedly, 'alone held the torch of learning and civilization bright and shining before the western world',[1] and it was this glow that helped to light the way for Europe's progress in music.

[1] S. Lane-Poole, *The Moors in Spain* (London, 1890), p. 43.

BIBLIOGRAPHY

GENERAL

AMBROS, A. W.: 'Die Musik der Culturvölker des Orients', 'Die Musik bei den Naturvölkern'. *Geschichte der Musik.* 3rd edition, edited by B. von Sokolowsky, i (Leipzig, 1887), pp. 341–567.

BEHN, F.: *Musikleben im Altertum und frühen Mittelalter* (Stuttgart, 1954).

COMBARIEU, JULES: *Musique et la magie.* Étude sur les origines populaires de l'art musical, son influence, et sa fonction dans les sociétés (Paris, 1909).

HORNBOSTEL, E. M. VON: 'Melodie und Skala'. *Jahrbuch der Musikbibliothek Peters,* xix (1912), pp. 11–23.

—— 'Die Probleme der vergleichenden Musikwissenschaft'. *Zeitschrift der internationalen Musikgesellschaft,* vii (1905/6), pp. 85–97.

KUNST, JAAP: *Ethno-Musicology.* A study of its nature, its problems, methods and representative personalities (The Hague, 1955).

LACH, R.: *Studien zur Entwicklungsgeschichte der ornamentalen Melopöie* (Leipzig, 1913).

LACHMANN, R.: 'Musik der außereuropäischen Natur- und Kulturvölker', in Bücken, *Handbuch der Musikwissenschaft* (Potsdam, 1931).

—— *Musik des Orients* (Breslau, 1929).

LAVIGNAC, A., and LA LAURENCIE, L.: *Encyclopédie de la musique,* 1re partie i and v (Paris, 1913 and 1922).

SACHS, C.: 'Die Musik der Antike' in Bücken, *Handbuch der Musikwissenschaft* (Potsdam, 1932).

—— *Musik des Altertums* (Breslau, 1924).

—— *The History of Musical Instruments* (New York, 1940).

—— *The Rise of Music in the Ancient World* (New York, 1943).

SCHAEFFNER, P. A.: *Les Origines des instruments de musique* (Paris, 1936).

SCHNEIDER, M.: *Geschichte der Mehrstimmigkeit.* I. Die Naturvölker (Berlin, 1934).

WALLASCHEK, R.: *Primitive Music* (London, 1893).

WELLESZ, E. 'Probleme der musikalischen Orientforschung'. *Jahrbuch der Musikbibliothek Peters,* xxiv (1917), pp. 1–18.

CHAPTER I

PRIMITIVE MUSIC

(i) *Ethnology*

ARNDT, R. F. W.: 'Die Religion der Nad'a'. *Anthropos,* xxvi (1931).

BÄCHTOLD-STÄUBLI, H.: *Handwörterbuch des deutschen Aberglaubens,* v (Berlin, 1932/3).

BAUMANN, H.: 'Afrikanische Wild- und Buschgeister'. *Zeitschrift für Ethnologie,* lxx (1938).

BEECHAM, J.: *The Ashanti* (London, 1841).

BROWN, A. R.: *The Andaman Islanders* (London, 1933).

BÜCHER, K.: *Arbeit und Rhythmus* (Sitzungsberichte d. Kgl. Sächsischen Gesellschaft d. Wissenschaften. Leipzig, 1896. 6th edition, 1924).

CODRINGTON, R. H.: *The Melanesians,* vii (Oxford, 1891).

EBOUÉ, M.: *Les Peuples du Ouranghi-Chari* (Paris, 1933).

EMSHEIMER, E.: 'Zur Ideologie der lappischen Zaubertrommel'. *Ethnos*, ix (1944).
FROBENIUS, L.: *Spielmannsgeschichten der Sahel* (Jena, 1921).
FUHRMANN, E.: *Tlinkit und Haida* (Hagen, 1923).
GRANET, M.: *Danses et légendes de la Chine ancienne*, i (Paris, 1926).
HERZOG, G.: 'Speech Melody and Primitive Music'. *Musical Quarterly*, xx (1934).
HEWITT, J. N. B.: 'Orenda'. *American Anthropology*, iv (1902).
KOCH, K.: 'Totemismus und Zweiklassenkultur in Neu-Guinea'. *Zeitschrift für Ethnologie*, lxxi (1931).
LEENHARDT, M.: *Arts de l'Océanie* (Paris, 1947).
MENGES, L., and POTAPOV, P.: *Materialien zur Volkskunde der Turkvölker des Altay* (Mitteilungen des Seminars für orientalische Sprachen) (Berlin, 1934).
MENGHIN, O.: *Geschichte der Steinzeit* (Vienna, 1931).
PREUSS, TH.: *Religion und Mythologie der Uitoto* (Leipzig, 1921).
—— *Die Nayarit-expedition*, i (Leipzig, 1912).
RATTRAY, R. S.: *The Ashanti* (Oxford, 1923).
—— *Reports of the Cambridge Anthropological Expedition to Torres Straits*, vi (Cambridge, 1908).
SCHAEFFNER, P. A.: 'Zur Initiation im Wagi Tal (Bismarck Archipelago)'. *Anthropos*, xxxiii (1938).
SCHMIDT, J. G.: 'Neue Beiträge zur Ethnologie der Nor-Papuas'. *Anthropos*, xxviii (1933).
STREHLOW, C.: *Die Aranda und Loritjastämme* (Frankfurt, 1907).
STUMPF, C.: 'Musikpsychologie in England'. *Vierteljahrsschrift für Musikwissenschaft*, i (1885).
WESTERMANN, D.: 'So, der Gewittergott der Ewe'. *Zeitschrift für Ethnologie*, lxx (1938).
WIRZ, P.: *Die Marind-anim*, i (Hamburg, 1922).

(ii) *Books and Articles on general features of Primitive Music*

BIBLIOTECA CANARIA: *El lenguaje silbado en la Gomera.*
DANCKERT, WERNER: 'Musikwissenschaft und Kulturkreislehre', *Anthropos*, xxxii (1937).
DINCSER, O.: *Die Probleme der Varianten in der Musikforschung* (Geneva, 1947).
HEINITZ, W.: 'Probleme der afrikanischen Trommelsprache', *Beiträge zur Kolonial-forschung*, lv (1942).
HORNBOSTEL, E. M. VON: 'Musikalische Tonsysteme', in Geiger and Scheel, *Handbuch der Physik*, viii (Berlin, 1927).
LABOURET, H.: 'Le Langage tambouriné et sifflé'. *Bulletin du comité d'études de l'Afrique occidentale française* (1923).
LACH, R.: *Studien zur Entwicklungsgeschichte der ornamentalen Melopöie* (Leipzig, 1913).
—— 'Die vergleichende Musikwissenschaft, ihre Methoden und Probleme'. *Sitzungsberichte der Akademie der Wissenschaften in Wien, Bd. 200* (Vienna, 1924).
MONTANDON, G.: *La Généalogie des instruments de musique* (Geneva, 1919).
NADEL, S.: *Marimbamusik* (Vienna, 1931).
RICARD, R.: *A propos du langage sifflé des Canaris* (Hesperis, 1932).
SACHS, CURT: *Geist und Werden der Musikinstrumente* (Berlin, 1929).
—— *Handbuch der Musikinstrumentenkunde* (Leipzig, 1920).
—— *Reallexikon der Musikinstrumente* (Berlin, 1913).
SCHNEIDER, M.: *El origen musical de los animales símbolos* (Barcelona, 1946).
—— 'Wandernde Melodien'. *Archiv für Musikforschung*, iii (1938).

SCHNEIDER, M.: 'Ethnologische Musikforschung', in Preuss and Trimborn, *Lehrbuch der Völkerkunde* (2nd edition, Stuttgart, 1956).

—— *La Danza de espadas y la tarantela* (Barcelona, 1948).

—— 'Los Cantos de lluvia'. *Anuario musical*, iv (1949).

—— 'Die Bedeutung der Stimme in den alten Kulturen'. *Tribus* (*Jahrbuch des Lindenmuseums*), ii–iii (Stuttgart, 1953).

—— *Singende Steine* (Kassel, 1955).

—— *La Philosophie de la musique chez les peuples non européens* (Paris, 1956).

—— 'Die historischen Grundlagen der musikalischen Symbolik'. *Die Musikforschung*, iv (1951).

STUMPF, C.: *Die Anfänge der Musik* (Leipzig, 1911).

WALLASCHEK, R.: *Primitive Music* (London, 1893).

(iii) *Books and Articles on the Music of particular Peoples or Regions*

D'ANGULO, J., and D'HARCOURT, E.: 'La Musique des Indiens de la Californie du Nord'. *Journal des Américanistes*, xxiii (1931).

BELAIEV, V.: 'The Folk-Music of Georgia'. *The Musical Quarterly*, xix (1933).

DENSMORE, FRANCES: *Chippewa Music* (Bureau of American Ethnology Bulletin 45) (Washington, 1910).

—— *Nootka and Quileute Music* (Bulletin 124) (Washington, 1939).

—— *Mandan and Hidatsa Music* (Bulletin 80) (Washington, 1923).

—— *Papago Music* (Bulletin 90) (Washington, 1929).

—— *Music of the Indians of British Columbia* (Bulletin 136) (Washington, 1943).

—— *Pawnee Music* (Bulletin 93) (Washington, 1929).

—— *Menominee Music* (Bulletin 102) (Washington, 1932).

EMSHEIMER, E.: 'Schamanentrommel und Trommelbau'. *Ethnos* ix (1946).

HORNBOSTEL, E. M. VON: 'Die Musik auf den Nordwestlichen Salomon Inseln'. R. Thurnwald, *Forschungen auf den Salomon Inseln* (Berlin, 1912).

KIRBY, P.: 'The Musical Practices of the Bushmen'. *Bantu Studies*, x (1936).

—— *The Musical Instruments of the Native Races of South Africa* (Oxford, 1936).

KUNST, J.: *Music in Nias* (Leiden, 1939).

—— *Music in Flores* (Leiden, 1942).

MAYER, R. F. H.: 'Sonnenverehrung in Neu-Guinea'. *Anthropos*, xxviii (1933).

SCHMIDT, W.: 'Über Musik und Gesänge der Karesau-Papuas'. *Kongressbericht der internationalen Musikgesellschaft* (Vienna, 1910).

SCHNEIDER, M.: 'Gesänge aus Uganda'. *Archiv für Musikforschung*, ii (1937).

—— 'A propósito del influjo árabe'. *Anuario Musical*, i (1946).

—— 'Lieder ägyptischer Bauern'. *Festschrift für Kodály* (Budapest, 1942).

—— 'La Canción de cuna'. *Anuario Musical*, iii (1948).

—— 'Phonetische u. metrische Korrelationen bei gesprochenen u. gesungenen Ewe Texten'. *Archiv für vergleichende Phonetik* (1941).

—— 'La Relation entre la musique et le langage dans la chanson chinoise'. *Anuario Musical*, v (1950).

—— 'Zambomba und Pandero'. *Spanische Forschungen*, i (1954).

—— 'Über die Verbreitung afrikanischer Chorformen'. *Zeitschrift für Ethnologie*, lxix (1937).

—— 'Zur Trommelsprache der Duala'. *Anthropos*, xlvii (1952).

SPECK, G.: *Ceremonial Songs of the Creek and Yuchi Indians* (Philadelphia, 1911).

STEINMANN, A.: 'Über anthropomorphe Schlitztrommeln in Indonesien'. *Anthropos*, xxxiii (1938).

TESSMANN, G.: *Die Bubi auf Fernando Po* (Darmstadt, 1923).

VAISAENEN, A. O.: *Wogulische und ostjakische Melodien* (Helsinki, 1937).
WIORA, W.: 'Alpenländische Liedweisen der Frühzeit'. *Festschrift für John Meier* (Lahe, 1949).
WITTE, P.: 'Lieder und Gesänge der Ewe-Neger'. *Anthropos*, i (1906).

CHAPTER II

(Numbers in brackets, other than dates, refer to serial entries in the Glossary of Characters, p. 190. Entries not mentioned in the text are marked †.)

(*a*) SOURCES AND TRANSCRIPTIONS

CHEN, C. H. and S. H.: *The Flower Drum and other Chinese Songs* (New York, 1943).
Chingshan Chynpuu (137) (1673).
COLLECTION PELLIOT, No. 3808, Bibliothèque nationale de France (a Tarng musical MS.).
GRAVES, S. M., and FARLEY, M. F.: *Min River Boat Songs* (New York, 1946).
JACOBS, A. G.: *The Chinese-American Song and Games Book* (New York, 1944).
JIANG KWEI: *Bairshyr Dawren Gecheu, Syh Jiuann, Syhbuh Tsongkan* (83) (Shanghai, 1929).
JU SHII: *Yilii Jingjuann Tongjiee Shyyueh Pian* (110). Melodies for 12 of the Songs, reprinted in the *Yueh Dean* (168) of Hwang Tzuoo (1692).
JU TZAYYUH: *Yuehliuh Chyuanshu* (85) (1595).
†KORNFELD, P. FRITZ: *Die tonale Struktur chinesischer Musik*; *St. Gabrieler Studien*, 16 (Mödling bei Wien, 1955).
LIU SHYA-AN [*sic*]: *Three Songs* (Tokyo, 1935).
Ming Dawtzanq (167).
NIING WANG: *Chyushian Shernchyi Mihpuu* (135) (1425).
†PICKEN, L.: 'Twelve Ritual Melodies of the T'ang Dynasty'. *Studia Memoriae Belae Bartók Sacra* (Budapest, 1956), pp. 147–73.
SHYONG PERNGLAI: *Sehpuu* (198).
Wugaang Chynpuu (136) (1546).

(*b*) BOOKS AND ARTICLES

(* indicates presence of musical examples.)

*AALST, J. VAN: *Chinese Music* (Shanghai, 1884).
*AMIOT, PÈRE: *Mémoire sur la musique des Chinois tant anciens que modernes* (Paris, 1779).
BAZIN AINÉ, A. P. L.: *Théâtre chinois* (Paris, 1838).
—— *Le Siècle des Youen* (Paris, 1854).
*BOSE, F.: *Musikalische Völkerkunde* (Freiburg i. Br., 1953).
*CHAO WEI-PANG: 'Yang-ko, the Rural Theatre in Ting-hsien, Hopei'. *Folklore Studies*, iii (Peiping, 1944), pp. 17–40.
*CHIANG UN-KAI: *K'ouen K'iu—le théâtre chinois ancien* (Paris, 1932).
COURANT, M.: *La Langue chinoise parlée* (Paris, 1914).
*—— 'Essai sur la musique classique des Chinois avec un appendice relatif à la musique coréenne'. *Encyclopédie de la musique* (Lavignac and L. de La Laurencie), 1re partie, i (Paris, 1913), pp. 77–241.
CREEL, H. G.: *The Birth of China* (New York, 1937), p. 99.
*CROSSLEY-HOLLAND, P. C.: 'Chinese Music'. *Grove's Dictionary of Music and Musicians* (ed. E. Blom), ii (London, 1954), pp. 219–48.

*DECHEVRENS, A.: 'Étude sur le système musical chinois'. *Sammelbände der internationalen Musikgesellschaft*, ii (1901), pp. 484–551.

EASTLAKE, F. W.: 'The "Sho" or Chinese Reed Organ'. *China Review*, xi (Hong Kong, 1882–3), pp. 33–41.

ECKARDT, H.: 'Chinesische Musik, II. Vom Ende der Han-Zeit bis zum Ende der Sui-Zeit (220–618). Der Einbruch westlicher Musik'. *Die Musik in Geschichte und Gegenwart*, ii (ed. F. Blume) (Kassel and Basel, 1952), cols. 1205–7; 'III. Die T'ang-Zeit (618–907). Die Rolle der westländischer (Hu-) Musik. Die Zehn Orchester. Die Musik der Zwei Abteilungen. Akademien und Konservatorien'. Ibid., cols. 1207–16.

FARMER, H. G.: 'Reciprocal influences in music 'twixt the Far and Middle East'. *Journal of the Royal Asiatic Society* (London, 1934), pp. 327–42.

FERNALD, H. E.: 'Ancient Chinese Musical Instruments'. *Museum Journal* (Philadelphia, 1936); reprinted in Hsiao Ch'ien, *A Harp with a Thousand Strings* (London, 1944), pp. 395–440.

*FISCHER, E.: *Beiträge zur Erforschung der chinesischen Musik* (Leipzig, 1911); reprinted in *Sammelbände der internationalen Musikgesellschaft*, xii (1911), pp. 153–206.

GIBSON, E. H.: 'Music and Musical Instruments of Shang'. *Journal of the North China Branch of the Royal Asiatic Society*, lxviii (Shanghai, 1937), pp. 8–18.

GOODRICH, L. C.: 'The Chinese Shêng and Western Musical Instruments'. *China Magazine*, xvii (New York, 1941), pp. 10, 11, 14.

GRANET, M.: *Fêtes et chansons anciennes de la Chine* (Paris, 1919).

GROUSSET, R.: *L'Asie orientale des origines au XVe siècle* (Paris, 1946).

GULIK, R. H. VAN: *The Lore of the Chinese Lute* (Tokyo, 1940).

—— 'Brief Note on the Cheng, the Chinese Small Cither'. *Tōyō Ongaku Kenkyū*, ix (Tokyo, 1951), pp. 10–25.

†—— 'The Lore of the Chinese Lute'. *Monumenta Nipponica*, vii, 1/2 (Tokyo, 1951), pp. 300–10.

HOFFMANN, A.: *Die Lieder des Li Yü* (Cologne, 1950).

*HORNBOSTEL, E. M. VON: 'Ch'ao-t'ien-tze (Eine chinesische Notation und ihre Ausführungen)'. *Archiv für Musikwissenschaft*, i (1919), pp. 477–98.

*HSIAO SHUSIEN: 'La Chanson populaire chinoise'. *Sinologica*, i (Basel, 1947), pp. 65–86.

IN FAALUU: 'Tarng-Sonq Dahcheu jy Laiyuan jyi chyi Tzuujy'. *Wuuchang Hwajong Dahshyue Gwoshyue Yanjiou Luennwen Juankan*, i. 4 (Tali, 1945) (104).

KARLGREN, B.: 'The Date of the Early Dong-so'n Culture'. *Bulletin of the Museum of Far Eastern Archaeology*, xiv (Stockholm, 1942), pp. 1–28.

KUTTNER, F. A.: 'The Musical Significance of Archaic Chinese Jades of the *Pi*-Disk Type'. *Artibus Asiae*, xvi. 1/2 (Ascona, 1953), pp. 25–50.

LEU BUHWEI (15): *Leu-Shy Chuenchiou* (14), v *Guuyueh* (61); vi *Inliuh* (63).

*LEVIS, J. H.: *The Foundations of Chinese Musical Art* (Peiping, 1936).

†LIOU CHERNGFUU: *Dictionary of Music* (in Chinese) *Inyueh Tsyrdean* (Shanghai, 1936).

LIOU SHI: *Shyming* (46).

†*MA HIAO-TS'IUN: 'La Musique chinoise'. *La Musique des origines à nos jours* (Norbert Dufourcq) (Paris, 1946), pp. 438–46.

MAHILLON, V. CH.: *Catalogue descriptif et analytique du musée instrumental du Conservatoire Royal de Bruxelles* (Ghent, 1880 and 1893).

—— *Annuaire du Conservatoire Royal de Bruxelles* (Ghent, 1886 and 1890). (Contains the conclusion of the catalogue and an account of experiments on the *liuhleu*.)

MOULE, A. C.: 'A list of the Musical and other Sound-Producing Instruments of the Chinese'. *Journal of the North China Branch of the Royal Asiatic Society*, xxxix (Shanghai, 1908), pp. 1–160.

*MOULE, G. E.: 'Notes on the Ting-chi, or half-yearly sacrifice to Confucius (with an appendix on the music by A. C. Moule)'. *Journal of the North China Branch of the Royal Asiatic Society*, xxxiii (Shanghai, 1901), pp. 37–73.

NORLIND, T.: 'Beiträge zur chinesischen Instrumentengeschichte'. *Svensk Tidskrift för Musikforskning*, xv (1933), pp. 48–83.

PICKEN, L.: 'The Origin of the Short Lute'. *Galpin Society Journal*, viii (London, 1955), pp. 32–42.

REINHARD, K.: *Chinesische Musik* (Eisenach and Kassel, 1956).

ROBINSON, K.: 'Chinesische Musik, I. Geschichtliche Entwicklung von der Frühzeit (Shang-Dynastie) bis zum Ende der Han-Zeit (1523 a. Chr. bis 206 p. Chr.) (Deutsche Übers. und Bearb.: Hans Eckardt)'. *Die Musik in Geschichte und Gegenwart*, ii (ed. F. Blume) (Kassel and Basel, 1953), cols. 1195–1205.

SHIAH CHERNGDAO: 'Bairshyr Gecheu Parngpuu Biann'. *Yannjing Shyuebaw* (113) (Peiping, 1932).

Shujing (91): *Shuenn Dean* (92); *Yushu Yihjyi* (93).

SOUEN K'AI-TI: 'L'origine et le développement du théâtre des marionnettes chinoises'. *Bulletin du centre franco-chinois d'études sinologiques* (194), i (Pekin, 1944), pp. 81–105 (in Chinese with summary in French).

*SOULIÉ DE MORANT, G., and GAILHARD, A.: *Théâtre et musique modernes en Chine* (Paris, 1926).

STANLEY, A.: 'Putoshan'. *Journal of the North China Branch of the Royal Asiatic Society*, xlvi (Shanghai, 1915), pp. 1–18.

SYMAA CHIAN (16): *Shyyjih* (17), xxiv, f. 37 v°. Translated in R. H. van Gulik: *The Lore of the Chinese Lute* (Tokyo, 1940).

*TANABE, H.: *Nihon Ongaku Kōwa* (Tokyo, 1926).

TREFZGER, H.: 'Das Musikleben der Tang-Zeit'. *Sinica*, xiii (Stuttgart, 1938).

*T'UNG FEI: *Fundamentals of Chinese Music* (195) (Shanghai, 1927) (in Chinese).

WALEY, A.: *The Book of Songs* (London, 1937).

—— *The Life and Times of Po-Chü-I* (London, 1949), pp. 150–5.

*WANG KWANG-CHI: 'Über die chinesische klassische Oper 1530–1860'. *Orient et Occident, Bibliothèque Sino-Internationale* (Geneva, 1934).

WATERMAN, R. A., LICHTENWANGER, W., HERRMANN, V. H., POLEMAN, H. I., and HOBBS, C.; 'Bibliography of Asiatic Musics, Eleventh and Twelfth Instalments, D. China'. *Notes*, vii, 3 and 4 (New York, 1950), pp. 415–23, 613–21.

*YANG INLIOU: *Jonggwo Inyueh Shyygang* (Shanghai, 1953).

Yilii (37), vii.

CHAPTER III

(Numbers in brackets, other than dates, refer to serial entries in the Glossary of Characters, p. 190. Entries not mentioned in the text are marked †.)

(*a*) TRANSCRIPTIONS

DAVISON, A. T., and APEL, W.: *Historical Anthology of Music*, i (Cambridge, Massachusetts, 1947).

GIRONCOURT, G. DE: 'Motifs de chants cambodgiens'. *Bulletin de la Société des Études indochinoises*, Nouvelle Série, xvi, No. 1 (Saïgon, 1941), pp. 51–105.

GRONEMAN, J., and LAND, J. P. N.: *De Gamělan te Jogjåkartå* (Amsterdam, 1890).

HASLUND-CHRISTENSEN, H., and EMSHEIMER, E.: *The Music of the Mongols* (Stockholm, 1943).

KEH, C. S.: 'Die koreanische Musik'. *Sammlung musikwissenschaftlicher Abhandlungen*, xvii (Strasbourg, 1935).

KIYOSE, Y.: *Six Japanese Folk Songs from Shinano District* (Tokyo, 1937).

KONOYE, H. and N.: *Etenraku* (180) (Tokyo, 1935).

MCPHEE, C.: *Balinese Ceremonial Music Transcribed for Two Pianos, Four Hands: Pemoengkah; Gambangan; Taboe Teloe* (New York, 1940).

MATSUDAIRA, Y.: *Seven Japanese Songs from Nambu District* (Tokyo, 1937).

SAIONJI, Y.: Nihon Minyō Taikan, Kantō-hen (Tokyo, 1953).

SEELIG, P. J.: *Siamesische Musik* (Bandoeng, 1932).

STUMPF, C.: 'Mongolische Gesänge'. *Sammelbände für vergleichende Musikwissenschaft*, i (1922), pp. 107–12.

TAKEDA, C.: 'The Songs of the Mongols, Notations and Explanations'. *Tōyō Ongaku Kenkyū*, ix (Tokyo, 1951), pp. 147–54; and x–xi (Tokyo, 1952), pp. 67–73 (in Japanese).

TEACHERS' TRAINING COLLEGE: *Kashmirī Mūsiqī*, i (Srinagar, n.d.) (in Urdū).

TOKYO ACADEMY OF MUSIC: *Collection of Japanese Koto Music* (Tokyo, 1888).

TORHOUT, N. DE, and HUMBERT-SAUVAGEOT: 'Dix-huits chants et poèmes mongols'. *Bibliothèque musicale du musée Guimet*, 1re série, iv (Paris, 1937).

TRICON, A., and BELLAN, CH.: *Chansons cambodgiennes* (Saïgon, 1921).

(*b*) BOOKS AND ARTICLES

(* indicates presence of musical examples.)

AUBOYER, J.: 'L'Indochine'. *L'Asie orientale des origines au XVe siècle* (R. Grousset) (Paris, 1941).

*BOSE, F.: *Musikalische Völkerkunde* (Freiburg i. Br., 1953).

CHARDIN, P. T., DE, and PEI WEN-CHUNG: *Le Néolithique de la Chine* (Pekin, 1944).

CONDOMINAS, G.: 'Le Lithophone préhistorique de Ndut Lieng Krak'. *Bulletin de l'école française de l'extrême orient*, xlv (Paris, 1951), pp. 359–92.

*COURANT, M.: 'Essai historique sur la musique classique des Chinois avec un appendice relatif à la musique coréenne'. *Encyclopédie de la musique* (Lavignac and L. de La Laurencie) 1re partie, i (Paris, 1913), pp. 211–20.

—— 'Japon, Notice historique'. Ibid., pp. 242–56.

COVARRUBIAS, M.: *Island of Bali* (London, 1937).

*CROSSLEY-HOLLAND, P. C.: 'Tibetan Music'. *Grove's Dictionary of Music and Musicians*, viii (London, 1954), pp. 456–64.

*DEMIÉVILLE, P.: *Hōbōgirin* (Tokyo, 1930); see article 'Bombai'.

*ECKARDT, A.: 'Koreanische Musik'. *Mitteilungen der deutschen Gesellschaft für Natur- und Völkerkunde Ostasiens*, xxiv B (Tokyo, 1930).

ELLIS, A. J.: 'Musical Scales of Various Nations'. *Journal of the Society of Arts*, 27 March (London, 1885).

*EMSHEIMER, E.: 'Über das Vorkommen und die Anwendungsart der Maultrommel in Sibirien und Zentral-Asien'. *Ethnos*, vi (Stockholm, 1941), pp. 109–27.

FITZGERALD, C. P.: *The Tower of Five Glories* (London, 1941).

*FRANCKE, A. H.: 'La musique au Thibet'. *Encyclopédie de la musique* (Lavignac and L. de La Laurencie), 1re partie, v (Paris, 1922), pp. 3084–93.

FÜRER HAIMENDORF, C. VON: *The Naked Nagas* (Calcutta, 1946).

*GIRONCOURT, G. DE: 'Recherches de géographie musicale en Indochine'. *Bulletin de la Société des Études indochinoises*, Nouvelle Série, xvii, No. 4 (Saïgon, 1942), pp. 7–174.

GOLOUBEW, V.: 'L'Âge du bronze au Tonkin et dans le Nord-Annam'. *Bulletin de l'école française de l'extrême orient*, xxix (Hanoy, 1929), pp. 1–46.

†*HARICH-SCHNEIDER, E.: 'Japanische Impressionen, I'. *Musica* (Kassel, 1949), No. 3, pp. 85–90.

†—— 'Japanische Impressionen, II'. Ibid., No. 4, pp. 129–36.

†—— 'Japanische Impressionen, III'. Ibid., No. 6, pp. 205–9.

†—— 'A Survey of the Remains of Japanese Court Music'. *Ethnos*, xvi (Stockholm, 1951), pp. 105–24.

†*—— 'Koromogae, one of the Saibara of Japanese Court Music'. *Monumenta Nipponica*, viii, 1/2 (Tokyo, 1952), pp. 398–406.

*—— 'The Present Condition of Japanese Court Music'. *The Musical Quarterly*, xxxix (1953), pp. 49–74.

†—— *The Rhythmical Patterns in Gagaku and Bugaku* (Leiden, 1954).

*HAYASHI, K.: *Swei-Tarng Yannyuehdiaw Yanjiou* (181) (Shanghai, 1936) (Chinese translation from the Japanese).

*HOOD, M.: *The Nuclear Theme as a Determinant of Paṭet in Javanese Music* (Groningen and Djakarta, 1954).

*HUMBERT-LAVERGNE, M.: 'La musique à travers la vie laotienne'. *Zeitschrift für vergleichende Musikwissenschaft*, ii (1934), pp. 14–19.

*HUTTON, J. H.: *The Sema Nagas* (London, 1921).

*HWANG YEOUDIH: 'Lienyang Yauren-di Inyueh'. *Minswu*, i (4) (Canton, 1942), pp. 28–35.

IN FAALUU: 'Tsorng Lihshyy-shanq Luenn Shinjiang Gewuu'. *Shanqhae Jongiang Ryhbaw* (172) (Shanghai, 12 December 1947).

*JAPANESE BUDDHIST MUSIC: See *Tōyō Ongaku Kenkyū*, xii–xiii (Tokyo, 1954).

*KNOSP, G.: 'Histoire de la musique dans l'Indo-Chine'. *Encyclopédie de la musique* (Lavignac and L. de La Laurencie), 1re partie, v (Paris, 1922), pp. 3100–46.

—— 'La Birmanie'. Ibid., pp. 3094–99.

*KOLINSKI, F. M.: 'Die Musik der Primitivstämme auf Malaka usw.'. *Anthropos*, xxv (Vienna, 1930), pp. 585–648.

*KUNST, J.: *A Study on Papuan Music* (Weltevreden, 1931).

—— *Over zeldsame Fluiten en veelstemmige Muziek in het Ngadaen Nageh-Gebied (West-Flores)* (Batavia, 1931).

—— *De Toonkunst van Java* (The Hague, 1934).

—— 'A Musicological Argument for Cultural Relationship between Indonesia—Probably the Isle of Java—and Central Africa'. *Proceedings of the Musical Association*, lxii (London, 1936), pp. 57–76.

—— 'Music in Nias'. *Internationales Archiv für Ethnographie*, xxxviii (Leiden, 1940), pp. 1–89.

—— 'Music in Flores'. Ibid., supplement to vol. xlii (Leiden, 1942).

—— *Music in Java* (2 vols.) (The Hague, 1949).

—— 'Kulturhistorische Beziehungen zwischen dem Balkan und Indonesien'. *Mededeeling No. CIII, Afdeling Culturele en Physische Anthropologie No. 46 Koninklijk Instituut voor de Tropen* (Amsterdam, 1953).

*KUNST, J. and KUNST-WELY, C. J. A.: *De Toonkunst van Bali* (Weltevreden, 1925).

*KUROSAWA, T.: 'The Musical Bow of the Bununs [*sic*] Tribe in Formosa and Suggestion as to the Origin of the Pentatonic Scale'. *Tōyō Ongaku Kenkyū*, x–xi (Tokyo, 1952), pp. 18–32.

KUTTNER, F. A.: 'Nochmals die Steinzeit-Lithophone von Annam'. *Die Musikforschung*, vi (1953), pp. 1–8.

*LANGE, D. DE, and SNELLEMAN, J. F.: 'La Musique et les instruments de musique dans les Indes orientales néerlandaises'. *Encyclopédie de la musique* (Lavignac and L. de La Laurencie), 1re partie, v (Paris, 1922), pp. 3147–78.

*MCPHEE, C.: 'The Balinese *wajang koelit* and its music'. *Djawa*, xvi (Jogjåkartå, 1936).

—— '*Angkloeng gamelans* in Bali'. Ibid. xvii (Jogjåkartå, 1937).

—— *A House in Bali* (New York, 1944).

—— 'The Five-Tone Gamelan Music of Bali'. *The Musical Quarterly*, xxxv (1949), pp. 250–81.

*MOREUX, S.: 'La Musique japonaise'. *La Musique des origines à nos jours* (Norbert Dufourcq) (Paris, 1946), pp. 446–54.

*MUELLER, L.: 'Einige Notizen über die japanische Musik'. *Mitteilungen der deutschen Gesellschaft für Natur- und Völkerkunde Ostasiens in Tokio*, i. 6 (Tokyo, 1874), pp. 13–20; i. 8 (Tokyo, 1875), pp. 41–48; i. 9 (Tokyo, 1876), pp. 19–35.

*MYERS, C. S.: 'A Study of Sarawak Music'. *Sammelbände der internationalen Musikgesellschaft*, xv (1914), pp. 296–308.

NIPPOLD, W.: *Rassen- und Kulturgeschichte der Negrito-Völker Südost-Asiens* (Göttingen, 1936).

PERI, N.: 'Études sur le drame lyrique japonais'. *Bulletin de l'école française de l'extrême orient*, ix (Hanoy, 1909), pp. 251, 707, and succeeding volumes.

*—— 'Essai sur les gammes japonaises'. *Bibliothèque musicale du musée Guimet*, 2e série, i (Paris, 1934).

*PHRA CHEN DURIYANGA: *Siamese Music* (Bangkok, n.d.).

*PIGGOTT, F. T.: *The Music and Musical Instruments of Japan* (Yokohama and London, 1893 and 1909).

PLAYFAIR, A.: *The Garos* (London, 1909).

RAFFLES, T. S.: *The History of Java*, i (London, 1817), p. 472.

*ROCK, J. F.: 'The Romance of ²K'A-²MÄ-¹GYU-³MI-²GKYI'. *Bulletin de l'école française de l'extrême orient*, xxxix (Hanoy, 1939), pp. 1–152.

*SACHS, C.: 'Les Instruments de musique de Madagascar'. *Travaux et mémoires de l'institut d'ethnologie*, xxviii (Paris, 1938).

SAVINA, F.: *Histoire des Miao* (Hong Kong, 1924).

SCHAEFFNER, A.: 'Une importante découverte archéologique: Le Lithophone de Ndut Lieng Krak (Vietnam)'. *La Revue de musicologie*, xxxiii° année, N.S.: Nos. 97–98 (1951), pp. 1–19.

SCHLESINGER, K.: *The Greek Aulos* (London, 1939).

*SICHEL, A.: 'Histoire de la musique des Malgaches'. *Encyclopédie de la musique* (Lavignac and L. de La Laurencie), 1re partie, v (Paris, 1922), pp. 3226–33.

*SOMERVELL, T. H.: 'The Music of Tibet'. *Musical Times*, lxiv (1923), p. 108.

SOUEN K'AI-TI: 'L'origine et le développement du théâtre des marionnettes chinoises'. *Bulletin du centre franco-chinois d'études sinologiques*, i (Pekin, 1944), pp. 81–105 (194).

*STUMPF, C.: 'Tonsystem und Musik der Siamesen'. *Sammelbände für vergleichende Musikwissenschaft*, i (1922), pp. 129–77.

*TANABE, H.: *Nihon Ongaku Kōwa* (Tokyo, 1926) (in Japanese).

—— *Japanese Music* (Tokyo, 1936).

TRAYNOR, L. M., and KISHIBE, S.: 'On the Four Unknown Pipes of the Shō (Mouth Organ) used in Ancient Japanese Court Music'. *Tōyō Ongaku Kenkyū*, ix (Tokyo, 1951), pp. 22–53.

*Tucker, A. N.: *Tribal Music and Dancing in the Southern Sudan* (*Africa*) (London, n.d.).

Waddell, L. A.: *The Buddhism of Tibet or Lamaism* (Cambridge, 1934).

Waley, A.: *The Nō Plays of Japan* (London, 1921).

—— *The Book of Songs* (London, 1937).

Waterman, R. A., Lichtenwanger, W., Herrmann, V. H., Poleman, H. I., and Hobbs, C.: 'Bibliography of Asiatic Musics, Ninth Installment, iv. South-east Asia, A. General, B. Burma, C. Siam, D. Indo-China, E. Malay and Malay Archipelago (East Indies), F. Philippine Islands'. *Notes*, vii. 1 (New York, 1949), pp. 84–98.

—— 'Ibid., Tenth Installment, v. Central East Asia, A. General, B. Japan, C. Korea'. *Notes*, vii. 2 (New York, 1950), pp. 265–79.

—— 'Ibid., Thirteenth Installment, vi. Central Asia and Siberia, A. General, B. Tibetans, C. Mongols, D. Turkic Peoples, E. Palaeo-Siberian, Samoyeds, Tungus, and Manchus'. *Notes*, viii. 1 (New York, 1950), pp. 100–18.

—— 'Ibid., Fourteenth Installment, Addenda, I. General, II. Southwest Asia, III. India, IV. Southeast Asia, V. Central East Asia, VI. Central Asia and Siberia'. *Notes*, viii. 2 (New York, 1950), 99. 322–9.

Zoete, B. de, and Spies, W.: *Dance and Drama in Bali* (London, 1938).

CHAPTER IV

THE MUSIC OF INDIA

(i) *Texts*

Dâmodara: *Saṃgîtadarpaṇa.* First two chapters, introduction, text and English translation by Arnold A. Bake. *Bibliothèque musicale du Musée Guimet* (Paris, 1930).

Nandikeśvara: *Abhinayadarpaṇa.* Text and translation edited by Manmohan Ghosh, Calcutta Sanskrit Series, v (Calcutta, 1934).

Râmâmâtya: *Svaramelakalânidhi.* Edited with introduction and translation by M. S. Ramaswami Aiyar (Annamalai University, 1932).

Śârngadeva: *Sangîtaratnâkara.* Sanskrit text with two commentaries and translation of the beginning of the first book by C. Kunhan Raja (Adyar Library, Madras, 1945).

Somanâtha: *Râgavibodha.* Edited with introduction and translation by M. S. Ramaswami Aiyar (Madras, 1923).

Simon, A.: '*Das Puṣpasûtra.* Mit Einleitung und Übersetzung'. *Abhandlungen der Kgl. Bayrischen Akademie der Wissenschaften*, i. Kl., xxiii (1909).

(ii) *Notations*

Rabindranath Tagore: *Twenty-six Songs.* With introduction by Arnold A. Bake and Philippe Stern. Bibliothèque musicale du Musée Guimet (Paris, 1935).

Ratan Devi: *Thirty Indian Songs from the Panjab and Kashmir.* With an introduction and translations by Ananda K. Coomaraswamy and a foreword by R. Tagore (London, 1913).

Simon, R.: 'Die Notationen des Somanatha'. *Sitzungsberichte d. philos.-philol. u. d. histor. Klasse d. Kgl. Bayerischen Akademie d. Wissenschaften* (Munich, 1903).

Sourendro Mohun Tagore: *Six Principal Ragas.* With a brief view of Hindu Music (Calcutta, 1877).

(iii) *General*

ABRAHAM, O., and v. HORNBOSTEL, E. M.: 'Phonographierte indische Melodien'. *Sammelbände der internationalen Musikgesellschaft*, v (1903–4).
CLEMENTS, E.: *Introduction to the Study of Indian Music* (London, 1913).
DANIÉLOU, A.: *Northern Indian Music*. 2 vols. (London, 1949 and 1954).
FOX STRANGWAYS, A. H.: *The Music of Hindostan* (Oxford, 1914).
—— 'Indian Music'. *Grove's Dictionary of Music and Musicians*, 5th edition, iv (London, 1954), pp. 456–60 (revised by A. A. Bake).
—— 'Music'. *The Legacy of India*, ed. by G. T. Garratt (Oxford, 1937).
FYZEE-RAHAMIM, A. B.: *The Music of India* (London, 1926).
GROSSET, J.: 'Inde, histoire de la musique depuis l'origine jusqu'à nos jours'. *Encyclopédie de la Musique* (Lavignac and L. de La Laurencie), 1re partie, i (Paris, 1913), pp. 257–376.
MUKERJI, D. P.: *Indian Music: An Introduction* (Bombay, 1945).
PINGLE, B. A.: *Indian Music* (Bombay, 1898).
POPLEY, A. H.: *The Music of India* (London, 1921).
RANADE, G. H. *Hindustani Music* (Poona, 1939).
SHRIPADA BANDOPADHYAYA: *The Music of India* (Bombay, 1945).

(iv) *Special Subjects*

(*a*) *Vedic*

FADDEGON, B.: 'Studies on the Sâmaveda'. Part I. Verhandelingen der Kon. Ned. Akad. v. Wetensch. Nieuwe Reeks, lvii, No. 1 (Amsterdam, 1951).
FELBER, E., and GEIGER, B.: 'Die indische Musik der vedischen und klassischen Zeit'. *Sitzungsberichte der Kais. Akademie d. Wissenschaften in Wien*. Philosophisch-historische Klasse, 170. Bd., 7. Abhandlung (Vienna, 1912).
HAUG, M.: 'Über das Wesen und den Wert des vedischen Akzentes'. *Abhandlungen d. Bayer. Akademie d. Wissenschaften*, xiii. 2. (1874).
HOOGT, J. M. VAN DER: *The Vedic Chant studied in its textual and melodic forms* (Wageningen, 1929).

(*b*) *Scales*

DANIÉLOU, A.: *Introduction to the Study of Musical Scales* (London, 1943).
FOX STRANGWAYS, A. H.: 'The Gândhâra Grâma'. *Journal of the Royal Asiatic Society* (1935), pp. 689–96.
MEHTA, MANHARRAM: *Twenty-two Shrutis and two Gramas of Indian Music* (Bombay, 1938).
RAMASWAMI AIYAR, M. S.: 'The Question of Grâmas'. *Journal of the Royal Asiatic Society* (1936), pp. 629–39.
SHRIPADA BANDOPADHYAY: *The Origin of Raga* (Delhi, 1946).
STERN, P.: 'La musique indoue. Les Ragas'. *Revue Musicale*, iii (1923).

(*c*) *Instruments*

MARCEL-DUBOIS, C.: *Les instruments de musique de l'Inde ancienne* (Paris, 1941).
SACHS, C.: 'Die Musikinstrumente Indiens und Indonesiens'. *Handbücher der Staatlichen Museen zu Berlin*. (Berlin, 2nd ed., 1923).

CHAPTER V

ANCIENT MESOPOTAMIA[1]

(i) *Sources (Iconography)*

BANKS, E. J.: *Bismaya* (New York, 1912).
BUDGE, E. A. WALLIS: *Assyrian Sculptures in the British Museum . . . Reign of Ashur-Nasir-Pal*, 885–860 B.C. . . . (London, 1914).
GALPIN, F. W., *The Music of the Sumerians and their Immediate Successors, the Babylonians and Assyrians* (Cambridge, 1937).
KINSKY, GEORG: *Geschichte der Musik in Bildern* (Leipzig, 1929).
LANGDON, STEPHEN: *Excavations at Kish* (London, 1925).
MORGAN, J. DE: *Délégation en Perse* (Paris, 1901).
OPPENHEIM, M. F. VON: *Tell Ḫalaf* (London, 1933).
WOOLLEY, LEONARD: *Ur Excavations* (London, 1934).

(ii) *Books and Articles*

DUCHESNE, J., and GUILLEMIN, M.: 'La Harpe en Asie occidentale ancienne'. *Revue d'Assyriologie*, xxxiv (1937).
—— ——: 'Sur l'origine asiatique de la cithare grecque', *L'Antiquité Classique*, iv (1935).
FARMER, Henry George: 'The Music of the Sumerians'. *Journal of the Royal Asiatic Society* (1939).
—— 'Persian Music'. *Grove's Dictionary of Music*, 5th edition, vi (London, 1954), pp. 676–82.
—— '*Pandur* or *Pantur*'. *Grove's Dictionary of Music*, vi, p. 535.
—— '*Pandoura*'. *Grove's Dictionary of Music*, vi, p. 534.
GALPIN, F. W.: *The Music of the Sumerians* . . . (Cambridge, 1937).
—— 'The Sumerian Harp of Ur'. *Music and Letters*, x (1929).
—— 'Babylonian Music'. *Grove's Dictionary of Music* i, pp. 282–3.
GENOUILLAC, H. DE: 'Hymnes Sumériens . . .'. *Revue d'Assyriologie* (1929).
LANGDON, STEPHEN: *Babylonian Liturgies* (Paris, 1913).
—— *Sumerian and Babylonian Psalms* (Paris, 1909).
—— *Tammuz and Ishtar* (Oxford, 1914).
—— *Sumerian Liturgies and Psalms* (Philadelphia, 1919).
—— 'Babylonian and Hebrew Musical Terms'. *Journal of the Royal Asiatic Society*, 1921.
—— *Babylonian Penitential Psalms* (Paris, 1927).
PÉLAGAUD, FERNAND: 'Syriens et Phrygiens'. *Encyclopédie de la musique* (Lavignac and L. de La Laurencie), 1re partie, i (Paris, 1913), pp. 49–66.
PINCHES, T. G.: 'Babylonian and Assyrian Music'. *Hastings' Encyclopedia of Religion and Ethics* (Edinburgh, 1917).
SACHS, CURT: 'Die Entzifferung einer babylonischen Notenschrift'. *Sitzungsberichte der Preußischen Akademie der Wissenschaften*, Phil.-hist. Klasse, xviii (1924).
—— 'Ein babylonischer Hymnus'. *Archiv für Musikwissenschaft*, vi (1925).
—— *Geist und Werden der Musikinstrumente* (Berlin, 1929).
—— 'The Mystery of the Babylonian Notation'. *Musical Quarterly*, xxvii (1941).

[1] A very complete bibliography is to found in the *Music Library Association Notes*, v (Washington, 1948), pp. 178–86.

STAINER, JOHN: *The Music of the Bible . . . with Additional Illustrations and Supplementary Notes by F. W. Galpin* (London, 1914).
THUREAU-DANGIN, F.: 'Le Rituel du Kalu'. *Revue d'Assyriologie* (1920).
VIROLLEAUD, C., and PÉLAGAUD, F.: 'Assyrie-Chaldée. La Musique Assyro-Babylonienne'. *Encyclopédie de la musique* (Lavignac and L. de La Laurencie), 1re partie, i (Paris, 1913), pp. 35–48.
WEGNER, MAX: *Die Musikinstrumente des alten Orients* (Münster, 1950).
WOOLLEY, LEONARD: *Ur Excavations* (London, 1934).

CHAPTER VI

ANCIENT EGYPT

(i) *Sources (Iconography)*

BORCHARDT, L.: *Denkmäler des alten Reiches* (Berlin, 1927).
CAPART, JEAN: *Documents pour servir à l'étude de l'art égyptien* (Paris, 1927 et seq.).
CHAMPOLLION, J. F.: *Monuments de l'Égypte et de la Nubie* (Paris, 1835–45).
KINSKY, GEORG: *Geschichte der Musik in Bildern* (Leipzig, 1929).
KLEBS, LUISE: (i) 'Die Reliefs des alten Reiches'; (2) 'Die Reliefs und Malereien des mittleren Reiches'; (3) 'Die Reliefs und Malereien des neuen Reiches'. *Abhandlungen d. Heidelberger Akademie d. Wissenschaften.* Phil.-hist. Klasse, (Heidelberg, 1915 et seq.)
ROSELLINI, IPPOLITO: *I Monumenti dell' Egitto e della Nubia* (Florence, 1832–44).
SACHS, CURT: *Die Musikinstrumente des alten Ägyptens* (Berlin, 1921).
STEINDORFF, G.: *Die Kunst der Ägypter* (Leipzig, 1928).
WEIGALL, ARTHUR: *Ancient Egyptian Works of Art* (London, 1924).

(ii) *Books and Articles*

BAILLET, AUGUSTE and JULES: 'La Chanson chez les Égyptiens'. *Mélanges Maspero*, i, *Orient ancien* (Cairo, 1934).
BORCHARDT, L.: 'Die Rahmentrommel im Museum zu Kairo'. *Mélanges Maspero*, i, *Orient ancien* (Cairo, 1934).
CAPART, JEAN: *Les Débuts de l'art en Égypte* (Brussels, 1903).
CLOSSON, E.: 'Une Nouvelle Série de hautbois égyptiens antiques'. *Festschrift für Guido Adler* (Berlin, 1930).
ERMAN, ADOLF: *Die Literatur der Ägypter* (Leipzig, 1923).
FARMER, HENRY GEORGE: 'Ancient Egyptian Instruments of Music'. *Transactions: Glasgow University Oriental Society*, vi (1931).
—— 'The Evolution of the Ṭunbur or Pandore'. *Transactions: Glasgow University Oriental Society*, v (1925).
—— 'Egyptian Music'. *Grove's Dictionary of Music*, 5th edition, ii (London, 1954), pp. 891–7.
FAULKNER, R. A.: 'The Lamentations of Isis and Nephthys'. *Mélanges Maspero*, i, *Orient ancien* (Cairo, 1934).
HERON-ALLEN, E.: *The 'Nefer' Sign. Concerning the hitherto accepted identification of an Egyptian hieroglyph as an instrument of music* (Selsey, 1941).
HICKMANN, H.: 'La Trompette dans l'Égypte ancienne'. *Supplément aux Annales du Service des Antiquités de l'Égypte* (Cairo, 1946).

HICKMANN, H.: 'Miscellanea Musicologica'. *Annales du service des antiquités de l'Égypte*, xlviii (1948), l (1950).

—— 'Ägyptische Musik'. *Die Musik in Geschichte und Gegenwart*, i (Kassel, 1949–51), cols. 92–106.

—— 'Les harpes de l'Égypte Pharaonique'. *Bulletin de l'Institut d'Égypte*, xxxv, (1953).

—— 'Quelques considérations sur la danse . . . dans l'Égypte pharaonique'. *Cahiers d'histoire égyptienne*, v (Cairo, 1953).

—— 'Le métier de musicien au temps des Pharaons'. *Cahiers d'histoire égyptienne*, vi (Cairo, 1954).

—— 'Dieux et déesses de la musique'. *Cahiers d'histoire égyptienne*, vi (Cairo, 1954).

—— 'Terminologie musicale de l'Égypte ancienne'. Ibid. xxxvi (1955).

—— 'Le Problème de la notation musicale dans l'Égypte ancienne'. Ibid. (1955).

—— *Musique et vie musicale sous les Pharaons*. 3 vols. (Paris, 1956).

LICHTHEIM, MIRIAM. 'The Song of the Harper'. *Journal of Near Eastern Studies*, iv (1945).

LORET, VICTOR: 'Les Flûtes égyptiennes antiques'. *Journal Asiatique* (1889).

—— 'Les Cymbales égyptiennes'. *Sphinx*, v (1902).

—— 'Note sur les instruments de musique de l'Égypte ancienne'. *Encyclopédie de la musique* (Lavignac and L. de La Laurencie), 1re partie, i (Paris, 1913), pp. 1–30.

LYLE, ROBERT: 'The Music of the Ancient Egyptians: A Conjectural Sketch.' *Musical Monthly Record*, lxxviii (1948).

NASH, W. L.: 'A Wooden Handle for Small Cymbals, from Egypt'. *Proceedings of the Society of Biblical Archaeology*, xxii (1900).

PULVER, JEFFREY: 'Israel's Music-Lesson in Egypt'. *Musical Times*, lvi (1915).

—— 'The Music of Ancient Egypt'. *Proceedings of the Musical Association* (1921–2).

SACHS, CURT: 'Die Namen der altägyptischen Musikinstrumente'. *Zeitschrift für Musikwissenschaft*, i (1919).

—— 'Die Tonkunst der alten Ägypter'. *Archiv für Musikwissenschaft*, ii (1920).

—— 'Altägyptische Musikinstrumente'. *Der alte Orient*, xxi (Leipzig, 1920).

—— *Die Musikinstrumente des alten Ägyptens* (Berlin, 1921).

—— 'Zweiklänge im Altertum'. *Festschrift für Johannes Wolf* (Berlin, 1929).

—— 'Eine ägyptische Winkelharfe'. *Zeitschrift für ägyptische Sprache*, lxix (1933).

SCHÄFER, H.: *Die Lieder eines ägyptischen Bauern* (Leipzig, 1903).

SCOTT, NORA E.: 'The Lute of the Singer Ḥar-Mosĕ'. *Bulletin of the Metropolitan Museum of Art* (1944).

SOUTHGATE, T. L.: 'On a Pair of Ancient Egyptian Double Flutes'. *Proceedings of the Musical Association* (1890–1).

—— 'Communication on the Ancient Egyptian Scale'. *Proceedings of the Musical Association* (1890–1).

—— 'The Recent Discovery of Egyptian Flutes'. *Musical Times*, xxxi (1890).

—— 'Some Ancient Musical Instruments'. *Musical News*, xxv (1903).

—— 'Ancient Flutes from Egypt'. *Journal of Hellenic Studies*, xxxv (1915).

STRICKLAND-ANDERSON, L.: 'A Sketch of the Origin and Development of Egyptian Music'. *Calcutta Review*, ii (1924).

WHYTE, E. T.: 'Egyptian Musical Instruments'. *Proceedings of the Society of Biblical Archaeology*, xxi). (1899).

CHAPTER VII

MUSIC IN THE BIBLE

(i) *Music of the Bible*

OESTERLEY, W. O. E.: 'Music of the Hebrews'. *The Oxford History of Music*, Introductory Volume (Oxford, 1929), pp. 33–65.

PRINCE, J. D.: 'Music'. *Encyclopaedia Biblica*, iii (New York, 1902), cols. 3225–43.

VARIOUS AUTHORS. 'Musik und Gesang'. *Die Religion in Geschichte und Gegenwart*, iv, 2nd ed. (Tübingen, 1930), cols. 294–306.

(ii) *Hebrew and early Jewish Music*

ELBOGEN, I.: *Der jüdische Gottesdienst in seiner geschichtlichen Entwicklung* (Leipzig, 1913).

FINESINGER, S. B.: 'Musical Instruments in the Old Testament'. *Hebrew Union College Annual*, iii (Cincinnati, 1926), pp. 21–76.

GRESSMANN, H.: 'Musik und Musikinstrumente'. *Religionsgeschichtliche Versuche und Vorarbeiten* (Giessen, 1903).

IDELSOHN, A. Z.: *Jewish Music in its Historical Development* (New York, 1929).

OESTERLEY, W. O. E.: *A Fresh Approach to the Psalms* (New York, 1937).

THACKERAY, H. ST. JOHN: *The Septuagint and Jewish Worship* (London, 1921).

WERNER, E.: 'The Conflict between Hellenism and Judaism in the Music of the Early Christian Church'. *Hebrew Union College Annual*, xx (1947), pp. 407–70.

(iii) *New Testament and early Christian Music*

BOUSSET, W.: *Kyrios Christos* (Göttingen, 1921).

DÖLGER, F. J.: *Sol Salutis* (Münster, 1925).

DUCHESNE, L.: *Christian Worship: its Origin and Evolution*. 5th ed. (London, 1927).

DUGMORE, C. W.: *The Influence of the Synagogue upon the Divine Office* (London, 1927).

KROLL, J.: *Die christliche Hymnodik bis zu Klemens von Alexandrien, Braunschweiger Vorlesungsverzeichnis* (Königsberg, 1921).

OESTERLEY, W. O. E.: *The Jewish Background of the Christian Liturgy* (Oxford, 1925).

QUASTEN, J.: *Musik und Gesang in den Kulten der heidnischen Antike und christlichen Frühzeit* (Münster, 1930).

WELLESZ, E.: *Aufgaben und Probleme auf dem Gebiete der byzantinischen und orientalischen Kirchenmusik* (Münster, 1923).

WERNER, E.: 'The Conflict between Hellenism and Judaism in the Music of the Early Christian Church', *Hebrew Union College Annual*, xx (1947), pp. 407–70.

(iv) *Literary Criticism of the Bible*

BULTMANN, R. K.: *Die Geschichte der synoptischen Tradition*. 2nd ed. (Göttingen, 1931).

DIBELIUS, M.: *A Fresh Approach to the New Testament and Early Christian Literature* (London, 1936).

GUNKEL, H.: *Einleitung in die Psalmen*, in the *Handkommentar zum Alten Testament* (Göttingen, 1933).
PFEIFFER, R. H.: *Introduction to the Old Testament* (New York, 1941).
STAERK, W.: 'Lyrik', in *Die Schriften des Alten Testaments* (Göttingen, 1920).
WELCH, A. C.: *The Work of the Chronicler* (London, 1939).

(v) *The Dead Sea Scrolls*

BURROWS, M. (ed.): *The Dead Sea Scrolls of St. Mark's Monastery*, i (New Haven, 1950).
—— *The Dead Sea Scrolls* (New York, 1955).

CHAPTER VIII

THE MUSIC OF POST-BIBLICAL JUDAISM

(i) *Sources*

BAER, A.: *Baal Tefilla* (Der praktische Vorbeter) (Frankfurt a. M., 1877).
IDELSOHN, A. Z.: *Thesaurus of Hebrew Oriental Melodies* (10 vols.) (Leipzig–New York–Jerusalem, 1914–32).
KAHLE, P.: *Masoreten des Ostens* (Leipzig, 1913).
—— *Masoreten des Westens* (Stuttgart, 1927).
LACHMANN, R.: *Jewish Cantillation and Song in the Isle of Djerba* (Jerusalem, 1941).
MARCELLO, B.: *Êstro armonico-poetico* (Venice, 1704).
NAUMBOURG, S.: *Agudath Schirim* (Recueil de chants religieux, &c.) (Paris, 1874).
—— *Zemiroth Israel* (Paris, 1847).
PORTALEONE, A.: *Shilte ha-gibborim* (Heb.) with Latin translation in B. Ugolinus, *Thesaurus Antiquitatum*, xxxii (Venice, 1744–67).
REBOURS, J. B.: *Traité de Psaltique* (Paris, 1906).
REUCHLIN, J.: *De accentibus linguae Hebraicae libri III* (Hagenau, 1518).
ROSSI IL EBREO, S. DE': *Shir hashirim asher Lishlomo* (with preface by Rabbi Juda Leon da Modena) (Venice, 1623).
—— new edition in score by S. Naumbourg (Paris, 1877).
WERNER, E., and SONNE, I.: 'The Philosophy and Theory of Music in Judaeo-Arabic Literature'. *Hebrew Union College Annual*, xvi, xvii (Cincinnati, 1941–3).

(ii) *General Subjects*

BIRNBAUM, E.: *Liturgische Übungen* (Berlin, 1906).
CONSOLO, F.: *Libro dei Canti d'Israele* (Florence, 1891).
GASTOUÉ, A.: *Les Origines du Chant Romain* (Paris, 1907).
—— 'Chant Juif et Chant Grégorien'. *Revue du Chant Grégorien* (1930–1).
GRADENWITZ, P.: *The Music of Israel* (New York, 1949).
IDELSOHN, A. Z.: *Jewish Music in its Historical Development*, 2nd edition (New York, 1944).
SACHS, C.: *Rhythm and Tempo* (New York, 1952).
WACHSMANN, K.: *Untersuchungen zum vorgregorianischen Gesang* (Regensburg, 1935).

WAGNER, P.: *Gregorianische Melodien*, 3 vols. (Leipzig, 1911–21).
WELLESZ, E.: *Aufgaben und Probleme auf dem Gebiet der byzantinischen und orientalischen Kirchenmusik* (Münster, 1923).
—— *Eastern Elements in Western Chant* (Oxford, 1947).
—— *Byzantine Music and Hymnography* (Oxford, 1949).
WERNER E.: *The Sacred Bridge* (Studies on the liturgical and musical interdependence of Synagogue and Church) (London-New York, 1956).
—— 'The Common Ground in the Chant of Synagogue and Church'. *Atti del Congresso* (Rome, 1951).
—— 'Preliminary Notes on Jewish and Catholic Musical Punctuation'. *Hebrew Union College Annual*, xv (1940).
—— 'Jewish Music'. *Grove's Dictionary of Music and Musicians*. 5th edition, iv (London, 1954), pp. 615–36.
—— 'Church, Music of the Early'. Ibid. ii, pp. 283–91.

(iii) *Special Subjects*

BIRNBAUM, E.: *Jüdische Musiker am Hof von Mantua* (Vienna, 1893).
BURROWS, M.: *The Dead Sea Scrolls* (New York, 1955).
FARMER, G. H.: *Sa'adya Gaon on the Influence of Music* (London, 1943).
—— *Maimonides on Listening to Music* (Bearsden, 1941).
HØEG, C.: *La Notation ecphonétique* (Paris and Copenhagen, 1935).
IDELSOHN, A. Z.: 'Die Maqamen der arabischen Musik'. *Sammelbände der internationalen Musikgesellschaft*, xv (1914).
—— 'The *Mogen Ovos* Mode'. *Hebrew Union College Annual*, xiv (1939).
KAHLE, P.: *The Cairo Geniza* (London, 1947).
LOEWENSTEIN, H.: 'Eine pentatonische Bibelweise in der deutschen Synagoge'. *Zeitschrift für Musikwissenschaft*, xii (1930).
NE'EMAN, J. L.: *Tzliley ha-miqra* (Hebr.) (Jerusalem, 1955).
NETTL, P.: *Alte jüdische Musiker und Spielleute* (Prague, 1923).
ROTH, C.: *L'Accademia musicale del Ghetto di Venezia* (Florence, 1928).
SCHÖNBERG, J.: *Die traditionellen Gesänge des israelitischen Gottesdienstes in Deutschland* (Nuremberg, 1926).
SINGER, J.: *Die Tonarten des traditionellen Synagogengesanges* (Vienna, 1886).
SUKENIK, M.: *Megillot Genuzot* (Hebr.) (Jerusalem, 1950).
WELLESZ, E.: 'Studien zur äthiopischen Kirchenmusik'. *Oriens Christianus*. N.S., ix, pp. 79–106 (Leipzig).
WERNER, E.: 'The Origin of the Eight Modes of Music'. *Hebrew Union College Annual*, xxi (1948).
—— 'The Psalmodic Formula Neannoe', *Musical Quarterly*, xxviii (1942).
—— 'Die hebräischen Intonationen des B. Marcello'. *Monatsschrift für Geschichte und Wissenschaft des Judentums* (Breslau, 1937).
—— 'The Origin of Psalmody'. *Hebrew Union College Annual*, xxv (1954).

CHAPTER IX

GREEK MUSIC

I. ANCIENT SOURCES (selected for non-specialists in chronological order).

(i) *Art of Music*

HOMER. Text: T. W. Allen (Oxford, 1906 and 1931).
PINDAR. Text, English translation and commentary: L. R. Farnell (London, 1932).

EURIPIDES. *Bacchae.* Text and commentary (with metrical analysis): E. R. Dodds (Oxford, 1944).

ARISTOPHANES. Text, English translation and commentary: B. B. Rogers (London, 1902–6).

PLATO (especially passages in *Republic, Laws, Phaedo, Symposium, Philebus Gorgias, Laches, Protagoras, Timaeus*). Text: J. Burnet (Oxford, 1905–10). Translations: B. Jowett, 4th edition (revised) (Oxford, 1953). Commentaries: on *Phaedo*: J. Burnet (Oxford, 1911), R. S. Bluck (London, 1955); on *Timaeus*: A. E. Taylor (Oxford, 1928).

ARISTOXENUS. Text, English translation and commentary: H. Macran (Oxford, 1902).

—— *Elementa Harmonica.* Text, Italian translation and commentary: R. da Rios, 2 vols. (Rome, 1954).

—— Further fragments. Text and German commentary: F. Wehrli, *Aristoxenos* (vol. ii of *Die Schule des Aristoteles*) (Basle, 1945).

TIMOTHEUS. U. von Wilamowitz-Moellendorff, *Die Perser* (Leipzig, 1903).

DIEHL, E. (ed.): *Anthologia Lyrica Graeca.* 2nd edition (Leipzig, 1942).

POWELL, J. U. (ed.): *Collectanea Alexandrina.* Oxford, 1925.

(ii) *History of Music* (as reconstructed in and after the fourth century B.C.).

ATHENAEUS (especially Book XIV). Text and English translation (Loeb edition, revised). C. B. Gulick (Harvard, 1950).

[PSEUDO-]PLUTARCH: *De musica.* Text, French translation, and commentary: H. Weil and T. Reinach (Paris, 1900).

—— Text, Translation and Commentary: F. Lasserre (Lausanne, 1954).

(iii) *Harmonic Science* (after Aristoxenus)

PTOLEMY: *Harmonics.* Text: I. Düring (Göteborg, 1930), with Porphyry (ibid., 1932), and German translation and commentary (ibid., 1934).

JAN, C. VON (ed.): *Musici Scriptores Graeci* (Euclid, minor theorists, sundry excerpts, some musical fragments). Text and Latin prolegomena, &c., Biblioteca Teubneriana (Leipzig, 1895). *Supplementum* of musical fragments, ibid. (Leipzig, 1899).

ARISTIDES QUINTILIANUS. Text: A. Jahn (Berlin, 1882).

PHILODEMUS. Text: J. Kemke, Biblioteca Teubneriana (Leipzig, 1884).

THEON OF SMYRNA. Text: E. Hiller, ibid. (Leipzig, 1878).

Anonymi Scriptio de musica. Bacchii senioris introductio artis musicae. Text and commentary: F. Bellermann (Berlin, 1841).

GEVAERT, F. A., and VOLLGRAFF, C.: *Problèmes musicaux d'Aristote.* Text, French translation and commentary (Ghent, 1903).

(iv) *Musical Documents* (see also pp. 363–76 and notes).

JAN, C. VON: op. cit. (§ iii).

REINACH, T.: appendix to *La Musique grecque* (Paris, 1926).

MOUNTFORD, J. F.: 'Greek Music in the papyri and inscriptions'. Powell and Barber, *New Chapters in Greek Literature*, 2nd series (Oxford, 1929) and 3rd series (Oxford, 1933).

—— 'A new fragment of Greek music in Cairo'. *Journal of Hellenic Studies*, li (1936).

GRANDE, C. DEL: 'Nuovo frammento di musica greca in un papiro del museo di Cairo'. *Aegyptus*, v (1936).

MARTIN, E.: *Trois Documents de musique grecque* (Paris, 1953).

WINNINGTON-INGRAM, R. P. (with S. Eitrem and L. Amundsen): 'Fragments of Unknown Greek Tragic Texts', *Symbolae Osloenses*, xxxi (1955).

(v) *Notation*

BELLERMANN, F.: *Die Tonleitern und Musiknoten der Griechen* (Berlin, 1847).
FORTLAGE, K.: *Das musikalische System der Griechen in seiner Urgestalt* (Leipzig, 1847).
SACHS, C.: 'Die griechische Instrumentalnotenschrift' and 'Die griechische Gesangsnotenschrift'. *Zeitschrift für Musikwissenschaft*, vi and vii (1924).
WESTPHAL, R.: *Griechische Harmonik und Melopöie*, chapter VIII (Leipzig, 1886).

(vi) *Instruments*

REINACH, T.: 'Lyra', 'Tibia', &c. Daremberg-Saglio, *Dictionnaire des Antiquités* (Paris, 1873–1917).
SCHLESINGER, K.: *The Greek Aulos* (London, 1939).
WEGNER, M.: *Das Musikleben der Griechen* (Berlin, 1949).

No full collection of archaeological evidence exists.

II. MODERN WORKS

(i) *General*

ABERT, H.: *Die Lehre vom Ethos in der griechischen Musik* (Leipzig, 1899).
BOWRA, C. M.: *Greek Lyric Poetry from Alcman to Simonides* (Oxford, 1936).
EMMANUEL, M.: 'Grèce'. *Encyclopédie de la musique* I (Lavignac and L. de La Laurencie), 1re partie, i (Paris, 1913), pp. 377–540.
—— *La Danse grecque antique* (Paris, 1895).
GALILEI, VINCENZO. *Dialogo della musica antica e moderna* (Florence, 1581).
GEVAERT, F. A.: *Histoire et théorie de la musique d'antiquité* (Ghent 1875–81).
—— *La Mélopée antique* (Ghent, 1885).
GRAND, C. DEL: *Espressione musicale dei poeti greci* (Naples, 1932).
JAEGER, W.: *Paideia: The Ideals of Greek Culture* (Oxford, 1946).
LALOY, L.: *Aristoxène de Tarente et la musique d'antiquité* (Paris, 1904).
MARROU, H.: *Histoire de l'éducation dans l'antiquité* (Paris, 2nd ed., 1950).
—— *St. Augustin et la fin de la culture antique* (Paris, 1949).
—— *Μουσικος Ανηρ* (Grenoble, 1937).
PICKARD-CAMBRIDGE, A. W.: *Dithyramb, Tragedy, and Comedy* (Oxford, 1927).
—— *The Dramatic Festivals of Athens* (Oxford, 1953).
REINACH, T.: *La Musique grecque* (Paris, 1926).
—— 'Musica'. Daremberg-Saglio, *Dictionnaire des antiquités* (Paris, 1873–1917).
RIEMANN, H.: *Handbuch der Musikgeschichte*, i (Leipzig, 2nd ed., 1919).
SÉCHAN, L.: *La Danse grecque antique* (Paris, 1930).
VETTER, W.: 'Musik'. Pauly and Wissowa, *Real-Encyclopädie der klassischen Altertumswissenschaft* (1894—still in progress).
WESTPHAL, R.: *Aristoxenos*. I. Commentary (Leipzig, 1883), II. Text (Leipzig, 1893).
WILAMOWITZ-MOELLENDORFF, U. VON: *Griechische Verskunst* (Leipzig, 1921).

(ii) *Special points of History or Theory*

BAPP, C. A.: *De fontibus quibus Athenaeus in rebus musicis enarrandis usus sit* (Leipzig, 1885).

Dale, A. M.: *The Lyric Metres of Greek Drama* (Cambridge, 1948).
Denniston, J. D.: 'Metre, Greek'. *Oxford Classical Dictionary* (Oxford, 1949).
—— 'Some Recent Theories of the Greek Modes'. *Classical Quarterly*, vii (1913).
Düring, I.: 'Studies in Musical Terminology in Fifth-Century Literature'. *Eranos*, xliii (1945).
Garrod, H. W.: 'The Hyporcheme of Pratinas', *Classical Review*, xxxiv (1920).
Gombosi, O.: *Tonarten und Stimmungen der antiken Musik.* (Copenhagen, 1939).
Marrou, H.: '*Μελογραφία*', *L'antiquité classique*, xv (1946).
Martellotti, G.: *Mesomede* (Rome, 1929).
Monro, D. B.: *Modes of Ancient Greek Music* (Oxford, 1894).
Mountford, J. F.: 'Greek Music and its Relation to Modern Times'. *Journal of Hellenic Studies*, xl (1920).
—— 'The Musical Scales of Plato's Republic'. *Classical Quarterly*, xvii (1923).
—— 'The Harmonics of Ptolemy and the Lacuna in ii, 14'. *Transactions of the American Philological Association*, lvii (1926).
Page, D. L.: *Alcman: The Partheneion* (Oxford, 1951).
Reinach, T.: 'La Musique des sphères'. *Revue des études grecques*, xiii (1900).
Ruelle, C. E.: 'Le musicographe Aristide Quintilien'. *Sammelbände der internationalen Musikgesellschaft*, ix (1907).
Stiles, F. H. E.: 'An Explanation of the Modes or Tones in the Ancient Greek Music'. *Philosophical Transactions of the Royal Society*, li (1760).
Vetter, W.: 'Musikalische Sinndeutung des antiken Nomos'. *Zeitschrift für Musikwissenschaft*, xvii (1935).
Winnington-Ingram, R. P.: *Mode in Ancient Greek Music* (Cambridge, 1936).
—— 'The Spondeion Scale'. *Classical Quarterly*, xxii (1928).
—— 'Aristoxenus and the Intervals of Greek Music'. *Classical Quarterly*, xx (1926).
—— 'The Pentatonic Tuning of the Greek Lyre: a theory examined'. *Classical Quarterly*, new series, vi (1956).

CHAPTER X

ROMAN MUSIC

(i) *General Histories and Encyclopedias*

(A) Most of the older histories of music include something about Roman music in their sections on Greece. Burney devotes a chapter to the subject and there are valuable remarks in Gevaert, *Histoire et théorie de la musique d'antiquité* (Ghent, 1875–81).

Bartholinus: *De tibiis veterum et earum antiquo usu libri tres* (Rome, 1677).
Chappell, W.: *History of Music.* I. From the earliest records to the fall of the Roman Empire (London 1874).
Degani: *La Musica nella preistoria e nelle antiche civiltà* (Reggio Emilia, 1939).

(B) Useful works of reference include the catalogue of the German Archaeological Institute of Rome, Nairn's *Classical Hand-list*, and *l'Année philologique.*

Abert, A. in Friedländer: *Darstellungen aus der Sittengeschichte Roms.* 9th edition (Leipzig, 1921–3).
Behn, F. 'Die Musik im römischen Heere'. *Mainzer Zeitschrift*, vii (1912), p. 36.

DAREMBERG-SAGLIO: *Dictionnaire des antiquités grecques et romaines d'après les textes et les monuments* (1877–1919).

PAULY and WISSOWA: *Real-Encyclopädie d. klassischen Altertumswissenschaft* (1894—still in progress).

(ii) *For the Etruscans and their connexions with Rome*

FELL, R. A. L.: *Etruria and Rome* (Cambridge, 1924).

GIGLIOLI, G. Q.: *L'Arte etrusca* (Milan, 1935).

McCARTNEY, E. S.: 'Military indebtedness of Early Rome to Etruria'. *Memoirs of the American Academy in Rome*, i, p. 121.

SOLARI, A.: *Vita pubblica e privata degli Etruschi* (Florence, 1931).

(iii) *For the Theatre*

BIEBER, M.: *The History of the Greek and Roman Theater* (Princeton, 1939).

(iv) *For Roman art and Hellenistic painting*

HERRMANN, P. (ed.): *Denkmäler d. Malerei d. Altertums* (in progress from 1906).

REINACH, S.: *Répertoire des reliefs grecs et romains*, i–iii (Paris, 1909–12).

—— *Répertoire des peintures grecques et romains* (Paris, 1922).

RIZZO, G. E.: *La Pittura ellenistico-romana* (Milan, 1929).

STRONG, E.: *La scultura romana da Augusto a Costantino*. 2 vols. (Florence, 1923–6).

—— *Art in Ancient Rome* (Ars Una) (London, 1929).

Mostra Augustea della Romanità. Catalogue and separate bibliographies and index (Rome, 4th ed., 1939). Section lxx is devoted to music.

(v) *The Aquincum organ*

HYDE, W. W.: *Transactions and Proceedings of the American Philological Association*, lxix (1938), p. 392.

KUZSINSKY, V.: *Aquincum* (Budapest, 1934). The site of the *schola centonariorum* where the organ stood is site 30 of plan I.

MERCURELLI, C.: *Rivista di Archeologia cristiana*, xv (1938), p. 73.

NAGY, L.: *Die Orgel von Aquincum* (Budapest, 1934).

—— *Laureae Aquincenses*, ii (1941), p. 182 for the building, pl. xli shows the museum case with the remains on show.

(vi) *Papyri*

It is not easy to find one's way about the specialized literature. A number of musicians' contracts are collected in Tenney Frank's *Economic Survey of Rome*, volume devoted to Egypt, p. 299 (cf. p. 694 for musicians in public games). The latest list of teaching contracts is in Taubenschlag, *Law of Greco-Roman Egypt in the light of the papyri* (New York, 1944), p. 284. For the tax on trades see the appropriate sections of Wallace, *Taxation in Egypt* (Princeton, 1938) and *Michigan papyri*, v, Tebtunis II, p. 321 for a tax on piper and musician. There is an important article by Westermann in the *Journal of Egyptian Archaeology* (1932), p. 16, on entertainments in villages. Two new papyri throw light on the variety of musical instruments: Knudtzon, *Bakchiastexte* (1946), no. 2 for a list of temple musical instruments in A.D. 188, including a monochord; Petropoulos, *Papyri Societatis Archaeologicae Atheniensis* (1939), 43^{v}, second century A.D., includes references to the bagpipes and the funeral pipes.

CHAPTER XI

THE MUSIC OF ISLAM

(i) *Sources*

AL-HEFNI, M.: *Ibn Sina's Musiklehre, hauptsächlich an seinem 'Naġāt' erläutert, nebst Übersetzung u. Herausgabe des Musikabschnittes des 'Naġāt'* (Berlin, 1931).

AL-HUJWĪRĪ: *The Kashf al maḥjūb, the oldest Persian treatise on Ṣūfism.* Translated by R. A. Nicholson (London, 1911).

AL-MAQQARĪ: *The History of the Mohammedan Dynasties in Spain* . . . Translated by Pascual de Gayangos (London, 1840–3).

AL-MAS'ŪDĪ: *Maçoudj: Les Prairies d'or.* Texte et traduction par Barbier de Meynard et Pavet de Courteil (Paris, 1861–77).

CARRA DE VAUX, B.: *Le Traité des rapports musicaux ou l'épître à Scharaf ed-Dîn, par Safi ed-Dîn 'Abd el-Mumin Albaghdâdî* (Paris, 1891).

D'ERLANGER, R.: *La Musique arabe, Tome I, Al-Fārābī . . . Grand traité de la musique . . . Livres i et ii* (Paris, 1930).

—— *La Musique arabe, Tome II, Al-Fārābī . . . Livre III, et Aviçenne . . . Kitābu'š-Šifā'* . . . (Paris, 1935).

—— *La Musique arabe. Tome III, Ṣafiyu-d-Dīn al-Urmawī: I, Aš-Šarafiyyah . . .: II, Kitāb al-adwār* (Paris, 1938).

—— *La Musique arabe, Tome IV, I, Traité anonyme . . . II, Al-Lādhiqī, Traité al-Fatḥiyah* (Paris, 1939).

FARMER, H. G.: *An Old Moorish Lute Tutor: Being Four Arabic Texts from Unique Manuscripts . . .* (Glasgow, 1933).

—— *Al-Fārābī's Arabic Latin Writings on Music: In the 'Iḥṣā' al-'ulūm' . . ., 'De scientiis' . . ., and 'De ortu scientiarum'* (Glasgow, 1934).

—— *Turkish Instruments of Music in the Seventeenth Century, as described in the 'Siyāḥat nāma of Ewliyā Chelebī'* (Glasgow, 1937).

—— *The Organ of the Ancients: From Eastern Sources (Hebrew, Syriac and Arabic)* (London, 1939).

—— 'The Sources of Arabian Music. An Annotated Bibliography of Arabic Manuscripts which deal with the Theory, Practice, and History of Arabian Music'. *Records of the Glasgow Bibliographical Society*, xiii (1939). Issued separately in 1940.

—— *Music: The Priceless Jewel. From the 'Kitāb al-'iqd al-farīd' of Ibn 'Abd Rabbihi (d. 940)* (Bearsden, 1942).

—— *Sa'adyah Gaon on the Influence of Music* (London, 1943).

—— 'The Minstrels of the Golden Age of Islam' (from the *'Iqd al-farīd*). *Islamic Culture*, xvii–xviii (1943–4).

—— 'An Anonymous English-Arabic Fragment on Music'. *Islamic Culture*, xviii (1944).

—— 'The Song Captions in the Kitāb al-aghānī'. *Transactions: Glasgow University Oriental Society*, xv (1955).

HANOCH AVENARY: 'Abu 'l-Salṭ's Treatise on music'. *Musica Disciplina*, vi (1952).

IBN KHALDŪN: *Prolégomènes d'Ebn Khaldoun* (Notices et extraits des manuscrits de la Bibliothèque du Roi, xix–xxi) (Paris, 1862–8).

IKHWĀN AL-ṢAFĀ': [*Risālat al-mūsīqī*] *Die Propaedeutik der Araber im zehnten Jahrhundert* (F. Dieterici) (Berlin, 1865).

KOSEGARTEN, J. G. L.: *Alii Ispahanensis Liber Cantilenarum Magnus* (Greifswald, 1840).

LACHMANN, ROBERT, and MAHMUD EL-HEFNI: *Ja'qūb Ibn Isḥāq al-Kindī: Risāla fī ḫubr ta'līf al-alḥān: Über die Komposition der Melodien* (Leipzig, 1931).

MACDONALD, D. H.: 'Emotional Religion in Islām as affected by music and singing. Being a translation of a book of the 'Iḥyā 'ulūm ad-dīn' of Al-Ghazzālī'. *Journal of the Royal Asiatic Society* (1901–2).

ROBSON, JAMES: *Ancient Arabian Musical Instruments: As described by Al-Mufaḍḍal ibn Salama (9th century) in the . . . 'Kitāb al-malāhī' . . .* (Glasgow, 1938).

—— *Tracts on Listening to Music: Being 'Dhamm al-malāhī' by Ibn Abi'l-Dunyā and 'Bawāriq al-ilmā'' by Majd al-Dīn al-Ṭūsī al-Ghazālī* (London, 1938).

UNVALA, JAMSHEDJI MANECKJI: *The Pahlavi Text: King Ḫusraw and his Boy* (Paris, 1921).

(ii) *Books and Articles*

BARBIER DE MEYNARD: 'Ibrahim, fils de Mehdi. Fragments historiques, scènes de la vie d'artiste au IIIe siècle de l'hégire . . .'. *Journal Asiatique* (1869).

BARTÓK, BÉLA: 'Die Volksmusik der Araber von Biskra und Umgebung'. *Zeitschrift für Musikwissenschaft*, ii (1919–20).

BELAIEV, VIKTOR: *Muzīkalnïe instrumenti Uzbekistana* (Moscow, 1933).

—— 'Turkish Music'. *Musical Quarterly*, xxi (1935).

—— 'Formi Uzbekskoy Muzïki'. *Sovetskaya Muzīka* (July–August, 1935).

—— 'Three Eastern Pieces'. *Monthly Musical Record*, lvii (1927).

—— 'Turkomanian Music'. *Pro musica* (1927).

—— and USPENSKY, V.: *Turkmenskaya Muzīka* (Moscow, 1928).

CAUSSIN DE PERCEVAL, A.: 'Notices anecdotiques sur les principaux musiciens arabes des trois premiers siècles de l'Islamisme'. *Journal Asiatique* (1873).

CHOTTIN, A.: 'Les Genres dans la Musique marocaine'. *La Revue musicale du Maroc* (1930).

—— *Corpus de Musique marocaine*, I, *Nouba de Ochchāk . . .* (Paris, 1931).

—— *Corpus de Musique marocaine*, II, *Musique et danses berbères du Pays Chleuh* (Paris, 1933).

CHRISTENSEN, ARTHUR: 'La Vie musicale dans la civilisation des Sassanides'. *Bulletin de l'Association Française des amis de l'Orient* (Paris, 1936).

COLLANGETTES, XAVIER M.: 'Étude sur la musique arabe'. *Journal Asiatique* (1904, 1906).

The Encyclopaedia of Islām (Leiden, 1913–38). s.v. 'Būḳ', 'Duff', 'Ghinā', 'Kītāra', 'Mi'zaf', 'Mizmār', 'Mūsīqī', 'Rabāb', 'Nawba', 'Ṣandj', 'Ṭabl', 'Ṭabl Khāna', 'Ṭunbūr', ''Ud', 'Urghan', as well as the leading singers, instrumentalists, and theorists.

FARMER, HENRY GEORGE: 'Clues for the Arabian Influence on European Musical Theory'. *Journal of the Royal Asiatic Society* (1925) = *The Arabian Influence on Musical Theory* (London, 1925).

—— 'The Arabic Musical Manuscripts in the Bodleian Library'. *Journal of the Royal Asiatic Society* (1925).

—— 'The Old Persian Musical Modes'. *Journal of the Royal Asiatic Society* (1926).

—— *A History of Arabian Music to the XIIIth Century* (London, 1929).

—— 'The Influence of Music: From Arabic Sources'. *Proceedings of the Musical Association*, 52nd Session (1925–6).

—— *Historical Facts for the Arabian Musical Influence* (London, 1930).

—— 'Greek Theorists of Music in Arabic Translation'. *Isis*, xiii (1930).

FARMER, HENRY GEORGE: 'Histoire abrégée de l'échelle de la musique arabe'. *Recueil des travaux du Congrès de musique arabe . . . Caire . . . 1932* (Le Caire, 1934).

—— *Studies in Oriental Musical Instruments*, 1st series (London, 1931); 2nd series (Glasgow, 1939).

—— [Persia.] 'An Outline History of Music and Musical Theory'. A. U. Pope's *A Survey of Persian Art* (London, 1938).

—— 'The Jewish Debt to Arabic Writers on Music'. *Islamic Culture* (1941).

—— *The Minstrelsy of the Arabian Nights. A Study of the Music and Musicians in the Arabic 'Alf Laila was Laila'* (Bearsden, 1945).

—— 'Ghosts: An Excursus on Arabic Musical Bibliographies'. *Isis*, xxxvi (1946).

—— 'Crusading Martial Music'. *Music and Letters*, xxx (1949).

—— *Oriental Studies: Mainly Musical* (London, 1953).

—— See also *Grove's Dictionary of Music*, 5th ed. (London, 1954), s.v. 'Arabian Music', 'Berber Music', 'Egyptian Music', 'Iraquian and Mesopotamian Music', 'Maghribī Music', 'Mohammedan Music', 'Moorish Music', 'Persian Music', 'Ṣūfī and Darwīsh Music', 'Syrian Music', 'Turkestānī Music'.

HORNBOSTEL, ERICH VON: 'Phonographierte tunesische Melodien'. *Sammelbände der internationalen Musikgesellschaft*, viii (1906–7).

—— and LACHMANN, R.: 'Asiatische Parallelen zur Berbermusik'. *Zeitschrift für vergleichende Musikwissenschaft*, i (1933).

HUART, CLÉMENT: 'Étude biographique sur trois musiciennes arabes'. *Journal Asiatique* (1884).

IDELSOHN, A. Z.: 'Die Maqamen der arabischen Musik'. *Sammelbände der internationalen Musikgesellschaft*, xv (1913–14).

KIESEWETTER, R. G.: *Die Musik der Araber* (Leipzig, 1842).

KOSEGARTEN, J. G. L.: 'Die moslemischen Schriftsteller über die Theorie der Musik'. *Zeitschrift für die Kunde des Morgenlandes*, v (Bonn, 1844).

LACHMANN, ROBERT: 'Die Musik in den tunisischen Städten'. *Archiv für Musikwissenschaft*, v (1923).

LAND, J. P. N.: 'Recherches sur l'histoire de la gamme arabe'. *Actes du Sixième Congrès International des Orientalistes tenu en* 1883 *à Leide* (Leiden, 1885).

—— 'Remarks on the earliest development of Arabic music'. *Transactions of the Ninth Congress of Orientalists*, 1892, ii (London, 1893).

—— 'Tonschriftversuche und Melodieproben aus dem muhammedanischen Mittelalter'. *Vierteljahrsschrift für Musikwissenschaft*, ii (1886).

LOEWENTHAL, A.: *Honein Ibn Ishāk, Sinnsprüche der Philosophen . . . ins Deutsche übertragen und erläutert* (Berlin, 1896).

—— *Musik des Orients* (Breslau, 1929).

MITJANA, RAFAEL: 'La musique en Espagne'. *Encyclopédie de la musique* (Lavignac and L. de La Laurencie), 1re partie, iv (Paris, 1920), especially pp. 1920–5.

—— 'L'Orientalisme musical et la Musique arabe'. *Le Monde Oriental* (Uppsala, 1906).

POPE, A. U.: *A Survey of Persian Art from Prehistoric Times to the Present* (Oxford, 1938).

RA'ŪF, YEKTĀ BEY: 'La Musique turque'. *Encyclopédie de la musique* (Lavignac and L. de La Laurencie), 1re partie, v (Paris, 1922), pp. 2945–3064.

—— *Dār al-alḥān kulliyyāt* (Constantinople, n.d.). Contains the compositions of the old Turkish composers.

RIBERA, JULIÁN: *La Música de las Cantigas* (Madrid, 1922).

—— *Music in Ancient Arabia and Spain; Being 'La Música de las Cantigas' ... translated and abridged by Eleanor Hague and Marion Leffingwell* (Stanford University Press, U.S.A., 1929).

—— *La Música andaluza medieval en las canciones de trovadores, troveros y minnesinger* (Madrid, 1923–5).

—— *Historia de la música árabe medieval y su influencia en la española* (Madrid, 1927).

ROUANET, JULES: 'La Musique arabe'. *Encyclopédie de la musique* (Lavignac and L. de La Laurencie), 1re partie, v (Paris, 1922), pp. 2676–2939.

—— and YAFIL, E. N.: *Répertoire de musique arabe et maure: Collection d' Ouvertures, Mélodies, Noubet, Chansons, Préludes, Danses, etc.* (Algiers, 1904 et seq.).

SIRAJUL HAQ: 'Samāʿ and Raqṣ of the Darwishes'. *Islamic Culture* (1944).

VILLOTEAU, G. A.: *La Description de l'Égypte: État moderne* (Paris, 1809–26).

WERNER, E., and SONNE, I.: 'The Philosophy and Theory of Music, in Judaeo-Arabic Literature'. *Hebrew Union College Annual*, xvi, xvii (Cincinnati, 1941, 1943).

LIST OF CONTENTS OF *THE HISTORY OF MUSIC IN SOUND* VOLUME I

The History of Music in Sound is a series of volumes of gramophone records, with explanatory booklets, designed as a companion series to the *New Oxford History of Music*. Each volume covers the same ground as the corresponding volume in the *New Oxford History of Music*, and is designed as far as possible to illustrate the music discussed therein. The records are issued in England by The Gramophone Company (H.M.V.) and in the United States by R. C. A. Victor, and the booklets are published by the Oxford University Press. The editor of Volume I of *The History of Music in Sound* is Egon Wellesz.

CHINA

THREE ANCIENT MELODIES

LP		*78*	
Side I	*Band* 1 (*a*)	*Side* 1 (*a*)	Tzuey Ueng Charn (The Strumming of an Elderly Gentleman in a State of Refined Intoxication)
	(*b*)	(*b*)	Lanq Taur Sha (Waves Washing the Beach)
	(*c*)	(*c*)	Nan Jinn Gong (Entering the Palace)

INSTRUMENTAL AND DRAMATIC MUSIC

	Band 2 (*a*)	*Side* 2 (*a*)	The Poet Rides
	(*b*)	(*b*)	Meihua San Nonq (Plum Blossom)
	Band 3	(*c*)	Duet from *Sheau Fanqniou* (The Little Shepherd)
	Band 4 (*a*)	(*d*)	Excerpt from *Muudan Tyng* (The Peony Pavilion)

OPERA

	(*b*)	*Side* 3 (*a*)	Excerpt from *Bair Sheh Juann* (The White Serpent)
	Band 5	(*b*)	Excerpt from *Wuu Jia Po* (Lady Precious Stream)
	Band 6	(*c*)	Excerpt from *Yuanmen Jaan Tzyy* (Beheading a Son)
	Band 7	(*d*)	Excerpt from *Tsao Chyau Guan* (Thatched Bridge Pass)

TIBET

Side II	*Band* 1 (*a*)	*Side* 4 (*a*)	Lamaist Instrumental Ensemble
	(*b*)	(*b*)	Lamaist Chanting
	(*c*)	(*c*)	Hymn by Two Nuns

CAMBODIA

	Band 2	*Side* 5 (*a*)	Bampe (Lullaby)

MADAGASCAR

LP		*78*	
	Band 3	*Side* 5 (*b*)	Raivo (Hair-cutting ceremony)

LAOS

	Band 4 (*a*)	*Side* 6 (*a*)	Song of Nam-Ngum Bargeman
	(*b*)	(*b*)	Mẹngphoutomdok (Buzzing of Bees)
	(*c*)	(*c*)	Laoh-Tenh (old dance)
	(*d*)	(*d*)	Thoum (Court of Love)

BALI

	Band 5 (*a*)	*Side* 7 (*a*)	Tjroektjoek Poenjah
	(*b*)	(*b*)	Excerpt from *Tjalonarang*
	(*c*)	*Side* 8 (*a*)	Excerpt from a Gamboeh

TAHITI

	Band 6 (*a*)	(*b*)	Paoa (primitive song)
	(*b*)	(*c*)	Aue Aue (modern dance)

JAPAN

Side III	*Band* 1	*Side* 9 (*a*)	Gagaku (Court Music): Dance of the Great Peace
	Band 2	(*b*)	Rokudan (Nos. 1, 3, and 6)
	Band 3	(*c*)	Chidori-no-Kyoku (Song of the Sea Plovers)

INDIA

FOLK MUSIC

	Band 4 (*a*)	*Side* 10 (*a*)	Rice-transplanting song (Western Ghats)
	(*b*)	(*b*)	Harvest Processional song (Western Ghats)
	(*c*)	(*c*)	Toda song (Nilgiri Mountains)
	(*d*)	(*d*)	Death Wail (Cape Comorin)
	Band 5 (*a*)	*Side* 11 (*a*)	Afridi song (Khyber Pass)
	(*b*)	(*b*)	Marathi Weaver's song (Hyderabad)
	(*c*)	(*c*)	Bhajan (Marathi Villagers' Prayer) (Hyderabad)

CLASSICAL MUSIC

	Band 6 (*a*)	*Side* 12 (*a*)	Sundari Nann'indarilo (Telugu) (Carnatic devotional song)
	(*b*)	(*b*)	Pahâdî (Dhun) (Sârangî with tablâ)
	(*c*)	(*c*)	Kâñkariyé jî na Mâro (Hindi)
	Band 7	*Side* 13	Râga Kedâra (shannâi)

JEWISH MUSIC

Side IV	*Band* 1 (*a*)	*Side* 14 (*a*)	Lamĕnassêah àl Haǧǧitît (Psalm 8)
	(*b*)	(*b*)	Mŏhôlêl Kôl Weḫôl Joḫôl (Hymn for Hasha'na Rabba)
	(*c*)	(*c*)	'Al Năhărôt Bob̮al Hoseḫoh (Paraphrase of Psalm 137)

ANCIENT GREECE

LP	*78*	
Band 2	*Side* 15 (*a*)	First Delphic Hymn
Band 3	(*b*)	Epitaph of Seikilos

MUSIC OF ISLAM

NEAR EAST

Band 4	*Side* 16 (*a*)	Muezzin's Call to Prayer
Band 5	(*b*)	Taqsīm Bayātī (Turkish)
Band 6	(*c*)	Bedouin song (from El Fayum)

IRAQ

Band 7	*Side* 17 (*a*)	Tahher Fouadaka Bil-Rāhāt (His image)
Band 8	(*b*)	Ya Naees el-Tarfe (Oh you with the dreaming eyes)

THE MAGHRIB

Band 9	*Side* 18 (*a*)	Oomri Alayki (I spent my life) (Moroccan)
Band 10	(*b*)	Alhazo Zabi (Could it be that your eyes?) (Tunisian)
Band 11	(*c*)	Fah el-banafseg (The narcissus flower is blooming) (Aigerian)

INDEX